Judges
1–12

VOLUME 6D

THE ANCHOR YALE BIBLE is a project of international and interfaith scope in which Protestant, Catholic, and Jewish scholars from many countries contribute individual volumes. The project is not sponsored by any ecclesiastical organization and is not intended to reflect any particular theological doctrine.

THE ANCHOR YALE BIBLE is committed to producing commentaries in the tradition established half a century ago by the founders of the series, William Foxwell Albright and David Noel Freedman. It aims to present the best contemporary scholarship in a way that is accessible not only to scholars but also to the educated nonspecialist. Its approach is grounded in exact translation of the ancient languages and an appreciation of the historical and cultural context in which the biblical books were written, supplemented by insights from modern methods, such as sociological and literary criticism.

John J. Collins
General Editor

THE ANCHOR YALE BIBLE

Judges
1–12

A New Translation with
Introduction and Commentary

JACK M. SASSON

THE ANCHOR YALE BIBLE

Yale UNIVERSITY PRESS

New Haven & London

Published with assistance from the foundation established in memory of
Amasa Stone Mather of the Class of 1907, Yale College.

Yale University Press books may be purchased in quantity for educational, business,
or promotional use. For information, please e-mail sales.press@yale.edu (U.S. office)
or sales@yaleup.co.uk (U.K. office).

Designed by Lindsey Voskowsky.
Set in Garamond and Centennial types by Newgen North America.
Printed in the United States of America.

Library of Congress Cataloging-in-Publication Data
Bible. Judges. English. Sasson. 2013.
  Judges 1–12 / a new translation with introduction and commentary
Jack M. Sasson.
    pages cm. — (The Anchor Yale Bible ; v. 6D)
  Includes bibliographical references and index.
  ISBN 978-0-300-19033-5 (hardback)
1. Bible. Judges—Commentaries.   I. Sasson, Jack M.   II. Title.
BS1303.S27 2013
222'.32077—dc23
                                                                        2013008305

A catalogue record for this book is available from the British Library.

This paper meets the requirements of ANSI/NISO Z39.48–1992 (Permanence of Paper).
                              10 9 8 7 6 5 4 3 2 1

David Noel Freedman
זכרונו לברכה

Contents

II. NOTES AND COMMENTS: ARGUMENTS

III. NOTES AND COMMENTS: THE JUDGES

Foreword

More than thirty-five years have passed since the publication of the existing Anchor Bible commentary on the book of Judges by Robert Boling. The landscape of scholarship on early Israel has changed beyond recognition during that period. When Boling wrote, it was still possible to defend the substantial historicity of the biblical text. Now it must be recognized as a literary artifact, in which nuggets of historical information are incidental.

The new commentary by Jack M. Sasson remains true to the spirit of the older commentary, and that of the Anchor Bible series, in fundamental ways. This is a commentary that seeks to illuminate the Hebrew text of Judges by drawing on the archeology and literature not only of ancient Israel, but also of the ancient Near East. Sasson, however, is more concerned with literary patterns than with historical reconstruction. For example, he uses the Sumerian King List to illuminate the structure of the biblical book. The commentary is distinguished by its use of illustrations from the archives of ancient Mari, a source in which Sasson is an expert. The commentary is considerably more extensive than that of Boling. This commentary covers only half the biblical book but is longer than Boling's commentary on the entire book. Some of the increased detail is due to the need to cover and interact with the scholarship of the intervening period (notably the theory that early Israel developed as a revolt of peasants against their Canaanite overlords), but mainly it is due to Sasson's greater erudition in the literature of the ancient Near East. The commentary also displays extensive knowledge of postbiblical Jewish tradition.

In recent years, the pendulum of biblical scholarship has swung toward literary and theological readings that are not informed in significant ways by the literature of the ancient Near East. Sasson's commentary on Judges is a refreshing corrective to that trend, and a plea for recognition of the importance of the literary and historical contexts from which the biblical text emerged.

John J. Collins
General Editor, Anchor Yale Bible

Acknowledgments

On the completion of any work that had years of gestation and months of writing, there are so many to acknowledge and thank that this note cannot adequately fulfill the obligation. My fascination with Judges began long before I entered my academic career, for on Sabbath days I would follow synagogal chanting of excerpts from its chapters. On a yearly basis, Deborah and Jephthah brought Israel's enemies to their knees, and Samson's mighty feats beckoned, albeit in their preconceived state (see "The Book of Judges in Contemporary Liturgy" in the Introduction). I have on occasions taught seminars covering the Judges period in North Carolina and at Vanderbilt, absorbing much good exegesis from my students. This commentary itself began to take shape only in recent years, mostly since a 2005 sabbatical in New York found me by the fine libraries of Columbia University (incorporating that of the Union Theological Seminary) and of the Jewish Theological Seminary. An invitation by Jean-Marie Durand and Thomas Römer to deliver lectures at the Collège de France in 2009 helped me outline issues beyond exegetical annotations. A major impetus to completing this work occurred when John J. Collins, editor of the Anchor Yale Bible, accepted my proposal to publish the first of two volumes on Judges.

I owe most, however, to Vanderbilt and its community. If its Heard Library is well-stocked, the staff of its Divinity Library is beyond compare, from its chief librarian, Bill Hook, to the many people working there, not least among them Christopher Benda, unparalleled solver of bibliographic cruxes, and Jim Toplon, head of the Interlibrary Loan Services. I must acknowledge the largely anonymous horde of computer experts who have posted an enormous literature on Judges on the Internet, among them scholarly items that are buried in collections of difficult access. It is true that their contribution has complicated my task, forcing me to confront arguments that would have been lost to me a generation ago; but if scholarship is also a conversation among peers across the centuries, then I am indeed very fortunate to have participated in the séances.

In the years since I have joined its faculty, the Vanderbilt Divinity School and its dean, James Hudnut-Beumler, have been generous with their support. My colleagues in Hebrew Bible studies, Annalisa Azzoni, Douglas Knight, and Herbert Marbury, are models for cooperation and enriching conversations. I have had a number of research assistants over the years, among them Christopher Paris and Ryan Davis, who have been helpful in reviewing the pages I have written. The brunt of overseeing final inspection of the manuscript, however, has fallen on Michael Biggerstaff. He has done me a great service—controlling inconsistencies in transliteration, correcting lapses in references, taming the hirsute bibliography, and generating the indexes—and I am glad to acknowledge it. Ljubica Jovanovic kindly proofed the citation of Greek material.

I cannot begin to thank the lucky stars that guided John J. Collins to assign Susan Ackerman of Dartmouth College, a member of the Anchor Yale Bible Board, as a content reviewer of the manuscript. She is just tops! Susan was good not just at forcing me to correct philological trespasses and to bolster flabby arguments, but also at widening my awareness of issues that had skipped my attention. Her comments came sharply edged, but also were witty and chatty—such that during the summer (2011) in which her emails reached me, they morphed into virtual visits by a respected colleague. In the pages that follow, you will find me citing a number of her opinions ("S. Ackerman, private communication"); no doubt I should have mentioned more.

I must also thank Vadim Staklo, reference editor at Yale University Press; Susan Laity, senior manuscript editor; and their staff for shepherding this volume through the many stages it takes to turn an ungainly manuscript into the handsome volume you now have in your hands. I am very fortunate to have had Jessie Dolch copyedit the manuscript; she wielded the pen lightly but precisely, skillfully sharpening ideas, clarifying thoughts, establishing stylistic consistency, and finding better homes for seemingly orphaned comments. I pray I have lived up to her editing standards, but likely I did not. Jenya Weinreb interceded several times to improve the flow of words.

I am dedicating this volume of Judges to the memory of David Noel Freedman (1922–2008). The years are not long gone since he single-handedly edited every volume of the Anchor Bible Series—and so much else besides. I bonded with him when we worked on the Anchor Bible of Jonah, receiving from him dozens of erudite, pedagogic, yet chatty pages, in a type as clean as the prose he crafted. I would see David (that's what he asked me to call him) at the annual SBL meetings, and during the score of years I knew him he was always the same frail presence, slightly shrunken by the large leather bag he carried everywhere. Over meals, he talked about many subjects, academic or not, with enthusiasm, urgency, and humor. He commissioned me to write Judges a while ago, sensing that the book would easily reward an additional examination for the series he was lovingly editing. I imagine him inspecting this volume now and cherish the hope that he might find his mentoring not in vain.

Abbreviations

AB	Anchor Bible
ABD	*Anchor Bible Dictionary*; see Freedman 1992
ANET[3]	*Ancient Near Eastern Texts Relating to the Old Testament*; see Pritchard 1969
ARM	Archives royales de Mari (in transliteration and translation, listed by editors)
	1: See Dossin 1950
	2: See Jean 1950
	3: See Kupper 1950
	4: See Dossin 1951
	5: See Dossin 1952
	6: See Kupper 1954
	8: See Boyer 1958
	10: See Dossin and Finet 1978
	11: See Burke 1963
	14: See Birot 1974
	21: See Durand 1983
	26/1: See Durand 1988
	26/2: See Charpin et al., 1988
	27: See Birot 1993
	28: See Kupper 1998
AYB	Anchor Yale Bible

BDB	*Hebrew and English Lexicon of the Old Testament*; see Brown, Driver, and Briggs 1907
BHQ 7	*Biblia Hebraica Quinta Edition*; see Marcos 2011
BHS	*Biblia Hebraica Stuttgartensia*; see Kittel et al. 1990
CAD	*The Chicago Assyrian Dictionary*; see M. Roth et al., 1956–2011
CANE	*Civilizations of the Ancient Near East*; see Sasson, Baines, Beckman, and Rubinson 1995
COS	*The Context of Scripture*; see Hallo and Younger 1997–2003
CTA	*Corpus des tablettes en cunéiformes alphabétiques*; see Herdner 1963
CTH	*Catalogue des textes Hittites*; see Laroche 1971
DAGR	*Dictionnaire des antiquités grecques et romaines*; see Daremberg and Saglio 1877
DDD	*Dictionary of Deities and Demons in the Bible*; see van der Toorn et al., 1995
DNWSI	*Dictionary of North-West Semitic Inscriptions*; see Hoftijzer and Jongeling 1995
EA	El-Amarna tablets; see Moran 1992
EB	*Encyclopaedia Biblica*; see Cheyne and Black 1899–1903
EncJud	*Encyclopaedia Judaica*; see C. Roth 1972
ETCSL	*Electronic Text Corpus of Sumerian Literature* (http://etcsl .orinst.ox.ac.uk/)
FM	*Florilegium marianum*
	2: See Charpin and Durand 1994
	4: See Ziegler 1999
	5: See Charpin and Ziegler 2003
	7: See Durand 2002a
	8: See Durand 2005
	10: See Marti 2008
	11: See Chambon 2009
	12: See Jacquet 2011
GKC	*Gesenius' Hebrew Grammar*; see Gesenius 1910
HALOT	*The Hebrew and Aramaic Lexicon of the Old Testament*; see Koehler, Baumgartner, and Stamm 1994–1999
IDB	*The Interpreter's Dictionary of the Bible*; see Buttrick 1962
IDBSup	*Interpreter's Dictionary of the Bible: Supplementary Volume*; see Crim 1976

KTU	*Die keilalphabetischen Texte aus Ugarit*; see Dietrich, Loretz, and Sanmartín 1976
LÄ	*Lexikon der Ägyptologie*; see Helck and Otto 1972–92
LAB	Pseudo-Philo's *Liber antiquitatum biblicarum*; see Jacobson 1996
LAPO 16–18	Littératures anciennes du Proche-Orient; see Durand 1997–2000
M.R. no.	Sigla used in the *ABD* (see vol. 1, xlvii–xlviii) to locate sites in Israel and Jordan, coordinated with maps on the inside front cover of each *ABD* volume. Similar (but not the same) scheme at the *OEANE*.
NABU	*Nouvelles assyriologiques brèves et utilitaires*
NEAEHL	*The New Encyclopedia of Archaeological Excavations in the Holy Land*; see E. Stern 1993
NETS	*New English Translation of the Septuagint*; see Pietersma and Wright 2007
NJPS	See *TNK*, below
OBTR	*The Old Babylonian Tablets from Tell Al Rimah*; see Dalley, Walker, and Hawkins 1976
OEAE	*Oxford Encyclopedia of Ancient Egypt*; see Redford 2000
OEANE	*The Oxford Encyclopedia of Archaeology in the Near East*; see E. Meyers 1997
RAI	Rencontre Assyriologique Internationale
RIMA	The Royal Inscriptions of Mesopotamia, Assyrian Periods; see Grayson 1987, 1991, 1996
RIMB	The Royal Inscriptions of Mesopotamia, Babylonian Periods; see Frame 1995
RlA	*Reallexikon der Assyriologie und vorderasiatischen Archäologie*; see Ebeling 1928–
RS	"Ras Shamra," followed by a number: abbreviation for tablets from Ugarit
SAI	*The Shemshāra Archives*; see Eidem and Læssøe 2001
TDOT	*Theological Dictionary of the Old Testament*; see Botterweck, Ringgren, and Fabry 1974–2006
TH	"Tell Hariri," followed by a number: abbreviation for some tablets from Mari
TLOT	*Theological Lexicon of the Old Testament*; see Jenni and Westermann 1997

TNK   *The Jewish Bible: Tanakh: The Holy Scriptures—The New JPS Translation According to the Traditional Hebrew Text: Torah * Nevi'im * Kethuvim* (New York: Jewish Publication Society, 1985)

Other abbreviations not listed here follow Patrick H. Alexander, John F. Kutsko, Shirley Decker-Lucke, James D. Ernest, and David L. Petersen, eds., *The SBL Handbook of Style for Ancient Near Eastern, Biblical, and Early Christian Studies* (Peabody, MA: Hendrickson, 1999).

INTRODUCTION

There is a delicious anecdote about Hillel the Elder, who lived in Roman-occupied Palestine as the millennia turned into the Common Era. Once, a pagan agreed to convert to Judaism if Hillel would teach him the entire Torah while he remained standing on one foot. "What is hateful to you, do not do to another," Hillel answered. "This is all the Torah, entirely—the rest is its commentary."[1]

This bit of wisdom is preserved in the Talmud (*bShabbat* 31a). With many generations separating the event from its earliest recording, several questions have surfaced about it. Whether it occurred at all is one of them, its authenticity not at all helped by the many other charming tales of pagans bringing questions to Hillel. There is also the way the event was turned into a drama pitting two formidable sages. The man had first gone to Shammai, Hillel's rival, with the same request; but wielding a builder's stick, Shammai had shooed him away. The story, therefore, means to contrast their grasp of what was at the core of Israel's teaching. Yet Hillel was not trivializing Judaism's heritage, for although he apparently does convert the pagan, he also gives him major guidance: It is not enough to dwell on how not to hurt others; the convert (and all others as well) must also "go and study" the many ways the Torah develops that precious principle.

The Rest in a Commentary

This much is obvious from surface analysis. The story is featured in many sermons and drives home teachings that hardly need much elaboration. Yet it was much too pithy for scholars to leave it alone, so they naturally developed a commentary around it. To begin with, a variant has the pagan asking to be made a high priest as a condition. One more story is attributed to Akiva, another worthy ancestor—but this time about a century later than Hillel. That version (*Avot of Rabbi Nathan* A16) is more prolix, featuring Akiva's challenger as seeking to learn Torah "at once" rather than when balancing on one leg. A similar saying was attributed to Ben Bag Bag, "Delve into [the Torah] again and again, for everything is in it" (*Avot* 5.25). As this Ben Bag Bag may have been a disciple of Hillel as well as a proselyte, some commentators found it attractive to concretize the anecdote.

Even more scholarly comments developed after Mordecai Kaplan, the founder of the Reconstructionist movement in Judaism, observed that the "foot" (*regel* in Hebrew) on which the pagan wished to stand could be an aural pun on Latin *regula*, meaning "a measuring stick" but also a "rule, model, principle." The pagan, therefore, wants Hillel to package Judaism into one rule. Suddenly, the story took on many more nuances, attracting attention not just to Hillel's simple rule of conduct, but also to the stick that Shammai was brandishing. Kaplan's proposal was very attractive; but why, it might be asked, would any Hillel contemporary reference a Latin word when Greek and Aramaic were (excuse the pun) the ruling languages of Palestine? The concerns therefore could no longer be just on the anecdote and its many meanings, but were also on reconstructing the contexts of its creation, transmission, and reception. Some readers might recoil at the determined academic peeling of a tale with such an ostensibly simple message, but others might appreciate the scholarly effort to endow a story with more range and depth than seemingly meet the eye.

The lesson here is that in reacting to any writing from the past, it may not be enough to let the writing speak for itself; rather, we might prod it for the meaning(s) of its language, the techniques that advance its objectives, the impulses behind its composition, the motivations behind its preservation, the diversity of interpretations during its transmission, and the learned attention it has gathered over time in faith traditions. When attached to a longer text, such as any extract from the Hebrew Bible, this kind of program fits snugly into what we term "a commentary." At its best, the exercise should turn into a passport to a fuller understanding of how texts meant in antiquity and how they continue to mean over the centuries. It is with such goals in mind that I offer you this first of a two-volume Anchor Yale Bible Commentary to the book of Judges.

The Book "Judges"

In Jewish tradition, following the *Tôrâ* (Pentateuch, or Five Books of Moses) and preceding the corpus of literary and wisdom texts assembled under the title *kĕtûvim* (Writings) is a compilation of books labeled *nĕvî'îm* (Prophets). This collection first rehearses the history of Israel from the conquest of the Promised Land to its brutal loss (*nĕvî'îm ri'šônîm*, former prophets). It then gathers the oracles that prophets delivered largely during that interval (*nĕvî'îm 'aḥarônîm*, later prophets). The exploits of Israel under Moses's attendant, Joshua, open the first of these collections. His tales feature a flawed capture of land by a people that has not achieved the perfection that God wished for it. Immediately following are narratives that, at their core, feature leaders commissioned to set this people on the right path. What propels this telling is the spiral of successes that these rescuers, judges, are said to achieve and the speedy stumbling on the part of the people that follows. The series of rescuing judges continues into the book that follows (1 Samuel), where both Eli and his acolyte, Samuel, are cited as such; but their rules differ from those of their predecessors in many ways, most obviously in how they come to their office, in their lack of specific military tasks, in their attachment to cultic duties, and in their presumption that their children could inherit their posts.[2]

Eventually, the blocks at either side of the core series of narrated exploits encouraged a perception of completeness, allowing the whole to constitute a book in itself. This step must have been set before the third century BCE, but how much earlier is for speculation. It is difficult, too, to ascertain how far into the past to trace the judgment that the prophet Samuel set Judges (and Ruth as well) in writing (*bBava Batra* 14b). Perhaps it was because of this last conviction on the Samuel authorship of Judges that there has never been any doubt about its place within the Jewish and Christian canons. Still, not until the Common Era do we have information about the label that was applied to the book.

The Label "Judges"

In the Talmudic tractate *bAvodah Zarah* (25a) references to Judg 17:6 are said to be taken from *sēfer hayyāšār* ("Book of the Upright"), but the phrase seems attributable to other narratives featuring Israel's heroes. In *bBava Batra* 14b, the second book in that middle division was called *šōfĕṭîm*. That Hebrew title may have been plucked from its use in Judg 2:16 and 18. As we shall soon learn, however, the word *šōfĕṭîm* is not easy to translate (see the Introductory Remarks to IIA2). Our own English name for the book, Judges, actually is derived from the Vulgate, *Liber Judicum*, itself dependent on the Septuagint κριταί.

It is difficult to ascertain, too, how far back to trace the title *šōfĕṭîm*. Writing in the second century BCE about the deeds of ancestors, Ben Sirach (Ecclesiasticus) refers to "the judges, each with his own name, whose heart did not commit fornication and who did not turn away from the LORD." While he sandwiches them between Joshua and Samuel, he does not cite the name of the book carrying their story. In the first century CE, Josephus speaks only of an interval in Israel's government as "the judges." He too does not give the book a name. The same can be said about Pseudo-Philo, who composed his wildly expansive *Biblical Antiquities* in the early second century CE. (Both of these authors will be discussed more below.)

The earliest reference to an actual name for the book comes from the first century CE. On finding an allegory in Gideon's destruction of Penuel (Judg 8:8–9), Philo refers to "the tower the name of which is displayed in the book that is entitled *the Book of Judgment*" (*Conf.*, 1.128). We need to go to the third century CE, so slightly before our Talmudic reference, to find Origen citing a book called Σαφατειμ (obviously an approximation of *šōfĕṭîm*), so confirming that the label was widespread by then. From a slightly later period (there is wide scholarly discrepancy about its date) is the pseudepigraphic *Lives of the Prophets*. It speaks of the "days of anarchy as written in Spharphotim [*sēfer šōfĕṭîm*?], that is, in the Book of Judges."[3]

The Texts of Judges
THE HEBREW TEXT

The Hebrew text of Judges has come to us in fairly good condition. In the present commentary, I have relied on both the Leningrad and the Aleppo codices. The former has grounded the critical edition of the *Biblia Hebraica Stuttgartensia* (Rüger 1990), the fourth edition in the Deutsche Bibelgesellschaft series. A fascicle of Judges for the fifth edition (*BHQ* 7, Marcos 2011) reached me too late for more than superficial use. The Aleppo Codex is the skeleton for a new edition of the *Miqra'ot gedolot*, consisting of the Targum Jonathan and the observations of a number of traditional Jewish exegetes (M. Cohen 1992).[4] Except for Judg 5, which contains what has come to be known as the Song or Poem of Deborah, the book is couched in prose of relatively straightforward comprehension. The poem, however, presents hirsute problems; yet it cannot be said that it has suffered inordinately from corruption. Together with the story of Ehud in chapter 3, it displays a rather high density of words that are unique to their contexts, forcing us into a higher mode of speculation than is normal. Yet none of these *hapax legomena* compromises a full grasp of the narrative.[5] Hebrew manuscripts of the complete Judges are comparatively "late," and they show inconsequential differences (Moore 1895; note to xliii–xliv). In them, scribal corrections (*tiqqune soferim*) are few and hardly distinctive (see at 1:27, 6:5, 7:13, 7:21, and 11:37). The few examples of passages or clauses that are duplicated in other biblical books (mostly Joshua) suggest stability in transmission. At the least, this constancy might save us from investing energy into "establishing the earliest form of the text."

The earliest extant copies of the Hebrew texts were recovered from Qumran (Ulrich 2009: 254–58, see 2011; conveniently also in Amit 1999b: 17–18).

They are few and fragmentary; nevertheless, they have provoked far-reaching claims about their implication (Trebolle Barrera 1995). There is reason to suggest that among them are copies made by inexpert scribes, dampening any urge to speculate about their effect on textual research (see the Notes to 6:7–10).

TRANSLATIONS FROM ANTIQUITY

Over the centuries, Judges has had its fair share of exegetical attention. First came the translations into the languages of the Hellenistic and Roman periods (Greek, Aramaic, and Latin), before the flood of renderings into other languages, mostly for Christian usages (Syriac, Peshiṭta, Coptic, Gothic, Armenian, Arabic—excluding Saadia's—Ethiopic, and so forth). The earliest renderings did not always share our attachment to a faithful transfer of thoughts and descriptions into a target language; rather, major goals included clarifying perceived obscurity, expanding apparent shortcomings, and neutralizing potential anthropomorphizing of the Hebrew God.[6]

Greek and Latin

From the late third century BCE on (perhaps slightly later), there were many efforts, by many hands, to translate the Hebrew and Aramaic Bible to Greek, with diverse results deceptively subsumed under the label Septuagint, or LXX. Currently there are competing proposals on reconstructing their origins, import, influence, and application.[7] As far as Judges is concerned, a number of manuscripts have suggested at least two major divergent versions (receptions?), each with disputed precursors. Accordingly, Rahlfs (1935; reprint 1979) printed both, side by side. One of them (I label it Rahlfs B; in the literature one finds LXX[B], or simply B) is based on a fourth-century CE manuscript in the Vatican. The other (Rahlfs A, also LXX[A], or A) relies on a fifth-century CE document in the British Library (Codex Alexandrinus). Since Rahlfs's edition, however, both versions have been shown to be composites that may (or may not) be dependent on antecedents, among them the Old Greek (OG).[8] The issues are too intricate for me to fully develop here, but I invite you to sample some of them in Philip Satterthwaite's fine introduction to facing translations of each version (2007). My own understanding has been enhanced by Harlé and Roqueplo's detailed commentary of 1999, with commendable comparisons between the receptions.[9] Suffice it to say that the recent findings have complicated enormously our capacity to reconstruct their move from any presumed Hebrew original(s). Already in 1895 (xliii–xlvi), Moore had come to the same conclusion.

The Latin translations hardly illumine the Hebrew Judges. That of Jerome (the Vulgate) is dependent on a Hebrew text that, albeit unvocalized, cleaves closely to our text; yet it was far from literal (W. Smelik 1995: 299–315). It superseded an Old Latin translation that was based on diverse Greek editions. In some cases, such as at 8:13, Jerome favored the Targum's reading for a place name over the Greek's. In others (7:1, 3; 12:4), he followed the Greek in re-arranging a series of verbs. He simply omitted some difficult phrases, as at 5:2 and 4, and adroitly finessed potential polytheism at 5:8.

Aramaic Targum

For centuries on both sides of the Common Era, creative knowledge of Hebrew among all but the learned elite (among them many at Qumran) was declining. As Jews were congregating in synagogues, Aramaic came to be the language by which to understand Scripture.[10] *Targûm* means "a translated text," in this case into Aramaic, and the achievement (at least) for the *nĕvî'îm* segment of the Bible is traditionally assigned to Jonathan ben Uzziel (*bMegillah* 3a), said to be a disciple of Hillel the Elder. Naturally, this is disputed, but it need only concern us here that the Targum on Judges is typical of others: expansive, with midrashic lore galore attached to translated verses, disciplined in deflecting all potential anthropomorphisms, and consistent in avoiding reference to the ineffable divine name.

I rely on W. Smelik's massive edition (1995) of the Targum of Judges. Its annotations to the Aramaic text bristle with informative notes while many of its pages offer a meticulous review of contemporary issues in Targumic studies.[11] A definite plus is a chapter (pp. 189–322) that compares the Targum of Judges with their Peshiṭta, Greek, and Vulgate equivalents. While less attached to the Hebrew original than is the Targum, the Peshiṭta seems to shun the latter's fondness for expansion; but their relationship is sharply disputed in the literature, as are the circles in which the Peshiṭta originated. I have checked into it (Dirksen 1972), as well as into other renderings, but without consistency.

The Assessment of Judges
JUDGES AND THE CONSTRUCTION OF THE PAST[12]

According to its own estimate in the received Hebrew, Judges covers several centuries, with 111 years of subjugation and 299 of independence.[13] This calculation does not include the intervals before the inauguration of Othniel, the first judge (so before 3:8), and after the death of Samson, the last judge to be named in the book.[14] But Hebrew chronography was driven by considerations other than a slavish charting of its past. Rather, there is manifest concern to impose a precharted order on the collection of traditions without particular attention to chronological or topical disjunctions. There is also concern to demonstrate authority over lore by signaling shifts in practices or in the naming of places (see the Notes on *'ad hayyôm hazzê* at 1:21; see also 20:27–28). Control of the past is starkly displayed in wielding four *bayyāmîm hāhēm* ("in those days"; at 17:6, 18:1, 19:1, and 21:25) to underscore anarchic situations that, ostensibly, would be reversed when kingship is established.[15] Such tactics fit nicely within antiquarianism, an intellectual effort that can be followed deep into the Near Eastern past, so much before it reached it richest deployment in the Neo-Babylonian period (Beaulieu 1994). Rubio (2009) nicely grasps that "collecting is not the object of antiquarianism, but rather a symptom of nostalgia as the melancholy of dispersion and loss" (157). Yet the ideology that shaped the structure and framing of historical writing was developed much earlier and might caution us about stipulating a time frame for such creations. A well-known Mesopotamian document, the Sumerian King List (SKL), may help us focus on some of these considerations as they concern Judges (see further the Introductory Remarks to IIIB).

Just under four thousand years ago, a Mesopotamian scribe by the name of Nūr-Ilabrat (NIN.ŠUBUR) collected diverse traditions into his own recension of a cuneiform document recalling past dynasties, since labeled the SKL.[16] For him, no less than for the redactors of Judges, historical accuracy was hardly the major goal; rather, it was the bolstering of self-images. He invoked two dozen cities, recalled 140 kings, and chronicled hundreds of millennia. While his historical reliability is (to say the least) suspect, we must not doubt his success in generating meaning from his compilation. A threefold conceit inspired his effort: His first assumption is that kingship was instituted about 275,000 years ago as a creative act by the gods, presumably eager to share with humans an institution that partook of their divinity. The second is that the gods would never offer kingship to more than one city at any one time, although the mechanism for transfer is war and not divine fiat. The third holds that no earthly power could be dominant forever.

First Conceit: Creation and History

Despite Israel's attachment to the supremacy of one God and its capacity to broaden an argument when relying on leather scrolls rather than on clay tablets, similar assumptions about the past are deployed in the SKL and in the book of Judges. In what came to be the received form of the Pentateuch, a God who obsesses almost exclusively about Israel observes a seventh-day respite from crafting the world, thus inspiring the Sabbath, an institution that was unique to Israel. By forging a creation etiology that had meaning only through their experience, the Hebrews launched a narrative in which they were destined to take ownership of history. The process was not presented linearly. As it concerned control of land that was promised, Israel's historiography displays a pragmatism that is surprising for accounts with theological inspiration. The patriarchal age is characterized as a period of infiltration, in which a relatively small band of Hebrews moves into a region that reacts to their arrival. Pockets of lands are acquired through purchase (Gen 23) or peacemaking (Gen 27). Moments of violence are registered (Gen 14 and 34 among them), and they too end in some territorial gains. The exodus and the conquest are foreshadowed early on (Gen 12). When they do occur, under Moses and Joshua, they involve extraordinary numbers of Hebrews, thus forcing Canaanites into a reactive violence that, in turn, justifies appropriation of their land. Judges will draw on these diverse traditions as precedents.

Second Conceit: Sequential Transfer of Divine Authority

The second of Nūr-Ilabrat's conceits is that the gods would not want power to be owned by more than one city, although they might quite readily see it more than once in that same city. In Judges, we find an adaptation of this notion. Once the election of leaders becomes the focus of Judges, power is sequentially transferred twelve times, equivalent to the idealized number of tribes.[17] (See Table I.) But rather than coming from all twelve tribes, judges are said to originate from just eight of them (Judah, Benjamin, Joseph, Naphtali, Issachar, Asher, Zebulun, and Dan), perhaps ten if we do not subsume Ephraim, Manasseh, and Gilead under Joseph, their eponymous ancestor. Ephraim and Gilead each repeats twice; the rest are restricted to one. The tribes that receive judgeship are drawn from the matriarchs Leah and Rachel, wives of Jacob, and include their surrogates Zilpah and Bilhah; yet a good half of the leaders are assigned to Joseph or his descendants (Manasseh and Ephraim). There is also reference to Israel's traditional enemies: Canaanites, Philistines, Amalekites, Moabites, and Midianites. For good measure, we have Aram-naharayim and it might reflect Syro-Aramaic powers.

It is probable that in drawing up the list of tribes that contributed judges, the effort was to broaden the selection as much as possible. Missing from the roster are Reuben, Simeon, Levi, and Gad. Reuben, Simeon, and Levi are the first three children of Leah, and they famously lost to Judah, their fourth brother, the opportunity to produce a king for Israel. Gad does not appear in Judges, and Simeon (at Judg 1) and Reuben (at Judg 5:15–16) have minor mention. Brief anecdotes are attached to five of these judges: Tola, Jair, Ibzan, Elon, and Abdon. What we are told about them basically replays a fixation on the number of children they had and the number of donkeys they owned. The remaining seven judges (eight if one includes Baraq) receive sustained narratives, each self-contained and complete, requiring no background from what precedes and delivering no justification for what succeeds. As such, with minimal adjustment they could easily be shuffled from one context to another without

Table I. The Judges of Israel[a]

[J]udge (šōfeṭ) [R]escuer (môšîʿaʿ)	Tribe	Trait	Adversary	Enemy nation	Oppression (yrs)	Peace (yrs)	Text
Othniel [R/J]	Judah	"Warrior"	Cushan-rishatayim	Aram-naharayim	8	40 (Rahlfs A: 50)	3:7–11
Ehud [R]	Benjamin	"Tyranicide"	Eglon	Moab + Ammon/Amalek	18	80	3:12–30
[Shamgar [R]][b]	"Ben-Anath"	Canaanite?		Philistines			3:31]
Deborah [J] Baraq	[Ephraim] Naphtali	"Mantic" Unmotivated	Jabin/Sisera	Canaan/Hazor Haroshet-haggoyim	20	40	4:1–5:31
Gideon/Jerubbaal [R]	Manasseh	"Skeptic"	Oreb/Zeeb Zebah/Zalmunna	Midian/Amalek	7	40	6:1–8:32
Abimelech[c]	Manasseh/Shechem	Fratricide		Intra (Shechem)		3	9:1–57
Tola [R/J]	Issachar					23	10:1–2
Jair [J]	Gilead	30 sons on 30 colts; 30 villages				22	10:3–5
Jephthah [J]	Gilead	Landless		Ammon/Ephraim	18	6 (Rahlfs B: 60)	11:1–12:7
Ibzan [J]	Asher?	30 sons; 30 daughters				7	12:8–10
Elon [J]	Zebulun					10	12:11–12

(continued)

Table I. The Judges of Israel (Continued)

[J]udge (šōfēṭ) [R]escuer (môšîʿaʿ)	Tribe	Trait	Adversary	Enemy nation	Oppression (yrs)	Peace (yrs)	Text
Abdon [J] (Bedan?; LXX: Baraq)	Ephraim	40 sons; 30 grandsons; 70 colts				8	12:13–15 (1 Sam 12:11)
Samson [R/J]	Dan	"Dolt"		Philistines	40	20+	13:1–16:31
					Total: 111	Total: 299+ (Rahlfs A: 309; Rahlfs B 353)	

aTable lists judges in the book of Judges. For judges featured in the book of Samuel, see the Introduction.

bSee IIIB, Notes to Judg 3:31, for why Shamgar does not belong in a list of judges.

cSee IIIE2, Notes to Judg 9:22 and IIIF, Notes to Judg 10:1 for Abimelech's status. For Shechem, he is a king.

seriously harming the overall compilation. Striking is the observation that no judge shares the personality or characteristic of the others: Othniel is a warrior; Ehud is a terrorist; Deborah is an augur, and a woman at that; Baraq is a diffident leader; Gideon is a skeptic in the mold of Abram/Abraham; Abimelech is an opportunist and a brute; Jephthah has self-doubts galore, inciting him to unhappy acts; and Samson seems a mindless hulk.[18] These observations on the characters of the major judges might tell us something about those editing inherited tales. Above all, however, they reinforce sustained traits about the Hebrew God: a divine unpredictability and the capacity to empower the unexpected.

Third Conceit: Earning the Promise

The third of Nūr-Ilabrat's assumptions proposes that no earthly power could be dominant forever. Invariably, after it is bestowed to one city, kingship is withdrawn and awarded to another city. Hebraic theology, however, suppresses overt hints of polytheism, and its literature upholds the conviction that any covenant must be eternal because it comes from the only God that ever exists, hence that ever matters. Throughout Scripture, there is the exhortation to love God fiercely because he alone is a god; yet incongruously there is also the call to resist the lure of other gods because, as is warned, Israel's God is jealous and unforgiving. This is stated succinctly in Deut 6:12–15, but the lesson is found at most layers of Hebraic lore. There is also this remarkable passage in Deuteronomy (31:16–21):

> The LORD said to Moses: You are soon to lie with your fathers. This people will thereupon go astray after the alien gods in their midst, in the land that they are about to enter; they will forsake me and break my covenant that I made with them. Then my anger will flare up against them, and I will abandon them and hide my countenance from them. They shall be ready prey; and many evils and troubles shall befall them. And they shall say on that day, "Surely it is because our God is not in our midst that these evils have befallen us" . . . Therefore, write down this poem and teach it to the people of Israel; put It in their mouths, in order that this poem may be my witness against the people of Israel. . . . For I know what plans they are devising even now, before I bring them into the land that I promised on oath.

In this and similar passages, we may find a parallel to Nūr-Ilabrat's belief in the fragility of power and the inevitability not so much of change as of succession. Yet, for all of Israel's inconstancy and its incapacity to keep to the one true God, its faults are not premeditated; rather, they derive from a character that its own God stamped into its DNA.[19] We might wonder about such a Calvinistic expression of predestination; but if we are (heaven forbid!) into psycho-history, we might propose that by making Israel's deficiencies primordial, its historians sought to explain why God's chosen could hardly compete with pagan neighbors. The argument is that God did make an eternal promise of land in Canaan, but Israel must keep earning it, repeatedly and painfully, long after its ancestors succeeded in capturing portions of it.

The book of Judges affirms this Sisyphean goal, by setting events in a spiral: Israel sins, generally said as a whole; an angry God unleashes enemies; Israel begs for mercy; God empowers a combative leader who occasionally rallies a few tribes to battle; Israel takes control but soon weakens its devotion, with the expected divine reaction. In this arrangement, the enemy is but a pawn, and its own reaction to acting as God's rod before becoming a punching bag is hardly ever at issue. The second chapter of Judges gives a pithy formulation for this sequence, but the idea is embedded elsewhere in Scripture and likely depends on an absorbed tradition.[20] Here we are struck by how obtrusive the narrator has chosen to be, potentially compromising our interest in tales with predictably unhappy outcomes. Even more remarkable, too, are the hints that the condition is not just for Israel, but for its God as well. In Judges, just as Israel repents but is bound to transgress, its God also punishes but is bound to forgive—for what choices are open to a God whose reputation rides on Israel's success?[21] Pivotal to the argument in Judges is the one moment (see at Judg 10:13–14) when God decides to resist saving Israel once more, with major consequences on how Israel reconstructed its institutional history. In the Comments to Judg 11–12, their significances are broached, but there will be ample reason to expand on these matters in volume 2 of this commentary.

JUDGES IN THE HEBREW BIBLE

The stories in Judges survived not just because they carried versions of history that were important to Israel, but because they were accessible, as narratives, as theology, and as examples. Specimens of traditional literature in all its senses, these stories absorbed and transmitted inherited lore over many generations. Through our received Hebrew text, we are heirs to this lore, and we find echoes of it beyond the verses that will soon be familiar to us. There is the opening of the book of Ruth (1:1), which sets a story "when the judges were ruling" (*vayyĕhî bîmê šĕfōṭ haššōfĕṭîm*). A family is shown as escaping God's Promised Land in time of famine. Famines are instruments of God's punishment, and even if none is mentioned in our received version of Judges, penitence rather than evasion of consequence is surely the desired lesson. The predictable catastrophe follows, but upon the return of a remnant to Bethlehem a miraculous reversal of fortune is told in some of Scripture's most lyrical verses. The tale is about ordinary people achieving extraordinary ends when they care for each other; but if it be noticed that Ruth is also a subtle parable for rising from ashes, the linkage with Judges and its many near-perdition experiences might be apparent.

Ruth came to be so closely attached to Judges, in fact, that in the Greek canon of Scripture, the book is set immediately following Judges.[22] Josephus follows this cue by locating the famine in the days of Eli (*Ant.* 5.318). Chronologically more sparing, the *Seder Olam* (see below) of a few generations later sets the whole in the days of Ehud, likely exploiting lore that connects Ruth to Eglon (see the Notes to Judg 3:12).

There is also an allusion of a different sort to the "days of the judges" at 2 Kgs 23:22–23. During the reign of King Josiah (the second half of the seventh century BCE), Judah moved vigorously to revitalize convictions and institutions deemed to have been drafted at Sinai. Among them was the Passover sacrifice, whose ritual was said to have been neglected "in that manner since the time when judges ruled Israel [*mîmê haššōfĕṭîm ʾăšer šāfĕṭû ʾet-yiśrāʾēl*], including when kings ruled Judah and Israel." As far as the received Hebrew text, this notice in 2 Kings had it technically correct, and we have to go back to the book of Joshua (5:10–11) to locate in Hebrew lore the previous celebration of Passover.[23] This notice confirms the tradition that the judges era was not thought to be suited for carrying on divinely set rituals. Moreover, the sequence it cites implies that Eli and Samuel were not fully distanced from the other judges.

JUDGES IN LATE ANTIQUITIES

Until fairly recently, after the triumph of biblically inspired monotheism in western Asia and Europe, Judges was not so much interpreted as applied. There was hardly any reason to question its essential historicity; rather, the arguments in the opening chapters for the spiral of events were convincing as an explanation for the unfolding of events. Jewish, Christian, and to a lesser degree Muslim reflections on its narratives drew teaching lessons from the actions of each and all personalities. In doing so, there was much opportunity for allegorical and typological applications, validating the conviction that Scripture is indeed an eternal charter for human behavior.

To assess from its citation in the New Testament, Apocrypha, and Pseudepigrapha, Judges was a source of modest inspiration. In the Notes and Comments of this volume, I refer to those known to me. I have also done the same for selected references in the Talmud and the church fathers. Those from the former corpus are relatively few and are accessible in a narrated form in Ginzberg (2003: 855–85). Those from the latter corpus are (as far as I know) not yet collected or fully reviewed, but a nice study on Gideon from patristic sources is available in Légasse (1985; see also 1991). Second- and third-century CE synagogal prayers, Jewish in origin but Christian in final garb, invoke the help God had given a number of judges, despite manifest shortcomings.[24] The implication is that God might do the same for us.

Rewritten Judges

Two avenues for drawing or enlarging on biblical narratives developed as the millennium was forging into the Common Era. The first of these need not concern us here. It included many narratives that set freshly imagined stories into the biblical period, embedding personalities known from Scripture. Familiar examples, because they found a place in the LXX, would include Judith, Susanna, and Tobit. Less known (but no less interesting) are such "novellas" as *Joseph and Aseneth*, the *Martyrdom of Isaiah*, and the *Testament of Abraham*.[25]

There is also another category of reactions to Scripture; in this case, the familiar is rewritten, with passages reshaped, the sequence reset, and gaps filled (Nickelsburg 1984: 89–156). Most importantly, its message is redirected. Debatable is whether or not to include here those books that experience radical genre change through judicious insertions. *The Genesis Apocryphon*, which covers the first fifteen chapters of the Torah, can be cited as an example. The Greek Esther, in all its versions, makes for another fine illustration, moving from travesty (serious subject, lightly treated) in the Hebrew version, to apocalypse (hidden knowledge, later resolved) in one of the Greek versions. In the case of Judges, I have liberally cited in the Notes and Comments from two major redrafts of episodes in the book because they sporadically disclose interesting readings of the Scripture on which they relied. More importantly, these efforts reveal an interest in reaching new audiences.

JOSEPHUS AND HIS *JEWISH ANTIQUITIES*

Writing toward the end of the first century CE, Josephus had in mind a non-Jewish readership. For this reason, he offers explanations for institutions peculiar to Judaism (the Sabbath, circumcision, and the like), occasionally reshuffles material for a smoother narrative (for which he apologizes to fellow Jews), dampens egregiously challenging miraculous events (Jonah in the fish, for example), and includes clarifications not in the text, especially as they concern bizarre Jewish laws. Expansions (such as in the story of Joseph) play on elements in the Hellenistic novel or advance the cause of Hebraic aristocracy, among them presenting Moses as a prince in Egypt, the fodder for the Hollywood treatment of the subject.

As concerns Judges, in Book 5 Josephus is frontal about bringing out lessons that could easily be grasped. Immediately after opening on chapters in which, as in the Hebrew text, Israel is haltingly successful against the entrenched inhabitants of the Promised Land, Josephus moves directly to the closing chapters. Israel had become effeminate and wanted only to enjoy what it had achieved. Indolence brought internal strife, directly leading to the horrors described in Judg 19–21 and, not incidentally, giving the tribe of Benjamin ample time to recuperate. Yet God is merciful, and when external threats occur, he sends Othniel to rally Israel. In this way, Josephus loops back to the heroes and can now focus on their nobility of character. (The same approach is taken by the *Seder Olam Rabbah*; see below.) In his hand, the story of Ehud is paradigmatic. A warrior with unusual skills—here Josephus has better insights on Ehud's talent than a good number of scholars—Ehud is motivated to seek liberty for his people. Diplomatic and brave, he confronts Eglon and kills him by driving a dagger into his heart (not his belly). He rules longer than any other judge. Given a Roman audience that has had its fill of imperious queens (Cleopatra), combative Jews, and uppity Jewish women (Berenice), Josephus omits the Song of Deborah and diminishes her role in favor of Baraq's.

Gideon is another of Josephus's heroes, a paragon of Jewish leadership, his piety not besmirched by any construction of pagan paraphernalia. Gideon's destruction of pagan altars is minimized, lest it offend. Less understandable is the omission of the execution of Midianite kings, since Romans made such acts a focus for ceremonial triumphs. (Think of what happened to Vercingetorix!) More nuanced is Josephus's portrayal of Jephthah. He is brave and resolute yet also the maker of foolish vows, for which he is roundly condemned. Samson gets a haircut, morally and ethically. He is handsome and wise; his father is a leader, but faulted for his jealousy; his mother is exceedingly beautiful. His name means "strong," and he is slated to be a prophet. Samson takes credit for discomfiting his enemies in skirmishes and, despite his noble traits, succumbs to the weakness of flesh. Yet it all leads to a redemptive death. With Samson's demise, Josephus can move directly into the judgeship of Eli, told in the first chapters of 1 Samuel.

In citing Josephus, I have used Whiston's translation (Whiston 1960). Far from being current, it has the advantage instead of wide posting on the Web. I have also relied on Feldman's massive assessment of Josephus's art (1998).

PSEUDO-PHILO'S *LIBER ANTIQUITATUM BIBLICARUM*

Another late-first-century work, the *Liber antiquitatum biblicarum* (*LAB*), is attributed to Philo; hence its author is commonly cited as Pseudo-Philo, and I continue to use this mislabel. I have relied on Jacobson's fine edition (1996), but also Harrington's translation (1985).[26] The copies of the *LAB* that have reached us are in Latin, but many presume a Hebrew original for it. The author takes up Israel's history through the death of Saul, with eccentric shrinkage of interest. The patriarchs are treated in one brief segment (§8). The legal material sandwiched between the exodus and the conquest also gets short shrift, the accent being on confrontations, mostly between God and his people (for example, the golden calf and the Korah insurrection), with an all-powerful God ready to punish idolatry and linkage with idolaters. Given a predilection for midrashic expansions on relatively confined narratives, Pseudo-Philo grooves on Judges, with fully a third of the *LAB* devoted to its affairs as well as with bravura augmentations. On Kenaz (Cenez), father of Othniel, there are four chapters (25–28).[27] Zebul occurs next, with much debate in the scholarly literature about his identity, for nothing about his actions reminds of those of Ehud. An Eod, normally Greek for Ehud, occurs later, but he is an entirely evil character. Pseudo-Philo has a pronounced affection for the women of Judges, Deborah and Jephthah's daughter especially—so much so that there is good speculation that a woman is behind the text (DesCamp 1997: 76–80).

Another spurious attribution to Philo is *On Samson* (*De Sampsone*), a Jewish sermon preserved in Armenian only. In the next volume of this commentary on Judges, I will cite it from Siegert and de Roulet (1999).

JUDGES IN THE QUR'AN

No character from Judges is directly recalled in the Qur'an; however, an incident involving Ṭâlût (likely Saul) is evocative of one involving the biblical Jephthah (Judg 12:1–6). Ṭâlût is selected to lead Israel. On his way to meet Jâlût (Goliath), he tests his followers,

> saying, "Allah will surely test you at a river. Whoever drinks its water is not mine—and whoever does not drink is mine—except he who takes it in the hollow of his hand." So they all drank it, except a few of them. When Ṭâlût and the believers with him had crossed the river, they said, "We do not have power now to face Jâlût and his armies." Those who were certain of meeting Allah [that is, of dying] said, "Many a times has a smaller group overcome a bigger group by Allah's grace." Allah is indeed with the steadfast. (Sura 2 [*The Cow*]: 249–51)

Still, Ṭâlût's followers rise to the occasion, among them Dâwûd (David), who kills Jâlût.[28]

In later Muslim lore, only Samson (Shamshûn) among the judges seems to have provoked much interest (Takim 2004). In Sîra literature, however, the Battle at Badr—a turning point in the fortunes of Muhammad—is preceded by a dream manifested in the camp of the enemy, likely inspired by Judg 7:4–8 (see Von Mžik 1915). Muslim historiographers who strove to achieve universal histories, however, did consult the biblical testaments and made reference to a number of personalities in Judges (Sokolow 1979). An interesting commentator is al-Yaʿḳūbī, a Shiʿî from the ninth century, and I cite him from Ebied and Wickham (1970).

The Book of Judges in Contemporary Liturgy[29]

The Book of Judges is a modest source for liturgical application:

1. Among *Orthodox and Conservative Jews*, three extracts from Judges are linked to Sabbath readings from the Pentateuch, a like number of excerpts as are taken each from Joshua and the books of Samuel.[30] How early this conjunction between Torah and the Prophets took place is hard to say. Acts 13:1 and Luke 4:16–20 remain our earliest sources for the practice of linking the Sabbath readings of segments from the Torah and the Prophets. There are conjectures (see the *EncJud*, 16: 1342–45) that the practice began during the persecutions that led to the Hasmonean revolt.

2. No readings from Judges are attached to the *Roman Catholic* lectionary for Sundays and major feasts. The weekday masses follow a two-year cycle. During Advent–Christmas and Lent–Easter, the first reading comes from the Gospels or, during Easter, from the Acts of the Apostles. For the remainder of each year, reading alternates between semicontinuous readings from Old Testament books and New Testament books other than the Gospels. On Monday through Thursday of week 20 in Year One, the first reading is Judg 2:11–19 (divine selection of judges), Judg 6:11–24a (Gideon selected as rescuer), Judg 9:6–15 (Jotham's fable), and Judg 11:29–39a (Jephthah and his daughter). For Friday and Saturday of that week the readings are selections from the first two chapters of Ruth.

3. There is little reading from the Old Testament in the Sunday divine liturgy of *Orthodox churches*, and none from Judges. In the vespers service for Theophany (January 6), celebrating the baptism of Jesus Christ and the revelation of the Holy Trinity, the sign of the fleece delivered to Gideon (Judg 6:36–40) is one Old Testament reading.[31]

4. The Consultation on Common Texts provides options for the Old Testament readings in the Revised Common Lectionary of *Anglican and Protestant* communions, thus accommodating different understandings of linkage between the testaments. While most employ a typological understanding, and thus selection, of Old Testament passages in relation to gospel passages during the special seasons of the year (that is, Advent–Christmas and Lent–Easter), some continue this typological approach for the remainder of each year as well. Judges 4:1–7 is one of the options for the first reading on a Sunday toward the very end of Year A of a three-year cycle (numbered "Proper 28" in nearly all the church lectionaries).

The Study of Judges in the Modern Era

> The whole is a treasure hunt where the treasure is time and the hiding place the past. . . . The key to the problem of reestablishing the past turns out to be the key of art.
> —*Vladimir Nabokov, on Proust's* À la recherche du temps perdu[32]

Absorption with the Bible is a very humanistic enterprise. In the West, few documents from the past have remained under inspection so consistently and for so long. Evaluating the import of its pages has promoted conversations over the ages, eventually crossing religious, cultural, and language divides. Since late antiquity and through the Middle Ages, Judges has gathered its share of exegetical attention from leaders of individual confessions. With opportunity to derive devotional instruction from Judges remaining scarce, allegorical, typological, and mystical readings stoked piety and inspired homilies.[33] Jewish sages annotated Judges, explicating individual words or phrases rather than commenting on the book's construction. Midrash readily buttressed their readings, and their pedagogic goal was moral rather than historical or anthropological. Many of these commentators are gathered in the *Miqra' ot gedolot*. Beyond finding inspiration in the occasional sermon, Christians could turn to decoration (mostly paintings) at monumental buildings for nicely prescribed interpretation. As far as I know, Judges did not inspire any medieval mystery plays.

The Renaissance, the Reformation, the Christian reacquaintance with the Hebrew Bible, the invention of printing, and a renewed search for lost tribes in the newly "discovered" worlds are among many factors contributing to a fuller detailing of Judges. For our purposes, however, none of these occasions generated as urgent an impetus as the more precise control of biblical languages, the critical assessment of the Hebrew text, the West's renewed exposure to biblical lands, and the decipherment of the lost languages of the ancient Near East. In consequence, the more "modern" commentaries to Judges began to be printed during the past two centuries.

To this day, a good number of commentaries continue to forward confessional objectives, and I have consulted several for their traditional understanding of a narrative in which the role of God as a major mover of events is apt to be primary. However, I have relied most on contributions from the modern period in which Scripture is treated as a human confection and as a literary product of its time, both propositions inviting countless reactions. Such commentaries wrestle with critical issues about the received Hebrew words, among them comparing variant readings, fixing their meanings past and present, and speculating on their fusion into the present form. In the most recent generations, several by-forms and derivatives of these methods have enriched scholarship, each sharpening the focus on specific problems by multiplying the questions or enlarging the perspectives from which to answer them. (Post)modernist, (post)structuralist, postcolonial, and feminist perceptions are among the more imaginative veins that are explored.[34] Below, I survey representative commentaries that stress scholarly undertakings.

ACCENT ON SOURCES[35]

The traditional attribution of Judges to the pen of the prophet Samuel—or at least to his circle—was not challenged meaningfully until the early nineteenth century. Especially in Germany, components of Judges were assigned to a full palette of sources, familiar to us now under the sigla JEDP, each with multiple manifestations.[36] Increasingly since then, what Israel wished to be recalled about the interval covered in Judges and how modern scholarship assesses the same period came to be distinct constructs. The Yahwist and Elohist had been assigned a large part of Joshua, so it was natural that globs of Judges were similarly allotted. This was the position of Budde (1890), whose commentary had great authority and was more or less followed by Moore (1895), the finest of its genre. True, the Deuteronomist was said to have left marks (2:6–3:6), and not a few commentators (Lagrange [1903] among them) found themselves ready to give his circle firm control of most of the introductory material. The Priestly circles, too, had their contributions to make, especially in diverse notices about land fought for and lost in the opening chapters and in the events involving Gibeah. There were earnest debates about how much of the Song of Deborah reflected the event itself. Many were persuaded that its rhetoric and language are evidence of uncontaminated transmission. Inevitably, strands were disentangled, allowing for the recovery of traditions thought to once have been separate. Many followed Holzinger's notion that originally Jephthah pursued separate wars against Ammon and Moab (Burney 1970: 299). Once separate traditions, they eventually congealed into the present account.

A major transition in the academic study of Judges occurred in the commentary of Burney (1918 and 1920). Burney participated in the effort to find in Judges an application of the documents shaping the Hexateuch (Genesis to Joshua) but demurred from any Deuteronomistic contribution, assigning instead much to an "Ephraimite school of prophetic teachers" (1970: xii–xiii). With him, however, the debate about the role of foundational sources in the crafting of a fused version of Judges had reached its peak.[37] Nonetheless, what distinguished Burney's commentary from those of his predecessors is its unprecedented investment in ancient Near Eastern history. Ostensibly focusing on Canaan, Burney devotes dozens of pages to the Western Mediterranean, following the Semites from their entry (as it was then imagined) into the arena through the exodus (in its many possible settings). In this regard, he was a fine reader of the archeologist Hugo Winckler (whom he cites), who was among the first to situate Israel's history within those of its neighbors. Yet, I cannot say that Burney does much with all that, and his accent on the interval separating Hammurabi from Solomon is beyond need for correction; but in focusing many pages on the Amarna period, with its rich details about the Habirus (then as now with debated linkage to Hebrew ancestors), he was crafting a much imitated backdrop for Judges.

ACCENT ON REDACTION HISTORY

A newer phase of research on Judges was inspired by a refinement in the study of the forms and contexts for the redaction of biblical works. As shaped by Gunkel, the approach was much invested in oral transmission: Any biblical tradition had a potential prehistory, thus compromising the proximate dating source criticism promoted for it. Ironically enough, the premise gave investigators the freedom to reassess the development of traditions, seeking clues not just from linguistic features or from the progressive elaboration of its institutions, but from Israel's version of its history. During the Second World War, Noth proposed that Judges belonged to a sequence of material that was compiled a generation or so after the fall of Jerusalem in 586 by a historiographer he would label the "Deuteronomistic Historian."[38] Since his epoch-making study, several competing theories developed on how and why this material was processed over centuries. Some simply offer minor adjustments to Noth's hypothesis;[39] others want to dispense with it, precisely because in their opinion Judges does not fit.[40] Most influential were the proposals of Richter (1963 and 1964), who suggested an evolution for Judges that discriminated between northern narratives centering on local *môšî'îm*, "saviors," from those with *šōfĕṭîm*, "judges."[41] Revisions were undertaken in several redactions, each leaving a sign of its own investment in Israel's moral background (its sins, its capacity to absorb retribution, its propensity for apostasy, and the like) or in its attitude to the monarchy (Becker 1990), and so delivering a final product with the consequent fault lines. These redactors, however, leave clues of single-minded interest: Some are historians (DtrH), some are nourished by prophetic ideals (DtrP), some are keen to advance legalistic arguments (DtrN), and some have purely priestly interests.[42]

The current trend within this approach, however, is to find multiple phases of Deuteronomistic manipulations and editing. They are said to be affected by the political situation then in effect—from Assyrian hegemony to Macedonian control—and are heavily influenced by their literary styles. The covenantal phraseology in the book of Deuteronomy is said to draw on late-Assyrian treaties, and the military descriptions in Joshua are said to be inspired by Assyrian reports. Judges is discussed as a pastiche, its language and ideology betraying centuries of manipulations, since the last days of the Northern Kingdom until the Hellenistic era.[43] Its core, however, is thought to be set in Achaemenid Yehud, when Judahites regrouped in their land but lacked their own monarchs. These proposals offer shifting contexts for any tradition and generally privilege polyglot, cosmopolitan, yet impressionable Hebrew narrators or redactors, with much too easy access to the same ancient historical lore (to use or to reject) that is now amassed in our library shelves. Yet, when it comes to knowledge about their own past, these redactors seem to be aware of nothing beyond the same scriptural traditions that have survived to our own days. These premises certainly complicate, but do not make impossible, any effort to set dates for the many phases in the composition, transmission, and editing of Judges.

ACCENT ON CULTURAL AND SOCIAL CONTEXTS

Commentaries and studies on Judges continue to appear, and while none but those oriented to a confessional audience ignores concerns such as those just raised, the trend is toward highlighting meaning and reception, often accompanied by marked attention to the book's social context, that is, to the milieu in which it was generated. Also in them is a willingness to absorb the results of specialized literary studies of Judges, with striking achievements, a number of which will be cited in the Notes and Comments. An interesting example is Amit's commentary to Judges (1999b), with ideas distilled from a major study (Hebrew, 1992; English, 1999a) on how the book of Judges was edited into the version familiar to us. In her opinion, editors (eventually authors) aimed not so much to preserve traditions or historical truth, but to transmit lessons from the narrated past to future generations. "Signs," portending divine guidance or intervention, and "leadership," displayed in the series of recurring acts of success and failure, are two major characteristics in tandem with the process that was likely undertaken in reaction to the fall of the Northern Kingdom; "Judges reflect the literary materials that influenced the shaping of Deuteronomy and its school, and that its own composition preceded the reign of Josiah" (1999a: 364; see also Amit 2009). To me, all this is vaguely reminiscent of the Richter school, whose tenets Amit with some success vigorously contests. She is syncretistic rather than atomistic, proposing steps on how diverse strands emerged by x-raying the book as a fulfilled unit so as to better expose its anatomy.

Soggin has offered Judges commentaries (1981a, 1987) that do not ignore issues raised on the many layers of Deuteronomistic redactions across the great exile divide. He makes a solid contribution that avoids concrete theorizing about the production of Judges.[44] Olson (1998) is joined by others (Oeste 2011b; Levin 2012: 315–16) in pursuing the theme of an increasingly corrupt Israel as one of the schemes for the edited Judges. Block (1999) accepts the infallibility of Scripture; nonetheless, he rejects a single authorship in favor of a product informed by the stream of Mosaic theological and literary tradition.[45] The book illustrates the danger of assimilation, for, despite the participation of divinely commissioned judges, Israel sinks progressively deeper into Canaanization, a term that for him can only have negative connotations. Brettler (2002) has Judges replay the confrontations between the lines of Saul and of David and display a sharp preference for Judah over Israel (see Wong 2005 and Frolov 2007). Butler (2009) places the audience of Judges as a witness to the division of the kingdom; its tales allow it "to decide which king to follow and which sanctuary to recognize as the true center of worship" (lxxiv). He reckons that Judah wins this audience's approbation. Butler's study is an excellent source for diverse readings and previous opinions. Oeste (2011a) tests Judg 9 for an unprejudiced notion of kingship. There, Abimelech's regional rule is faulted, with an implied approval of a centralized monarchy. Irwin (2012) thinks the book reflected postexilic anxiety on who will lead in troubled times. Swanson (2012) finds wholesale parody in Judges, with leadership—its failure and absence—as its main target. Remarkable in such suggestions is how much they wed the Hebrew imagination of centuries ago to just the material in our received Scripture.

ACCENT ON ARCHEOLOGICAL EVIDENCE

Burney's passion for historicizing Judges was a harbinger. Largely ignored in its day, his commentary was reissued in 1970 with an affirming "Prolegomenon" by William Albright. Boling's Anchor Bible volume (1975), too, is anchored in the knowledge of Bronze Age history and archeology (see below). Boling turned to the then imperfectly grasped Middle-Euphrates Mari documents that date to the eighteenth century BCE to resolve cruxes in Judges.[46] He also advanced a proposal for the growth of Judges.[47] Yet he was keenest to demonstrate that the stories in Judges, "stemming from the early days were fixed in all their essentials before they were employed in telling the authoritative story of Israel's life in Canaan" (1975: 29).

In the Notes and Comments of the present commentary there will be ample occasions to discuss proposals to set Judges within a history of Late Bronze and Early Iron Age Western Asia (see especially under Judges Deborah [IIIC] and Gideon [IIID]). Suffice it to say here that the challenges are at least threefold. The first is internal to the Hebrew Bible and has to do with reconciling the interval for Judges as given in its verses (Hebrew Bible, 410; Rahlfs A, 420; Rahlfs B, 464) with the notice in 1 Kgs 6:1 that has 480 years separating the exodus from the construction of the temple. When other biblical records are computed, however, this gap stretches almost a century longer.[48]

The second complication has to do with evaluating what is regarded as contrasting memory of how Israel came into Canaan after leaving Egypt. Joshua is said to give a Blitzkrieg version of the conquest, while the first chapters of Judges present it as a series of hiccuppy skirmishes between native groups and diverse elements that later coalesce into Israel. The notion is broadly repeated in the literature, more for investing credibility in at least one biblical version of the occupation of Canaan than for any certain confirmation through archeological or textual means. A third approach, launched in early-twentieth-century America (Wallis 1912) but achieving initial credibility half a century later (Mendenhall 1962; but especially in Gottwald 1979), proposes that economic lack and zeal for the god Yʜᴠʜ prompted indigenous, communitarian peasants to confederate and overpower hierarchical and urbanized Canaanites. Lack of adequate evidence for internal revolts, a much too uncontaminated notion of Yahwism in early Israel, and assignment of crucial texts to a later period have undermined this theory. However, even those who reject it for its anachronistic insurgency ideology have retained its reliance on social scientific perspectives. This research component is now thoroughly integrated in recent discussions, as will be obvious in inspecting the third challenge to calibrating the historical worth of Judges.

This third difficulty has to do with the relatively restricted spans most historians and archeologists allot for the formation of Israel, at the conquest and during the Judges era. They circumstantially set it to follow the collapse of Egyptian and Canaanite domination in the wake of incursions by Sea Peoples. This seminal stage *should* archeologically correspond with Iron I (1200–1000 BCE), yet the fit between the biblical material and the largely nonepigraphic archeological surveys does not make for a persuasive match. After a painstaking review of the evidence, here is what Bloch-Smith and Nakhai (1999) conclude about the conquest stage: "Were it not for the Bible, no late thirteenth–early twelfth century Israelite invasion would be suspected. For the most part, language, dress, pottery, architecture, and cultic features demonstrate continuity from the LBA [Late Bronze Age] into the Iron Age. Early 'Israelite' access to perennial water sources necessitated a working relationship with the autochthonous population. While towns and cities were destroyed in the appropriate period, they do not necessarily correspond to the cities allegedly destroyed by the 'Israelites.' In addition, no one can prove that the 'Israelites' were the agents of destruction" (118–19). Nonetheless, Bloch-Smith and Nakhai rely on the Judges account to explain an increase in population in the highlands.[49] Finkelstein treats the same evidence as "part of a long-term, cyclic mechanism of alternating processes of sedentarization and nomadization of indigenous groups in response to changing political, economic, and social circumstances . . . the early Israelites were, in fact, Canaanites" (in Finkelstein, Mazar, and Schmidt 2007: 83). Much scholarly literature gravitates toward versions of these arguments. Yet, without uncovering a nice cache of reliable extrabiblical records, arriving at convincing reconstructions will remain a challenge.[50] There is also the question of how far to entrust historians and archeologists with arbitrating many matters in Judges that are impervious to historical research.

ACCENT ON THE EPIC STYLE

Boling's Anchor Bible commentary also argued a role for folklore in the shaping of Judges. Following David's success, an epic worthy of Israel's past was forged out of strands of inherited lore about Israel's ancestors. The whole was updated and revised subsequently, but fragments of the epic remained embedded in Judges. Until the 1960s, application of the term "epic" to biblical lore had been haphazard, occasional, tentative, elastic, and accommodating. It received stronger affirmation in the writings of F. M. Cross (1973, 1998), who offered it as a ballast in Israel to the forging of myths in Canaan. The argument was forcefully rejected by Talmon. In two essays (collected in 1993; see also Alter 1981: 25–26), Talmon pointed out that the use of prose in biblical narrative defuses most of the proposed arguments for an epic style.[51] Nonetheless, a generation later, the idea of an epic as a form of biblical historiography informs Niditch's attractive recent commentary (2008; see also Niditch 2010). For her, Judges depicts heroes who are brave and bold, who find divine help, and who might use guile—all epic traits according to some folklorists. Yet, even when these elements are granted, it is difficult to apply them uniformly to most judges without overlooking gross shortcomings.[52] Missing in Judges, too, are basic elements in epic style, among them the journey and the transformation of the hero. The judges of Judges mostly stay put and, despite their absorption of divine splendor, hardly gain introspectively.[53]

ACCENT ON THE RECEPTION OF JUDGES

For centuries, Scripture has nourished the artistic imagination. In novels, the theater, and poetry, as well as in film, video, oratorio, and opera, the artist exploits core biblical texts to fill gaps, expand action, and thicken characters. On the canvas or through a plastic medium, the eye tends to be reductive, capturing a series of biblical moments or episodes into one image that sharpens their essence.[54] Not all characters in the book of Judges quickened artistic inspiration equally. Hardly noticed were the deeds of Othniel, Achsah, Ehud, Shamgar, Abimelech, Micah, or, not surprisingly, of any of the five "minor" judges. However, Deborah, Gideon, Jephthah, and Samson were nicely represented. In the art of the church and even in some oratorios, some features in their stories replayed typologies associated with the (alleged) obstinacy of the synagogue or the passion of Christ. There is a large critical literature on the artistry of such creations and on the contexts in which they were produced; only in recent days, however, has biblical scholarship entered into a dialogue with these achievements. A delightful volume is Gunn (2005), now sold under the title *Judges Through the Centuries*. With a light touch, it surveys centuries of reactions, responses, and readings (from and into) Judges, in print, in art, and in children's illustrations. Given the immense material available, it cannot be comprehensive, but it is hard to match its lucidity and the liveliness of its style. I found in it chestnuts galore and report on some of them in the Notes and Comments.[55]

Studies of recent vintage are bringing the biblical text(s) in dialogue with the arts. Some appear in collections (among them, Barton, Exum, and Oeming 2005; Exum and Nutu 2007; and Exum 2007) and others in journals increasingly devoted to such examinations (such as *Prooftexts* [1981–], *Biblical Interpretation* [1993–], and *Biblical Reception* [2012–]). In these pages, what the biblical text has meant to its readers down the centuries is the subject of scholarly attention. In just one year (2007), several essays explored Deborah's victory over Canaan and Jael's murder of Sisera: Christianson (2007) explored how one genre of cinema (the film noir) shares with the biblical account "a remarkably similar rhetoric of ambiguity" (169); Leneman (2007) studied Pizzetti's *Debora e Jaele*, an opera that reconfigures biblical characters, amplifying "the moral ambiguities found in the original narrative" (428); and Exum (2007) focused on a Dutch painting of 1635, Salomon de Bray's *Deborah, Jael, and Barak*, to problematize their roles in the biblical text.

A CONCLUDING REMARK

The most obvious impression that might be drawn from the above cursory inspection of generations of Judges commentaries is how wedded their critical inspirations are to the major scholarly trends evolving over recent generations: from source analysis in the second half of the nineteenth century to the literary evaluations (of all sorts) at the threshold of the twenty-first. Equally obvious is how, over time, regnant critical schemes shatter and are supplanted by an ever-expanding abundance of resources and methodologies. Loprieno (1996) relies on the study of ancient Egyptian literature to chart a humanistic shift in the past century from historiocentric to reception models when analyzing cultural remains. The reasons for this development as it applies to the Bible are worthy of speculation elsewhere, but they must include the splintering of European-centered biblical exegesis, the investment of non-Protestants in recovering themes central to the Hebrew Bible, the vigorous interpretive reaction (especially in North America) of conservative (even "fundamentalist") scholarship, the easy access to (and often lightly absorbed adaptation of) approaches current in the humanities and the social sciences, and—by no means least—the immense contributions of the archeology of ancient Israel.

The corollary to all this persistent fragmenting or regrouping of convictions on the formation of Judges is that what is proposed even by the finest minds on the origin and adaptation of Judges traditions is not likely to garner unanimous or long-lasting acceptance. Yet, to say that vexing issues are beyond definitive resolution, now and in the future, should not lead to dejection or cynicism. Rather, it might encourage a deeper appreciation of the procreative nature of scholarship as it tackles seemingly intractable matters. We might also keep in mind that each methodology, even when it fails to achieve lasting solutions, generates new vocabularies and grammars, indeed new discourses that stimulate enriching perspectives by which to reinspect the Bible, the greatest of gifts that Israel—indeed, the ancient Near East—has willed us.

This Anchor Yale Bible Judges

In 1975, the Anchor Bible series, then published by Doubleday, offered Robert Boling's fine commentary to Judges (AB 6A). I have already cited his skill as a scholar (he also coauthored the AB Joshua) and archeologist (Tananir, Shechem) but need to mention here his finely tuned ear for contemporary idiom and his deployment of snappy lines that often ended in exclamation points ("Yahweh is with you, aristocrat!," at Judg 6:12). A bonus is the set of archeological maps and illustrations that help make the narratives more concrete. In one volume, Boling's effort remains a handy commentary to consult. Still, there is now this volume of the Anchor Yale Bible, and it behooves me to tell you what you will find in it.

This commentary is to the Hebrew version of Judges, as received in our days. In it, I try to fulfill goals as developed above: to expand comprehension of the Hebrew text by explaining its meaning, exploring its contexts, and charting its effect over time. I therefore accept the challenge of illuminating the words as are now printed in our oldest codices ("Leningrad" and "Aleppo"; see above), together with their vowels, accents, and punctuation. You will soon find out, however, that I do not shy away from citing variant or divergent readings in the few Hebrew fragments from Qumran and that I readily call on testimonies from diverse Greek, Aramaic, and Latin renderings when explaining passages. They will have a place in the Notes and will receive much attention as valuable exegetical witnesses. What I do not do is prefer one reading over another or assume that one reading is based on a better text than another. I do not emend the text, even when it is obviously crotchety; I do not remove material that might be interpolated; I do not draw from other sources to inject language ostensibly lost in transmission.

I am not attached to the Masoretic Text (MT) out of religious orthodoxy or pious conviction but because I take it as my task to comment on the Hebrew

Judges that has survived the centuries rather than the better text that ought to have reached us. Though it is quite likely that ancient translators once worked from Hebrew texts with less cranky passages, it is just as likely that they struggled over the same problematic verses that are before us now. One reason for their difficulty may have to do with the fact that the Hebrew they knew gravitated toward the mishnaic and so differed sensibly from the grammar that controlled the production of the consonantal Judges.[56] I therefore treat each version as a testament to its own understanding of a passage. In the process, rather than reducing a comprehension of Judges to reconstructed verses, I hope to explore a richer interpretive vein as over the centuries translators and expositors felt obligated to instruct and edify even when facing difficult or mystifying passages.

The translation I offer is neither literal (word-for-word correspondence) nor equivalent (matching what is deemed to be the intent); rather, it strives for easy comprehension without disregarding the original Hebrew construction. When sense is advanced, I have (rarely) expanded on the original Hebrew text either between parentheses or by resorting to *italics*.

CONTENTS

A commentary is not a thesaurus and should not be a dumping site for previous notions. Still, it will be obvious that I deploy a vast array of documentation and instruments in my pages, even on issues and matters in which I am not invested. Much of the annotation is internal to the discussion on Judges and reports on judgments in commentaries, articles, surveys, and biblical dictionaries. But it does include a fair sampling from ancient Near Eastern documents to illumine a biblical passage or to bolster an interpretation of a context. I do not appeal to ancient lore to re-create or complete a biblical scene, but to illustrate how actions or events unfolded elsewhere under comparable circumstances. Earlier in this Introduction, I turned to the early-second-millennium Mesopotamian Sumerian King List to clarify the structuring principles that underlie the book of Judges. In the pages that follow, I will draw on the archives of many neighboring cultures from across the centuries to illustrate, explain, or develop certain matters raised in Judges. However, I will favor most those from Mari, not least because I have some familiarity with them. Although I do not dismiss the many centuries that severed direct linkage between Mari and Israel, I find it appealing that the narrative style of its Amorite-spiked Akkadian letters comes closest to that of Hebrew prose, in its thick incrustation of anecdotes as well as its care of presentation and timing of utterances. Furthermore, its documentation affords much insight into living contexts, among them days of war and peace, settings urban and tribal, and activities of the privileged and the disadvantaged.[57]

FORMAT

I happily follow the format of the Anchor Bible series. It is always a judgment call on how to apportion the annotated biblical text into a sequence of commentary sections. Perfectly reasonable is to follow the chapter division scheme as inherited since the Middle Ages, such as in Niditch's recent Old Testament Library contribution (2008). Block (1999) gathers it all into three portions, with a script that focuses on what he considers to be the progressive "Canaanization" of Israel: (1) the background, (2) God's response, and (3) climax.[58] Boling divides the same material into twenty-eight segments. I have done it in twenty, taking as a frequent inspiration (conveniently rather than slavishly) a likely pre-Masoretic allocation of texts set between *pětûḥôt* (represented by the symbol פ).[59] The consequence is that the commentary to earlier segments covers fewer verses than the latter ones.

Following this Introduction is a bibliography. Elaborate though it may be, it is but a fraction of the immense scholarly labor on Judges, enhanced by appeal to Near Eastern documentation. A translation is then offered that is justified in the Notes, and both are followed by Comments. The layout of the translation follows that of the Hebrew, with a few modifications, such as in the occasional opening of a new paragraph after a *sětûmâ*, "closed section" (see the Notes to 1:8–11). The Notes are the heart of the commentary. For all but two of the twenty segments, I have heralded each by an Introductory Remark that identifies an issue of religious, social, cultural, or historical significance appropriate to the unit I am examining. In so doing, I hope to provide a background to the annotations and a frame for the exposition in the concluding Comments.

The method I follow in the Notes is to comment on practically every phrase rather than on individual terms. Lexical notices, citations of witnesses, references to illuminating biblical passages, and relevant snippets from Near Eastern archives are woven into a single narrative, as much to explain why differences arose as to demystify this aspect of our research. The hope is to create a developing argument for how words sequence into phrases and phrases build into narratives. To counter what could be a thickening of grammatical or lexical discussions, I have adopted a chatty but I hope not a verbose style. I am conscious that in some passages this art will fail me (the Song of Deborah admittedly is a challenge), but I trust that it will bring readers a better awareness of how biblical narratives work. Keeping in mind that for most of its readers and over the centuries Judges was a repository of terrific—if not always edifying—stories rather than a source for testing history or reconstructing institutions, I have refrained from getting sucked into the many competing notions of how

Judges reached its present form. In the Comments, I often rephrase the results of my philological inspections into readable prose. I adopt, as best as I can, the perspective (historiographic or theosophic) of the narrator to enlarge on issues raised in the segment just annotated. I also engage the narrator on how characters are made to behave and how events are plotted.

CHARACTERISTICS OF THE ANNOTATIONS
On Transliteration

Against a trend that cites the Hebrew text through vowelless (and accentless) consonants, I continue the practice of transliterating it. I do so because not every reader of this commentary will have mastered the Hebrew script and because there might be interest in approximating the current pronunciation of the text. I follow the system adopted in scholarship; but to better reflect contemporary (but not necessarily ancient) pronunciation, I render spirantized *bêt* as *v* and *pê* as *f*. I also transliterate the *wāw* by means of a *v*. *gîmel*, *dālet*, *kāf*, and *tāv*, however, remain the same, even when spirantized. In the few cases where this system may mask a Hebrew pun on consonants (as at Judg 7:3), I cite the consonantal Hebrew in parentheses. I have not transliterated the Greek extracts, hoping that they would prove less of a challenge for those wishing to mouth them. In marking vowels, I have generally adopted the convention for the "academic style" (5.1.1) in the *SBL Handbook of Style* (P. Alexander et al., eds.; Peabody, MA: Hendrickson, 1999).

On Biblical References

Normally, biblical references match in both Hebrew and English editions. Sporadically, they do not, and in such cases I give the references to the Hebrew version but also include citations from the Revised Standard Version (RSV), for example, Joel 3:3 (2:30 RSV). This should work for the majority of English translations. Inadvertently, I might have let slip a few such concordances.

On Citing the Name of the Hebrew God

Hebrews wrote out the name of their god using four consonants (the Tetragrammaton): Yhvh. Abbreviated forms can also occur when constructing personal names, either as a *prefixed* YHV, as in *yĕhônātan* (Jonathan), and YV, as in *yô'ēl* (Joel), or *suffixed* YH and YHV, as in *yirmĕyâ(h)* or *yirmĕyāhû* (Jeremiah), and probably also as just *suffixed* V, as in *yitrô* (Jethro), or H, as in *šĕlōmōʰ* (Solomon). The sounding of God's name is not known, but based on reconstructed verbal forms or on comparisons with divine names from West Semitic cultures, many will give it as "Yahweh" or "Yahveh," and in my comments I am likely to use either form. But because such spellings remain conjectural, and also to avoid needlessly offending those who would not welcome informal mention of the divine name, in the translations I have opted for the "the Lᴏʀᴅ," a solution as old as the LXX, where it frequently occurs as κύριος. An exception is at 6:22, and I offer there an explanation why. Inconsistently, however, I follow others in referring to "Yahwism" (rather than "Yahvism").

On Gendering the Hebrew God

The Hebrew god was famously not to be represented by any figure. Whether or not this was so at all times during Israel's history is fiercely discussed, more so after the discoveries at Kuntillet el-ʿAjrud.[60] In the Hebrew text, that god is assigned masculine adjectives and pronouns. Debated is whether this is because that god was perceived as masculine in form and gender or because masculine indicators are the default in Hebrew, a language that lacked a neuter subject. Nonetheless, I would gladly have avoided gender markings associated with God, had I perfected an attractive way to do so. Evasive tactics strained my command of English, so on many occasions, I simply had to let go of the effort.

On Ethnic Labels

In the plural and attached to the name of a nation, a tribe, or an eponymous ancestor, the word *bēn*, normally "son," takes the meaning of "member of" that unit. The same construction applies to *bat*, "daughter," but relatively rarely (as in Gen 27:46 and Judg 21:21).[61] In many translations, this is taken literally, with awkward formulations, as in "children/sons of Israel," or as an ethnic label, "the Israelites." I have avoided the first usage and restricted the second. Instead, and depending on the context, I have called on "the people of Israel" but as often also simply on "Israel" when a string of dependent words might clutter comprehension, as at Judg 3:2: "These are the nations that the Lᴏʀᴅ kept whole . . . , just to give generations of Israel experience [*raq lĕmaʿan daʿat dōrôt bĕnê-yiśrāʾēl*]."

BIBLIOGRAPHY

Abel, Félix-Marie

1933–38: *Géographie de la Palestine.* 2 vols. Paris: Librairie Lecoffre, J. Gabalda et cie.

Abou-Assaf, Ali, Pierre Bordreuil, and Alan Millard

1982: *La Statue de Tell Fekherye et son inscription bilingue assyro-araméenne.* Paris: Éditions Recherche sur les Civilisations.

Abraham, Karen

1993: "The Dowry Clause in Marriage Documents from the First Millennium B.C.E." Pp. 311–20 in D. Charpin and F. Joannès, eds. *La circulation des biens, des personnes et des idées dans le Proche-Orient ancien.* 38 Rencontre Assyriologique Internationale; Paris: Éditions Recherche sur les Civilisations.

Abrahami, Philippe

1992: "La circulation militaire dans les textes de Mari: La question des effectifs." Pp. 157–66 in D. Charpin and F. Joannès, eds. *La circulation des biens, des personnes et des idées dans le Proche-Orient ancien.* 38 Rencontre Assyriologique Internationale; Paris: Éditions Recherche sur les Civilisations.

Achenbach, Reinhard

2012: "Divine Warfare and YHWH's Wars: Religious Ideologies of War in the Ancient Near East and in the Old Testament." Pp. 1–26 in Gershon Galil, Ayelet Gilboa, Aren M. Maeir, and Dan'el Kahn, eds. *The Ancient Near East in the 12th–10th Centuries BCE: Culture and History. Proceedings of the International Conference held at the University of Haifa, 2–5 May, 2010.* Alter Orient und Altes Testament, 392; Münster: Ugarit Verlag.

Ackerman, James S.

1975: "Prophecy and Warfare in Early Israel: A Study of the Deborah-Barak Story." *Bulletin of the American Schools of Oriental Research* 220: 5–13.

Ackerman, Susan

1998: *Warrior, Dancer, Seductress, Queen: Women in Judges and Biblical Israel.* New York: Doubleday.

2000: "What If Judges Had Been Written by a Philistine?" *Biblical Interpretation* 8: 33–41.

2002: "Why Is Miriam Also Among the Prophets? And Is Zipporah Among the Priests?" *Journal of Biblical Literature* 121: 47–80.

Ackroyd, Peter R.

    1952: "The Composition of the Song of Deborah." *Vetus Testamentum* 2: 160–62.

Adamthwaite, Murray R.

    1992: "Lab'aya's Connection with Shechem Reassessed." *Abr-Nahrain* 30: 1–19.

Aharoni, Yohanan

    1967: *The Land of the Bible: A Historical Geography.* London: Burns and Oates.

    1970: "New Aspects of the Israelite Occupation in the North." Pp. 254–67 in J. A. Sanders, ed. *Near Eastern Archaeology in the Twentieth Century: Essays in Honor of Nelson Glueck.* New York: Doubleday.

    1975: "Hazor and the Battle of Deborah: Is Judges 4 Wrong?" *Biblical Archaeology Review* 1/04: 3–4, 26.

    1979: *The Land of the Bible: A Historical Geography.* London: Burns and Oates.

Aḥituv, Shmuel

    2008: *Echoes from the Past: Hebrew and Cognate Inscriptions from the Biblical Period.* Jerusalem: Carta.

Ahlström, Gösta W.

    1977: "Judges 5:20 f. and History." *Journal of Near Eastern Studies* 36: 287–88.

Ahn, John J., and Stephen L. Cook, eds.

    2009: *Thus Says the LORD: Essays on the Former and Latter Prophets in Honor of Robert R. Wilson.* Library of Hebrew Bible/Old Testament Studies, 502; New York: T. and T. Clark.

Akimoto, Kazya

    2010: "Ante-Aesopica: Fable Traditions of the Ancient Near East." Ph.D. dissertation, Vanderbilt University.

Albright, William F.

    1936: "The Song of Deborah in the Light of Archaeology." *Bulletin of the American Schools of Oriental Research* 62: 26–31.

    1960: "Discussion." Pp. 94–123 in C. H. Kraeling and R. M. Adams, eds. *City Invincible: A Symposium on Urbanization and Cultural Development in the Ancient Near East.* Chicago: University of Chicago Press.

    1963: "Jethro, Hobab, and Reuel in Early Hebrew Tradition." *Catholic Biblical Quarterly* 25: 1–11.

    1966: *The Proto-Sinaitic Inscriptions and Their Decipherment.* Harvard Theological Studies, 22; Cambridge: Harvard University Press.

    1968: *Yahweh and the Gods of Canaan: A Historical Analysis of Two Contrasting Faiths.* Jordan Lectures 1965; London: Athlone.

    1970: "Prolegomenon to C. F. Burney, *The Book of Judges.* . . ." Pp. 1–38 in Burney 1970.

Alexander, Philip S.

    1992: "Early Jewish Geography." *ABD* 2: 977–88.

Alfrink, B.

    1943: "L'Expression *šākab ʿim ʾăbôtāyw.*" *Oudtestamentische Studiën* 2: 106–18.

    1948: "L'Expression *ne ʾĕsap ʾel ʿammāyw.*" *Oudtestamentische Studiën* 5: 118–31.

Alt, Albrecht

    1940–41: "Meros." *Zeitschrift für die alttestamentliche Wissenschaft* 58: 244–47.

Alter, Robert
  1981: *The Art of Biblical Narrative*. New York: Basic Books.
  1985: *The Art of Biblical Poetry*. New York: Basic Books.
Altman, Amnon
  2010: "Tracing the Earliest Recorded Concepts of International Law. (5) The Near East 1200–330 BCE." *Journal of the History of International Law* 12: 101–53.
Amit, Yairah
  1989: "The Story of Ehud (Judges 3:12–30): The Form and the Message." Pp. 97–112 in Exum 1989.
  1992: *The Book of Judges: The Art of Editing* (in Hebrew). Biblical Encyclopaedia Library, 6; Jerusalem: Mosad Bialik.
  1999a: *The Book of Judges: The Art of Editing*. Leiden: E. J. Brill.
  1999b: *Shoftim: 'im mavo u-ferush*. Mikra le-Yisra'el; Tel Aviv: 'Am 'oved.
  2000a: "Bochim, Bethel and the Hidden Polemic (Judges 2:1–5)." Pp. 121–31 in G. Galil and M. Weinfeld, eds. *Studies in Historical Geography and Biblical Historiography Presented to Zecharia Kallai*. Leiden: E. J. Brill.
  2000b: *Hidden Polemics in Biblical Narrative*. Leiden: E. J. Brill.
  2004: "Judges." Pp. 508–57 in Berlin, Brettler, and Fishbane 2004.
  2009: "The Book of Judges—Dating and Meaning." Pp. 297–322 in Gershon Galil, Mark Geller, and Alan Millard, eds. *Homeland and Exile: Biblical and Ancient Near Eastern Studies in Honour of Bustenay Oded*. Vetus Testamentum Supplement, 130; Leiden: E. J. Brill.
Anbar, Moshé
  1988: "La 'reprise.'" *Vetus Testamentum* 38: 385–98.
  1991: *Les Tribus amurrites de Mari*. Orbis Biblicus et Orientalis, 108; Freiburg: Universitätverlag Freiburg Schweiz.
Anbar, Moshe, and Nadav Na'aman
  1986–87: "An Account Tablet of Sheep from Ancient Hebron." *Tel Aviv* 13–14: 3–12.
Anderson, Gary A.
  1987: *Sacrifice and Offerings in Ancient Israel: Studies in Their Social and Political Importance*. Harvard Semitic Monographs, 41; Atlanta, GA: Scholars.
Ap-Thomas, D. R.
  1940: "The *Ephah* of *Meal* in Judges vi 19." *Journal of Theological Studies* 41: 175–77.
Arbeitman, Yöel L.
  1988: "Iranian 'Scribe,' Anatolian 'Ruler,' or Neither: A City's Rare Chances for 'Leadership.'" Pp. 1–101 in Y. L. Arbeitman, ed. *FUCUS: A Semitic/Afrasian Gathering in Remembrance of Albert Ehrman*. Amsterdam: J. Benjamin's.
Arnaud, Daniel
  1991: *Textes syriens de l'Âge du Bronze récent*. Aula Orientalis Supplement, 1; Sabadell: Editorial AUSA.
Artzy, Michal, and Daniel Hillel
  1988: "A Defense of the Theory of Progressive Soil Salinization in Ancient Southern Mesopotamia." *Geoarchaeology* 3: 235–38.

Asen, Bernhard A.

    1997: "Deborah, Barak and Bees: *Apis mellifera*, Apiculture and Judges 4 and 5." *Zeitschrift für die alttestamentliche Wissenschaft*: 514–33.

Assante, Julia

    2007: "What Makes a 'Prostitute' a Prostitute? Modern Definitions and Ancient Meanings." *Historiae* 4: 117–32.

Assis, Elie (Eliyahu)

    2005a: "The Hand of a Woman: Deborah and Yael. (Judges 4)." *Journal of Hebrew Scriptures* 5/19 http://ejournals.library.ualberta.ca/index.php/jhs/article/viewFile/5744/4797 [= Ehud Ben Zvi, ed. *Perspectives on Hebrew Scriptures* 2. Piscataway, NJ: Gorgias, 2007].

    2005b: *Self-Interest or Communal Interest: An Ideology of Leadership in the Gideon, Abimelech, and Jephthah Narratives. Judg. 6–12.* Vetus Testamentum Supplement, 106; Leiden: E. J. Brill.

Astour, Michael C.

    1959: "Benê-Iamina et Jéricho." *Semitica* 9: 5–20.

    1964: "Amarna Age Forerunners of Biblical Anti-royalism." Pp. 6–17 in Lucy Davidowicz, ed. *For Max Weinreich on His Seventieth Birthday; Studies in Jewish Language, Literature and Society.* The Hague: Mouton.

    1965: "The Origin of the Terms 'Canaan,' 'Phoenician,' and 'Purple.'" *Journal of Near Eastern Studies* 24: 346–50.

Ataç, Mehmet-Ali

    2010: *The Mythology of Kingship in Neo-Assyrian Art.* Cambridge: Cambridge University Press.

Auffret, Pierre

    2002: "En ce jour-là Debora et Baraq chantèrent: Étude structurelle de Jg 5, 2–21." *Scandinavian Journal of the Old Testament* 16: 113–50.

Aufrecht, Walter

    1989: *A Corpus of Ammonite Inscriptions.* Ancient Near Eastern Texts and Studies, 4; Lewiston, NY: E. Mellen.

Auld, A. Graeme

    1989: "Gideon, Hacking at the Heart of the Old Testament." *Vetus Testamentum* 39: 257–67.

Aurenche, Olivier

    1981: *La maison orientale: L'architecture du Proche Orient ancien des origines au milieu du quatrième millénaire.* Bibliothèque archéologique et historique, 109; Paris: Librairie orientaliste P. Geuthner.

Avalos, Hector

    1995: "Legal and Social Institutions in Canaan and Ancient Israel." Pp. 615–31 in Sasson, Baines, Beckman, and Rubinson, eds., 1995.

Avner, Uzi

    2001: "Sacred Stones in the Desert." *Biblical Archaeological Review* 27: 31–35.

Bahat, Dan

    1997: "Jerusalem." *OEANE* 3: 224–38.

Bal, Mieke

    1988a: "Tricky Thematics." *Semeia* 42: 133–55.

1988b: *Death and Dissymmetry: The Politics of Coherence in the Book of Judges.* Chicago: University of Chicago Press.

1992: *Murder and Difference: Gender, Genre, and Scholarship on Sisera's Death.* Bloomington: Indiana University Press.

Barr, James

1961: *The Semantics of Biblical Language.* London: Oxford University Press.

1990: "Mythical Monarch Unmasked? Mysterious Doings of Debir King of Eglon." *Journal for the Study of the Old Testament* 48: 55–68.

Barré, Michael L.

1991: "The Meaning of *pršdn* in Judges III 22." *Vetus Testamentum* 41: 1–11.

Barron, Amy E.

2010: "Late Assyrian Arms and Armour: Art Versus Artifact." Ph.D. dissertation, University of Toronto. https://tspace.library.utoronto.ca/bitstream/1807/24677/8/Barron_Amy_E_201006_PhD_thesis.pdf.

Bartelmus, Rüdiger

1985: "Die sogennante Jothamfabel: Eine politisch-religiöse Parabeldichtung." *Theologische Zeitschrift* 41: 97–120.

Barthélemy, Dominique

1982: *Critique textuelle de l'Ancien Testament 1. Josué, Juges, Ruth, Samuel, Rois, Chroniques, Esdras, Néhémie, Esther.* Orbis biblicus et orientalis, 50/1; Göttingen: Vandenhoeck and Ruprecht.

Bartlett, J. R.

1969: "The Use of the Word ראש as a Title in the Old Testament." *Vetus Testamentum* 19: 1–10.

1978: "The Conquest of Sihon's Kingdom: A Literary Re-examination." *Journal of Biblical Literature* 97: 347–51.

Barton, John, J. Cheryl Exum, and Manfred Oeming

2005: *Das Alte Testament und die Kunst: Beiträge des Symposiums "Das Alte Testament und die Kultur der Moderne" anlässlich des 100. Geburtstags Gerhard von Rads. 1901–1971, Heidelbert, 18.–21. Oktober 2001.* Münster: Lit.

Basser, Herbert W.

2005: "History of Interpretation to Judges 5:4–5, with Special Attention to Rabbi Yosef Kara." *Revue des Études Juives* 164: 9–32.

Batto, Bernard Frank

1974: *Studies in Women at Mari.* Baltimore, MD: Johns Hopkins University Press.

Bauks, Michaela

2007: "Traditionsgeschichtliche Erwägungen zur Namenlosigkeit von Jiftachs Tochter. Ri 11,29–40." *Lectio Difficilior* 1/2007. http://www.lectio.unibe.ch.

2010: *Jephtas Tochter: Traditions-, religions- und rezeptionsgeschichtliche Studien zu Richter 11,29–40.* Forschungen zum Alten Testament, 71; Tübingen: Mohr Siebeck.

2011: "Jephtas Gelübde und die Unabwendbarkeit seiner Einlösung." Pp. 27–40 in Kristin De Troyer and Armin Lange, eds. *The Qumran Legal Texts Between the Hebrew Bible and Its Interpretation.* Contributions to Biblical Exegesis and Theology, 61; Leuven: Peeters.

Baumgarten, Elisheva
2007: "'Remember that glorious girl': Jephthah's Daughter in Medieval Jewish Culture." *Jewish Quarterly Review* 97: 180–209.

Beal, Richard H.
2002: "Gleanings from Hittite Oracle Questions on Religion, Society, Psychology and Decision Making." Pp. 11–37 in Piotr Taracha, ed. *Silva Anatolica: Anatolian Studies Presented to Maciej Popko on the Occasion of His 65th Birthday.* Warsaw: Agade.

Beal, T. K., and D. Gunn
2009: "Judges, Book of." Pp. 637–47 in John H. Hayes, ed. *Dictionary of Biblical Interpretations.* Nashville, TN: Abingdon.

Beaulieu, Paul-Alain
1994: "Antiquarianism and the Concern for the Past in the Neo-Babylonian Period." *Bulletin of the Canadian Society for Mesopotamian Society* 28: 37–42.

Bechmann, Ulrike
1989: *Das Deboralied zwischen Geschichte und Fiktion: Eine exegetische Untersuchung zu Richter.* Dissertationen—Theologische Reihe, 33; St. Ottilien: EOS Verlag.

Beck, John A.
2008: "Dew, and the Narrative-Geographical Shaping of Judges 6:33–40." *Bibliotheca Sacra* 165: 28–38.

Becker, Uwe
1990: *Richterzeit und Königtum: Redaktionsgeschichtliche Studien zum Richterbuch.* Zeitschrift für die alttestamentliche Wissenschaft Beiheft, 192; Berlin: De Gruyter.

Becker-Spörl, Silvia
1998: *Und sang Debora an jenem Tag: Untersuchungen zu Sprache und Intention des Deboraliedes. (Ri 5).* Frankfurt: Peter Lang.

Beckman, Gary
1996: *Hittite Diplomatic Texts.* SBL Writings from the Ancient World, 7; Atlanta, GA: Scholars Press.

Bedenbender, Andreas
1997: "Biene, Fackel, Blitz: Zur Metaphorik der Namen in der Deborageschichte (Ri 4–5)." *Texte and Kontexte* 76: 43–48.

Beem, Beverly
1991: "The Minor Judges: A Literary Reading of Some Very Short Stories." Pp. 146–72 in K. Lawson Younger, Jr., William H. Hallo, and Bernard F. Batto, eds. *The Biblical Canon in Comparative Perspective: Scripture in Context, IV.* Ancient Near Eastern Texts and Studies, 11; Lewiston, NY: Edwin Mellen.

Beeston, Alfred Felix Landon
1979: "Hebrew *šibbolet* and *šobel*." *Journal of Semitic Studies* 14: 175–77.
1988: "*šibbolet*: A Further Comment." *Journal of Semitic Studies* 33: 259–61.

Bekkum, Koert van
2011: *From Conquest to Coexistence: Ideology and Antiquarian Intent in the Historiography of Israel's Settlement in Canaan.* Culture and History of the Ancient Near East, 45. Leiden: E. J. Brill.

Benz, Frank L.

1972: *Personal Names in the Phoenician and Punic Inscriptions: A Catalog, Grammatical Study and Glossary of Elements*. Studia Pohl, 8; Rome: Biblical Institute Press.

Benzinger, Immanuel

1894: *Hebräische Archäologie*. Leipzig: J. C. B. Mohr, Paul Siebeck.

Berlin, Adele, Marc Zvi Brettler, and Michael Fishbane

2004: *The Jewish Study Bible*. New York: Oxford University Press.

Berquist, John L., and Alice Hunt

2012: *Focusing Biblical Studies: The Crucial Nature of the Persian and Hellenistic Periods: Essays in Honor of Douglas A. Knight*. The Library of Hebrew Bible/Old Testament Studies, 544; New York: T & T Clark International.

Bertman, Stephen

1964: "A Note on the Reversible Miracle." *History of Religions* 3: 323–27.

Beyerlin, Walter

1963a: "Geschichte und Heilsgeschichtliche Traditionsbildung im Alten Testament: Ein Beitrag zur Traditionsgeschichte von Richter VI–VIII." *Vetus Testamentum* 13: 1–25.

1963b: "Gattung und Herkunft des Rahmens im Richterbuch." Pp. 1–29 in E. Würthwein and O. Kaiser. eds. *Tradition und Situation: Studien zur alttestamentlichen Prophetie*. Göttingen: Vandenhoeck and Ruprecht.

Bird, Phyllis

2006: "Prostitution in the Social World and the Religious Rhetoric of Ancient Israel." Pp. 40–58 in Christopher A. Faraone and Laura K. McClure, eds. *Prostitutes and Courtesans in the Ancient World*. Madison: University of Wisconsin Press.

Birot, Maurice

1974: *Lettres de Yaqqim-Addu, gouverneur de Sagarâtum*. ARM, 14; Paris: Librairie orientaliste P. Geuthner.

1993: *Correspondance des gouverneurs de Qaṭṭunân*. ARM, 27; Paris: Éditions Recherche sur les Civilisations.

Bledstein, Adrien J.

1993: "Is Judges a Woman's Satire on Men Who Play God?" Pp. 34–54 in Brenner, ed., 1993.

Blenkinsopp, Joseph

1961: "Ballad Style and Psalm Style in the Song of Deborah: A Discussion." *Biblica* 42: 61–76.

1997: "The Family in First Temple Israel." Pp. 48–103 in Leo G. Perdue, Joseph Blenkinsopp, John J. Collins, and Carol L. Mayers, eds., *Families in Ancient Israel*. Louisville, KY: Westminster John Knox.

Bloch-Smith, Elizabeth

2003: "Israelite Ethnicity in Iron I: Archaeology Preserves What Is Remembered and What Is Forgotten." *Journal of Biblical Literature* 122: 401–25.

Bloch-Smith, Elizabeth, and Beth Albert Nakhai

1999: A Landscape Comes to Life: The Iron Age I." *Near Eastern Archaeology* 62: 62–92, 101–27.

Block, Daniel I.

    1994: "Deborah Among the Judges: The Perspective of the Hebrew Historian." Pp. 229–53 in A. R. Millard, James Karl Hoffmeier, and David W. Baker, eds., *Faith, Tradition, and History: Old Testament Historiography in Its Near Eastern Context*. Winona Lake, IN: Eisenbrauns.

    1999: *Judges, Ruth*. New American Commentary; Nashville, TN: Broadman and Holman.

    2009: *Judges*. Zondervan Illustrated Bible Background Commentary, 2: 94–241; Grand Rapids, MI: Zondervan.

Bluedorn, Wolfgang

    2001: *Yahweh Versus Baalism: A Theological Reading of the Gideon-Abimelech Narrative*. Journal for the Study of the Old Testament Supplement, 329; Sheffield: Sheffield Academic Press.

Bodi, Daniel

    2005: *The Michal Affair: From Zimri-Lim to the Rabbis*. Hebrew Bible Monograph, 3; Sheffield: Sheffield Phoenix Press.

    2010: *The Demise of the Warlord: A New Look at the David Story*. Hebrew Bible Monograph, 26; Sheffield: Sheffield Phoenix Press.

Bodine, Walter R.

    1980: *The Greek Text of Judges: Recensional Developments*. Harvard Semitic Monographs, 23; Chico, CA: Scholars Press.

Boling, Robert G.

    1963: "'And Who Is Š-K-M?' Judges IX 28." *Vetus Testamentum* 13: 479–82.

    1975: *Judges: A New Translation with Introduction and Commentary*. AB, 6A; Garden City, NY: Doubleday.

    1983: "Enigmatic Bible Passages: Jericho Off Limits." *Biblical Archaeologist* 46: 115–16.

Boling, Robert G., and G. Ernest Wright

    1982: *Joshua: A New Translation with Introduction and Commentary*. AB, 6; Garden City, NY: Doubleday.

Bonechi, Marco

    1991: "Relations amicales syro-palestiniennes: Mari et Haṣor au XVIIIᵉ siècle av. J.C." *FM*, 1: 9–22.

Boogaart, Thomas A.

    1985: "Stone for Stone: Retribution in the Story of Abimelech and Shechem." *Journal for the Study of the Old Testament* 32: 45–56.

Borowski, Oded

    1998: *Every Living Thing: Daily Use of Animals in Ancient Israel*. Walnut Creek, CA: Altamira.

Botterweck, G. Johannes, Helmer Ringgren, and Heinz-Josef Fabry

    1974–2006: *Theological Dictionary of the Old Testament*. Grand Rapids: MI: Eerdmans.

Boyer, Georges

    1958: *Textes juridiques et administratifs*. ARM, 8; Paris: Librairie orientaliste P. Geuthner.

Braude, William G., and Israel J. Kapstein

    1981: *Tanna Debe Eliyyahu*. Philadelphia: Jewish Publication Society of America.

Brenner, Athalya

1990: "A Triangle and a Rhombus in Narrative Structure: A Proposed Integrative Reading of Judges IV and V." *Vetus Testamentum* 40: 129–38 [= Brenner 1993: 98–109].

Brenner, Athalya, ed.

1993: *A Feminist Companion to Judges.* Sheffield: JSOT Press.

1999: *A Feminist Companion to Judges, Second Series.* Feminist Companion to the Bible, 4: Sheffield: JSOT Press.

Brettler, Marc Z.

1989: "Jud 1,1–2,10: From Appendix to Prologue." *Zeitschrift für die alttestamentliche Wissenschaft* 101: 433–35.

1991: "Never the Twain Shall Meet? The Ehud Story as History and Literature." *Hebrew Union College Annual* 62: 285–304.

2002: *The Book of Judges.* Old Testament Readings; London: Routledge.

Bright, John

2000: *A History of Israel.* 4th edition, with an Introduction and Appendix by William P. Brown; Louisville, KY: John Knox.

Brock, Sebastian

2011: "A *Soghitha* on the Daughter of Jephtha, by Isaac." *Hugoye: Journal of Syriac Studies* 14: 3–25.

Brockhaus, Monika

2011: "Achsah: Who Ever Saw Her Was Angry with His Wife: Achsah in the Bible and Bavli Temurah 16a." *Lectio Difficilior* 2/2011, http://www.lectio.unibe .ch/11_2/brockhaus_monika_2011.html.

Brown, F., G. R. Driver, and C. A. Briggs

1907: *A Hebrew and English Lexicon of the Old Testament.* Oxford: Oxford University Press.

Brunner, Christopher J.

1980: "The Fable of the Babylonian Tree." *Journal of Near Eastern Studies* 39: 191– 202, 291–302.

Buccellati, Giorgio

1990: "From Khana to Laqê: The End of Syro-Mesopotamia." Pp. 229–53 in Ö. Tunca, ed. *De la Babylonie à la Syrie, en passant par Mari. Mélanges offerts à Monsieur J. R. Kupper à l'occasion de son 70e anniversaire.* Liège: Université de Liège.

1995: "Ethics and Piety in the Ancient Near East." Pp. 1685–86 in Sasson, Baines, Beckman, and Rubinson, eds., 1995.

Budde, D. Karl

1890: *Die Bücher Richter und Samuel: Ihre Quellen und ihr Aufbau.* Giessen: J. Ricker'sche Buchhandlung.

Burchard, C.

1985: "Joseph and Aseneth (First Century B.C.–Second Century A.D.)." Pp. 177– 247 in Charlesworth, ed., 1985.

Burke, Madeleine Lurton

1963: *Textes administratifs de la salle 111 du palais.* ARM, 11; Paris: Librairie orientaliste P. Geuthner.

Burnette-Bletsch, Rhonda

    1998: "At the Hands of a Woman: Rewriting Jael in Pseudo-Philo." *Journal for the Study of the Pseudepigrapha* 17: 53–64.

Burney, Charles Fox

    1970: *The Book of Judges, with Introduction and Notes; and Notes on the Hebrew Text of the Book of Kings, with an Appendix.* Library of Biblical Studies. New York: Ktav. (Originally published as *The Book of Judges, with Introduction and Notes,* 1918; 2nd edition, 1920.)

Buth, Randall

    1994: "Methodological Collision Between Source Criticism and Discourse Analysis: The Problem of 'Unmarked Temporal Overlay' and the Pluperfect/Nonsequential *wayyiqtol.*" Pp. 138–54 in Robert D. Bergen, ed. *Biblical Hebrew and Discourse Linguistics.* Winona Lake, IN: Eisenbrauns.

Butler, Trent C.

    2009: *Judges.* Word Biblical Commentary; Nashville, TN: Thomas Nelson.

Buttrick, George Arthur

    1962: *The Interpreter's Dictionary of the Bible. An Illustrated Encyclopedia.* 4 vols. Nashville, TN: Abingdon.

Camp, Claudia V.

    1981: "The Wise Women of 2 Samuel: A Role Model for Women in Early Israel." *Catholic Biblical Quarterly* 43: 14–29.

Canby, Jesse V.

    1976: "The Stelenreihen at Assur, Tell Halaf, and *maṣṣebôt.*" *Iraq* 38: 113–28.

Cantrell, Deborah J.

    2011: *The Horsemen of Israel: Horses and Chariotry in Monarchic Israel.* Winona Lake, IN: Eisenbrauns.

Caquot, André

    1986: "Les tribus d'Israël dans le Cantique de Débora (*Judges* 5, 13–17)." *Semitica* 36: 47–70.

Cartledge, Tony

    1992: *Vows in the Hebrew Bible and the Ancient Near East.* Journal for the Study of the Old Testament Supplement, 147; Sheffield: JSOT Press.

Cassin, Elena

    1968: *La splendeur divine: Introduction à l'étude de la mentalité mésopotamienne.* Civilisations et Sociétés, 8; Paris: Mouton.

Castelbajac, Isabelle de

    2001: "Histoire de la rédaction de Juges IX: Une solution." *Vetus Testamentum* 51: 166–85.

Cavigneaux, Antoine

    1994: "Magica mariana." *Revue d'Assyriologie* 88: 155–61.

Cazelles, Henri

    1958: Review of Jean-Robert Kupper, *Les nomades en Mésopotamie au temps des rois de Mari.* Bibliothèque de la Faculté de philosophie et lettres de l'Université de Liège, 142; Paris: Les belles letters, 1957; *Vetus Testamentum* 8: 316–20.

    1974: "Déborah (Jud. V 14), Amaleq et Mâkîr." *Vetus Testamentum* 24: 235–38.

Chambon, Grégory
    2009: *Les archives du vin à Mari*. *FM*, 11; Mémoires de NABU, 12; Paris: SEPOA.
Charlesworth, James H., ed.
    1983: *The Old Testament Pseudepigrapha*, Vol. 1. *Apocalyptic Literature and Testaments*. New York: Doubleday.
    1985: *The Old Testament Pseudepigrapha*, Vol. 2. *Expansions of the "Old Testament" and Legends, Wisdom and Philosophical Literature, Prayers, Psalms, and Odes, Fragments of Lost Judeo-Hellenistic Works*. New York: Doubleday.
Charpin, Dominique
    1984: "Inscriptions votives d'époque assyrienne." *Mari: Annales de recherches interdisciplinaires* 3: 41–77.
    1993: "Données nouvelles sur la poliorcétique à l'époque paléo-babylonienne." *Mari: Annales de recherches interdisciplinaires* 7: 193–203.
    1997: "Manger un serment." Pp. 85–96 in S. Lafont, ed. *Jurer et maudire: Pratiques politiques et usages juridiques du serment dans le Proche-Orient ancien* [= *Méditerranées, Revue de l'association Méditerranées* 10–11]. Paris: L'Harmattan.
    2003: "La 'toponymie en miroir' dans le Proche-Orient amorrite." *Revue d'Assyriologie* 97: 3–34.
    (forthcoming): "Guerre et paix dans le monde amorrite et post-amorrite." In H. Neumann, ed. *Krieg und Frieden im Alten Vorderasien*. 52 RAI; Wiesbaden: Harrassowitz.
Charpin, Dominique, and Jean-Marie Durand
    1994: *Recueil d'études à la mémoire de Maurice Birot*. *FM*, 2; Mémoires de NABU, 3; Paris: SEPOA.
Charpin, Dominique, and Nele Ziegler
    2003: *Mari et le Proche-Orient à l'époque amorrite. Essai d'histoire politique. FM*, 5; Mémoires de NABU, 6; Paris: SEPOA.
Charpin, Dominique, Francis Joannès, Sylvie Lackenbacher, and Bertrand Lafont
    1988: *Archives épistolaires de Mari, I/2*. ARM, 26/2; Paris: Éditions Recherche sur les Civilisations.
Cheyne, Thomas Kelly, and J. Sutherland Black
    1899–1903: *Encyclopaedia Biblica: A Critical Dictionary of the Literary, Political and Religion History, the Archeology, Geography and Natural History of the Bible*. New York: Macmillan.
Childs, Brevard
    1963: "A Study of the Formula, 'Until This Day.'" *Journal of Biblical Literature* 82: 279–92.
Christianson, Eric S.
    2003: "A Fistful of Shekels: Scrutinizing Ehud's Entertaining Violence. Judges 3: 12–30." *Biblical Interpretation* 11: 53–78.
    2007: "The Big Sleep: Strategic Ambiguity in Judges 4–5 and in Classic *film noir*." Pp. 169–94 in Exum 2007 [= *Biblical Interpretation* 15: 519–48].
Civil, Miguel
    1999–2000: "Reading Gilgameš." Pp. 179–89 in M. Molina, Joaquín Sanmartín, and Ignacio Márquez Rowe, eds. *Arbor Scientiae. Estudios del Próximo Oriente*

Antiguo dedicados a Gregorio del Olmo Lete con ocasión de su 65 aniversario [= *Aula Orientalis*, 17–18]. Sabadell: Editorial AUSA.

Clines, David J. A., and Ellen van Wolde

2011: *A Critical Engagement: Essays on the Hebrew Bible in Honour of J. Cheryl Exum*. Sheffield: Sheffield Phoenix Press.

Cody, Aelred

1966: "When Is the Chosen People Called a Goy?" *Vetus Testamentum* 16: 1–6.

Cohen, Abraham

1924: "Studies in Hebrew Lexicography." *American Journal of Semitic Languages and Literatures* 40: 153–85.

Cohen, Menachem, ed.

1992: *Joshua—Judges*. Ramat-Gan: Bar-Ilan University [*Mikra'ot Gedolot 'Haketer.'* A Revised and Augmented Scientific Edition of 'Mikra'ot Gedolot'; based on the Aleppo Codex and Early Medieval MSS.]

Cohen, Shaye J. D.

2010: *The Significance of Yavneh and Other Essays in Jewish Hellenism*. Texts and Studies in Judaism, 136; Tübingen: Mohr Siebeck.

Collins, Billie Jean

2007a: *The Hittites and Their World*. Archaeology and Biblical Studies, 7; Atlanta, GA: Society of Biblical Literature.

2007b: "The Bible, the Hittites, and the Construction of 'Others.'" Pp. 153–61 in Detlev Groddek and Marina Zorman, eds. *Tabularia Hethaeorum: Hethitologische Beiträge; Silvin Košak zum 65. Geburtstag*. Dresdner Beiträge zur Hethitologie, Bd. 25; Wiesbaden: Harrassowitz.

Collins, John J.

2003: "The Zeal of Phinehas: The Bible and the Legitimation of Violence." *Journal of Biblical Literature* 122: 3–21.

2005: *The Bible After Babel: Historical Criticism in a Postmodern Age*. Grand Rapids, MI: Eerdmans.

Collon, Dominique, and Andrew George, eds.

2005: *Nineveh: Papers of the XLIXe Rencontre Assyriologique internationale, London, 7–11 July 2003*. London: British School of Archaeology in Iraq [= *Iraq* 66 (2004) and 67/1 (2005)].

Coogan, Michael D.

1978: "A Structural and Literary Analysis of the Song of Deborah." *Catholic Biblical Quarterly* 40: 143–66.

Cook, Stanley A.

1927: "The Theophanies of Gideon and Manoah." *Journal of Theological Studies* 28: 368–83.

Cook, Stephen L., and Sara C. Winter, eds.

1999: *On the Way to Nineveh: Studies in Honor of George M. Landes*. Atlanta, GA: Scholars Press.

Cook, Steve

2009: "Habakkuk 3, Gender, and War." *Lectio difficilior* 1/2009: 1–12. http://www.lectio.unibe.ch/09_1/steve_cook_habakkuk_3.html.

Cooke, George A.

1892: *The History and Song of Deborah: Judges IV and V*. Oxford: Horace Hart.

1913: *The Book of Judges in the Revised Version*. Cambridge Bible for Schools and Colleges. Cambridge: Cambridge University Press.

Cooper, Jerrold S.

2002: "Virginity in Ancient Mesopotamia." Pp. 91–112 in S. Parpola and R. M. Whiting, eds. *Sex and Gender in the Ancient Near East. Proceedings of the 47th Rencontre Assyriologique Internationale, Helsinki, July 2–6, 2001*. 47 Rencontre Assyriologique Internationale; Helsinki: SAA Publications.

2006: "Prostitution." *RlA* 11: 12–21.

Craig, Kenneth M., Jr.

1998: "Bargaining in Tov. (Judges 11, 4–11): The Many Directions of So-called Direct Speech." *Biblica* 79: 76–85.

Craigie, Peter C.

1969: "The Song of Deborah and the Epic of Tukulti-Ninurta." *Journal of Biblical Literature* 88: 253–65.

1972: "A Reconsideration of Shamgar Ben Anath (Judg 3:31 and 5:6)." *Journal of Biblical Literature* 91: 239–40.

Crenshaw, James L.

1971: *Prophetic Conflict: Its Effect upon Israelite Religion*. Zeitschrift für die alttestamentliche Wissenschaft Beiheft, 124; Berlin: Walter de Gruyter.

Crim, Keith

1976: *The Interpreter's Dictionary of the Bible. An Illustrated Encyclopedia, Supplementary Volume*. Nashville, TN: Abingdon.

Cross, Frank M.

1973: *Canaanite Myth and Hebrew Epic: Essays in the History of the Religion of Israel*. Cambridge, MA: Harvard University Press.

1998: *From Epic to Canon: History and Literature in Ancient Israel*. Baltimore: Johns Hopkins University Press.

Dafni, Amots, Shay Levy, and Efraim Lev

2005: "The Ethnobotany of Christ's Thorn Jujube (*Ziziphus spina-christi*) in Israel." *Journal of Ethnobiology and Ethnomedicine* 1: 8. http://www.ncbi.nlm.nih.gov/pmc/articles/PMC1277088/.

Dahood, Mitchell

1979: "Scripio defectivia in Judges 1, 19." *Biblica* 60: 570.

Dalley, Stephanie, and Beatrice Teissier

1992: "Tablets from the Vicinity of Emar and Elsewhere." *Iraq* 54: 83–111.

Dalley, Stephanie, C. B. F. Walker, and J. D. Hawkins

1976: *The Old Babylonian Tablets from Tell al Rimah*. London: British School of Archeology in Iraq.

Dam, Cornelis van

1997: *The Urim and Thummim: A Means of Revelation in Ancient Israel*. Winona Lake, IN: Eisenbrauns.

Danelius, Eva

1963: "Shamgar Ben Anath." *Journal of Near Eastern Studies* 22: 191–93.

Daremberg, Charles, and Edmond Saglio

    1877: *Dictionnaire des antiquités grecques et romaines, d'après les textes et les monuments*. Paris: Librairie Hachette. http://dagr.univ-tlse2.fr/sdx/dagr/index.xsp.

Daube, David

    1956: "Gideon's Few." *Journal of Jewish Studies* 7: 155–61.

Daviau, P. M. Michèle

    1993: *Houses and Their Furnishings in Bronze Age Palestine: Domestic Activity Areas and Artefact Distribution in the Middle and Late Bronze Ages*. JSOT/American Schools of Oriental Research Monograph Series, 8; Sheffield: JSOT Press.

Davidson, Edith T. A.

    2008: *Intricacy, Design, and Cunning in the Book of Judges*. Bloomington, IN: Xlibris.

Davies, G. Henton

    1963: "Judges VIII 22–23." *Vetus Testamentum* 13: 151–57.

Day, John

    1993: "Bedan, Abdon or Barak in 1 Samuel XII 11?" *Vetus Testamentum* 43: 261–64.

Day, Peggy L.

    1989: "From the Child Is Born the Woman: The Story of Jephthah's Daughter." Pp. 58–74 in Day, ed., 1989.

Day, Peggy L., ed.

    1989: *Gender and Difference in Ancient Israel*. Minneapolis: Fortress.

Dearman, J. A., ed.

    1989: *Studies in the Mesha Inscription and Moab*. Atlanta, GA: Scholars Press.

Deist, Ferdinand

    1996: "Murder in the Toilet (Judges 3:12–30): Translation and Transformation." *Scriptura* 58: 263–72.

Del Monte, Giuseppe F.

    2005: "The Hittite ḫerem." Pp. 21–45 in L. Kogan and S. Loesov, eds. *Babel und Bibel*, Vol. 2. *Memoriae Igor M. Diakonoff*. Winona Lake, IN: Eisenbrauns.

Dempster, S. G.

    1978: "Mythology and History in the Song of Deborah." *Westminster Theological Journal* 41: 33–53.

Demsky, Aaron

    2004: "The Boundary of the Tribe of Dan (Joshua 19:41–46)." Pp. 261–84 in Chaim Cohen, Avi Hurvitz, and Shalom M. Paul, eds. *Sefer Moshe: The Moshe Weinfeld Jubilee Volume*. Studies in the Bible and the Ancient Near East, Qumran, and Post-Biblical Judaism. Winona Lake, IN: Eisenbrauns

DesCamp, Mary Therese

    1997: "Why Are These Women Here? An Examination of the Sociological Setting of Pseudo-Philo Through Comparative Reading." *Journal for the Study of the Pseudepigrapha* 16: 53–80.

Dieleman, Jacco

    2005: *Priests, Tongues, and Rites: The London-Leiden Magical Manuscripts and Translation in Egyptian Ritual (100–300 CE)*. Religions in the Graeco-Roman World, 153; Leiden: E. J. Brill.

Dietrich, Manfred

    2003: "Salmanassar I. von Assyrien, Ibirānu (VI.) von Ugarit und Tudḫalija IV. von Ḫatti." *Ugarit—Forschungen* 35: 103–39.

Dietrich, Manfred, Oswald Loretz, and Joaquín Sanmartín

    1976: *Die keilalphabetischen Texte aus Ugarit*. Alter Orient und Altes Testament, 24; Neukirchen-Vluyn: Neukirchener Verlag.

Dirksen, P. B.

    1972: *The Transmission of the Text in the Peshiṭta Manuscripts of the Book of Judges*. Monographs of the Peshiṭta Institute, 1; Leiden: E. J. Brill.

    2005: *1 Chronicles*. Historical Commentary on the Old Testament; Leuven: Peeters.

Doak, Brian R.

    2011: "'Some Worthless and Reckless Fellows': Landlessness and Parasocial Leadership in Judges." *Journal of Hebrew Scriptures* 11/2. http://www.arts.ualberta.ca/JHS/Articles/article_149.pdf.

Dobbs-Allsopp, Frederick William

    1993: *Weep, O Daughter of Zion: A Study of the City-Lament Genre in the Hebrew Bible*. Biblica et orientalia, 44; Rome: Pontifical Biblical Institute.

    2000: "Darwinism, Genre Theory, and City Laments." *Journal of the American Oriental Society* 120: 625–30.

Dorsey, David A.

    1991: *The Roads and Highways of Ancient Israel*. Baltimore, MD: Johns Hopkins University Press.

Dossin, Georges

    1950: *Correspondance de Šamši-Addu et de ses fils*. ARM, 1; Paris: Imprimerie nationale = Geuthner.

    1951: *Correspondance de Šamši-Addu et de ses fils*. ARM, 4; Paris: Imprimerie nationale = Geuthner.

    1952: *Correspondance de Iasmaḫ-Addu*. ARM, 5; Paris: Librairie orientaliste P. Geuthner.

    1955: "L'inscription de fondation de Iaḫdun-Lim, roi de Mari." *Syria* 32: 1–28.

    1956 : "Une lettre de Iarîm-Lim, roi d'Alep, à Iašub-Iaḫad, roi de Dêr." *Syria* 33: 63–69.

    1957: "Une *lectio difficilior* dans Juges, IX, 31." Pp. 163–67 in *L'Ancien Testament et l'Orient*. Louvain: Institut Orientaliste, Université de Louvain, Publications Universitaires.

    1982: "Kushan Rishʿatayim." Pp. 9–11 in G. van Driel, Th. J. H. Krispijn, and Marten Stol, eds. *Zikir šumim. Assyriological Studies Presented to F. R. Kraus on the Occasion of His Seventieth Birthday*. Leiden: E. J. Brill.

Dossin, Georges, and André Finet

    1978: *Correspondance féminine*. ARM, 10; Paris: Librairie orientaliste P. Geuthner.

Drews, Robert

    1989: "The 'Chariots of Iron' of Joshua and Judges." *Journal for the Study of the Old Testament* 45: 15–23.

Driver, G. R.

    1957: "Problems of Interpretation in the Heptateuch." Pp. 66–76 in *Mélanges bibliques, rédigés en l'honneur de André Robert*. Travaux de l'Institut Catholique de Paris, 4; Paris: Bloud et Gay.

Driver, Samuel Rolles

1998: *A Treatise on the Use of the Tenses in Hebrew and Some Other Syntactical Questions*. 4th edition. Biblical Resource Series; Grand Rapids, MI: William B. Eerdmans.

Dumbrell, William J.

1975: "Midian: A Land or a League?" *Vetus Testamentum* 25: 323–37.

Durand, Jean-Marie

1983: *Textes administratifs des salles 134 et 160 du Palais de Mari: Transcrits, traduis et commentés*. ARM, 21. Paris: Librairie orientaliste P. Geuthner.

1988: *Archives Épistolaires de Mari, I/1*. ARM, 26/1; Paris: Éditions Recherche sur les Civilisations.

1990: "Problèmes d'eau et d'irrigation au royaume de Mari: L'apport des textes anciens." Pp. 101–42 in B. Geyer, ed. *Techniques et pratiques hydro-agricoles traditionelles en domaine irrigué*. Institut d'Archéologie du Proche Orient, Bibliothèque Archéologique et Historique, 136, Vol. 1. Paris: Paul Geuthner.

1991a: "L'emploi des toponymes dans l'onomastique d'époque amorrite (1). Les noms en *mut*." *Studi epigrafici e linguistici* 8: 81–97.

1991b: "Précurseurs syriens aux protocoles néo-assyriens: Considérations sur la vie politique aux Bords de l'Euphrate." Pp. 13–72 in D. Charpin and F. Joannès, eds. *Marchands, Diplomates et Empereurs: Études sur la civilisation mésopotamienne offertes à Paul Garelli*. Paris: Éditions Recherche sur les Civilisations.

1992: "Unité et diversités au Proche-Orient à l'époque amorrite." Pp. 97–128 in Dominique Charpin and Francis Joannès, eds. *La circulation des biens, des personnes et des idées dans le Proche-Orient ancien*. Actes de la XXXVIIIᵉ Rencontre Assyriologique Internationale, Paris, 8–10 juillet 1991; Paris: Éditions Recherche sur les Civilisations.

1993: "Le combat entre le Dieu de l'orage et la Mer." *Mari: Annales de recherches interdisciplinaires* 7: 41–70.

1997: *Documents épistolaires du palais de Mari, 1*. Littératures anciennes du Proche-Orient, 16; Paris: Les Éditions du Cerf.

1998: *Documents épistolaires du palais de Mari, 2*. Littératures anciennes du Proche-Orient, 17; Paris: Les Éditions du Cerf.

2000: *Documents épistolaires du palais de Mari, 3*. Littératures anciennes du Proche-Orient, 18; Paris: Les Éditions du Cerf.

2002a: *Le Culte d'Addu d'Alep et l'affaire d'Alaḫtum*. FM, 7; Mémoires de NABU, 8; Paris: SEPOA.

2002b: "La vengeance à l'époque amorrite." *FM*, 6: 39–50.

2005: *Le Culte des pierres et les monuments commémoratifs en Syrie amorrite*. FM, 8; Mémoires de NABU, 9; Paris: SEPOA.

2008: "Environnement et occupation de l'espace: Les nomades." *Supplément au Dictionnaire de la Bible* 14 : 298–324.

Durand, Jean-Marie, and Lionel Marti

2003: "Chroniques du Moyen-Euphrate 2. Relecture de document d'Ekalte, Émar et Tuttul." *Revue d'Assyriologie* 97: 141–80.

2004: "Les Textes hépatoscopiques d'Émar (I)." *Journal Asiatique* 292: 1–53.

Ebeling, Erich, et al.,

1928–: *Reallexikon der Assyriologie und vorderasiatischen Archäologie.* Berlin: W. de Gruyter.

Ebied, R. Y., and L. R. Wickham

1970: "Al-Yaʿḳūbī's Account of the Israelite Prophets and Kings." *Journal of Near Eastern Studies* 29: 80–98.

Echols, Charles L.

2008: *'Tell Me, O Muse': The Song of Deborah (Judges 5) in the Light of Heroic Poetry.* Library of Hebrew Bible/Old Testament Studies, 487; New York: T. and T. Clark.

Ehrlich, Arnold B.

1968: *Randglossen zur hebräischen Bibel; Textkritisches, Sprachliches und Sachliches,* Vol. 3. *Josue, Richter, I. u. II. Samuelis.* Hildesheim: G. Olms (originally published 1910).

1969: *Mikrâ ki-pheschutô,* Vol. 2. *Dibrê sôferîm.* Library of Biblical Studies; New York: Ktav (originally published 1899–1901).

Eidem, Jesper

2011: *The royal Archives from Tell Leilan: Old Babylonian Letters and Treaties from the Lower Town Palace East.* Publications de l'Institut historique-archéologique néerlandais de Stamboul (PIHANS), 117; Leiden: Netherlands Institute for the Near East.

Eidem, Jesper, and Jørgen Læssøe

2001: *The Shemshāra Archives.* Historisk-filosofiske skrifter, 23; Copenhagen: Kongelige Danske Videnskabernes Selskab.

Eissfeldt, Otto

1925: *Die Quellen des Richterbuches, in synoptischer Anordnung ins Deutsche übersetzt, samt einer in Einleitung und Noten gegebenen Begründung.* Leipzig: J. C. Hinrichs.

1966: "Gottesnamen in Personennamen als Symbole menschlicher Qualitäten." Pp. 110–17 in Kurt Rudolph, ed. *Festschrift Walter Baetke: Dargebracht zu seinem 80. Geburtstag am 28. März 1964.* Weimar: Böhlau.

Elgavish, David

2000: "Did Diplomatic Immunity Exist in the Ancient Near East?" *Journal of the History of International Law* 2: 73–90.

Ellis, Richard S.

1995: "Mühle. B, Archäologisch." *RlA* 8: 401–4.

Emerton, John

1976: "Gideon and Jerubbaal." *Journal of Theological Studies* 27: 289–312.

1978: "The 'Second Bull' in Judges 6:25–28." Pp. 52–55 in M. Haran, ed. *H. L. Ginsberg Volume.* Eretz-Israel, 14; Jerusalem: Israel Exploration Society.

1985: "Some Comments on the Shibboleth Incident (Judges XII 6)." Pp. 149–57 in André Caquot, Simon Légasse, and Michel Tardieu, eds. *Mélanges bibliques et orientaux en l'honneur de M. Mathias Delcor.* Neukirchener: Butzon and Bercker Kevelaer.

Eph'al, Israel

2009: *The City Besieged: Siege and Its Manifestations in the Ancient Near East.* Culture and History of the Ancient Near East, 36; Leiden: E. J. Brill.

Eras, V. J. M.

1957: *Locks and Keys Throughout the Ages.* Amsterdam: H. H. Fronczek.

Eshel, Hanan

1990: "Isaiah VIII 23: An Historical-Geographical Analogy." *Vetus Testamentum* 40: 104–9.

Evans, Carl D.

1983: "Naram-Sin and Jeroboam: The Archetypal *Unheilsherrscher* in Mesopotamian and Biblical Historiography." Pp. 97–125 in W. W. Hallo, J. Moyer, and L. Perdue, eds. *Scripture in Context II: More Essays on the Comparative Method.* Bloomington: Indiana University Press.

Exum, J. Cheryl

1985: "'Mother in Israel': A Familiar Figure Reconsidered." Pp. 73–85 in Letty M. Russell, ed. *Feminist Interpretation of the Bible.* Philadelphia: Westminster John Knox.

1989: "The Tragic Vision and Biblical Narrative: The Case of Jephthah." Pp. 59–83 in Exum, ed., 1989.

1993: "On Judges 11." Pp. 131–44 in Brenner, ed., 1993.

1995: "Feminist Criticism: Whose Interests Are Being Served." Pp. 65–90 in Yee 1995.

2007: "Shared Glory: Solomon de Bray's Jael, Deborah and Barak." Pp. 1–37 in Exum and Nutu 2007.

Exum, J. Cheryl, ed.

1989: *Signs and Wonders: Biblical Text in Literary Focus.* Semeia Studies; Atlanta, GA: Society of Biblical Literature.

2007: *Retellings: The Bible in Literature, Music, Art and Film.* Leiden: E. J. Brill.

Exum, J. Cheryl, and Ela Nutu

2007: *Between the Text and the Canvas: The Bible and Art in Dialogue.* Bible in the Modern World, 13; Sheffield: Sheffield Phoenix Press.

Faber, Alice

1992: "Second Harvest: *šibbōlɛθ* Revisited (Yet Again)." *Journal of Semitic Studies* 37: 1–10.

Feigin, Samuel

1931: "Some Cases of Adoption in Israel." *Journal of Biblical Literature* 50: 186–200.

Feldman, Louis H.

1998: *Studies in Josephus' Rewritten Bible.* Journal for the Study of Judaism, Supplement 58; Leiden: E. J. Brill.

Fensham, F. Charles

1961: "Shamgar Ben Anath." *Journal of Near Eastern Studies* 20: 197–98.

1977: "The Numeral Seventy in the Old Testament and the Family of Jerubbaal, Ahab, Panammuwa and Athirat." *Palestine Exploration Quarterly* 109: 113–15.

Fewell, Danna Nolan

    1995: "Deconstructive Criticism: Achsah and the (E)razed City of Writing." Pp. 119–45 in Yee 1995.

Fiensy, D. A., and D. R. Darnell

    1985: "Hellenistic Synagogal Prayers (Second to Third Century A.D.)." Pp. 671–97 in Charlesworth, ed., 1985.

Fink, Amir Sumaka'i

    2008: "Levantine Standardized Luxury in the Late Bronze Age: Waste Management at Tell Atchana (Alalakh)." Pp. 165–95 in A. Fantalkin and A. Yasur-Landau, eds. *Bene Israel: Studies in the Archaeology of Israel and the Levant During the Bronze and Iron Ages in Honour of Israel Finkelstein.* CHANE 31; Leiden: E. J. Brill.

Finkelstein, Israel, Amihai Mazar, and Brian B. Schmidt

    2007: *The Quest for the Historical Israel: Debating Archaeology and the History of Early Israel.* Atlanta, GA: Society of Biblical Literature.

Finkelstein, Israel, and Lily Singer-Avitz

    2009: "Reevaluating Bethel." *Zeitschrift des Deutschen Palästina-Vereins* 125: 33–48.

Finkelstein, Jacob J.

    1962: "Mesopotamia." *Journal of Near Eastern Studies* 21: 73–92.

    1988: *The Archaeology of the Israelite Settlement.* Jerusalem: Israel Exploration Society.

Fishbane, Michael

    1985: *Biblical Interpretation in Ancient Israel.* Oxford: Oxford University Press.

Fleming, Daniel

    1992: *The Installation of Baal's High Priestess at Emar: A Window on Ancient Syrian Religion.* Harvard Semitic Studies, 42; Atlanta, GA: Scholars Press.

    1998: "Mari and the Possibilities of Biblical Memory." *Revue d'Assyriologie* 92: 41–78.

    2012: *The Legacy of Israel in Judah's Bible.* Cambridge: Cambridge University Press.

Floyd, Michael H.

    1980: "Oral Tradition as a Problematic Factor in the Historical Interpretation of Poems in the Law and the Prophets." PhD dissertation, Claremont Graduate School.

Fögen, Thorsten

    2009: *Tears in the Graeco-Roman World.* Berlin: Walter de Gruyter.

Fokkelman, Jan P.

    1995: "The Song of Deborah and Barak: Its Prosodic Levels and Structure." Pp. 595–628 in David P. Wright, David Noel Freedman, and Avi Hurvitz, eds. *Pomegranates and Golden Bells: Studies in Biblical, Jewish, and Near Eastern Ritual, Law, and Literature in Honor of Jacob Milgrom.* Winona Lake, IN: Eisenbrauns.

Foley, Helene P.

    2005: "Women in Ancient Epic." Pp. 105–18 in J. Foley 2005.

Foley, John Miles, ed.

    2005: *A Companion to Ancient Epic.* Oxford: Blackwell.

Foster, Benjamin R.

    1996: *Before the Muses: An Anthology of Akkadian Literature.* 2 vols. Bethesda, MD: CDL.

Fowler, Jeaneane D.

    1988: *Theophoric Personal Names in Ancient Hebrew: A Comparative Study.* Journal for the Study of the Old Testament Supplement, 49; Sheffield: JSOT Press.

Frame, Grant

    1995: *Rulers of Babylonia: From the Second Dynasty of Isin to the End of Assyrian Domination (1157–612 BC).* RIMB, 2; Toronto: University of Toronto Press.

Franke, Sabina

    1995: "Kings of Akkad: Sargon and Naram-Sin." Pp. 831–41 in Sasson, Baines, Beckman, and Rubinson, eds., 1995.

Franklin, Naomi

    2003: "The Tombs of the Kings of Israel: Two Recently Identified 9th-Century Tombs from Omride Samaria." *Zeitschrift des Deutschen Palastina-Vereins* 119: 1–11.

Freedman, David Noel, ed.

    1980: *Pottery, Poetry, and Prophecy: Collected Essays on Hebrew Poetry.* Winona Lake, IN: Eisenbrauns.

    1992: *The Anchor Bible Dictionary.* New York: Doubleday.

Freeman, Sarah Elizabeth

    1943: "A Copper Dagger of the Middle Bronze Age in Baltimore." *Bulletin of the American Schools of Oriental Research* 90: 28–30.

Frick, Frank S.

    1978: *The City in Ancient Israel.* SBL Dissertation Series, 36; Missoula, MT: Scholar's Press.

    1992: "Palestine, Climate of." *ABD* 5: 119–26.

Fritz, Volkmar

    1982: "Abimelech und Sichem in Jdc. Ix." *Vetus Testamentum* 32: 129–44.

    2000: "Die Grenzen des Landes Israel." Pp. 14–34 in Gershon Galil and Moshe Weinfeld, eds. *Studies in Historical Geography and Biblical Historiography Presented to Zechariah Kallai.* Vetus Testamentum Supplement, 81; Leiden: E. J. Brill.

    2011: *The Emergence of Israel in the 12th and 11th Centuries BCE.* SBL Encyclopedia Series, 2; Atlanta, GA: Society of Biblical Literature.

Frolov, Serge

    2007: "Fire, Smoke, and Judah in Judges: A Response to Gregory Wong." *Scandinavian Journal of the Old Testament* 21: 127–38.

Frymer-Kensky, Tikvah

    1998: "Virginity in the Bible." Pp. 79–96 in Victor H. Matthews, Bernard M. Levinson, and Tikva Frymer-Kensky, eds. *Gender and Law in the Hebrew Bible and the Ancient Near East.* Journal for the Study of the Old Testament Supplement, 262; Sheffield: Sheffield Academic Press.

Fuchs, Andreas

    1998: *Die Annalen des Jahres 711 v. Chr. nach Prismenfragmenten aus Ninive und Assur.* State Archives of Assyria Studies, 8; Helsinki: Neo-Assyrian Text Corpus Project.

Fuchs, Esther
  1989: "Marginalization, Ambiguity, Silencing: The Story of Jephthah's Daughter." *Journal of Feminist Studies in Religion* 5: 35–45.

Garbini, Giovanni
  1978: "Il Cantico di Debora." *La Parola del Passato* 33: 5–31.

Garsiel, Moshe
  1993: "Homiletic Name-Derivations as a Literary Device in the Gideon Narrative: Judges vi–viii." *Vetus Testamentum* 43: 302–17.

Gass, Erasmus
  2005: *Die Ortsnamen des Richterbuchs in historischer und redaktioneller Perspektive*. Abhandlungen des Deutschen Palästina-Vereins, 35; Wiesbaden: Harrassowitz.

George, Andrew R.
  1999: Review of Marc van de Mieroop's *The Ancient Mesopotamian City*. *Bulletin of the School of Oriental and African Studies, University of London*, 62: 550–52.
  2007: "The Civilizing of Ea-Enkidu: An Unusual Tablet of the Babylonian Gilgameš Epic." *Revue d'Assyriologie* 101: 59–80.

Gerbrandt, Gerald Eddie
  1986: *Kingship According to Deuteronomistic History*. SBL Dissertation Series, 87; Atlanta, GA: Scholars Press.

Gerhards, Meik
  2009: "Die biblischen 'Hethiter.'" *Die Welt des Orients* 39: 145–79.

Gerstein, Beth
  1989: "A Ritual Processed: A Look at Judges 11.40." Pp. 175–93 in Mieke Bal, ed. *Anti-Covenant: Counter-Reading Women's Lives in the Hebrew Bible*. Journal for the Study of the Old Testament Supplement, 81 [= Bible and Literature Series, 22]; Sheffield: JSOT Press.

Gesenius, Wilhelm
  1910: *Gesenius' Hebrew Grammar*, as edited and enlarged by the late E. Kautzsche. 2nd English edition, by A. E. Cowley. Oxford: Clarendon.

Geus, C. H. J. de
  1976: *The Tribes of Israel*. Assen: Van Gorcum.

Gevirtz, Stanley
  1958: "The Hapax Legomenon תרמה (Judg. 9:31)." *Journal of Near Eastern Studies* 17: 59–60.
  1963: "Jericho and Shechem: A Religio-Literary Aspect of City Destruction." *Vetus Testamentum* 13: 52–62.

Ghouti, Michael
  1991: "*Sapâdum, bakûm* et la déploration à Mari." *NABU* 27, pp. 21–23.

Gibson, Arthur
  1976: "*ṣnḥ* in Judges I 14: NEB and AV Translations." *Vetus Testamentum* 26: 275–83.

Gilan, Amir
  2008: "Were There Cannibals in Syria? History and Fiction in an Old Hittite Literary Text." Pp. 267–84 in Ettore Cingano and Lucio Milano, eds. *Papers on Ancient Literatures: Greece, Rome and the Near East: Proceedings of the "Advanced Seminar in the Humanities," Venice International University 2004–2005*.

Quaderni del Dipartimento di Scienze dell'Antichità e del Vicino Oriente, Università Ca' Foscari, Venezia, 4; Padua: S.A.R.G.O.N. Editrice e Libreria.

Gilead, Chaim
1988–89: "סיפור מלחמת דבורה וברק בסיסרא כפשוטו." *Beit Mikra* 116–19: 292–301.

Ginsberg, Harold L.
1969: "Aramaic Proverbs and Precepts." Pp. 427–30 in Pritchard 1969.

Ginzberg, Louis
2003: *Legends of the Jews*. 2nd edition. New York: Jewish Publication Society.

Glaser, O.
1932: "Zur Erzählung von Ehud und Eglon. Ri. 3, 14–26." *Zeitschrift des deutschen Palästina-Vereins* 55: 81–82.

Glassner, Jean-Jacques
1987–90: "Mahlzeit." *RlA* 7: 259–70.
2004: *Mesopotamian Chronicles*. Writings from the Ancient World, 19; Atlanta, GA: Society of Biblical Literature.

Globe, Alexander
1974: "The Literary Structure and Unity of the Song of Deborah." *Journal of Biblical Literature* 93: 493–512.
1975: "Judges V 27." *Vetus Testamentum* 25: 362–67.

Goodwin, Donald Watson
1969: *Text-restoration Methods in Contemporary U.S.A. Biblical Scholarship*. Pubblicazioni del Seminario di semitistica, Ricerche, 5; Naples: Istituto orientale di Napoli.

Goren, Y., Israel Finkelstein, and Nadav Na'aman
2003: "The Expansion of the Kingdom of Amurru According to the Petrographic Investigation of the Amarna Tablets." *Bulletin of the American Schools of Oriental Research* 329: 2–11.

Gottwald, Norman K.
1979: *The Tribes of Yahweh: A Sociology of the Religion of Liberated Israel, 1250–1050 B.C.E.* Maryknoll, NY: Orbis.

Graesser, Carl F.
1972: "Standing Stones in Ancient Palestine." *Biblical Archaeologist* 35: 33–63.

Gray, John
1977: "A Cantata of the Autumn Festival: Psalm LXVIII." *Journal of Semitic Studies* 22: 2–26.

Grayson, Albert Kirk
1987: *Assyrian Rulers of the Third and Second Millennia BC to 1115 BC*. RIMA, 1; Toronto: University of Toronto Press.
1991: *Assyrian Rulers of the Early First Millennium BC, I. 1114–859 BC*. RIMA, 2; Toronto: University of Toronto Press.
1996: *Assyrian Rulers of the Early First Millennium BC, II. 858–745 BC*. RIMA, 3; Toronto: University of Toronto Press.

Green, Douglas J.
2010: "I Undertook Great Works": *The Ideology of Domestic Achievements in West Semitic Royal Inscriptions*. Forschungen zum Alten Testament. 2 Reihe, 41; Tübingen: Mohr Siebeck.

Greenberg, Moshe
    1993: "Is There a Mari Parallel to the Israelite Enemy-*ḥerem?*" Pp. 49–53 in
        S. Aḥituv and B. A. Levine, eds. *Avraham Malamat Volume* (in Hebrew). Eretz-
        Israel, 24; Jerusalem: Israel Exploration Society.
Greenberg, Raphael
    1987: "New Light on the Early Iron Age at Tell Beit Mirsim." *Bulletin of the Ameri-
        can Schools of Oriental Research* 265: 55–80.
Greenstein, Edward, and David Marcus
    1976: "The Akkadian Inscription of Idrimi." *Journal of the Ancient Near Eastern
        Society of Columbia University* 8: 59–96.
Grimme, Hubert
    1896: "Abriss der biblisch-hebräischen Metrik." *Zeitschrift der Deutschen Morgen-
        landschen Gesellschaft* 50: 529–84.
Gross, Walter
    2009: *Richter.* Mit Karten von Erasmus Gass. Herders Theologischer Kommentar
        zum Alten Testament; Freiburg im Breisgau: Herder.
Grossfeld, Bernard
    1973: "A Critical Note on Judg 4, 21." *Zeitschrift für die Alttestamentliche Wissen-
        schaft* 85: 348–96.
Grottanelli, Cristiano
    1989: "The Roles of the Guest in the Epic Banquet." Pp. 272–332 in C. Zac-
        cagnini, ed. *Production and Consumption in the Ancient Near East.* Budapest:
        Egyptology Department of the University.
    1994: "Aspetti symbolici del latte nella bibbia." Pp. 381–97 in L. Milano, ed. *Drink-
        ing in Ancient Societies: History and Culture of Drinks in the Ancient Near East.
        Papers of the Symposium Held in Rome, May 17–19, 1990.* HANE/S, 6. Padua:
        Sargon.
    1999: *Kings and Prophets: Monarchic Power, Inspired Leadership, and Sacred Text in
        Biblical Narrative.* New York: Oxford University Press.
Guest, P. D.
    1998: "Can Judges Survive Without Sources? Challenging the Consensus." *Journal
        for the Study of the Old Testament* 78: 43–61.
Guggenheimer, Heinrich W.
    1998. *Seder Olam: The Rabbinic View of Biblical Chronology.* Northvale, NJ: Jason
        Aronson.
Guichard, Michaël
    1999: "Les aspects religieux de la guerre à Mari." *Revue d'Assyriologie* 93: 27–48.
    2011 : "Un David raté ou une histoire de habiru à l'époque amorrite. Vie et mort
        de Samsī-Ērah, chef de guerre et homme du peuple." Pp. 29–93 in Jean-Marie
        Durand, Thomas Römer, and Michael Langlois, eds. *Le jeune héros: Recherches
        sur la formation et la diffusion d'un thème littéraire au Proche-Orient ancien.
        Actes du colloque organisé par les chaires d'Assyriologie et des Milieux bibliques du
        Collège de France, Paris, les 6 et 7 avril 2009.* Orbis Biblicus et Orientalis, 250;
        Göttingen: Vandenhoeck and Ruprecht.
Guillaume, Philippe
    2000: "Deborah and the Seven Tribes." *Biblische Notizen* 101: 18–21.

2001: "Dating the *Negatives Besitzverzeichnis* (Judges 1,27–34): The Case of Sidon." *Henoch* 23: 131–37.

2004: *Waiting for Josiah: The Judges*. London: T. and T. Clark International.

Gunn, David M.

2005: *Judges*. Blackwell Bible Commentaries; Malden, MA: Blackwell.

Güterbock, Hans G.

1938: "Die historische Tradition und ihre literarische Gestaltung bei Babyloniern und Hethitern." *Zeitschrift für Assyriologie* 44: 45–149.

Haag, Herbert

1967: "Gideon-Jerubbaal-Abimelech." *Zeitschrift für die alttestamentliche Wissenschaft* 70: 305–12.

Haak, Robert D.

1982: "A Study and New Interpretation of *qṣr npš*." *Journal of Biblical Literature* 101: 161–67.

Hackett, Jo Ann

1985: "In the Days of Jael: Reclaiming the History of Women in Ancient Israel." Pp. 15–38 in Clarissa W. Atkinson, Constance Buchanan, and Margaret R. Miles, eds., *Immaculate and Powerful: The Female in Sacred Image and Social Reality*. Boston: Beacon.

Hallo, William W.

1995: "Lamentations and Prayers in Sumer and Akkad." Pp. 1871–881 in Sasson, Baines, Beckman, and Rubinson, eds., 1995.

2004: "New Light on the Story of Achsah." Pp. 330–35 in John Kaltner and Louis Stulman, eds. *Inspired Speech: Prophecy in the Ancient Near East, Essays in Honor of Herbert B. Huffmon*. Edinburgh: T. and T. Clark.

Hallo, William W., and K. L. Younger

1997–2003: *The Context of Scripture*, Vol. 1, 1997; Vol. 2, 2000; Vol. 3, 2003; Leiden: E. J. Brill.

Halpern, Baruch

1978: "The Rise of Abimelek Ben-Jerubbaal." *Hebrew Annual Review* 2: 79–100.

1983a: "The Resourceful Israelite Historian: The Song of Deborah and Israelite Historiography." *Harvard Theological Review* 76: 379–402.

1983b: *The Emergence of Israel in Canaan*. SBL Monographs Series, 29; Chico, CA: Scholars Press.

1988a: *The First Historians: The Hebrew Bible and History*. San Francisco: Harper and Row.

1988b: "The Assassination of Eglon: The First Locked-Room Murder Mystery." *Bible Review* 4: 33–41, 44.

Hamlin, E. John

1985: "The Significance of Bethel in Judges 1:22–26." *Eastern Great Lakes and Midwest Biblical Societies, Proceedings* 5: 67–72.

Hamori, Esther J.

2010: "The Spirit of Falsehood." *Catholic Biblical Quarterly* 72: 15–30.

Handy, Lowell K.

1992: "Uneasy Laughter: Ehud and Eglon as Ethnic Humor." *Scandinavian Journal of the Old Testament* 6: 233–46.

Haran, Menaḥem

    1969: "*Zebaḥ hayyamîm.*" *Vetus Testamentum* 19: 11–22.

Harlé, Paul, and Thérèse Roqueplo

    1999: *Les Juges: Traduction des textes grecs de la Septante.* La Bible d'Alexandrie, 7; Paris: Les Éditions du Cerf.

Harrington, Daniel J.

    1985: "Pseudo-Philo (First Century A.D.)." Pp. 297–377 in Charlesworth, ed., 1985.

Harris, Rivkah

    1964: "The *Nadītu* Women." Pp. 106–35 in J. A. Brinkman, ed. *Studies Presented to A. Leo Oppenheim, June 7, 1964.* Chicago: University of Chicago Press.

Harter, Stephanie, Françoise Bouchet, Kosta Y. Mumcuoglu, and Joe E. Zias

    2004: "Toilet Practices Among Members of the Dead Sea Scrolls Sect at Qumran (100 BC–68 CE)." *Revue de Qumran* 21: 579–84.

Hartmann, Thomas A.G.

    2000: "גמד in Richter 3,16 oder die Pygmäen im Dschungel der Längenmasse." *Zeitschrift für Althebraistik* 13: 188–93.

Harvey, Julien

    1962: "Le 'Rîb-Pattern,' réquisitoire sur la rupture de l'alliance." *Biblica* 43: 172–96.

Haupt, Paul

    1909: "Midian und Sinai." *Zeitschrift der Deutschen Morgenländischen Gesellschaft* 63: 506–30.

Hauser, Alan J.

    1975: "The 'Minor Judges': A Re-Evaluation." *Journal of Biblical Literature* 94: 190–200.

    1987: "Two Songs of Victory: A Comparison of Exodus 15 and Judges 5." Pp. 265–84 in E. R. Follis, ed. *Directions in Hebrew Poetry.* Journal for the Study of the Old Testament Supplement, 40; Sheffield: Sheffield Academic Press.

Hawkins, J. David

    1983: "The Hittite Name of Til-Barsip: Evidence from a New Hieroglyphic Fragment from Tell Aḥmar." *Anatolian Studies* 33: 131–36.

Heimpel, Wolfgang

    2003: *Letters to the King of Mari: A New Translation, with Historical Introduction, Notes, and Commentary.* Mesopotamian Civilizations, 12; Winona Lake, IN: Eisenbrauns.

Helck, Wolfgang, and Eberhard Otto

    1972–92: *Lexikon der Ägyptologie.* Wiesbaden: Harrassowitz.

Hendel, Ronald S.

    1996: "Sibilants and *šibbōlet* (Judges 12:6)." *Bulletin of the American Schools of Oriental Research* 301: 69–75.

Herdner, Andrée

    1963: *Corpus des tablettes en cunéiformes alphabétiques découvertes à Ras Shamra-Ugarit de 1929 à 1939.* Institut français d'Archéologie de Beyrouth. Bibliothèque archéologique et historique, 79; Mission de Ras Shamra, 10; Paris: P. Geuthner.

Hess, Richard S.

    1997: "The Dead Sea Scrolls and Higher Criticism of the Hebrew Bible: The Case of 4QJudg[a]." Pp. 122–28 in Stanley E. Porter and Craig A. Evans, eds. *The Scrolls and the Scriptures: Qumran Fifty Years After*. Journal for the Study of Pseudepigrapha Supplement, 26; Sheffield: Sheffield Academic Press.

    1999: "Judges 1–5 and Its Translation." Pp. 142–60 in Porter and Hess 1999.

Hoffman, Yair

    1999: "The Deuteronomistic Concept of the *ḥerem*." *Zeitschrift für die Alttestamentliche Wissenschaft* 111: 196–210.

Hoftijzer, J., and K. Jongeling

    1995: *Dictionary of North-West Semitic Inscriptions*. Leiden: E. J. Brill.

Hogeterp, Albert L. A.

    2010: "Daniel and the Qumran Daniel Cycle: Observations on 4QFour Kingdoms[A–B] (4Q552–553)." Pp. 173–91 in Mladen Popović, ed. *Authoritative Scriptures in Ancient Judaism*. Journal for the Study of Judaism Supplement, 141; Leiden: E. J. Brill.

Holder, John

    1988: "The Presuppositions, Accusations, and Threats of 1 Kings 14:1–18." *Journal of Biblical Literature* 107: 27–38.

Holm, Tawney L.

    2008: "The Fiery Furnace in the Book of Daniel and the Ancient Near East." *Journal of the American Oriental Society* 128: 85–104.

Honeyman, A. M.

    1953: "The Salting of Shechem." *Vetus Testamentum* 3: 192–95.

Horowitz, Wayne, and Aaron Shaffer

    1992: "A Fragment of a Letter from Hazor." *Israel Exploration Journal* 42: 165–67.

Horowitz, Wayne, Takayoshi Oshima, and Seth Sanders

    2006: *Cuneiform in Canaan: Cuneiform Sources from the Land of Israel in Ancient Times*. Jerusalem: Israel Exploration Society.

Houston, Walter J.

    1997: "Misunderstanding or Midrash: The Prose Appropriation of Poetic Material in the Hebrew Bible (Part II)." *Zeitschrift für die alttestamentliche Wissenschaft* 109: 534–48.

Hubbard, Robert L.

    1984: "The Hebrew Root *pgʿ* as a Legal Term." *Journal of the Evangelical Theological Society* 27: 129–33.

Hübner, Ulrich

    1987: "Mord auf dem Abort? Überlegungen zu Humor, Gewaltdarstellung und Realienkunde in Richter 3,12–30." *Biblische Notizen* 40: 130–40.

Hughes, Dennis D.

    1991: *Human Sacrifice in Ancient Greece*. London: Routledge.

Irwin, Brian P.

    2012: "Not Just Any King: Abimelech, the Northern Monarchy, and the Final Form of Judges." *Journal of Biblical Literature* 131: 443–54.

Isaac, Ephraim

    1983: "1, Ethiopic Apocalypse of Enoch. Second Century B.C.–First Century A.D." Pp. 5–89 in Charlesworth, ed., 1983.

Ishida, T.

    1979: "The Structure and Historical Implications of the Lists of Pre-Israelite Nations." *Biblica* 60: 461–90.

Israel Museum

    1971: *The Israel Museum. A Brief Guide.* Jerusalem: Israel Museum (Muze'on Yiśra'el).

Jackson, Kent

    1983: *The Ammonite Language of the Iron Age.* Harvard Semitic Monographs, 27; Chico, CA: Scholars Press.

Jacobsen, Thorkild

    1983: "Lad in the Desert." *Journal of the American Oriental Society* 103 [= J. M. Sasson, ed. *Studies in Literature from the Ancient Near East, by Members of the American Oriental Society, Dedicated to Samuel Noah Kramer.* New Haven, CT: American Oriental Society]: 193–200.

Jacobson, Howard

    1992: "The Judge Bedan (1 Samuel xii 11)." *Vetus Testamentum* 42: 123–24.

    1994: "Bedan and Barak Reconsidered." *Vetus Testamentum* 44: 108–9.

    1996: *A Commentary on Pseudo-Philo's Liber Antiquitatum Biblicarum, with Latin Text and English.* 2 vols. Arbeiten zur Geschichte des antiken Judentums und des Urchristentums, 31; Leiden: E. J. Brill.

Jacquet, A.

    2002: "Lugal-meš et *malikum*: Nouvel examen du *kispum* à Mari." *FM*, 6: 51–68.

    2011: *Documents relatifs aux dépenses pour le culte.* *FM*, 12; Paris: SEPOA.

    2012: "Funerary Rites and Cult of the Ancestors During the Amorite Period: The Evidence of the Royal Archives of Mari." Pp. 123–36 in P. Pfälzner, ed. *(Re-)Constructing Funerary Rituals in the Ancient Near East.* Wiesbaden: Otto Harrassowitz.

Jans, Edgar

    2001: *Abimelech und sein Königtum: Diachrone und synchrone Untersuchungen zu Ri 9.* Arbeiten zu Text und Sprache im Alten Testament, 66; St. Ottilien: EOS-Verlag.

Janzen, David

    2005: "Why the Deuteronomist Told About the Sacrifice of Jephthah's Daughter." *Journal for the Study of the Old Testament* 29: 339–57.

Janzen, J. Gerald

    1987: "A Certain Woman in the Rhetoric of Judges 9." *Journal for the Study of the Old Testament* 38: 33–37.

Jassen, Alex P.

    2011: "Re-Reading 4QPesher Isaiah A. 4Q161. Forty Years after DJD 5." Pp. 57–90 in George J. Brooke and Jesper Høgenhaven, eds. *The Mermaid and the Partridge: Essays from the Copenhagen Conference on Revising Texts from Cave Four.* Studies on the Texts of the Desert of Judah, 96; Leiden: E. J. Brill.

Jastrow, Marcus

    1950: *A Dictionary of the Targumim, the Talmud Babli and Yerushalmi, and the Midrashic Literature.* New York: Pardes.

Jean, Charles-François
1950: *Lettres diverses*. ARM, 2; Paris: Imprimerie nationale = Geuthner
Jeffrey, David Lyle, ed.
1992: *A Dictionary of Biblical Tradition in English Literature*. Grand Rapids, MI: W. B. Eerdmans.
Jenni, Ernst, and Claus Westermann
1997: *Theological Lexicon of the Old Testament*. 3 vols. Peabody, MA: Hendrickson.
Jeyes, Ulla
1989: *Old Babylonian Extispicy: Omen Texts in the British Museum*. Uitgaven van het Nederlands Historisch-Archaeologisch Instituut te İstanbul, 64; Istanbul: Nederlands Historisch-Archaeologisch Instituut te İstanbul.
Joannès, Francis
1994: "L'eau et la glace." *FM*, 2: 133–50.
Jobling, David
1989: "Right-Brained Story of Left-Handed Man: An Antiphon to Yairah Amit." Pp. 125–31 in Exum, ed., 1989.
Jongeling, Karel
2005: "'And It Came to Pass' Again." Pp. 291–329 in L. Kogan and S. Loesov, eds. *Babel und Bibel* 2. *Memoriae Igor M. Diakonoff*. Winona Lake, IN: Eisenbrauns.
Josephus, Flavius. See Whiston, William, trans.
Jospe, Raphael
1990: "Hillel's Rule." *Jewish Quarterly Review* 81: 45–57.
Jost, Renate
1997: "Achsahs Quellen; feministisch-sozialgeschichtliche Überlegungen zu Josua 15,15–20/Ri 1,12–15." Pp. 110–25 in Rainer Kessler, Kerstin Ulrich, Milton Schwantes, and Gary Stansell, eds. *"Ihr Völker alle, klatscht in die Hände!" Festschrift für Erhard S. Gerstenberger zum 65. Geburtstag*. Münster: LIT.
Joüon, Paul, and T. Muraoka
1996: *A Grammar of Biblical Hebrew*. 2 vols. Rome: Pontifical Biblical Institute.
Jull, Tom A.
1998: "מקרה in Judges 3: A Scatological Reading." *Journal for the Study of the Old Testament* 81: 63–75.
Kalimi, Isaac
1980: "On Three Assumptions in the Study of the Kenites." *Beth Mikra* 83: 367–72.
1988: "Three Assumptions About the Kenites." *Zeitschrift für die alttestamentliche Wissenschaft* 100: 386–93.
Kallai, Zecharia
1986: "The Settlement Traditions of Ephraim." *Zeitschrift des Deutschen Palästina-Vereins* 102: 68–74 [= Kallai 1998: 202–10].
1998: *Biblical Historiography and Historical Geography: Collection of Studies*. Frankfurt am Main: Peter Lang.
Kasher, Aryeh
1981: "The Historical Background of 'Megillath Antiochus.'" *Proceedings of the American Academy for Jewish Research* 48: 207–30.

Katz, Dina

1993: *Gilgamesh and Akka*. Groningen: STYX.

Kaufmann, Yeḥezqel

1953: *The Biblical Account of the Conquest of Palestine*. Jerusalem: Magnes.

1960: *The Religion of Israel, from Its Beginnings to the Babylonian Exile*. Translated and abridged by Moshe Greenberg. Chicago: University of Chicago Press.

1962: *Sefer Shofṭîm*. Jerusalem: Qiryat Sefer.

Keith, A. L.

1924: "The Taunt in Homer and Vergil." *Classical Journal* 19: 554–60.

Kempinski, Aharon, and Ronny Reich, eds.

1992: *The Architecture of Ancient Israel: From the Prehistoric to the Persian Periods—in Memory of Immanuel (Munya) Dunayevsky*. Jerusalem: Israel Exploration Society.

King, Philip J., and Lawrence Stager

2001: *Life in Biblical Israel*. Louisville, KY: Westminster John Knox.

Kitchen, Kenneth A.

2007: "Moab in Egyptian and Other Sources: Fact and Fantasy." *Göttinger Miszellen* 212: 119–28.

Kittel, Rudolph, Karl Elliger, Wilhelm Rudolph, and Hans Peter Rüger

1990: *Torah, Nevi'im u-Khetuvim*. Biblia Hebraica Stuttgartensia, Ed. 4; Stuttgart: Deutsche Bibelgesellschaft.

Klein, Lillian R.

1988: *The Triumph of Irony in the Book of Judges*. Journal for the Study of the Old Testament Supplement, 68; Sheffield: Almond Press.

1993a: "A Spectrum of Female Characters in the Book of Judges." Pp. 24–33 in Brenner, ed., 1993.

1993b: "The Book of Judges: Paradigm and Deviation in Images of Women." Pp. 55–71 in Brenner, ed., 1993.

1999: "Achsah: What Price This Prize?" Pp. 18–26 in Brenner, ed., 1999.

Knauf, Ernst Axel

1988: *Midian: Untersuchungen zur Geschichte Palästinas und Nordarabiens am Ende des 2. Jahrtausends v. Chr*. Wiesbaden: Harrassowitz.

1991: "Eglon and Ophrah: Two Toponymic Notes on the Book of Judges." *Journal for the Study of the Old Testament* 51: 25–54.

2010: "History in Judges." Pp. 140–49 in Lester L. Grabbe, ed. *Israel in Transition: From Late Bronze II to Iron IIa (c. 1250–850 B.C.E.)*, Vol. 2. *The Texts*. Library of Hebrew Bible/Old Testament Studies, 521; European Seminar in Historical Methodology, 8: New York: T. and T. Clark.

Knights, C. H.

1993: "Kenites = Rechabites?: 1 Chronicles II 55 Reconsidered." *Vetus Testamentum* 43: 10–18.

Knoppers, Gary N.

1993: "Treaty, Tribute List, or Diplomatic Letter: KTU 3.1 Reexamined." *Bulletin of the American Schools of Oriental Research* 289: 81–94.

Kochavi, Moshe

1974: "Khirbet Rabûd = Debir." *Tel Aviv* 1: 2–33.

2000: "Hébron: Archéologie." Pp. 51–56 in A. Lemaire, ed. *Les routes du Proche-Orient. Des séjours d'Abraham aux caravanes de l'encens*. Paris: Desclée de Brouwer.

Koehler, Ludwig, Walter Baumgartner, and Johann Jakob Stamm
1994–99: *The Hebrew and Aramaic Lexicon of the Old Testament*. Leiden: E. J. Brill.

Kogan, Leonid
2005: "Comparative Notes in the Old Testament (I)." Pp. 731–37 in L. Kogan and S. Loesov, eds. *Memoriae Igor M. Diakonoff*. Babel and Bibel, 2; Winona Lake, IN: Eisenbrauns.

Koller, Aaron J.
2013: *The Semantic Field of Cutting Tools in Biblical Hebrew: The Interface of Philological, Semantic, and Archaeological Evidence*. The Catholic Biblical Quarterly Monograph Series, 49; Washington, DC: Catholic Biblical Association of America.

Kooij, A. van der
1995: "'And I also said': A New Interpretation of Judges II 3." *Vetus Testamentum* 45: 294–306.
1996: "On Male and Female Views in Judges 4–5." Pp. 135–52 in Bob Becking and Meindert Dijkstra, eds. *On Reading Prophetic Texts: Gender-Specific and Related Studies in Memory of Fokkelien van Dijk-Hemmes*. BibInter, 18; Leiden: E. J. Brill.

Koppen, Frans van
2007: "Syrian Trade Routes of the Mari Age and Mb II Hazor." Pp. 367–74 in Manfred Bietak and Hermann Hunger, eds. *The Synchronisation of Civilisations in the Eastern Mediterranean in the Second Millennium B.C., III*. Contributions to the Chronology of the Eastern Mediterranean, 9; Österreichische Akademie Der Wissenschaften, Denkschriften der Gesamtakademie, 37; Vienna: Verlag der Österreichische Akademie Der Wissenschaften.

Kraeling, E. G.
1935: "Difficulties in the Story of Ehud." *Journal of Biblical Literature* 54: 205–10.

Krafeld-Daugherty, Maria
1994: *Wohnen im Alten Orient: Eine Untersuchung zur Verwendung von Räumen in altorientalischen Wohnhäusern*. Altertumskunde des vorderen Orients, 3; Münster: Ugarit Verlag.

Kramer, Phyllis Silverman
1999: "Jephthah's Daughter: A Thematic Approach to the Narrative as Seen in Selected Rabbinic Exegesis and in Artwork." Pp. 67–92 in Brenner, ed., 1999.

Kugel, James
1981: *The Idea of Biblical Poetry: Parallelism and Its History*. New Haven, CT: Yale University Press.

Kupper, Jean-Robert
1950: *Correspondance de Kibri-Dagan, gouverneur de Terqa*. ARM, 3; Paris: Imprimerie nationale = Geuthner.
1954: *Correspondance de Baḫdi-Lim, préfet du palais de Mari*. ARM, 6; Paris: Imprimerie nationale = Geuthner.
1998: *Lettres royales du temps de Zimri-Lim*. ARM, 28; Paris: Éditions Recherche sur les Civilisations.

Kutsko, John F.

    2000: *Between Heaven and Earth: Divine Presence and Absence in the Book of Ezekiel.* Biblical and Judaic Studies from the University of California, San Diego, 7; Winona Lake, IN: Eisenbrauns.

Lafont, Bertrand

    1987: "Les filles de roi de Mari." Pp. 113–21 in J.-M. Durand, ed. *La Femme dans le Proche-Orient Antique.* XXXIIIe Rencontre Assyriologique Internationale, Paris, 7–10 juillet 1986; Paris: Éditions Recherche sur les Civilisations.

    1991: "Un homme d'affaires à Karkemiš." Pp. 275–86 in D. Charpin and F. Joannès, eds. *Marchands, Diplomates et Empereurs: Études sur la civilisation mésopotamienne offertes à Paul Garelli.* Paris: Éditions Recherche sur les Civilisations.

    2001a: "Relations internationales, alliances et diplomatie au temps des royaumes amorrites. Essai de synthèse." *Amurru* 2: 213–328.

    2001b: "Fortunes, héritages et patrimoines dans la haute histoire mésopotamienne; à propos de quelques inventaires de biens mobiliers." Pp. 295–313 in C. Breniquet and C. Kepinski, eds. *Études mésopotamiennes: Recueil de textes offert à Jean-Louis Huot.* Paris: Éditions Recherche sur les Civilisations.

Lafont (Démare), Sophie

    1997: "Un 'cas royal' à l'époque de Mari." *Revue d'Assyriologie* 91: 109–19.

    2000: "L'arbitrage en Mésopotamie." *Revue de l'arbitrage* 4: 557–90.

Lagarde, Paul de

    1870: *Onomastica Sacra.* 1st edition. Gottingae: Rente.

Lagrange, Marie-Joseph

    1903: *Le livre des Juges.* Études bibliques; Paris: V. Lecoffre.

Lambert, Wilfred G.

    2007: *Babylonian Oracle Questions.* Mesopotamian Civilizations, 13. Winona Lake, IN: Eisenbrauns.

Landers, Solomon

    1991: "Did Jephthah Kill His Daughter?" *Bible Review* 7/4: 23–31, 42.

Lanoir, Corinne

    1997: "Le livre des Juges, l'histoire et les femmes." *Foi et Vie* 96/4: 55–71.

Lapp, Paul W.

    1968: "Bab edh-Dhra,' Perizzites and Emim." Pp. 1–25 in *Jerusalem Through the Ages: The Twenty-Fifth Archaeological Convention, October 1967.* Jerusalem: Israel Exploration Society.

LaRocca-Pitts, Elizabeth C.

    2001: *"Of Wood and Stone": The Significance of Israelite Cultic Items in the Bible and Its Early Interpreters.* Harvard Semitic Monographs, 61; Winona Lake, IN: Eisenbrauns.

Laroche, Emmanuel

    1971: *Catalogue des textes Hittites.* Études et commentaires, 75; Paris: Klincksieck.

Latvus, Kari

    1998: *God, Anger and Ideology: The Anger of God in Joshua and Judges in Relation to Deuteronomy and the Priestly Writings.* Journal for the Study of the Old Testament Supplement, 279; Sheffield: Sheffield Academic Press.

Layton, Scott C.

    1990: *Archaic Features of Canaanite Personal Names in the Hebrew Bible.* Harvard Semitic Monographs, 47; Atlanta, GA: Scholars Press.

    1997: "Yael in Judges 4: An Onomastic Rejoinder." *Zeitschrift für die alttestamentliche Wissenschaft* 109: 93–94.

Lebeau, Marc

    2005: "Eau et sanitaires à l'étage." *Subartu* 16: 99–105.

Légasse, Simon

    1985: "Le cycle de Gédéon (Juges, 6–13), commenté par les Pères de l'Eglise." *Bulletin de Littérature Ecclésiastique* (Toulouse) 86: 163–97.

    1991: "Le cycle de Gédéon (Juges, 6–13), d'après l'ancienne littérature juive." *Bulletin de Littérature Ecclésiastique* (Toulouse) 92: 163–80, 243–58.

Lemaire, André

    1981: "Galaad et Makîr: Remarques sur la tribu de Manassé à l'est du Jourdain." *Vetus Testamentum* 31: 39–61.

    1985: "L'incident du *sibbolet* (Jg 12,6): Perspective historique." Pp. 275–81 in André Caquot, Simon Légasse, and Michel Tardieu, eds. *Mélanges bibliques et orientaux en l'honneur de M. Mathias Delcor.* Neukirchen-Vluyn: Butzon and Bercker Kevelaer.

Lemche, Niels P.

    1985: *Early Israel.* Vetus Testamentum Supplement, 37; Leiden: E. J. Brill.

    1998: "Greater Canaan: The Implication of a Correct Reading of EA 151:49–67." *Bulletin of the American Schools of Oriental Research* 310: 19–24.

Lemos, Tracy M.

    2006: "Shame and Mutilation of Enemies in the Hebrew Bible." *Journal of Biblical Literature* 125: 225–41.

    2010: *Marriage Gifts and Social Change in Ancient Palestine: 1200 BCE to 200 CE.* Cambridge: Cambridge University Press.

Leneman, Helen

    2007: "Re-visioning a Biblical Story Through Libretto and Music: *Debora e Jaele* by Ildebrando Pizzetti." Pp. 87–113 in Exum 2007 [= *Biblical Interpretation* 15: 428–63].

Lenzi, Alan

    2008: *Secrecy and the Gods: Secret Knowledge in Ancient Mesopotamia and Biblical Israel.* State Archives of Assyria Studies, 19; Helsinki: Neo-Assyrian Text Corpus Project.

Le Roux, Nicolas

    2006: *Un Régicide au nom de dieu. L'assassinat d'Henri III, 1ᵉʳ août 1589.* Paris: Gallimard.

Lesko, Barbara S., ed.

    1989: *Women's Earliest Records from Ancient Egypt and Western Asia. Proceedings of the Conference on Women in the Ancient Near East, Brown University, Providence Rhode Island, November 5–7 1987.* Atlanta, GA: Scholars Press.

Levin, Yigal.

    2012: "Ideology and Reality in the Book of Judges." Pp. 309–26 in Gershon Galil, Ayelet Gilboa, Aren M. Maeir, and Dan'el Kahn, eds. *The Ancient Near East in the 12th–10th Centuries BCE: Culture and History. Proceedings of the Interna-*

tional Conference Held at the University of Haifa, 2–5 May, 2010. Alter Orient und Altes Testament, 392; Münster: Ugarit Verlag.

Levine, Baruch A.

2000: *Numbers 21–36.* AYB, 4A; New Haven, CT: Yale University Press.

2009: "Religion in the Heroic Spirit: Themes in the Book of Judges." Pp. 28–42 in Ahn and Cook 2009.

Levinson, Bernard

1997: *Deuteronomy and the Hermeneutics of Legal Innovation.* Oxford: Oxford University Press.

Levison, Jon R.

1995: "Prophetic Inspiration in Pseudo-Philo's '*Liber Antiquitatum Biblicarum.*'" *Jewish Quarterly Review* 85: 297–329.

Lewis, Theodore J.

1996: "The Identity and Function of El/Baal Berith." *Journal of Biblical Literature* 115: 401–23.

Lichtheim, Miriam

1973: *Ancient Egyptian Literature,* Vol. 1. *The Old and Middle Kingdom.* Berkeley: University of California Press.

1976: *Ancient Egyptian Literature,* Vol. 2. *The New Kingdom.* Berkeley: University of California Press.

1980: *Ancient Egyptian Literature,* Vol. 3. *The Late Period.* Berkeley: University of California Press.

Liedke, Gerhard

1971: *Gestalt und Bezeichnung alttestamentlicher Rechtssätze. Eine formgeschichtlich-terminologische Studie.* Wissenschaftliche Monographien zum Alten und Neuen Testament, 39; Neukirchen-Vluyn: Neukirchener Verlag.

Lindars, Barnabas

1971: "Some Septuagint Readings in Judges." *Journal of Theological Studies* 22: 1–14.

1973: "Jotham's Fable: A New Form-Critical Analysis." *Journal of Theological Studies* 24: 355–66.

1986: "A Commentary on the Greek Judges?" Pp. 167–200 in *VI Congress of the International Organization for Septuagint and Cognate Studies. Jerusalem 1986.* SBL-SCSS, 23; Atlanta, GA: Scholars Press.

1995: *Judges 1–5: A New Translation and Commentary.* Edinburgh: T. and T. Clark.

Lion, Brigitte

2001: "Le gouverneurs provinciaux du royaume de Mari à l'époque de Zimri-Lîm." *Amurru* 2: 141–209.

Lion, Brigitte, and Cécile Michel

1997: "Criquets et autre insectes à Mari." *Mari: Annales de recherches interdisciplinaires* 8: 707–24.

Lion, Brigitte, Cécile Michel, and Pierre Villard, eds.

1997: *Enfance et éducation dans le Proche-Orient ancien.* Ktèma 22, Dossier 1; Strasbourg: Université Marc Bloch.

Lisella, A. R.

2005: "'La donna alla finestra': Una rappresentazione iconografica sugli avori del I millennio a.C." Pp. 97–120 in Alessandro Di Ludovico and Davide Nadali, eds.

Studi in onore di Paolo Matthiae presentati in occasione del suo sessantacinquesimo compleanno. Contributi e Materiali di Archeologia Orientale 10; Rome: Università degli Studi "La Sapienza."

Liver, J.

    1967: "The Wars of Mesha, King of Moab." *Palestine Exploration Quarterly* 99: 14–31.

Liverani, Mario

    1990: *Prestige and Interest: International Relations in the Near East ca. 1600–1100 B.C.* Padua: Sargon.

    2005: *Israel's History and the History of Israel.* London: Equinox.

Livingston, David

    1994: "Further Considerations on the Location of Bethel at el-Bireh." *Palestine Exploration Quarterly* 126: 154–59.

Logan, Alice

    2009: "Rehabilitating Jephthah." *Journal of Biblical Literature* 128: 665–85.

Loprieno, Antonio

    1996: "Defining Ancient Egyptian Literature: Ancient Texts and Modern Theory." Pp. 39–58 in Antonio Loprieno, ed. *Ancient Egyptian Literature: History and Forms.* Leiden: E. J. Brill.

Maccoby, Hyam

    1982: *The Sacred Executioner: Human Sacrifice and the Legacy of Guilt.* New York: Thames and Hudson.

MacDonald, Burton

    2000: *"East of the Jordan": Territories and Sites of the Hebrew Scriptures.* Boston: American Schools of Oriental Research.

MacDonald, Burton, and Randall W. Younker, eds.

    1999: *Ancient Ammon.* Studies in the History and Culture of the Ancient Near East, 17; Leiden: E. J. Brill.

Machinist, Peter

    2000: "Biblical Traditions: The Philistines and Israelite History." Pp. 53–83 in E. D. Oren, ed. *The Sea Peoples and Their World: A Reassessment.* University Museum Monograph 108; University Museum Symposium Series, 11. Philadelphia: University Museum, University of Pennsylvania.

Magness, Jodi

    1998: "Two Notes on the Archaeology of Qumran." *Bulletin of the American Schools of Oriental Research* 312: 37–44.

Maeir, Aren M.

    2011: "The Archaeology of Early Jerusalem: From the Late Proto-Historic Periods (ca. 5th Millennium BCE) to the End of the Bronze Age (ca. 1200 BCE)." Pp. 171–88 in K. Galor and G. Avni, eds. *Unearthing Jerusalem: 150 Years of Archaeological Research in the Holy City.* Winona Lake, IN: Eisenbrauns.

Maier, Samuel A.

    2000: "Diplomacy and International Marriages." Pp. 165–73 in Raymond Cohen and Raymond Westbrook, eds. *Amarna Diplomacy: The Beginnings of International Relations.* Baltimore, MD: Johns Hopkins University Press.

Malamat, Abraham

1953: "The War of Gideon and Midian: A Military Approach." *Palestine Exploration Quarterly* 85: 61–75.

1954: "Cushan Rishathaim and the Decline of the Near East Around 1200 B.C." *Journal of Near Eastern Studies* 13: 231–42.

1971: "The Egyptian Decline in Canaan and the Sea People." Pp. 23–38 in Benjamin Mazar, ed. *Judges. The World History of the Jewish People: Ancient Times, 3.* New Brunswick, NJ: Rutgers University Press.

1989: *Mari and the Early Israelite Experience.* Schweich Lectures of the British Academy, 1984. Oxford: Clarendon.

2004: "The Punishment of Succoth and Penuel by Gideon in the Light of Ancient Near Eastern Treaties." Pp. 69–71 in Chaim Cohen, Avi Hurvitz, and Shalom M. Paul, eds. *Sefer Moshe: The Moshe Weinfeld Jubilee Volume.* Studies in the Bible and the Ancient Near East, Qumran, and Post-biblical Judaism. Winona Lake, IN: Eisenbrauns.

Maly, Eugene

1960: "The Jotham Fable: Anti-monarchical?" *Catholic Biblical Quarterly* 22: 299–305.

Mann, Thomas W.

1977: *Divine Presence and Guidance in Israelite Traditions: The Typology of Exaltation.* Johns Hopkins Near Eastern Studies; Baltimore, MD: Johns Hopkins University Press.

Marais, Jacobus

1998: *Representation in Old Testament Narrative Texts.* Biblical Interpretation Series, 36; Leiden: E. J. Brill.

Marchesi, Gianni

2010: "The Sumerian King List and the Early History of Mesopotamia." Pp. 231–48 in M. G. Biga and M. Liverani, eds. Ana turri gimilli. *Studi dedicati al Padre Werner R. Mayer, S.J.* Quaderno di Vicino Oriente, 5; Rome: University of Rome.

Marcos, Natalio Fernández

2003: "The Hebrew and Greek Texts of Judges." Pp. 1–16 in Adrian Schenker, ed. *The Earliest Text of the Hebrew Bible: The Relationship Between the Masoretic Text and the Hebrew Base of the Septuagint Reconsidered.* SBL Septuagint and Cognate Studies, 52; Atlanta, GA: Society of Biblical Literature.

2011: שפטים *Judges.* Biblia Hebraica Quinta editione; Fascicle 7. Stuttgart: Deutsche Bibelgesellschaft.

Marcus, David

1986: *Jephthah and His Vow.* Lubbock: Texas Tech Press.

1989: "The Bargaining Between Jephthah and the Elders (Judges 11:4–11)." *Journal of the Ancient Near Eastern Society of Columbia University* 19: 95–100.

1992: "Ridiculing the Ephraimites: The Shibboleth Incident (Judg 12:6)." *Maarav* 8: 95–105.

Marello, Pierre

1997: "Liqtum, reine de Burundum." *Mari: Annales de recherches interdisciplinaires* 8: 455–59.

Margalit, Baruch

   1995: "Observations on the Jael-Sisera Story (Judges 4–5)." Pp. 629–41 in David P. Wright, David Noel Freedman, and Avi Hurvitz, eds. *Pomegranates and Golden Bells: Studies in Biblical, Jewish, and Near Eastern Ritual, Law, and Literature in Honor of Jacob Milgrom*. Winona Lake, IN: Eisenbrauns.

Margalith, Othniel

   1988: "The Hivites." *Zeitschrift für die Alttestamentliche Wissenschaft* 100: 60–70.

Marti, Lionel

   2008: *Nomades et sédentaires à Mari: La perception de la taxe-*sugâgûtum. *FM*, 10; Mémoires de NABU, 11; Paris: SEPOA.

   2011: "Pierres levées et monuments commémoratifs: L'apport des textes de l'Euphrate syrien." Pp. 191–200 in Tara Steimer-Herbet, ed. *Pierres levées, stèles anthropomorphes et dolmens*. Oxford: Archaeopress.

Martin, Lee Roy

   2011: "The Spirit of Yahweh in the Book of Judges." *Journal for Semitics* 20: 18–43.

Martino, Stefano de

   2004: "Pork Meat in Food and Worship Among the Hittites." Pp. 49–57 in Cristiano Grottanelli and Lucio Milano, eds. *Food and Identity in the Ancient World*. History of the Ancient Near East, Studies, 9; Padua: S.A.R.G.O.N. Editrice e Libreria.

Maryon, H., R. M. Organ, O. W. Ellis, R. M. Brick, R. Sneyers, E. E. Herzfeld, and F. K. Naumann, eds.

   1961: "Early Near Eastern Steel Swords." *American Journal of Archaeology* 65: 173–84.

Matthews, Victor, and Don Benjamin

   1992: "Jael: Host or Judge?" *Bible Today* 30: 291–96.

Maxwell-Hyslop, R.

   1946: "Daggers and Swords in Western Asia: A Study from Prehistoric Times to 600 B.C." *Iraq* 8: 1–65.

Mayer, Walter

   1995: *Politik und Kriegskunst der Assyrer*. Abhandlungen zur Literatur Alt-Syrien-Palastinas und Mesopotamiens, 9; Münster: Ugarit Verlag.

Mayes, A. D. H.

   1969: "Historical Context of the Battle Against Sisera." *Vetus Testamentum* 19: 353–60.

Mazar, Amihay

   1990: *Archaeology of the Land of the Bible, 10,000–586 B.C.E.* New York: Doubleday.

Mazar (Maisler), Benjamin

   1934: "Shamgar ben 'Anat." *Palestine Exploration Quarterly* 66: 192–94.

   1965: "The Sanctuary of Arad and the Family of Hobab the Kenite." *Journal of Near Eastern Studies* 24: 297–303.

McCarthy, D. J.

   1978: *Treaty and Covenant: A Study in Form in the Ancient Oriental Documents and in the Old Testament*. Rev. ed., AB 21A; Rome: Pontifical Institute.

McDaniel, Thomas F.

    1983: *Deborah Never Sang: A Philological Study on the Song of Deborah (Judges Chapter V), with English Translation and Comments*. Jerusalem: Makor.

    2003: *The Song of Deborah: Poetry in Dialect*. http://daniel.eastern.edu/seminary/tmcdaniel/Volume%20One%20By%20Chapter.htm.

McKenzie, Steven L., and Stephen R. Haynes, eds.

    1993: *To Each Its Own Meaning: An Introduction to Biblical Criticisms and Their Application*. Louisville, KY: Westminster John Knox.

McMahon, Gregory

    1997: "Instructions to Priests and Temple Officials (1.83)." Pp. 217–21 in Hallo and Younger 1997–2003.

McNutt, Paula M.

    1994: "The Kenites, the Midianites, and the Rechabites as Marginal Mediators in Ancient Israelite Tradition." *Semeia* 67: 109–32.

Meek, Theophile James

    1929: "Some Emendations in the Old Testament." *Journal of Biblical Literature* 48: 162–68.

Mendenhall, George E.

    1962: "The Hebrew Conquest of Palestine." *Biblical Archaeologist* 25: 66–87. [Reprinted with slight revisions in Edward F. Campbell and David Noel Freeman, eds. *The Biblical Archaeologist Reader*, 3, pp. 100–20. Garden City, NY: Anchor/Doubleday, 1970.]

Mettinger, Tryggve N. D.

    1971: *Solomonic State Officials: A Study of the Civil Government Officials of the Israelite Monarchy*. Lund: Gleerup.

    1976: *King and Messiah: The Civil and Sacral Legitimation of the Israelite Kings*. Lund: Gleerup.

    1995: *No Graven Image? Israelite Aniconism in Its Ancient Near Eastern Context*. Stockholm: Almquist and Wiksell International.

Meyers, Carol

    1991: "Of Drums and Damsels: Women's Performance in Ancient Israel." *Biblical Archaeologist* 54/1: 16–27.

Meyers, Eric M., ed.

    1997: *Oxford Encyclopaedia of Archaeology in the Near East*. New York: Oxford University Press.

Michalowski, Piotr

    1983: "History as Charter: Some Observations on the Sumerian King List." *Journal of the American Oriental Society* 103 [= J. M. Sasson, ed. *Studies in Literature from the Ancient Near East, by Members of the American Oriental Society, Dedicated to Samuel Noah Kramer*. New Haven, CT: American Oriental Society]: 237–48.

    1989: *The Lamentation over the Destruction of Sumer and Ur*. Mesopotamian Civilizations, 1; Winona Lake, IN: Eisenbrauns.

    2011: *The Correspondence of the Kings of Ur: An Epistolary History of an Ancient Mesopotamian Kingdom*. Mesopotamian Civilizations, 15; Winona Lake, IN: Eisenbrauns.

Michel, Cécile

    2004: "The *Perdum*-mule: A Mount for Distinguished Persons in Mesopotamia During the First Half of the Second Millennium BC." Pp. 190–200 in Barbro Santillo Frizell, ed. *PECUS. Man and Animal in Antiquity*. Proceedings of the conference at the Swedish Institute in Rome, September 9–12, 2002. Rome: Swedish Institute in Rome. http://www.svenska-institutet-rom.org/pecus/michel.pdf.

    2009: "Les filles consacrées des marchands assyriens." *Topoi* 10: 145–63.

Midden, Piet van

    2001: "A Hidden Message? Judges as Foreword to the Book of Kings." Pp. 77–86 in Janet W. Dyk, ed. *Unless Some One Guide Me . . . Festschrift for Karel A. Deurloo*. Amsterdamse Cahiers voor Exegese van de Bijbel en zijn tradities, Supplement Series, 2: Maastricht: Shaker.

Milano, Lucio

    1995: "Mühle. A. 1. In Mesopotamien." *RlA* 8: 393–400.

Miles, Johnny

    2008: "'Who are you calling "stupid"?' Ethnocentric Humour and Identity Construct in the Colonial Discourse of Judges 3.12–30." *Bible and Critical Theory* 4/1: 1–16.

Miller, Barbara

    2005: *Tell It on the Mountain: The Daughter of Jephthah in Judges 11*. Collegeville, MN: Liturgical Press.

Miller, Geoffrey P.

    1996a: "Verbal Feud in the Hebrew Bible: Judges 3:12–30 and 19–21." *Journal of Near Eastern Studies* 55: 105–17.

    1996b: "The Song of Deborah: A Legal-Economic Analysis." *University of Pennsylvania Law Review* 144/5: 2293–320.

    2011: *The Ways of a King: Legal and Political Ideas in the Bible*. Journal of Ancient Judaism Supplements, 7; Göttingen: Vandenhoeck and Ruprecht.

Miller, J. Maxwell

    1974: "Jebus and Jerusalem: A Case of Mistaken Identity." *Zeitschrift des Deutschen Palastina-Vereins* 90: 115–27.

Miller II, Robert D.

    2005: *Chieftains of the Highland Clans: A History of Israel in the Twelfth and Eleventh Centuries B.C.* Grand Rapids, MI: Eerdmans.

    2008: "When Pharaohs Ruled: On the Translation of Judges 5:2." *Journal of Theological Studies* 59: 650–54.

Minunno, Giuseppe

    2008: "La mutilation du corps de l'ennemi." Pp. 247–51 in P. Abrahami and L. Battini, eds. *Les armées du Proche-Orient ancient (IIIe–Ier mill. Av. J.–C.) Actes du colloque international organisé à Lyon les 1er et 2 décembre 2006. Maison de l'Orient et de la Méditerranée*. BAR International Series 1855; Oxford: John and Erica Hedges.

Mitchell, T. C.

    1969: "The Meaning of the Noun *ḥōtēn* in the Old Testament." *Vetus Testamentum* 19: 93–112.

    2000: "Camels in the Assyrian Bas-Reliefs." *Iraq* 62: 187–94.

Mittmann, Siegfried

    1977: "Ri 1,16f und das Siedlungsgebiet der kenitischen Sippe Hobab." *Zeitschrift des Deutschen Palästina-Vereins* 93: 213–35.

Mobley, Gregory

    2005: *The Empty Men: The Heroic Tradition of Ancient Israel*. Anchor Bible Reference Library; New York: Doubleday.

Moor, Johannes Cornelis de

    1993: "The Twelve Tribes in the Song of Deborah Journal." *Vetus Testamentum* 43: 483–94.

    1995: "Standing Stones and Ancestor Worship." *Ugarit-Forschungen* 27: 1–20.

    1997: *The Rise of Yahwism: The Roots of Israelite Monotheism*. Leuven: University Press, Uitgeverij Peeters.

Moore, George F.

    1895: *A Critical and Exegetical Commentary on Judges*. International Critical Commentary; Edinburgh: T. and T. Clark.

    1898a: "Shamgar and Sisera." *Journal of the American Oriental Society* 19: 159–60.

    1898b: *The Book of Judges: A New English Translation, Printed in Colors Exhibiting the Composite Structure of the Book*. Holy Bible Polychrome Edition; Sacred Books of the Old Testament, 7; New York: Dodd, Mead.

Moran, William L.

    1992: *The Amarna Tablets*. Baltimore, MD: Johns Hopkins University Press.

Mosca, Paul G.

    1984: "Who Seduced Whom? A Note on Joshua 15:18 || Judges 1:14." *Catholic Biblical Quarterly* 46: 18–22.

Mouton, Alice

    2004a: "Une épreuve pour différencier l'homme du dieu: Le 'texte des cannibales' hittite (KBo 3.60) et quelques rapprochements, ou comment reconnaît-on un dieu hittite?" *Altorientalische Forschungen* 31: 303–19.

    2004b: "Le rituel de Walkui (KBo 32.176): Quelques réflexions sur la déesse de la nuit et l'image du porc dans le monde hittite." *Zeitschrift für Assyriologie* 94: 85–105.

Mulder, M. J.

    1995: "Baal-berith." Pp. 266–72 in *DDD*.

Mullen, E. Theodore, Jr.

    1982: "The 'Minor Judges': Some Literary and Historical Considerations." *Catholic Biblical Quarterly* 44: 185–201.

    1984: "Judges 1:1–36: The Deuteronomistic Reintroduction of the Book of Judges." *Harvard Theological Review* 77: 33–54.

Müller, H.-J.

    1995: "Chemosh." Pp. 356–62 in *DDD*.

Müller, Jens-Oliver, Eva Ehninger, and Eike Fess

    2005: "Das Alte Testament in Bildender Kunst, Musik und Film des 20. Jahrhunderts." Pp. 227–52 in Barton, Exum, and Oeming 2005.

Murphy, Frederick J.

    1988: "Retelling the Bible: Idolatry in Pseudo-Philo." *Journal of Biblical Literature* 107: 275–87.

    1993: *Pseudo-Philo: Rewriting the Bible*. New York: Oxford University Press.

Myers, Jacob M.

1953: "The Book of Judges." Pp. 675–876 in George Arthur Buttrick, ed. *The Interpreter's Bible*, Vol. 2. New York: Abingdon.

Na'aman, Nadav

1986a: *Borders and Districts in Biblical Historiography*. Jerusalem: Simor.

1986b: "Ḫabiru and Hebrews: The Transfer of a Social Term to the Literary Sphere." *Journal of Near Eastern Studies* 45: 278–85.

1986c: "Hezekiah's Fortified Cities and the *LMLK* Stamps." *Bulletin of the American Schools of Oriental Research* 261: 5–21.

1988: "Canaanites and Perizzites." *Biblische Notizen* 45: 42–47.

1990: "Literary and Topographical Notes on the Battle of Kishon (Judges IV–V)." *Vetus Testamentum* 40: 423–36.

1994a: "The Canaanites and Their Land: A Rejoinder." *Ugarit-Forschungen* 26: 397–418.

1994b: "The 'Conquest of Canaan' in the Book of Joshua and in History." Pp. 218–81 in I. Finkelstein and N. Na'aman, eds. *From Nomadism to Monarchy: Archaeological and Historical Aspects of Early Israel*. Washington, DC: Biblical Archaeology Society.

1996: "The Contribution of the Amarna Letters to the Debate on Jerusalem's Political Position in the 10th Century B.C.E." *Bulletin of the American Schools of Oriental Research* 304: 17–27.

1999: "Four Notes on the Size of Late Bronze Age Canaan." *Bulletin of the American Schools of Oriental Research* 313: 31–37.

2000: "Ḫabiru-Like Bands in the Assyrian Empire and Bands in Biblical Historiography." *Journal of the American Oriental Society* 120: 621–24.

2004: "The ṣuḫāru in Second-Millennium BCE Letters from Canaan." *Israel Exploration Journal* 54: 92–99.

2009: "Saul, Benjamin and the Emergence of 'Biblical Israel' (Part 1)." *Zeitschrift für die Alttestamentliche Wissenschaft* 121: 211–24.

Nabokov, Vladimir Vladimirovich

1980: *Lectures on Literature*. New York: Harcourt Brace Jovanovich.

Nachmanides (Ramban)

1974: *Commentary on the Torah: Leviticus*. New York: Shilo.

Neef, Heinz-Dieter

1994: "Deboraerzählung und Deboralied: Beobachtungen zum Verhältnis von Jdc. IV und V." *Vetus Testamentum* 44: 47–59.

1995: "Meroz: Jdc 5, 23a." *Zeitschrift für die alttestamentliche Wissenschaft* 107: 118–22.

1999: "Jephta und seine Tochter (Jdc xi 29–40)." *Vetus Testamentum* 49: 206–17.

Neis, Rachel

2012: "'Their Backs Toward the Temple, and Their Faces Toward the East': The Temple and Toilet Practices in Rabbinic Palestine and Babylonia." *Journal for the Study of Judaism* 43: 328–68.

Nelson, R. D.

2007: "Ideology, Geography, and the List of Minor Judges." *Journal for the Study of the Old Testament* 31: 347–64.

Neudecker, Richard

1994: *Der Pracht der Latrine: Zum Wandel öffentlicher Bedürfnisanstalten in der kaiserzeitlichen Stadt.* Studien zur antiken Stadt, 1; München: Verlag Dr. Friedrich Pfeil.

Neumann, Hermann Michael

2002: "Taanach und Megiddo: Überlegungen zur strukturell-historischen Situation zwischen Saul und Salomo." *Vetus Testamentum* 52: 93–102.

Niccacci, Alviero

1982: "Egitto e Bibbia sulla base della stele di Piankhi." *Liber Annuus Studii Biblici Franciscani* 32: 7–58.

Nicholson, E. R.

1977: "The Problem of צנח." *Zeitschrift für die Alttestamentliche Wissenschaft* 89: 259–65.

Nickelsburg, George W. E.

1984: "Stories of Biblical and Early Post-Biblical Times" and "The Bible Rewritten and Expanded." Pp. 33–87 and 89–156, respectively, in Stone 1984.

Niditch, Susan

1989: "Eroticism and Death in the Tale of Jael." Pp. 43–57 in Day, ed., 1989.

2005: "The Challenge of Israelite Epic." Pp. 277–87 in Foley, ed., 2005.

2008: *Judges.* Old Testament Library; Louisville, KY: Westminster John Knox.

2010: "Epic and History in the Hebrew Bible: Definitions, 'Ethnic Genres,' and the Challenges of Cultural Identity in the Biblical Book of Judges." Pp. 86–102 in David Konstan and Kurt A. Raaflaub, eds. *Epic and History.* Chichester, West Sussex: Wiley-Blackwell.

Niehr, Herbert

1986: *Herrschen und Richten: Die Wurzel špḥ im Alten Orient und im Alten Testament.* Forschung zur Bibel, 54; Würzburg: Echter Verlag.

2006: "שפט." *TDOT* 15: 411–31.

Nielsen, Eduard

1955: *Shechem. A Traditio-Historical Investigation.* Copenhagen: G.E.C. Gad.

Niesiołowski-Spanò, Łukasz

2005: "Where Should One Look for Gideon's Ophra?" *Biblica* 86: 478–93.

Nissinen, Martti

2000: *Prophecy in Its Ancient Near Eastern Context: Mesopotamian, Biblical, and Arabian Perspectives.* SBL Symposium Series, 13; Atlanta, GA: Society of Biblical Literature.

2003: "Fear Not: A Study on an Ancient Near Eastern Phrase." Pp. 122–61 in Marvin A. Sweeney and Ehud Ben Zvi, eds. *The Changing Face of Form-Criticism for the Twenty-First Century.* Grand Rapids, MI: Eerdmans.

Noegel, Scott B.

2007: *Nocturnal Ciphers: The Allusive Language of Dreams in the Ancient Near East.* American Oriental Studies, 89; New Haven, CT: American Oriental Society.

Noort, Ed

1999: "Numbers 27,21: The Priestly Oracle Urim and Tummim and the History of Reception." Pp. 109–16 in H. J. L. Vanstiphout, ed. *All Those Nations . . .*

Cultural Encounters Within and with the Near East: Studies Presented to Hans Drijvers at the Occasion of His Sixty-fifth Birthday by Colleagues and Students. GroniComers/ICOG Communications, 2: Groningen: Styx.

Noth, Martin

    1953: *Das Buch Josua.* 2nd edition. Tübingen: J. C. B. Mohr.

    1981: *The Deuteronomistic History* (translation of *Überlieferungsgeschichte des Pentateuch*, 1943, 2nd edition, 1957). Journal for the Study of the Old Testament Supplement, 182; Sheffield: JSOT Press.

Nylander, Carl

    1980: "Who Mutilated 'Sargon's' Head?" Pp. 271–72 in Bendt Alster, ed. *Death in Mesopotamia.* 26 RAI, Mesopotamia, 8; Copenhagen: Academisk forlag.

O'Brien, Mark A.

    1989: *The Deuteronomistic History Hypothesis: A Reassessment.* Orbis biblicus et orientali, 92; Freiburg: Vandenhoeck and Ruprecht.

O'Connell, Robert H.

    1996: *The Rhetoric of the Book of Judges.* Vetus Testamentum Supplement, 63; Leiden: E. J. Brill.

O'Connor, Michael P.

    1980: *Hebrew Verse Structures.* Winona Lake, IN: Eisenbrauns.

Oded, Bustenai

    1996: "Cushan-Rishathaim (Judges 3:8–11): An Implicit Polemic." Pp. 89*–94* in Michael V. Fox and Victor Avigdor Hurowitz, eds. *Texts, Temples, and Traditions: A Tribute to Menahem Haran.* Winona Lakes: IN: Eisenbrauns.

Oeste, Gordon K.

    2011a: *Legitimacy, Illegitimacy, and the Right to Rule: Windows on Abimelech's Rise and Demise in Judges 9.* Old Testament Studies, 546; New York: T. and T. Clark.

    2011b: "Butchered Brothers and Betrayed Families: Degenerating Kingship Structures in the Book of Judges." *Journal for the Study of the Old Testament* 35: 295–316.

Ogden, Daniel

    2002: *Magic, Witchcraft, and Ghosts in the Greek and Roman Worlds: A Sourcebook.* New York: Oxford University Press.

Ogden, Graham S.

    1994: "Poetry, Prose, and Their Relationship: Some Reflections Based on Judges 4 and 5." Pp. 111–30 in Ernst R. Wendland, ed. *Discourse Perspectives on Hebrew Poetry in the Scriptures.* New York: United Bible Societies.

Olmo Lete, Gregorio del

    1995: "El molk púnico: Interpretación de un ritual." Pp. 9–22 *in La problemática del infanticidio en las sociedades fenicio-púnica.* IX Jornadas de Arqueología fenicio-púnica, Eivissa, 1994; Trabajos del Museo Arqueológico de Ibiza, 35; Eivissa: Museo Arqueológico de Ibiza y Formentera.

    2000: *La Biblia Hebrea en la Literatura Moderna: Guía temática y bibliográfica.* Textos Docents; Barcelona: Universidad de Barcelona.

Olson, Dennis T.

    1998: "The Book of Judges." Pp. 721–888 in Leander E. Keck, ed., *The New Interpreter's Bible*, Vol. 2. Nashville, TN: Abingdon.

Olyan, Saul M.

    2010: "What Do We Really Know About Women's Rites in the Israelite Family Context?" *Journal of Ancient Near Eastern Religions* 10: 55–67.

Orlinsky, Harry M.

    1942: "Critical Notes on Gen 39 14, 17, Jud 11 37." *Journal of Biblical Literature* 61: 87–97.

Otto, Eckart

    1976–80: "Jerusalem." *RlA* 5: 278–81.

    1996: "Krieg und Religion im Alten Orient und im alten Israel." Pp. 37–47 in J. Hermann, ed. *Glaubenskriege in Vergangenheit und Gegenwart*. Veröffentlichung der Joachim-Jungius-Gesellschaft, 83; Göttingen: Vandenhoeck and Ruprecht.

Parker, Simon B.

    1979: "The Vow in Ugaritic and Israelite Narrative Literature." *Ugarit Forschungen* 11: 693–700.

Parpola, Simo

    1980: "The Murderer of Sennacherib." Pp. 171–82 in B. Alster, ed. *Death in Mesopotamia: Papers Read at the XXVIᵉ Rencontre assyriologique internationale*. Copenhagen: Akademisk Forlag.

Perrot, Charles

    1969: "*Petuḥot et Setumot*: Études sur les alinéas du Pentateuque." *Revue Biblique* 76: 50–91.

Pietersma, Albert, and Benjamin G. Wright

    2007: *A New English Translation of the Septuagint: And the Other Greek Translations Traditionally Included Under That Title*. New York: Oxford University Press.

Philo of Alexandria

    1993: *The Works of Philo, Complete and Unabridged*. Peabody, MA: Hendrickson.

Pinnock, Frances

    1997: "Tipologia di un pugnale rituale del III millennio a.C." Pp. 463–93 in P. Matthiae, ed. *Studi in memoria di Henri Frankfort (1887–1954)*. Contributi e Materiali di Archeologia Orientale, 7; Rome: University of Rome.

Pintore, Franco

    1978: *Il matrimonio interdinastico nel Vicino Oriente durante i secoli XV–XIII*. Orientis Antiqui Collectio, 14; Rome: Istituto per l = Oriente.

Pisano, Stephen

    1984: *Additions or Omissions in the Books of Samuel: The Significant Pluses and Minuses in the Massoretic, LXX and Qumran Texts*. Orbis biblicus et orientalis, 57; Göttingen: Vandenhoeck and Ruprecht.

Poethig, Eunice Blanchard

    1985: "The Victory Song Tradition of the Women of Israel." Ph.D. dissertation, Union Theological Seminary.

Pongratz-Leisten, Beate

    2002: "'Lying King' and 'False Prophet': The Intercultural Transfer of a Rhetorical Device Within Ancient Near Eastern Ideologies." Pp. 215–43 in A. Panaino and G. Pettinato, eds. *Ideologies as Intercultural Phenomena: Proceedings of the Third Annual Symposium of the Assyrian and Babylonian Intellectual Heritage*

Project. *Held in Chicago, USA, October 27–31, 2000.* Melammu Symposia, 3; Milan: Università di Bologna and IsIao.

Poorthuis, M. J. H. M.

1998: "Rebekah as a Virgin on Her Way to Marriage: A Study in Midrash." *Journal for the Study of Judaism* 29: 438–62.

Porter, Stanley E., and Richard S. Hess

1999: *Translating the Bible: Problems and Prospects.* Journal for the Study of the New Testament Supplement, 173; Sheffield: Sheffield Academic Press.

Potts, Dan T.

1990: "Lock and Key in Ancient Mesopotamia." *Mesopotamia* 25: 185–92.

Powell, Marvin A.

1985: "Salt, Seed, and Yields in Sumerian Agriculture: A Critique of the Theory of Progressive Salinization." *Zeitschrift für Assyriologie* 75: 7–38.

Pritchard, James B.

1969: *Ancient Near Eastern Texts Relating to the Old Testament.* 3rd edition. Princeton, NJ: Princeton University Press.

Pseudo-Philo

1976: *Les antiquités bibliques.* Paris: Les Éditions du Cerf.

Pury, Albert de, Thomas Römer, and Jean-Daniel Macchi, eds.

2000: *Israel Constructs Its History: Deuteronomistic Historiography in Recent Research.* Journal for the Study of the Old Testament Supplement, 306; Sheffield: Sheffield Academic Press.

Rabin, Chaim

1955: "Judges 5:2 and the "Ideology" of Deborah's War." *Journal of Jewish Studies* 6: 125–34.

Rabinowitz, Isaac

1984: " '*āz* Followed by Imperfect Verb-Form in Preterite Contexts: A Redactional Device in Biblical Hebrew." *Vetus Testamentum* 34: 53–62.

Rad, Gerhard von

1991: *Holy War in Ancient Israel.* Translated and edited by Marva J. Dawn and John H. Yoder. Grand Rapids, MI: W. B. Eerdmans.

Radner, Karen

2005: *Die Macht des Namens: Altorientalische Strategien zur Selbsterhaltung.* SANTAG, 8; Wiesbaden: Harrassowitz.

2010: "Gatekeepers and Lock Masters: The Control of Access in Assyrian Palaces." Pp. 269–80 in Heather D. Baker, Eleanor Robson, and Gábor Zólyomi, eds. *Your Praise Is Sweet: A Memorial Volume for Jeremy Black from Students, Colleagues and Friends.* London: British Institute for the Study of Iraq.

Rahlfs, Alfred

1979: *Septuaginta.* Reprint edition. New York: American Bible Society.

Rainey, Anson F.

1983: "Toponymic Problems (cont.): Harosheth-hagoiim." *Tel Aviv* 10: 46–48.

1996: "Who Is a Canaanite? A Review of the Textual Evidence." *Bulletin of the American Schools of Oriental Research* 304: 1–15.

2006: "Looking for Bethel: An Exercise in Historical Geography." Pp. 269–73 in Seymour Gitin, J. Edward Wright, and J. P. Dessel, eds. *Confronting the Past:*

Archaeological and Historical Essays on Ancient Israel in Honor of William G. Dever. Winona Lake, IN: Eisenbrauns..

    2008: "Shasu or Habiru: Who Were the Early Israelites?" *Biblical Archaeology Review* 34/06: 51–55.

Rainey, Anson F., and R. Steven Notley

    2006: *The Sacred Bridge*. Carta's Atlas of the Biblical World; Jerusalem: Carta.

Rake, Mareike

    2006: *"Juda wird aufsteigen!": Untersuchungen zum ersten Kapitel des Richterbuches*. Zeitschrift für die alttestamentliche Wissenschaft Beiheft, 367; Berlin: de Gruyter.

Reculeau, Hervé

    2008a: "Late Bronze Age Rural Landscapes of the Euphrates According to the Emar Texts." Pp. 129–40 in Lorenzo d'Alfonso, Yoram Cohen, and Dietrich Sürenhagen, eds. *The City of Emar Among the Late Bronze Age Empires: History, Landscape, and Society. Proceedings of the Konstanz Emar Conference, 25–26.04 2006*. Alter Orient und Altes Testament, 349; Neukirchen: Ugarit Verlag.

    2008b: "Environnement et occupation de l'espace: Les sédentaires." *Supplément au Dictionnaire de la Bible* 14: 325–357.

Redford, Donald B.

    1992: *Egypt, Canaan, and Israel in Ancient Times*. Princeton, NJ: Princeton University Press.

    1997: "Textual Sources for the Hyksos Period." Pp. 1–44 in Eliezer D. Oren, ed. *The Hyksos: New Historical and Archaeological Perspectives*. University Museum Symposium Series, 8; Philadelphia: University Museum, University of Pennsylvania.

    2000: *Oxford Encyclopedia of Ancient Egypt*. 3 vols. New York: Oxford University Press.

Rehm, Ellen

    2004: "Abschied von der Heiligen Hure: Zum Bildmotiv der 'Frau am Fenster' in der phönizisch-nordsyrischen Elfenbeinschnitzkunst." *Ugarit Forschung* 35: 487–519.

Reiner, Erica

    1969. "Akkadian Treaties from Syria and Assyria." Pp. 531–41 in Pritchard 1969.

    1998: "Apodoses and Logia." Pp. 651–54 in M. Dietrich and I. Kottsieper, eds. *"Und Mose schrieb dieses Lied auf": Studien zum Alten Testament und zum Alten Orient. Festschrift für Oswald Loretz zur Vollendung seines 70. Lebensjahres mit Beiträgen von Freunden, Schülern und Kollegen*. Münster: Ugarit Verlag.

Reis, Pamela Tamarkin

    1997: "Spoiled Child: A Fresh Look at Jephthah's Daughter." *Prooftexts* 17: 279–98.

    2005: "Uncovering Jael and Sisera: A New Reading." *Scandinavian Journal of the Old Testament* 19: 24–47.

Rendsburg, Gary A.

    1988: "The Ammonite Phoneme /Ṭ/." *Bulletin of the American Schools of Oriental Research* 269: 73–79.

1998–99: "Confused Language as a Deliberate Literary Device in Biblical Hebrew Narrative." *Journal of Hebrew Scriptures* 2, http://www.jhsonline.org/Articles/ article_12.htm.

2003: "Hurvitz Redux: On the Continued Scholarly Inattention to a Simple Principle of Hebrew Philology." Pp. 104–28 in Ian Young, ed. *Biblical Hebrew: Studies in Chronology and Typology*. Journal for the Study of the Old Testament Supplement, 369; London: T. and T. Clark.

Rendsburg, Gary A., and William M. Schniedewind

2010: "The Siloam Tunnel Inscription: Historical and Linguistic Perspectives." *Israel Exploration Journal* 60: 188–203.

Revell, E. J.

1996: *The Designation of the Individual: Expressive Usage in Biblical Hebrew.* Kampen: Kok Pharos.

Reviv, Hanoch

1966: "The Government of Shechem in the El-Armana Period and in the Days of Abimelech." *Israel Exploration Journal* 16: 252–57.

Richter, Wolfgang

1963: *Traditionsgeschichtliche Untersuchungen zum Richter-buch.* Bonner biblische Beiträge, 18; Bonn: P. H. Hanstein.

1964: *Die Bearbeitungen des "Retterbuches" in der deuteronomischen Epoche.* Bonner biblische Beiträge, 21; Bonn: P. H. Hanstein.

Ridley, R. T.

1986: "To Be Taken with a Pinch of Salt: The Destruction of Carthage." *Classical Philology* 81: 140–46.

Ritner, Robert Kriech

2009: *The Libyan Anarchy: Inscriptions from Egypt's Third Intermediate Period.* Writings from the Ancient World, 21; Atlanta, GA: Society of Biblical Literature.

Rollston, Christopher A.

2006: "Scribal Education in Ancient Israel: The Old Hebrew Epigraphic Evidence." *Bulletin of the American Schools of Oriental Research* 344: 47–74.

Römer, Thomas C.

1998: "Why Would the Deuteronomists Tell About the Sacrifice of Jephthah's Daughter?" *Journal for the Study of the Old Testament* 77: 27–38.

2005: *The So-Called Deuteronomistic History.* London: T. and T. Clark.

Rooke, Deborah W.

2012: *Handel's Israelite Oratorio Libretti: Sacred Drama and Biblical Exegesis.* Oxford: Oxford University Press.

Rösel, H. N.

1976: "Studien zur Topographie der Kriege in den Büchern Josua und Richter." *Zeitschrift des Deutschen Palastina-Vereins* 92: 10–46.

Roth, Cecil, ed.

1972: *Encyclopaedia Judaica.* Jerusalem: Keter (2nd edition, Gale Publishing, 2006).

Roth, Martha T.

1989a: *Babylonian Marriage Agreements: 7th–3rd Centuries B.C.* Alter Orient und Altes Testament, 222; Neukirchen-Vluyn: Neukirchener Verlag.

1989b: "Marriage and Matrimonial Prestations in First Millennium B.C. Babylonia." Pp. 245–55 in Lesko 1989.

1997: *Law Collections from Mesopotamia and Asia Minor*. 2nd edition. Writings from the Ancient World, 6; Atlanta, GA: Scholars Press.

Roth, Martha T., et al., eds.

1956–2011: *The Assyrian Dictionary of the Oriental Institute of the University of Chicago*. Chicago: Oriental Institute of the University of Chicago.

Routledge, Bruce

2004: *Moab in the Iron Age: Hegemony, Polity, Archaeology*. Philadelphia: University of Pennsylvania Press.

Rubio, Gonzalo

2009: "Scribal Secrets and Antiquarian Nostalgia: Tradition and Scholarship in Ancient Mesopotamia." Pp. 155–82 in Diego Barreyra Fracaroli and Gregorio del Olmo Lete, eds. *Reconstructing a Distant Past: Ancient Near Eastern Essays in Tribute to Jorge R. Silva Castillo*. Aula Orientalis Supplement, 25; Sabadell: Editorial AUSA.

Rudman, Dominic

2000: "The Second Bull in Judges 6:25–28." *Journal of Northwest Semitic Languages* 26: 97–103.

Rüger, Hans Peter

1990: *Torah, Nevi'im u-Khetuvim*. Biblia Hebraica Stuttgartensia. 4th edition. Stuttgart: Deutsche Bibelgesellschaft.

Ryan, Roger

2007: *Judges*. Sheffield: Sheffield Phoenix Press.

Sakenfeld, Katharine Doob

2008: "Whose Text Is It?" *Journal of Biblical Studies* 127: 5–18.

Sasson, Jack M.

1966: "Canaanite Maritime Involvement in the Second Millennium B.C." *Journal of the American Oriental Society* 86: 126–38.

1978: "A Genealogical 'Convention' in Biblical Chronography?" *Zeitschrift für die alttestamentliche Wissenschaft* 90: 171–85.

1980: "The 'Tower of Babel' as Clue to the Redactional Structuring of the Primeval History [Gen. 1–11:9]." Pp. 211–19 in Gary Rendsburg, ed. *The Bible World: Essays in Honor of Cyrus H. Gordon*. New York: Ktav.

1985: "Yarim-Lim's War Declaration." Pp. 237–55 in J.-M. Durand and J.-R. Kupper, eds. *Miscellanea Babyloniaca. Mélanges offerts à Maurice Birot*. Paris: Editions Recherches sur les Civilisations.

1987: "On Mesha's Sacrifice of His Son: A Response." *Biblical Archeology Review* 13: 12–15, 60.

1989: *Ruth: A New Translation. With a Philological Commentary and a Folkloristic-Formalist Interpretation*. Revised edition. Sheffield: Almond Press.

1990: *Jonah: A New Translation with Introduction, Commentary and Interpretations*. AB, 24b; New York: Doubleday.

1994a: "The Posting of Letters with Divine Messages." Pp. 299–316 in D. Charpin and J.-M. Durand, eds. *Recueil d'études à la mémoire de Maurice Birot*. FM, 2; Mémoires de NABU, 3; Paris: SEPOA.

1994b: "The Blood of Grapes: Viticulture and Intoxication in the Hebrew Bible." Pp. 399–419 in Lucio Milano, ed. *Drinking in Ancient Societies: History and Culture of Drinks in the Ancient Near East*. Padua: Sargon.

1997: "The Vow of Mutiya, King of Shekhna." Pp. 483–98 in G. D. Young, M. W. Chavalas, and R. E. Averbeck, eds. *Crossing Boundaries and Linking Horizons: Studies in Honor of Michael C. Astour on His 80th Birthday*. Bethesda, MD: CDL.

1998a: "About 'Mari and the Bible.'" *Revue d'Assyriologie* 92: 97–123.

1998b: "The King and I: A Mari King in Changing Perceptions." *Journal of the American Oriental Society* 118: 453–70.

2001a: "On Reading the Diplomatic Letters in the Mari Archives." *Amurru* 2: 329–38.

2001b: "Ancestors Divine?" Pp. 413–28 in W. H. van Soldt, J. G. Dercksen, N. J. C. Kouwenberg, and Th. J. H. Krispijn, eds. *Veenhof Anniversary Volume: Studies Presented to Klaas R. Veenhof on the Occasion of His Sixty-Fifth Birthday*. Leiden: Nederlands Instituut voor het Nabije Oosten.

2001c: "Absalom's Daughter: An Essay in Vestige Historiography." Pp. 179–96 in J. Andrew Dearman and M. Patrick Graham, eds. *The Land That I Will Show You: Essays on the History and Archaeology of the Ancient Near East in Honor of J. Maxwell Miller*. Journal for the Study of the Old Testament Supplement, 343; Sheffield: Sheffield Academic Press.

2002: "Ritual Wisdom? On 'Seething a Kid in Its Mother's Milk.'" Pp. 294–308 in Ulrich Hübner and Ernst Axel Knauf, eds. *Kein Land für sich allein: Studien zum Kulturkontakt in Kanaan, Israel/Palaestina und Ebirnâri für Manfred Weippert zum 65. Geburtstag*. Orbis biblicus et orientalis, 186; Freiburg: Universitätsverlag.

2004: "Doeg's Job." Pp. 317–22 in *Scriptura: International Journal of Bible, Religion and Theology in Southern Africa 3* [*Festschrift Yehoshua Gitay*].

2006a: "The Servant's Tale: How Rebekah Found a Spouse." *Journal of Near Eastern Studies* 65: 241–65.

2006b: "Mari and the Holy Grail." Pp. 186–98 in Stanley W. Holloway, ed. *Orientalism, Assyriology and the Bible*. Sheffield: Sheffield Phoenix Press.

2007: "Scruples: Extradition in the Mari Archives." Pp. 453–73 in *Festschrift für Hermann Hunger, zum 65. Geburtstag gewidmet von seinen Freunden, Kollegen, und Schülern* [= *Wiener Zeitschrift für die Kunde des Morgenlandes* 97]. Wien: Institut für Orientalistik.

2008: "Oracle Inquiries in Judges." Pp. 149–68 in Chaim Cohen, Victor Avigdor Hurowitz, Avi Hurvitz, Yochanan Muffs, and Baruch J. Schwartz, eds. *Birkat Shalom: Studies in the Bible, Ancient Near Eastern Literature, and Postbiblical Judaism Presented to Shalom M. Paul on the Occasion of His Seventieth Birthday*. Winona Lake, IN: Eisenbrauns.

2009: "Ethically Cultured Interpretations: The Case of Eglon's Murder (Judges 3)." Pp. 571–95 in Gershon Galil, Mark Geller, and Alan Millard, eds. *Homeland and Exile: Biblical and Ancient Near Eastern Studies in Honour of Bustenay Oded*. Vetus Testamentum Supplement, 130; Leiden: E. J. Brill.

2010: "Coherence and Fragments: Reflections on the SKL and the Book of Judges." Pp. 361–73 in Sarah C. Melville and Alice L. Slotsky, eds. *Opening the Tablet Box: Near Eastern Studies in Honor of Benjamin R. Foster. Leiden: E. J. Brill.

2011: "'A Breeder or Two for Each Leader': On Mothers in Judges 4 and 5." Pp. 333–55 in Clines and van Wolde 2011.

2013a: *"It is for this reason that I have not come down to my lord . . .*": Visit Obligations and Vassal Pretexts in the Mari Archives." *Revue d'Assyriologie* 107: 119–29.

2013b: "Jephthah: Chutzpa and Overreach in the Portrayal of a Hebrew Judge." In D. Vanderhooft and A. Winitzer, eds. *Literature as Politics, Politics as Literature: Essays on the Ancient Near East in Honor of Peter Machinist.* Winona Lake, IN: Eisenbrauns.

(forthcoming): "Casus belli in the Mari Archives." In H. Neumann, ed. *Krieg und Frieden im Alten Vorderasien.* 52 RAI; Wiesbaden: Harrassowitz.

(forthcoming): "Siege Mentality: Fighting at the City Gate in the Mari Archives" (contribution to a Memorial Volume).

Sasson, Jack M., John Baines, Gary Beckman, and Karen S. Rubinson, eds.

1995: *Civilizations of the Ancient Near East.* New York: Scribner (reprinted as two-volume edition, Peabody, MA: Hendrickson, 2000).

Satran, David

1995: *Biblical Prophets in Byzantine Palestine: Reassessing the* Lives of the Prophets. Leiden: E. J. Brill.

Satterthwaite, Philip

2007: "Judges." Pp. 195–238 in Pietersma and Wright 2007.

Savran, George W.

2003: "Theophany as Type Scene." *Prooftexts* 23: 119–49.

Sawyer, John F. A.

1981: "From Heaven Fought the Stars." *Vetus Testamentum* 31: 87–89.

Sawyer, John F. A., and David J. A. Clines, eds.

1983: *Midian, Moab and Edom: The History and Archaeology of Late Bronze and Iron Age Jordan and North-West Arabia.* Journal for the Study of the Old Testament Supplement, 24; Sheffield: JSOT Press.

Scherer, Andreas

2005: "Gideon: Ein Anti-Held? Ein Beitrag zur Auseinandersetzung mit dem sog. 'flawed-hero approach' Am Beispiel Von Jdc. Vi 36–40." *Vetus Testamentum* 55: 269–73.

2007: "Die 'kleinen' Richter und ihre Funktion." *Zeitschrift für die Alttestamentliche Wissenschaft* 119: 190–200.

Schloen, J. David

1993a: "Caravans, Kenites, and Casus Belli: Enmity and Alliance in the Song of Deborah." *Catholic Biblical Quarterly* 55: 18–38.

1993b: "The Exile of Disinherited Kin in KTU 1.12 and KTU 1.23." *Journal of Near Eastern Studies* 52: 209–20.

Schmitz, Philip

2008: "Deity and Royalty in Dedicatory Formulae: The Ekron Store-Jar Inscription Viewed in the Light of Judges 7:18, 20 and the Inscribed Gold Medallion from the Douïmès Necropolis at Carthage, (*KAI* 73)." *Maarav* 15: 165–73.

Schöpflin, Karin
  2004: "Jotham's Speech and Fable as Prophetic Comment on Abimelech's Story: The Genesis of Judges 9." *Scandinavian Journal of the Old Testament* 18: 3–32.
Schulman, A. R.
  1979: "Diplomatic Marriage in the Egyptian New Kingdom." *Journal of Near Eastern Studies* 38: 177–93.
Schwartz, Baruch J.
  2004: "Reexamining the Fate of the 'Canaanites' in the Torah Traditions." Pp. 151–70 in Chaim Cohen, Avi Hurvitz, and Shalom M. Paul, eds. *Sefer Moshe: The Moshe Weinfeld Jubilee Volume*. Studies in the Bible and the Ancient Near East, Qumran, and Post-Biblical Judaism. Winona Lake, IN: Eisenbrauns.
Schwartz, Glenn M.
  1995: "Pastoral Nomadism in Ancient Western Asia." Pp. 249–58 in Sasson, Baines, Beckman, and Rubinson, eds., 1995.
Schwemer, Anna Maria
  1995: *Studien zu den frühjüdischen Prophetenlegenden Vitae Prophetarum*. 2 vols. Tübingen: J. C. B. Mohr.
Seale, Morris S.
  1962: "Deborah's Ode and the Ancient Arabian Qasida." *Journal of Biblical Literature* 81: 343–47.
Seebass, Horst
  1982: "Machir im Ostjordanland." *Vetus Testamentum* 32: 496–503.
Seeman, Don
  2004: "The Watcher at the Window: Cultural Poetics of a Biblical Motif." *Prooftexts* 24: 1–50.
Segond, Albert
  1900: *Le Cantique de Débora: Étude exégétique et critique*. Genève: W. Kündig.
Selms, A. van
  1964: "Judge Shamgar." *Vetus Testamentum* 14: 294–309.
Shalev, Sariel
  2004: *Swords and Daggers in Late Bronze Age Canaan*. Prähistorische Bronzefunde, 4/13; Stuttgart: Franz Steiner Verlag.
Shalom-Guy, Hava
  2010: "Three-Way Intertextuality: Some Reflections of Abimelech's Death at Thebez in Biblical Narrative." *Journal for the Study of the Old Testament* 34: 419–32.
Shanks, Hershel
  2012: "Privies and Privacy." *Biblical Archaeology Review* 38/2: 6, 64–65.
Sharon, Diane
  2006: "Echoes of Gideon's Ephod: An Intertextual Reading." *Journal of the Ancient Near Eastern Society of Columbia University* 30: 89–102.
  2007: "Choreography of an Intertextual Allusion." Pp. 249–69 in Kathryn F. Kravitz and Diane M. Sharon, eds. *Bringing the Hidden to Light: The Process of Interpretation. Studies in Honor of Stephen A. Geller*. Winona Lake, IN: Eisenbrauns.
Shaw, Joseph W.
  1989: "Phoenicians in Southern Crete." *American Journal of Archaeology* 93: 165–83.

Shea, William H.

2004: "Jabin and Sisera at Megiddo." *Biblical Historian* 1/2: 24–27.

Shemesh, Yael

2011: "Jephthah—Victimizer and Victim: A Comparison of Jephthah and Characters in Genesis." *Journal of the Ancient Near Eastern Society of Columbia University* 32: 117–31.

Shupak, N.

1989: "New Light on Shamgar ben ʿAnath (Judg 3:31 and 5:6). *Biblica* 70: 517–25.

Siegert, Folker, and Jacques de Roulet

1999: *Prédications synagogales. Pseudo-Philon; traduction, notes et commentaire.* Sources chrétiennes, 435; Paris: Les Éditions du Cerf.

Sima, Alexander

2001: "Nochmals zur Deutung des Hebräischen Namens ʿOṭnîʾēl." *Biblische Notizen* 106: 47–50.

Simon, Uriel

1964: "The Parable of Jotham (Judges 9:8–15): The Parable, Its Application and Their Narrative Framework." *Tarbiz* 34: 1–34.

Simpson, Cuthbert A.

1957: *The Composition of the Book of Judges.* Oxford: Basil Blackwell.

Simpson, William Kelly, Edward F. Wente, and Raymond O. Faulkner, eds.

1972: *The Literature of Ancient Egypt: An Anthology of Stories, Instructions, and Poetry.* New Haven, CT: Yale University Press.

Singer, Itamar

2002: *Hittite Prayers.* Writings from the Ancient World, 11; Atlanta, GA: Society of Biblical Literature.

Smelik, Klaas A. D.

1991: *Writings from Ancient Israel: A Handbook of Historical and Religious Documents.* Louisville, KY: Westminster John Knox.

1992: *Converting the Past: Studies in the Ancient Israelite and Moabite Historiography.* Oudtestamentische Studiën, 27; Leiden: E. J. Brill.

Smelik, Willem F.

1995: *The Targum of Judges.* Oudtestamentische Studiën, 36; Leiden: E. J. Brill.

Smith, Clyde C.

1977: "Jehu and the Black Obelisk of Shalmaneser III." Pp. 71–105 in A. L. Merrill and T. W. Overholt, eds. *Scripture in History and Theology: Essays in Honor of J. C. Rylaarsdam.* Pittsburgh, PA: Pickwick.

Smith, Mark S.

1995: "Anat's Warfare Cannibalism and the West Semitic Ban." Pp. 368–86 in S. W. Holloway and L. K. Handy, eds. *The Pitcher Is Broken: Memorial Essays for Gösta W. Ahlström.* Journal for the Study of the Old Testament Supplement, 190; Sheffield: Sheffield Academic Press.

2009: "What Is Prologue Is Past: Composing Israelite Identity in Judges 5." Pp. 43–58 in Ahn and Cook 2009.

Snyman, S. D.

2005: "Shamgar ben Anath: A Farming Warrior or a Farmer at War?" *Vetus Testamentum* 55: 125–29.

Soggin, J. Alberto

1973: "Bemerkungen zur alttestamentlichen Topographie Sechems mit besonderem Bezug auf Jdc. 9." *Zeitschrift des Deutschen Palästina-Vereins* 83: 183–98.

1981a: *Judges: A Commentary*. Philadelphia: Westminster John Knox.

1981b: "Bemerkungen zum Deboralied, Richter Kap 5: Versuch einer neuen Übersetzung und eines Vorstosses in die älteste Geschichte Israels." *Theologische Literaturzeitung* 106: 625–39.

1987: *Le livre des Juges*. Commentaire de l'Ancien Testament, 5b; Genève: Labor et Fides.

Sokolow, Moshe

1979: "The Book of Judges in Medieval Muslim and Jewish Historiography." *Journal of the Ancient Near Eastern Society of Columbia University* 11: 113–30.

Sparkes, B. A.

1975: "Illustrating Aristophanes." *Journal of Hellenic Studies* 95: 122–35.

Speiser, E. A.

1967: "The Shibboleth Incident: Judges 12:6." Pp. 143–50 in J. J. Finkelstein and M. Greenberg, eds. *Oriental and Biblical Studies: Collected Writings of E. A. Speiser*. Philadelphia: University of Pennsylvania [= *Bulletin of the American Schools of Oriental Research* 85; 1942: 10–13].

Spronk, Karl

2001: "A Story to Weep About: Some Remarks on Judges 2:1–5 and Its Context." Pp. 87–94 in Janet W. Dyk, ed. *Unless Some One Guide Me . . . Festschrift for Karel A. Deurloo*. Amsterdamse Cahiers voor Exegese van de Bijbel en zijn tradities, Supplement Series, 2; Maastricht: Shaker.

Stager, Lawrence

1985: "The Archaeology of the Family in Ancient Israel." *Bulletin of the American Schools of Oriental Research* 260: 1–35.

1988: "Archeology, Ecology, and Social History: Background Themes to the Song of Deborah." Pp. 221–34 in J. Emerton, ed. *Congress Volume: Jerusalem 1986*. Vetus Testamentum Supplement, 40; Leiden: E. J. Brill.

1989: "The Song of Deborah: Why Some Tribes Answered the Call and Others Did Not." *Biblical Archaeology Review* 15: 50–64.

1998: "Forging an Identity: The Emergence of Ancient Israel." Pp. 90–131 in Michael Coogan, ed. *The Oxford History of the Biblical World*. New York: Oxford University Press.

1999: "The Fortress-Temple at Shechem and the 'House of El, Lord of the Covenant.'" Pp. 228–49 in Prescott H. Williams, Jr., and Theodore Hiebert, eds. *Realia Dei: Essays in Archaeology and Biblical Interpretation in Honor of Edward F. Campbell Jr., at His Retirement*. Durham, NC: Duke University Press.

2003a: "Key Passages." Pp. 240–45 in Israel Eph'al, Amnon Ben-Tor, and Peter Machinist, eds. *Hayim and Miriam Tadmor Volume*. Eretz-Israel, 27; Jerusalem: Israel Exploration Society.

2003b: "The Shechem Temple Where Abimelech Massacred a Thousand." *Biblical Archeology Review* 29/4: 26–35, 66–69.

Stamm, Johann Jakob

1967: "Hebräische Frauennamen." Pp. 301–39 in *Hebräische Wortforschung. Festschrift zum 80. Geburtstag von Walter Baumgartner.* Vetus Testamentum Supplement, 16; Leiden: E. J. Brill.

1980: *Beiträge zur Hebräischen und altorientalischen Namenkunde.* Göttingen: Vandenhoeck and Ruprecht.

Staubli, Thomas

1991: *Das Image der Nomaden im alten Israel und in der Ikonographie seiner sesshaften Nachbarn.* Orbis biblicus et orientalis, 107; Freiburg: Universitätsverlag.

Steinberg, Naomi

1999: "The Problem of Human Sacrifice in War: An Analysis of Judges 11." Pp. 114–35 in Cook and Winter 1999.

Stern, Efrayim

1993: *The New Encyclopedia of Archaeological Excavations in the Holy Land.* 4 vols. Jerusalem: Carta.

Stern, Philip D.

1991: *The Biblical ḥerem: A Window on Israel's Religious Experience.* Brown Judaic Studies, 211; Atlanta, GA: Scholars Press.

Sternberg, Meir

1987: *The Poetics of Biblical Narrative.* Bloomington: Indiana University Press.

Stieglitz, Robert R.

1991: "The City of Amurru." *Journal of Near Eastern Studies* 50: 45–48.

Stolper, Matthew W.

1997: "Flogging and Plucking." *Topoi orient-occident,* Supplément 1: 347–50.

Stone, Michael E., ed.

1984: *Jewish Writings of the Second Temple Period: Apocrypha, Pseudepigrapha, Qumran, Sectarian Writings, Philo, Josephus.* Compendia rerum Iudaicarum ad Novum Testamentum, 2; Literature of the Jewish People in the Period of the Second Temple and the Talmud, 2; Assen: Van Gorcum.

Storch, W.

1970: "Zur Perikope von der Syrophonizierin." *Biblische Zeitschrift* 14: 256–57.

Streck, Michael P.

2008: "Salz, Versalzung. A. Nach Schriftquellen," *RlA* 11: 592–99.

Sumner, W. A.

1968: "Israel's Encounters with Edom, Moab, Ammon, Sihon, and Og According to the Deuteronomist." *Vetus Testamentum* 18: 216–28.

Suter, Claudia

1992: "Die Frau am Fenster in der orientalischen Elfenbeinschnitzkunst des frühen 1. Jahrtausends v. Chr." *Jahrbuch der Staatlichen Kunstsammlungen in Baden-Württemberg* 29: 7–28.

Swanson, Kristin A.

2012: "What Happens When We Read Judges in the Persian Period?" Pp. 92–106 in Berquist and Hunt 2012.

Sweeney, Marvin A.

1997: "Davidic Polemics in the Book of Judges." *Vetus Testamentum* 47: 517–29.

Szuchman, Jeffery, ed.

2009: *Nomads, Tribes, and the State in the Ancient Near East: Cross-disciplinary Perspectives.* Oriental Institute Seminars, 5; Chicago: Oriental Institute of the University of Chicago.

Tadmor, Hayim, Benno Landsberger, and Simo Parpola

1989: "The Sin of Sargon and Sennacherib's Last Will." *State Archives of Assyria, Bulletin* 3/1: 3–51.

Takim, Liaqat

2004: "Samson." *Encyclopaedia of the Qur'ān* 4: 525–26.

Talmon, Shemaryahu

1978: "The Presentation of Synchroneity and Simultaneity in Biblical Narratives." Pp. 9–26 in Joseph Heinemann and Samuel Werses, eds. *Studies in Hebrew Narrative Art Throughout the Ages.* Scripta Hierosolymitana; Jerusalem: Magnes.

1993: "The Comparative Method in Biblical Interpretation: Principles and Problems" and "Did There Exist a Biblical National Epic?" Pp. 11–49 and 91–111, respectively, in *Literary Studies in the Hebrew Bible: Form and Content.* Jerusalem: Magnes.

Tatu, Silviu

2006: "Jotham's Fable and the Crux Interpretum in Judges IX." *Vetus Testamentum* 56: 105–24.

Taylor, J. G.

1982: "The Song of Deborah and Two Canaanite Goddesses." *Journal for the Study of the Old Testament* 23: 99–108.

Thelle, Rannfrid I.

2002: *Ask God: Divine Consultation in the Literature of the Hebrew Bible.* Beiträge zur biblischen Exegese und Theologie; Frankfurt am Main: Peter Lang.

Timm, Stefan

1989: *Moab zwischen den Mächten: Studien zu historischen Denkmälern und Texten.* Ägypten und altes Testament, 17; Wiesbaden: Otto Harrassowitz.

Tomback, Richard S.

1978: *A Comparative Semitic Lexicon of the Phoenician and Punic Languages.* Dissertation Series, 32; Missoula, MT: Scholars Press.

Toorn, Karel van der

1985: *Sin and Sanction in Israel and Mesopotamia: A Comparative Study.* Studia Semitica Neerlandica, 22; Assen: Van Gorcum.

1992: "Mill, Millstones." *ABD* 4: 831–32.

1995: "The Domestic Cult at Emar." *Journal of Cuneiform Studies* 47: 35–49.

Toorn, Karel van der, Bob Becking, and Pieter W. van der Horst, eds.

1995: *Dictionary of Deities and Demons in the Bible.* Leiden: E. J. Brill.

Tournay, Raymond J.

1996: "Le Cantique de Débora et ses relectures." Pp. 195–207 in Michael V. Fox, Victor A. Hurowitz, Avi Hurvitz, Michael L. Klein, Baruch J. Schwartz, and Nili Shupak, eds. *Texts, Temples, and Traditions: A Tribute to Menahem Haran.* Winona Lake, IN: Eisenbrauns.

Tov, Emanuel

1978: "The Textual History of the Song of Deborah in the A Text of the LXX." *Vetus Testamentum* 28: 224–32.

2012: *Textual Criticism of the Hebrew Bible*. 3rd edition. Minneapolis, MN: Fortress.

Trebolle Barrera, Julio

1989: "Textual Variants in 4QJudg^a and the Textual and Editorial History of the Book of Judges." *Revue de Qumran* 14: 229–45.

1991: "Edition préliminaires de 4Juges^b: Contribution des manuscrits qumrâniens des *Juges* à l'étude textuelle et littéraire du livre." *Revue de Qumran* 15: 79–100.

1995: "49. 4QJudg^a"; "50. 4QJudg^b"; "54. 4QKgs." Pp. 161–64, 165–69, and 171–83, respectively, in Ulrich, Cross, Crawford, Duncan, Skehan, Tov, and Trebolle Barrera, eds. 1995.

Trible, Phyllis

1984: *Texts of Terror: Literary-Feminist Readings of Biblical Narratives*. Overtures to Biblical Theology; Philadelphia: Fortress.

Tsevat, Matitiahu

1983: "Two Old Testament Stories and Their Hittite Analogues." *Journal of the American Oriental Society* 103: [= J. M. Sasson, ed. *Studies in Literature from the Ancient Near East, by Members of the American Oriental Society, Dedicated to Samuel Noah Kramer*. New Haven, CT: American Oriental Society]: 321–26.

Ulrich, Eugene

2011: "The Evolutionary Production and Transmission of the Scriptural Books." Pp. 47–64 in Hanne von Weissenberg, Juha Pakkala, and Marko Marttila, eds. *Changes in Scripture: Rewriting and Interpreting Authoritative Traditions in the Second Temple Period*. Zeitschrift für die alttestamentliche Wissenschaft Beiheft, 419; Berlin: De Gruyter.

Ulrich, Eugene, ed.

2009: *The Biblical Qumran Scrolls: Transcriptions and Textual Variants*. Vetus Testamentum Supplement, 134; Leiden: E. J. Brill.

Ulrich, Eugene, Frank Moore Cross, Sidnie White Crawford, Julie Ann Duncan, Patrick W. Skehan, Emanuel Tov, Julio Trebolle Barrera, eds.

1995: *Qumran Cave 4, IX: Deuteronomy, Joshua, Judges, Kings*. Discoveries in the Judaean Desert, 14. Oxford: Clarendon.

Ünal, Ahmet

1993: "Ritual Purity Versus Physical Impurity in Hittite Anatolia: Public Health and Structures for Sanitation According to Cuneiform Texts and Archaeological Remains." Pp. 119–39 in Takahito Mikasa, ed. *Essays on Anatolian Archaeology*. Wiesbaden: Harrassowitz.

Vanderkam, James C.

1995: "Prophecy and Apocalyptics in the Ancient Near East." Pp. 2083–94 in Sasson, Baines, Beckman, and Rubinson, eds., 1995.

Van Seters, John

1972: "The Conquest of Sihon's Kingdom: A Literary Examination." *Journal of Biblical Literature* 91: 182–97.

1980: "Once Again: The Conquest of Sihon's Kingdom." *Journal of Biblical Literature* 99: 117–19.

1983: *In Search of History: Historiography in the Ancient World and the Origins of Biblical History*. New Haven, CT: Yale University Press (reprinted, Eisenbrauns 1997).

1984: "Joshua 24 and the Problem of Tradition in the Old Testament." Pp. 139–58 in W. Boyd Barrick and John R. Spencer, eds. *In the Shelter of Elyon: Essays on Ancient Palestinian Life and Literature in Honor of G. W. Ahlström*. Journal for the Study of the Old Testament Supplement, 31; Sheffield: Almond Press.

Vaux, Roland de

1961: *Ancient Israel: Its Life and Institutions*. Translated by John McHugh. London: Darton, Longman and Todd.

1970: "The Settlement of the Israelites in Southern Palestine and the Origins of the Tribe of Judah." Pp. 108–34 in H. T. Frank and W. L. Reed, eds. *Translating and Understanding the Old Testament: Essays in Honor of Herbert Gordon May*. Nashville, TN: Abingdon.

1978: *The Early History of Israel*. Translated by David Smith. Philadelphia: Westminster John Knox.

Vernes, Maurice

1892: "Le cantique de Débora." *Revue des études juives* 24: 52–67, 225–55.

Veijola, Timo

1984: "David in Keila: Tradition and Interpretation in 1 Samuel 23, 1–13." *Revue Biblique* 91: 51–87.

Veldhuis, Nick

1999: "All Those Signs." Pp. 161–74 in H. J. L. Vanstiphout, ed. *All Those Nations . . . Cultural Encounters Within and with the Near East: Studies Presented to Hans Drijvers at the Occasion of His Sixty-fifth Birthday by Colleagues and Students*. GroniComers/ICOG Communications, 2: Groningen: Styx.

Viberg, Åke

1992: *Symbols of Law: A Contextual Analysis of Legal Symbolic Acts in the Old Testament*. Coniectanea Biblica OT Series, 34: Stockholm: Almqvist and Wiksell.

Vidal, Jordi

2009: "The Siege of Razama: An Example of Aggressive Defence in Old Babylonian Times." *Altorientalische Forschungen* 36: 365–71.

Vincent, Mark A.

2000: "The Song of Deborah: A Structural and Literary Consideration." *Journal for the Study of the Old Testament* 91: 61–82.

Von Mžik, Hans

1915: "Die Gideon-Saul-Legende und die Überlieferung der Schlacht bei Badr: Ein Beitrag zur ältesten Geschichte des Islām." *Wiener Zeitschrift für die Kunde des Morgenlandes* 29: 371–83.

Waldman, Nahum M.

1989: "The Imagery of Clothing, Covering and Overpowering." *Journal of the Ancient Near Eastern Society* 19: 161–70.

Wallhead, Celia

2001: "The Story of Jael and Sisera in Five Nineteenth- and Twentieth-Century Fictional Texts." *Atlantis* 23: 147–66.

Wallis, Louis
  1912: *Sociological Study of the Bible.* Chicago: University of Chicago Press.
Waltisberg, Michael
  1999: "Zum Alter der Sprache des Deboraliedes Ri 5." *Zeitschrift für Althebraistik*
    12: 218–32.
Watke, Bruce K., and M. O'Connor
  1990: *An Introduction to Biblical Hebrew Syntax.* Winona Lake, IN: Eisenbrauns.
Watson, W. G. E.
  1984: *Classical Hebrew Poetry: A Guide to Its Techniques.* Journal for the Study of the
    Old Testament Supplement, 26; Sheffield: Almond Press.
Webb, Barry G.
  1987: *The Book of Judges: An Integrated Study.* Journal for the Study of the Old
    Testament Supplement, 46; Sheffield: Almond Press.
Weinfeld, Moshe
  1967: "The Period of the Conquest and the Judges as Seen by the Earlier and Later
    Sources." *Vetus Testamentum* 17: 93–113.
  1983a: "The Extent of the Promised Land: The Status of Transjordan." Pp. 59–75
    in G. Stecker, ed. *Das Land Israel in biblischer Zeit.* Göttingen: Vandenhoeck
    and Ruprecht.
  1983b: "Divine Intervention in War in Ancient Israel and in the Ancient Near East."
    Pp. 121–47 in H. Tadmor and M. Weinfeld, eds. *History, Historiography and In-
    terpretation: Studies in Biblical and Cuneiform Literatures.* Jerusalem: Magnes.
  1988: "The Ban on the Canaanites and Its Development in Israelite Law" (in He-
    brew). *Zion* 53: 135–47.
  1993: "The Ban on the Canaanites in the Biblical Codes and Its Historical Devel-
    opment." Pp. 142–60 in André Lemaire and Benedikt Otzen, eds. *History and
    Traditions of Early Israel: Studies Presented to Eduard Nielsen, May 8th 1993.*
    Leiden: E. J. Brill.
Weippert, Manfred
  1976–80: "Kanaan." *RlA* 5: 352–55.
  2001: "Ich bin Jahwe—Ich bin Ištar von Arbela. Deuterojesaja im Lichte der
    neuassyrischen Prophetie." Pp. 31–59 in B. Huwyler and H.-P. Mathys, eds.
    Prophetie und Psalme: Festschrift für Klaus Seybold Zum 65. Geburtstag. Mün-
    ster: Ugarit Verlag.
  2010: *Historisches Textbuch zum Alten Testament; mit Beiträgen von Joachim Friedrich
    Quack, Bernd Ulrich Schipper und Stefan Jakob Wimmer.* Grundrisse zum Al-
    ten Testament. Das Alte Testament Deutsch, Ergänzungsreihe, 10: Göttingen:
    Vandenhoeck and Ruprecht.
Weitzman, Michael P.
  1999: *The Syriac Version of the Old Testament: An Introduction.* University of Cam-
    bridge Oriental Publications, 56. Cambridge: Cambridge University Press.
Welten, P.
  1965: "Bezeq." *Zeitschrift des Deutschen Palästina-Vereins* 81: 138–65.
Wellhausen, Julius
  1994: *Prolegomena to the History of Israel; with a reprint of the article Israel from
    the Encyclopaedia Britannica.* Scholars Press Reprints and Translations Series.

Atlanta, GA: Scholars Press (reprint of 1885 English edition; first published as *Geschichte Israels*, 1878, then as *Prolegomena zur Geschichte Israels*, 1882).

Wendel, Alfred

1931: *Das israelitisch-jüdische Gelübde*. Berlin: Philo-Verlag.

Wenham, G. J.

1971: "The Deuteronomic Theology of the Book of Joshua." *Journal of Biblical Literature* 90: 140–48.

1972: "Betulah: 'A Girl of Marriageable Age.'" *Vetus Testamentum* 22: 326–48.

Westbrook, Raymond

1988: *Old Babylonian Marriage Law*. Archiv für Orientforschung, 23; Horn, Austria: F. Berger.

1991: *Property and the Family in Biblical Law*. Journal for the Study of the Old Testament Supplement, 113; Sheffield: JSOT Press.

Westbrook, Raymond, ed.

2003: *A History of Ancient Near Eastern Law*. Handbook of Oriental studies. Section 1, The Near and Middle East, 72; Leiden: E. J. Brill.

Westenholz, Aage, and Walther Sallaberger

1999: *Akkade-Zeit und Ur III-Zeit*. Orbis biblicus et orientalis, 160–63; Annäherungen, 3; Göttingen: Vandenhoeck and Ruprecht.

Westenholz, Joan Goodnick

1983: "Heroes of Akkad." *Journal of the American Oriental Society* 103: [= J. M. Sasson, ed. *Studies in Literature from the Ancient Near East, by Members of the American Oriental Society, Dedicated to Samuel Noah Kramer*. New Haven, CT: American Oriental Society]: 327–36.

1997: *Legends of the Kings of Akkade: The Texts*. Mesopotamian Civilizations, 7; Winona Lake, IN: Eisenbrauns.

Whiston, William, trans.

1960: *The Complete Works of Josephus*. Grand Rapids, MI: Kregel.

White (Crawford), Sidney A.

1992: "In the Steps of Jael and Deborah: Judith as Heroine." Pp. 5–16 in J. C. Vanderkam, ed. *"No One Spoke Ill of Her": Essays on Judith*. Early Judaism and Its Literature, 2; Atlanta, GA: Scholars Press.

Whiting, Robert M.

1987: *Old Babylonian Letters from Tell Asmar*. Assyriological Studies, 22; Chicago: Oriental Institute.

1995: "Amorite Tribes and Nations of Second-Millennium Western Asia." Pp. 1231–42 in Sasson, Baines, Beckman, and Rubinson, eds., 1995.

Whitman, James Q.

1995: "At the Origins of Law and the State: Supervision of Violence Mutilation of Bodies, or Setting of Prices?" *Symposium on Ancient Law, Economic and Society*, II [= *Chicago-Kent Law Review* 71/1]: 41–84.

Wilcke, Claus

1989: "Genealogical and Geographical Thought in the Sumerian King List." Pp. 557–71 in Hermann Behrens, Darlene Loding, and Martha Tobi Roth, eds. DUMU-E$_2$-DUB-BA-A. *Studies in Honor of Åke W. Sjöberg*. Occasional Publications of the Samuel Noah Kramer Fund, 11; Philadelphia: University Museum.

Wilkie, John M.

    1951: "The Peshiṭta Translation of Ṭabbur Ha'areṣ in Judges ix 37." *Vetus Testamentum* 1: 144.

Wilkinson, Elizabeth

    1983: "The *hapax legomenon* of Judges IV 18." *Vetus Testamentum* 33: 512–13.

Willesen, Folker,

    1958: "The אפרתי of the Shibboleth Incident." *Vetus Testamentum* 8: 97–98.

Williamson, Joanne

    1999: *Hittite Warrior*. Bathgate, ND: Bethlehem Books.

Willis, T. M.

    1997: "The Nature of Jephthah's Authority." *Catholic Biblical Quarterly* 59: 33–44.

Wills, Lawrence M.

    1995: *The Jewish Novel in the Ancient World*. Ithaca, NY: Cornell University Press.

Winter, Irene

    1980: *A Decorated Breastplate from Hasanlu, Iran*. Hasanlu Special Studies I; Philadelphia: University Museum.

Woestenburg, Els, and Bram Jagersma

    1992: "The Continuing Story of Sippar-Amnānum = Sippar-rabûm." *NABU* 28, pp. 24–25.

Wolde, E. van

    1995: "Yael in Judges 4." *Zeitschrift für die alttestamentliche Wissenschaft* 107: 240–46.

Wolf, C. Umhau

    1947: "Traces of Primitive Democracy in Ancient Israel." *Journal of Near Eastern Studies* 1947: 98–108.

Wong, Gregory T. K.

    2005: "Is There a Direct Pro-Judah Polemic in Judges?" *Scandinavian Journal of the Old Testament* 19: 84–110.

    2006: *The Compositional Strategy of the Book of Judges: An Inductive, Rhetorical Study*. Leiden: E. J. Brill.

    2007: "Song of Deborah as Polemic." *Biblica* 88: 1–22.

Wright, George E.

    1946: "The Literary and Historical Problem of Joshua 10 and Judges 1." *Journal of Near Eastern Studies* 5: 105–14.

Wright, Jacob L.

    2011: "War Commemoration and the Interpretation of Judges 5:15b–17." *Vetus Testamentum* 61: 505–21.

Wulff, Hans E.

    1966: "Door Locks in Persia." *Technology and Culture* 7: 497–503.

Yadin, Yigal

    1963: *The Art of Warfare in Biblical Lands in the Light of Archaeological Study*. New York: McGraw-Hill.

    1968: "'And Dan, Why Did He Remain in Ships?'" *Australian Journal of Biblical Archaeology* 1: 9–23.

Yee, Gale A.

    1993: "By the Hand of a Woman: The Metaphor of the Woman Warrior in Judges 4." *Semeia* 61: 99–132.

1995: *Judges and Method: New Approaches in Biblical Studies.* Minneapolis, MN: Fortress.

Young, Ian M.

1998a: "Israelite Literacy: Interpreting the Evidence: Part I." *Vetus Testamentum* 48: 239–53.

1998b: "Israelite Literacy: Interpreting the Evidence: Part II, *Vetus Testamentum* 48: 408–22.

Younger, K. Lawson, Jr.,

1991: "*Heads! Tails! Or the Whole Coin?!*: Contextual Method and Intertextual Analysis—Judges 4 and 5." Pp. 109–46 in K. Lawson Younger, Jr., William W. Hallo, and Bernard F. Batto, eds. *The Biblical Canon in Comparative Perspective: Scripture in Context IV*. Ancient Near Eastern Texts and Studies, 11; Lewiston, NY: Edwin Mellen Press.

1994: "Judges 1 in Its Near Eastern Literary Context." Pp. 207–27 in Alan Millard, James K. Hoffmeier, and David W. Baker, eds. *Faith, Tradition, and History: Old Testament Historiography in Its Near Eastern Context.* Winona Lake, IN: Eisenbrauns.

1995: "The Configuration of Judicial Preliminaries: Judges 1.1–2.5 and Its Dependence on the Book of Joshua." *Journal for the Study of the Old Testament* 68: 75–92.

2000: "The Panamuwa Inscription." Pp. 148–60 in Hallo and Younger 2000.

Zadok, Ran

1988: *The Pre-hellenistic Israelite Anthroponymy and Prosopography.* Orientalia Lovaniensia Analecta, 28; Leuven: Uitgeverij Peeters.

Zakovitch, Yair

1972: "*ypth̬ = bdn.*" *Vetus Testamentum* 22: 123–25.

1981: "Siseras Tod." *Zeitschrift für die alttestamentliche Wissenschaft* 93: 364–74.

Zertal, Adam

2002: "Philistine Kin Found in Early Israel." *Biblical Archaeology Review* 28: 18–31, 60–61.

Zettler, Richard L.

1987: "Sealings as Artifacts of Institutional Administration in Ancient Mesopotamia." *Journal of Cuneiform Studies* 39: 197–240.

Ziegler, Nele

1999: *Le Harem de Zimri-Lim. FM*, 4; Mémoires de NABU, 5; Paris: SEPOA.

Zimmermann, Frank

1952: "Reconstructions in Judges 7:25–8:25." *Journal of Biblical Literature* 1952: 111–14.

TRANSLATION

Judges 1–12

I. Prelude

1 ¹After the death of Joshua, the people of Israel inquired of the Lord, "Who should march for us against the Canaanites at first, to attack them?" ²The Lord said, "Judah must march; I have already handed him the land." ³Judah, however, said to his kin Simeon, "Come along with me, in my lot, and we will both attack the Canaanites. I will then go with you myself, in your lot." So, Simeon went with him. ⁴Judah went up, and the Lord handed them the Canaanites and the Perizzites. They defeated them at Bezeq—ten thousand men. ⁵They found Adoni-bezeq in Bezeq and attacked him, defeating the Canaanites as well as the Perizzites. ⁶When Adoni-bezeq fled, they pursued him. Seizing him, they severed his thumbs and toes. ⁷Adoni-bezeq said, "Once seventy kings, all with severed thumbs and toes, were scrapping under my table; as I had done, God has repaid me." They brought him to Jerusalem and there he died.

⁸The people of Judah attacked Jerusalem and captured it. They put it to the sword and set fire to the city. ⁹Afterward, the people of Judah went down to attack the Canaanites who inhabited the upland, the Negev, and the foothills as well. ¹⁰Judah moved against the Canaanites who lived in Hebron (earlier, Hebron was called Qiryat-arba) and they defeated Sheshay, Ahiman, and Talmay. ¹¹From there, he went against the inhabitants of Debir (earlier, Debir was called Qiryat-sefer).

¹²Caleb then announced, "To him who defeats Qiryat-sefer and captures it, I give him Achsah, my daughter, as wife." ¹³Othniel son of Kenaz (brother of Caleb, who was younger than him) defeated it; so he gave him Achsah, his daughter, as wife. ¹⁴On arriving, she convinced him to request the field from

her father. As she dismounted from the donkey, Caleb asked her, "What's with you?" ¹⁵She answered him, "Hand me a present! You have given me away as if Negev-land; so you must now give me basins of water." Caleb gave her Upper Gullot as well as Lower Gullot.

¹⁶The descendants of the Kenite, the father-in-law of Moses, marched with those of Judah from the City of Palms to the wilderness of Judah, in the Negev of Arad. Having gone there, he settled among the inhabitants. ¹⁷Judah went with Simeon his brother and they attacked the Canaanites dwelling in Zephat. They vowed it for *ḥērem*-obliteration, so that the town was called Hormah. ¹⁸Judah captured Gaza and its territory, Ashkelon and its territory, and Ekron and its territory. ¹⁹The LORD was with Judah, so he took over the hill country; but displacing the people of the plain was not to happen, for they had chariots of iron. ²⁰Hebron was given to Caleb, as Moses had promised, from there expelling all three Anak descendants. ²¹As to the Jebusites dwelling in Jerusalem, Benjamin could not displace them; so the Jebusites have shared Jerusalem with Benjamin to this day.

²²The House of Joseph for their part marched against Bethel, the LORD being with them. ²³As the House of Joseph watched Bethel—previously the town was named Luz—²⁴the guards noticed a man leaving the city. They told him, "Show us an entry into town and we will treat you well." ²⁵He showed them an entry into the town and they put it to the sword; but they released the man and his entire family. ²⁶This man went to Hittite territory and founded a town, calling it Luz, its name to this day.

²⁷Manasseh did not occupy Beth-shean and its dependent states, Taanach and its dependencies, the inhabitants of Dor and its dependencies, the inhabitants of Ibleam and its dependencies, or the inhabitants of Megiddo and its dependencies. In this region, Canaanites were determined to remain. ²⁸Whenever Israel was dominant it would impose tribute on the Canaanites, without displacing them. ²⁹As to Ephraim, it did not displace the Canaanites that inhabited Gezer, so in Gezer itself the Canaanites lived among them.

³⁰Zebulun did not displace the inhabitants of Qitron and the inhabitants of Nahalol. The Canaanites lived alongside but were subject to tribute.

³¹Asher did not displace the inhabitants of Akko, the inhabitants of Sidon, Ahlab, Achzib, Helbah, Aphek, and Rehov. ³²So the people of Asher lived among the Canaanites who settled the land, for Asher could not displace them.

³³Naphtali did not displace the inhabitants of Bet-Shemesh and the inhabitants of Bet-Anat, but dwelled among the Canaanites settling the land; the inhabitants of Bet-Shemesh and Bet-Anat were subject to pay them tribute.

³⁴The Amorites pushed the Danites toward the hills, for they would not let them move down toward the valley. ³⁵The Amorites were determined to remain

in Har-Heres, Ayyalon, and Shaalabim; but when the House of Joseph compelled them, they were subject to tribute. ([36]Amorite territory stretched from Maale-Akrabim, through Sela, and upwards.)

II. Arguments

2 [1]Coming up to Bochim from Gilgal, the LORD's emissary said, "When leading you out of Egypt and bringing you to the land that I pledged to your ancestors, I said, 'I shall never annul my covenant with you. [2]For your part, you must make no covenant with the inhabitants of this land. You must raze their altars.' But you have not obeyed me. How could you have done that? [3]I have decided therefore not to drive them out before you, so that for you they will become foes, their gods snares." [4]As the emissary of the LORD spoke these words to all Israel, the people broke into loud weeping. [5]So they called that place Bochim, and they offered sacrifices there to the LORD.

[6]When Joshua dismissed the people, each person in Israel went to take possession of his allotted land. [7]The people served only the LORD during the full lifetime of Joshua as well as the full lifetime of all the elders who outlived Joshua and who had witnessed every great deed that the LORD had done for Israel. [8]Joshua son of Nun, the servant of the LORD, died at 110 years of age [9]and was buried within his allotted land, at Timnath-heres in Mount Ephraim, north of Mount Gaash. [10]Eventually, when members of this entire generation were gathered to their fathers, the generations of people born after them hardly acknowledged the LORD or even the deeds he had done for Israel.

[11]The people of Israel did what was offensive to the LORD: They worshiped the many Baals; [12]they forsook the LORD, God of their fathers, who had brought them out of the land of Egypt; they committed to other gods, from among those of people around them, bowing down to them. So they provoked the LORD [13]by forsaking the LORD and worshiping Baal and the Ashtaroth. [14]Incensed against Israel, the LORD abandoned them to raiders, who plundered them and turned them over to their enemies on all sides, such that they could no longer resist their foes. [15]Everywhere they marched to battle, the LORD would intervene to hurt them, as the LORD declared and as the LORD avowed to them. They therefore suffered terribly. [16]The LORD would then install judges, and they would rescue them from their plunderers. [17]Yet, the people would not heed their own judges, for they would lust after other gods, falling prostrate before them. They swiftly retreated from the path their fathers had followed, in no way acting to obey the commandments of the LORD. [18]Whenever the LORD would install judges for them, the LORD would sustain the judge who would rescue them from their enemies during that judge's entire tenure; for the LORD would be moved to pity by their groaning, because of their tormentors and oppressors.

[19]At the death of the judge, however, they would once again act more corruptly than their own parents, by following other gods, serving them, and falling prostrate before them; they omitted none of their practices or their obstinate ways.

[20]Incensed against Israel, the LORD decided, "Since the people of this nation violated the covenant that I urged on their fathers and did not heed my command, [21]I will certainly no longer displace before them even a single person from those nations that Joshua left whole when he died, [22]so as to use them for testing Israel: Whether or not they can keep to the LORD's way, guiding themselves as their ancestors had done." [23]Thus the LORD kept those nations whole, without displacing them hastily, and did not turn them over to Joshua.

3   [1]These are the nations that the LORD kept whole, using them to test all those in Israel who had not experienced all the wars in Canaan, [2]just to give generations of Israel experience, teaching them about war, only because previously they did not experience them: [3]The (lands of) the five rulers of the Philistines and all Canaanites, Sidonians, and Hivvites who inhabited the hill region of the Lebanon, from Mount Baal-Hermon to Lebo-Hamath. [4]They were there to test Israel, to determine whether they would heed the commandments that the LORD had urged on their fathers through Moses. [5]So the people of Israel settled among the Canaanites, Hittites, Amorites, Perizzites, Hivvites, and Jebusites. [6]They took for themselves their daughters in marriage, giving their own daughters to their sons, as well as worshiping their gods.

III. The Judges
OTHNIEL

[7]The people of Israel did what was offensive to the LORD: They forgot the LORD their God and worshiped the many Baals and Asherahs. [8]Incensed against Israel, the LORD turned them over to Cushan-rishatayim, king of Aram-naharayim. For eight years, the people of Israel served Cushan-rishatayim. [9]When the people of Israel pleaded with the LORD, the LORD installed a rescuer for the people of Israel, to rescue them: Othniel son of Kenaz (brother of Caleb who was younger than him). [10]Endowed with zeal for the LORD, he became judge in Israel. When he set out in battle, the LORD gave Cushan-rishatayim, king of Aram, over to him so that he brought Cushan-rishatayim under his control. [11]The land had peace for forty years. Then Othniel son of Kenaz died.

EHUD

[12]The people of Israel resumed offending the LORD; so the LORD emboldened Eglon, king of Moab, against Israel because its people did what was offensive to the LORD. [13]He brought Ammon and Amalek to his side, intent to defeat Israel;

together, they occupied the City of Palms. [14]For eighteen years, the people of Israel served Eglon, king of Moab. [15]When the people of Israel pleaded with the LORD, the LORD provided them a rescuer: Ehud son of Gera, of Benjamin, a man with a hindered right arm. Through him, the people of Israel sent tribute to Eglon king of Moab.

[16]Ehud made for himself a two-edged dagger, a forearm in length, girding it at his right thigh under his tunic. [17]Then he presented the tribute to Eglon king of Moab—Eglon himself was an imposing man. [18]Once he completed presenting the tribute, he dismissed the people carrying it. [19]Having just come back from the hewn images near Gilgal, he said, "I have a secret message for you, O King." Eglon said, "Hush!" All those serving him left his presence. [20]As Ehud was approaching him, he was sitting on the raised chamber of the reception hall that was his, all by himself. So as Ehud said, "I have a divine message for you," he rose from his throne. [21]Reaching with his left hand, Ehud drew the dagger from his right thigh and stuck it in his belly. [22]Even the hilt sunk with the blade, the fat closing over the blade such that he could not yank the dagger out of his belly and the bowels spilled out.[a] [23]Slipping out toward the *colonnade*, Ehud shut and bolted the doors of the raised chamber behind him.

[24]No sooner did he leave than his servants came in. When they saw that the doors of the platform were bolted, they said, "He must be relieving himself in the chamber of the reception hall." [25]They got embarrassed waiting, for he was not opening the doors of the raised chamber. So they took the key and when they unlocked there was their lord fallen dead on the floor!

[26]Throughout their hemming and hawing, Ehud was escaping. He moved beyond the hewn images and was escaping toward Seirah. [27]As soon as he got there, he sounded the ram's horn all over Mount Ephraim and all of Israel joined him in coming down the mountain, with him in the lead. [28]"Pursue behind me," he told them, "for the LORD has handed you Moab, your enemy." They came down with him and captured all the fords of the Jordan leading to Moab, allowing no one to cross. [29]On just this occasion, they killed about ten thousand men; they were all stout and prominent, yet not a single man escaped. [30]From that time on, Moab fell under Israel's power. The land had peace for eighty years.

SHAMGAR

[31]After him[b] was Shamgar son of Anat, who slew six hundred Philistines with an oxgoad. He too rescued Israel.

---

a. Or: he slipped out toward the vestibule.
b. Or: Next to him.

DEBORAH

4 ¹With Ehud dead, the people of Israel resumed offending the Lord, ²so the Lord turned them over to Jabin, king of Canaan, who ruled from Hazor. His army commander was Sisera, who operated from Haroshet-haggoyim. ³The people of Israel cried out to the Lord; for he had nine hundred chariots of iron and oppressed Israel brutally for twenty years.

⁴Deborah was a woman prophet, a wielder of flames.ᶜ It was she who was judging Israel at that time. (⁵She would sit beneath the "Palm of Deborah," between Ramah and Bethel in Mount Ephraim, and the people of Israel would come up to her for judgment.) ⁶She conveyed a message to Baraq son of Abinoam of Kedesh in Naphtali, telling him, "The Lord, God of Israel, has commanded: 'Plan to deploy at Mount Tabor, taking with you ten thousand men of Naphtali and Zebulun. ⁷At Wadi Kishon, I will deploy against you Sisera, Jabin's army commander, with his chariots and his infantry; but I will hand him over to you.'" ⁸Baraq said to her, "If you go with me, I will go; if you do not go with me, I will not go." ⁹"Very well, I will go with you," she answered; "but any glory for you will not come from the course you take, for the Lord will turn Sisera over to a woman."

Deborah arose, setting out for Kedesh to be with Baraq.ᵈ ¹⁰Baraq then mustered Zebulun and Naphtali at Kedesh. Ten thousand men marched behind his steps, with Deborah joining him. (¹¹Now Heber the Kenite had separated himself from other Kenites, from the descendants of Hobab, the father-in-law of Moses, pitching his tent as far as the Oak at Bezaanannim,ᵉ which is near Kedesh.) ¹²Sisera was informed that Baraq son of Abinoam had gone up to Mount Tabor. ¹³Sisera mustered all his chariotry—nine hundred chariots of iron—and all the troops he had, *setting forth* from Haroshet-haggoyim toward Wadi Kishon.

¹⁴Deborah told Baraq, "Up! This is the moment the Lord has delivered Sisera into your power, for the Lord has already taken your lead." With Baraq charging down Mount Tabor, ten thousand men behind him, ¹⁵the Lord flustered Sisera, his chariotry, and his army, at the edge of the sword, ahead of Baraq.ᶠ Sisera dropped from his chariot and fled on foot. ¹⁶Baraq chased after the chariots and the army as far as Haroshet-haggoyim. Everyone in Sisera's army fell to the sword; not even one man survived.

¹⁷Sisera himself fled on foot to the tent of Jael, wife of Heber the Kenite; for there was a peace accord between Jabin, king of Hazor, and the House of Heber

---

c. Or: wife of Lappidoth.

d. Or: So Deborah arose and accompanied Baraq to Kedesh.

e. *Ketiv*: The Oak at Bazeannim (see the Notes at Judg 4:11).

f. Or: *they were routed* at the edge of the sword by Baraq (see the Notes at Judg 4:15).

the Kenite. ¹⁸Jael came out to greet Sisera, saying to him, "Turn this way, my lord; turn toward me and have no fear." So he turned toward her, and into the tent. She covered him with a blanket. ¹⁹He said to her, "Do let me have some water; I am thirsty." She opened a skin of milk, gave him drink, and covered him. ²⁰He said to her, "Stand at the entrance of the tent. If anybody comes to ask you if there is any man here, just say 'There is not!'" ²¹Jael, wife of Heber, took hold of a tent peg and grasped a mallet in her hand. Approaching him cautiously, through his temple^g she hammered the peg till it punched the ground. He was fast asleep from exhaustion, and so he died.

²²Baraq just then was tracking Sisera. Jael went out to meet him, saying, "Come, I will show you the man you are seeking." When he reached her, there was Sisera sprawling dead, with a peg in his temple.^h

²³From that day on, God made Jabin, king of Canaan, submit to the people of Israel. ²⁴Their pressure against Jabin, king of Canaan, became increasingly aggressive until they annihilated Jabin, king of Canaan.

Poem

5   ¹Sang Deborah and Baraq son of Abinoam, on that very day:
        ²For seizing leadership in Israel,
        For people in full devotion,
                Bless the LORD!
        ³Kings, listen! Rulers, be alert!
        I—to the LORD, I would sing
                Would exalt the LORD, god of Israel.

        ⁴LORD, as you head out from Seir
                March from Edom territory
        Earth quakes; heaven itself dissolves;
                Clouds too dissolve into water,
            ⁵Mountains melt, because of the LORD
                The One of Sinai—
                Because of the LORD, god of Israel.

        ⁶In the days of Shamgar son of Anat,
            In the days of Jael,
        Trails are unused,
            Wayfarers take twisting trails.
        ⁷Hamlets vanish in Israel; simply vanish

---

g. Or: jaw.
h. Or: jaw.

Till I,ⁱ Deborah, arise
      Arise, a mother in Israel.

⁸As God selects new *leaders*^j
      War is at the gate:
      Shield is hardly seen, or a spear
          Among forty thousand in Israel.

⁹My heart is with Israel's magistrates.
The devoted among the people
      Do bless the Lord!

¹⁰You who ride gleaming she-asses
You who sit on *woven rugs*^k
And you wayfarers—Proclaim it!
¹¹Through the din of archers,
      Between watering sites,
There, they rehearse the Lord's vindication,
      Vindication for his hamlets in Israel.

Just as the Lord's people march down to the gates,
¹²Up, up, Deborah!
      Up, up and utter a song!
Go on, Baraq,
And gather your spoils, Son of Abinoam!
¹³Then a survivor triumphs
      Over the mightiest people.

The Lord triumphs for me,
Over the warriors.

¹⁴From **Ephraim**, *men* with roots in Amalek;
      After you,^l **Benjamin**, among your kin
From **Machir**, down come the magistrates,
      From **Zebulun**, too, such as hold the scribe's rod.
¹⁵And in **Issachar**, commanders are with Deborah

---

i. Or: you.
j. Or: When (*Israel*) selects new gods.
k. Or: at a tribunal; or: on saddles.
l. Or: Behind you, Benjamin.

As Baraq, so is Issachar
　　　—Into the valley, sent on foot.
Among the ranks of **Reuben**,
Notables are resolved of heart:
¹⁶Why then would you stay between the folds,
　　　Listening to the bleating of flocks?ᵐ
Among the ranks of Reuben,
　　　Notables are searching souls.
¹⁷**Gilead** camps beyond the Jordan
　　　And **Dan**—why would he dwell on ships?
Asher stays by the shore of the sea,
　　　And camps by its wharfs
¹⁸**Zebulun**, a people taunting itself to die,
　　　Naphtali also, on high terrain.

¹⁹Come the kings, set to fight:
　　　As Canaan's kings fight,
At Taanach, by the streams of Megiddo,
　　　No silver in plunder they gain.
²⁰From heaven they attack—
　　　The stars from their courses, they attack Sisera;
²¹Torrent Kishon sweeps them away
　　　A primordial torrentⁿ—the Torrent Kishon.

March on, my forceful soul!

²²Just then hammer the hooves of horses
　　　At the galloping, galloping of his steeds.

²³Curse Meroz, said the LORD's messenger
　　　Curse bitterly its inhabitants
Because they came not to the aid of the LORD,
　　　To the aid of the LORD, among the warriors.

²⁴Blessed among women be Jael
　　　Wife of Heber the Kenite;
Among women in tents may she be blessed.

---

m. Or: to the piping for the flocks.
n. Or: a raging torrent.

^{25}Water he wants, milk she gives

In a princely beaker she offers soured milk.
^{26}Her hand reaches for the peg,

Her right, for the workmen's hammer.
She hammers Sisera, crushes his head,

Smashing, splitting his temple.
^{27}Between her feet he bends, drops, sprawls.

Between her feet he bends, drops;

Where he bends, there he drops—crushed.

^{28}Through the window

She leans and frets, Sisera's mother,

through the lattice:
Why is his chariotry delayed in coming?

Why so tardy the rattles of his chariots?
^{29}Her wisest ladies would answer;

(But she answers herself in reply):
^{30}They must be dividing the spoil they find:

A breeder or two for a leader,
Spoil of dyed garments for Sisera;

Spoil of dyed garments, embroidered

A dyed garment, doubly embroidered,

Round the necks of spoil.°

^{31}So may all your enemies perish, LORD
But may those loving him be as the sun on its mighty rise!

The land had peace for forty years.

GIDEON

6 ^{1}The people of Israel did what was offensive to the LORD, so he abandoned them to Midian for seven years. ^{2}Midian so ruthlessly controlled Israel that, because of Midian, the people of Israel made for themselves *dens* that were in the mountains, so caves and fissures. ^{3}Thus it was that whenever Israel seeded its land, Midian would rise, together with Amalek and Qedem tribesmen, to gang up against it. ^{4}Setting up camp opposite them, they would ravage whatever the land was yielding, as far as Gaza, leaving nothing edible in Israel,

---

o. Or: From the necks of spoil; or (with emendation): For his [Sisera's] neck, as spoil; For my [Sisera's mother] neck, as spoil.

including sheep, cattle, or donkeys. ⁵They and their livestock would come up, together with their tents, swarming like locusts. They and their camels were beyond reckoning, penetrating the land just to ravage it. ⁶Because of Midian, Israel was brought so low that its people pleaded with the LORD.

⁷As Israel was beseeching the LORD on account of Midian, ⁸he sent them a man, a prophet who told them, "This is what the LORD, the God of Israel, says: It is I who brought you out of Egypt, freeing you from a house of bondage. ⁹I delivered you from Egypt and from all those oppressing you. I drove them from before you and gave you their land. ¹⁰I would say to you, 'I am the LORD your God. Do not fear the gods of the Amorites, in whose land you live'; but you would not listen to me."

¹¹An angel of the LORD came and sat under the oak at Ophrah belonging to Joash of Abiezer. His son Gideon was then beating out the wheat in a winepress to stash it away from the Midianites. ¹²The angel of the LORD became visible to Gideon and said, "The LORD be with you, warrior." ¹³"Please, sir," Gideon replied, "if the LORD is with us, how could all this be happening to us? Where are all those marvelous deeds of his that our ancestors related when telling us that the LORD brought us out of Egypt? The LORD has now abandoned us, handing us over to Midian." ¹⁴The LORD faced him and said, "Go in this strength of yours and rescue Israel from Midian's control. I am empowering you." ¹⁵"Please, lord," he said to him, "with what do I rescue Israel? My clan is the weakest in Manasseh, and I am the youngest in my family." ¹⁶The LORD answered him, "I will certainly be with you, and you will trounce Midian as one person." ¹⁷"If you favor me," he replied, "give me a sign that it is to me you speak. ¹⁸Just don't move from here until I come back to set before you the offering I bring out." "I will wait until you return," he replied. ¹⁹When Gideon came *home*, he prepared a young goat and an ephah of unleavened wheat bread. Putting the meat in a basket and its broth in a pot, he presented them to him under the oak tree as he approached. ²⁰The angel of God said to him, "Take the meat and the unleavened bread and set them on the boulder over there, but pour out the broth." He did so. ²¹The angel of the LORD extended the tip of the staff he held, touching the meat and the unleavened bread. As fire shot out of the rock, consuming the meat and the bread, the angel of the LORD vanished from his sight. ²²Gideon realized that it was the angel of the LORD, and he exclaimed, "Ahah, Lord YHVH; inasmuch as I have seen the angel of the LORD face to face!" ²³But to him said the LORD, "Be at peace and do not fear; you will not die." ²⁴Gideon built there an altar to the LORD, naming it "LORD Peace." (To this day it still stands in Ophrah of Abiezer.)

²⁵That same night the LORD said to him, "Take the sacrificial ox belonging to your father and, with another that is seven years old, tear down the Baal

altar belonging to your father and cut down as well the *asherah* over it. ²⁶Build a *properly arrayed* altar to the LORD your God at the peak of the fortification, then take the second ox and make a burnt offering with the wood of the *asherah* that you will cut down." ²⁷So Gideon took ten of his servants and did as the LORD told him. However, fearing his father's household and the townsfolk, he worked at night rather than during the day. ²⁸In the morning, the townsfolk awoke to a razed altar of Baal, a cut-down *asherah* (that was) over it, and the second ox sacrificed on the newly built altar. ²⁹They asked each other, "Who did this?" After inquiry and investigation, they concluded, "Gideon son of Joash did it." ³⁰The townsfolk demanded of Joash, "Bring out your son. He must die, because he has razed Baal's altar and cut down the *asherah* over it." ³¹But Joash replied to those standing by him, "Is it for you to plead Baal's cause? Are you trying to save him? Whoever pleads for him shall be put to death by morning! If he is God, let him plead for himself when someone razed his altar." ³²On that very day, he called him Jerubbaal, meaning, "Let Baal rebuke him because he razed his altar."

³³All Midian, Amalek, and Qedem tribesmen joined forces. They crossed over and camped in the Jezreel Valley. ³⁴Zeal for the LORD sheathed Gideon. He sounded the ram's horn and Abiezer rallied behind him. ³⁵He sent messengers throughout Manasseh, and it too rallied behind him. He then sent messengers through Asher, Zebulun, and Naphtali, and they came up to meet them.

³⁶Gideon said to God himself, "If you intend me to be the rescuer of Israel, as you once said, ³⁷I am setting this woolen fleece on the threshing floor. If dew is on just the fleece when the entire ground is dry, I will know that you will rescue Israel through me, as you once said." ³⁸So it was: When he rose early the next day, he squeezed the fleece and wrung dew from it—a bowlful of water. ³⁹Gideon said to God himself, "Do not be angry with me for speaking yet again. Let me make just one more test through the fleece: Let the fleece be dry, while there is dew all over the ground." ⁴⁰That night, God did exactly that: The fleece only was dry, but all over the ground there was dew.

7 ¹Next morning, Jerubbaal—that is, Gideon—and all the troops with him encamped by Harod Spring. From his angle, the camp of Midian was to the north, at Moreh Hill, in the valley. ²The LORD said to Gideon, "You have too many people with you for me to deliver Midian into their hands; Israel might take credit from me, boasting, 'My own might rescued me.' ³Therefore, tell the people openly, 'Anyone scared or anxious should turn back by taking flight from Mount Gilead.'" Among the people, twenty-two thousand turned back while ten thousand remained.

⁴The LORD said to Gideon, "The people are too many. Lead them to water and I will cull them for you there. Anyone of whom I tell you, 'This one goes

with you,' that one shall go with you; and anyone of whom I tell you, 'This one is not to go with you,' that one shall not go." ⁵When he led the people to water, the Lord said to Gideon, "Set apart all those who lap up water with the tongue, as does a dog, *from* all those who bend down on their knees to drink." ⁶Three hundred was the number of lappers, with hand to their mouth, while the rest of the people bent down on their knees to drink water. ⁷Then the Lord said to Gideon, "With these three hundred lappers I will rescue you and deliver Midian to you. The people may all go home." ⁸The provisions of the people were collected, their ram's horns as well. He sent off every man from Israel, each to his tent, keeping just the three hundred men. The camp of Midian was below him, in the valley.

⁹That same night the Lord said to him, "Be ready to go down into the camp, for I have turned it over to you. ¹⁰Should you fear going down, then go down with your attendant Purah toward the camp. ¹¹Once you hear what they say, you will take courage and go down into the camp." So he went down with his attendant Purah to the outpost of those girded for battle in the camp. ¹²Midian, Amalek, and all Kedem were swarming on the valley plain, as many as locusts. Their camels were beyond count, as many as sand on the seashore. ¹³Gideon came there just as one man was relating a dream to another, "I just had a dream: There was a *round loaf* of barley bread tumbling in the Midian camp. It reached the tent, falling as it struck it. It spun it upwards, and the tent crumpled."ᵖ ¹⁴His companion answered, "This can be nothing but the sword of Gideon son of Joash, from Israel. God is turning Midian and the entire camp over to him."

¹⁵When Gideon heard the dream told and interpreted, he bowed low. Returning to the camp of Israel, he said, "Be ready, for the Lord has turned the camp of Midian over to you!" ¹⁶He divided the three hundred men into three units, equipping them all with ram's horns and empty jars, with torches in the jars. ¹⁷He told them, "Observe my action to do the same. When I reach the outpost of the camp, simply do whatever I do. ¹⁸As I and all those with me blow the ram's horn, you too will blow your ram's horn from all around the camp, saying, 'For the Lord and for Gideon!'"

¹⁹Gideon and the hundred men with him arrived at the outposts of the camp, at the start of the middle watch, barely after the sentries were posted. They blew the ram's horns and crashed the jars they had. ²⁰The men in three units blew their horns and broke their jars. Grasping torches in their left hands and in their right hands the ram's horns for blowing, they shouted, "A sword for the Lord and for Gideon!" ²¹While everyone circling the camp stood his

---

p. Or: "Reaching the tent, it struck it and it fell—when it threw it upwards, the tent collapsed."

ground, the whole camp began running, howling, and scampering. [22]Just as the
three hundred ram's horns were sounded, everywhere in the camp the LORD
set one sword against the other. The entire host fled toward Zererah as far as
Beth-shittah, then as far as the outskirts of Abel-meholah by Tabbath. [23]From
Naphtali, from Asher, from Manasseh, men from Israel were summoned and
they rushed after Midian. [24]The messengers Gideon sent all over the hills of
Ephraim conveyed: "Come down to face Midian, but capture ahead of them
the waterways along the Jordan up to Beit-barah." All the men of Ephraim
rushed and captured the waterways along the Jordan up to Beit-barah. [25]They
captured Midian's two commanders, Oreb and Zeeb. They executed Oreb at
Oreb Rock and they executed Zeeb at Zeeb Winepress, and kept after Midian.
They brought Gideon the heads of Oreb and Zeeb from across the Jordan.
8 [1]The men of Ephraim censured him severely by telling him, "How could
you treat us like this by not calling us when you went to fight Midian?" [2]He
answered them, "Have I done anything so far comparable to you? Ephraim's
gleanings are better than Abiezer's vintage! [3]To you God turned over Midian's
commanders, Oreb and Zeeb; what did I achieve that matches you?" Their
resentment against him abated once he addressed them in this way.
[4]Gideon moved toward the Jordan; he crossed *it* and with him were three
hundred men, exhausted yet pursuing. [5]He told the people of Succoth, "Please
give some loaves of bread to the people who follow me as they are exhausted; I
am pursuing Zebah and Zalmunna, the kings of Midian." [6]The chiefs of Succoth replied, "Are the palms of Zebah and Zalmunna already in your hand
that we should give bread to your troops?" [7]Gideon said, "Just for that, when
the LORD turns Zebah and Zalmunna to me, I will flail your flesh with desert thorns and briers." [8]From there he went up to Penuel and made the same
request of them; but the people of Penuel answered the same as the people of
Succoth. [9]So he also told the people of Penuel: "On my safe return, I will demolish this citadel!"
[10]Zebah and Zalmunna were at Karkor. The army they had was about
15,000—all that remained of the entire camp of the Qedem tribesmen, for the
fallen numbered 120,000 swordsmen. [11]Gideon marched up the road of the tent
dwellers, up to the east of Nobah and Jogbehah, and routed the camp, which
was off guard. [12]Zebah and Zalmunna took to flight, with Gideon in pursuit.
He captured Zebah and Zalmunna, the two kings of Midian, and threw the
whole army into panic.
[13]On his way back from the battle through Potsherd Heights, Gideon son
of Joash [14]captured a youth[q] from the people of Succoth and interrogated him.

---

q. Or: an administrator.

He wrote for him the names of the commanders and elders of Succoth, seventy-seven in number. ¹⁵Then he came to the people of Succoth and said, "Here are Zebah and Zalmunna, about whom you taunted me, saying, 'Are the palms of Zebah and Zalmunna already in your hand that we should give bread to your tired men?'" ¹⁶He took the town's elders and desert thorns and briers as well, and had the people of Succoth experience them. ¹⁷As for Penuel, he razed its citadel, killing the town's population.

¹⁸He then asked Zebah and Zalmunna, "Where are the men you killed in Tabor?" "May the same happen to you," they replied, "each had the bearing of princes." ¹⁹"They were my brothers," he said, "sons of my mother; as the LORD lives, had you spared them, I would not kill you." ²⁰He told his eldest son Jether, "Go ahead and kill them!" The youth would not draw his sword, for he was fearful, being still young. ²¹Zebah and Zalmunna then said, "Go ahead and cut us down, for manhood defines the person!" So Gideon went ahead and killed Zebah and Zalmunna. He took the crescents that were on the necks of their camels.

²²Everyone in Israel said to Gideon, "Rule over us—you, as well as your son and your grandson; for you have rescued us from Midian." ²³But Gideon told them, "I will not rule over you myself and my son will not rule over you; the LORD alone shall rule over you." ²⁴Gideon said to them, "I have a request to make of you: Each of you give me a ring from his plunder." (They had gold rings because they were of Ishmael.) ²⁵"Gladly," they replied. They spread out a garment and everyone tossed in it a ring from his plunder. ²⁶The weight of the gold he had requested came to 1,700 (shekels) of gold; this was apart from the crescents and the pendants and the purple robes worn by the kings of Midian or from the collars on the necks of their camels. ²⁷Gideon turned it into an ephod and set it up in his own town of Ophrah. All Israel lusted after it; for Gideon and his house, it became a snare. ²⁸Thus Midian was humbled before the people of Israel, and could not recover. The land had peace for forty years in Gideon's days.

²⁹Jerubbaal son of Joash went to live in his own house. ³⁰Seventy sons were Gideon's—all of them his issue, for he had many wives. ³¹When also his concubine,ʳ who lived in Shechem, bore him a son, he set his name as Abimelech. ³²Gideon son of Joash died at a ripe old age and was buried in the tomb of his father Joash at Ophrah of Abiezer.

³³Once Gideon died, Israel again lusted after the many Baals, setting up Baal-berith as God. ³⁴Israel had no memory for the LORD their God who delivers them from all the enemies around them. ³⁵They did not show solidarity

---

r. Or: secondary wife.

with the House of Jerubbaal-Gideon despite the good that he had done for Israel.

ABIMELECH

9 ¹Abimelech son of Jerubbaal traveled to Shechem to meet with his maternal uncles. Speaking to them and to the whole clan of his mother's family, he said, ²"Speak openly to all the leaders of Shechem: Which is better for you, seventy men—sons of Jerubbaal, all—ruling you or just one man ruling you? Keep in mind that I am your own bone and flesh." ³His maternal uncles spoke openly on his behalf to all the leaders of Shechem, and they resolved to support Abimelech for they reasoned, "He is our brother." ⁴They gave him 70 shekels from the temple of Baal-berith. Abimelech used them to hire some rootless and reckless men, and they followed him. ⁵He came to his father's house in Ophrah and executed on one stone his brothers, the sons of Jerubbaal, seventy men. Only Jotham, the youngest son of Jerubbaal, survived because he went into hiding.

⁶All the leaders of Shechem assembled along with all Beth-millo. They went and installed Abimelech as king by the *firmly set* oak at Shechem. ⁷When Jotham was informed, he climbed to the summit of Mount Gerizim and he called out to them in a loud voice, "Listen to me, leaders of Shechem, so God may listen to you."

> ⁸The trees set out to anoint a king over themselves. They said to the olive tree, "Reign over us." ⁹But the olive tree replied, "Have I stopped yielding my wealth of oil, with which through me gods and men are honored, that I should go hold sway over the trees?" ¹⁰The trees said to the fig tree, "Do come and reign over us." ¹¹But the fig tree replied, "Have I stopped yielding my deliciously sweet fruit that I should go hold sway over the trees?" ¹²The trees said to the vine, "Do come and reign over us." ¹³But the vine replied, "Have I stopped yielding my wine, which gladdens gods and men, that I should go hold sway over the trees?" ¹⁴Then all the trees said to the thorn, "Do come and reign over us." ¹⁵The thorn said to the trees, "If in good faith you are anointing me king over you, come and find shelter in my shade; but if not, may fire issue from the thorn and consume the cedars of Lebanon."

¹⁶"Now then, if you have acted completely in good faith when making Abimelech king, if you have done right by Jerubbaal and his house, and if you have repaid him for his favors, ¹⁷as when my father fought for you, casting his life aside, to save you from Midian; ¹⁸yet you rose against my father's house that day, you killed his sons—seventy men—on one stone, and set up Abimelech, the son of his handmaid as king above the leaders of Shechem because he is your brother. ¹⁹So, if you have acted completely in good faith toward Jerubbaal and

his house on this very day, then rejoice in Abimelech and may he also likewise rejoice in you. ²⁰But if not, may fire issue from Abimelech and consume the leaders of Shechem and Beth-millo, but may fire also issue from the leaders of Shechem and Beth-millo and consume Abimelech!" ²¹With that, Jotham fled; he escaped toward Beer and lived there, away from his brother Abimelech.

²²For three years, Abimelech wielded authority over Israel. ²³Then God cast such ill will between Abimelech and the leaders of Shechem that the leaders of Shechem betrayed Abimelech, ²⁴so that the violence against the seventy sons of Jerubbaal could be revisited and their bloodguilt could rest on their brother Abimelech—because he had executed them—as well as on the leaders of Shechem—because they had encouraged him to execute his brothers. ²⁵The leaders of Shechem set ambushes against him on mountaintops. They robbed whoever passed by them on the road. Word of this reached Abimelech.

²⁶Gaal son of Ebed came, together with his brethren, and they moved into Shechem, and the leaders of Shechem trusted him. ²⁷They went out into the fields, harvested and trod their grapes, and had celebrations. They entered their temples and after eating and drinking, they cursed Abimelech. ²⁸Gaal son of Ebed said, "Who is Abimelech and who is Shechem that we should serve him? Did not this son of Jerubbaal and his agent Zebul once serve the men of Hamor, ancestor of Shechem? Why should we serve him? ²⁹Were I given command over this people, I would get rid of Abimelech!" He then challenged Abimelech, "Increase your forces and head out."

³⁰When Zebul, the town's governor, heard the words of Gaal son of Ebed, he was furious. ³¹He sent messages to Abimelech at Tormahˢ to say, "Gaal son of Ebed and his brethren have come to Shechem and they are inciting the town against you. ³²Therefore, set out tonight with the forces you have with you and lie in wait in the open country. ³³Next morning at sunrise, make an early rush on the town; but once he and his people move out against you, do with him as you see fit." ³⁴Abimelech and all the people with him moved out by night and set up four divisions in ambush against Shechem. ³⁵When Gaal son of Ebed came out to post himself at the entrance to the town's gate, Abimelech and the people with him moved out from the ambush. ³⁶Gaal saw the people and said to Zebul, "People are marching down from the hilltops!" But Zebul said to him, "You mistake shadows made by hills for men." ³⁷Gaal spoke up again, "People are now coming down from the core of the earth and one division is heading from the direction of Soothsayers Oak." ³⁸Zebul told him, "Where is now your boast, 'Who is Abimelech that we should serve him?'? There is the people you belittled—go out there and fight him!"

---

s. Or: secretly.

³⁹So, in front of the leaders of Shechem, Gaal went out to fight Abimelech. ⁴⁰When Abimelech rushed at him, he ran away from him. Many fell wounded, all the way to the entrance of the gate. ⁴¹With Abimelech staying in Arumah, Zebul drove out Gaal and his brethren from Shechem where they could no longer stay. ⁴²The next day, when people went to the fields, Abimelech was informed. ⁴³Taking his people, he partitioned them into three units, posting them in ambush in the fields. Whenever he saw people leaving town, he pounced on them and struck them down. ⁴⁴Abimelech and the men in his unit fanned out into position at the entrance of the town's gate. Two other units rushed against all those out in the field, striking them down. ⁴⁵All during that day, Abimelech fought against the town. He captured the town, killing the people in it. He razed the town and sowed it with salt.

⁴⁶When all leaders of Citadel Shechem heard about it, they went into the chamber of the El-berith temple. ⁴⁷Abimelech was told that all the leaders of Citadel Shechem had gathered. ⁴⁸Abimelech went up Mount Zalmon, along with all the people with him. Grasping some axe in his hand, Abimelech chopped off a tree limb, then lifting it, he set it on his shoulder. He then said to the people near him, "What you have seen me do, quickly copy me." ⁴⁹Each of them having also chopped a limb, they all followed Abimelech. They piled them about the chamber and set it on fire over them. In this way, all the people of Citadel Shechem also died, about a thousand men and women.

⁵⁰Abimelech went to Thebez; he encamped at Thebez and captured it. ⁵¹There was a fortified citadel in the center of the town. Men and women, as well as the town's leaders, hurried into it. Locking up behind them, they climbed up to the citadel's roof. ⁵²Abimelech reached the citadel and attacked it. He moved up to the gate of the citadel to set it on fire; ⁵³but some woman hurled an upper millstone on Abimelech's head, shattering his skull. ⁵⁴Immediately, he shouted to the attendant, his arms-bearer, "Draw your sword and kill me, lest it is said about me that a woman killed him." His attendant stabbed him and he died.

⁵⁵When the men of Israel saw that Abimelech was dead, everyone went home. ⁵⁶Thus God turned back on Abimelech the evil he had done to his father by killing his seventy brothers. ⁵⁷As to the evil acts by the people of Shechem, God brought them on their own head. The curse of Jotham son of Jerubbaal had indeed fallen on them.

TOLA

10 ¹Stepping up to rescue Israel after Abimelech was Tola son of Puah son of Dodo, of Issachar. He lived at Shamir in the hills of Ephraim. ²He was judge in Israel for twenty-three years. He died and was buried at Shamir.

JAIR

³After him, Jair of Gilead stepped up and was judge in Israel for twenty-two years. ⁴He had thirty sons who rode on thirty colts. Thirty villages were theirs. To them even now is applied the name "Hovels of Jair," in the territory of Gilead. ⁵Then Jair died and was buried at Kamon.

⁶The people of Israel resumed offending the Lord: They worshiped the many Baals and Ashtaroth, as well as the gods of Aram, the gods of Sidon, the gods of Moab, the gods of the Ammonites, and the gods of the Philistines. They forsook the Lord and did not worship him. ⁷Incensed against Israel, the Lord turned them over to the Philistines and to the men of Ammon. ⁸They crushed and oppressed the people of Israel in that year for eighteen years—all the people of Israel across the Jordan—in the Amorite territory of Gilead.

⁹The men of Ammon crossed the Jordan to make war on Judah, Benjamin, as well as the House of Ephraim. Israel suffered terribly. ¹⁰The Israelites pleaded with the Lord, "We have sinned against you, by forsaking our God and worshiping many Baals."

¹¹The Lord said to the people of Israel, "Was it not that when Egypt, the Amorites, the Ammonites, the Philistines, ¹²the Sidonians, Amalek, and Maon oppressed you, you cried out to me and I indeed rescued you from them? ¹³Yet you have abandoned me and worshiped other gods. Just for that, I will not keep on rescuing you. ¹⁴Go and beseech the gods you have chosen; these might rescue you in this time of trouble." ¹⁵But the people of Israel told the Lord: "We have sinned. Do to us whatever you wish; only save us just now!" ¹⁶They removed the alien gods from their midst and worshiped the Lord; but he lost patience with Israel's behavior.

¹⁷The men of Ammon were summoned and camped in Gilead while the men of Israel assembled and camped by Mizpah. ¹⁸Among the people, the commanders of Gilead said to each other, "Whoever is first to fight against Ammon shall be chief over all the inhabitants of Gilead."

JEPHTHAH

11 ¹Jephthah of Gilead was well-born, the son of a harlot; Gilead begot Jephthah. ²Gilead's wife bore him sons and when the wife's sons grew up, they drove Jephthah out, telling him, "You must not share in our father's property, for you are the son of another woman." ³So Jephthah fled from his brothers and settled in the Tob Land. Rootless men were drawn to Jephthah and they joined with him.

⁴Soon after, Ammon attacked Israel. ⁵And just as Ammon was attacking Israel, the elders of Gilead went to fetch Jephthah from Tob Land. ⁶They said

to Jephthah, "Come be our general so that we can fight Ammon." ⁷Jephthah told the elders of Gilead, "Did you not hate me and drive me out of my father's house? Why would you come to me now, just when you are in trouble?" ⁸The elders of Gilead told Jephthah, "Just so! We now are turning to you. Go with us and fight Ammon; you will then be our chief, over all the people of Gilead." ⁹Jephthah said to the elders of Gilead, "If you are bringing me back to fight Ammon, once the LORD delivers them to me, I am to be a chief for you." ¹⁰The elders of Gilead told Jephthah, "The LORD is witness between us that we will do just as you have said." ¹¹So Jephthah went with the elders of Gilead. The people made him chief and general over them. Jephthah repeated all terms pertaining to him before the LORD at Mizpah.

¹²Jephthah then sent messengers to the king of Ammon, saying, "What have you to do with me that you come against me, to fight in my land?" ¹³The king of Ammon replied to Jephthah's messengers, "Well, Israel seized my land when coming out of Egypt, from the Arnon to the Jabbok, as far as the Jordan. Now, then, restore all of it peaceably." ¹⁴Jephthah once again sent messengers to the king of Ammon, ¹⁵saying to him,

> Thus says Jephthah: Israel did not seize the land of Moab or the land of Ammon. ¹⁶For, as they left Egypt, Israel followed the desert to the Red Sea and on to Kadesh. ¹⁷Israel then sent messengers to the king of Edom, saying "Allow me to pass through your country." But the king of Edom would not approve. Israel also sent (messengers) to the king of Moab; but he refused. So Israel remained at Kadesh. ¹⁸Then, taking the desert, Israel skirted the land of Edom and the land of Moab. Keeping to the east of the land of Moab, Israel camped across the Arnon. So, with the Arnon as Moab's border, Israel never went within Moab's territory.
>
> ¹⁹Next, Israel sent messengers to Sihon, king of the Amorites and king of Heshbon. Israel said to him, "Allow us to pass through your land to my place." ²⁰Sihon would not trust Israel to cross his border.ᵗ Instead, Sihon rallied all his people, camping by Jahza. He then attacked Israel. ²¹But the LORD, the God of Israel, handed Sihon and all his people over to Israel, and they defeated them. Israel occupied all the land of the Amorites, the inhabitants of that land. ²²So *the people of Israel* occupied all the territory of the Amorites, from the Arnon to the Jabbok, from the desert to the Jordan.
>
> ²³Therefore, now that the LORD, the God of Israel, displaced the Amorites on behalf of his people Israel, are you to occupy it? ²⁴Whatever your god Chemosh displaces for you, you must surely occupy. So too, whatever the LORD our god has displaced on our behalf, we must occupy. ²⁵Moreover, are you any better than Balak son of Zippor, king of Moab? Did he start a quarrel with Israel let alone go to war against them? ²⁶With Israel now having settled for three hundred years in Heshbon and its dependencies, in Aroer and its

---

t. Or: to pass through his territory.

dependencies, and in all the towns along the Arnon, why has none of you regained *them* at any time then? ²⁷While I have not wronged you, you are doing me harm to fight against me. The LORD is the judge to decide now between the people of Israel and the people of Ammon!

²⁸But the king of the Ammon would not listen to the words that Jephthah sent him.

²⁹Endowed with zeal for the LORD, Jephthah crossed Gilead and Manasseh, passed through Mizpeh of Gilead, and from Mizpeh he marched into Ammon. ³⁰Jephthah made the following vow to the LORD, "If you deliver Ammon into my hands, ³¹then whoever comes out, leaving the doors of my home to meet me on my safe return from Ammon, will be the LORD's and I will have him offered as a burnt victim."

³²When Jephthah marched into Ammon to fight against it, the LORD handed its people to him. ³³From Aroer as far as Minnith, he devastated some twenty towns, all the way to Abel-keramim—a crushing blow. Ammon was humbled because of Israel. ³⁴When Jephthah approached his home in Mizpah, there was his daughter coming out to meet him, with drums and dances. There was only her, a beloved child; beside her, he had no son or daughter.ᵘ ³⁵On seeing her, he rent his clothes and said, "Ahah, daughter! You have devastated me utterly and are among those tormenting me! For I have opened my mouth to the LORD and I cannot turn back." ³⁶"Father!" she said to him, "you have opened your mouth to the LORD; do with me as has come out of it, now that the LORD has executed vengeance for you against your enemies from Ammon." ³⁷She said to her father, "This should be done for me: Leave me be for two months as I go away. I will move down the hills and there weep over my maidenhood, my companions and I." ³⁸He said, "Go" and sent her on for two months. She went—she and her companions—and bemoaned her maidenhood upon the hills. ³⁹At the end of two months, when she returned to her father, he did to her as he had vowed. She had never known a man. So it became a tradition in Israel:ᵛ ⁴⁰At set moments, daughters of Israel would go out four days a year to commemorate the daughter of Jephthah of Gilead.

12 ¹Ephraim was summoned to a man and crossed the Jordan to Zaphon. They said to Jephthah, "Why did you move to fight Ammon and us you did not call to go with you? We will set your house on fire with you in it!" ²Jephthah answered them, "I was intensely in conflict with Ammon—my people and I. I pleaded with you, but you would not rescue me from them. ³When I realized that you are no rescuer, I took life in hand and moved against Ammon. The

---

u. MT reads *mimmennû*, so "from him, there was no (other) son or daughter."

v. Or: she set an example in Israel.

LORD handed them over to me. So why do you rise against me just now to fight me?" ⁴Jephthah gathered all the men of Gilead and fought Ephraim. Gilead defeated Ephraim, for having said, "You are but survivors from Ephraim, Gilead, in the midst of Ephraim as in Manasseh's." ⁵Gilead barred the fords of the Jordan from Ephraim. Should a survivor from Ephraim say, "Let me cross," the men of Gilead would ask him, "Are you an Ephraimite?" Should he say "No," ⁶they would tell him, "Say Shibbolet!" "Sibbolet," he would say, not managing to voice it that way. Seizing him, they would slaughter him by the fords of the Jordan. In that instance alone, from Ephraim forty-two thousand fell.

⁷Jephthah was judge in Israel for six years. When Jephthah of Gilead died, he was buried in the towns of Gilead.

IBZAN

⁸Judging Israel after him was Ibzan of Bethlehem. ⁹He had thirty sons. He sent thirty daughters beyond *the area* and had thirty daughters brought for his sons from beyond *the area*. He was judge in Israel for seven years. ¹⁰Then Ibzan died and was buried in Bethlehem.

ELON

¹¹Judging Israel after him was Elon of Zebulon; he was judge in Israel for ten years. ¹²Then Elon of Zebulon died and was buried in Ayyalon, in the territory of Zebulon.

ABDON

¹³Judging Israel after him was Abdon son of Hillel of Pirᶜaton. ¹⁴He had forty sons and thirty grandsons, who rode on seventy colts; he was judge in Israel for eight years. ¹⁵Then Abdon son of Hillel of Pirᶜaton died. He was buried in Pirᶜaton, in the territory of Ephraim, on Amalek Hill.

I. NOTES AND COMMENTS
Prelude

IA

The Southern Tribes

---

1. Adoni-bezeq (Judg 1:1–7)

1 ¹After the death of Joshua, the people of Israel inquired of the LORD, "Who should march for us against the Canaanites at first, to attack them?" ²The LORD said, "Judah must march; I have already handed him the land." ³Judah, however, said to his kin Simeon, "Come along with me, in my lot, and we will both attack the Canaanites. I will then go with you myself, in your lot." So, Simeon went with him. ⁴Judah went up, and the LORD handed them the Canaanites and the Perizzites. They defeated them at Bezeq—ten thousand men. ⁵They found Adoni-bezeq in Bezeq and attacked him, defeating the Canaanites as well as the Perizzites. ⁶When Adoni-bezeq fled, they pursued him. Seizing him, they severed his thumbs and toes. ⁷Adoni-bezeq said, "Once seventy kings, all with severed thumbs and toes, were scrapping under my table; as I had done, God has repaid me." They brought him to Jerusalem and there he died. ⌂

NOTES
Introductory Remarks: Divining the Will of God[1]

When Saul tried desperately to learn what God had in store for him, "The LORD would not answer, whether through dreams [*ḥălōmôt*], casting lots [*'ûrîm*], or prophets [*nĕvî'îm*]" (1 Sam 28:6).[2] Other avenues were available, but in Israel they were condemned (see Deut 18:10–12; see also Hos 3:4 and Ezek 21:21 [26 RSV]). The technical idiom for consulting God is *šā'al be-*. This idiom must not be confused with other *šā'al* constructions involving God, even if some of them might have eventually called for oracular procedures, for example, *šā'al min* (+*'et/'im*), "requesting (something) from

God," as in Deut 18:16 (everything), 1 Sam 1:20, 27 (a son), 1 Sam 8:20 (a king), Isa 7:11 (a sign), Zech 10:1 (rain), and Ps 27:4 (one wish). The same can be said for *šāʾal le-*, as in 1 Sam 1:28 and 2:20 (a son).

The preposition in our idiom (*šāʾal be-*) refers to the instrument by which an answer is sought, normally from God (Yhvh or Elohim).[3] Greek renderings generally use Num 27:21 to flesh out the picture. Moses, the last of the ancestors to meet God face to face, is receiving instruction on how his successor will learn the will of God: "[Joshua] should stand before the priest Eleazar who will inquire on his behalf for an Urim decision, the Lord being present. At his [God's] command the armies will go out and at his command, they will come back, he as well as all of Israel—that is, the whole community." The instruction God gives to Moses aims to reassure Israel on how to proceed militarily. Joshua not being Moses, to learn God's disposition he must make inquiry through a priest and by means of Urim, with God being present (how?) at the inquiry.

The Urim take the place of God's voice, in that they give answers to the question that Joshua poses. (Elsewhere the idiom is *šāʾal ʾet-pî YHVH*, "to ask for the Lord's opinion" [Josh 9:14], and *šāʾal bidbar hāʾĕlōhîm*, "to ask for a divine statement" [2 Sam 16:23].) The Urim is one of a pair that occurs as *ʾûrîm vĕtummîm* and is rendered since the King James Version (KJV) as "Urim and Thummim." Treated as a merismus (two opposites giving a whole), the phrase likely stood for "complete enlightenment." The pair were kept by the high priest in/on an ephod or in a *ḥōšen [ham]mišpāṭ*, "pouch of decision" (Exod 28:15, 29–30); they were probably distinctly shaped lots (generally called *gôrāl*) that, when cast or dropped, established a narrow answer ("yes" or "no") to a specific question.[4] The process could be tedious, as possibilities are eliminated seriatim until the right answer is provided. An illuminating example is available in Josh 7:16–18. Joshua is following God's instruction on how to identify the person who took for himself spoils of war devoted to God: "Early the next morning, Joshua had Israel come forward by tribe. The tribe of Judah was picked by the lot [*vayyillākēd šēveṭ yĕhûdâ*]. He then had the clans [*mišpāḥâ*] of Judah come forward. The clan of Zerah was picked. He then had the clan of Zerah come forward by households [*gĕbārîm*], and Zabdi was picked. Finally, he had each individual in the household come forward, and Achan son of Carmi son of Zabdi, son of Zerah, of the tribe of Judah, was picked."

The selection process seems straightforward enough, but as we know from similar operations beyond Israel, a dependable answer will hang on the quality and precision of the question. A single question may yield an equivocal response. To arrive at more certainty, it is possible to ask the same question on separate occasions in the hopes that the same answer repeats itself. Here is what David did to reassure his soldiers about fighting the Philistines (1 Sam 23:1–5):

> David was told that the Philistines were attacking Keilah and were just then plundering the threshing areas. David inquired of the Lord, asking, "Should I go and attack these Philistines?" The Lord told David, "Go ahead with attacking the Philistines to rescue Keilah." But David's men told him, "We are here in Judah already terrified; how much more so, then, if we go to Keilah, toward the Philistines' battlefront?" David once more inquired of the Lord, and the Lord answered him, "Go ahead, march down to Keilah; I am handing the Philistines to you myself." David and his men headed to Keilah. At-

tacking the Philistines, he carried off their cattle and inflicted on them a great defeat. So David rescued the people of Keilah. (Abiathar son of Ahimelek, having escaped to David at Keilah, brought with him the ephod.)[5]

Optimally, a series of questions will result in progressively more specific answers, leading to the only course of action. Thus, when Saul learns that David was in Keilah, he sought to trap him there. Sensing the snare, David inquires once more of God (1 Sam 23:9–13):

> [David] told Abiathar the priest, "Bring the ephod here." David then said, "LORD, God of Israel. Your servant has heard reliably that Saul seeks to come to Keilah to devastate the town because of me: Will the town's leaders shut me in, for his hand? Will Saul march down, as your servant has heard? LORD, God of Israel, please reveal it to your servant." The LORD replied, "He will march down." David repeated, "Will the leaders of Keilah shut me and my men in, for Saul's hand?" The LORD replied, "They will shut." David and his men, about six hundred men, went out of Keilah and moved out wherever they could.[6]

We notice here how David's original twofold query had to be rephrased into separate concerns: whether Saul will tighten the noose around Keilah, and whether the town's leaders will block David's escape route.[7] The point is that matters of deep importance required sophisticated inquiry, often multilayered, even repetitious. Above all, reliance on a seemingly clear answer from a narrowly framed question may not be the prudent thing. This is clearly set out in Judg 20:18–28 using vocabulary that is hauntingly similar to what we read in our passage (see below). We shall need to know whether, despite the apparent early success, Israel's casual reliance on God's response may not have had unfortunate consequences.

After Joshua

1 1. *vayyĕhî ʾaḥărê môt yĕhôšuaʿ*. Not unlike scrutinizing the opening sequence of a fine movie or play, noticing the way a book in Hebrew Scripture begins can give clues on how to evaluate the ensuing narrative. Inspecting closely the words in the first verses also can expose the attitude of the teller (let us not worry about his or her gender at this stage) toward all those characters that will soon crowd the canvas.

The word *vayyĕhî* opens a number of biblical books. Because its subject is impersonal, the verbal form finds equivalence in our "there once was," or the like. (See Jongeling 2005 for a recent study on its use.) But it must not be thought that by using it Hebrews doubted the historical accuracy of what they were about to tell or read. When the exact passage of time needs to be recorded, Hebrew readily uses *vayyĕhî ʾaḥărê kēn*, "afterwards," or *vayyĕhî ʾaḥărê haddĕbārîm (hāʾēllê)*, "after these matters." For more precise coordination of events, a noun or verbal form that is specific to a preceding action follows *vayyĕhî ʾaḥar(ê)*, for example, "after the plague" (Num 25:19 [26:1 RSV]) or "after they wheeled the ark around" (1 Sam 5:9); "after he buried [the man of God]" (1 Kgs 13:31); and "On Amaziah's coming from defeating the Edomites" (2 Chr 25:14).

In contrast, narrators are rather spare in turning to the phrase *vayyĕhî ʾaḥărê môt* (+name).[8] We hear about it just four times. In Gen 25:11, "after the death of Abraham" plays Janus as it looks back on the deeds of the great patriarch and looks forward to the story of Isaac, the only Hebrew to be born, raised, married, and settled in the Promised Land before it was delivered by conquest. In the same way, the other three occurrences open on new experiences even as they keep memory and knowledge of previous events: on the death of Moses (Josh 1:1), of Joshua (Judg 1:1), and of Saul (2 Sam 1:1).[9] Why it is that, since Hellenistic times, traditions opened new "books" at the occurrence of the phrase in all but the first occasion (Gen 25:11) is a mystery not easily solved. If we recall that the chapter and verse numbering did not prevail until the Christian era, a case might have been made to split Genesis at precisely this point.

The four examples display interesting distinctions in how their tales unfold. In the Genesis passage, once we are told "after the death of Abraham, God blessed his son Isaac," we expect to learn about the many ways God's favor made Isaac prosper. We do not. The rest of the verse tells us that "Isaac lived by Beer Lehai Ro'i" as the narrative stagnates by listing Ishmael's descendants. It then picks up on Rebekah's difficult conception and delivery, on the first of Jacob's deceptions, and on Isaac's placing his wife in danger—all this before we read about Isaac's heart breaking by Jacob's second deception and by Esau's unacceptable marriages. The second book of Samuel, which opens with "after the death of Saul, when David had returned from defeating Amalek," in fact remains haunted by the authority of the slain king. David (conveniently) establishes, by example, the principle that the blood of God's anointed (so his own no less than Saul's) cannot be shed by mortals, and then launches on one of the most powerful elegies to come from the ancient world (2 Sam 1:17–27).

It is common in Judges commentaries to link the two remaining examples, in the first verses of Joshua and Judges, because they both mention the death of leaders and they both allude to God's actions on Israel's behalf, to the point that some (for example, the *BHS*) have suggested reading "Moses" rather than "Joshua." The effect is to find in our chapter a reprise of what obtained in Joshua. But the resemblances are superficial and the distinction striking. In Josh 1:1, continuity of goals for Israel's new leader is girded by balancing the status of Moses as "the Lord's servant" (*'ebed YHVH*) with that of Joshua, "Moses's lieutenant" (*mĕšārēt mōšê*). Moreover, in Josh 1 God seizes control of history when, unsolicited, he gives Joshua a vision of the Promised Land that Israel will control. This contrasts sharply with the way Judges opens. God does not volunteer instruction; so with no charter on how to proceed, Israel has to provoke God into telling the tribes what to do. This silence of God, which is broken only after specific appeal, will be emblematic of the course of events that we will pursue in our book. In Judg 1:1, the phrase also proves consequential, for it will display the lack of understanding with which Israel assimilates God's directives. Perhaps it is because Jewish exegetes sensed something was awry that they lumped our passage with all other *vayyĕhî* openings as presaging sorrow or trouble (Midrash *Esther Rabbah*, Prologue 11).

The Inquiry

*vayyiš'ălû bĕnê yiśrā'ēl ba*YHVH. It is interesting to note that addressing a Greek-reading audience, Josephus (*Ant.* 5.120) picks up his narrative with Josh 24:33, stating that "after the death of Joshua and Eleazar, Phineas prophesied that according to God's will they should commit the government to the tribe of Judah." Among others, Boling (1975: 51) unfurls the first of a series of pluperfects (also at 2:6 and 2:8), "There was a time, after Joshua's death, when the Israelites had asked Yahweh," to resolve the issue of linkage between Joshua and Judges.

As posed, Israel's query is halting (literally, "who should march for us, toward the Canaanites, at first, to battle against them?") where the "parallel" formulation of Judg 20:18 seems syntactically more natural ("Who will march for us at first, in battle against the Benjaminites?"), gaining flow by placement of the adverb immediately after the verb and shift of the enemy to the end of the phrase, thus not requiring the use of a resumptive pronominal suffix (*bô*). Whether or not the choppy effect means to convey hesitation on the part of Israel is up to us to decide.

mî yaʿălê-llānû . . . lĕhillāḥem. When concerned with troop movements, the idiom *ʿălâ lĕhillāḥem,* "to go up for battle [+ *ʿal*, against]," need not partake of the basic meaning of the verb *ʿălâ,* implying topographical shift from a lower to higher terrain. It conventionally refers to the march of troops as they invade land, no matter the direction. As such, it occurs widely in Scripture (for example, Josh 8:3 and Judg 20:23). The opposite idiom, *yārad lĕhillāḥem* (see at 1:9), which is less attested, behaves similarly. (In Akkadian, Gilgamesh "descends" [*warādum*] to the Cedar Forest, even if it is located on a mountain.) In such matters, the vocabulary seems to emulate verbs found in the definition and description of borders within Israel, including *yāṣāʾ,* "to move out"; *sābab* (Niphal), "to turn around"; and *ʿābar,* "to cross" (see Alexander 1992).

By inserting *lānû,* "for us," in its inquiry, Israel has asked God to select one (or more) of its tribes to initiate the struggle against the Canaanites. Because of the placement of the adverb (see below) it is not clear whether it connotes on our behalf ("so we do not have to do it ourselves") or among us ("eventually we will all have to do it"). The use of *lānû* in the phrase *mî yaʿălê-llānû* of Deut 30:11–14 implies an impossible task that cannot be fulfilled ("Who will climb for us toward Heaven to get [God's law] for us so that when he has us hear it, we may observe it?").[10]

CANAAN

hakkĕnaʿănî. The Hebrew uses the singular, for the noun and for the possessive suffix ("against the Canaanite . . . to attack him?"), and thus invests unity to the foe that Israel must face. The effect also personalizes the struggle between two opposite camps, even if Canaan included a number of cities and people that did not always act in concert. (On this collective usage, see Revell 1996. 221–29.) I render (with many others) as plural because this collective sense is conveyed in the Hebrew Bible, where the plural is only rarely used (Obad 1:20, Neh 9:24). Greek (most manuscripts) translate as plural Χαναναίους (accusative masculine), here and at 1:3. In other Judges references in Greek, however, the singular is used, as in Hebrew.

The name is old and found in extrabiblical sources from the eighteenth century BCE on, but under different spelling: in the Mari archives, *Kinaḫnum;* in Alalah (level IV), *Kinʾani;* in Mesopotamian letters in the Amarna archives, *Kinaʾa/i;* in Egyptian hieroglyphs, *Kinaʿnu;* in Ugarit, *Kinʾa/i* (syllabic) and *knʿn* (consonantal); and so forth.[11] The extrabiblical sources reinforce the notion that Canaan was a geographic rather than a national name, but they also fail to give us its territorial limits, with much debate emerging from a reference in El Amarna 151.[12]

In biblical texts, the borders of Canaan are described in Num 34:1–12 and Ezek 47:15–20, 48:1–28. The information they give is interesting. (See Aharoni 1967:

61–72, and Map 4, p. 64). The southern border goes from the "Wilderness of Zinn" (south of the Dead Sea) to the "Brook of Egypt" (Wadi el-'arish), so north of Edom. As it happens, this line matches that of Judah as given in Josh 15:1–4. To the west is the Mediterranean Sea. The northern border is a bit vaguer to pinpoint, but it seems to stretch from just north of modern Tripoli (Lebanon) to just south of Homs (Syria). The eastern border seems to bulge out into the Anti-Lebanon before turning back to the Jordan at the southern tip of the Sea of Galilee. Whether or not these demarcations matched non-Hebraic notions about Canaan is not relevant to us.[13] Suffice it to say that in the Bible the Canaanites, whatever their ethnic identity, are clearly distinguished from such neighbors as Philistines, Moabites, and Edomites but more ambiguously so from such people as Amorites, Perizzites, Hivvites, Girgashites, Jebusites, and the like (see Gen 10:16–18, 34:2; Deut 1:7; Josh 5:1; and Table 2 at IIA3).

We do not know the meaning behind the name "Canaan" in any of its forms. Scholars used to connect the geographical name with a Ḫurrian word for a dye and its color (*kinaḫḫu/kinaḫḫena*), while rather anachronistically attaching the word "purple" to both. They are more reticent to do so now, even if the production of the dye from sea mollusks was known to the Mediterranean of around 2000 BCE. More interesting for us is to notice that the Hebrews readily derived a meaning for the name from their root *kn*ʿ, attested only in the reflexive ("to abase oneself") and the causative ("to humble"), and so linking the fate of Canaan and its land to a curse Noah launched right after the flood (Gen 9:26–29): "Accursed be Canaan; he shall serve his brothers as the lowest slave. May the LORD, God of Shem be blessed; may Canaan become a slave to him. May God give breadth to Japheth, for him to dwell in the tent of Shem, with Canaan becoming their slave." The root *kn*ʿ is not found in any other West Semitic language, and so we must ask ourselves whether the verbal usage in Hebrew is dependent on the geographic name and not the other way around.

The word *battĕḥillâ* essentially deals with temporal priority rather than of place or status, so the beginning of the harvest (Ruth 1:22), of a journey (Gen 13:3), or of settlement (2 Kgs 17:25). The adverb can, by extension, be used to speak of the inception of a prayer (Dan 9:23) or of wisdom (Prov 9:10). It is absent from Gen 1:1, where is found *bĕrēʾšît*, initiating a series of events. We do not learn from its use whether Israel is motivated by cowardice ("Let me not be the one, please") or bravery ("I hope I get selected").

The Response

1 2. *wayyōʾmer YHVH*. . . . God's response is decisive, yet too ample for what is expected in oracular responses. We notice how much shorter is God's answer in the "parallel" formula at Judg 20:18 ("Israel proceeded up to Bethel and inquired of God, 'Who shall march first for us to battle against the Benjaminites?' The LORD answered, 'Judah, first.'") We also notice that here, *battĕḥillâ* is not repeated, as there; God is simply ignoring whatever reason motivated Israel to shape its inquiry as above. God's assurance that he has already delivered the land to Judah may seem unsolicited, in fact shortening the process by making it unnecessary for Israel to reassure itself about success by multiplying the questions. Yet, as we shall see in the Comments, this line will prove generative. A rendering that uses the past perfect "Yahweh had said" (Boling 1975: 54), even if prompted by concern for redaction history, seriously misunderstands the oracular process.

The land (*'ereṣ*) that God promises (*dibbēr, šābaʿ*) to the patriarchs (often in Genesis, for example, 12:7, 13:14–17, 15:4–8) *and* wants to deliver (*nātan [bĕyad-]*) to Israel, if it proves worthy of it, as its heritage (*naḥălâ*) or possession (*'ăḥuzzâ*), is a major theme in Hebrew historiography. It includes land that God owns (Lev 25:23) but is now under control of Canaanites (see Exod 3:17, Num 34:2) or of the Amorites (Deut 1:7). How much area it covers differs, from the largest (the Nile to the Euphrates, at Gen 15:18 and generally in Deuteronomy) to the more modest (often expressed as "from Dan to Beersheva"; see the fine overview by M. Ottosson, *TDOT* 1: 400–405; Weinfeld 1983a; Fritz 2000).

1 3. *vayyōʾmer yĕhûdâ lĕšimʿôn ʾāḥîv.* In Hebrew lore as arranged by later historiographers, Simeon and Judah were sons of the same mother, Leah, the prolific but less loved wife of Jacob. Leah gave them names she deemed appropriate to her searing battles with her sister Rachel. "Simeon" is supposed to recall that God heard the appeal of the unloved (verb *šāmaʿ*, Gen 29:33) and "Judah" is in praise (Hiphil of *yādâ*, Gen 29:35). Few scholars accept these etymologies, but nothing much better has been offered for Simeon and too many fanciful suggestions have been made for Judah, none improving on the folk etymologies in the Bible.[14]

Judah calls Simeon "*'āḥ.*" It may not be necessary to read more than the basic meaning, "brother," for *'āḥ* in our passage. However, in Hebrew (as in many other languages), "brother" has a broader meaning than blood brothers, members of an extended family, or even a nation. In Amorite society of the Middle Bronze Age, political and power metaphors were constructed from the vocabulary of kinship. When to use which term for what kind of political relationship was controlled by an elaborate protocol, with harsh retaliation for infraction or misuse (see comments in Sasson 1998b: 462–64). In that world, "brother" was used by people who deemed themselves equal in power and prestige or who were in an alliance to fight a common foe. The usage may be applicable here as well, for the relationship of the tribes of Judah and Simeon were particularly close, at least as far as Hebrew traditions were concerned.

One of the many burdens of the book of Genesis is to justify why kings eventually came from both sons of Rachel (Saul from Benjamin and the kings of Israel from Joseph, via Ephraim), but from just the fourth of Leah's sons, Judah, skipping over the older Reuben, Simeon, and Levi. Explanations for this leapfrogging are given in stories of violence against their own father: Reuben, by violating Bilhah (Gen 35:22), and Simeon with Levi, by creating enmity with Shechem (Gen 34). (See their less than generous recall in Jacob's testament, Gen 49:3–7.)

While genealogies and lists for the tribe of Simeon are recorded often enough (for example, at Exod 6:15, frequently in Numbers, and in Josh 19), the blessing of Moses (Deut 33) does not mention Simeon. Ezekiel could only hope for its restoration (48:24–25), and the Chronicler had lost track of its territory, locating it among northern tribes (2 Chr 15:9, 34:6). Yet, Judah and Simeon are given crucial roles in the cruel games Joseph plays on his brothers (Gen 42–43), foreshadowing their fate as sharers of common territory (see below). The material, therefore, is written to reflect a first-millennium reality—that the tribes of Judah and Simeon shared land (see de Vaux 1970). What actually transpired is much harder to pin down.

On the theory (just that!) that place names have a way of surviving ethnic shifts (think of such names as Los Angeles and Manhattan), the entity known as Judah (*yĕhûdâ*) may have preceded the settlement of the tribe by that name; for aside from nouns that readily associate with whoever occupies a specific area (such as *'ereṣ* and *'admat*, "territory of [X],"), about Judah we hear of *har/hārê*, "mountain(s)" (for example, at Josh 11:21, 2 Chr 21:11); *midbar*, "wilderness"; and *negev*, "desert" (Judg 1:16, 1 Sam 27:10, 2 Sam 24:7).

It is difficult to establish the territory of individual tribes just before the creation of the monarchy, first because we practically have nothing on this topic from extrabiblical sources and second because by the time the biblical material gelled in its present form, what used to be known about the tribes of Judah and Simeon had already been heavily compromised by the historiographic vision of the kingdom of Judah. For these reasons, we are at the mercy of (learned) speculations, many of which have been influenced by the suggestions of Noth (1981). In Noth's opinion, Judah was but a consolidation or confederation of smaller tribes such as Caleb, Kenaz, Keni, and Jerahmeel, a number of which we shall meet later on. (See the excellent overview of H.-J. Zobel, *TDOT* 5: 482–99). Simeon, too, may have belonged to this confederation, for even as described in Josh 19:1–6, it seems about to be absorbed by Judah. This close connection between Judah and Simeon explains why in our passage Judah invites Simeon to make Canaan an enemy in common.

'ālê 'ittî bĕgôrālî. There may be no significance that the idiom for joining forces for battle (*'ālâ* + preposition *'et*) is attested only in Judges (here and at 4:10). Elsewhere is found the slightly better attested *'ālâ 'im*.[15] In offering to "go with" (*hālak* + preposition *'et*) Simeon, Judah is using a much more common idiom. Simeon, adds the narrator, "went with" him.

Judah is inviting Simeon to join him in his *gôrāl*. Above, we have seen how "lots" were likely cast when God's choice was sought. Judah could not be implying that God's directive was incomplete, hence shortsighted (but see the Comments). So, in inviting Simeon to "come along with me, in my lot," Judah is actually telling him to share the territory that their joint victory would yield. Here, as commentators have pointed out (for example, Lindars 1995: 13–14), there is reference to Josh 19:1–9. In Shiloh, Joshua allotted lands to seven tribes that had yet to receive their territory:

> The second lot [*gôrāl*] to come out was for Simeon, for the Simeon tribe, by clans. Their patrimony [*nāḥălâ*] was within the patrimony of Judah. Belonging to their patrimony were: Beersheba, Sheba, and Moladah; Hazar-Shual, Balah, and Ezem; Eltolad, Betul, and Horma; Ziqlag, Bet-Hammarkabot ("Chariot-City"), and Hazar-susa ("Horse-Coral"); Bet-lebaoth and Sharuhen—thirteen towns, plus their villages; Ayin, Rimmon, Eter, and Ashan—four towns and their villages; plus all the villages around these towns as far as Baalat-beer, Ramat-Negev—All this being the patrimony of the Simeon tribe, by clans. The patrimony of Simeon came out of the portion of Judah for, as the allotment of Judah was too large for its people's own use, Simeon tribesmen took patrimony within theirs.

As it happens, there is a pair of interesting Mari letters that are nearly duplicates in contents and are presumed to belong to a broadcast that King Zimri-Lim sent to a great number of potential allies. I quote the version sent to kings Abi-samar and Ikšud-lašēmēšu (ARM 28 148; see also LAPO 16 #247, pp. 386–88): "The entire land has reverted to its destined lot [*ana isqīša itūr*] and everyone has occupied the throne of his father. I heard it said, 'The land of Idamaraṣ, wherever he took hold of fortresses, heeds Zimri-Lim.' Write me then; I will come and solemnly take (this) holy oath for you, 'Hand over the city to me and I will give it to its master.' As for you all, I will show you as well as your property the place of choice that you will tell me." The letter was posted at the dawn of a new age in the region, at the collapse of the powerful kingdom created by Samsi-Addu, and at the wholesale reoccupation by ousted rulers of many centers that had been committed to him. *isqum*, "lot," can have an abstract meaning ("fate" or the like), but it applies to inheritance or share assigned by lot and so reminds of our context here.

1 4. *wayyaʿal yĕhûdâ*. The narrative will henceforth ignore Simeon's participation in the war against the Canaanites until it brings it back for syntactic purposes in 1:17. Henceforth, plurals attached to nouns and verbal forms seem associated solely with Judah and its warriors, possibly in the form *bĕnê yĕhûdâ*, "Judah folk" (from 1:8). Some commentators regard this verse as superfluous; "except the ten thousand slain—a round number for which we need hardly seek an historical source—it tells us nothing which we do not read in the context" (Moore 1895: 13–14). Yet this verse does report on the fulfillment of God's promise, drawing emphasis not just by repeating the vocabulary of the pledge (*nātan* [enemy] *bĕyād-*), but by clarifying that the Promised Land included Perizzites as well.

THE PERIZZITES

Who the Perizzites (Greek, Φερεζαῖος; Latin, *Ferezeus*) were remains unsolved, despite the abundance of theories. The name, in the singular, always occurs preceded by a definite article, thus denoting an ethnic or national group (GKC 406 [§126l]). There are about two dozen mentions of the name (two more also in the Apocrypha), never without association with other groups, generally referring to folks that Israel confronted as it settled in the Promised Land (see Table 1 at IB1). Joshua 11:3 lumps Amorites, Hittites, Perizzites, and Jebusites in "the mountains." In a somewhat contrasting passage, Josh 17:15 places the Perizzites and the Rephaim in the "woodlands" (*yāʿar*) rather than in the "Ephraim mountains." Four passages link the Canaanites and the Perizzites, always in this sequence. (See also the Greek of Josh 16:10). Genesis 13:7 and 34:30 treat them as the two main groups occupying the land, while our passage and Judg 1:5 speak of their defeat in future Judah territory.

Our extensive records from Late Bronze Palestine have failed (as yet) to locate any people by that name, and derivations of their names (and so presumably also their lineage) from such languages as Ḫurrian, Hittite, Anatolian, and Sumerian are all half-hearted (see P. Artzi, *EncJud* 13: 288), as are the speculations based on archeology (see Lapp 1968).[16] The likelihood is that the term is Hebraic in origin, created on the root **prz* that in a number of instances (Esth 9:19, Ezek 38:11, Zech 2:8) refers to unforti-fied settlements or to their inhabitants (Esth 9:19, Deut 3:5, I Sam 6:18). The doubling of the third consonant of the root (*zayin*), reflected in the MT but not the Greek, is doubtless to keep the preceding vowel short (see GKC 234 [§84k]). It may well be, therefore, that "Perizzites" primarily referred to people who had no access to fortified areas. Only secondarily did it come to refer to a people, in effect, the reverse of what happened to "Canaanite," an ethnicon that came to mean "merchants."[17]

Bezeq is where Saul mustered Israel to counter the threat of the Ammonites, thus proving his mettle as a potential king (1 Sam 11:8–11). In this narrative, Bezeq lies close to Jabesh-Gilead and perhaps also to Gibeah of Saul. Following Eusebius (de Lagarde 1870: 105, 237), a connection with Tell/Khirbet Ibzīq, north of Shechem almost halfway to Beth-shean, has been proposed, at least since medieval times. Because this tell shows little evidence of settlement before the seventh century BCE and because it is located in a terrain ill-suited for the gathering of troops (but why not at nearby Ras Ibziq?), A. Zertal has favored linking Khirbet Salhab with Bezeq.[18]

Whether or not we are dealing with another Bezeq in our passage is at issue in the literature, the reason being that Eusebius's Bezeq seems too far north of Jerusalem (about 30 miles or so distant) where the rout of the Canaanites took place and where the unfortunate Adoni-bezeq was brought to die. Many sites with names that are reminiscent of "Bezeq" and are close to Jerusalem have therefore been proposed in the literature, none convincingly so (Moore 1895: 14–15 gives many choices). But there is no compelling reason to make Jerusalem central to the search, since Adoni-bezeq could have headed there for shelter when he was caught.

ʿăśeret ʾălāfîm ʾîš, "ten thousand" is conventional for an impressive number of soldiers (Judg 4:6, 20:34; 1 Kgs 5:28 [14 RSV, workers]), prisoners (2 Kgs 14:7, Jerusalemites), or victims (Judg 3:29, Moabites; 2 Kgs 14:7, Edomites). The word *ʾelef* should not be translated "contingent" (Boling 1975: 55) or "companies" (Hess 1999: 144) as long as we do not establish how large a group is meant. In Mari, where engagements could pit five thousand to ten thousand men (Abrahami 1992: 166), there were units of ten (led by a *waklum*) and of fifty (led by a *laputtûm*). There were also a *pirsum* (section) of one hundred men, a *lētum* (corps) of two hundred, and an *ummānum* (army) of one thousand. But I also suspect that a realistic scenario for what transpired at Bezeq most certainly would not have been the goal of Hebrew tellers eager to give God credit for remarkable achievements, so forcing them to be realistic would be a serious misreading of Scripture as well as a treacherous treading on historicizing.

1 5. *vayyimṣeʾû ʾet-ʾădōnî bezeq bĕbezeq*. Whether *ʾădōnî bezeq* (at 1:7 *ʾădōnî-bezeq*) is a name or a title is at issue. On the face of it, it looks like a title: *ʾādôn*, differing from *baʿal* in reflecting authority rather than possession, and its *yôd* a vestigial of a construct ending (GKC 253 [§90l]; Layton 1990: 116–18). So we have here "Lord of Bezeq," and this is how Josephus understood it.[19] The verb *māṣāʾ* (BDB, 593) often involves an unexpected discovery or good fortune, as in the case of Jonah finding the perfect ship with which to escape God (Jonah 1:3). Its use here gives a nice touch to the unfolding scene, implying that Judah and Simeon surprised the king of Bezeq, who, with his large army, had not expected to be battling in his own territory. They pinned him down and destroyed a good chunk of his army. Subsequently, he tried to escape but succeeded only in contributing to the motif, nicely displayed in Josh 10 and in Judg 4, of an enemy vainly escaping the Hebrews and their God.

But all other witnesses took *ʾădōnî bezeq* as a name, probably because other Canaanite kings are about to be mentioned (see 1:10) and because the anecdote that we shall soon read is best understood when naming a character. I have therefore translated it as such; but because most modern commentators also take it as a personal name but are not content with its construction, a number of hypotheses offer suggestions such as the following:

1. That in our passage the place name Bezeq is secondary, extracted from the name of the victim Adoni-bezeq;
2. That in the name "Adoni-bezeq" the second element must be the name of a god and not of a city (as in Adonijah [for YHVH] and Adoni-zedeq [potentially a Canaanite deity]), even if no known god from antiquity is called "Bezeq";
3. That the story was calqued on an account in Josh 10, where the Israelites defeated an Adoni-zedeq (Adoni-bezeq in Vaticanus Greek![20]), king of Jerusalem, so explaining why Judah's victim was taken to die in Jerusalem. Yet no textual witness gives any reading that differs from the Hebrew, except for Josephus, who has a metathesized second element, Adonizebekos.[21]

All this speculation is unnecessary. To begin with, names constructed on toponyms (cities, rivers, mountains, etc.) are well-known in Amorite personal names, especially in the phrase *mut-* ("man/hero of") + toponym, so very reminiscent of our *'ădôn-* (see listing in Durand 1991a). While names that are composed of *'ădôn* + a geographical name are not known from the Hebrew Bible, we do have people whose names match that of a place (for example, Hebron) or are constructed from a gentilic (for example, Happuti); see the list in Zadok 1988: 387.

Second, the element *bezeq* in the name of its king need not refer to a god, but to a noun or a verbal form, as in the names Adoniram (Ezra 2:13, 8:13; Neh 7:18) and Adonikam (1 Kgs 4:6, 5:28). The dictionaries for West Semitic (BDB; Hoftijzer 1995: 149–50; Jastrow 1950: 154) give us meanings for a root **bzq* (dealing with pebbles, rocks, and the like) that might suitably explain the name Adoni-bezeq without exploiting the lexical riches of Arabic, Akkadian, and other Semitic languages.[22]

As to the accounts in Josh 10 about Adoni-zedeq and in Judg 1:4–9 about Adoni-bezeq, they are hardly equivalent to each other, even if they both relate victories for Israel. It is unreasonable to presume that there existed in ancient Israel only those traditions now preserved in Joshua and Judges from which to establish the true historiography of what had happened at Bezeq.

1 6. A ruler fleeing at the rout of his troops is a realistic event and is well-reported in narratives and annals. In biblical lore, the flight of rulers (verb: **nws*) sets the scene for a follow-up episode most often an anecdote that establishes a context for their demise after capture (from hiding or not), from which to derive lessons. We shall soon report on Judg 4:15 (Sisera) and 8:10–21 (Zebah and Zalmunna), but other examples include kings of the Amorite coalition against Gibeon (Josh 10:3) and the fate of Agag (minus flight) in 1 Sam 15.

MUTILATION

vayyĕqaṣṣĕṣû 'et-bĕhōnôt yādā'v vĕraglā'v. Mutilation of defeated enemies was frequent in the past and continues to be reported in modern warfare. If not the full head from the neck up, the organs of senses (eyes, nose, ears, lips, tongues, and hands) as well as the sexual organs are often the target (Lemos 2006; Minunno 2008). The mutilation of captives differs from punishment controlled by *lex talionis*, "eye for an eye, tooth for a tooth," principles that are well-known in ancient law, whether we judge them realistic or not (on which, see Whitman 1995). They also differ from disfigurement that the gods inflict as punishment, as when the divine ferryman Nemty, often appearing as a falcon, is punished for disobeying Re by the removal of his toes, compromising his ability to perch (Lichtheim 1976: 218); or when the gods mutilate the fingers of a princess for disrespecting her father (ARM 26 312: 36′–39′).[23]

Mutilation can be "cosmetically" applied (ears, earlobes, nose, even eyes) to brand a male captive destined for slavery without compromising his usefulness. (Female captives were less likely to be defaced, for hardly happy reasons.) It can also degrade the elite (2 Sam 10:1–5, parallels for which are in Stolper 1997), disqualifying them from their occupations, as was the case of the servant of a high priest whose ear was lopped off (Mark 14:47). Mutilation can also be applied capriciously, to instill pain and humiliation on the victim and fear on those who might resist the victors, the last a favored goal for first-millennium Assyrian rulers. A governor of Suḫu in the Middle Euphrates proudly proclaims cutting off the hands and lower lips of captured enemies before freeing them to broadcast his greatness (Frame 1995, 293: 38; see below, notes to 1:7). The maiming can precede death (as in our passage) or even succeed it, as when David executes the murderers of Ishboshet, their severed limbs displayed by the pools of Hebron (2 Sam 4:12).[24]

AUTO DA FÉ?

The mutilation of Adoni-bezeq, however, is related for a purpose other than punishment or the spread of fear. In calling on classical texts (Aelian, Caesar, Valerius Maximus) as sources for somewhat similar mutilations of captives, some commentators (among them Moore 1895: 17–18; Burney 1970: 6; Lindars 1995: 18; Boling 1975: 55) explain that mutilation prevented the victims from wielding weapons (partially correct) or from running away (partially incorrect). For a more relevant explanation, we need, however, to look at the next verse.

1 7. *šibʿîm mĕlākîm . . . hāyû mĕlaqqĕṭîm taḥat šulḥānî.* The number "seventy" (a multiple of two independently significant numbers, seven and ten) evokes completion, whether it refers to a block of years (Ps 90:10, a human lifetime; Isa 23:15–17, change in Tyre's fortune; Jer 25:11–12, 29:10; Dan 9:24; Zech 1:12, 7:5; 2 Chr 36:21, change in Judah's fortunes), to a span of days (Gen 50:3, mourning for Jacob), or to a collection of human beings. Jacob's family consists of seventy when it enters Egypt, potentially a full nation (Gen 46:27, Exod 1:5, Deut 10:22); Moses is to collect a contingent of seventy elders (Exod 24:1, 9; Num 11:16, 24–25; see Ezek 8:11); and Gideon had seventy sons (Judg 8:30 and following), Abdon had seventy descendants (Judg 12:14), and Ahab had seventy "sons," that is, vassals (2 Kgs 10:1). Josephus (*Ant.* 5.123) increases the number to seventy-two, nobody knows why, but see also Luke 10:1, citing a similar number (Ehrlich 1968: 68).

I do not think that the number is selected here to evoke the political council of a once mighty king (Boling 1975: 55). Nor should it make us place Adoni-bezeq at Jerusalem rather than at Bezeq (Lindars 1995: 15).[25] Rather, it is used to convey Adoni-bezeq's sense that he once had control of his whole world, its kings having lost their authority to him. Thumbless, his victims can no longer firmly grasp; toeless, they cannot keep their balance. And so in their haste not to lose morsels to other victims, they fed like dogs, using their mouths to pick up food dropped from Adoni-bezeq's table.[26]

(Until very recently, in the Levant, dogs were scavengers rather than pets; in fact, they were the sewers of antiquity.) The image of royalty behaving like scavengers sets us up for the main lesson of Adoni-bezeq's fate. Here again, Josephus (*Ant.* 5.123), who obviously enjoyed the imagery, expands: "Nay, indeed," Adoni-bezeq is quoted to say, "I was not always to lie concealed from God, as I find by what I now endure, while I have not been ashamed to do the same to seventy-two kings."

ka'ăšer 'āśîtî kēn šillam-lî 'ĕlōhîm. There is nothing specifically Canaanite about the venerable and lasting sentiment that people are repaid in kind; hence it cannot be cited as ironic of Israel's behavior (Block 1999: 90–91). People want good deeds repaid to their benefactors (Ruth and Orpah, Ruth 1:8; Hiram of Tyre, 2 Chr 2; ambiguous, Prov 24:29) and evil deeds returned on their perpetrators (Samson and Philistines, in a tit-for-tat, Judg 15:10–11; see also Obad 1:15 and Lev 24:19). Samuel chides Agag for bereaving women before turning his mother into a bereaver (1 Sam 15:33). But there is also the notion that such repayments—whether for individuals (see Josh 7:15, the execution of Achan) or nations (Obad 1:15, Edom; Jer 50:29, Babylon; Lam 3:64, Jerusalem; Joel 4:4–8 [3:4–8 RSV], Phoenicians)—are left for God to carry out, for they are but manifestations of the divine justice that is powerfully described in Ps 94. We shall soon see a fine example at Judg 9:56–57: "Thus God turned back on Abimelech the evil he had done to his father by killing his seventy brothers. As to the evil acts by the men of Shechem, God brought them on their own head. The curse of Jotham son of Jerubbaal had indeed fallen on them."

Of interest here is whether or not Adoni-bezeq is attributing to the Hebrew God this dispensation of justice when citing *'ĕlōhîm* (rather than Yhvh). In ancient Near Eastern literature, it is quite common to find the word *nṯr* (Egypt) or dingir/*ilum* (Mesopotamia), "god," invoked for a specific, albeit unnamed, god, and it should be translated "God." In such instances, the verbal form attached to the activity of that "God" is commonly not plural. In our passage, however, the verb controlled by *'ĕlōhîm* is in the singular, when a Canaanite ruler should have had little qualm in assigning retribution to his "gods" (**kēn šillemû-lî 'ĕlōhîm*).[27] So we must imagine that whether in a moment of spiritual illumination or to elicit sympathy from his captors, Adoni-bezeq is said to confer on the Hebrew God the power to balance justice. Something similar, minus the irony, may be at stake in the other narrative that brings together Canaanites, divine justice, and the dispensing of food under tables. As told in Matt 15:26–27 (Mark 7:27–28), a Canaanite woman seeks healing for her daughter from Jesus, and when he replies that he cures Jews only, the woman earns a miracle when she answers, "even puppies eat the scraps that fall from their master's table" (see Storch 1970). Whether in his candor Adoni-bezeq was playing on the root **šlm*, which occurs also in the name "Jerusalem" (see below), is a plausible speculation.

Also worthy of notice is Adoni-bezeq's seemingly unsolicited introspection. Elsewhere, we wait until the moment of death before a repartee brings out the relevant truth. When Jether, Gideon's child, shrinks from executing Zebah and Zalmunna, they taunt Gideon, "Go ahead and cut us down, for manhood defines the person!" (Judg 8:21). Agag, about to suffer Samuel's blow, exclaims, "So, now bears down bitter death" (1 Sam 15:32; other renderings possible). But Adoni-bezeq had miles to go before expiring, and his task was to proclaim the greatness of the Hebrew God at the gate of Jerusalem. A governor from Suḫu in the Middle Euphrates (eighth century BCE) uses the defeated similarly, when he writes: "I fell upon [tribesmen] and killed 1716 of their men. I defeated them from the well of Makiru as far as the well of Gallabu and the well Suribu and filled the wadis with their skulls. I removed the arms and lips of 80 of their men and released them (to propagate my) glory."[28]

vayyēbî'uhû yĕrûšālayim vayyāmot šām. A plural verbal form with an indefinite subject may be rendered by the English passive ("he was brought to Jerusalem"); but to apply the principle here might compromise the storyline that has Judah capturing Adoni-bezeq and the confession that requires him to learn the humility of the captured (see Moore 1895: 18, contra Webb 1987: 231). Likewise missing the point would be attributing Adoni-bezeq's transport to his own people (see Block 1999: 91). Despite his infirmity, Adoni-bezeq was promenaded, as is the case of the agonized victim as reported in ARM 26 434: 36–44. If the notice is playing on a triumphal practice of transporting leaders before their execution, as known from Sumer (Ibbi-Sin taken to die in Elam) to Rome (Vercingetorix ritually garroted there), then it must mean that Jerusalem is already captured even if we will not learn of that momentous event until the next verse; if so, this notice would be an excellent case of anticipatory *hysteron proteron* ("the latter first"), a rhetorical device in which an idea is advanced that is fleshed out only later.[29]

Adoni-bezeq died from his wounds, in Jerusalem, where Judah was to war next (contra Ehrlich 1969: 44). Josephus had the Hebrews kindly bury, rather than expose, him.[30] (On Jerusalem, see below at 1:8).

For פ (and ס), see "Conquests in the Hills" below.

COMMENTS

> R. Adda b. R. Hanina said: Had Israel not sinned, only the Penta-
> teuch and the Book of Joshua would have been given to them, because
> (Joshua) records the disposition of Palestine (among the tribes). How
> is this known? "For wisdom increases with anger" (Eccl 1:18).
> —bNedarim *22b*

Testing the Trust

For anyone reading the book of Judges as a chapter in the continuing saga of the Hebrew people, its opening lines must startle. We had come to its verses expecting continued unity, stability, and order. True, the trajectory in Joshua was not straight. But lessons were learned, above all on how to trust God. Joshua had opened on an unfolding display of communal resolve to trust God's choices. From Shittim, spies were sent out who, unlike an infamous precedent (Num 13), unanimously reported panic at a surging Israel. The Jordan was forded through a replay of the miracle at Yam Suf (Exod 14–15). At Gilgal, Israel learned how to remove the shame of Egypt from its body through circumcision. After celebrating the Passover, it weaned itself from manna, a food it did not produce (Josh 5). At Jericho, facing its first test, Israel showed how to proceed correctly with the conquest. It consulted God at every step and stayed true to his instruction, however bizarre or unorthodox. As a result, Jericho fell, and Israel made its initial inroads into the Promised Land.

However, in attacking its next target, Ai, Israel had not consulted God and therefore was not alerted to the sacrilege committed in its midst (Josh 7:1–5), compromising its future success. Israel suffered an initial defeat, but it recovered quickly, learning to use the lots to extirpate the crime from its midst (Josh 7:13–26). And once it learned from God the proper military tactics ("set up an ambush against the town, from behind it," Josh 8:2; "Stretch out the javelin you are holding toward Ai, for I am delivering it to you," Josh 8:18), success was assured. Surprisingly, Israel did not consult with God when it granted Gibeon a peace treaty ("The men [of Israel] partook from their food, having failed to ask God's opinion," Josh 9:14). Although this treaty quickened a major war (and a glorious victory) against an Amorite coalition, Gibeon itself provided a haven for non-Israelites within the Promised Land, and its fate had dire consequences on Saul and his dynasty (see 2 Sam 21).

Promises Fulfilled

Sandwiched between two statements on Joshua's old age (Josh 13:1 and 23:1) is a fleeting (but portentous) account of the "land not yet subdued" (Josh 13:1–7), a long report on the allotment of promised territory (Josh 13:8–19), and a briefer listing of privileged cities (Josh 13:20–21). Afterwards comes a soothing coda (Josh 21:41–43), with its fitting and positive conclusion to the restoration of a land that was once promised (and largely delivered) to Abraham and Isaac. The tribulation and pain of a half millennium of enslavement in Egypt, which followed on Jacob's emotionally fathomable but politically unwise decision to settle near his beloved Joseph, is now behind Israel, thanks to Moses and to Joshua: "The LORD delivered to Israel the entire land he had promised to give their ancestors; they took it over and settled in it. The LORD made peace for them all around, fulfilling all that he had promised their ancestors. Not one among their enemies stood in their way, the LORD having handed them all their enemies; not one of the many good promises that the LORD had made to the House of Israel failed to materialize. Everything was fulfilled."

In the final chapters (Josh 23–24), Joshua delivers not one, but two powerful summations that rehearse the covenant God graciously offered the ancestors, thus giving Israel one more chance to focus on its terms. True, there are reminders of a brutal loss of privileges for those who forsake this covenant (Josh 23:16, 24:20), but the offer is so generous (complete dominance and eternal peace) and its stipulations so minimal (worship no one but the Lord) that with unity and harmony achieved, the chances for rejecting the terms rightly seemed remote.

Forcing God to Act

So, given the circumstances of Joshua's death, we might have expected the book of Judges to open on God selecting the next leader and charging him with keeping Israel focused on its primary goal of keeping the faith. Or we might have had Israel consulting with God about the tribe—even the individual from a tribe—to whom primacy should be given. Rather, we open on a stilted act. Israel does not intend to act as a unit. In posing its request so narrowly (see the Introductory Remarks), Israel was giving God little choice in choreographing the brutal phase of the next battle against the Canaanites, who, emboldened by the death of a great military ruler, were likely to give stiffer opposition to the occupation of the vast chunks of promised territory still under their control (Josh 13:2–6).[31] God selects Judah and assures him of victory, but there is evident discomfort on all sides. In his response, God omits mention of "at first" and so establishes no time limit to the brunt Judah is to bear; Israel fails to redraft its inquiry so as to derive more precision about tactics or foes; Judah lacks faith in God's message, and so he asks Simeon to join his battles; Simeon fails to clarify its agreement, and so when the two conquer Zephat/Hormah (Judg 1:17), the town is shared by both (Josh 15:30) rather than falling wholly to Simeon (Josh 19:4, 1 Chr 4:30).

This lack of unreserved trust between God and one of his chosen tribes becomes paradigmatic for the remaining narratives in Judges. Yet both sides are willing to keep the contacts from sundering beyond repair. Judah's victory at Bezeq is displayed almost formulaically: There is a battle, an enemy is defeated, (huge) casualty is reckoned, and death or execution of leaders ensues (see 1 Sam 4:10–12; 2 Sam 18:6–17; and Webb 1987: 84–85). Yet Adoni-bezeq, alone to be mentioned by name, breaks out from this cliché to deliver the lesson that becomes emblematic for the succeeding narratives: The God who gives glory to one leader can also deliver it to his enemy. This conviction is certainly Israelite, and Israel's people must have been pleased to have it broadcast by one who has not yet learned all about the Hebrew God. But it was also available to any Canaanite, for we find its burden delivered in the prophecy the god Addu of Aleppo (Ḥalab) communicated early in the second millennium BCE to Zimri-Lim of Mari:

> I had given all the land [of your kingdom] to your father and because of my weapons, he had no opponents. But when he abandoned me, I took his land away and gave it to his enemy. But then I restored you to your father's throne and handed you the weapons with which I battled the Sea. I rubbed your body with oil from my own numinous glow so that no one could ever stand up to you. Now therefore listen to my only wish: Whenever anyone appeals to you for judgment, saying, "I am aggrieved," be there to decide his case and to give him satisfaction. This is all that I desire of you.[32]

2. Achsah (Judg 1:8–15)

1   [8]The people of Judah attacked Jerusalem and captured it. They put it to the sword and set fire to the city. [9]Afterward, the people of Judah went down to attack the Canaanites who inhabited the upland, the Negev, and the foothills as well. [10]Judah moved against the Canaanites who lived in Hebron (earlier, Hebron was called Qiryat-arba) and they defeated Sheshay, Ahiman, and Talmay. [11]From there, he went against the inhabitants of Debir (earlier, Debir was called Qiryat-sefer).

[12]Caleb then announced, "To him who defeats Qiryat-sefer and captures it, I give him Achsah, my daughter, as wife." [13]Othniel son of Kenaz (brother of Caleb, who was younger than him) defeated it; so he gave him Achsah, his daughter, as wife. [14]On arriving, she convinced him to request the field from her father. As she dismounted from the donkey, Caleb asked her, "What's with you?" [15]She answered him, "Hand me a present! You have given me away as if

Negev-land; so you must now give me basins of water." Caleb gave her Upper Gullot as well as Lower Gullot. פ

NOTES

Introductory Remarks: Political Marriages

Once, a prince of Egypt was destined to die violently from any of three fates. Taking charge of his life and hoping to avoid his fate, the prince set forth from his protected castle: "He went northward across the desert, following his heart and living on the best of all the desert game. He reached the Prince of Nahrin [Upper Mesopotamia]. Now the Prince of Nahrin had no children except one daughter. For her a house had been built whose window was seventy cubits away from the ground. He had sent for all the sons of all the princes of Khor [Syria] and told them: 'He who reaches the window of my daughter, his wife she shall be'" (from *The Doomed Prince*, translated in Lichtheim 1976: 201). Needless to say, the prince got the prize; the girl, an only child (see at 11:34), turned out to be a true "woman of valor," saving her husband from at least one of his cruel fates.

This story is preserved among other tales and copies of love songs on one hieratic papyrus dating to the end of the second millennium BCE (so not too removed from the period the Hebrews set for their own Judges stories). It is not alone in antiquity in preserving the theme of the competitive warrior winning his destined bride. Although the end of this tale is missing, we should not doubt (as do some Egyptologists) that the prince will overcome his fate and succeed his father as pharaoh. We are here in the realm of folktales and fairytales, but while "real world" rulers are not likely to bet their daughters on frivolous dares, they do offer them as reward to faithful vassals and rising chieftains or as cement for tribal or dynastic accords.[1] In a bizarre affair, a king of Emar (fourteenth century BCE) gives four of his daughters and much precious metal to a Ḫurrian king threatening his capital.[2] Naturally, during such moments of dynastic unions, gifts are exchanged all around (see the Comments). A tablet from Shemshara of around 1800 BCE even informs us that at such occasions territory may be ceded to the bride. A powerful king writes to a potential vassal: "You and I—our coming together is overdue. Let me order the making of golden statues of you and me, one set to embrace the other. I shall give you my own daughter, and I shall give you (the city of) Shusharra and the land of [. . .] as bridal gift for my daughter."[3]

We know from the behavior of Rachel, Leah, and Michal toward their fathers that bartered brides were not simply pawns in games for adult males, but their reactions were set in literature. We recover the voices of actual brides in Mari letters exchanged among King Zimri-Lim, his daughters, and palace administrators.[4] A number of these daughters report on sad marriages, in which they never gain the affection of their husbands or a mastery over their own courts.[5] A particularly tragic story is revealed in the letters of Kirum, the second of two daughters of Zimri-Lim given to the same vassal.

Of interest for us here, however, are the dossiers of the sisters Inbatum ("Little Grape") and Tiṣpatum. The first married Atamrum, an imposing king of Andarig, the second Ili-Ištar of Šuna. Both rulers had been rewarded with princesses for their allegiance to Zimri-Lim when they had other choices. For reasons beyond our grasping, both of these sisters managed to quickly take control of their new environment (surprising in the case of Tiṣpatum, who was a mere teenager). They became primary wives and reigning queens as well as acting monarchs during their husbands' absences, occasionally (Inbatum) even carrying on correspondence with other monarchs. Self-confident and eager to bolster their standing with their husbands, the sisters solicited land or cities from their father. I give an excerpt from one letter each. Noticeable is how Inbatum finds a way to calm her father's threat to punish her husband's appropriation of a city and how Tiṣpatum tries to shame her dad into doing the right thing.[6]

Here is Inbatum to her father, Zimri-Lim (ARM 10 84 = LAPO 18 #1232, pp. 448–50):[7]

> I have listened to the tablet my father conveyed to me. My father has written me long and in detail about the town Amaz. The town Amaz for a while now has depended on a [leader] from my husband's land; but when this town broke away from my husband, your servant [general] Ḫimdiya acted to restore it to my husband. He made this land submit and installed an officer of my husband as its manager. In no way did he plunder this town. I/He had no idea that this town, in fact, depended on you! Once my husband returns here, discuss it between you and my husband, and if this town is yours, then my husband should certainly give it back to you.
>
> Now about what my father wrote (threateningly) to me, "As for me, I will do what needs to be done." Why has my father written so to me? When you and my husband conferred, my husband, heading to Babylon, entrusted to you Andarig, town and country, so that the land of Yamutbal is now your land and the town of Andarig is your town. The land is yours to protect; but do what seems right to you. Why did my father write this to me and so has pained me?

And here is Tiṣpatum to Zimri-Lim (ARM 10 98 = LAPO 18 #1239, pp. 459–60):

> If in truth my lord loves the city Šuna and (regards) Ili-Ištar his servant, do hurry here a hundred soldiers and your trustworthy officer and do save your city and servant. Else, the enemy will seize the city. I swear it, there could be the following opinion about [Ili-Ištar], "How could it be that he is married to the daughter of Zimri-Lim and that he is obedient to him?" My father and lord should reflect on all these matters.

That elite brides could harangue their fathers on behalf of their husbands is useful to keep in mind as we read about Caleb, Achsah, and Othniel.

Conquests in the Hills

1 8–11. These verses could easily belong to the previous section. In many manuscripts, after v. 7 there is a *pĕrāšâ pĕtûḥâ*, "open section" (represented by a "פ"), indicating that a new line needs to begin at this point. A gap that does not necessitate moving to a new line will have a *pĕrāšâ sĕtûmâ*, "closed section" (symbolized by a "ס"). The two markers (פ and ס) are not found in Hebrew manuscripts and codices, but they are inserted in certain scholarly editions of the Hebrew Bible, such as the Biblia Hebraica series (Kittel, Stuttgartensia, and Quinta [*BHQ*]).[8] In the translated segments preceding the Notes—

but not in the Translation at the beginning of this book—I follow the codification of the *BHQ*.

What is interesting is that these two signals on segmenting (hence interpreting) passages are not new with the Masoretes but are already implied in Qumran manuscripts. Unfortunately, so far we do not have enough Judges material from Qumran to confirm its application there.[9] In apportioning materials to diverse chapters of this commentary, and especially in the early moments of Judges, I have taken a cue from this allotment of material and justify the instances when I deviate from them. I have kept these symbols in the translation, if only to draw attention to a very ancient tradition of scanning the book of Judges.

In this particular instance, adhering to the traditional division allows vv. 8–11 to play Janus, looking backward to Judah's continued assault on the Canaanites, but also looking forward to involving diverse groups that come to be part of Judah.

JERUSALEM

1 8. The first time a reader of the received Scripture meets with *yĕrûšālayim*, the future capital of a united Israel (and its greatest city), is in Josh 10:1, when Adoni-zedeq, king of Jerusalem, panics at the success of the Hebrew forces and mounts a coalition to punish Gibeon for allying itself with them.[10] Not until Josh 18:28 (but suggested at Josh 15:8 and repeated at Judg 19:10) is the name of Jerusalem associated with "Jebus" (*yebûs*), thereby harking back to the many pentateuchal passages in which God promises the land of the Jebusites to the Israelites. Nowhere in Joshua is the city said to fall to the Hebrews, despite the defeat of its king. Indeed, Josh 15:63 conspicuously sets unconquered Jerusalem apart from the territory said to be allotted to Judah. There is also mention of Benjamin having failed to completely dispossess the Jebusites in Jerusalem (Judg 1:21, on which, see below), although in Josh 18:28 Jerusalem is reckoned as belonging to Benjamin. Later on, David is credited with bringing it into the fold (2 Sam 5:6–12; 1 Chr 11:4–9).

Josh 15:63	*Judg 1:21*
As to the Jebusites who lived in Jerusalem, Judah could not drive them out; so the Jebusites are still today living in Jerusalem with Judah.	As to the Jebusites who lived in Jerusalem, Benjamin could not drive them out, so the Jebusites are still today living in Jerusalem with Benjamin.

We know nothing about the Jebusites from extrabiblical sources, and so there are many theories about them, some more fanciful than others, claiming them to be Anatolians, Ḥurrians, or some other non-Semites.[11] Jerusalem may be cited as Rushlamimu (or the like) in the Egyptian execration texts (eighteenth century BCE), but it is definitely mentioned as Urusalim in the Amarna records (fifteenth to fourteenth centuries BCE; EA 285–90, possibly also 291).[12] The consonants of the name (*yrvšlm*) are traditionally vocalized as a dual in Hebrew (pronounced *yĕrûšālayim*).[13] The LXX spelling Ἱερουσαλήμ, however, suggests that in the Hellenistic period the dual either was not heard or was heard differently. (Note also "Yerûšlem" in biblical Aramaic.) While the scholarly consensus now is that the name incorporated the god Shalem, no clear meaning is available for the first element **yr(v)*.

The topography of earliest Jerusalem is not clear, although it was likely bound to a narrow oval (the Ophel), defensible on all but a narrow saddle where it linked with a larger plateau. By Middle Bronze II (circa eighteenth century BCE), it was fortified, although its dimensions are not clearly delineated. A few tombs that are dated to the Late Bronze Age show prosperous elite. But the Amarna tablets reveal the area to be unstable, thinly populated, and attractive mostly to raiders and bandits. With Nubian soldiers there undermining his authority, Jerusalem's ruler Abdi-Ḥeba sends desperate letters begging the pharaohs (Amenhotep III and Akhenaton) to secure his stability and to help him against Ḥabirus, thus rewarding his loyalty. With the decline of Egyptian prestige, especially after the havoc created by the Sea Peoples, we learn little about Jerusalem until Hebrew historiography takes over (see Bahat 1997: 224–38; Na'aman 1996, for Iron Age Jerusalem).

Its Capture   As punctuated by the Masoretes, the warfare around Jerusalem is given in two modes: overview (attack and capture, *vayyillāḥămû . . . bîrûšālayim vayyilkĕdû 'ōtāh*) and detail (slaughter and burning, *vayyakkûhā lefî-ḥāreb vĕ'et-hā'îr šillĕḥû bā'ēš*). Yet the vocabulary does not propose a total destruction. When construed with the verb *nākâ* (to a much lesser extent *hārag* and, rarely, *ḥālaš*), the phrase *lĕfî-ḥereb* (literally, "at the mouth of the sword") occurs often in Scripture, implying slaughter, but not necessarily total.[14] This is crucial to keep in mind, for fighting, capturing, sacking, or burning a city (no matter how brutal the slaughter of its citizens) does not necessarily imply permanent possession of it. To promote that sense, the phrase needs to be associated with some forms of the verb *yrš (see below at 1:20) or with the Hiphil of *hāram* ("to place under the ban"; see below), either directly (Josh 6:21, 1 Sam 15:8) or in circumlocution (Deut 13:16; Josh 10:28, 10:35–39, 11:11–12).

Burning is also associated with the taking of towns, with '*ēš*, "fire," construed indirectly with *śāraf*, "to burn," or with the Piel of *šālaḥ* (hence pluralizing its targets), the latter more often found in poetry. Here too the results are not cataclysmic, because burnt towns have a way of quickly resurrecting: For example, destroyed Laish is settled by the Danites (Judg 18:27–29). Ziklag is burned down (1 Sam 30:3), yet it remained occupied by David (2 Sam 1:1). Pharaoh burns Gezer, but he gives it as a gift to his son-in-law, Solomon (1 Kgs 9:16–17). In fact, even Shechem, which Abimelech attacks and captures—slaughtering (*hārag*) its inhabitants, razing its walls, and sowing salt on its earth (Judg 9:45)—remains viable under Rehoboam (1 Kgs 1:1) and a citadel under Jeroboam (1 Kgs 12:25). Jerusalem, said to have been destroyed and burned by the Babylonians (2 Kgs 24:10), remained a major center. The examples drawn from antiquity for the resurrection of cities after their alleged destruction are legion.

The point of the above annotation is that regardless of the historical reality (which is likely beyond recovery), the Hebrew narrator was not conveying an irreversible destruction of Jerusalem. So to hold him in contradiction with material cited above (Josh 15:63, Judg 1:21, and 2 Sam 5:6–12) is to give evidence of artless reading of martial reports. Still, it is touching to notice that the import of 1:8 was so troubling in antiquity that Josephus offered a solution: "they besieged Jerusalem; and when they had taken the lower city, which was not under a considerable time, they slew all the inhabitants; but the upper city was not to be taken without great difficulty, through the strength of its walls, and the nature of the place" (*Ant.* 5.124).

1 9. *vĕʾaḥar yārĕdû bĕnê yĕhûdâ.* This verse anticipates the Judahite campaigns that will be detailed through v. 20 (perhaps also v. 21), and in it the verb *yārad*, "to go down," controls the troop maneuvers that will bring the region under tribal control. The adverb *ʾaḥar* does not specify the length of time before the fulfillment of an act. In most cases, it occurs immediately after the preceding act, but in others the length of the interval is not relevant (for example, in Josh 2:16) or can be unfolding over a long span (for example, at Gen 10:18). How long it took Judah to accomplish its goal, therefore, is left unexpressed.

Judah attacks the Canaanites who live in the uplands (*hāhār*), in the dry region to the south (*hannegeb*), and, depending on where you stand, the "foothills" or "lowlands" (*haššĕpēlâ*), the last a term that generally refers to the region between the Judean hills and coastal plains toward the Mediterranean. These three areas are reckoned to be part of Judah, and only a sliver of the Aravah (occasionally *midbar*), referring to the rift valley north of the Dead Sea, is missing from land that becomes traditionally Judah, probably because it was sparsely inhabited (see Deut 1:7–8; Josh 10:40, 11:16, 12:8 [includes also their slopes, *ʾăšēdôt*, "cliffs"]).

HEBRON . . .

1 10. *vayyēlek yĕhûdâ ʾel-hakkĕnaʿănî hayyôšēb bĕḥebrôn.* Here and at v. 11 the idiom is *hālak ʾel+*, rather than the previous *ʿālâ ʾel+* or *yārad le+*, and it is not always associated with military campaigns. The impression one gets from its usage is of a routine march from one battlefield to the next.

Hebron has had a long history in Hebrew traditions. There was an oak at nearby Mamre where Abram was said to build an altar (Gen 13:18). Hebron is famously associated with the burial of patriarchs and matriarchs in a cave with a double chamber (Machpelah), first in Gen 23, but then also at 25:9–10 and 35:27–29. Joshua is reported to have destroyed Hebron after hanging its king, Hoham (Josh 10:26, 36–37). The region was divided into segments, two of which (the walled area and the pastureland) were given over as a place of refuge (Josh 21:9–13, 1 Chr 6:42). Two others, the arable fields and villages, were Caleb's. Hebron becomes deeply associated with Hebrew royalty, with David (2 Sam 2:11, 5:5) and Absalom (2 Sam 15:10) beginning their careers there. We are told that Hebron was fortified under Rehoboam (2 Chr 11:10).

The earliest extrabiblical mention of a city named Hebron does not appear until the (late) eighth century BCE in the formula *lmlk/ḥbrn*, "for the king/Hebron area," etched on jars or stamped on jar handles from Lachish and Gath (see Israel Museum 1971: 45–46, 95–97; nos. 80–81). So we do not know how far back to retroject a name that is likely derived from an Amorite word referring to a tribal unit, *ḥibrum*, although the *-ôn* ending on names of people and places reflects a shift from a Canaanite *-ān*.[15] The modern Arabic name al-Khalil, "the Friend," may well be a translation of a name based on *ḥābēr*, in later Hebrew meaning "friend" and so attaching it to Abraham, in Muslim traditions, *ḫalīl ʾallâ/ar-raḥmān*, "Friend of God/the Merciful" (see Isa 41:8, Jub 19:9) (on all this see Cazelles, *TDOT* 4:193–97).

. . . AND QIRYAT-ARBA

vĕšēm-ḥebrôn lefānîm qiryat-ʾarbaʿ. According to Num 13:22 (see also below), Hebron was founded seven years before Zoan (probably Tanis) in Egypt. This biblical datum is difficult to assess, not just because "founding a city" is a fluid notion in Near Eastern lore—rulers commonly claim originating cities when they only repair their fortifications—but for its unusual linkage of births for a national and a foreign city.[16] The archeology of Hebron, however, shows it to have deeper foundations, and it may already have been a fortress during the Hyksos period. Although it is now doubted that the Amarna letters written by a Šuwardata came from Hebron (more likely Keilah or Gath), there is nevertheless reason to believe that it was a fortified area also in the Late Bronze Age.[17]

The Greek rendering for this information differs here in a number of ways from the Hebrew and from different manuscripts. To begin with, it seems to have duplicated the consonants *pnym, for a number of Greek manuscripts have καὶ ἐξῆλθεν Χεβρὼν ἐξ ἐναντίας, "and Hebron went against him" (or the like). It is not useful to speculate why. Additionally, it gives the name of the town as Καριαθαρβοξεφερ/Καριαθαρβοκσεφερ ("Καριατηαρβοκσεφερ"), which is the result of joining the Hebrew of qiryat-ʾarbaʿ from this verse and qiryat-sēfer of the following verse. Elsewhere, the Greek version transcribes qiryat-ʾarbaʿ by Καριαθαρβοκ (Josh 21:11, Neh 11:25), but also the literal πόλις Αρβοκ in Josh 14:15.[18]

There are many suggestions for the name Qiryat-arba, said to have once been the name of Hebron. Some are based on Josh 14:15 (after Arba, said to be the greatest/biggest among the Anak, primordial and gigantic inhabitants of Canaan) or on Josh 15:13 and 21:11 (after Arba, said to be the father of Anak/Anok).[19] Other explanations are traditional (the three patriarchs and Adam were buried there; Abraham and his Canaanite allies of Gen 14:24 had made reputations there),[20] "logical" (it was once divided into four sections, just as Qiryatayim, for example, at Num 32:37, had two parts), or scholarly (it brought together the clans of Caleb, Kenaz, Jerahmeel, and Keni). Following Mendenhall, Arbeitman (1988: 895–900) has sought a Hittite etymology for ʾarbaʿ, allegedly because ḥebrôn and ʾarbaʿ (mamrēʾ too for that matter) must carry the same meaning, but in different languages. This observation is not well-taken: Would anyone impose the same meanings for Paris/Ville lumière, for Chicago/Windy City, or for New York/The Big Apple just because each set of names refers to the same city? In any case, ʾarbaʿ is a limpidly Semitic word, with its characteristically Semitic ʿayin.

Truth to tell, we do not know why and how Qiryat-arba got its name, but a number of other places have names constructed with qiryâ, "village": Aside from Qiryatayim, we have Qiryat-hussot (Num 22:39) and Qiryat-yeʾarim (Josh 9:17, said to also be called Qiryat-Baal in Josh 15:60). What is remarkable is that the Hebrews, more so than any of their neighbors, were willing, in fact eager, to keep a record of changes in the names of towns (in Judg 1:23 soon also about Bethel/Luz) when their neighbors simply renamed them and promptly ignored any previous appellation. Why this is so will be broached below under the Comments.

Three Defeated Kings

We presume that the three kings šēšay . . . ʾāḥîman . . . talmāy (Rahlfs B, Σεσσι—Αχινααν—Θολμιν; Rahlfs A, Σεσι—Αχιμαν—Θολμι) had power in each of the three regions mentioned above from long ago. The trio is bound together eternally in diverse passages, and their defeat is credited to two different (albeit harmonizable) opponents:

Num 13:22	Josh 15:14	Josh 1:10	Judg 1:20
[Israel] went up into the Negev and came to Hebron—Ahiman, Sheshay, and Talmay, the descendants of Anak, being there.	Caleb drove out from there the three sons of Anak, Sheshay, Ahiman, and Talmay, the descendants of Anak.	Judah marched against the Canaanites who lived in Hebron (earlier Hebron was called Qiryat-arba) and they defeated Sheshay, Ahiman, and Talmay.	Hebron was given to Caleb, as Moses had promised, and he removed from there the three sons of Anak.

Rhyming names occur frequently in Hebrew lore, possibly because of their mnemonic value, and so often attracting doubts about authenticity. (See below about Cushan-rishatayim, king of Aram-naharayim.) In lists, the names that rhyme are often paired or set in sequence—such as Uz and Buz (Gen 22:21), Muppim and Huppim (Gen 46:21), Mahlon and Chilion (Ruth 1:2), and Hemdan, Eshban, Yitran, and Keran (Gen 36:26)—and so are they in our group in Num 13:22. As to the meaning of these names, people have needlessly looked for esoteric linguistic background for one or all of them: Ḥurrian, Hyksos, "pre-Philistine" Sea Peoples, and the like (see Boling and Wright 1982: 374, with bibliography; Redford 1992: 257 n. 2). In fact, there is no reason to look beyond Semitic roots construed with perfectly respectable Hebrew *-ayy* and *-an* endings.[21] Talmay occurs also as the name of a king of Geshur and father of one of David's wives (2 Sam 3:3, 13:37–38). A Levite by the name of Ahiman is known from 1 Chr 9:17.

Greek adds γεννήματα τοῦ Ενακ, "offspring of Enak," from Josh 15:14.

DEBIR . . .

1 11. *vayyēlek miššām ʾel-yôšĕbê dĕbîr.* Although not identified as in the previous verse, the inhabitants of Debir are also Canaanites. The noun *dĕbîr* applies to the rear portion of a building, generally a temple, and it may be that topographically the town was deemed to be so within a specific region. (Some defend an etymology from *dābār*, "word," hence something like "oracle.") The name is perfectly Semitic; yet once more, Arbeitman (1988; following Mendenhall) needlessly imposes a Hittite etymology on it (allegedly *dabara*) to have it parallel Debir's other name, Qiryat-sefer (allegedly "Scribe City"; see below).

Debir, one of three cities bearing this name in Hebrew Scriptures, was a royal center according to Josh 10:39 and 12:13. Its capture is reported on three occasions:

Josh 10:38–39	Josh 15:15–19	Judg 1:11–15
Joshua turned back toward Debir and, with all of Israel, he attacked it. He captured it, together with its king and its towns. They put them to the sword and utterly destroyed every person in it, leaving none alive.[22]	(Involves Othniel; see below)	(Involves Othniel; see below)

Until recently, it was common to situate Debir at Tell Beit Mirsim, largely because of W. F. Albright (see now R. Greenberg 1987). Following a suggestion by K. Galling, M. Kochavi (1974) once proposed Khirbet Rabûd as a better candidate, because of its location (a better distance from Hebron and Jerusalem), size (12 acres), stratigraphy (alone regionally besides Jerusalem to produce Late Bronze remains), and topography (cisterns and the nearby wells of Alaqa; but see below). More recently, Kochavi (2000) favored Tell Rumeyde, partly on the summit of the mountain of the same name, a site that is occasionally identified with ancient Hebron. Still, without a reliable ancient itinerary to situate Debir geographically and without documentary evidence to confirm the identification, the issue of location remains unsettled.

. . . AND QIRYAT-SEFER

Qiryat-sefer may mean something like "Inscriptions Village" rather than "Town of Records" or "Town of Scribes," presumably because the area had many inscribed monuments.[23] The puzzler is what to do with yet another name for Debir, Qiryat-sannâ (Josh 15:49). Easiest is to claim that the last name is but a copying error of deep antiquity. This is possible, especially since the Greek text expands by explaining Καριαθσωφαρ (for Qiryat-sefer) by means of πόλις γραμμάτων, "Documents City" (reflected also in the next verse). Hardest is to find semantic equivalence between *sefer* and *sannâ*, especially when the latter has an obscure meaning. Perhaps it is best to let the matter rest unresolved (but see Moore 1895: 26–27).

Fewell (1995: 131–33) labels the Hebrews Luddites for destroying a city named after records or writing. An amusing charge, for who would declare warriors to be tee-totalers for attacking Gath ("Winepress")?

The Challenge

CALEB

1 12. *vayyō'mer kāleb*. The rather stark appearance of Caleb at this juncture contrasts sharply with how he is introduced in the other account retelling of the fall of Qiryat-sefer, Josh 15:13–19.

From the tribe of Judah, Caleb, son of Jephunneh, had earned great prestige when, among twelve vanguards sent to reconnoiter Canaan, he and Joshua urged the conquest of the Promised Land.[24] For this, God made Caleb two promises (Num 14:24; see also 26:65 and Deut 1:36): He will enter the land, and his descendants will inherit it. Caleb, therefore, may have earned his name ("Dog") for his resilience and doggedness.[25] When time for the apportionment came, octogenarian Caleb reminded Joshua of the promise made through Moses and demanded the opportunity to possess a land inhabited by Anakim ("giants") and peppered with fortresses. After a detour to describe the inheritance of Judah, and not incidentally to situate Caleb's portion within it, we are given details on how Caleb harvested the promise but also found means to expand his influence on neighboring Qiryat-sefer (Debir) (Josh 15:13–19). In the compilation below, differences between this version and that of Judges are in boldface type. Curly brackets alert to material in Judges that is not in Joshua.

Joshua [see 14:13–15] gave to Caleb son of Jephunneh a portion within Judah according to the LORD's command to Joshua: Qiryat-'arba (ancestor of Anak), it being Hebron. {Caleb} dispossessed from there the three Anakites: Sheshay, Ahiman, and Talmay, heirs of Anak. From there he **marched against** [*vayyaʿal miššām ʾel*] the inhabitants of Debir (earlier, Debir was called Qiryat-sefer). Caleb announced, "To him who defeats Qiryat-sefer and captures it, I give him Achsah, my daughter, as wife." Othniel son of Kenaz (brother of Caleb {*who was younger than him*}), defeated it; so he gave him as wife Achsah, his daughter. On arriving, she convinced him to request [*lisʾōl*] from her father **a** {*the*} field. As she dismounted from the donkey, Caleb asked her, "What's with you?" She answered {*him*}, "**Give me** [*tĕnâ-llî*] {Hand me [*hāvâ-llî*]} a present. You have given me away as if Negev-land; so you must now give me basins of water." He {*Caleb*} gave her Uppermost Gullot [*gullōt ʿilliyôt*] as well as Lowest Gullot [*gullōt taḥtiyyôt*].

ACHSAH

vĕnātattî lô ʾet-ʿaksâ bittî lĕʾiššâ. We are not told why Caleb could not himself storm Qiryat-sefer (Debir). Is it because his allotted territory was limited to the area around Hebron? It is also not at all evident that Caleb is offering the brave soldier who attacks and defeats Qiryat-sefer more than a bond forged through marriage, although a number of commentators assume that the fallen city was also part of the prize. (Saul thinks it is enough to offer a daughter for killing Philistines; 1 Sam 18:17.) Here we must make a distinction between the anecdote's internal logic and coherence (holding the information necessary for its explanation) and its meaning and import when set within a narrative (for which, see the Comments). That the story was favored among Hebrews can be gathered not only from its repetition (almost verbatim) in two contexts, but from the need of the Chronicler to devote to Achsah an entry in his genealogical list. The incident might also have invited emulation, as when the Chronicler has David offer a choice position to anyone capturing Jebusite Jerusalem (1 Chr 11:4–8). Still, commenting on Gen 24:13, the Midrash *Genesis Rabbah* (60:3) was not pleased with Caleb's promise: "Four asked improperly: three were granted their request in a fitting manner, and the fourth, in an unfitting manner. They are: 'Eliezer' (Abraham's servant), Caleb, Saul, and Jephthah." The four had needlessly initiated vows when God was certain to deliver on promises. We shall visit Jephthah's case soon.

The name of Caleb's daughter, Achsah, is derived from an ornament, as was for Zillah and Adah, daughters of Lamech (Gen 4:19).[26] It is harmless, though not necessary, to make a connection between the meaning of the name and the playfulness that Achsah will soon display. The issue is complicated by the Greek versions, in which there is metathesis into Asca. The rabbis (*bTemurah* 16a; see Brockhaus 2011) explained the name through a pun: Achsah was so beautiful that whoever saw her got angry (root: *kʿs*) at his own wife. Who knows whether these sages were serious? It is also harmless to presume that she was an adolescent. Yet, women in the ancient Near East married at all stages of life, and especially when of elite or wealth status, found attractive mates even when divorced or widowed. Still, it is hardly useful to find for Achsah a parallel in the goddess Anat, allegedly for a shared petulance (Niditch 2008: 41).

1 13. Othniel makes his debut in this anecdote, as reported in Joshua and here. The name *'otnî'ēl* is given as Γοθονιηλ in Greek ("Othonihel" in the Vulgate) and so suggests that the initial phoneme was a *ghayin* rather than a *'ayin*. It is natural to take the name as a nominal sentence of the type "my *x* is El," and so does Zadok (1988: 54). He connects it to an Amorite root, **ḥutn-*, rendering it "God/El is my strength." The orthography of the name, however, masks many other potential meanings. An argument has been made to treat it as a verbal sentence, with an "Edomite" verbal root, **ġvṭ*, and a first-person accusative suffix, and so "God has helped me" (Sima 2001). The hunt for a plausible etymology is likely to continue for generations.

There is discrepancy in the information about Othniel as given in Josh 15:17 and Judg 1:13, in that the latter is more detailed. In both, Othniel is said to be *ben-qĕnaz 'aḥî kālēb*. Since Caleb is known as the son of Jephunneh or of Hezron (or even of Hur) but never of Kenaz, the assumption is that the brother of Caleb is Kenaz and not Othniel.[27] In Hebraic lore, Kenaz is associated with Edomite tribal groups (Gen 36 and elsewhere) that were eventually absorbed into Judah.[28] What "brother" means in this context has been discussed in the literature, some scholars not satisfied to read it as a kinship term. Thus, on the basis of an (alleged) Mari usage, Boling (1975: 56) rather incongruously thinks that *'aḥ* should refer to a "military confederate."[29] There are also term discrepancies in the Greek versions, and this has encouraged some scholars to offer some convoluted proposals (see, for example, Lindars 1995: 28).

So, Othniel is Caleb's nephew, and Judg 1:13 merely adds *haqqāṭōn mimmennû*, "younger than him," probably to widen the age gap between Othniel and the aged Caleb. Luckily, not much rides on Othniel's true affiliation (see also below at 3:9–10) and we move to the anecdote, a remarkably layered story taking up just four verses. But contrary to Albright (1968: 42–43, followed by Boling 1975: 56), there is nothing poetic about any of them. (If vv. 14–15 can be made metrical, then nothing else is safe for prose.) Albright had sought to give the anecdote antiquity because it is poetic, a very questionable premise no less than application.

Achsah's Dare

1 14. *vayyĕhî bĕbô'â*. Here we must imagine a cortège bringing the bride to the groom, as is occasionally attested in the documents involving elite marriages (the Targum uses *mê'ālâ*, "coming in"; W. Smelik 1995: 338).[30] We are told this detail to sharpen Achsah's will, perhaps also her chutzpah, in making demands even before she has had time to enter her new life.

vattĕsîtēhû liš'ōl mē'ēt-'ābîhā haśśādê (*śādê* in Joshua). From Caleb a specific field is being asked; but there is some debate about who is doing the asking, not just because there are discrepancies between the Greek and the Hebrew "parallel" versions of the episode in Josh 15 and Judg 1, but also because of differences within the Greek manuscript traditions. In some of them, Achsah directly solicits her father for the land; in others (such as Rahlfs B, where his name is explicitly inserted), Othniel asks his bride to do so.[31] Naturally, the reading of each version would require us to interpret differently what transpired, the Greek (possibly influenced by Hellenistic culture) generally restricting Achsah's motivation and initiative. For our purposes, it is convenient to concentrate on the Hebrew version of events.

The Hebrew verb at stake (*svt*; for which, see G. Wallis in *TDOT* 10: 207–10) is itself fairly well-represented in Scripture, always occurring in the Hiphil. Most often, it describes individuals steering others into acts that are unacceptable (such as worshipping false gods, Deut 13:7), foolish (such as undertaking a doomed campaign, 2 Chr 18:2), or untraditional (such as misappropriating property, 1 Kgs 21:25). As it happens, when the consequences of this incitement are recorded, they tend to be negative, but the verb itself is neutral about the intentions of subjects, as happens in our case. Interestingly, the Targum has a verbal form that also is quite neutral, *mĕlaktê*, "she advised him," but there are other readings too (see W. Smelik 1995: 339).[32]

In urging Othniel to request a field from her father, Achsah is prodding her groom to go beyond the family bonds established by marriage.[33] We need to recognize here that a number of sectors come together to form a town. Located within a walled area are a stronghold (*migdāl*), several streets (*šûq*), several living quarters (*ḥûṣôt*), and a gate or gates (*šaʿar*), fronted by an open area (*rĕḥōb*). Beyond this fortified area, however, there were cultivated fields (*śādê*), pastureland (*migrāš*), outlying districts (*ḥāṣēr*), encampments (*ṭîrâ*), and diverse water resources, including springs, wells, cisterns, streams, and, rarely, canals (see Frick 1978: 78–91). It is possible to have diverse sectors of a city under different control. We recall that when Hebron was conquered, Caleb was left in control of its fields and the outlying districts (*ʾet-śĕdēh hāʿîr veʾet ḥăṣērêhā*) but not of the walled area or the surrounding pasturelands (*ʾet-qiryat ʾarbaʿ. . . . veʾet migrāšêhā sĕbîbōtêhā*) (Josh 21:11–12).

So at the urging of Achsah, Othniel is emboldened to request a field (but how large?) from Caleb, whether as part of the dowry is not made clear. It is also left unclear whether the field is one Caleb controlled around Hebron or one from the Debir (Qiryat-sefer) region.[34] Although this lack of information may disturb the historian in us, it has no consequence for unraveling the rest of the story. From the rest of the verse, however, we have the impression that her father fulfilled his son-in-law's request.

Othniel may have had his qualms about his bride's instruction, for Achsah boldly turned to her father. Yet, they treat each other ambiguously. We are told that when *vattiṣnaḥ mēʿal haḥămôr* her father asked her, *māh-llāk*. The phrase is brief (also in Greek, τί ἐστίν σοι), and while it literally means "what + for you," in Hebrew literature it carries many shades of meaning:

—"What do you want?" asks David of Bathsheba as she comes to warn him about Adonijah (1 Kgs 1:16)
—"What troubles you?" or "What is the problem?" asks the angel solicitously of Hagar (Gen 21:17; see also 2 Sam 14:5, 2 Kgs 6:28, Esth 5:3, Ps 114:5)
—"What good does it do you?" Israel is asked sarcastically when seeking Egypt's help (Jer 2:18)
—"How dare you?" God berates the nervy wicked (Ps 50:16)

But for us the most relevant nuance for *māh-llāk* may occur in Judg 18:23–24, when the armed men of Dan, stunned by Micah's temerity in pursuing them, ask him, "How could you be so foolish as to have rallied (your men)?" (*māh-llĕkā kî nizʿāqtā*). Something of the same response occurs in Isa 22:1 (the prophet lambasts a doomed Jerusalem for rejoicing) and in Jonah 1:6 (the navigator is shocked at an oblivious Jonah). In our anecdote, Caleb seems not to be asking after the welfare of his daughter nor is he offering her his help. Rather, he is chiding her for inspiring Othniel into demanding land. But what was Achsah doing when her father was questioning her sanity?

THE DONKEY

Whatever Achsah was doing, it was done *(mē)ʿal haḥămôr*, "from a donkey's back"—so while either riding or dismounting the animal. Although riding donkeys is a sign of elite behavior (already so in Amorite culture, and see below at 5:10), I do not think that this motif is at stake here.[35] For reasons not yet clear to me, however, whenever narratives have cause to mention the riding of donkeys (the contexts for horses tend to be military), they discriminate between the male (*ḥămôr*) and the female (*ʾātôn*) of the species.[36] A nice anecdote involves the jenny that teaches Balaam a lesson about the presence of God (Num 22); and a whole story about David's marriage to Abigail, widow of the brutish Nabal (a Caleb descendant!), is choreographed within two donkey rides (1 Sam 25).

What Achsah was doing, however, is hidden by the phrase *vattiṣnaḥ min-*, occurring only in this episode as told in Joshua and Judges. Another idiom involving the same verb but a different preposition (and hence often wrongly treated as the same) occurs at Judg 4:21, where Jael, using a hammer to drive a peg into Sisera's temple, forces it into the ground (*vattiṣnaḥ bĕ-*). In this last context, the image is derived from setting up a tent. But in our anecdote, it is not at all clear what Achsah was up to. The matter has puzzled since antiquity, leaving its trace on the versions (nicely reviewed in Barthélemy 1982 and Lindars 1995: 29–31). The Targum has *vĕʾitrĕkênat mēʿal*, "she dismounted," which seems reasonable enough. But the LXX has many readings, some of them rather expansive, all allowing Achsah to get her father's attention: καὶ ἐγόγγυζεν καὶ ἔκραξεν ἀπὸ τοῦ ὑποζυγίου, "she grumbled and cried out from her draft animal" in Judg 1:14; καὶ ἐβόησεν ἐκ τοῦ ὄνου, "she yelled from her donkey," in Josh 15:18.[37] Some rabbinic texts, in fact, convey a like notion,[38] as do renderings that translate (dependent on a dubious use of Arabic) "she clapped her hands" (Soggin 1981a: 22; Jost 1997; Bal 1988a: 146–55).[39] It is plausible to imagine, as found in other narratives (Abigail before David, 1 Sam 15:23; the woman of Shunem before Elisha, 2 Kgs 4:22–27), that she dismounted her donkey to fall at the feet of her father (Klein 1999: 24–25); seeking favor from a powerful man, Abigail curtsies to David immediately after she dismounts (1 Sam 25:23). A notorious and heavily critiqued suggestion by G. Driver (1957: 75–76, picked up in the New English Bible [NEB] and Authorized Version [AV]) has a contemptuous Achsah farting loudly enough to catch Caleb's attention, with comic potential.[40]

When all is said and done, however, we are left to our own devices to imagine what Achsah was doing on/from her donkey when she entered into discussion with her father. Luckily, our ignorance of her activity compromises our appreciation neither of the request from her father nor the wit with which she couched it.

THE REQUEST

1 15. *vattōʾmer lô hābâ-llî bĕrākâ*, "She answered him, 'Give me a gift.'" The parallel Joshua passage has minor differences: the absence of *lô*, "to him," and *tĕnâ-llî*, "give me," rather than *hābâ-llî*, the latter a rarer idiom. The verb **yhb* is often cited as Aramaic, when it is better to observe that in Hebrew its attestation is limited to the imperative, most of the contexts suggesting an urgency to the demand (as in Gen 29:21, 30:1, and 47:15). Occasionally, the request is also coarsely shaded, as in Prov 30:15, "The leech has two daughters, 'Give, give!' [*hav hav*]." I have opted to render it by the slightly unidiomatic, but also parasonantic, "Hand me!," a phrase that might well carry a pregnant meaning, as we shall soon observe. *Běrākâ*, "blessing," is well-attested in the sense of "present, gift" (Gen 33:11, where it plays on both meanings; 1 Sam 30:26; 2 Kgs 5:15), especially when consisting of edible material. As object of the verb *nātan* (in the Niphal), *běrākâ* also occurs in 1 Sam 25:27. While I translate it in our passage as "present," I acknowledge that Achsah may well have also sought a blessing, and so there may be a genuine double meaning here, as in Gen 33:11. Still another pun may also be at stake in that if vocalized *běrēkâ* the word means "pond, water reservoir" (Eccl 2:6, Song 7:5) (so, with Ehrlich 1968: 46 and Hallo 2004: 333).

kî 'ereṣ hannegeb nětattānî cannot be translated "for you have given Negev land to me" or the like (KJV, New Jerusalem Bible [NJB], Boling 1975), for which one would expect something like **nātattā (l)lî*, as in the clause immediately following (minus the conversive *vav*).[41] As far as the anecdote is concerned (and despite the mention of the "Negev of Caleb" in 1 Sam 30:14), Caleb has no business offering his daughter anything, let alone land unrelated to the conquest of Qiryat-sefer. Inspired by the Greek ὅτι εἰς γῆν νότου ἐκδέδοσαί με ("because you have set/assigned me in the south land"), a number of translations give a less implausible "since you have set me in the land of the Negev";[42] but here too, one would likely need *kî *bě'ereṣ hannegeb nětattānî*. But what would the happy couple be doing in the Negev?

The verbal form in our clause, which features the perfect of *nātan* with a personal suffix, is nicely represented in the Hebrew Bible. Psalms 118:18 reads, "The LORD has severely punished me, but did not hand me over to Death" (*vělammāvet lō' nětānānî*) (similarly, Ps 124:6, Lam 1:13–14, and other examples with the imperfect). They uniformly give the impression of someone doing something to someone else, and this understanding is nicely reflected in the Tanakh translation of our phrase, "You have given me away as Negev-land." I have adopted it.

WATER SOURCES

In asking for *gullōt mayim* Achsah is at once specific and vague. The word *gullâ*, plural *gullôt*, normally refers to a basin or bowl; but it goes back to a root (**gll*) that describes rolling or heaping, and it is not just from Caleb's response that we conclude that she was asking for water resources rather than a water vessel (but see the Comments below).[43] This is bolstered by the contrast Achsah is drawing on the "Negev," an arid region, as well as on a potential pun on the *běrākâ* (see above). But in what form this water was stored is so unclear that the Targum gives it simply as *'ătar bêtšiqyâ' děmayā'*, "a watering place." Greek translators were also mystified. In the Joshua version of the passage they simply transliterated (Γολαθμαιν), and in Judges they read a form of the verb **g'l* (λύτρωσιν ὕδατος "a [singular!] redemption of water"). In Israel, water was drawn from rivers, lakes, and springs, and aquiferous water was reached through shafts; but it could also be rainwater collected in reservoirs, cisterns, wells, or even basins or bowls.

Whatever Achsah was requesting, her father responded with a set of them. For unknown reasons, in Judges (but not in Joshua) many Greek manuscripts add κατὰ τὴν καρδίαν αὐτῆς, "as per her heart," that is, as she wished. The phrase may well have been supplied by the Greek translator, but if it had been original to some of the Hebrew texts, then the suggestion (adopted by Boling 1975: 57) that it presupposes *klbh (with a fetching pun on Caleb's name) is plausible despite Lindars's objection (1995: 32).

The problem is what to do with the gifts that Caleb granted his daughter. That they are place names Upper and Lower Gullot (rather than, say, water-retaining objects) is suggested by the absence of articles on the attribute, in this case "upper/lower" (*'illît/ taḥtît*) (see GKC 409–10 [§126y]). There is a discrepancy in how these attributes are handled in the parallel versions of the anecdote. In Judges, *'illît/ taḥtît* is a singular noun, suggesting that *gullōt*, whatever its original meaning, was deemed a singular.[44] For this reason Moore (1895: 30) suggests that the word should end in *-at*, as do many place names (Zephat, Baalat, etc.). This would reinforce the notion that the gift to Achsah was land rather than pools of water; and if this is so, then whether we locate Debir near water basins, underground reservoirs (and so at Tell Beit Mirsim), or cisterns (and so at Khirbet Rabûd) may in fact be an irrelevant criterion.[45]

COMMENTS

In this segment of Judg 1 we have inspected but a few verses, yet a number of matters are raised by what they report. We first wonder about the kind of intention that provokes a Hebrew narrator to record two sets of names for conquered towns. In this section, for example, Hebron and Debir are said to have once gone under the names of Qiryat-arba and Qiryat-sefer (elsewhere also even Qiryat-sannâ). This phenomenon occurs readily in Scripture, and we shall meet with a number of examples in Judges.[46] It must not, however, be confused with (1) renaming conquered places after ancestors (for example, Dan and Nobah), (2) citing the new but not the old names (as in Num 32:38), (3) attaching to them the name of the leader who fortified them (for example, Gibeat Shaul), or (4) establishing a particular etiology (Beer lehai-ro'i, Gen 16:14; Esek, Gen 26:20). Nor is it similar to places that are given variants (a number in Gen 14, among them "Valley of Shaveh, that is, Valley of the King," Gen 14:17), equivalence in different languages (for example, "Jegar-sahadutha" [Aramaic], Gal-ed [Hebrew], the latter also called Mitzpah, Gen 31:47–48), or doubling (for example, Adami-[han]Nekeb in Josh 19:33).[47]

Variance in Naming Places

Biblical narratives are so generous in dispensing examples for the preservation of before and after for place names that we may be lulled into imagining its prevalence in other Near Eastern lore. Until the Hellenistic period when the Macedonians and later the Romans took control of the region, most places in the Levant retained their names for centuries, even if occupied by folks from different ethnic or linguistic affiliation. (Romans might rename cities to perpetuate lessons. For example, in the wake of the Bar Kokhba revolt Hadrian renamed Jerusalem [*Colonia*] *Aelia Capitolina*, after his family and Jupiter.) Economic and judicial documents avoided registering differences in names lest it muddle the circumstances, creating potential legal difficulties later on.[48] In their monuments and annals, kings imagined having founded cities when they renamed them and would register their ancient name only if they persisted in local usage. Adad-nirari II (around 900 BCE) talks of attacking "Gidara, which the Arameans call Raqamatu" (Radammatu a few lines later) (see RIMA 2: 150). Reporting on his third-year campaigns (for example, at RIMA 3/2: 19, 64, 74), Shalmaneser III speaks of (Ana-)Aššur-utēr-aṣbat, a town allegedly "founded" by his ancestor Tiglath-pileser I. But the local population continued to call it Pit(tu)ru/a more than a century later. We know of one town, Masuwari, that was given an Aramaic name (Til-Barsip) before the Assyrians renamed it Kar-Shalmaneser (see Hawkins 1983).

This is not at all what obtains in the Hebrew narratives, where, as far as we can tell, the cited original name seldom had a long life. Moreover, there is even reason to doubt the narrator's knowledge of name changes. For example, Jerusalem was called Urusalim centuries before the Hebrews took it over. As far as we can tell, it never had a name remotely like Jebus (Judg 19:10–11, 1 Chr 11:4), forcing us to base it on inhabitants not documented beyond the Bible. While the absence of evidence cannot be a criterion from which to decide the reliability of narrators (Hebrews or others), nevertheless we can cautiously suggest that in insisting on recording two names for the same locale, the Hebrew was interested less in preserving history than in keeping his readers or audience focused on a major premise of Hebrew historiography: The land that was promised was not a wasteland, to be occupied without resistance; rather, it was a choice land that had given much prosperity and stability to those inhabiting it previously. Names such as Qiryat-sefer and Qiryat-arba (however we translate them) are comments on that success, but they are also reminders to the Hebrews of the tough choices God made in delivering that land to them. It follows that the anecdotes are also exhortations to remain worthy of that choice.

The Achsah Episode

We are also struck by how suddenly the divinely inspired marches of warriors ceased, shifting focus to a drama of wills. Much has been written recently about the Achsah episode. Some have dealt with the grammatical problems associated with the story (Mosca 1984), mostly along the lines discussed in the Notes. Others have imaginatively mined the differences between the Joshua and Judges accounts (Fewell 1995; Marais 1998: 78–79) or discussed its potential satiric purpose (Bledstein 1993). There is interest also on how the story of Achsah unlocks the structure of a book in which women are prominently featured (for example, Lanoir 1997), promoting a vision of women in Hebrew Scripture that may be symbolic (Klein 1988: 173) and socially more balanced (Jost 1997; Klein 1993a: 25; Klein 1999). Yet it seems to me that the discussions have not adequately explored what it is that Achsah ended up obtaining from her father.

Caleb vowed Achsah as a trophy to the conqueror of Qiryat-sefer (Debir). Such an offer can have happy consequences (as was the case in the Egyptian tale of *The Doomed Prince*), but it can also turn sour, as was the case when Saul's Michal first sided with her husband before losing respect for him. In this story, however, matters turned out fine, and Othniel was lucky in acquiring land and bride. Yet, this is essentially a heroic view of how things are done, for marriages, if based solely on the premise of bravery or chivalry, are bound to falter—think of the problems Michal's marriage created for David no less than for Saul. For such marriages to survive healthily in a world in which polygyny, concubinage, and divorce ride on the whim of male elites, they needed to be bolstered by measures that make the bride valuable, not just to her father and husband, but to herself as well. How Achsah managed to buttress a potentially tenuous marriage is the burden of this episode.

If we proceed (as we should) from the conviction that a story must deliver in its verses all the elements for its decipherment, we are left to imagine that Othniel was to receive nothing besides the hand of Achsah. Admittedly, Achsah was no mean prize as she would have given him entry to the family of Caleb, an old warrior who personally knew Moses and Joshua and who had earned God's gratitude by confirming the wisdom of promising Canaan. The anecdote does not dwell on Othniel (it will do so a bit later), but here attention is all on Achsah and her schemes.

It is well to remember that marriages, especially among the elite, were occasions for multiple gift-givings, the two most basic among them being the "bridewealth" (*mōhār*), which is the groom's gift to his father-in-law, and the "dowry" (*šillûḥîm*), which is the father's gift to his daughter. In Mesopotamia and elsewhere, among the elite the two gifts tended to approximate each other in value. In addition to jewelry, dowries included many items that were practical—pots and pans, furniture, maidservants.[49] There could also be gifts by the groom to the bride and, according to Mari documents, gifts for the bride's mother and brothers (see Sasson 2006a, on Gen 24).

According to the version in the Hebrew of Judges (by no means duplicated in the Greek accountings and in those of Joshua in either language), Achsah resolves to remedy the situation on two fronts. She first incites her (future) husband to request arable land from her father. Such gifts are not usual in cultures that hoard land for male descendants (the story of Zelophehad's daughters gives relevant testimony, Num 27 and 36); yet the shifting of land to a daughter given as bride is known among rulers of antiquity, as when Pharaoh gives Gaza in dowry to his daughter (1 Kgs 9:16).[50] It must be understood that the land would belong to the bride, and ultimately to her children from the union; but as long as there is a marriage, it is added to the husband's holding. In fact, the shifting of substantial land as part of a marriage agreement can guarantee continuity for a marriage, as husbands are reluctant to give up its control by initiating a divorce. Furthermore, as we learned from the fate of Mari princesses (see above), the stronger their espousal of their husband's causes, the more secure their status is likely to be. This may be why Caleb, though miffed by Achsah's connivance ("What's with you?"), was likely open to the request she failed to inspire Othniel into making.

We also realize that philology makes it unlikely that Achsah herself was assigned any land, in the Negev or elsewhere (see the Notes to v. 15), an observation that allows us to turn to the second of Achsah's demands; this one, she herself presses on her father. She softens any potential resistance by assuming an accusatory tone: You have treated me as wasteland, she tells him. Her reproach must certainly have stung Caleb, for he had offered nothing to the victor but her hand. Her demand deliciously recaps the words her father had used when he bartered her (v. 12: *věnātattî lô . . . . lěʾiššâ*; v. 15: *věnātattâ lî gullōt mayim*). She asks for "basins of water." Whether or not she had in mind vessels with which to transport water (not unknown in lists of dowries for brides) need only pique our curiosity. Her father (and the readers of Judges) understood her request geopolitically. As a result, Achsah and her lucky husband, Othniel, benefited much from the quick wit displayed in Hebrew lore yet again by a woman.

3. Chariots of Iron (Judg 1:16–21)

1 ¹⁶The descendants of the Kenite, the father-in-law of Moses, marched with those of Judah from the City of Palms to the wilderness of Judah, in the Negev of Arad. Having gone there, he settled among the inhabitants. ¹⁷Judah went with Simeon his brother and they attacked the Canaanites dwelling in Zephat. They vowed it for *ḥērem*-obliteration, so that the town was called Hormah. ¹⁸Judah captured Gaza and its territory, Ashkelon and its territory, and Ekron and its territory. ¹⁹The Lord was with Judah, so he took over the hill country; but displacing the people of the plain was not to happen, for they had chariots of iron. ²⁰Hebron was given to Caleb, as Moses had promised, from there expelling all three Anak descendants. ²¹As to the Jebusites dwelling in Jerusalem, Benjamin could not displace them; so the Jebusites have shared Jerusalem with Benjamin to this day. ס

NOTES
Introductory Remarks: Holy Wars[1]

Wars are conducted for many reasons. But when nations reflect on why they entered them, few will offer more than one side of the story or admit to a lack of justification. When rehearsed in a retelling of the past in which deities are major shapers, wars are said to be successful because gods (or God) will them to be so. In fact, most conflicts in antiquity made room for the gods: divination shaped military strategies; prayers, sacrifices, and rituals emboldened fighters; and divine statues or emblems (for Israel an ark) accompanied armed hosts. In this sense, the majority of aggressive conflicts rehearsed in Scripture (and for that matter in Near Eastern annals and hymns) may be labeled "holy wars."[2] The crucial ingredient, however, is what is done with their spoils.

Wars result in much loss and destruction, but also often in much plunder, and the benefit from those spoils (land, slaves, animals, goods) is reason for leaders and soldiers to take their chance on long journeys and risky undertakings. A king of Qatna tells his son-in-law, Yasmaḥ-Addu of Mari: "Time is propitious for your coming up here. Feed your troops spoils so they will bless you. These three towns are hardly fortified and we can take them in one day" (ARM 5 16 = LAPO 17 #443, p. 11). Division of the loot, especially among the elite and their allies, is highly choreographed, with brutal consequences for defaulters; but no ally is more demanding of shares than the divinity guaranteeing a victory. This is so in all cultures from antiquity, and Israel partook of most of the same institutions. Because Israel has told its story as one of election, of divine involvement in its battles, and of delivering a Promised Land, one of its major components is the right of God to demand (and impose) a division of spoils that may seem unbalanced or one-sided.

This is the *ḥērem*, the irrevocable devolution to God of most or all plunder from one campaign. The practice compromises all possibility of exchange (of captured soldiers, inhabitants, and booty) or of securing loyalty on the basis of a victor's generosity, themselves major features of postwar activities in antiquity. The imbalance between delivering what is owed a god and keeping what fighters think they earned can be a source of traditions, such as how Israel's conquest was almost stopped at Ai (Josh 7) and how Saul lost his kingship (1 Sam 15).[3] Yet, in the many wars reported in Scripture, it is not often clear why some result in *ḥērem* and most do not; the level of divine participation in any war was hardly ever the major incentive.

The process for *ḥērem* can be expressed by means of the causative (1 Chr 26:27) and factitive (Jer 6:4, Joel 4:9 [3:9 RSV], Mic 3:5) of the verb *qdš*, to "dedicate, sanctify." Most often, however, it is expressed through the causative of *ḥrm*, "to consecrate something or someone" to God. As it applies to war contexts, what is delivered to God may differ: It could include all living beings, but exclude female virgins; it could include movable property (animals and goods), but not always. While the enemy in distant lands must be given the chance to accept enslavement (Deut 20:10–20), those from the seven nations whose lands Israel was to occupy (Hittites, Girgashites, Amorites, Canaanites, Perizzites, Hivvites, and Jebusites) are expressly set for obliteration.[4] Wars against these "nations" are launched by God, but they can also start when men take a vow, so involving God (Num 21:1–3; perhaps also Judg 1:17). Yet, some towns that experience the severest of punishments—such as Laish (Judg 18:27) and Bethel (Judg 1:25)—are not said to be in *ḥērem*. As we shall see, several of the battles reported in Judges are fought personally by the Hebrew God, but they too are not treated as *ḥērem*.

Inconsistent sources no less than modern sensibility have kept pertinent a number of issues about the *ḥērem* and its place in Israel's history. The practice could not have originated just when Israel began to write, yet scholars have sought to chart its evolution from within our inherited texts. Weinfeld (1988, 1993) is among those who offer a rather precise development, depending on the verbs used in diverse textual layers (*grš* in JE; Hiphil of *yrš* in P; Hiphil of *ḥrm* in D). This sequence allows him (as it does others) to conveniently declare the practice as enunciated in Deuteronomy as unrealistic and "utopian," a relief to readers of Scripture who find its savagery disconcerting.[5] Scholars who claim with some justification to find evidence for a holy war in neighboring lands often force precision on the comparison by adopting an elastic definition of its application (M. Smith 1995), or they compile the evidence from literary documents in which ideology and vibrancy trump historical accuracy (Niccacci 1982, regarding Egypt). Sometimes, a connection with the Hebrew *ḥērem* is invested into ancient sources whenever towns are turned into wasteland or space is vowed to a deity (Del Monte 2005, regarding Hittite practices). What remains lacking is often a divine injunction to make them so.

The best control on whether or not the *ḥērem* was a realistic institution, however, must come from the records of martial activities by Israel's neighbors. Given that literary texts (hymns and annals) construct war as mirroring cosmic events and craft combat as testing the resolve (and faith) of leaders, we must be wary when turning to them for comparative insights.[6] For example, we read in a ninth-century BCE Moabite inscription that King Mesha butchered the Hebrew populations of two conquered towns. It fits the genre, however, when the same text says that Hebrew prisoners were set to work on Mesha's building projects.[7]

More useful for assessing the reality of holy wars would be references in nonliterary texts, such as administrative documents and letters. The Mari archives are well-endowed with such material, and scholars have mined their contents. A few references to the *asakkum* (normally a demon, here possibly an herb, but understood to mean "taboo" when associated with gods and kings) seem to refer to objects that are set aside for gods, so that "eating the *asakkum*" meant "violating a taboo." Following B. Landsberger, Malamat (lastly 1989) developed the correspondences between the Mari and Hebrew material. But his interpretation has been criticized from the Hebrew side by Greenberg (1993). Moreover, from the Akkadian side, it looks like the concept is closer to an ordeal than to a divine edict.[8]

The latest study to find *ḥērem* aspects in the Mari records (Guichard 1999) also cites earlier research. In the records, there are allusions to gods inspiring leaders to war and supporting the efforts of warriors. There are references to demands from the gods for booty and prisoners, and there is information about deliveries of spoils to them or to their temples.[9] An individual who partook of booty reserved for one god was unmasked and fined (ARM 5 72 = LAPO 17 #462, pp. 37–39), but unlike Achan (Josh 7), he and his family escaped the ultimate punishment. There is the sense that unexpected deaths can be due to gods who were robbed of consecrated objects (ARM 26 280). Relatively few, but nevertheless known, are examples of the mass killing of soldiers, the murder of all males of a conquered village, and the total devastation of a town. Yet such episodes are not tied to divine commands.

When all is said and done, nothing from daily records, of Mari or elsewhere, gives evidence to fully parallel the Hebrew *ḥērem*, in which God is said to inspire combats that end in a complete liquidation of spoils. In our age of brutal devastations, yet also of sensitivity to human misery, we are likely to continue pondering the reality behind such events as the annihilation of Hormah and the instructions on the *ḥērem* as detailed in Deuteronomy, the last a highly motivational tractate that addresses a people whose opportunity and resources to fulfill the goals of a *ḥērem* had become severely restricted.

Allies

1 16. *ûbĕnê qênî ḥōtēn mōšê.* *Qênî* is a gentilic adjective, referring to a "Kenite," and as such would normally have had an article, as is the case for about a dozen scriptural attestations, a number of which we shall meet in Judges (4:11, 17; 5:24). Still, another anomalous attestation cautions against hasty emendations.[10] 1 Samuel 15:6 tells us that after Saul alerted the Kenites to move out from Amalek territory, lest they too suffer his attacks, "the Kenite pulled away from Amalek [*vayyāsar qênî mittôk 'ămālēq*]." Somewhat similar is the case of *ḥōrî* in Gen 36:22 (1 Chr 1:39).

A *ḥōtēn/ḥātān* is a man related to another by marriage, so father-, brother-, or son-in-law. (The same ambiguity is attached to the Greek γαμβρός and πενθερός.) Because we are told that the *qênî* was a *ḥōtēn* of Moses, in antiquity most versions found it useful to insert the name of someone who is reckoned as a Kenite, but they differed in their selection. One Greek manuscript (Rahlfs B) connects it with Jethro, known as the father of Zipporah in Exod 3:1 (also as Reuel in Exod 2:18) and gives οἱ υἱοὶ Ιοθορ τοῦ Κειναιου τοῦ γαμβροῦ Μωυσέως, "the sons of Jothor [= Jethro], the Kenite, Moses's father-in-law." Rahlfs A, however, took its cue from what is later said in Judg 4:11 about a Hobab, kin (but not clear how) to Moses, and so has οἱ υἱοὶ Ιωβαβ τοῦ Κιναίου πενθεροῦ Μωυσῆ. In Num 10:29, we are told about a "Hobab son of Reuel, the Midianite, *ḥōtēn mōšê*," which can be rendered either as father-in-law or brother-in-law of Moses, depending on how we parse the sentence and vocalize the relevant word.

Similar ambiguity exists in Rahlfs A. The Targum goes its own way with *ûbĕnê šalmāʾâ ḥāmûhî dĕmōšê*, "the sons of Shalmaʾa, father-in-law of Moses." Shalmaʾa was the north Arabian tribe identified in the Hellenistic period with the Kenites.[11]

KENITES

Who the Kenites were is difficult to resolve, as Hebrew lore about them is not always harmonious. In the covenant God makes with Abram (Gen 15), the Kenites (and two other people sharing *qôf*, *nûn*, and *yôd* in their names) are listed among the ten nations promised to his descendants, and so they were involuntarily cursed by Balaam, who linked them with the Amalekites (Num 24:21–22; see 1 Sam 15:4–6). But in Num 10: 29–32, Moses offers Hobab of Midian (who may have been a Kenite) a share in the Promised Land if he helps the Hebrews negotiate the wilderness.[12] And our verse implies cooperation between the Kenites and Judah.

Well into the twentieth century, scholars wove imaginatively on the fate and influence of the Kenites. It does not help that we have no extrabiblical records on them, although some Nabatean and Sabean personal names are coined on verbal roots they hold in common. Numerous speculations have arisen concerning them: (1) that they were deemed itinerant smiths, because the root **qyn* in Arabic and in some Aramaic dialects may be connected to metalwork, because smiths are featured among Cain's descendants, and because Middle Kingdom Egyptian tomb paintings display nomads with anvils (contra Kalimi 1980, 1988); (2) that they inspired the Hebrews to monotheism, because of Jethro's influence on Moses and because of their alleged influence on the Rechabites (see B. Mazar 1965; McNutt 1994); and (3) that they were attached to the Midianites (because of Jethro, priest of Midian, reckoned as a *ḥanîf*, a pagan with monotheistic convictions), the Amalekites (see 1 Sam 15:6), and the Rechabites (1 Chr 2:55; see Knights 1993). We shall come back to them (at Judg 4:11ff.) when discussing Jael and Sisera. Suffice it to say here that our passage implies an alliance with Judah.

ʿālû mēʿîr hattĕmārîm definitely implies that the journey began from the "City of Palms." Both Deut 34:3 and 2 Chr 28:15 use the City of Palms as epithet of Jericho. While Greek renderings (ἐκ [τῆς] πόλεως τῶν φοινίκων) do not differ from the Hebrew, the Targum simply gives it as *qartāʾ yĕrîḥô*, "Jericho Town." Earlier scholars have nevertheless looked to place it elsewhere, most often at the Tamar ("Date Palm") of Ezek 47:19 and 48:28 (see Moore 1895: 33 and the review of the literature in Gass 2005: 30–40). Aharoni (1979: 215) thinks of Zoar at the southern tip of the Dead Sea, since in the Talmud (*mYevamot* 16.7) it is called "City of Palms." But we shall soon meet with another reference (Judg 3:13) that makes just north of the Dead Sea seem the best location for this town.

The specific region of the Wilderness of Judah cited as *midbar yĕhûdâ ʾăšer bĕnegev ʿărād* lies west of the Dead Sea, sandwiched between the hills and the Negev of Judah. The region is forbidding but not beyond settling, as we are told of a number of towns within a wilderness, likely of Judah (Josh 15:61–62). David escaped Saul there (Ps 63:1, regarding 1 Sam 22–24), and close by John the Baptist found spiritual reinforcement (Matt 3:1; see also Matt 4 for an account of Jesus's time there).

Arad was reputedly destroyed by Joshua (Josh 12:14), in partial payment for the success its king had had against the Hebrews as they wandered in the desert (Num 21:1). But that passage continues to say that the Hebrews destroyed the town, calling it Hormah ("Rubbles"), one of many bearing this name (see below). Yet, the king of Arad was still there to hound them later (Num 33:40). While excavations at modern Tell Arad have yielded documents that confirm that it held the same name in antiquity, stratigraphic problems have led some scholars to locate Canaanite Arad elsewhere in the region, based on the literature for the candidacy of several tells (el-Milḥ, Masos, and Ira), all within kilometers of each other. For our purpose, therefore, we need not be more precise than that.

Our problem, however, is syntactic. Is the verse telling us that the Kenites accompanied the Judeans to the Wilderness of Judah and settled there with them, the region being called the "Negev of Arad"?[13] Or must we transpose its clauses to obtain something like the NJPS's "and they went and settled among the people in the Negeb of Arad"? Many proposals are based on readings from the versions (Greek gives "toward the slopes [κατάβασις = Hebrew *môrād?*] of Arad").[14] Some cut out a sequence of words (generally *yĕhûdâ ʾăšer bĕnegev*), so bringing the Kenites to the *midbar ʿărād*, "Wilderness" (rather than the Negev) "of Arad."

As to the people the Kenites joined, by adopting the implication of 1 Sam 15:6 (see above), "Amalekites" is either inserted after *vayyēšeb ʾet-hāʿām* or, following some Greek manuscripts, restored from an alleged apocopation of **bʿmlqy*, to avoid linking the commendable Kenites with the despised Amalekites (see Barthélemy 1982: 73–74). When all the above is taken into consideration, Moore (1895: 34) gives us the clearest formulation of the reconstructed verse: "Hobab the Kenite, brother-in-law of Moses went up with the Judites from Palm Town to the Wilderness of Arad. He went and dwelled with the Amalekites."[15] Here, the accent is on assimilation rather than the dispossession required of Hebrews. But if we follow Moore, we would no longer be dealing with the received Hebrew that, I claim, is reasonably understandable.

Success (Partial) for Leah Tribes

HORMAH

1 17. Mittmann (1977) gives a seamless reconstruction of 1:16–17: "The sons of Hobab, the Kenites, went up from the city of Palms . . . on the slope from Arad . . . (17) . . . and they defeated the Canaanites, who inhabited Zephath and utterly destroyed it, and named the city Hormah." But v. 17 actually rehearses information provided earlier on Judah making common cause with Simeon. It thus strives to textually leapfrog the material on Adoni-bezeq and on Achsah sandwiched between 1:4 and 1:16. If etymology is any guide (and occasionally it is), Zephat stood on a height (root **sph*, as in Mizpah). Unfortunately, we cannot be precise about it (see Gass 2005: 46–57). The place is cited just here so that we have two different Greek transcriptions of the name: Sephek (Rahlfs B) and Sepheth (Rahlfs A). A valley of Zephata, also unplaced but obviously not the same place, occurs in 2 Chr 14:9 (10 RSV). There are proposals where to site it, generally somewhere near Arad, so more or less in the same selection as we saw above, at tells el-Milḥ, Masos, Mashash, and Ira.

About Zephat's fate, we are told that Judah and Simeon *vayyaḥărîmû ʾôtāh*, one of a few occasions (another is in Num 21:2, a vow by Israel) in which the devastation of a place had not been demanded by God. We need not be told how severely it was treated, given the name it acquired. Hormah is crafted from the G (Qal) of **ḥrm* and so conveys the sense of a place that was once utterly destroyed, from assets to living creatures. (In Greek, Ἀνάθεμα, "Devoted to a Curse" [Rahlfs B], and Ἐξολέθρευσις, "Destruction" [Rahlfs A].)[16] In Hebrew narratives Hormah was the new name for a town that was so treated, and so it is applied to Arad after its ruin (Num 21:1–3, but already so named in Num 14:45 = Deut 1:44). In Josh 12:14, Hormah and Arad are listed among captured towns, so we must imagine that the list-maker had Zephat in mind. The town was allotted to Simeon (Josh 19:4, 1 Chr 4:30) but sited within Judah (Josh 15:30). It continued to exist in David's time (1 Sam 30:30).

PHILISTINE TOWNS

1 18. Gaza, Ashkelon, and Ekron are three of five confederated Philistine cities, the others being Gath and Ashdod. Each of these towns was ruled by an oligarchy headed by a *seren*, "tyrant," who controlled a number of other towns with a different degree of subordination (*ḥăṣērîm*, "villages," and *bānôt*, "suburbs"). The conquest of these three cities brings the roster of defeated towns to a fortuitous seven: Jerusalem, Hebron, Debir, Zephat, Gaza, Ashkelon, and Ekron. The accuracy of this statement about their defeat, however, is challenged by the Greek, which adds the adverb οὐκ, "not," before the verb it normally uses in Judges for the H(iphil) of *yāraš* (κληρονομέω, "gain possession of") rather than for *lākad* (normally [κατα]λαμβάνω, see below). It is possible that the Greek was mindful of other traditions, such as that the conquest of Philistia had to await David; so it is at this point, rather than in the next verse, that the listing of unconquered territory begins. Ashdod (Ἄζωτος) is even added to the cities not conquered, and so we are coming closer to agreement with what is said in Judg 3:3 (see below) and Josh 13:1–3: "When Joshua had grown old, full of years, the LORD told him, 'You have grown old, full of years; yet there is much land that has yet to be taken over. This is the country remaining: All the Philistine and Geshur regions (from Shihor, just by Egypt, to the territory of Ekron northward) is reckoned as Canaanite, so all five Philistine lords, namely of Gaza, Ashdod, Ashkelon, Gath, and Ekron, as well as the Avvim toward the south.'"

DISPOSSESSION

1 19. Hebrew is rather spare in using the phrase *vayyĕhî YHVH ʾet*-[someone]: once about Ishmael (using *ʾĕlōhîm*, Gen 21:20), twice about Joseph (Gen 39:2, 21), once about Joshua (Josh 6:27), and once (here) about Judah. The phrase initiates narratives that detail successes, and so in our context, it follows with the summary statement, "He took over the hill country."[17] Yet it must be with certain irony that this brief reference to success actually opens in the Hebrew text the rehearsal of territory that had not been conquered.

kî lōʾ lĕhôrîš. The syntax of the negative adverb followed by an infinitive construct is unusual but is found also elsewhere (BDB 518b), yielding a sense of "must not" or "cannot," for example, 1 Chr 15:2: "David then said, 'The ark of God must not be carried except by the Levites.'" The intent, then, is to tell us not about Judah's failure, but about the limits imposed on his conquest. For this reason, we should not imagine that originally the phrase read **kî lōʾ yākōl lĕhôrîš*, "[Judah] could not supplant," as proposed by Burney (1970: 19) and others (Mullen 1984: 50 n. 59).[18]

The verb at stake, *yāraš*, occurs about two dozen times in Judges, a third of them in this and the following section, as well as another third in Jephthah's reflection on Sihon's fate (at 11:19–28). In the Qal, it has to do with occupying a territory. When conjugated in the Hiphil and construed with *min* (from), it is about expelling from an area; with *mippěnê* (someone), it names the group that benefits from the act. The Hiphil is also about emptying (when said of land) or replacing (when said of people), without always relying on other verbs to establish how the result is achieved (contra Schwartz 2004: 161–62, with bibliography). I have kept this distinction in my translations rather than stay consistently with one English verb (such as "dispossess") or phrase ("took possession," "drive out," or the like), lest I fail to convey distinct, albeit often coordinated, acts. In fact, ancient translations (Aramaic and Greek) often use different verbs when translating the form (see Lindars 1995: 46–47). In this verse (but not in the one immediately following) the spelling is "defective" (*yrš* versus *yvrš*).

Dispossession of land was a feature of many cultures that rely on military power to occupy wanted territory. In the Mari archives, when Zimri-Lim conquered the Mari area, the Sim'al tribes that placed him in power simply pushed out the population then in control and took over the emptied territory. Its leaders, however, had to pay him a tax (*sugāgūtum*) for the privilege of occupying the newly cleared regions (on this, see Marti 2008: 14–16). A parallel could be drawn with the conqueror being the Hebrew God rather than a king.

The reason for Judah's lack of success in the valley is its enemy's possession of *rekeb barzel*, "iron chariotry," that is, a unit of chariots that are protected by metal sidings and a horse or horses fitted with metal helmets. The enforcement added weight, giving the chariot better traction, hence also its rider a more secure platform from which to wield weaponry (Cantrell 2011: 63 n. 8). The combination of terrain and weaponry in this passage has led to much speculation about the strategy of using chariots in open land warfare. From monuments and texts, the war chariot can be documented since the third millennium BCE. It was not especially fleet then because it was drawn by ox or onager. In the mid-second millennium, however, horses gave the chariot speed; yet most specialists think that the combination was not used for offensive warfare. Rather, it gave archers a platform from which to volley arrows at a moving enemy front. (Whether the horses of a chariot also served to panic or trample foot soldiers is debated.) When galloping at full speed, horses are not easily maneuverable, and chariots often levitate off the ground. Also, when spooked, horses can be hard to control, so taking them into enemy space risks overturned chariots, precariously stranding highly trained riders. One problem solved by the Assyrians in the eighth century BCE was the creation of a braking device, giving added control of even heavy chariots. But it was apparently not until the final days of the Assyrian Empire (say, the mid-seventh century) that technological innovation permitted the use of iron in the manufacture of wheel rims and of the protruding blades that made them such fearsome martial instruments, especially in classical accounts and in Hollywood movies. By then, however, the cavalry had become the instrument of choice for cutting down marching armies. (On all this, see the *ABD* contribution, "Chariot," by Littauer and Crouwel; Drews 1989; and Cantrell 2011.)

The research of military historians, therefore, indicates that no matter how we explain the metal armaments, the "iron chariots" in our passage, as elsewhere (Josh 17:18;

Judg 4:3, 13), are likely anachronistic and cannot report on the true reason for the Hebrews's failure to conquer the plains. Even so, the narrator has not really introduced these fearsome machines as an excuse, for when he reports on Sisera's mighty chariotry (Judg 4:3, 13), there is premonition for a great victory against the Canaanites. Moreover, the received text of Josh 17:17–18 makes it explicit that such weaponry cannot slow the conquest: "Joshua told the House of Joseph—to Ephraim and Manasseh—, 'You are a large population and have great power, so you must not have just one allotment, but the hill country should be yours as well. Because it is forest land, clear it and its furthest limits shall become yours; for you will supplant the Canaanites even when they are strong by having chariots of iron.'" In fact, for our verse in Judges, the Greek versions (but not Josephus!) give quite a different reason for the failure: ὅτι Ρηχαβ διεστείλατο αὐτήν/αὐτοῖς, "because Rekhab had prevented it," so possibly alluding to a Rechabite warning against contacts with the Canaanites (see Harlé and Roqueplo 1999: 79–80). What was at stake in the Hebrew of 1:19 will be discussed in the Comments.

AFTERTHOUGHT?

1 20. This verse may seem out of context, and some scholars have moved it after 1:10. But it does clarify that Hebron was Caleb's conquest, resolving potential discord in what is said in 1:10 (about Judah's conquest of Hebron) and in 1:12–15 (about Caleb and Qiryat-sefer/Debir). (See the Notes to these verses above.) Rahlfs B specifies "the three cities of the children of Anak [τὰς τρεῖς πόλεις τῶν υἱῶν Ενακ]."

The use of the plural *vayyittĕnû* gives an impersonal sense to the attribution of Hebron to Caleb. The allusion is to Num 14:24, where an angry God had said, "As for my servant Caleb, because a different spirit was in him and was loyal to me, I will have him come into the land that he reaches and his offspring will take it over."

Letdown (Partial) for a Rachel Tribe

1 21. On the problems of Jerusalem, its Jebusites, and its allotment and (non)conquest, see the Notes to 1:8. Medieval exegetes generally solved the problem of attribution (Benjamin or Judah, see Josh 15:63) by fixing Jerusalem on their common border, hence giving each a share in the success or failure, leaving its "fortress" unconquered until David's days. With sharper pens, modern scholars occasionally emend either the Joshua or the Judges passage to bring them into harmony.[19] Yet, as Lindars and others have observed, the introductory material to the story of the judges features Judah, Benjamin, and soon, Joseph, each of whom provided Israel with its future kings. Perhaps more relevant, then, is the placement of information about Benjamin just before the narrator turned his attention to the House of Joseph, for in some passages, the former is made part of the latter. For example, in 2 Sam 19:21 (20 RSV), Shimei of Benjamin refers to himself as belonging to the House of Joseph.

'ad hayyôm hazzê (with variations and occasionally with plural nouns; see Jenni, *TLOT* 2: 531–32) occurs very frequently in the narrative portions, but most densely in Joshua (fifteen times) and Judges (seven times).[20] Literally it means "until the present day," and it can be used to confirm the validity of an inherited tradition or etiology (Childs 1963: 292). Yet, if I had courage of conviction, I would translate the phrase "*since* that time," for it certainly cannot suggest that events or situations stopped being so either at the featured period (here, the Judges era) or at the time of writing (when-

ever Judges was written or edited; traditionally by Samuel who, as Radaq pointed out, did not know of David's conquest). We notice how the ancient translations (Targum, Greek, and Vulgate) keep this formula even when its information was in most cases irrelevant to their situation.

COMMENTS

The narrative begins to fragment at this point, not at all shocking for a book that concatenates a number of episodes of diverse lengths and goals when aiming for a unified whole. Our segment begins with the story of the Kenites, decent people with leaders who acted honorably with Israel when it was crucial. Moses so appreciated their help that he offered them a place in the Promised Land. (Did he consult with God when he made his proposal?) At that time, they declined, choosing to remain in their native areas. But now we find them moving with Judah into areas (not clear which) that are clearly promised to Israel. The significance of this tidbit, however, goes beyond what it says. Willingly, Israel is permitting people with the barest blood connection to the patriarchs to enter their territory. It is true that they are not among those proscribed and so we should not expected that their people will turn into foes or their gods into snares (below at 2:3). Yet one of their clans does, allying itself with the Canaanites (4:17); and while we do not hear about Kenites actively joining Jabin of Hazor as he oppressed Israel for a generation, it could not be comforting to know that allies that are given trust for the most reasonable reasons can nevertheless end up giving aid and comfort to enemies. So much for not consulting God when offering to share land that was his to give.

We have a momentary return to an alliance that ostensibly had divine support (but see the Comments to IA1, Judg 1:1–7), this time Judah coming to Simeon's side. Together they capture Zephat, turning it into Hormah, named after its fate. We may imagine that this is precisely what God had wanted Judah and Simeon to do with Canaanite territory, but we are missing a divine command for them to do so. This observation may seem unsupported were it not for what the Greek of 1:18 has to say. There, the Hebrew text records Judah's capture of Gaza, Askelon, and Ekron; but the Greek translators knew better, for Israel never took control of these cities, not then, not incontestably ever, but also certainly not at the turn of the millennium (Aharoni 1979: 218). And so the translators were more honest by declaring that these Philistine cities went beyond Judah's grasp.

The Greek also prepares us better for the next statement (1:19); for even as we read that with God's help Judah conquered the hill region, we are not startled at all to learn that, in fact, the success was minimal, as Judah was kept from the more fertile region of Palestine. There is also a somewhat sinister touch to the declaration of failure, for, as observed above, the syntax of a crucial phrase in 1:19 ($k\hat{\imath}$ $l\bar{o}'$ $l\check{e}h\hat{o}r\hat{\imath}\check{s}$) moves the failure from the human (Judah could not conquer) to the divine (Judah was not to conquer) and so increases our suspicion that there is already resistance on the part of God to fulfill his plans for Israel. With the notice about Benjamin (Judah according to Josh 15:63) having to share Jerusalem with the Jebusites (1:21), we have reached the nadir of unacceptable compromises on the parts of those tribes that will later form the nucleus of the Southern Kingdom. A low point to be sure, but also an appropriate one from which to begin surveying further compromises, this time on the part of northern tribes.

IB

The Northern Tribes

1. Stratagems and Reality (Judg 1:22–36)

1   ²²The House of Joseph for their part marched against Bethel, the LORD being with them. ²³As the House of Joseph watched Bethel—previously the town was named Luz—²⁴the guards noticed a man leaving the city. They told him, "Show us an entry into town and we will treat you well." ²⁵He showed them an entry into the town and they put it to the sword; but they released the man and his entire family. ²⁶This man went to Hittite territory and founded a town, calling it Luz, its name to this day. ס

²⁷Manasseh did not occupy Beth-shean and its dependent states, Taanach and its dependencies, the inhabitants of Dor and its dependencies, the inhabitants of Ibleam and its dependencies, or the inhabitants of Megiddo and its dependencies. In this region, Canaanites were determined to remain. ²⁸Whenever Israel was dominant it would impose tribute on the Canaanites, without displacing them. ס ²⁹As to Ephraim, it did not displace the Canaanites that inhabited Gezer, so in Gezer itself the Canaanites lived among them. ס

³⁰Zebulun did not displace the inhabitants of Qitron and the inhabitants of Nahalol. The Canaanites lived alongside but were subject to tribute. ס ³¹Asher did not displace the inhabitants of Akko, the inhabitants of Sidon, Ahlab, Achzib, Helbah, Aphek, and Rehov. ³²So the people of Asher lived among the Canaanites who settled the land, for Asher could not displace them. ס

³³Naphtali did not displace the inhabitants of Bet-Shemesh and the inhabitants of Bet-Anat, but dwelled among the Canaanites settling the land; the inhabitants of Bet-Shemesh and Bet-Anat were subject to pay them tribute. ס ³⁴The Amorites pushed the Danites toward the hills, for they would not let

them move down toward the valley. [35]The Amorites were determined to remain in Har-Heres, Ayyalon, and Shaalabim; but when the House of Joseph compelled them, they were subject to tribute. ([36]Amorite territory stretched from Maale-Akrabim, through Sela, and upwards.) פ

NOTES

Introductory Remarks: The Amorites[1]

Who the Amorites are is an interesting problem, complicated by our knowledge of three major corpora that either mention the term or refer to activities of people labeled as such. Our earliest documentation comes from the mid to late third millennium (Fara, Agade, and Ur III periods). It becomes most informative in the Middle Bronze Mari archives of the eighteenth century BCE. There, *amurrû* (Sumerian mar.tu) is

1. The name of a scimitar-wielding god, frequently invoked in the creation of personal names.
2. The name of a Semitic dialect, and as such it identifies individuals (for example, singers from Hazor!)[2] who are fluent in it.
3. An ethnic marker, often contrasting with Akkadian, and so discriminating between those who claim tribal roots and those who (against reality) identify with East Semitic urbanism. Among those Amorites are Yaminites and Sim'alites (there are others), each with major subtribes and cultural differences. In the literature, one finds (plausible) conjectures about eventual tribal migration of remnants of the Yaminites into Benjamin territory of the Jordan Valley (Astour 1959; somewhat similar, Fleming 1998; 2012: 140–41).
4. A cardinal point, generally the west, and as such can refer to an area with a number of independent states that may or may not deem themselves united.

The second corpus of information on the Amorites comes from the Late Bronze Age, their story told in the Amarna tablets and in the records from Ugarit. Beginning from a modest seat around Tripoli in Lebanon, under Abdi-aširta and his son Aziru, Amurru eventually carved out for itself a territory on the western slope of the Lebanon chain in the Middle Orontes Valley. It endured for almost two centuries (Goren, Finkelstein, and Na'aman 2003). The name of the country was attached to a town in the region (like Ṣumur), and it may have been kept alive as such until at least the ninth century BCE (Stieglitz 1991).

The final cluster of testimony comes from the Hebrew Bible, and it is the most challenging because it is evoked as a memory of a Transjordan folk with many power centers, among them two (at Heshbon and Bashan, ruled respectively by Sihon and Og) that failed to stop the move of Israel into the Promised Land. This moment was so signal that it was recalled repeatedly in Hebrew lore.[3] Yet in the many references to the Amorites, we find them in areas that match what is assigned to Canaanites: on the west coast of the Dead Sea (Gen 14:7), in Hebron (Gen 14:13), in Shechem (Gen 48:22), in Gilead and Bashan (Deut 3:10), in Gibeon (2 Sam 21:2), and by Mount Hermon (Deut 3:8, 4:47–48). They are mentioned in many catalogues of pre-Israelite inhabitants of Palestine, sometimes alongside the Canaanites, sometimes not (see Table 2, under "Emori"). There is the famous statement that Israel's father was a "fugitive Aramean"

(Deut 26:5), and Ezekiel (16:3) claims that Jerusalem was Canaanite, with an Amorite father and a Hittite mother.

How these three corpora mesh is difficult to pin down. In sets of biblical reference, since the late nineteenth century it has been common to presume (rather than show) this continuity. Occasionally, an article is written that describes the move of pastoralists from the inland regions along the Euphrates to the coastal regions (Buccellati 1990), yet the material we have from each corpus differs in what is labeled "Amorite." I do not believe people in Mari called themselves Amorites, although an individual could be termed one. They did claim, however, that some tribes moved easily in such areas (see Charpin and Ziegler 2003: 30–32). Amurru as a Late Bronze Age power acquired the name punctually, and it is difficult to say whether it had a political prehistory there.

The material from the Bible recalls quasi-mythical folks, gigantic in stature (Deut 3: 11, Amos 2:9) and associated with nations that have left no trace in nonbiblical records. In previous scholarship, when Hebrews were thought never to consciously utter contradictory, gratuitous, or repetitious material, Amorites and Canaanites were assigned to separate sources (respectively E/D and J), but this is now recognized as a doubtful and unnecessary distinction. We are discovering that "Canaanites" was a term that was applied to communities by outsiders eager to lump stretches of land into a convenient unit. Until a fortunate discovery brings them forcefully into reality, the same may be said for "Amorites." For the Hebrews, however, Amorites and Canaanites were both equally iniquitous and equally missionary in their zeal to seduce the Hebrews into betraying the only true God. They were, therefore, equally deserving of dispossession.

Success

1 22. Unlike references in Genesis to *bêt yôsēf*, "Joseph's palace" (Gen 43:18–19) or "Joseph's household" (Gen 50:8), beginning with Josh 17:17 the phrase applies mostly to a dynasty established by the patriarch. From the late second millennium, the stringing of *bêt* ("House of") to the name of an ancestor was used to refer to a tribe. But already in the Mari age, and likely as a consequence of tribal settlements into urban centers, Akkadian *bītum* had come to refer to the royal family, especially when attached to its seat of government. In this sense, King Samsi-Addu could write his son (ARM 1 77 = LAPO 18 #1005, pp. 169–70): "I will take for you a young woman, the daughter of Išḫi-Addu (of Qatna). The House of Mari is of good repute, as is the House of Qatna." In the Mari world, to begin a reign is often expressed *ana kussi bīt abim erēbum* (with variations), "to occupy [literally, 'enter'] the throne of the father's House"—the word "father" not always to be taken literally, as it also refers to a political sponsor.[4]

As it concerns the Hebrews, we find the merging of these two constructions, in that when "House" is attached to the name of an ancestor, it reflects a reigning dynasty and, by extension, the land it rules.[5] "The House of Omri" (*bīt Ḫumri*) is how Israel was known to the Assyrians, and "the House of David" (*byt dwd*) is how Judah was labeled to the rulers of Damascus. This usage is readily found in Judges, as well. In addition to the "House of Joseph," we will meet with the "House of Jerubbaal-Gideon" (Judg 8:35) and the "House of Ephraim" (Judg 10:9). Yet, because the terminology does not fit an evocation of a period in which kingship was yet to be, there may be irony in that what it will describe is mostly land not taken.[6]

For *bêt yôsēf*, many Greek copies give either "sons of Israel" (likely picking up on 1:1) or "sons of Joseph," the last a reference to the tribe of Joseph that is itself well-attested in the Hebrew Bible (among examples, Num 26:37, 36:1, 5; Josh 14:4, 17:14, 16; 18:11; 1 Chr 7:29). In the remaining narratives (six references), rather than referring just to Ephraim and Manasseh (tribes named after Joseph's sons), the phrase collectively designates the northern tribes. In the prophets (twice) it stands for the Northern Kingdom without implying dynastic continuity within it. In contrast, Hebrew editors were careful not to use the "House of Judah" until David is said to have taken the throne (2 Sam 2:4). Interestingly enough, *benê yôsēf*, "sons of Joseph," ceases to be used beyond the book of Joshua. I fail to see why some scholars believe that the phrase "House of Joseph" is used as a polemic against Judah (de Geus 1976: 70–96; Lemche 1985: 284).

laʿălôt ʾel (+ city) can have martial implications, even when an explicitly martial verb is not linked to it (as in 1:1). It is possible (but not likely) that the idiom intentionally foreshadows an impious act, such as a pilgrimage to the sinful Bethel (Hamlin 1985). We notice simply that *gam-hēm* (conjunction + third-person pronoun) has several functions, depending on context: "they too," as in competitions (Exod 7:11); "in the same way," as in a sequence of acts (Num 4:22, Deut 3:20); "neither they nor you" (Num 18:3); and intensively, "even they" (Ps 38:11 [10 RSV]). In our context, *gam-hēm* implies "in the same way," and this is picked by all ancient translations, presumably matching what was said above (at 1:1) about Judah. Medieval commentators long ago noticed how its insertion shifts the focus from Judah to Joseph. But this insertion can also imply that their activities, while separate and individual, were also simultaneous. If so, the narrator may have sought to negate any implication that Judah (together with Simeon) had priority when God launched attacks against those who occupied the Promised Land.

This observation is reinforced by *vaYHVH ʿimmām*, "the LORD being with them," replaying the sentiments expressed about Judah in 1:19 and, earlier, in 1:4. It is hard to assess whether the phrase explains the impulse to go against Bethel (hence looks backward) or foreshadows their success (hence looks forward). The phrase itself has rather limited use in Scriptures, occurring at the tail end of a thought, reinforcing anticipatorily virtues already expressed: David and his many skills (1 Sam 16:18, 18:14), Israel when led by a virtuous king (2 Chr 20:17), Israel when grasping the Promised Land (Num 14:9, with *ʾet* rather than *ʿim*). Still, a number of Greek texts (Rahlfs Λ among them) read καὶ Ιουδας μετ' αὐτῶν ("Judah being with them"), so completely miss the shift of focus from Judah to Joseph. Lindars (1995: 53) gives an accounting of scholars who favor this reading as "original."

BETHEL

Bethel (Greek, Βαιθηλ) enters center stage here. While the meaning of its name is transparent, "House of El/god" (meaning "temple"), the traditions about Bethel are complex, with diverse narratives about how it acquired its name. Complicating matters is the discovery of first-millennium BCE documents and inscriptions that allude to a god by that name (see W. Röllig in *DDD*, 331–33). Scholars, in fact, cite a number of biblical passages in which Bethel is best understood as a god rather than as a place, but they differ in their selection. Among the more likely attestations of the god Bethel are

Jer 48:13, where there is a contrast with the god Chemosh; Zech 7:2, where it forms the name Bethel-sharezer; and Hos 10:15, where the wrath of Bethel, obviously a deity, is cited.[7]

With the possible exception of a Bethel near Ziklag in Judah (1 Sam 30:27; see Josh 19:4 and 1 Chr 4:30), the vast majority of biblical references are to a Bethel that lay north of Jerusalem. (There is debate among scholars whether the Bethel of 1 Sam 30:27 is a different town.) Bethel had a storied history. Hebrew lore attached it and its environs to the patriarchs (in Genesis) but also to the Canaanites (in Joshua). In his earliest encounters with the Promised Land, Abram is said to zigzag between Bethel and Ai, where he built altars to God, before (Gen 12:8) and after (Gen 13:3) he entered Egypt. Not surprisingly, the language of his itinerary reminds of what is said about Joshua's entry into Canaan (Josh 8:9, 12; 12:9, 16), itself a *reconquest* of land partially delivered to the patriarchs. Tradition is also very insistent on crediting Jacob with fixing a new name on a town then known as Luz after his encounter with the divine (Gen 28:19; 31:13; 35:6–7; 35:7, 15). The explanation there for the town's name ("House of Elohim") is transparent and much more appropriate to the circumstance than what obtains from the Judges passage under current discussion.

Whether or not Bethel was built around a shrine or took its name from a famous shrine in its environs has been the subject of debate, some scholars maintaining that Canaanites ordinarily built holy sites within city walls but that the Hebrews, because of their nomadic practices, outside city walls (contrast Na'aman 1988 and Kallai 1986: 131). In fact, at least among the Amorites of Mari, worship of the same deity took place on both sides of a fortified area. For example, the goddess Annunitum had shrines in the palace area (*ša libbi ālim*, ARM 26 214: 5) as well as [*ša*] *kawâtim*, "beyond the walls" (ARM 26 216: 1′–2′; 229: 6–7), and we know of many such outside sanctuaries from Emar. A similar condition seems to obtain in Dan, with potentially a *bāmâ* within the town and several stelas beyond the gates (see Biran in the *ABD*).

We will soon have other occasions to speak of Bethel and of other traditions about it (see below, at Judg 4:5; 9:46; 20:18, 26, 31; and 21:2), some of which are obviously anticipating the center for worshiping false manifestations of God (1 Kgs 12–13). Since the mid-nineteenth century, Bethel has been sited at the modern Beitin (Bētīn), about 10 miles (17 kilometers) north of Jerusalem, as much because of its location as for the aural similarity between the Hebrew and Arabic names.[8] Excavations begun there by Albright and continued into 1960 by Kelso have provided mixed information. Yet there are doubts (see W. Dever in *OEANE* 1: 300–301) about conclusions such as A. Mazar's (1990): "At Bethel, a fortified Late Bronze Canaanite city was destroyed toward the end of the period and was rebuilt in Iron Age I as an Israelite town. This is one of the few cases where archaeology might confirm a conquest tradition" (333).

Whatever its precise location and its archeological history, Bethel stood on the edge of two worlds—that of Ephraim (hence the Northern Kingdom), to which it belonged, and that of Judah (hence the Southern Kingdom)—and at the crossroads of major route systems between east (from Jericho) and west (toward Aphek) and between south (from Bethlehem) and north (toward Shechem) (see Dorsey 1991: 134–35, 139–40). Not surprisingly, the traditions have Bethel allocated to both the South (Benjamin, Josh 18:22) and the North (our passage). Later, Bethel is absorbed into Judah (2 Chr 13:19, Ezra 2:28, Neh 7:32).

We are told that God was with the House of Joseph, no doubt to balance what had been said about the warring southern tribes. As it happens, Bethel remains the only success for the North, the remaining notices reporting on territory not conquered or, at best, reaching an advantageous modus vivendi (see at 1:34–46). This is in sharp contrast with the success the South had over seven cities. As usual, the Targum expands to "the word of God being helpful to them." Rahlfs A is one of a number of Greek manuscripts, however, that reads καὶ Ιουδας μετ᾽ αὐτῶν, "Judah joining them," encouraging many scholars (among them Boling and Eissfeldt) to follow suit, arguing that orthographically, Hebrew יהודה, "Judah," and יהוה, "Yнvн," are easily mistaken for each other.[9] Aside from inserting Judah into unattested activities, the reading misses a major opportunity to derive a good lesson about the God who tests his flock by giving them seemingly easy victories.

1 23. What is implied by the verb *vayyātîrû* when describing the action at Bethel is not easy to ascertain, the difficulty leading Greek translators (Rahlfs B) to use two verbs, καὶ παρενέβαλον καὶ κατεσκέψαντο Βαιθηλ, "they set up camp and kept watch on Bethel," and the Targum simply to revert to an old motif, *ušlaḥû mĕ᾽allelin dĕbêt yôsēf*, "then Joseph sent spies." The Qal of *twr* clearly means "to roam," literally as in the story of men sent to scout the Promised Land (Num 13:2, 21, 32; 14:34; Ezek 20:6) or figuratively (said of the heart, but negatively, Num 15:39, Eccl 2:3). The Hiphil occurs elsewhere only in Prov 12:26, unfortunately a difficult passage (*TNK*, "A righteous man gives his friend direction [*yātēr mērē᾽ēhû ṣaddîq*], but the way of the wicked leads astray"). My translation is contextual, inspired by cases in which an army camps at the city gate and watches patiently for opportunity, as described in an eighteenth-century BCE Mari letter reporting a campaign near Qadesh in Syria: "We have camped at Raḥiṣum (Amarna Ruḫizzi), by the city of Dubba, about which I have often written my lord . . . rootless men [*ḫabbātū*] and men from Canaan are set in Raḥiṣum. We and they—we simply watch each other."[10]

LUZ

A number of traditions were known about Luz, none inspiring confidence regarding Israel's real knowledge of the town's past.[11] The change of names from Luz to Bethel is credited to Jacob as he moved in and out of the Promised Land (at Gen 28:19 and 35:6; see also 48:3). Joshua 16:2 (but not 18:13) seems to differentiate between Bethel and Luz(ah) ("From Bethel [the Joseph–Benjamin frontier] ran to Luz and passed on to the territory of Erech at Ataroth"), a problem the Greek translation solves by dropping Luz. It does not help that we have as yet no mention of this town from nonbiblical sources. Conjectures are many, with some definitely less inspired (see T. K. Cheyne in the *EB*, s.v.) than others, including the proposal that Bethel designated the temple compound at Luz, eventually becoming the dominant name (see Gass 2005: 76–82).

In Hebrew lore "Land of the Hittites" is not the region in Anatolia that scholars have come to know from second-millennium cuneiform and (Egyptian) hieroglyphic archives; rather, it is the Syria of the first millennium, more or less equivalent to the Neo-Assyrian *māt Ḥatti*, as described in Josh 1:4 (different in the LXX): "Your territory shall be bounded from the wilderness and from the Lebanon to the Great River, the River Euphrates on the east—so all the land of the Hittites, up to the Mediterranean Sea on the west."[12] Not surprisingly, all individuals whom the Bible labels as

Hittites have lovely Semitic names: Ephron (Gen 23, etc.), Beeri (Gen 26:34), Elon (Gen 26:34, 36:2), Ahimelech (1 Sam 26:6), and Uriah (2 Sam 11).

Luz likely received its name from its "almond" groves (in this meaning, it is also associated with Jacob [Gen 30:37]), but Boling (1975: 59) prefers to connect it with the same root that verbally refers to "turning aside," so "Deception," a name allegedly generated by the plot. But why would its residents carry such a negative name when founding the city anew?

1 24–26. A number of motifs combine to shape this particular notice about Luz:

1. Capturing a fortified city by stealth is well-known in the literature, from Egypt ("The Capture of Joppa," Simpson, Wente, and Faulkner 1972: 81–84) to Greece (*The Iliad*), and it depends on the belief that cunning ranks only slightly behind courage as a military trait. Among the inquiries on the safety of a city as set before the gods Šamaš (justice) and Adad (executor) was whether "an influential citizen might communicate with an enemy army, open the lock of a town's gate, expel the garrison of Marduk and King Samsu-ditana, son of Ammi-ṣaduqa, and allow the enemy army in" (adapted from Lambert 2007: 27–29). In Mari letters, we read about activities that to us might seem less than honorable, such as an enemy making a breach in a wall while ostensibly observing a truce (A. 2417, about which see LAPO 17 #607, pp. 271–73). How David captured Jerusalem is told in a famously obscure passage at 2 Sam 5:6–7, but it was also done by unorthodox means (see below).

2. The person facilitating the fall of the town may well be a traitor to his people (treated as such by Josephus), but in fact he served to give them continuity by transplanting his immediate household from a town doomed to fall to the God-inspired Israel. Here too we are meeting with a motif that can be fodder for epics; for example, an escapee from Troy, Aeneas, founds Rome.[13]

3. Finally, there is the motif of victorious warriors treating kindly a person who gave them help, more or less what is told about Rahab of Jericho.

This concatenation of motifs may encourage us to look into future episodes that may link with ours; but unlike what we will learn about the founding of Dan (Judg 18), alas there seems to be no narrative about Luz beyond this single episode.

The *šōmĕrîm* are simply guards, not scouts, patrols, or spies; they are there when opportunity strikes. (In Song 3:3 and 5:7, *haššōmĕrîm hassōvĕvîm bāʿîr* refers to different groups, watchmen and patrols.) The man they apostrophize is not a prisoner or a warrior, simply someone going about his business. The air of normalcy in such events is eerie, more like cats and mice at a distance from each other. The Greek, however, felt the need to be more aggressive: "they seized him" (καὶ ἔλαβον αὐτὸν; perhaps reflecting a form of the verb ʾḥz). What they ask of the man is for access into the citadel that is not normally available. Many fortified cities had entries ("postern gates") beside the main gate, often rather narrow, permitting movements of individuals rather than groups and thus serving the needs of citizens trying to reach their fields.[14] Because it remains difficult to imagine that such entries would have been kept open or unguarded when an enemy was within sight, it might be that the man showed the soldiers a water-shaft (*ṣinnôr*) that connected springs to the inner citadel, as perhaps occurred when David took over the Jebusite stronghold Jerusalem (2 Sam 5:8, admittedly a difficult passage).

Radaq charmingly suggested that the secret entrance began in the hidden hollow of an almond tree, hence the name Luz.[15]

There is some irony here about the fate of the man that is played out textually: In 1:8 almost the same vocabulary is used to describe the fate of Jerusalem, "[Judah] . . . put [Jerusalem] to the sword and set fire to the city," except that the verb šālaḥ (Piel) is here not construed with "fire." (What a difference a word makes!) There may also be a lesson in that the man chose to set roots in 'ereṣ haḥittim, describing Hittite territory that God had promised the Hebrew people (Josh 1:4).

The Land Not Taken

For the northern tribes, here begins the litany of native dwellers that, despite God and Joshua, remained in control of their own lands (see Kallai 1986). Some will keep total sovereignty; others will pay tribute, either monetary or in servitude. The series was already featured earlier, when Benjamin was said to have failed in supplanting the Jebusites (1:21). In the literature about the first chapter of Judges, there is much discussion about all those areas within the Promised Land that could not be conquered. In Judges the language was mostly that a tribe "would not displace" the inhabitants of a specific area whereas in Joshua the phrase was sharper: they "could not displace." Table 1 offers a harmony of citations.

Readily observable is the major discrepancy about Jerusalem, its fate, and which tribe (Judah or Benjamin) might (or might not) have let it escape Israel's clutches. Also noticeable is that what is said about Manasseh and Ephraim in both Judges and Joshua more or less matches, but there are minor differences in content and language. Dan's failure is reported in Judges but only in the Greek of Joshua. In Joshua, no fiascos are reported for Zebulun, Asher (but see under Manasseh), and Naftali; so essentially the last half dozen verses of chapter 1 have no equivalents in Joshua. Which book has priority is naturally an important issue, but opinions are all over the place, and they do not stay put, for they depend on conjectures, some more inspired than others. Some argue in zigzag, assigning some priority for some notices to Judges and others to Joshua. (See the Notes under each appropriate verse.) There was always the possibility that the compilers of both books had access to material from a third source, and this was also discussed, but especially sharply by Albrecht Alt (1940–41). He termed such notices *negativen Besitzverzeichnis* ("catalogue of nonoccupied places"), arguing that their terseness likely made them ancient, even reliable. In this he was followed by Noth, who argued that the whole first chapter was a compilation of inherited traditions. Reactions were not muted, and it was soon argued that the notices can hardly be called lists and so could not be plucked from any ancient register. They were simply composed as part of the narrative. All this is told nicely in Rake (2006: 20–73; see also Guillaume 2001); less attractive is her suggestion that these notices are evocative of conditions in the Persian period, with an allocation of material in Judges that reflects interest in Yehud (Judah) first and then Samaria (Joseph). (See also the Comments to IIA1 [2:1–5]).

JOSEPH TRIBES

1 27–29. Josephus took the opportunity to streamline what he imagined to be the incoherence of Judges. He had assigned the capture of Bethel to Ephraim, and, ignoring

Table 1. Lands Not Taken

Judges	*Joshua*
[**1:8** The people of Judah attacked Jerusalem and captured it. They put it to the sword and set fire to the city.] **1:21** As to the Jebusites dwelling in Jerusalem, Benjamin could not displace them; so the Jebusites have shared Jerusalem with **Benjamin** to this day.	**15:63** As to the Jebusites who lived in Jerusalem, **Judah** could not drive them out; so the Jebusites have shared Jerusalem with **Judah** to this day. [**18:28** Zela, Eleph, and Jebus—that is, Jerusalem—Gibeath and Kiriath: fourteen towns, with their villages. That was the portion of the Benjaminites, by their clans (*TNK*).]
1:27–28 Manasseh did not occupy Beth-shean and its dependencies, Taanach and its dependencies, the inhabitants of Dor and its dependencies, the inhabitants of Ibleam and its dependencies, or the inhabitants of Megiddo and its dependencies. In this region, Canaanites were determined to remain. 28Whenever Israel was dominant it would impose tribute on the Canaanites, without displacing them.	**17:11–13 Within Issachar and Asher**, Manasseh possessed Beth-shean and its dependencies, Ibleam and its dependencies, the inhabitants of Dor and its dependencies, **the inhabitants of En-dor and its dependencies**, the inhabitants of Taanach and its dependencies, and the inhabitants of Megiddo and its dependencies: **these three districts**. The people of Manasseh could not occupy these towns, so the Canaanites stubbornly remained in that land. Whenever the people of Israel dominated, they turned the Canaanites into tribute givers; but they never could displace them.
1:29 As to Ephraim, it did not displace the Canaanites that inhabited Gezer, so in Gezer itself the Canaanites lived among them.	**16:10** However, [Ephraim] did not displace the Canaanites who dwelt in Gezer; so the Canaanites remain by Ephraim to this day. But they had to perform forced labor.
1:34 The Amorites pushed the Danites toward the hills, for they would not let them move down toward the valley.	**Greek 19:47a** And the sons of Dan did not force out the Amorrite who was oppressing them in the mountain, and the Amorrites did not permit them to go down into the valley, and they reduced from them the boundary of their portion.
1:35 The Amorites were determined to remain in Har-Heres, Ayyalon, and Shaalabim; but when the House of Joseph compelled them, they were subject to tribute.	**Greek 19:48a** And the Amorrite continued to dwell in Elom and in Salamin, and the hand of Ephraim was heavy upon them, and they became as tribute to them.

Note: Boldface indicates obvious textual discrepancies.

Manasseh, at length (*Ant.* 5.136–74) brings here the story of the Levite from Ephraim and the consequent war against Benjamin that in our received Bible does not open until chapter 19. Josephus also takes the occasion to editorialize, paraphrasing from indictments to be featured in our chapter 2:

> After this, the Israelites grew effeminate as to fighting any more against their enemies, but applied themselves to the cultivation of the land, which producing them great plenty and riches, they neglected the regular disposition of their settlement, and indulged themselves in luxury and pleasures; nor were they any longer careful to hear the laws that belonged to their political government: whereupon God was provoked to anger, and put them in mind, first, how, contrary to his directions, they had spared the Canaanites; and, after that, how those Canaanites, as opportunity served, used them very barbarously. But the Israelites, though they were in heaviness at these admonitions from God, yet were they still very unwilling to go to war; and since they got large tributes from the Canaanites, and were indisposed for taking pains by their luxury, they suffered their aristocracy to be corrupted also, and did not ordain themselves a senate, nor any other such magistrates as their laws had formerly required, but they were very much given to cultivating their fields, in order to get wealth; which great indolence of theirs brought a terrible sedition upon them, and they proceeded so far as to fight one against another, from the following occasion. (*Ant.* 5.132–35)

Manasseh[16]   Israel is powerless to dislodge the inhabitants of five major cities: Beth-shean (the Greek refers to the city's Hellenistic name by adding "a city of Scythians" [ἥ ἐστιν Σκυθῶν πόλις, 2 Macc 12:29]), Taanach (see Judg 5:19), Ibleam, Megiddo, and Dor (En-Dor in Josh 17:11, not at all the same place), each with its dependent state. All were centers with deep histories, with their dependencies occupying a fair chunk of what ostensibly would have been Manasseh's territory west of the Jordan. The reason given for this failure is lame, the relevant verbal phrase, *vayyōʾel . . . lāševet*, implying a stubborn resistance or a strong wish (Exod 2:21, Judg 17:11), so much so that both the Greek (ἤρξατο) and the Targum (*věšārî*) offer "the Canaanites *began* to dwell in the land," an illogical rendering, given that the Canaanites were there already.

There is insistence on Israel's failure in 1:28 (*věhôrēš lōʾ hôrîšô*), but also an attempt to save face. Whenever Israel (so not just Manasseh) became strong (so likely during the united monarchy), it subjected these cities to a *mas*. In usage, this term (like *sēbel*) is somewhat ambiguous, covering a broad category of impositions demanded by a central administration, be it from its citizens, vassals, or conquered. The phrasing for *mas* is slippery in that it can be a direct, but most often indirect (even doubly indirect), object to such verbs as *nātan* (in Josh 17:13), *śym* (our passage), *ʿālâ* (Hiphil), or *hāyâ*. When linked to *ʿōvēd*, "worker," *mas* likely means forced labor; but it is prudent to translate it in our context as "tribute" (as did the Targum) since this last term is broad enough to include the unwilling disposal of human labor as well as durable goods. (On these matters, see Mettinger 1971: 128–39.) Whatever the precise benefits, payment, or labor, God did not condone subjecting foes to a *mas* when they were to be dispossessed (Weinfeld 1967).

Ephraim[17]   Gezer was an imposing site at the foothills of the Judean range, and it came under Israel's control only when the Egyptians gave it to Solomon as a wedding present (1 Kgs 9:16). The idiom *lāšēv bĕqerev* implies harmonious dwelling, whether joyfully or not, and the Greek seems incongruous when adding καὶ ἐγένετο εἰς φόρον, "became tributary," possibly from Josh 16:10 but more likely harmonizing with what will be said in the next verse.

LEAH TRIBES

Zebulun   **1** 30. A lower Galilee tribe with frontiers delineated in Josh 19:10–16, Zebulun will come to the fore twice in Judges, when it answers Baraq's appeal (4:10) and when it produces the judge Elon (12:12). Despite their evocative names, the towns that escape Zebulun's control, Kitron ("Incense") and Nahalol ("Streamy"), are not particularly well-known to us, so guesses on where to locate them are rife and are mostly based on speculative connection with modern names of tells (see the dictionaries). The latter occurs as one of the Levite cities (Josh 21:35, with a slightly different spelling but is recalled differently in Greek versions: Ενααλα (Rahlfs A) and Δωμανα (Rahlfs B). That the Canaanites are said to continue to live among the Israelites, yet were tributary, is, as said above, incongruous; but until the twentieth century, Jews and Christians lived in peace among Muslims, to whom they paid a special tax.

Asher   **1** 31–32. Asher (Leah, via Zilpah) occupied the hills of the western Galilee, almost reaching the coastline (see Josh 19:25–31), a region praised for its agricultural bounty (Gen 49:20, Deut 33:24) and its access to the sea (Judg 5:17). The cities said to be beyond its control are mostly along the coastline, but we have difficulty in identifying all of them. Akko is doubtless the port that is well-known to us, even if this is its only appearance in Scripture.[18] Sidon is the famous Phoenician port city, and it never fell to Hebrew control. Both Aphek and Rehob have names shared by a number of towns, and the common speculation is that they are to be sought near Akko. The last three towns (Ahlab, Achzib, and Helbah) are difficult to locate, especially since they are spelled quite differently in the Greek versions, and there is speculation that they may in fact simply be consonantal replays of each other.[19] What is interesting here is that Asher is said to share space with these Canaanites, rather than the other way around, as if Asher's presence is tolerated by the Canaanites, declared *yōšĕvê hā'āreṣ*, a phrase normally applied to those in control of a territory.

RACHEL TRIBES

Naphtali   **1** 33. Naphtali (Rachel, via Bilhah), settled in the eastern segments of the upper Galilee, will soon produce the great warrior Baraq (Judg 4–5) as well as the leaders that join Gideon against the enemy (Judg 6:33–35). The towns they could not control, Bet-Shemesh and Bet-Anat, were likely centers for Canaanite shrines (respectively to the Sun and to Anat; see below at 3:31). Where to locate them is a problem (in the former case complicated by mention of homonyms), and the many solutions are mostly speculative. Suffice it to say that we are in the upper Galilee. The same reversal of subservient status, as is the case of Asher, is found here, but this time there is an expanded notion (however unreasonable) about these towns paying tribute to Naphtali.

Dan   **1** 34–35. The Amorites give Dan (Rachel, via Bilhah) the worst treatment. The tribe (most commonly cited as *bĕnê-dān*) does not simply fail to control its promised area (Josh 19:40–46), but also it is confined to hilly areas, likely not a very productive region (see Demsky 2004). What is interesting is that there is less a desire here to give us a sense of Danite territory (in fact, the previous tribal progression from south to north is interrupted here) than to flesh out information about the Amorites. The verb used here, *lāḥaṣ*, conveys intense pressure, for us best exposed in Num 22:25 when, upon sighting an angel, Balaam's jenny "pressed herself against the wall, crushing Balaam's foot against the wall" (*vattillāḥēṣ 'el-haqqîr vattilḥaṣ 'et-regel bil'ām 'el-haqqîr*). The towns the Amorites refused to abandon are not easily identified: Har-Heres, meaning "Potsherd Hill," occurs only here, so some scholars identify it with Bet-Shemesh because *haḥarsâ* is a poetic word for "Sun" (Judg 14:18) and because of Josh 19:41.[20] Ayyalon ("Deer Park") is better attested as being near the Philistine border. Later it will have the tomb of the judge Elon (Judg 12:12), but by then it will belong to Zebulun. Shaalbim ("Fox Hill") is mentioned elsewhere (1 Kgs 4:9, Josh 19:42) but cannot be located on a map. Greek witnesses give a double dose of names with interpretation, so at their most expansive (Rahlfs B) reading, "And the Amorite began to dwell in the mountain of shards, where there are bears and foxes [ἐν τῷ ὄρει τῷ ὀστρακώδει ἐν ᾧ αἱ ἄρκοι καὶ ἐν ᾧ αἱ ἀλώπεκες], in Myrsinon, and in Thalabin."[21] Worth noting here, as in the case of Ephraim above, Josephus (*Ant.* 5.175–78) uses the resistance of the Amorites (he calls them Canaanites) as background to telling of the migration of Dan, a story that will not come into our received Hebrew and Greek texts until chapter 18.

Despite their success, the Amorites had to submit to Joseph, whose control (*yad*) pressed on them (*vattikvad*). The idiom is well-attested elsewhere, among them describing the punishment God meted out to the Philistines (1 Sam 5:6, 11). Yet Rake (2006: 62–64) gives it an opposite meaning: Unlike Judah, Joseph was slow to move against his enemies. However, subjugation is clearly indicated by the phrase that follows, *vayyihĕyû lāmas*, "they were subject to tribute."

The roster of tribes presented here is not as complete a set as one finds elsewhere. (See Table 5 at IIC2.) The Rachel (and Bilhah) tribes are set out in full, although allocated to South (Benjamin) and North (Manasseh, Ephraim, Naphtali, and Dan). Missing from the roster of Leah tribes are Reuben, Levi, Issachar, and Gad (via Zilpah). Levi was not to inherit land, and Reuben and Gad settled territory east of the Jordan. The oddity is the absence of Issachar. Indeed, while Issachar will be attached to Deborah and Baraq (see under Judg 5:25), this tribe is conspicuously missing from the narratives about Gideon. I have no explanation for it—if one is needed, that is.

Amorites

1 36. "Amorite" is often treated in Scripture as an ethnic or regional designation (see the Introductory Remarks). Exceptionally, at Josh 13:4 it refers to the "frontier of Amorites," implying a kingdom. Here we are given some specifics about its boundary, though it is not clear at all with what intent. The matter is muddled by Rahlfs A, which attaches ὁ Ιδουμαῖος, "the Edumeian," to "the territory of the Amorites," encouraging scholars to presume that the text originally read Edomite. That Akrabim ("Scorpions Height") and Sela ("Cliff") can be associated with Edom has sharpened this conviction (see Moore 1895: 54–55). Whether we are dealing with Amorite or Edomite boundaries, however, this sentence in no way contributes to our knowledge of how the conquest was proceeding (Lindars 1995: 72–73).

COMMENTS

In two chapters in the book of Joshua (10–11), a numbers of segments are patched into a sequence to chart the conquests in the south (chapter 10) and then in the north (chapter 11) of the Promised Land. Yet after an impressive list of defeated city-states (chapter 11), we are given a general overview of globs of land that had not yet come under Hebrew control (Josh 13:1–6). "When Joshua was old and was well-advanced in years," we are told, "the LORD said to him":

> You are very old, and there are still very large areas of land to be taken over. This is the land that remains: all the regions of the Philistines and of the Ge-shurites: from the Shihor River on the east of Egypt to the territory of Ekron on the north . . . ; from the south, all the land of the Canaanites, from Arah of the Sidonians as far as Aphek, the region of the Amorites, the area of the Gebalites; and all Lebanon to the east, from Baal Gad below Mount Hermon to Lebo Hamath. As for all the inhabitants of the mountain regions from Lebanon to Misrephoth Maim, that is, all the Sidonians, I myself will drive them out before the Israelites.

We notice that the quotation is attributed to God. As is conventional to Hebrew literature, God cannot be ignorant of what the future holds, and although he is often disappointed by some outcomes—Israel regularly dashes his hopes—in this case Joshua is to allot them land just the same, pending successes that will come after the leader's death. Yet, at some intervals (for example, at 13:13, 15:63, 16:10, 17:12–13, and 19:47) we are warned not to expect fulfillment of expectations.

This pattern is rehearsed compactly in Judg 1: Description of the South first is followed by review of what happened to the North. Pockets of failures (some replayed from Joshua) are then given seriatim rather than interspaced. But Judg 1 also has its own internal coherence. Each portion, South and North, opens on an anecdote before closing on disappointments in achieving control of land. In telling about the southern tribes, we are given rather lame excuses for failures (Judg 1:19, the enemy had chariots of iron; Judg 1:21, the enemy hunkered down), but the hope remains that a better appreciation of God's intents would broaden the conquests.[22]

As the narrative reports on the northern tribes, however, there is a shift from many achievements with an occasional stumble to one achievement with many potential failures. Even the conquest of Luz, an acknowledged but unchronicled success (it is not recorded in Joshua), is a deceptive achievement. God may well be with Joseph when its tribes move toward Luz, and God may even inspire its guards to trick the city into submission, but the prize, Bethel, will eventually turn out to be a snare (Amos 3:14, 5:6). What is embedded in Joshua about territory beyond the control of Israel—Manasseh (Josh 17:11–13, see 16:10), Zebulun (Josh 19:10–16), Asher (Josh 19:24–31), and Naphtali (Josh 19:32–39)—reads much more starkly in Judges. Rather than continuing to harvest from Joshua (19:47) a story on Dan's conquest of Leshem—and thus potentially creating a nice bracket for what is said about Luz—the narrator turns space over to the Amorites and to their victories over their Israelite enemy. The lesson this catalogue of failures strives to achieve is moral, not historical. Soon there will be opportunity for the latter (Judg 18), but at this point, the better goal is to prepare for the grievances God will have against his flock.

Arguments

IIA

What Went Wrong

---

1. Accusation (Judg 2:1–5)

2   ¹Coming up to Bochim from Gilgal, the LORD's emissary said, "When leading you out of Egypt and bringing you to the land that I pledged to your ancestors, I said, 'I shall never annul my covenant with you. ²For your part, you must make no covenant with the inhabitants of this land. You must raze their altars.' But you have not obeyed me. How could you have done that? ³I have decided therefore not to drive them out before you, so that for you they will become foes, their gods snares." ⁴As the emissary of the LORD spoke these words to all Israel, the people broke into loud weeping. ⁵So they called that place Bochim, and they offered sacrifices there to the LORD. פ

NOTES

> Tears lubricate love songs and love, weddings and funerals, public
> rituals and private pain, and perhaps no scientific study can capture
> their many meanings.
> —*Benedict Carey, "A good cry isn't for everyone"*[1]

Introductory Remarks: Angels and Messengers[2]

When God needed a message delivered, the available media and means were many. He could deliver the message to one individual or to a group. He might meet the target face to face, as is said explicitly about his interviews with Moses (Exod 33:11) and young Samuel (1 Sam 3:1–4). He could communicate indirectly, on mountains (Sinai/Horeb for one), near running waters (Gen 16:7, 32:23–33 [22–32 RSV]), at trees (Gen 12:6–7), through dreams (very common), and via natural phenomena, such as storms (lightning and thunder above all), winds (Ps 104:4), clouds in the shape of a

177

chariot (Hab 3:8), and smoke or fire (for example, Gen 15:17, "a smoking oven, a flaming torch"; Ps 104:4; or Joel 3:3 [2:30 RSV], "pillars of smoke").

We have seen in earlier Introductory Remarks to Judg 1:1–7 that lots (Urim and Thummim) and other instruments deemed less acceptable (tĕrāfîm, necromancy, and diverse forms of divination) were also available. Most often, however, God chose a mal'āk, human or supernatural, through which to communicate words that were barely distinguishable from God's own (see Exod 23:20–22). Mal'āk is normally rendered "messenger" or (less so) "representative," as it derives from the root *l'k, in Ugaritic meaning "to convey (messages)." In Hebrew (Aramaic and Phoenician as well) the root is frozen in such additional nouns as mĕlā'kâ and mal'ākût, "mission, work." In entrusting news, good or bad, to such emissaries, God is actually displaying grace, choosing to reveal rather than to hide decisions from his flock. Occasionally, however, we read that the dispatch of a mal'āk is a distancing act, done by a God who can no longer tolerate his people's repeated betrayals: "I will send an angel before you, and I will drive out the Canaanites, the Amorites, the Hittites, the Perizzites, the Hivvites, and the Jebusites . . . But I will not move out among you, because you are a stiff-necked people, lest I terminate you on the way" (Exod 33:2–3).

Biblical lore cites prophets (men and women) as the best-known human instruments, with a rich repertoire of terms applied to them, including nābî' ("prophet"), rō'ê ("seer"), ḥōzê ("visionary"), and 'îš (hā-)'ĕlōhîm ("God's man" [never "God's woman"!]). As a human envoy, mal'āk is applicable to kings (hyperbolically, about David, in 1 Sam 29:9 and 2 Sam 14:17), prophets (for example, Hag 1:13), and priests (Mal 2:7). The supernatural beings are presumably drawn from the circle of divine beings labeled "sons of God/gods" (bĕnê [hā]'ĕlōhîm, as in Gen 6:2–4 and Job 1:6, 2:1) or simply the "heavenly host" (ṣĕvā' haššāmayim, as in Deut 4:19, 17:3; 2 Kgs 17:16). They are never cherubic or cuddly, for when seen by humans (or by a prophet's donkey, Num 22), they make for an arresting presence.

The mission of the mal'ākîm is as simple as conveying a statement or as complex as shepherding Lot's family out of Sodom (Gen 19). They can be distinct and only represent God, or they can fade into the God who had commissioned them (Gen 18; see below at Judg 6). Thus while two of the mal'ākîm bringing tidings to Abraham make their way to Lot's Sodom, a third remains behind and is quickly identified as God.[3] When acting as adversary or promoting confusion, these beings can be called "spirit" ([hā]rûaḥ, as in 1 Kgs 22:19–22; also linked to šeqer, "deceit," or rā'â, "evil") or Satan (śāṭān, as in Zech 3). Our term for them, "angels," derives from the Greek (ἄγγελος), but unlike the Latin Vulgate or Targum Jonathan, which discriminates between supernatural (angelus, ml'kh) and human (nuntius, azgd') creatures, the Hebrew mal'āk does not. As we will soon see, this distinction is a source of problems.[4]

CHIDINGS

2 1. The construction (mal'ak-YHVH) suggests a definite subject ("the" rather than "an"). I translate mal'āk here neutrally, "emissary" ("messenger" might do as well), taking a cue from Targum Jonathan.[5] In most contexts, the distinction between human and angelic emissaries is clear even if not immediately so to the protagonists who meet them. In Judg 2:1, however, settling the matter is difficult. Greek and Latin versions both have

"angels"; the Targum gives "prophet," adding "on God's order." A clue to resolving our difficulty may be had from an episode involving Joshua. With his army bivouacking at Gilgal (see below) as it recovers from circumcision and celebrates the Passover, Joshua moves on to the site of his next battle. This is what happened (Josh 5:13–15):

> When Joshua was near Jericho, he looked up and saw a man standing before him, his drawn sword in hand. Joshua went up to him and asked him, "Are you for us or for our foes?" He replied, "No, but I am now come as commander of the LORD's host." Joshua threw himself face down to the ground and, prostrating himself, said to him, "What does my lord command his servant?" The commander of the LORD's host told Joshua, "Remove your sandals from your feet, for where you stand is holy." And Joshua did so.

This episode does not connect well with anything previous, except to enrich the parallels among the activities of Moses and Joshua. And in as much as this commander of the Lord will do nothing obvious at Jericho, the anecdote does not have much of a future either. What is interesting here is the difficulty in discriminating between the human and the divine. The figure does nothing unusual (as in the stories we shall soon inspect about Gideon and about Samson's parents) to substantiate its supernatural origins. Joshua sees a human in form, albeit of commanding posture, and it is only his faith in that being's statement that he behaves as if near holiness. Here, the difference between a human and a divine figure is above all played psychologically. We accept that Joshua saw an angel in human form because Joshua acts as if he did.[6]

Still, an insight by Savran (2003: 126–28) may be helpful in clarifying both the Joshua and the Judges passages.[7] In studying close to a score of examples of meetings with supernatural beings, Savran noted that the individuals involved tend to be separated from others, with no other participants to crowd their contact. The circumstance confers intimacy on their interaction; in some cases, as in Gen 32:23–33 (22–32 RSV), the encounter becomes emotionally fraught. The same isolation of characters promotes the potential that the narrator intended Joshua to meet an angel. As occurs in other contexts discussed by Savran (and will also be featured in Judg 6), Joshua's dialogue with the "man" will fade into one with God, corroborating the same inference. In contrast, because his harangue was heard by a multitude, we may have a clue that the narrator intended the *mal'āk* at Bochim to be a human messenger.

GILGAL

As edited in the received form, Judges presumes that events in the book of Joshua are known to readers, for Gilgal figures there prominently as a base of operations for the Hebrew armies (Josh 4:19ff.). In Hebrew, the name is almost always preceded by an article ("the Gilgal"), implying that it was descriptive, having to do with something rounded or in a circle. If so, rather than referring to anything "folkloristic," such as an association with "rolling away [verb: *gll*] Egypt's disgrace" (Josh 5:9), the name Gilgal might refer to its shrine, with rounds of stones or images (Josh 4:19–20, and below at 3:19). It might also allude to its topography, because it reminded of either a skull (*gulgōlet)* or columns (*gĕlîlôt*, in Josh 18:17 actually paralleling the Gilgal of 15:7!). The dictionaries discriminate among half a dozen towns named Gilgal. However, aside from looking for it near Jericho and Bethel, proposals to pinpoint the locations can be based on descriptive sympathy (Khirbet el-Mafjer, with a twelve-stone church) or aural harmony (Jiljulieh).

The thread of Hebrew historiography gives Gilgal prominence in the period immediately preceding the monarchy (Saul is crowned there, 1 Sam 11:14–15, echoed in David's recrowning in 2 Sam 19:15 [14 RSV]). Prophets (Amos, Hosea) condemn it as too accommodating to false gods. So when the messenger is said to come from Gilgal, he is leaving a site (as well as a moment) at which Israel and God had been in synch, working harmoniously to conquer the land that God promised and Israel deserved. The contrast between the two circumstances could not be made sharper, but the narrator succeeds in making it so by telling us from where the messenger reached *habbōkîm* to deliver his sermon.

"THE WEEPERS"

We notice that, as in Gilgal, an article is attached to the name of the messenger's destination, *habbōkîm* (it disappears in v. 5), implying that it was descriptive. *bōkîm* means "Weepers," and later on the name is linked to the reaction of the people to the messenger's severe words, "They broke into loud *weeping*."[8] Many scholars are not satisfied with such a (folk) etymology, and they connect *bōkîm* with a tree that shares its (Semitic) roots, so Allon-bacuth (allegedly "Weeping Oak") where Rebekah's nurse, Deborah, was said to be buried (Gen 35:8; see below). Others connect to the *bākā'* trees (balsam?) of 2 Sam 5:23–24 and to a valley named after them (Ps 84:7 [6 RSV]), even if the consonants are not compatible (see Lindars 1995: 76–77).

Some versions, among them Greek, try to be more specific by expanding, ἐπὶ τὸν Κλαυθμῶνα καὶ ἐπὶ Βαιθηλ καὶ ἐπὶ τὸν οἶκον Ισραηλ, "[an angel of the LORD went up from Galgal] to the Place of Weeping [plural in v. 5, Κλαυθμῶνες], and to Baithel, and to the House of Israel." Aside from specifically mentioning Bethel, so connecting backwards with the story of Luz and its capture, citing the "House of Israel" (rather than the more common "sons of Israel") sharpens connection with the "House of Joseph" of 1:23. A superficial connection with Israel assembling at Bethel later (at 20:26 and 21:2) has encouraged adoption of the Greek, with some translations (for example, the Jerusalem Bible) simply substituting Bethel for Bochim. Of course, it could be that the Greek reading is an accurate translation from a Hebrew manuscript now lost, and this is sometimes suggested because there is a space without a "ס" (פסקא) in the midst of the verse (see Kaufmann 1962: 92; with fine review in Barthélemy 1982: 75–76). It is more likely, however, that the LXX is simply trying to identify the location of a place otherwise unknown. (For more on Bochim, see below.)

PAST PLEDGE

As is normal, what the messenger delivers is understood as God's own words without having to say so; nonetheless, the Greek attaches "thus says the LORD." The first part reverses the normal formula that carries the condition of a covenant: the apotasis/apodosis ("then I shall do this") coming before the protasis ("if you do this"). There is another anomaly: God's words begin with a verb in the imperfect (*'a'ălê*, "I will lead you") when one would expect an expression of a past action. Most translations simply ignore the problem and translate with a past tense, perhaps encouraged by claims that we are dealing here with an unusual use of the imperfect (lastly in Watke and O'Connor 1990: 464, 498). Especially in nineteenth-century scholarship there were many proposals to expand for clarity or to emend the form as we have it (Lindars 1995: 77 and Moore 1895: 60–61 give samplings). However, this is not necessary for, as in many Semitic languages, the imperfect (especially in the first person) can be used to express a wish or intention that has carried from a moment distant in the past (GKC [§107], p. 317; perhaps *vāʾāvi*ʾ and *vāʾōmar* should be pointed *věʾavi*ʾ and *věʾōmar*).

God is recalling what he had promised to the ancestors long before Israel exited Egypt: He would never annul or cancel the covenant (*lěhāfēr běrît*—not the "break" of most translations, as it might imply volatility or arbitrariness), as it might lead to the disastrous results described in Lev 26:44: "Yet, even then, when they are in the land of their enemies, I will not reject them or spurn them so as to destroy them, annulling my covenant with them: for I the LORD am their God." But there was a condition to God's pledge.

WHAT COULD YOU BE DOING?

2 2–3. *věʾattem*, "as for you," introduces the stipulations for Israel to deserve God's loyalty. They include no political covenants with the conquered inhabitants and destruction of their altars. Although each condition is distinctive, in fact they can be related, for in the ancient world no pact was ever signed without cultic activities that included oaths, symbolic acts, presentation of a proposed treaty, sacrifice, and shared meals (even at long distance by shipping portions of the sacrifice).[9] Through these acts, a new relationship is established among all concerned (including their gods) that makes them (and their leaders) part of the same family.

The language is familiar from other contexts; *likrōt běrît lě*[x]-, literally "to cut an obligation/pledge with (someone)," means to conclude a treaty. Cross-cultural use of similar phraseology that links "cutting, splitting [*kārat*]" with "oath" (Phoenicia), calves (Sefire), and donkey foals (Mari) allows the reconstruction of a symbolic ritual in which a lesser power stood (or walked) between portions of a split animal.[10] Whatever its pristine origins, however, by the time it is invoked in the Hebrew Bible, the phrase had become idiomatic rather than descriptive, even if covenant ceremonies might include blood sacrifice.

The demand that Israel raze (*nātaṣ*) the altars of the enemy is metonymic for other acts of extirpation that are more fully developed in Deut 7:5: "You shall demolish their altars, smash their pillars [*maṣṣēvōtām*], cut down their sacred posts [*ʾăšērēhem*], and consign their images [*pěsîlêhem*] to the fire."[11] Greek (slightly differently in Rahlfs A and B) felt the need to alert against worship of other gods and to urge destroying their images.

Israel, of course, does not listen (*šāmaʿ*), which also means it does not obey—so a moral fault. It is obvious that the messenger is chiding when adding *mah-zzōʾt ʿăśîtem*. But precisely how is not clear. In Eccl 2:2, "I said of laughter, 'It is mad,' and of pleasure, 'What use is it?' [*mah-zzōh ʿōśâ*]," the phrase accentuates the futility of an act, and this is fairly obvious from other usage (Gen 3:13). In other contexts, however, it attributes deception (Gen 12:18, 26:10, Abra[ha]m; Gen 29:25, Laban; Gen 42:28, God; Exod 14:11, Moses; Judg 15:11, Samson) or exposes foolishness (Exod 14:5, Egyptians; Jonah 1:10, Jonah). Perhaps all three are implied here. Greek simply charges Israel with faults: You did not listen, "for you did these things" (ὅτι ταῦτα ἐποιήσατε).

After questioning Israel's sanity, the messenger comes back with God's resolve, and they follow closely on the two faults just enunciated. By making covenants with the inhabitants, Israel gives them comfort and support, enabling them to become adversaries.[12] Worse, their presence will invariably move Israel to worship their seductive gods, alienating the only God who might protect it. In this sense, these gods will actively turn into snares (idiom: *hâyâ lĕmôqēš lĕ+*), provoking more divine retaliation. How to assess the force of the conjunctive *vĕgam* is of interest. If it stands for "and now I say" (so Rashi), then it foreshadows the looming punishment that follows on misdeed; but if it means "I am also saying," then we are rehearsing sentiments expressed long ago, as in Exod 23:29. Van der Kooij (1995) favors the second approach.

Bochim

TEARS . . .

2 4–5. The image is vivid. Israel weeps loudly even as the words are spilling from the messenger's mouth, for the Hebrew encourages synchroneity here: *vayyĕhî kĕdabbēr mal'ak YHVH . . . . vayyiśśĕ'û hā'ām . . . 'et-qôlām*. The Greek and Targum versions, however, are less dramatic: Israel waits until the words are uttered before breaking down in tears.

Not unlike us, people of antiquity readily shed tears (verb: *bākâ*, accentuated by cries, *qōl*), because it is expected (such as at funerals, for Abner, 2 Sam 3:32; see 2 Sam 13: 36) or because they are touched by grief (Hagar, over the dying Ishmael, Gen 21:16; David and his men, on the destruction of Ziklag, 1 Sam 30:4), anger (Esau, deceived by his brother, Gen 27:38), alarm at potential loss (Naomi's daughters-in-law, Ruth 1:9, 14), or regret (Saul, about hounding David, 1 Sam 24:17).[13] They also wept out of sympathy (Job's friends, Job 2:12) or joy (Jacob on meeting Rachel, Gen 29:11). The same can be said for groups. They shed tears out of fear (on learning about powerful Canaan, Num 14:1), humiliation (1 Sam 11:4), or remorse (after almost wiping out Benjamin, Judg 21:2). But in antiquity, beyond the hurt and loss that led to private wails and sobs, weeping was also highly institutionalized. It was an element in formal commemorations, whether periodic, as during laments on the destruction of cities and temples, or whether it accompanied evocations of the deaths of gods (such as Dumuzi/ Tammuz).

No doubt a combination of emotions overtook the people when hearing God's chiding: They are fearful and contrite all right, but it could not hurt at all to display penitence, through tears but also through sacrifice. Whether or not the name Bochim was imposed right there and then by the sorrowful crowd depends on whether or not we make them the subject of *vayyiqrĕ'û šēm* ("they named that place Bochim") or treat the phrase impersonally ("the place was called Bochim"). Either can be argued, but as there is linkage between the naming and the offering of sacrifices, the narrator is definitely suggesting the former (contra Lindars 1995: 79). If this is the case, the narrative's investment in this episode is to have us accept that Bochim earned its name because of a specific tearful reaction to dreadful news, a goal only slightly compromised by its mention at 2:1. Sanctification of the spot, possibly as a shrine, may have followed on the people's next act.

The verb alluding to sacrifice, *zāvaḥ*, is one of many in Hebrew about slaughter; it can refer to both ritual and profane killings, depending on its contexts and connections with other substantives.[14] Here it is obviously the former, as what is killed is destined for God, *vayyizvĕḥû-šām laYHVH*. However, for all its references to warfare, oracles, and individual mayhem, Judges has few references to *zāvaḥ* or its congeners. There will soon be (at Judg 8) several mentions of *zevaḥ*, but they will allude to a Midianite king, likely named after a feast day. But if we switch to other nouns that refer to sacrifices (in this case *ʿōlôt* and *šĕlāmîm*), at Judg 20:26 and 21:2–4, we find Israel, unnerved by its engagements with Benjamin, going to Bethel to shed tears, fast, and offer sacrifices.[15] It will be another occasion in the book of Judges where "weeping" and sacrifices are linked. We shall soon have Jephthah's daughter weeping before her father accomplishes what he vows (11:37–39), but connecting the situation with ours will be a stretch.

COMMENTS

Whether delivered by an angel, a prophet, or simply an individual commissioned for the occasion, what God has to say could not have given comfort. This particular episode seems suspended in time, especially in the Hebrew version, so also in place. We certainly can presume that it was purposefully set after Israel reached the Promised Land, since it explains why the land was not fully conquered. But like many other episodes in Hebrew narratives (the Akedah in Gen 22 is a parade example), few are the details that attach it to its surroundings.[16] The episode occupies very few verses, but the drama it describes is integral and complete. The absence of specifics contributes to the parabolic tenor of the message: Entrance and exit are abrupt, disjunctive, and tense; yet they are conclusive, and none but scholars would demand that they deliver background or denouement.

The speech opens with an unexpected verbal form (an imperfect of *hēʿālôt*), effectively transferring God's thought into time immemorial. As formulated, long before Israel was on its way to the Promised Land, God had vowed to deliver a land to the elect. The conditions were also set then: God does not bequeath land to those who are ready to accommodate unworthy people or to undermine God's authority. But look at Israel now, God's message continues: It cannot fulfill these minimal expectations. Therefore, God is about to launch the sort of travails that are normal when enemies share the same land. Falsely, these hardships may be deemed punishment for recent shortcomings; in fact, these countermeasures had been preset long ago, when Israel and God were still courting each other.

The Greek versions of our episode are engrossed by the punctual aspect of the event and so try to be more specific about Bochim, linking it to Bethel. Many scholars sympathize with this drive to historicize and so give priority to the Greek witnesses (for example, Cooke 1913: 23: "There is little doubt we should substitute **to Beth-el**, following the LXX"). Amit (2000a: 125–26), who presumes that the Hebrew narrator is purposely refraining from mentioning Bethel, sets the episode just before Josiah's reform when narrators indulged in a "hidden polemic" against a paganizing city. This is far-fetched and depends on foregrounding political circles hardly known to us. Spronk

(2001: 90) follows her suggestion but makes the place a locus for cultic weeping for the dead.

But the biggest flaw in harmonizing between the Hebrew and Greek versions (whether by emending or by conjuring up veiled ideologies) is in not recognizing their dissimilar objectives. For the Greek, the mention of Bethel sets the story as the other bracket of what had happened at Luz. In this way, 2:15 comments on the northern tribes and explains why their efforts were bound to be foiled. The failures of Manasseh, Ephraim, Zebulun, Asher, Naphtali, and Dan to dislodge the enemy were not just the result of military failure, but also of moral if not also spiritual breakdown. The story, therefore, relies on short-term memory, is circumspect, has limited ambitions, and aims for clear-cut results.

In the Hebrew version, however, the emissary's trajectory sharpens the parabolic goal of the episode. The messenger moves from Gilgal where, under Joshua, Israel had charted the occupation and was resolved to fulfill its destiny. He appears before all of Israel at Bochim, a place otherwise unknown (to us) but with a name ("Weepers") that is conceived by all of Israel. He delivers a message to all of Israel and formulates a compact that must apply for all of Israel. The episode is commenting on all that had occurred previously and criticizing each and all tribes. The Hebrew version, therefore, has a longer memory of the Hebrew past and can prepare us to draw better lessons from the powerful indictments that will soon follow.

I have preferences for both versions, each in its own setting, and would not want to reshape either for the sake of consistency or coherence.

2. Judges for Israel (Judg 2:6–23)

2   ⁶When Joshua dismissed the people, each person in Israel went to take possession of his allotted land. ⁷The people served only the LORD during the full lifetime of Joshua as well as the full lifetime of all the elders who outlived Joshua and who had witnessed every great deed that the LORD had done for Israel. ⁸Joshua son of Nun, the servant of the LORD, died at 110 years of age ⁹and was buried within his allotted land, at Timnath-heres in Mount Ephraim, north of Mount Gaash. ¹⁰Eventually, when members of this entire generation were gathered to their fathers, the generations of people born after them hardly acknowledged the LORD or even the deeds he had done for Israel. ס

¹¹The people of Israel did what was offensive to the LORD: They worshiped the many Baals; ¹²they forsook the LORD, God of their fathers, who had brought them out of the land of Egypt; they committed to other gods, from among those of people around them, bowing down to them. So they provoked the LORD ¹³by forsaking the Lord and worshiping Baal and the Ashtaroth. ¹⁴Incensed against Israel, the LORD abandoned them to raiders, who plundered them and turned them over to their enemies on all sides, such that they could no longer resist their foes. ¹⁵Everywhere they marched to battle, the Lord would intervene to hurt them, as the LORD declared and as the LORD avowed to them.

They therefore suffered terribly. [16]The LORD would then install judges, and they would rescue them from their plunderers. [17]Yet, the people would not heed their own judges, for they would lust after other gods, falling prostrate before them. They swiftly retreated from the path their fathers had followed, in no way acting to obey the commandments of the LORD. [18]Whenever the LORD would install judges for them, the LORD would sustain the judge who would rescue them from their enemies during that judge's entire tenure; for the LORD would be moved to pity by their groaning, because of their tormentors and oppressors. [19]At the death of the judge, however, they would once again act more corruptly than their own parents, by following other gods, serving them, and falling prostrate before them; they omitted none of their practices or their obstinate ways.

[20]Incensed against Israel, the LORD decided, "Since the people of this nation violated the covenant that I urged on their fathers and did not heed my command, [21]I will certainly no longer displace before them even a single person from those nations that Joshua left whole when he died, [22]so as to use them for testing Israel: Whether or not they can keep to the LORD's way, guiding themselves as their ancestors had done." [23]Thus the LORD kept those nations whole, without displacing them hastily, and did not turn them over to Joshua. פ

NOTES

Their eyes became dim-sighted until another sheep arose and led them. Then, they would all return and their eyes became opened.
—*1 Enoch 89:41*[1]

Restore our judges as in former times and our counselors as at the beginning. Remove from us sorrow and groaning. Reign over us, you alone, O LORD, with benevolence, compassion, fairness, and justice. Blessed are you, O LORD, the King who loves righteousness and justice.
—*The eleventh benediction in the* Amidah[2]

Introductory Remarks: Translating the Title *šōfēṭ*—A Justification

In the following pages there will be several occasions to translate the word *šōfēṭ*, and I have knowingly chosen an English word, "judge," that cannot adequately represent what was meant by the Hebrew. The old line "translators are traitors" (*traduttore traditore* is the felicitous Italian adage) has as many variants as there are languages with the capacity to pun on the relevant verbs, but the sentiment it carries is never more true than when applied to vocabulary describing activities or vocations that are not easily duplicated across cultures. This is certainly the case when evolving societies create increasingly distinctive professions but apply to them inherited terminology. In our culture, a judge (eventually from Latin *judex*, "one who pronounces the law") is normally a court official with authority to hear and decide in legal cases. Our judges do not create law (although they can creatively interpret it), and they do not execute the judgment (but they might increase the penalty when angered). Other organs of government are allotted these tasks. But even within our culture, the term "judge" can have applications that are scarcely legal, for example, a judge in a beauty or sports contest. What is shared is the authority to impose an opinion. The point to keep is that the same title need not imply the same qualification or area of expertise.

The Hebrew word šōfēṭ (plural šōfĕṭîm) is a participle, so one engaged in the performance of a *špṭ act. Other words based on this root are mišpāṭ, "ordinance, decree," šĕfāṭîm (always in the plural but referring to a "judgment, decision"), and šĕfōṭ, with a similar sense but also implying "punishment." The verb šāfaṭ is ostensibly transparent (it certainly is not about unjust acts or results) but also is difficult to adequately pinpoint. It seems to cover two overlapping spheres of action.[3] One is about making a choice among alternatives, hence deciding legal cases, so closer to our sense of "judge," with ṣedeq, "righteousness," but also nĕqāmâ, "reprisal," as a goal. In this category, it stands in parallel with such verbs as *dîn, "to present/settle a legal case," and *rîb, "to accuse, contest (legally)." In Judges, the single reference to the title šōfēṭ with this specific sense is applied to God as the ultimate judge in political disputes (11:27).

The other meaning has to do with authority and control, even dominion. Here it matches such verbs as yš' (Hiphil), "rescue"; *plṭ (Piel), "deliver"; *nṣl (Hiphil) min, "deliver from"; and *šw', "save."[4] In Judges, this meaning is applied to leaders only in the preamble (Judg 2:16–19), about which, see the Comments. The image of God as a šōfēṭ, standing in the midst of an assembly (Ps 82), certainly partakes of both meanings. Perhaps the same can be said about Moses, who governs as well as decides cases (Exod 18:13).[5]

To evaluate the role of those titled šōfēṭ, we might also assess the company they keep.[6] Together with priests (Deut 17:9) and Levites (Deut 19:17–18), or with elders (Deut 21:2), they are charged with investigating (verb: dāraš) cases too difficult for local officials to solve, so a kind of inspector. The presumption is that the famous call to "pursue full justice" (ṣedeq ṣedeq tirdōf, Deut 16:20) applies to them. They can be linked with nontemple šōṭĕrîm, "clerks, record keepers," in such a way that they form a hendiadys (a single idea out of two nouns), so "notaries" or the like (Deut 16:18; 1 Chr 23:4, 26:29). Perhaps as such they are represented at major covenantal convocations (Josh 8:33, 23:2, 24:1). It is difficult to decide whether or not to treat similarly the mention of śar vĕšōfēṭ in Exod 2:14 (so "chief magistrate"—said mockingly of Moses) or the reference to šofĕṭîn and dayyānîn (Aramaic), so "board of judges" in Ezra 7:25. They may represent discrete functions. Finally, the term occurs in literary contexts, in one case (Isa 1:23) paralleling śar, "official," in another (Isa 1:26) matching yō'ēṣ "adviser." In Isa 3:2–4 it is embedded in a long string of functions. From this sampling, we can say that beyond operating on a legal or political level, the šōfēṭ also held decidedly bureaucratic functions, further compromising our search for its English equivalent.

The root *špṭ occurs in a number of cognate languages (among them Akkadian, Ugaritic, Aramaic, Amorite, and Phoenician) with meanings that are similarly broad. Once promising as a resource for shedding light on the biblical institution were the Mari archives, with their rich storehouse of information on the activities of the šāpiṭum and the office he held, the šāpiṭūtum. What made the documentation especially interesting is that it contained enormous details on the many individuals who held such offices, always as functionaries of the king, giving us a richer profile for the personalities and the posts they occupied. The dossier of such "governors" (our conventional name for their office) has them working for the palace, caring for fields and canals, policing and spying in and out of their area, attending to the local shrines, and resolving personal and tribal disputes. Taking the initiative was not their forte, so only superficially do they function as do our "judges." To approximate the authority of the Hebrew *šōfēṭ*, we would need to attach to the Mari *šāpiṭum* the power attributed to the *merḥûm*, a military leader of the tribal elements in the king's army.[7]

This brief exposition may be useful, but it has led to no happy solution. Hebrew usage for *šōfēṭ* and its cognates discourages locating for it a precise English term, and this is confirmed by sampling excellent translations of Scripture. For example the *TNK* [NJPS] has "magistrates" for *šōfēṭ* in most biblical contexts, reserving "chieftain" for *nāśî'*. In Judges, however, it gives "chieftain" for *šōfēṭ* (once also for *rō'š*, at 10:18), yet it retains the traditional "Judges" for the name of the book. "Leaders" (New International Version [NIV]) and "rulers" are perfectly reasonable if ambiguous renderings, but they risk being bland. Having failed to arrive at a better alternative, not wishing to give it as a transliteration of Hebrew ("Shofet," or the like), and lacking the temerity to demand that the Anchor Yale Bible change the title of this volume, I (reluctantly) stay with "judges," joining others (for example, the RSV, New King James Version [NKJV], Jerusalem Bible, and the like) who might have come to the same conclusion.

After Joshua

2 6–7. In the book of Joshua we learn about the dispatch of spies (to Jericho, 2:1), scouts (to Ai, 7:2), and inspectors (to uncover a crime, 7:22). People are sent on these missions that get filled within the lifetime of Joshua. In these cases, the verb is *šālaḥ*, and it has to do with setting off someone (among them messengers) or something (among them rods or bodily parts) toward a destination away from the subject. In our phrase *vayyěšallaḥ yěhôšū'*, however, we meet with the Piel of the same verb, so the meaning here is factitive: to make someone or something move out. The accent is on a displacement that is definitive, with no expectation of return to the dispatcher. Thus the verbal form is used when God expels Eve and Adam (Gen 3:23), Noah sends out birds from the ark (Gen 8), Moses demands release of the Hebrew slaves (for instance, Exod 7:16), scapegoats are thrust into the wilderness (Lev 16:22), and women are divorced (for instance, Deut 24:1). As it happens, the phrase *vayyěšallaḥ yěhôšū'*, as well as the information it initiates, replicates material in Josh 24:28–31. The relationship is evaluated in the Comments below.

For some translators, the replay of language from Joshua forces a decision on how to construe its reiteration. The Judges narrator could not have wished Joshua to die and be buried *after* the angel had made his visit to Bochim. A superficial "solution" is to translate all the verbs with the pluperfect, as does Boling (1975: 71; see also O'Connell 1996: 72) ("When Joshua had dismissed the people, each person in Israel had gone to take possession of his allotted land"). While markers for the pluperfect in Hebrew remain under debate, resorting to them in English translations almost always arrests narrative continuity or isolates events from their contexts. As rendered by Boling, this passage sits forlorn and unconnected. Yet, these verses cannot have been attached *secondarily* as final words to Joshua, for they make a convincing coda there to the drama for which he was the major protagonist. Nor could they have once opened Judges, for entire phrases at the end of one block of material are not repeated at the beginning of another simply to sustain continuity in events. To the contrary, what we now have at Judg 1:1, with its reference to the death of Joshua (see above), is a perfectly reasonable introduction to the next phase in the development of the narrative. This time, however, it is no longer about the conquest of land but about the loss of divine support—episodic and spasmodic though its propulsion may have been.

Joshua's Generation

During Joshua's long life and the many years that his generation lived beyond him, Israel never thought of shifting its allegiance to other gods. This notion is driven home by the phrase *he'ĕrîkû yāmîm*, "increasing the years," almost always associated with the longevity achieved by devotion to God (frequent in Deuteronomy) or to his commandments (Exod 20:12, Deut 5:16; for the reverse see Eccl 8:13). It does not matter that the virtues of Joshua's generation are linked to its firsthand experience of God's mighty acts, for as we shall soon see, there will be many opportunities for God to interfere physically on behalf of his people. Yet Israel will repeatedly display perplexing amnesia about the wonders it experienced, and it will no longer recall that there can be no fulfillment of promise when God feels rejected.

The Surviving Generation

2 8–9. The notice about Joshua's death and burial rephrases what is said in Josh 24:29–30 (see the Comments). Himself from the tribe of Ephraim (so from Joseph), Joshua lived 110 years, the same as Joseph (Gen 50:22, 26)—a parallel that is exploited in Josh 24 (but not here) by mention of the reburial of Joseph's bones. Although God frequently labels a patriarch, a prophet (Ahijah, Elijah, Isaiah), and a king (mostly David) "my servant," the title "the Lord's servant" (*'eved YHVH*) is limited to Moses and (less often) to Joshua. It is always applied posthumously; a good number of the examples in fact are located in Joshua.[8] As applied to Moses and to Joshua, the phrase is yet one more fragment in a parallel design that includes removal of shoes when meeting the divine (Josh 5:13–15 and Exod 3:2–5), miraculous crossings of major bodies of water (Josh 4:23 and Exod 15), assurance of God's support (Josh 1:5, 3:7; cf. 4:14), and mediating a covenant between Israel and God (Josh 24, Exod 20–24) (see Wenham 1971: 145–46).

Mount Ephraim

Mount Ephraim (*har 'efrāyim*) refers to a block of heights controlled by a number of tribes, including Benjamin, Ephraim, and Manasseh. Many translations offer "hill country of Ephraim" (or the like). There is a discrepancy, however, about where in Mount Ephraim Joshua's burial site was. In our passage, it is at Timnath-heres (*timnat-ḥeres*; Greek, Θαμναθαρες), the designation likely influenced by the mention of Har-Heres recorded just above (Judg 1:35). In Josh 24:30, however, the grave was at Timnath-serah (*timnat-seraḥ*, Greek, Θαμναθασαχαρα), likely following Josh 19:50 (Greek, Θαμνασαραχ). The metathesis (a switch in the order of the same consonants) is therefore contextual and hardly amenable to reconstructing an "original" reading. In the *ABD* (6: 557–58) H. R. Weeks treats both place names under Timnath-heres, more or less adopting a theory that the name in Joshua was cleansed to remove a potential cultic implication because *ḥeres* (see above) *might* mean "sun." As to location, since antiquity Joshua's tomb was venerated at Thamna (Josephus, Timnab; *Ant.* 5.119), a town with much history during the Hellenistic period, placed at today's Khirbet Tibneh (M.R. 160157), some 24 kilometers southwest of Nablus (Shechem). Nearby are many tombs cut in the rock, some with a dozen or more chambers. It does not help that Mount Gaash has yet to be identified.

One Generation to Another

2 10. The notice about the extinction of Joshua's generation returns to what was said about fealty to God but also prepares for the denunciation that is about to be launched. The phrase *haddôr hāhû'*, "that generation," is used with similarly ominous prospects in Exod 1:6, developing on what follows in Joseph's wake. Metaphoric for burial are the expressions "to be gathered to the ancestors" (*ne'ĕsāp 'el-'ăvôt-*, 2 Kgs 22:20, 2 Chr 34:28) and kindred phrases: *ne'ĕsāp 'el-'am-*, "to be gathered to one's people," and *šākab 'im 'ăvôt-*, "to rest with the ancestors." Nevertheless, they evoke an experience in which families engaged in a protracted act of devotion: After laying out the deceased in a hewn cave or burying the dead in a shallow grave ("to sleep with the ancestors," 1 Kgs 14:31, 2 Chr 12:16), the family awaits the body's reduction to bones before they are gathered and placed with those of other members of the clan. The sequence is brought out in 2 Chr 34:28 (slightly shorter in 2 Kgs 22:20), in which Huldah reassures Josiah regarding his personal fate: Because he was full of humility, "I will therefore gather you to your ancestors [*hinnĕnî 'ōsifkā 'el-'ăvōtêkā*] and you will be gathered into your tomb in peace [*vĕne'ĕsaftā 'el-qivrōtêkā bĕšālôm*]. Your eyes will not witness all the horror I am planning for this place and its inhabitants."[9] Eventually, after issues of resurrection began to surface during the Persian period, the bones of each individual were collected into an ossuary that, with or without a name, was set alongside others from the same family.[10] In Judges, however, we hear only of burial in family tombs (Gideon, 8:32; Samson, 16:31) or in tribal towns: Tola, in the Shamir hills of Ephraim, 10:2; Jair, in Kamon of Gilead, 10:5; Jephthah, in Gilead, 12:7; Ibzan, in Bethlehem of Zebulun, 12:10; Elon, in Ayyalon also of Zebulun, 12:12; and Abdon, in Pir'aton of Ephraim, 12:15.

Generational transition takes place at the extinction of those who experienced Joshua's leadership. The phrase *lō' yādĕ'û 'et-YHVH* is even harsher than its literal rendering, "they did not know the LORD." In fact they did, but they simply chose to ignore him, much as is said about the sons of Eli, who ostensibly were ministering at his altar (1 Sam 2:12). Too, their memory lapsed on the great victories that God had given them. Soon (at 3:1), this notion will be picked up before the consequences are detailed.

Backsliding

2 11–13. The roster of faults opens at Judg 2:11 with a formula that conveys the shift in fortune that Israel will experience. We shall meet slight variations of it at 3:7 and 6:1, as well as a more decorated version that sharpens Israel's outrageous behavior ("the people of Israel *resumed* offending the LORD") at 3:12, 4:1, 10:6, and 13:1. An obvious difference is whether or not specific provocations follow the expression, as it does here. It is not just that Israel's memory of God and of the deeds he wrought in its behalf was faulty, but that it actively pursued worship of the *bĕ'ālîm*, plural of *ba'al*, "owner, possessor." Here the word refers neither to the West Semitic god Haddad (normally *habba'al* in the Hebrew Bible or "Baal" in Ugaritic and Phoenician texts) nor to a combination of his many manifestations (Baal-Gad, Baal-Hazor, Baal-Hermon, Baal-Meon, Baal-Peor, or the like). Rather, *běʿālîm* is here generic for all false divinities, powers, or numina, of either sex, who might have swayed Israel away from the only God they needed to worship. In biblical lore, however, hardly ever is there any valid exposition for what attracts Israel to these powers. Is it their demonstrated success in bringing bounties to the faithful or their proven capacity to thwart enemies and achieve victories? Instead, we find blistering mockery of their impotence (1 Kgs 18), sarcasm of their human manufacture (Isa 44), and catalogues of activities associated with their worship, including charges of sexual license and human sacrifice that, fortunately, are not confirmed beyond dispute from contemporaneous sources.

The verb associated with this alienation is *ʿāzav*, "to abandon, to forsake," normally with some permanence. It is fairly standard in narratives about Israel's defections, but in Judges it is allocated to just two clusters: thrice in our segment (at 2:12, 13, and 21) and, as we shall see, thrice more in the crucial moment when God pledges to withdraw his favor before the rise of Jephthah (at 10: 6, 10, and 13). The oddity is the verb's use in 2:21, when Joshua is said to "leave behind" (an exceptional usage) all those unconquered nations that will haunt Israel. The play here is unmistakable, a sort of tit-for-tat: Israel forsakes God, and Joshua sets up the instruments for Israel's future punishment. Yet, it must not be imagined that God was innocent of this development, as we shall see at 2:23.

SEDUCTIVE DEITIES

The charge is developed in 2:12: How could Israel abandon a deity who was not only the God of ancestors (*ʾĕlōhê [hā]ʾăvôt*)[11] with whom a covenant was established (Exod 3:1–6, 6:2–8), but also a God who delivers from bondage (Exod 20:2, Deut 5:6)? Worse, how could Israel put its faith in the gods of people destined for obliteration, by definition therefore impotent gods? Naturally God is angered, and in 2:13 the narrator returns to the core of the affront: the worship of local gods. Here, male and female deities are mentioned in the merismus (a whole out of parts) linking *baʿal* (in the singular, so the Canaanite Baal) and the *ʿaštārôt* (in the plural, as always in Scriptures; but see Josh 21:27), his consort of many manifestations.[12] The idiom is different from what preceded; here it is *ʿāvad lĕ-*, rather than the more frequent *ʿāvad ʾet* that we just saw in 2:11. In Jer 44:3 the idiom does not seem to suggest a different meaning; but to judge from 1 Sam 4:9, in which Philistines are urged to fight lest they become slaves to the Hebrews, it is implied here that Israel has fallen victim to its neighbors, slaving at their shrines rather than simply worshiping their gods.[13]

For the Hebrews, Ashtoret-Astarte was the goddess of the Sidonians, so of their neighbor to the north. Occasionally, the name is given in the singular (2 Kgs 23:13; 1 Kgs 11:5 and 33, albeit with a plural referent), but most often we find the plural, as above.[14] Scripture can poetically invoke Ashtoret's name as a noun/adjective for the power she represented, in this case fertility, as in *ʿaštĕrōt ṣōʾnekā*, "your fertile sheep."[15] (Deut 7:13 and 28:51 are veritable compendia of such sentiments.) The Hebrew Bible also reports a shrine with multiple avatars of the goddess in Bashan (Deut 1:4; Josh 12:4, 13:12, 31; see Josh 9:10), near Qarnayim (Gen 14:5), and in Beth-shean, where Saul's armors are deposited in homage (1 Sam 31:10, see 1 Chr 10:10; the passage is often emended). In Ugaritic and Phoenician lore, Astarte can also be an avatar (but not a consort) of Baal.

The phrase and its congeners (we find also the plural of Baal, as in Judg 10:6, 1 Sam 7:4) do not convey a sophisticated appreciation of Canaanite theology; rather, they serve to condemn forbidden loyalty. Later on, in a line that gives a tightened version of what is expressed in 2:11–13 (see below), we find Israel worshiping the Baalim and the Asheroth (3:7). Asherah (Ugaritic's *'aṯrt* and Amarna Aširta) was the consort of El. In a Canaanizing tale found in the Hittite capital Ḫattuša (today's Boghaz Köy), she was not above seducing Baal. As her worship moved beyond Canaan, to Ramesside Egypt, for example, the goddess commonly morphed into other imported deities, such as Qadesh(et), Anat, and Astarte. (See the brief overview by John Day in *ABD* 1: 483–87.) For our purposes, it may suffice to observe that no Canaanite would confuse Astarte and Asherah; but for the point Israel is trying to make, there was no need to be fussy about identity, and we should not try to emend either passage to achieve harmony.

The Anger of God

2 14–15. The charge laid out in the preceding verses against Israel is powerful; in human terms, it is equivalent to treason, deliberate and remorseless. Whatever Israel had to say in its own defense is not recorded; at 2:1–5 (above), Israel was quick to accept the onus and to beg forgiveness. God is moved to anger (*vayyiḥar-'af YHVH*) for the first of four times in Judges (also at 2:20, 3:8, and 10:7). In the Comments, I review the linkage between the two attestations in this chapter. In this case, however, as in 3:8 and 10:7, the consequence is misery for Israel. The outcome is soon detailed, almost sequentially, but the narrator wants it known that each of these reverses is divinely orchestrated: God "gives them over" (*nātan běyad*), an expression with broad applications, but in military contexts always implying that people are left to the mercy of others.[16] The *šōsîm* (from an unstable root **šsh/śss/š's*) seems to designate pirate raiders. Working beyond the control of organized state powers (see 2 Kgs 17:20), their work is particularly cruel as it must be accomplished stealthily, quickly, and indiscriminately to avoid retaliation. Several scholars have tried to associate them with the Shasu/Shosu (*š3sw*) of Egyptian New Kingdom and Empire records, likely referring to a social class rather than an ethnic entity. The Shasu operated in southern Palestine across the Jordan, behaving much like the Habirus (Rainey 2008), often forcefully confronting Egypt. Much interest was focused on a list carved on Egyptian columns at Soleb (Amenhotep III) and Amarah (Seti or Ramses II) in which Shasu elements are attached to six areas, among them Seir. Another place, Yhw, is connected with the Hebrew God, and so the Shasus were also incongruously associated with formative Israel. (On all this, see also "Shasu" by W. A. Ward, *ABD* 5: 1165–67, as well as the articles of S. Rosen, E. van der Steen, and especially Th. Levy in Szuchman 2009.)

Next, God "sells" (*mākar běyad* [someone]) Israel, not for gain (what could Israel's enemy give him in payment?), but to affirm his total control over people deemed his property (*segullâ*; Deut 7:6, 14:2; Ps 135:4). With or without *běyad*, the verb shapes a theme that occurs often in Scripture (Deut 32:30, 1 Sam 12:9, Ps 44:13 [12 RSV], Isa 50:1, Ezek 30:12) and plays it like a leitmotif in Judges (3:8, 4:2, 10:7; also 4:9). With God no longer on its side, Israel cannot defend itself when the enemy swarms all around it. The last stage of God's assault is the cruelest of all, for God is not satisfied to coax enemies against Israel; rather, he actively frustrates its endeavor. The Hebrew is rather ambiguous, *běkōl ʾăšer yāṣěʾû* (verb: *yāṣāʾ*; oddly enough, πορνεύω, "to whore," in Rahlfs A), and may mean whatever kind of sortie they undertake or whatever places (so the Targum) they pitch their tents for battle. I translate with the latter, but the other rendering is also possible. Not grammatically accurate, however, is Boling's "whenever they ventured" (1975: 73).

But there is worse: The God who would battle the enemy is now battling his own people (the Targum says it is a plague); the scene seems a fulfillment of curses God promised to launch against a disloyal Israel: "The LORD will put you to rout before your enemies; you shall march out against them by a single road, but flee from them by many roads; and you shall become a horror to all the kingdoms of the earth" (Deut 28:25, *TNK*). Israel is powerfully hurt; the phrase *vattēṣer lāhem* will occur in Judg 10:9. Among other similar phrasings (at Gen 32:8 and 1 Sam 30:6, for example), it connotes distress that comes from being restricted in avenues or choices. Still, why we should not supply here "the children of Israel cried unto the LORD" (Burney 1970: 59; Lindars 1995: 105) is developed in the Comments.

Judges

2 16–17. The shift between the previous statement ("They therefore suffered terribly") and God's act is abrupt, with only a conjunction separating them. The causative (Hiphil) of the verb **qwm* (*hāqîm*) is fairly well-attested. It describes people setting up buildings, altars, tents, and siege towers, as well as rousing lions and helping animals to their feet. God (metaphorically) erects thrones (2 Sam 3:10), sets up the cosmos (Prov 30:4), and fulfills promises (as in Deut 9:5, Num 23:19). He brings to power what did not exist previously, among others, priests (1 Sam 2:35), prophets (Deut 18:15, 18), kings (Deut 28:36), and adversaries (*śāṭān*, 1 Kgs 11:14, 23). In the same way, he wills the formation of judges (Judg 2:16, 18), who are later equated with rescuers (*môšîʿaʿ*, Judg 3: 9, 15; 6:36; 12:3 [ironic]), with permanence of office distinguishing between the two. While "to raise" such leaders is the reasonable (and usual) English translation for the forms of *hāqîm*, I use "to install" because continuity, rather than just formation, is always at stake.

Worth noticing are references to judges in the plural (*šōfěṭîm*), three of them in two verses (2:16–17). Given that the argument being presented is that God sends just one judge at each eruption of compassion for Israel, this usage startles. One may treat these as examples of a distributive ("one judge for each group") or repetitive ("one judge after the other") use of the plural. More attractive to me is that the plural here moves the narrative from an actual recital of what has happened ("one judge came and then another judge came") to one that is to happen at the time of description ("judges would come"). The English modal "would" serves this purpose well, and I have used it for this sequence (2:16–19). A case can be made, however, to apply this construction from 2:14.

From 2:16 we learn about a major function of the "judge," which is to rescue (verb **yšʿ*, in the Hiphil) people. While this verb may indeed invest the act with a spiritual dimension ("to save" in the sense of "redeem" from sin or error) and while there are a fair number of passages in which "judging" in tandem with "rescuing" is attributed to God (Ps 36:7 [6 RSV], 72:4, 76:10 [9 RSV], 109:31; Isa 51:5; Ezek 34:22), it is useful to keep in mind that the judges do their work on earth, freeing people from immediate harm or danger by direct action. In fact, this is not the lesson the Greek drew from this passage, for it gives God credit for the liberation, καὶ ἔσωσεν αὐτοὺς κύριος, "and the LORD saved them" (Rahlfs B).[17]

CARNAL IGNORANCE

Israel's incapacity to bridle its passion for other gods is declared in carnal terms, so much so that this propensity for wickedness is displayed even as a judge is acting to stem God's anger (Kaufmann 1962: 97). Previously, they followed (*hālak ʾaḥăr*[*ê*]) false deities, implying a willingness just to assimilate and act as others do. This time, however, the verb is *zānâ ʾaḥăr*[*ê*], "to lust after," in a driven, unrestrained, perhaps also venal fashion. The metaphor is readily called upon elsewhere in Scripture (see the dictionaries), occasionally with the heart and eyes as subjects (Ezek 6:9), the object of desire being unspecified deities, *ʾĕlōhîm ʾăḥērîm* (as in here, Exod 34:15, Deut 31:16, 1 Chr 5: 25), the gods Molek (Lev 20:5) and the many Baals (Judg 8:33), diverse supernatural manifestations (Lev 17:7, 20:6) and instruments for divination (Judg 8:27).

2 18–19. In these verses, the above charge remains didactic, but the shortcoming is vividly illustrated. The accusation that Israel disobeyed its judges (2:17) is modified: Israel does indeed behave correctly during the tenure of the judge, so justifying God's change of heart (idiom: **nḥm* [N] *min*; but see Isa 1:24) because of Israel's groans (*neʾāqâ*, often resulting in good behavior, Exod 22:24, 6:5; but see Job 24:12).[18] The surcease is brief; come the judge's death, Israel once again loses its focus (the verb *šûb* is here in hendiadys (see Joüon and Muraoka 1996: 650 [§177b]) and becomes as corrupt (*věhišḥîtû*) as ever before. Here, there is a contrast between the *ʾāvôt* of two verses back (2:17), between ancestors always recalled as venerable and worthy and these particular *ʾāvôt*, the parents and grandparents who needed a judge to save them from deserved punishment. It is part of Israel's lore that the passing of one generation is enough to reverse hard-earned gains.

Justifications

2 20–22. This is our second meeting with God's anger (*vayyiḥar-ʾaf YHVH běyiśrāʾēl*), the first having just been displayed (at 2:14) and resulting in mayhem against Israel.[19] This time, the reference to God's antagonism against his people leads us to divine reflection that carries with it grave consequences for Israel's future. The anger is palpable, for God is scornful in labeling Israel "this *gôy*."[20] Now it is true that God can call Israel a *gôy* in very favorable contexts (Gen 12:2, 17:6, 18:18; Exod 19:6), but a plurality of the references (especially when in the plural *gôyîm*) are to the surrounding nations (Deut 15:6, 28:12, 36; Josh 23:4), evil in intent (Deut 9:4–5) and worshipers of false gods (Deut 18: 9, 2 Kgs 17:29, 2 Chr 33:2). The distinction between the usages is not categorical, and we have contexts such as Exod 33:13 (see also Deut 4:6–7) where Moses tells God, "Look this nation [*gôy*] is your people [*ʿam*]," the latter term more precisely referring to a group with ethnic bonds. A pejorative sense for *gôy* and especially for *gôyîm* ("gentile") crystallizes centuries after its biblical usage (see Cody 1966; on the anomalous use of the verb *ʿāzav*, see above, under 2:11–13).

How much of the statement to assign to God is difficult to establish. It could end at 2:22 or it could include that verse. The controlling verbal form in 2:22 is an infinitive (*lĕnassôt*) and so cannot easily be assigned to a specific voice. It is a judgment call. The RSV, KJV, and American Standard Version (ASV) treat 2:22 inclusively and so supply "that I [that is, God] may test" (or the like), which is not evident in the Hebrew. The matter is not aided by the previous clauses where in 2:20 the conjunction *yaʿan ʾăšer* sets the cause for God's anger without, however, following with an expected *lākēn*, "accordingly," to introduce the consequence. Rather, we find the particle *gam* (2:21), which normally introduces an emphasis or intensification. Still, the syntax we have here is not unprecedented (for example, Ezek. 5:11, *gam* followed by the imperfect, as in our verse; Ezek 16:43, by a perfect), and we may imagine that God is countering after much provocation rather than reacting in peeve.

A minor issue is the discord between the singular *derek*, "path, way," and the plural suffix in *bam*. Solutions are legion, with most Greek versions simply giving the singular, whether or not they depended on a Hebrew manuscript with the reading **bāh*. Boling (1975: 75) turns the phrase into a plural, "ways [**drky*] of the LORD," by doubling the initial *yôd* in YHVH. It is possible that we are dealing here with a distributive or repetitive use of the plural suffix, so something like "(keeping to the LORD's way), repeatedly/individually guiding themselves."

2 23. Earlier (at 2:17), we had noticed that when "[the Hebrews] swiftly retreated from the path their fathers had followed," God simply would no longer let them dispossess the land. Here, however, we learn that the *speed* by which Israel conquers the territory is a marker of God's reaction to its obduracy. Problematic, however, is the statement that justifies the survival of Israel's enemies. It implies that even as Joshua was directing a faithful Israel into battle against the enemy, God was sabotaging its success, in effect anticipating Israel's moral failure long before its seduction by foreign gods. Ehrlich (1968: 74; 1969: 47–48) is one of many commentators who propose replacing "Joshua" with "Israel."

COMMENTS

The Masoretes conceived this section as one unit, setting it between two *pĕtûḥôt* (פ); but they also divided it in two unequal portions by the insertion of just one *sĕtûmâ* (ס) at the close of v. 10. (On these symbols, see the Notes to 1:8–11.) But for the mention of "Joshua" at 1:1, *all* the remaining citations for him in the book of Judges are found in this unit. Three references are in the opening verses (6–8) and two others in the final verses (21, 23). These references brace material that tumbles at us in a disorderly fashion, not just in the series of episodes that lack a linear sequence—be they chronological or thematic—but even within each of these episodes. Among the many issues they raise, I comment on two: the nature of apostasy at the root of the conflict between God and Israel, and the complicated progress of the exposition in Judges.

Lusting After Foreign Gods

God's anger burns hottest when Israel indulges its lust for the gods of its neighbors. As disturbing as its fall for other gods is Israel's desertion of its ancestral God. For us, Israel's fickleness may seem senseless, given that these gods are patently false. We are never told what was in Israel's soul (not to say genes) that made its people so disposed to flirt with foreign gods. Did they imagine that their crops would be fuller and their animals more fecund if they served Baalim and Ashtarot? Did they feel more sophisticated, more part of the cultural mainstream, when worshiping the gods of established cultures? Or is it that having set roots in a new land, they simply wanted to assimilate into it? Perhaps they imagined that by recognizing the neighbor's gods, they might evade explaining their attachment to a God with a strange name, one who lacked a heavenly lineage, a recognizable form, a permanent domicile on earth, or a king to advance his cause.

Unanswerable questions, perhaps; still, it must be recalled that during the centuries in which Scripture was emerging as a testament to Israel's faith, embracing other gods did not require the crossing of steep psychological chasms. Israel never had to give up its God when adopting another, for in a polytheistic world, denial of deities was hardly ever a requirement.[21] Israel was not unique among its neighbors in shunning representation of its god, either anthropomorphically or symbolically, and it was not alone in listening to divine messengers, be they supernatural creatures or prophets.[22] True, eventually Israel did distinguish itself from its neighbors through its promotion of a monotheistic theology and adoption of several practices that were uniquely its own.[23] Yet, in matters that affected the pursuit of life and happiness, it was easy for Hebrews to minimize the consequences of such differences; for the gods of Canaan were equally eternal in their nature as well as in their capacity to create, control the cosmos, command destinies, protect, heal, and hurt. Neighboring deities eagerly championed those venerating them and fought battles for their favorites, with perhaps a better success rate than the Hebrew God. No less than Israel's god, those of Canaan (El, Baal, Astarte, Anat, Asherah, Chemosh) also demanded acknowledgment of the past, sought to inspire justice, and charted covenants defining the relationship between them and their flocks.[24] Their worship required prayers, sacrifice, personal service, and the fulfillment of vows. Their record for capriciousness or whimsy did not differ much from that of the Hebrew God.[25] This much is admitted in our segment, in which from the outset God is shown to seem oblivious to the futility of the regimen he created for Israel.

FICKLE DEVOTION

What is reported in our verses about the volatility of Israel's devotion is a major theme in Hebrew writings, especially in Deuteronomy. In Judges, however, these accusations—hardly ever disputed or refuted—give pulse to the remaining narratives and control the waves of episodes by setting events in spirals as evoked in the Introduction: Israel errs; God punishes; Israel seeks forgiveness; God provides it with a judge; Israel overpowers its enemy but soon surrenders to its gods' lures, with the expected consequences.[26] Recognizing that time and memory are seldom natural partners, the episodes in Judges advance shrewd insights: that Israel's concentration equals a flea's, that its heart cannot resist temptation, and that its determination rarely survives the devotion of its leaders. For all that, God has invested too much in Israel to let it wallow in its own weakness: divine judgment is harsh, but also just; punishment is painful, but hardly enduring. Through these trials, God and Israel learn much about how far each is willing to go to keep the covenant alive. In Judges, however, God is likely to blink first.

There is a certain peril, of course, for narrators to reveal early on the plot that will control the rest of their narrative; for this sort of intrusiveness not only risks deflating our hopes for a happy outcome every time a judge charges to the rescue, but it shakes our confidence in a God whose best efforts seem unlikely to turn Israel into the light to the nations he wishes it to be. Nonetheless, in setting Israel on a Sisyphean path, Judges has firmly affirmed that the "hero" of its story is neither the God whose expectations hardly modify despite Israel's obvious inadequacy nor the judges who will enter and leave the stage with unimpressive aftermaths; rather, it is Israel, whose repeated defiance is sending notice about a flawed alliance that must need major adjustment. Judges, in fact, will walk us through some of the necessary corrections.

Ruptured Commitments

ABANDONMENT

In 2:6–10, we are told that Joshua dismissed the people toward their inheritance. His generation was in full obedience and God its partner in glorious deeds. Joshua died and was buried, as well as his generation. The shift from one generation to another in 2:10 is natural enough, but not as much the abrupt move from loyalty to God to ignoring the experiences of elders. The shock of rejection is palpable, as the betrayal is told in at least five reiterations in three verses (2:11–13). In the scholarly literature, this segment is often argued as a new (or renewed) introduction to the book of Judges.[27] The reasoning is based on the observation that the phrase *vayyĕšallaḥ yĕhôšū*ᶜ, as well as the information it initiates, largely replicates what is found at the tail end of the book of Joshua:[28]

Josh 24:28–31	*Judg 2:6–9*
[28]Joshua then dismissed the people, each person to his allotted land. [29]After these events, Joshua son of Nun, the servant of the LORD, died at 110 years of age. [30]He was buried within his allotted land, at Timnath-***serah***, that was in Mount Ephraim, north of Mount Gaash. [31]Israel served [***vayyaʿăvōd yiśrāʾēl***] only the LORD the full lifetime of Joshua as well as the full lifetime of all the elders who outlived Joshua and who experienced [***yādĕʿû***] every great deed that the LORD had done for Israel. [*Burials of Joseph's bones and of Eleazar the priest follow.*]	[6]When Joshua dismissed the people, each person in Israel went to take possession of his allotted land. [7]The people served [***vayyaʿavdû hāʿām***] only the LORD during the full lifetime of Joshua as well as the full lifetime of all the elders who outlived Joshua and who had witnessed [***rāʾû***] every great deed that the LORD had done for Israel. [8]Joshua son of Nun, the servant of the LORD, died at 110 years of age [9]and was buried within his allotted land, at Timnath-***heres*** in Mount Ephraim, north of Mount Gaash.

When the two passages are compared, the rephrasing is obvious, yet the shuffling of material about Israel's devotion to God suggests a divergence in reasoning that is topical and internal to each book. This would argue against proposals that Judg 1:1–2:10 is a displaced appendix to Joshua, with Judg 2:6–9 picking up on what is now the ending of Joshua.[29] In Joshua, Israel's loyalty is sandwiched between two meritorious acts: the proper burial of Joshua and those of Joseph and Eleazar, the high priest, giving hope that such worthy acts will continue now that Israel is properly set on a mode of fine behavior. In Judges, however, Israel's commitment to God is stuck between statements about Joshua, his death, and burial, as if to underscore the momentary nature of Israel's piety. In fact, this line of argument is immediately bolstered by focus on Israel's wicked behavior (2:10–11). The backtracking about Joshua and his generation may have made better sense had it preceded the series of clashes that did not always go well for Israel; yet it brings nothing to illuminate this failure beyond what had already been presented in chapter 1 and explained at Bochim (2:1–5)—nothing, except to articulate why a new political institution was about to be offered to Israel. In sum, while this segment might well suggest a new launch for how Judges will unfold henceforth, it is not a new introduction to it.

SERIAL PUNISHMENT

At 2:14a, God's anger is revealed through the phrase *vayyiḥar-ʾaf YHVH bĕyiśrāʾēl*, "the LORD became incensed with Israel," which occurs also at 2:20a. The repetition of phrases with exact language can be accidental, especially because Hebrew prose shares neither the English style's dread of duplication nor its absorption with shaping seamless transitions. Yet, when set within relative proximity of each, renewed formulas may operate stylistically as resumptive phrases (*Wiederaufnahme*).[30] We have a choice on how to display their operation:

1. The two phrases can set forth *synchronous events*, each of which is presented immediately after stating "the LORD became incensed with Israel." The arrangement would suggest that God is taking two actions simultaneously. Even as God torments Israel by unleashing *outside* forces against its people (2:14–15), *inside* there remain forces potent enough to keep Israel at the *qui vive* (2:20–23). This first move is *open-ended* (at least for the coming generations), leading to a spiral of frustrations that, on the activation of a judge, turns into temporary success (2:16–19). In contrast, the second move is *punctual*, sustaining a policy already rehearsed in the final days of Joshua: Pockets of unconquered folks would remain as a permanent test of Israel's loyalty. With its references to Joshua's death (2:21) and to the lack of martial success (2:23), this segment loops back to 2:6–11.

2. The two phrases, however, can also bracket an *interpolation*—material that at one time was deemed tangential (perhaps even set in the margin) but eventually slipped into the body of the text, together with the resumptive phrase ("the LORD became incensed with Israel") that may have once served as a heading. In our context, it would suggest that 2:6–13 immediately ran into 2:20–23, forming a consecutive narrative that dwelled on Joshua. It reposted (from Josh 24) a notice about Joshua's death and burial and focused on the deteriorating state of affairs that followed. All this introduced a divine decision that had occurred when *Joshua was yet living*. In effect, the whole harked back to Josh 13:1–2, where are listed the many regions not yet conquered, significantly enough including the land under Philistine chieftains (Josh 13:3, Judg 3:13). The *interpolated segment*, therefore, would run from 2:14 to 2:19, covering the argument about the divine invention of a new institution: that of the judges. But it would also reveal how imperfect an institution it will prove to be. In effect, the insertion prepares us for its failure.

Whichever construction we choose—we might find advantages in either configuration—the information they both convey remains starkly obtrusive, none of it more so than what is forecast about Israel and its fate under the rule of judges. Why would anyone believe in the competence of the Hebrew god when whatever measures God takes on Israel's behalf are foredoomed to impermanent success? This is not at all the conclusion one might draw from reading what transpired at Bochim (2:1–5). There, some good sense was knocked into Israel, seemingly.

Tripartite Structure

Since antiquity, a tripartite division of Judges was always obvious to any discerning reader: A core with narratives about a series of judges (3:7–16:31) is flanked by a prelude (1:1–3:6) and a postlude (17:1–21:25), the last serving as a bridge to transitional judges, the judge-priest Eli, and the judge-prophet Samuel.[31] The prelude cherry picks from traditions about the settlements of tribes to spot future instability in both South and North. The core moves from the institution to the demise of a new institution, that of the judges. The postlude constructs an argument for what will occur in Samuel.

Long ago, too, it was noted that all the judges but Othniel (possibly also Ehud) operated in the Northern Kingdom of Israel. In western scholarship, the debate is mostly about how, when, and why these northern traditions were folded into a book that was set as a background to the rise of Davidic kingship. There have been many thoughtful suggestions, but in the past decades none stirred more interest that Richter's notion (1963, 1964) that a series of "deliverers" (*môšîᵃʿ*) stories were largely first compiled in the North.[32] That series was supplemented by another list, mostly about functionaries (so called "minor" judges) labeled *šōfēṭ*, recalled (if at all) through terse anecdotes or notices. When this collection reached Judah, an editor or a redactor—a difference, if any, in what they do is debated—gave these tales a divinely preordained destiny through a program set at 2:14–19; but whether to assign this activity to a pre-, intra-, or post-Deuteronomic or Deuteronomistic hand is endlessly debated.[33] Still, there is discrepancy between the program as set forth in 2:11–19 on how events were to unfold and what we meet in the tales. The program uniformly assigns the heroics to a *šōfēṭ*, "judge," while the tales (mostly) cite a *môšîᵃʿ* ("rescuer").

Startlingly, too, is the backgrounding of Israel's reaction. In most of the tales, Israel sheds tears to effectively placate God. Here, an impersonal notice alerts to God's shifting stance. Missing, then, is the intimacy that arises whenever Israel and God confront each other, tears and lectures notwithstanding. Instead, the accent is on God and the fluctuation of a preordained divine whim. In this preamble, once divine anger is kindled, all subsequent moves are God's: The dispatch of cruel foes is followed by the launching of judges, and the description of Israel's impotence is followed by that of its enemies. There is also the contradiction of a God being moved by Israel's groans to send rescuing judges (2:18) and Israel showing no respect for them (2:17). Such divergences between the preamble and what is told in the tales complicate our capacity to make trustworthy judgment on the ways they mesh together.

3. Lands Not Taken (Judg 3:1–6)

3 ¹These are the nations that the LORD kept whole, using them to test all those in Israel who had not experienced all the wars in Canaan, ²just to give generations of Israel experience, teaching them about war, only because previously they did not experience them: ³The (lands of) the five rulers of the Philistines and all Canaanites, Sidonians, and Hivvites who inhabited the hill region of the Lebanon, from Mount Baal-Hermon to Lebo-Hamath. [4]They were there to test Israel, to determine whether they would heed the commandments that the LORD had urged on their fathers through Moses. [5]So the people of Israel settled among the Canaanites, Hittites, Amorites, Perizzites, Hivvites, and Jebusites. [6]They took for themselves their daughters in marriage, giving their own daughters to their sons, as well as worshiping their gods. **ס**

NOTES
Introductory Remarks: Dispossessing the Nations

In Israel's traditions, which and how many nations Israel was to supplant are given in a form difficult to assess. Table 2 helps present the issues. As many as fourteen nations on this list are candidates for dispossession; eleven, if we remove Ammon, Moab, and Egypt as too anomalous for inclusion, as they reflect issues specific to the Ezra ideology regarding the Yehud community. We never find a list that covers all the remaining eleven; rather, the longest list occurs at Gen 15:18–21 and is made up of ten nations. But here too, this longest of lists could be trimmed as it opens on a unique sequence of three groups with rhyming names. We might also remove the mention of Rephaim (equated with the Anakim, Emim, Zuzim, or Zamzummim), reputed to be a race of primordial giants. While undoubtedly Israel accepted their primordial existence, searching for them in contemporaneous records will force us (as it has others) into surrealistic scholarship.

This leaves us with a core of six to seven nations. We notice that among this nucleus, the Canaanites, Hittites, and Amorites tend to take up the first slots in any of these lists. As we saw in earlier Notes (to 1:1, 1:4, and the Introductory Remarks to IB1 [Judg 1:22–36]), each of these names often stood for a region rather than for a specific nation-state. If we set them aside, the powers that remain are, in order of frequency, the Perizzites (see at 1:4), Jebusites (see at 1:8, 16), Hivvites, and Girgashites precisely those powers that have as yet to leave us uncontested evidence of their existence (see van Bekkum 2011: 129–42).

Summary: Why and Who

3 1–2. Reshuffling the initial words of 2:23, *vayyannaḥ YHVH 'et-haggôyim hā'ēllê*, the narrator opens his list of unconquered nations with *vĕ'ēllê haggôyim 'ăšer hinniaḥ YHVH*. One Greek text (Rahlfs A, followed by other Greek witnesses) gives Joshua (rather than God) credit for leaving unconquered some enemy nations. The reading is likely cosmetic, for with it, rather than being the pawn implied in 2:23, Joshua becomes an active participant in God's confrontation with Israel. Those being tested are the generations that did not experience *milḥāmôt kĕnā'an*, "the Canaan Wars" (see Exod 17:16), likely a more specific name for the better known *milḥāmôt YHVH*, "the LORD's Wars" (1 Sam 18:17, 25:28), themselves the subject of a (lost) book by that name (Num 21:14).

Despite parallels for *lĕma'an da'at* (Josh 4:24, 1 Kgs 8:60, Ezek 38:16), for good reasons some commentators find the language of v. 2 too overloaded or clumsy (details in Burney 1970: 81–82). Many delete the infinitive *da'at*, taking their cue from the Greek

Table 2. Lists of Nations Israel Is to Supplant

Nation

Location of list	Perizzi	Canaani	Hitti	Emori	Jebusi	Hivvi	Girgashi	Rephaim	Qeni	Kenizzi	Qadmoni	Ammoni	Moab	Egypt	Amalek	Anak
Gen 15:18–21 (covenant with Abram)	5	8	4	7	10		9	6	1	2	3					
Ezra 9:1 (forbidden marriages)	3	1	2	8	4							5	6	7		
Deut 7:1 (nations for conquest)	5	4	1	3	7	6	2									
Josh 3:10 (nations for conquest)	4	1	2	6	7	3	5									
Josh 24:11 (nations for conquest)	2	3	4	1	7	6	5									
Exod 3:8, 17 ("good land")	4	1	2	3	6	5										
Exod 23:23 (angel to lead)	3	4	2	1	6	5										
Exod 33:2 (angel to drive out)	4	1	3	2	6	5										
Exod 34:11 (nations for conquest)	4	2	3	1	6	5										
Deut 20:17, Josh 9:1 (fear of Israel)	4	3	1	2	6	5										
Josh 11:3 (called to battle)	4	1	3	2	5	6										

Josh 12:8 (defeat of kings)	4	3	1	2		6	5		1
Judg 3:5 (nations remaining)	4	1	2	3		6	5		
Neh 9:8–9 (confession)	4	1	2	3		5		6	
Num 13:28–29 (spy's report)	6	3	5	4					2
Exod 13:5 (good land)		1	2	3		5	4		
2 Chr 8:7 (Solomon levies)	3		1	2		5	4		
1 Kgs 9:20 (Solomon levies)	3		2	1		6	4		
Exod 23:28 (hornets drive out)		2	3				1		
Josh 17:15 (tribute/conquer)	1				2				
Gen 13:7 (Abram/Lot separate)	2	1							
Gen 34:30 (Jacob at Shechem)	2	1							
Judg 1:4, 5 (Judah wars)	2	1							

Note: The table is arranged as follows:

1. *Top to bottom:* The most expansive list is given first. If lists include the same number of nations, the order simply follows the sequence of books in the received Hebrew text.
2. *Left to right:* Nations with the most mentions are first (so Perizzites). Those with the same count are arranged alphabetically.
3. *Within each cell:* A numeral reflects the order of appearance in that particular list.

versions that seem to omit it (Ehrlich 1968: 74). Moore (1895: 77–78) offers broader changes, none particularly necessary since, albeit awkward, the sentence is intelligible as is. Albeit inspirational, the Hebrew Bible need not always carry inspired prose.

Some translations risk giving a false notion of what is at stake, suggesting that the enemy survived to increase Israel's travail; for example, see *TNK*: "These are the nations that the LORD left . . . so that succeeding generations of Israelites might be made to experience war." On the argument that the persistence of hostility keeps Israel healthily martial, see the Comments below.

3 3–6. The list of unconquered nations divides into two parts: those that remained independent, surviving to test Israel (v. 3), and those with whom Israel coexisted (v. 5). The last are essentially more treacherous to Israel's future since assimilation was feared as sapping its moral strength and undermining its special relationship with God. The two lists overlap:

Judg 3:3	*Judg 3:5*
Five Philistine rulers	
Canaanites	Canaanites
Sidonians	Hittites
	Amorites
	Perizzites
Hivvites	Hivvites
	Jebusites

PHILISTINES

The first list includes two groups (the Philistines and Sidonians) that were not normally accounted among those whose territory was promised. In Josh 13:3 the five Philistine cities are Gaza, Ashdod, Ashkelon, Gat, and Ekron. The oddity here is the mention of *sarnê pĕlištîm*, the "*seren*s of the Philistines," when all other references are to people or land. For this reason, some translate "principalities" (*TNK*, with the note "Lit. 'Lords'"), perhaps influenced by the Greek σατραπεία that refers to both an office and the territory ruled by that office. But the **seren* (always in the plural) is definitely a position, as we can surmise from 1 Sam 29 where *sarnê p.* alternates with *śārê p.*, "leaders, commanders" (admittedly, some have finessed the difference). While we occasionally read that the Philistines were ruled by kings (Gen 26:1, Jer 25:20), aside from 1 Sam 29:7 (where we have "leaders"), the **seren* seems to be the most senior official. There used to be a time when scholars (Burney 1970: 62) sought an Indo-European etymology for the term, equating it with the Greek τύραννος, "tyrant"; but the consensus nowadays is to declare it "Anatolian," so not just Indo-European.[1] Ultimately, the matter is hardly linguistic but is concerned with where to originate the Philistines, a murky issue at best but one that will be explored in detailing the Samson story (see for now Machinist 2000).

The Greek for Judges uses two different words in rendering "Philistines." Consistently in Rahlfs A, it uses (pejoratively) ἀλλόφυλοι, something like "foreigners, aliens," a term that can occasionally also apply to the Amalekites and Canaanites. In Rahlfs B, however, a few references (10:6, 7, 11; 13:1, 5; 14:2) give it as Φυλιστιμ, approximating the Hebrew. No one has offered a convincing reason for the difference, but both Harlé and Roqueplo (1999: 58–60) and Lindars (1995: 121) give good accountings of the phenomenon.

Sidon was only ambiguously (Josh 13:6) attached to territory destined for conquest, but it served to edge boundaries: of Canaan (Gen 10:19), Zebulun (Gen 49:13), and Asher (Josh 19:28). This is the second reference in Judges (see 1:31) to its escape from Israel's grasp. In fact, it remained independent, its daughters marrying Israel's kings (Solomon, 1 Kgs 11:1; Ahab, 1 Kgs 16:31).

With no unequivocal mention of them yet in ancient records, the Hivvites are yet another folk whose history or ethnic makeup cannot be pinpointed.[2] Scholarship has not helped by debating the relationship among, on the one hand, the Hivvites, the Horites, and Hittites of the Hebrew Bible and, on the other, the Hittites and Hurrians as known from Near Eastern sources.[3] In Scripture we are told that although individual Hivvites had Semitic names, the people were descended from Ham (Gen 10:17). Shechem (Gen 34:2) and Gibeon (Josh 9:7, 11:19) are given Hivvite connections, and we are told that they were finally subdued by Solomon (1 Kgs 9:20, 2 Chr 8:7–8). In this passage, they are said to dwell in the Lebanon range, to the north of Mount Baal-Hermon. This name may designate one of the three peaks of Mount Hermon in the Anti-Lebanon, today's Jebel el-Sheikh; or it could label one of the many shrines on its flank (as per Josh 13:5), so at Israel's northern frontier.[4] To the east the limit is set at Lebo-Hamath, either a frontier town (as taken here) to today's Hama in west central Syria on the Orontes (al-ʿAssi) River, or a region that opens into Hamath territory. To me, the last is less likely, despite the versions that so take it, as frontiers were loosely defined.

The second list (3:5) is much more inclusively Canaanite, and it includes a number of people we have already met. (See above, at 1:26 for Hittites; at 1:34–35 for Amorites; at 1:4 for Perizzites; and at 1:21 for Jebusites.)

Intermarriage

3 6. The sentiments against intermarriage are the same as in Deut 7:3. For the Hebrews of preexilic times, the exchange of daughters (not sons) as presented here is not strictly the religious complication (conversion or the like) that it eventually becomes in the Hellenistic period; rather, it was a weakening of ethnic bonds that might lead to consequent acceptance of pagan worship. This is especially a problem when Canaanite daughters enter a Hebrew household, bringing with them their deities (see Exod 34:16): "When you take their daughters as wives for your sons, their daughters will lust after their gods and seduce your sons to them." It is worth recalling that the matter comes to a head not simply during the exile, but also during the monarchy when, eager to establish connections with more powerful neighbors, Hebrew rulers (Solomon foremost among them) married foreign princesses and welcomed their gods into the palace.

COMMENTS

> The LORD was so angry with his people that he loathed his inheritance. He handed them over to nations who ruled them with hatred. When their enemies oppressed them, they wilted under their power. He would save them many times; but they would deliberately rebel,

sinking low by iniquity. Still, on hearing their shouts, the LORD would
see how distressed they were and, for their sake recalling his covenant,
he would relent in full kindness. He made all their captors have compassion toward them.

—*Ps 106:40–46*

When gods are angered by their own people, we learn from Near Eastern lore, they
abandon their shrines, thus inviting the enemy to gain the upper hand. This widespread notion is best captured from a category of Mesopotamian literature (mostly
in Sumerian) we label "Lamentations" that explains the devastations of major cities.[5]
Occasionally, as in the *Curse of Agade*, the fault for divine anger is attached to a leader
(Naram-Sin) for his inflated ego. (See also the discussion below under Abimelech,
IIIE2).[6] In this literature, however, justifying divine anger is hardly at stake; rather, the
accent is on the harrowing experience—physical, spiritual, and psychological—that
overwhelms a people when its god no longer defends it. The beauty of the Mesopotamian literature, with its haunted descriptions and embedded entreaties, is what kept it
alive in the scribal curriculum; but there was also the sense that commemorating such
events might stir the gods to concede the linkage between human suffering and the
health of the cosmos.

In this and the segments immediately previous in Judges, there is repeated warning
from a God who details the consequences of misbehavior—always in term of humiliation and subservience to cruel invaders. Divine anger is palpable in these verses, and it
is sharpened by its multiple invocations in a relatively brief space. Frustrated by Israel's
repeated obstinacy and the backsliding that invariably followed on reprieve, God unfolds a plan by which to keep Israel focused on the cost of defiance.

God's Anger

In Hebrew scripture, God gets angry. We are repeatedly told that it takes much provocation for God's anger to boil over and that contriteness can assuage or even revoke
divine wrath (Joel 2:12–13, for example).[7] This is true enough, yet God's ire is displayed
frequently and targeted broadly. Here is a sampling of its recipients:

Individuals: Nadav (Lev 10:2), Korah (Num 16:31–35), Aaron and Miriam
(Num 12:9–10), Uzzah (2 Sam 6:7), Saul's family (2 Sam 21:1), and Sennacherib (2 Kgs 19:28–37)

Groups, for abstract faults: Such as sin (Ps 7:12 [11 RSV], 21:9–10 [8–9 RSV];
Isa 3:8; Nah 1:2–3), injustice (Exod 21:22–24), and idolatry (Deut 32:
19–22, Josh 23:16, 2 Kgs 22:17, Isa 1:4)

Groups, for specific crimes: Impudent humanity (Gen 7:21–23, 11:8); Egypt,
for its obstinate Pharaoh (Exod 7–14); Sodom and Gomorrah (Gen 19:
24–25); disparaging the Promised Land (Num 14:37); apostasy (Exod 32:
35; many times in Numbers; 2 Sam 24); and unspecific crimes (Bet-
Shemesh) (1 Sam 6:19)

In the book of Judges, God's anger is rarely displayed against specific individuals
(Abimelech will be one exception); rather, it is against Israel—eventually also against
those sent to torment Israel. In these pages, a rather intimate drama is repeatedly played
out, with all sides expressing a desire for abiding attachment. Yet aspiration hardly ac-

cords with experience, and what Israel fulfills is never fully satisfying to God. It did not help that this God had pinned hopes for human improvement on a (relatively) minor folk whose self-esteem was too fragile (and its neighbors too intimidating) to stand by truths conveyed through a unique theology. Yet, for this folk, there was no escaping fate, for God hardly deviated from a premise starkly expressed elsewhere: "You alone have I singled out of all the families of the earth—That is why I will call you to account for all your iniquities" (Amos 3:2). Even as it crafted lore about Joshua successfully testing his arms against Canaanite nations, Israel recognized that an unhealthy cycle of error and terror was part of its inheritance, a deliberate scheme by which to keep it focused on its commitments. Why God did not deliver fully on the promise to the ancestors comes to be just one component of this stratagem.

The Enemy Within

In Judges and elsewhere are promoted at least three major explanations for why promised territory remained under enemy control.

1. CONTROLLING WILD BEASTS

> I will send forth my terror before you, and I will throw into panic all the people among whom you come, and I will make all your enemies turn tail before you. I will send a plague ahead of you, and it shall drive out before you the Hivvites, the Canaanites, and the Hittites. I will not drive them out before you in a single year, lest the land become desolate and the wild beasts multiply to your hurt. I will drive them out before you little by little, until you have increased and possess the land. (Exod 23:27–30; see also Deut 7:21–23)

Ostensibly an indication of God's solicitous regard for Israel (in fact, the above is embedded within blessings for obedience), this passage advances a "benign" explanation for the land not taken promptly enough. Given the huge numbers of Hebrews cited as coming out of Egypt (six hundred thousand adult men, not counting women and children, Exod 12:37, 38:26; Num 11:21) and the extravagant census numbers for the tribes at Sinai (Num 2), this argument might strain credulity. Yet it is balanced by a counternotion (featured in Lev 26:22, Deut 32:24, Jer 15:3, and Ezek 5:17) that wild beasts are one of four weapons God will unleash against offenders (the sword, famine, and pestilence being the others; Ezek 14:15).

2. MASTERING THE ART OF WAR

The argument offered in our segment of Judges is that God purposely kept enemies whole so that Israel could master combat. The notion may seem odd indeed, especially after the book of Joshua had revealed Israel as a honed instrument for war.[8] But, with Radaq (Kimḥi), this may precisely be the point. Citing Josh 23:10 ("A single person from among you can chase a thousand, for the LORD your God is himself battling for you, as he told you"; see also Lev 26:7–8), Radaq proposes that Israel must be disabused from relying on God for its victories. I cannot improve on his suggestion.

We may register here Josephus's exploitation of this notion in shaping an argument for Israel's woes during the Judges period. It was not simply that Israel had yet to master the art of war; rather, Israel grew "effeminate" (his term), turning to agriculture

Table 3. Testing Israel's Conviction

Josh 23:12–13	Judg 2:2–3	Judg 2:21–22	Judg 3:4–6
Should you revert and bond with the remnant of those nations—to those that are left among you—intermarrying with them and frequenting with each other, know for certain that the LORD your God will not continue to displace these nations before you; they shall become a snare and a trap for you, a scourge to your sides and thorns in your eyes, until you perish from this good land that the LORD your God has given you.	For your part, you must make no covenant with the inhabitants of this land. You must tear down their altars. But you have not obeyed me. How could you done that? I have decided therefore not to drive them out before you. Rather, they will turn into your foes, their gods into your snare.	I will certainly no longer displace before them even a single person from those nations that Joshua left as he died, using them to test Israel: Whether or not they keep to the LORD's way, therewith guiding themselves as their ancestors had done.	(These are the nations that the LORD kept whole . . .) They were there to test Israel, to determine whether they would heed the commandments which the LORD had urged on their fathers through Moses.

for enrichment. The tribute the people gathered from the nations Joshua conquered led them to lower their resistance to foreign gods (*Ant.* 5.132–35; text cited above, p. 171).

3. TESTING ISRAEL'S CONVICTION

Failure to achieve complete control of the Promised Land is most often presented as a test of Israel's faithfulness. The surprising observation resulting from Table 3 is in recognizing a deliberate development from Joshua to Judges. As presented in Josh 23:12, Joshua stands before Israel and delivers the message as a *warning* about potential failure rather than as one already proved by experience. The remarkable context and intricate syntax of Judg 2:1–5, however, show the theme poised in anticipation, suggesting that there is still time for the test to prove successful (see especially the Comments to IIA1, "Accusation"). This time it is a *mal'āk* (however it is translated) who delivers an *ultimatum*, and Israel wisely steps back from the edge. In its third manifestation (at Judg 2:21–22), the rupture is manifest and a *declaration of war* (normally sent after troops are in full move) is issued. If there is any test for Israel to pass, it can be set after this particular punishment has worked itself out.

The unhealthy condition, with a test that Israel can never pass, is presented in Judg 3:4–6. Rather than nations stubbornly remaining unconquered within Israel, Israel is resident in an ocean of foreigners. As their blood mixes, fervor for the single God dissipates. The warning of dire consequences delivered in Josh 23:12–13 is now fully realized. In fact, the promise for Israel to control the land can hardly be fulfilled. A fine prelude to the story of the judges is now complete.

III. NOTES AND COMMENTS
The Judges

Othniel (Judg 3:7–11)

3　[7]The people of Israel did what was offensive to the LORD: They forgot the LORD their God and worshiped the many Baals and Asherahs. [8]Incensed against Israel, the LORD turned them over to Cushan-rishatayim, king of Aram-naharayim. For eight years, the people of Israel served Cushan-rishatayim. [9]When the people of Israel pleaded with the LORD, the LORD installed a rescuer for the people of Israel, to rescue them: Othniel son of Kenaz (brother of Caleb who was younger than him). [10]Endowed with zeal for the LORD, he became judge in Israel. When he set out in battle, the LORD gave Cushan-rishatayim, king of Aram, over to him so that he brought Cushan-rishatayim under his control. [11]The land had peace for forty years. Then Othniel son of Kenaz died. פ

NOTES

Introductory Remarks: On Being Touched by the Divine

Othniel's greatest achievement does not unfold until after we are told that *wattĕhî ʿālāyv rûʷaḥ-YHVH* (3:10). While it is perfectly reasonable to translate this phrase literally (as is commonly done), "the spirit of the LORD was upon him," here and elsewhere in Judges I have sought to convey the consequent transformation by means of "endowed with zeal for the LORD." In this way I communicate that whatever change overtook Othniel (and all others), it was at once imposed on him ("endowed," a passive form implying investment by God) but also operated from within him ("zeal for the LORD").[1]

Our evidence on this subject is rich, but coming as it does from a broad variety of genres (diverse narratives and prophecies), as well as from different periods in Israel's literary history, it is not as precise as we might wish it to be. Truth to tell, however, we have but evocative information on what the Hebrews imagined this transformation entailed, so we may wonder: What happened when God's *rûʷaḥ* settled on individuals?

Did they bulge with vigor and personal magnetism or achieve enhanced persuasive power? Did they recognize the change affecting them? Did others immediately spot the conversion? Did it arouse in others enthusiasm or devotion? How long did the effect last? Did it manifest itself permanently or periodically? Was it ever forfeited? It might be noticed that in some accounts Assyrian rulers felt themselves bodily changed by divine interest in them. Here is how Adad-nārārī II (911–891 BCE) said it: "The great gods . . . altered my figure into a lordly one [*nabnītī ana nabnīti bēlūti uštennū*], perfected my appearance beautifully, and filled my lordly body with discernment [*tašīmtu*]. Once the great gods decreed (my destiny), handed me the staff to shepherd the people, elevated me over crowned kings, and crowned me with a royal nimbus [*melammu*; see below], they enhanced my supreme reputation over other lords. They assigned me the worthy name: Adad-nārārī, king of Assyria."[2]

The Hebrews were certain the change that overtook these heroes had to do with God's *rûʷaḥ* (Greek, πνεῦμα), a word with many meanings, from "wind" to "soul," each with multiple nuances, all conveying the nonpalpable, physically and spiritually.[3] I could not detect meaningful discrimination whether this *rûʷaḥ* was said to be YHVH's or *ʾĕlōhîm*'s, the biblical references being (unevenly) divided across books and genres, with at least twice as many formations with the former than with the latter. It must be noted, however, that *rûʷaḥ-YHVH* is the only phrasing found in Judges.[4] God's *rûʷaḥ* affected only some of the leaders (Joseph, Gen 41:38), judges (Othniel, Gideon, Jephthah, Samson), kings (Saul, 1 Sam 16–18; David, 2 Sam 23:2), prophets (Balaam, Num 24:2; Ezekiel, Ezek 11:5), or artists (Bezalel, Exod 31:3, 35:31). It overtook even messengers as a group (1 Sam 19:20).[5] But nowhere do we ever get the sense that individuals acquired divinity as a result of their encounter with this spark.

On receiving this spirit, an individual is said to be a changed person (Saul, 1 Sam 10:6), the alteration startling enough to be recognized from a distance by others (2 Kgs 2:15). Some of the possessed instantly turned violent: Samson tears apart a lion's cub (Judg 14:6), beats up on Philistines (Judg14:19), and breaks his chains (Judg 15:14); an angered Saul dismembers oxen (1 Sam 11:6–7). Ecstatic prophecy is another consequence that is immediate, with a seizure that is itself no less violent for being prophetically affecting: Saul (1 Sam 10:10, 19:24, after stripping naked), Ezekiel (Ezek 11:5), Azaria b. Oded (2 Chr 15:1), Jahaziel b. Zecharia (2 Chr 20:14), Zecharia b. Jehoiada (2 Chr 24:20). But other individuals simply become more persuasive (Othniel, Gideon, and Jephthah), mustering Israel toward victory. Occasionally, all that will happen is kept in anticipation, such as the first time the spirits settle on Samson (Judg 13:25), when David is anointed (1 Sam 16:13), or when we are told a future ruler will gather wisdom (Isa 11:2).

While *rûʷaḥ* mostly enhances the energy and authority of its holders, it could also flip on them, turning "evil" (*rāʿâ*) and driving them into foolish acts. Saul is the paradigmatic victim of such an "evil spirit" (1 Sam 16:14–18, 18:10, 19:9), the crucial shift occurring at 1 Sam 16:13–14, once Samuel anoints David, endowing him with zeal for the Lord, "the LORD's spirit moves out of [*sārâ mēʿîm*] Saul, and an evil spirit from the LORD tormented him."

The vocabulary for the transformation varies (see the dictionaries, under the words cited below). Most often, we find idioms that evoke a dynamic power from on high settling on individuals: *ḥāyâ ʿal-* ("being upon"), *ṣālaḥ ʿal/ʾel-* ("rushing upon"), *nāfal ʿal* ("falling on"), *šāfak ʿal* ("pouring over/on"), and, more gently, *nûʷaḥ ʿal-/be-* ("landing on/at," as by a bird). The impression is of an attack, the more gripping because unexpected or unprovoked, and its consequence can be brutal because, as it concerned some prophets, it may not have been at all welcome.[6] The reverse, implying removal of this authority, is told through such idioms as *sārâ mēʿim/mēʿal* (see above) or *ʿāvar min-* (1 Kgs 22:24 = 2 Chr 18:23). Quite arresting is the use of *pāʿam*, said about Samson's experience. The phrase *vattāḥel rûʷaḥ-YHVH lĕpaʿămô* centers on a unique form of the verb *pāʿam*, normally translated "to stir," but likely a denominative of the noun *paʿam* that refers to a unit of time, so implying pulsing bouts of zeal as Samson began his mission (Judg 13:25).

We also find other verbs, such as *lāvaš*, "to clothe" (said about Gideon) and *millēʾ* (Piel of *mālēʾ*), "to endow" (said about Bezalel). The sense is of complete investment in a divinely emitted power that reminds of the Mesopotamian *melammu* (from Sumerian me.lám), "radiance, effulgence, nimbus, aura" (or the like) in which divinities (occasionally also kings) are cocooned.[7] (Artistically, this is conveyed by enclosing a figure or its torso within jagged lines representing a nimbus.)

In some (postexilic) prophetic texts, this *rûʷaḥ* was deemed to reside within Israel (*ʿāmad bĕtôk-*), as part of God's covenant with his chosen folk (Hag 2:5), and it readily pours out on its people (Ezek 39:29, Joel 3:1 [2:28 RSV]). How it reached individuals is dramatically described in Num 11. The people complain about their manna diet, preferring to have flesh and vegetables. Moses appeals to God to have others share his burdens, and God accommodates him (Num 11:24–26, after *TNK*):

> Moses . . . gathered seventy of the people's elders and stationed them around the tent. Then the LORD came down in a cloud and spoke to him; he removed from the spirit that was on him and placed it on seventy elders. And when the spirit rested upon them, they spoke in ecstasy, but *did not continue*. Two men, one named Eldad and the other Medad, had remained in camp; yet the spirit rested upon them . . . and they spoke in ecstasy in the camp. . . . A youth ran out and told Moses, saying, "Eldad and Medad are acting the prophet in the camp!" Joshua son of Nun, Moses's attendant from his youth, spoke up and said, "My lord Moses, restrain them!" But Moses said to him, "Are you wrought up on my account? Would that all the LORD's people were prophets, that the LORD put his spirit upon them!"

The notion we gather from this powerful passage is of a hovering force (we cannot say whether radiant or not) that God, invisible within a cloud, draws upon (*vayyāʾṣel min-*) so as to place over (*nātan ʿal*) the elders. It is unclear whether the elders needed to accept its imposition, but the effect was instantaneous. No sooner did the spirit land on them (*kĕnôʷaḥ ʿălêhem*), than they began to prophesy. But then comes the mysterious *vĕlōʾ yāsāfû*, "and they did not continue/add," limiting the time in which they were in ecstatic transport.[8] Remarkable, too, is what we are told about two men who, albeit not among the selected elders, nonetheless were similarly transformed. The impression is of a blanket of power having fallen indiscriminately over a whole group within a specific confine, as well as inadvertently on a few beyond it. Rather than face punishment, the accidental recipients trigger formulation of the principle that all of Israel is candidate to host the divine spirit. The book of Judges will be a fine testing base for this principle.[9]

Backsliding

3 7–8a. The verbatim repeat of *vayya ʿăśû věnê-yiśrāʾēl ʾet-hāraʿ běʿênê YHVH* from where it occurs at 2:11 invites us to consider it a resumptive clue to the splicing of much material between its two occurrences. An earlier version might have taken us directly from the death of Joshua and the deterioration of faith among subsequent generations (2:6–10) to 3:7, with the consequences of adopting false gods. There is hardship, but it is followed by the rise of a rescuer (*môšîʿaʿ*) who "judges" Israel.

However, the reissue of practically the same formula at 6:1 weakens this conjecture. Instead, the clause initiates a compacted version of sentiments expressed earlier:[10]

3:7–8a	2:11–14b
[7]The people of Israel did what was offensive to the Lord: They forgot the Lord their God and worshiped the many Baals and Asherahs. [8]Incensed against Israel, the Lord turned them over to Cushan-rishatayim.	[11]The people of Israel did what was offensive to the Lord: **They worshiped the many Baals; [12]they abandoned the Lord, God of their fathers, who had brought them out of the land of Egypt; they committed to other gods, from among those of people around them, bowing down to them. So they provoked the Lord [13]**by forsaking the Lord and worshiping Baal and the Ashtaroth. [14]Incensed against Israel, the Lord . . . turned them over to their enemies on all sides.

The headers on Israel's failure are identical ("Israel did what was offensive to the Lord"), but the earlier notice also gives a gist for failures ("They worshiped the many Baals") that are detailed in 2:12. The sordid deeds reported in 3:7–8 are matched by what is told in 2:13–14, with minor differences. Earlier, Israel is said to abandon God (*vayya ʿazvû ʾet-YHVH*) before committing to false gods, male or female. Now, they forgot God (*vayyiškěḥû ʾet-YHVH*; a worse offense?) and so easily moved toward false ones. The pairing of Baal and Asherah (in the singular or plural) is fairly frequent in Scripture. It will occur three times in a Gideon episode (Judg 6:25–30) where the latter refers not to the goddess, but to a cultic object attached to the altar of Baal, whether in effigy or stylized.[11] Naturally, divine ire results, with its consequence: God turns them over (literally "sold them," as in 2:14) to their enemies for whom, in powerful imagery, they now slave (*vayya ʿavdû . . . ʾet* PN).

Cushan-rishatayim

The oppressor God chooses is Cushan-rishatayim, king of Aram-naharayim: in Hebrew *kûšan rišʿātayim melek ʾăram nahărāyim*, but in Greek Χουσαρσαθωμ (Rahlfs B, Χουσαρσαθαιμ) βασιλέως Συρίας ποταμῶν, "Khousarsathom/Khousarsathayim, king of Syria of the Rivers," "Syria" generally being the Greek rendering for Aram, especially in Genesis. Past and present, an enormous literature has gathered around this brief notice, resolved to make sense of Cushan-rishatayim's name, to identify the nation he ruled, and (significantly more academic) to delve into the historicity of the event.

HIS NAME

The name of the king has gathered attention since antiquity. As given in Hebrew, it is hardly a name that loving parents, especially if royal, would give a child. "Cushan" is obviously constructed on the element Cush with the "-an" ending that can be found on a number of names, for people (Azzan, Num 34:26; perhaps Achan, Josh 7; Bedan, 1 Sam 12:11; Bilshan, Ezra 2:2; Lotan, Gen 36:20, 22; Qeynan, Gen 5:9), for communities (Alvan, Gen 36:23; Aran, Gen 36:28), and for both (Canaan, Gen 10:6 and passim in the Hebrew Bible; Bilhan, Gen 36:27, 1 Chr 7:10). Cushan occurs as a place in Hab 3:7, possibly paralleling Midian. We recall that Cush of Scripture actually referred to three different places: Ethiopia in East Africa, the land of the Kassites in Mesopotamia, and an area near the Red Sea.[12]

But whereas "Cushan" is a perfectly plausible element in a name, "rishatayim" is less so.[13] As vocalized by the Masoretes, it is a dual, meaning "double wickedness" or the like. The Targum simply solved the problem by turning this element into a noun: Cushan is a *ḥāyāvâ*, a "sinner."[14] Al-Yaʿḳūbī (ninth century CE) makes him "the Wicked . . . the Giant of Moab" (Ebied and Wickham 1970: 84). Kimḥi is among other rabbis who explain that Cushan's is the second wickedness to strike Israel, the first being Balaam's. Scholars have shied away from such an unlikely nomenclature, proposing emendations such as *rōʾš ʿātayim*, "Chief of Atayim," or *rōʾš hattēmānî*, "Chief of Teman" (references in Lindars 1995: 133–34).

HIS LAND

The land he ruled, Aram-naharayim, is well-attested in Scripture. It consists of two elements: Aram, a region named after a tribal group, and naharayim, "Double River," a topographic designation for terrain limited by the three great bends of the Euphrates and bounded by its tributary the Balikh (some say the Khabur). Such cities as Harran, Nahor, and Pethor are found in this region. In most translations, this region is given as Mesopotamia, "Between Rivers," a term derived from the Greek rendering for the Aram-naharayim of Gen 24:10 but also for Paddan-Aram of Gen 28:2–6. The Greek sometimes expands by speaking of "Mesopotamia of Syria" (Gen 28:7), so elucidating why in our context the Greek gives "Syria of the Rivers" for Aram-naharayim. There are ancient Near Eastern references to Nahrina (Egyptian; possibly Amarna Na[ḫ]rima) and to *ebir nārim* or *ebirtim*, "Cross River" (cuneiform); and while they, too, seem to designate areas in upper Mesopotamia–Syria, they similarly fail to convey specific boundaries (see J. Finkelstein 1962, with comments on Aram-naharayim at 84–90).

THE CONTEXT

How to make this information yield history has been at issue. That a king from upper Mesopotamia would conquer Israel and that Othniel, a local chieftain, would defeat him have challenged our historical knowledge. Josephus (*Ant.* 5.182–84) turns it all into a fine romance:

There was one whose name was Othniel the son of Kenaz, of the tribe of Judah, an active man and of great courage. He had an admonition from God not to overlook the Israelites in such a distress as they were now in, but to endeavor boldly to gain them their liberty; so when he had procured some to assist him in this dangerous undertaking, (and few they were, who, either out of shame at their present circumstances, or out of a desire of changing them, could be prevailed on to assist him,) he first of all destroyed that garrison which Chushan had set over them; but when it was perceived that he had not failed in his first attempt, more of the people came to his assistance; so they joined battle with the Assyrians, and drove them entirely before them, and compelled them to pass over Euphrates. Hereupon Othniel, who had given such proofs of his valor, received from the multitude authority to judge the people; and when he had ruled over them forty years, he died.[15]

Modern scholarship has tried to resolve the problem in several ways. Easiest is to emend the passage by lopping off the "naharayim" element in the geographical name, so yielding Aram, generally designating areas around Damascus, therefore closer to Israel. In fact, this is precisely what happens in v. 10. (Ironically, a number of modern translations, such as the RSV, give "Mesopotamia," as in v. 8.) Because in Scripture there are enough occasions in which Aram could be confused for Edom, some scholars (see Lindars 1995: 133) have also proposed Edom as the seat of Cushan. Boling (1975: 81, 83) would push one consonant into the previous word, thus emending *'aram* **nahărāyim** into *'armôn hārîm*, "Fortress of the Mountain," allegedly a stronghold in southern Palestine. Somewhat related is the effort to treat the whole story as allegorical for events that will develop in Israel. Oded (1996) has it vaguely recalling hostilities between Kenizzite clans and nomadic elements, allegedly to argue against the future Saul of Benjamin. His effort, however, suffers from imagining that Hebrew narrators had access to no more lore than what is found in our received text.[16]

Imaginative Reconstructions   Another solution is to import wholesale into this passage imperfectly understood historical tidbits from Near Eastern documents. This approach goes back to our earliest recovery of cuneiform material (see Moore 1895: 85–86), but it is most highly developed in Malamat (1954), who sets our narrative in the late thirteenth century BCE, during the last and troubled days of the Nineteenth Dynasty. For him, Cushan-rishatayim may be a certain Yirsu, also known as Bay (or Beya), a high official who usurped the throne of Egypt before Setnakht, father of Ramses III, established the Twentieth Dynasty: "It is possible that Irsu . . . is identical with the first oppressor of Israel in the period of the Judges. Seemingly Cushan-rishatayim conquered the Israelite tribes while on his way to Egypt, and Israel's deliverance by Othniel followed the expulsion of the invaders from Egypt by Set-nakht" (234). The argument is fanciful, is wholly dependent on conjectures, and is steeped in qualifying language.[17] De Moor (1997: 208–70, following Knauf 1988: 135) weaves an (incredible!) romance from the same documentation to argue that Beya was Moses! Yet what is most interesting about de Moor's speculation is the accent it places on Egyptian revisionism. Much as it was done in post-Hyksos times, native historiographers highlighted the foreignness (*ḫ3rw*, "Asiatic") of a failed leader, blaming him for what upheavals Egypt experienced.

In truth, Beya/Yirsu had begun his career as a scribe, and he and his family may well have lived in Egypt for generations.

Othniel

3 9–10. What was conspicuously missing in the preceding accounts at 2:15–16 finds its place here. Between recall of Israel's sins, and God's redemptive act, we now have Israel pleading for help; for why would God help those who do not orally recant their vile behavior? The relevant idiom for Israel's appeal to God will be repeated in Judges as *zāʿaq ʾel YHVH* (at 3:9, 6:6–7, and 10:10) or *ṣāʿaq ʾel YHVH* (at 4:3 and 10:12).[18] Hebrew is particularly rich in verbs that describe uttered sound (at least twenty are mentioned by Albertz in *TLOT* 3: 1089–90), but none is more direct or emotive than the verb at the base of the idiom we find here, *zāʿaq ʾel-*, connoting as elsewhere an appeal that arises from oppression and outrage. When God responds, it is because he "hears" (that is, listens to) the pleas and "sees" (that is, recognizes) Israel's plight, leading him to rescue (verb: Hiphil of *yāšaʾ*), in this case by installing Othniel as judge.[19]

We have already met Othniel, the conqueror of Debir (Qiryat-sefer) and the winner of Achsah's heart (see IA2, "Achsah"). This episode takes us back to the narrative of conquests initiated by Judah and his ally Simeon, proposing that Othniel's victory over Debir was no fluke. On the transformation overtaking him when touched by God's *rûʷaḥ*, see the Introductory Remarks. While the Greek is literal, some Targumim tried for less charisma: *ušěrat ʾĕlôhî rûḥa gĕbûrâ/nĕbûʾâ min qŏdām YY*, "a spirit of strength/prophecy from God settled on him" (see W. Smelik 1995: 370). As a result, he begins his tenure as judge, presumably with enough prestige to muster the troops for his victory. Beyond Israel's triumph also came control (*vattāʿoz yādô ʿal*), the steps displayed as personal defeat for Cushan-rishatayim rather than just of his land. (For contrast, see below under 3:30.) For how long is debatable: Could it be for the full term of Othniel's forty-year rule? Historians might flinch at having to thread this chunky span into what we know of Levantine history, no matter what scenario or timeline they follow (see above). All others will accept it as a narrator's satisfying response to oppression.

The Reprieve

3 11. Prosopopoeia, also known as personification, is a rhetorical device in which abstractions or inanimate objects display human qualities or abilities, often through verbs that normally have humans as subjects. Fine examples in Scripture are those in which a ship "expected itself to crack up" (Jonah 1:4) or is commanded to howl (Isa 23:1). Fire, swords, and floods readily enter such constructions, as when they "eat" or "swallow." Earth, too, is said to sin (Ezek 14:13) or to vomit its inhabitants (Lev 18:25), but in our verse *hāʾāreṣ* refers to a political territory rather than either to "Earth" or to "the ground." This territory, namely Israel and the land it now controls, is said to be calm, quiet, and silent, the relevant phrase being a briefer version of the more complete *vĕhāʾāreṣ šāqĕṭâ mimmilḥāmâ*, "the land had rest from war," of Josh 11:23 and 14:15. We shall see a repeat of it at 3:30, 5:31, and 8:28.

This respite will last forty years, the number itself being a fine, conventional interval with multiple significances, covering a period at the end of which comes a major change, be it physical, spiritual, social, or martial.[20] At this age, men marry (Isaac, Gen 25:20; Esau, Gen 26:34) or come to leadership (Joshua, Josh 14:7; Ishbosheth, 2 Sam 2:10). There are also many testimonies about Israel's traipsing in the desert for forty years (Num 14:33, 32:13, etc.).[21] Forty years also cover the judgeship of Eli (1 Sam 4:18) and the reigns of David (for example, at 1 Kgs 2:11) and Solomon (2 Chr 9:30). So it is not surprising for the administration of Othniel, as well as that of Gideon (Judg 8:28) and of the Philistines (Judg 13:1), to last that long, nor that of Ehud to double this amount (Judg 3:30). Rahlfs A gives the number of years as fifty, possibly going back to a manuscript that recorded the number as Greek cipher: N (*nu*) for 50 rather than M (*mu*) for 40 (see Harlé and Roqueplo 1999: 95). The phrase about Othniel's death closes on a *pĕtûḥâ* (פ), giving us the sense that for the Masoretes (if not already at Qumran), his death was a major caesura. However, there is reason to suggest that this notice is set to open the next turn in Israel's fortunes (see below). Perhaps this particular case is playing Janus, ending a major episode and opening another.

Othniel does not completely disappear from our narratives henceforth. His descendants are given in 1 Chr 4:13b–14: "The sons of Othniel were Hathath and Meonothai, who begot Ophrah. Seraiah begot Joab father of Ge-harashim, so-called because they were craftsmen." The rabbis also added a few more tidbits. *bTemurah* 16a says: "It has been taught: A thousand and seven hundred *kal vaḥōmēr*, and *gĕzera šāvâ* [these are rabbinic hermeneutic principles] and numeric listings of the scribes were forgotten during the period of mourning for Moses. Said R. Abbahu, 'Nevertheless, Othniel son of Kenaz restored these forgotten teachings by dint of his deductive reasoning.'" The Targum too (1 Chr 2:55) credits Othniel with superior counsel and the power of prophecy (see W. Smelik 1995: 370–71).

Othniel's Death

3 11b. The Masoretes placed a strong disjunctive accent (an *'atnaḥ*) just before the notice about Othniel's death and (likely following traditional scribal formatting) began a new line (פ) to inaugurate the new cycle of sin and redemption. Given the fact that division into verses is a relatively recent phenomenon (High Middle Ages), it is up to us to decide whether to read the notice about the death of Othniel positively (during his lifetime, things went well for Israel) or forebodingly (happiness is over; now begins the dismal cycle). Perhaps we should adopt both postures, but I have opted for the latter interpretation, creating an explicit linkage between his death and the upsurge in Hebrew sinfulness. I am moved to do so because of a missing ingredient in the sequence of events said to unfold on the death of a judge. Here is a register for how these events are recorded in Judges:

> [—Judg 2:8, Joshua dies; (v. 9) burial; (v. 10) virtuous generation ends; (v. 11) sins resume]
> —Judg 3:11, Othniel dies; (v. 12) sins resume, Moabites prevail; (v. 15) Ehud is judge
> [—Judg 3:31, "After [Ehud] . . . ," Shamgar versus Philistines (see below)]
> —Judg 4:1, Sins resume, "Ehud having died"; (v. 2) Canaanites prevail; (v. 4) Deborah follows
> —Judg 6:1 (No death notices for Deborah or Baraq), sins resume, Midian prevails; (6:7–10) prophet warns; (6:11) Gideon's selection

—Judg 8:32, Gideon dies in old age and is buried with ancestors; (v. 33) sins resume "once Gideon died"

—Judg 9:54, Abimelech dies; (v. 55) Israel disbands; (vv. 56–57) lesson on his death; (10:1) Tola follows

—Judg 10:2, Tola dies and is buried; (v. 3) Ya'ir follows

—Judg 10:5, Ya'ir dies and is buried; (v. 6) sins resume; (6:7) Philistines and Ammonites prevail; (11:29) Jephthah is judge

—Judg 12:7, Jephthah dies and is buried; (v. 8) Ibzan follows

—Judg 12:10, Ibzan dies and is buried; (v. 11) Elon follows

—Judg 12:12, Elon dies and is buried; (v. 13) Abdon follows

—Judg 12:15, Abdon dies and is buried; (13:1) sins resume, Philistines prevail; (13:2) Samson follows

—Judg 15:20, Samson's rule ends; (16:30) Samson dies; (16:31) is buried

[—1 Sam 4:18, Eli's rule ends; (5:1) Philistines capture ark; (7:15) Samuel is judge]

[—1 Sam 8–10, Saul becomes king; (16:13) David is king; (25:1) Samuel dies and is buried]

Setting aside the judgeships of Eli and Samuel because they are embedded in elaborate narratives on the rise of kingship, we notice that the transfer of authority from one judge to another lacks a rigidly prescribed sequence of events. A full series would include these moments: death of a judge, burial, resumption of sin, control by an enemy, and investment of a new judge.[22] I will have occasion to return to these notices later; but as far as the one about Othniel is concerned, we lack mention of his burial, the element that more than any other in the series gives closure to the stewardship of each a judge. Perhaps the notice earlier (at 1:15) that his wife had land from her father was deemed enough information about his potential patrimony (S. Ackerman, personal communication).

COMMENTS

It is possible to acknowledge that the Cushan-rishatayim story is elusive yet to keep on searching for its proverbial historical kernel. Another approach, however, is to recognize that the material is steeped in imaginative language. The name Cushan-rishatayim could only be pejorative: He is not simply evil, but is doubly so. The nation with whom he is associated is distant, but its name rings nicely with its ruler, driven by aural euphony (rishatayim || naharayim). Still, if traditions are being reshaped for anecdotal purposes, we should not imagine that they are done so unwittingly; that is, we should not think that narrators recorded this information believing it to be authentic history. Rather, in such instances as this, when wit seems to be controlling the shape of delivered information, we may grant composers the capacity to strive for instruction that conveys sharper lessons than those derived from history.[23] This must certainly have been the case when formulating other patently moralizing royal names, which no proud parents would bestow on a crown prince, for example, the names Gen 14 assigns to the kings of Sodom (Bera, "In Evil"), Gomorrah (Birsha, "In Wickedness"), and their allies (Bela, "Swallower," likely king of Zoar). We shall soon (at 8:5) inspect the names of the Midianite kings Zebah and Zalmunna.

But why open the sequence of judges in such an anecdotal manner? If we recall that anecdotes hardly ever slight reality, but rather deal with plausible incidents in an amusing, occasionally humorous, yet also in an illustrative way, we may accept them as vehicles also for a different version of truth. Anecdotes and parables can belong to the same family, but the former are more likely to include historical (or historicizing) allusions while the latter are more likely to convey a moral. The anecdote about Othniel and how he bested Cushan-rishatayim compresses major themes that will replay in subsequent narratives: divine anger, bullying instruments of God's retribution, Israel coming to its sense, elevation and inspiration of a judge, reversal of fortune, and stability under God's protection. It also may be worth noticing that within this brief paradigm for disgrace and exaltation are embedded seven mentions of the divine name (Yhvh), a most significant number. In scholarship, this composition is most often attributed to Deuteronomists who, latching on to Judah-inspired material about Othniel, provided a pithy paradigm for a collection of northern-inspired tales about diverse deliverers who rise and disappear as Israel falters and then rises (see the Comments to IIA2, "Judges for Israel").

But there is more: The anecdote certainly illustrates how size and prestige alone cannot guarantee permanent dominance, not when God wishes to accept the pleas of the repentant. More importantly, by dragging Cushan-rishatayim from distant Aram-naharayim into land promised to Israel, the anecdote recalls patriarchal days when Amraphel of distant Shinar gathered his minions and struck deep into Palestine. Abram, modestly outfitted in all but divine grace, turned them back, thereby setting claims in the Promised Land (Gen 14). It is true that we still debate when to date that particular episode and how much historicity to confer on it.[24] Still, for an ancient Hebrew, Abram's stunning defeat of distant invaders and Othniel's triumph over outside forces simply reinforced one another, bolstering the plausibility of each no less than intensifying the messages they were meant to convey. Beyond all the lessons that will be absorbed from the stories in Judges, therefore, the trouncing of Cushan-rishatayim might give singular comfort to the many generations before and after the exile that bitterly experienced Mesopotamian power.

Ehud (Judg 3:12–31)

---

3 ^{12}The people of Israel resumed offending the Lᴏʀᴅ; so the Lᴏʀᴅ emboldened Eglon, king of Moab, against Israel because its people did what was offensive to the Lᴏʀᴅ. ^{13}He brought Ammon and Amalek to his side, intent to defeat Israel; together, they occupied the City of Palms. ^{14}For eighteen years, the people of Israel served Eglon, king of Moab. ס ^{15}When the people of Israel pleaded with the Lᴏʀᴅ, the Lᴏʀᴅ provided them a rescuer: Ehud son of Gera, of Benjamin, a man with a hindered right arm. Through him, the people of Israel sent tribute to Eglon king of Moab.

^{16}Ehud made for himself a two-edged dagger, a forearm in length, girding it at his right thigh under his tunic. ^{17}Then he presented the tribute to Eglon king of Moab—Eglon himself was an imposing man. ^{18}Once he completed presenting the tribute, he dismissed the people carrying it. ^{19}Having just come back from the hewn images near Gilgal, he said, "I have a secret message for you, O King." Eglon said, "Hush!" All those serving him left his presence. ^{20}As Ehud was approaching him, he was sitting on the raised chamber of the reception hall that was his, all by himself. So as Ehud said, "I have a divine message for you," he rose from his throne. ^{21}Reaching with his left hand, Ehud drew the dagger from his right thigh and stuck it in his belly. ^{22}Even the hilt sunk with the blade, the fat closing over the blade such that he could not yank the dagger out of his belly and the bowels spilled out.[a] ^{23}Slipping out toward the *colonnade*, Ehud shut and bolted the doors of the raised chamber behind him.

---

a. Or: he slipped out toward the vestibule.

²⁴No sooner did he leave than his servants came in. When they saw that the doors of the platform were bolted, they said, "He must be relieving himself in the chamber of the reception hall." ²⁵They got embarrassed waiting, for he was not opening the doors of the raised chamber. So they took the key and when they unlocked there was their lord fallen dead on the floor!

²⁶Throughout their hemming and hawing, Ehud was escaping. He moved beyond the hewn images and was escaping toward Seirah. ²⁷As soon as he got there, he sounded the ram's horn all over Mount Ephraim and all of Israel joined him in coming down the mountain, with him in the lead. ²⁸"Pursue behind me," he told them, "for the LORD has handed you Moab, your enemy." They came down with him and captured all the fords of the Jordan leading to Moab, allowing no one to cross. ²⁹On just this occasion, they killed about ten thousand men; they were all stout and prominent, yet not a single man escaped. ³⁰From that time on, Moab fell under Israel's power. The land had peace for eighty years. ס

³¹After him[b] was Shamgar son of Anat, who slew six hundred Philistines with an oxgoad. He too rescued Israel. ס

NOTES

Introductory Remarks: The Transfer of Leadership

Earlier (at 2:11–19; see IIA2, "Judges for Israel") we were coached to expect shifts in the leadership of Israel, the appointment of one judge after another itself a powerful recognition that deviant behavior was becoming the norm. An Israel that remained constant to the God of its forefathers would not need such leaders to unify it against foes: Its tribes would not harbor pockets of unconquered resistance, and its people would not sway toward the gods (not to say also toward the women) of remnant enemies. True, we are never given clear and pragmatic notions of how an uncorrupted Israel expected to rule itself. The proposition that seemed to suffice is of a pleased God guaranteeing the safety and peace of his folk.

What is interesting about the proposition that God installs a judge in response to Israel's confession of moral failure is not so much that God readily absolves a people with a dreadful record of lapses, but that alternate forms of guidance are not yet considered options. Thus, to guarantee continuity of purpose, there could have been a sustained investment of the divine *rûʷaḥ* in one family rather than in one individual, thus a dynasty that would endure no matter the frailty of its individual members. Or to ensure an overlap in the control of an enemy, this same *rûʷaḥ* could be endowed on more than one individual at any one time. The former solution will soon occur to Israel when kingship is established even if, with the selection of Saul of Benjamin, the first experiment proved less successful than could have been hoped. The second solution will also be tried (divided monarchy), but only half-heartedly, for a unique God

b. Or: Next to him.

could not risk assigning the fulfillment of an irrevocable pledge (the Promised Land) to potentially competing visions.

In fact, even in polytheistic cultures, when thinkers offered a judgment on the transfer of earthly power within Mesopotamia, they credited their gods with empowering just one city-state at a time. (See also the Introduction, "Judges and the Construction of the Past.") The notion there is that the gods are investing in an institution (in this case a kingship that duplicates on earth what works nicely in heaven) and not in a king. The shift of power from one city-state to another was a drama that unfolded in heaven, its consequence hardly influenced by human virtues or vices, jubilations or laments. Simply, time runs out for one city-state to keep control, and despite the prestige of its patron deity, the decision to empower another entity is inexorable. This point is brutally advanced in one Sumerian lament, when the moon-god Nanna is told about the fate of his city, Ur:

> The verdict of the [divine] assembly cannot be turned back,
> The word commanded by [the god] Enlil knows no overturning:
> Ur was granted kingship, it was not granted an eternal reign.
> Since days of yore when land was founded and people multiplied,
> Who has ever witnessed a reign of kingship that has maintained
>   preeminence?
> [Ur's] kingship has indeed been long, but is now drained.
> O my Nanna, do not exhaust yourself; just leave your city.[1]

Embedded as they are in a poetically crafted myth, the political sentiments expressed above could hardly have been taken realistically even by those who propagated them; nonetheless, they sustained the writing of such "historical" sources as the famous Sumerian King List, wherein one city-state (rather than one dynasty) was said to lose its turn of office before another power took it up. The same ideology informed a "prophet" when he communicated to Zimri-Lim of Mari the god Addu's warning about moving power from one favorite to another (cited in the Comments to IA1, "Adoni-bezeq").

The Tyrant

3 12. On whether the notice about Othniel's death (3:11b) leads into 3:12 is discussed in the previous chapter. Israel now resumes exasperating its god, and naturally he takes action to bring its people in line. The sequence is here reversed, in that the foe is prepared before God delivers Israel to his power. We are not told how long it took for this enemy to develop the needed coalition against Israel, but the first act takes place under God's own tutelage. In *vayyĕḥazzēq YHVH ʾet-ʿeglôn melek môʾāv ʿal-yiśrāʾēl*, the relevant verb is the Piel of *ḥāzaq*, "to strengthen, make tough." When construed in direct object with *zĕrôwaʿ*, "arm," it means to abet or embolden (Ezek 30:24, Hos 7:15); with *lēv*, "heart" (mostly about Pharaoh, Exod 9–14), or *pānîm*, "face" (Jer 5:3), it means to "turn stubborn"; with *yad*, "hand," it suggests encouragement (Judg 9:24, 1 Sam 23:16, Job 4:3).

What is implied when the direct object is a person is not as clear. In 2 Chr 29:34, it simply means to aid someone. So I have taken my cue from Exod 12:33, even if the verb there is Qal (in this verb often the same as Piel): "Egypt pressed the people [*vatteḥĕzaq miṣrayim ʿal-hāʿām*] to hurry and leave the land, thinking, 'We are all dying.'" The idea, therefore, is that for Moab to succeed against Israel, it needed to gather allies, and God was there to inspire it to do so.

Eglon's name has gathered comments.[2] That it is based on 'egel, the word for "calf," is very plausible, for we have plenty of names that are constructed on animals, in Hebrew lore as elsewhere, whether or not suffixes are attached to them[3] (in this case the diminutive -ôn, as in Abdon, from 'eved, "servant," or Samson, from šemeš, "sun," judges both).[4] Ours to decide is whether this is a real name or a mischievous sobriquet (see above under "Cushan-rishatayim") that tradition has attached to a Moabite king who dies under the knife. Generally, commentators who find satire in the story (and they are many) tend to read his name symbolically.[5] As to Eglon himself, rabbinic texts were fascinated with him, and he was placed center to a trio of Moabite worthies known to Scripture, each for an incidental devotion to God: "R. Jose b. Huna said: Ruth was the daughter of Eglon, the grandson of Balak, king of Moab."[6]

Moab, the country Eglon ruled, lay on the eastern side of the Dead Sea, sandwiched between a bulge called the Mīshor to the south of Gilead (Deut 3:10 and elsewhere) and Edom to the south at Wadi Zered (so today, at the southwest edge of the Hashemite Kingdom of Jordan). It is practically useless to be certain about Moab's demarcation, as its lines were porous to tribes and our sources (mostly biblical) have made it Moab's business to dispute certain areas claimed by Reuben and Gad. Mostly plateau, it gets decent enough moisture to make its strips of land fertile, less so for grain than for pasture; so much so that its kings are labeled sheep-breeders (2 Kgs 3:4). The area was populated from time immemorial and enters recorded history in the Late Bronze Age, when empire-period pharaohs (Ramses II) left mention of areas and towns that may be located in its region. But not until the ninth century BCE, with the famous Moabite Stone of King Mesha son of Kemoshyatti, does Moab contribute its own interpretation of its past. There are a fair number of references to Moabite rulers and events in Neo-Assyrian and Neo-Babylonian records.[7] Yet the Hebrew Bible material on Moab remains our largest source of information, and while the historical value of many of its statements cannot easily be checked against contemporary evidence, its historiographic value cannot be exaggerated. As befits a neighbor with mirror cultures and institutions, Moab's profile in Scripture is ambivalent, at once detestable and attractive.

There, Moab and Ammon are said to be children of incest, born to Lot's daughters (Gen 19:30–38). The pun given there on the name Moab (allegedly from mēʾāv, "from a father") is itself dreadful, if only because cuneiform spellings of the name give it as Maʾab, Maba, and Muʾaba, none suggesting the existence of the preposition min. (No plausible etymology for Moab has been offered.) The tradition stuck, earning the Moabite the cognomen "Children of Lot" (Deut 2:9). Moab was never promised to Israel, yet troubled relations between their people run like a leitmotif in Hebrew lore; from the desert wanderings when King Balak wished Israel harm (Num 22–24) to deep into Israel's monarchic period, Saul, David, and a number of Omrid kings controlled Moabite territory. On both sides, the struggle was couched as a duel between YHVH and Chemosh (Num 21:29, Jer 48:46, the Mesha Stone). Israel (almost) apostatized at Peor as it was reaching the Promised Land (Num 25:1–3), and Moabites were forever proscribed from joining Israel (Deut 23:3–4 [2–3 RSV]; Neh 13:1, 2). Still, Ruth was deemed from Moab and consequently also David, who once took his parents for refuge there (1 Sam 22:4).

It is difficult to assess the import of the last clause, "because its people did what was offensive to the LORD," since it does not supplement any previous information. The compound conjunction *'al kî* (*'al 'ăšer* also) simply gives an explanation for a previous statement.

3 13–14. In Judges, we may find internecine wars (spectacular examples are forthcoming), but when they are said to be launched by outside forces, they are never local. That is, when Philistines, Moabites, Ammonites, Amalekites, or Midianites attack, whatever tribe is their immediate victim, the clash will soon involve all of Israel. Historians may raise doubts about the probability of such broad arenas for the conduct of wars, especially when involving tribal forces and minor powers, but the principles driving their realization demanded wholesale defeats: It would simply not do for God to punish Israel's unfaithfulness regionally or piecemeal. Responsibility is always universal, and so are punishments and redemptions.

Vayye'ĕsōf 'ēlāᵛv 'et-bĕnê 'ammôn va'ămālēq vayyēlek vayyak 'et-yiśrā'ēl vayyîrĕšû 'et-'îr hattĕmārîm. The verbal forms stagger: *Eglon* gathers allies, *he* attacks, then *they* occupy, when to achieve their goal they should all attack at once.[8] Some translations (for example Boling's in AB) jump the gun by having all three proceed to attack Israel before reaching their goal. (Josephus, *Ant.* 5.185–86, has Eglon launch several battles.) Others take their cue from the LXX (and the versions, see Lindars 1995: 138), attributing all activities to Eglon. (So why bother with mentioning Ammon and Amalek?) Neither approach is necessary, for Hebrew is fairly tolerant of such allocation of subjects, especially when subjects and activities are set in a sequence. Still, with the verb *hālak* often used as an auxiliary to illustrate the consequent event, it makes sense that we are reading about Eglon's intentions as he crafts a coalition before we learn of their joint success.

Whatever the historical condition of the Moabite state in the Early Iron Age (most scholars doubt that it was much more than tribal territories), in launching this particular war, Eglon is shown to be quite realistic. Tactically, Moab is much too provincial (it hardly stretched to half the length of the Dead Sea's eastern shore) for it to attack over a broad front, and it invites the alliance of Ammon and Amalek. Ammon lay just to the north (bounded by the Zarqa [Jabbok] and Hasban wadis), and almost all of the extrabiblical information about it comes from the late Neo-Assyrian period, from which time we have an impressive list of tribal kings. (Conveniently, see *ABD* 1: 194–96, under "Ammon" and "Epigraphy, Transjordania.") It is tempting to imagine for Ammon (mostly *bĕnê 'ammôn* in Scripture) as for Moab, distinct but similarly evolutionary developments from tribal units, to tribal confederacy, to federated kingdoms, before reaching nation-state; but for Israel, they were practically twins, not just because in Hebrew lore they shared the same ancestor (Lot) and so were deemed kin, but because they often banded together against Israel (since Balak's days), because they worshiped gods (Chemosh and Milkom) that were so similar that Hebrew traditions would occasionally assign them indiscriminately, and because they were similarly excluded from participating in Yahweh's covenant. (For more on Ammon, see below.)

Unlike Moab and Ammon, which have left us extrabiblical traces, Amalek has so far escaped historical detection. Even in Scripture its people do not stay put. Linked to Edom in some traditions (Gen 36:12), they formed a power in southern Palestine

(Gen 14:7) where they ranged almost to the frontier of Egypt (Num 13:29, 14:43–45; 1 Sam 15:7). Amalek, therefore, can endanger Israel's southern flank. But our best cue for the meaning of Amalek's participation comes from Balaam's prophecy, "the best of nations, its fate is to utterly perish" (*rēʾšît gôyim veʾaḥărîtô ʿădê ʾōvēd*; Num 24:20). Its doom was set because, unprovoked, it attacked Israel at Rephidim, when its people had barely escaped the clutches of Pharaoh (Exod 17:8–13). They earned God's promise: "Inscribe this in a document as a reminder, and read it aloud to Joshua: I will utterly blot out the memory of Amalek from under heaven!" (Exod 17:14). So if Eglon's invitation to Ammon might make sense geographically (it broadened the front against Israel), bringing Amalek into the coalition simply sharpened the control that God had over these events. How could Israel not sense dire predicament when God is allowing its doomed enemy to triumph? Yet, how could Eglon expect success to be constant when his core ally is doomed?

The city that the coalition occupies, "City of Palms," is already known to us from 1:16. If it is another name for Jericho, then Eglon's (initial) success struck deep into Benjamin territory, if not also Israel's psyche, as Joshua had made Jericho a paradigm for the conquest of the Promised Land. Eglon's power move might be less impressive if it took place at Zoar, another site proposed for it (see the Notes to 1:16).

The number of years Eglon had control of Israel, eighteen, has a few significant parallels, only one of which might be of interest: Josiah had reigned for eighteen years when Hilkiya the Priest discovered the famous scroll of the laws (2 Chr 34:8, 14). Whether or not it is a scaled-up version of Cushan-rishatayim's eight years of oppression (Judg 3:8) is beyond us to assess.

The Champion

3 15. Enter Ehud; although he never gets to be "endowed with zeal for the LORD," we are told that God provided him as a rescuer (*vayyāqem YHVH lāhem môšîaʿ ʾet-ʾēhûd*). Ehud arrives equipped with no previous history, and the present story is hardly forthcoming about his life if less so about his personality.[9] In this regard, Hebrew narrators are treating him like the so-called minor judges, an unhelpful rubric that generations of scholars have attached to the briefly presented Shamgar, Tola, Jair, Ibzan, Elon, and Abdon. We know people from Benjamin had the same name (1 Chr 7:10), and a notice in another Benjamin list is commonly emended to locate him among descendants of Benjamin's son Bela. In the received Hebrew, 1 Chr 8:3 now reads, "Bela had sons: Addar, Gera, and Abihud"; but since the name Abihud is constructed with the element *ʾav*, "father," some scholars suggest translating, "Addar and Gera, *father of [E]hud.*"

Neither the name Ehud (Hebrew, *ʾēhûd*; Greek, Αωδ)[10] nor that of his father Gera (*gērāʾ*; Γηρα) can be confidently analyzed. Ehud is taken either as a shortened form Ahi/Abi-hôd, "my brother/father is Majesty," or a by-form for Ayyē-hôd, "where is the Majesty?" (On the latter, see Stamm 1980: 64, 69.)

Ehud's tribal affiliation is revealed next; the line *ben-gērāʾ ben-hayyĕmînî*, "the son of Gera, from Benjamin," itself is repeated exactly for Shimei, David's nemesis (2 Sam 19: 17 [16 RSV], 1 Kgs 2:8). There, as here, we should not take Gera as a clan rather than a person's name (Burney 1970: 69 and many others).[11] But the main point of the reference is to introduce us to a feature Ehud shared with other warriors from Benjamin (see below at Judg 20:16): Each is said to be 'iṭṭēr yad-yĕmînô. While the last two words are clear enough, "right arm/hand," the form of the first belongs to nouns that connote bodily defect, but also soundness. Exodus 4:11 gives a sequence that includes both: "The LORD said to [Moses], 'Who gives man speech? Who makes him dumb ['illēm] or deaf [ḥērēš], seeing [piqqēᵃḥ] or blind ['ivvēr]? Is it not I, the LORD?'" It is difficult to decide where 'iṭṭēr fits in this spectrum. Aside from its use in personal names (Ater in Ezra and Nehemiah), the root occurs in just one series of pleas to avoid catastrophes, including, "May the Pit [the netherworld] not tighten [te'ṭar] its mouth over me" (Ps 69:16 [15 RSV]).

HIS "HANDICAP"

My translation for the crucial phrase "(a man) with a hindered right arm" is as literal as possible to the Hebrew 'iṭṭēr yad-yĕmînô. But it must not be assumed that Ehud was infirm (as some translations have it),[12] and it must certainly not be translated as "left-handed" (a majority of translations) since such a rendering implies a genetic disposition to rely on the left hand. (1 Chr 12:2 gives us terms for right- and left-handed people, maymînîm and maśmi'lîm.) In itself, a correct translation for the phrase may seem trivial, were it not for the mushrooming literature on the sinister (Latin for "left") or the gauche (French for the same) world of left-handed people.[13]

We may find a clue to his "handicap" in a statement about men from Benjamin (!) who abandoned Saul for David: "They were warriors who can help win battles. Fixed to their bows, with either right or left hand, they were able to sling stones or shoot arrows" (1 Chr 12:1–2). The tribe of Benjamin, therefore, trains warriors to use either arm for fast discharge of arrows or stones. Such men required intensive training, and their numbers could not be large. In fact, Judg 20:16 relates that of the twenty-six thousand men Benjamin mustered for its fight against Israel, seven hundred were marked as 'iṭṭēr yad-yĕmînô such that each "could sling a stone at a hair and not miss." Hyperbolic though the numbers in that story may be, the ratio seems plausible: Just three of each one hundred men could fight without favoring their right arm. What we are dealing with here is not people who are left-handed by nature, but an elite group that operates well when their right arm could not or must not be used, whether for tactical reasons or because of potential war injuries during combat.[14] Whether this sort or training was special to Benjaminites or was developed by narrators eager to exploit the literal meaning of Benjamin, ben-yāmîn, "Son of the Right" (that is, "southerner"), cannot be safely judged, but the rich source of material on the Benjaminite tribes (dumu.meš yamina) in the Mari archives to my knowledge displays no similar propensity to play on etymology.

So Ehud was an elite warrior, well-trained for the task at hand. We cannot tell whether Israel knew of his specific plans when they sent him bearing tributes to Eglon.[15] That later on they rallied at the call of his shofar (v. 27) would lead us to suspect that they did. The fact that he was accompanied by a retinue (see 3:18) makes it unlikely that he was a "loner," whether or not God or Israel had inspired him to assassinate Eglon.

The Hebrew term for Ehud's tribute is minḥâ, a word of disputed etymology that operates in both secular and religious contexts. In the latter, it alludes to individuals bringing (hāvî) a minḥâ to God by presenting it (hiqrîv) to a priest, who then takes it (*higgîš*) to the altar (Lev 2:8, with variations in Num 5:25). In temporal settings, *minḥâ* is exchanged in goodwill among equals.[16] It also signals a vassal's continued allegiance to an overlord, hoping that it would propitiate (*kippēr*, Gen 32:21) a vastly more powerful individual.[17] Worth keeping in mind is that *hiqrîv* ("to present") controls *minḥâ* only in a cultic context, although in Ps 72:10 it is so used for a synonym, *'eškâr*.

HIS WEAPON

3 16. English has a large repertoire for weapons held by the hilt, differentiating them by their manufacture and use: sword, knife (normally single-edged), dirk, rapier, poniard, and the like. Hebrew, however, gives simply *ḥerev*. We have to select from the English inventory the term most appropriate to a context but must not doubt that Israel knew great diversity in the production of such weaponry.[18] In our particular passage, we are lucky to learn that it was sharp on both of its edges (so perfect for piercing) and that it was a *gōmed* in length. We know that double-edged weapons, from swords to daggers, had been in existence for a long time (the goddess Inanna used a serrated one to dispatch Ebiḫ)[19] and that their capacity to injure had become proverbial (Ps 149:6, Prov 5:4, Heb 4:12).[20] Unfortunately, how long a *gōmed* is and whether it applied to the whole weapon or just the blade cannot be decided. The word occurs only here in Scripture, and what the versions give are likely speculative. The Greek offers μάχαιραν δίστομον σπιθαμῆς τὸ μῆκος αὐτῆς, "a double-edged dagger (or sword), a span long." (Generally, the span is equivalent to the widest distance in an open palm.) The Targum has *garmîdā'*, generally a "cubit," the length between the elbow and a closed fist, and most translations give the same. (Hartmann [2000] gives it as 21 centimeters entire.) Who knows what is correct? If fixed on the outer part of the thigh, I would conjure up the ("Hyksos") dagger bought on the open market that was published long ago by Freeman (1943), even if it was centuries too early to have survived until Ehud's time and was made of copper rather than the bronze or iron dagger of Eglon's time. But it was 32 centimeters long, had a very fine grip, a 21-centimeter blade, and no cross-piece to separate them. A more compact version would fit nicely on the inner thigh of an average-sized man but would still be long enough to do its nasty job.

Ehud bound the dagger under his clothing, at his thigh. The compound preposition *mittaḥat lĕ-* gives the act a hint of a motion when it could easily have done without it by ignoring the *lĕ-*. This is a crucial bit of information, as it suggests an extraordinary measure: Warriors, we know, tied their weapons over their clothing, and if they had daggers, they likely attached them to their belts. It must have been particularly uncomfortable to have such a weapon stiff by one's thigh, but it also contributed to Ehud's ability to come by the king undetected. The item of clothing, *mad*, is one of many outer garments mentioned in Scripture, and it is cited either as singular or as plural, so suggesting multiple layers or segments when worn, obviously falling below the knees. (See the dictionaries, generally under "Clothing," "Dress and Ornamentation," or the like.) A priest may have a *mad* over other garments (Lev 6:3 [10 RSV]), but it seems to be something worn, perhaps as a body-length hauberk of thin leather, by warriors, among them ambassadors who likely wanted to look spiffy for the occasion (2 Sam 10:4, written *mādû*). There is a humorous story about David, the shepherd, who simply could not feel comfortable battling Goliath with Saul's *mad* on his body (1 Sam 17:38–39) and a more solemn one of him receiving Jonathan's (1 Sam 18:4).

The Setting

3 17. As noted above, the verbal form controlling Ehud's tribute, *hiqrîv*, normally conveys a cultic function. The bearing of tribute (*biltum*, *tamartum*, or *mandattum* in Akkadian) by a defeated enemy is not to be confused with the routine exchange of gifts among equals or the delivery of a *sīrum*-"tax" by a vassal eager to avoid an attack.[21] In Neo-Assyrian annals we hear much about kings imposing yearly or perpetual tributes on the defeated no less than those hoping to avoid becoming their victims. The famous and widely reproduced Black Obelisk that shows Jehu of Israel (or his representative) groveling at the feet of Shalmaneser III, with lines of tribute carriers in other panels, tells the story as well as any text.[22] This delivery was itself a quasi-ceremonial affair, since in antiquity it occurred at regular periods; Mari documents reveal that such deliveries coincided with religious festivals, such as those dedicated to Ištar. We may imagine that something ritual was at stake here, hence the use of *hiqrîv*.

Why we need to know about Eglon's physical condition is not immediately obvious. He is said to be *bārî' mĕ'ōd*, and in many translations he is "very fat," a condition deemed humorous, especially when associated with the future victim's name, meaning "calf-y." Sternberg (1987) remarks on his gluttony by (absurdly) harking back to a previous detail, "[Ehud's] undersized sword thus contrasts with the oversized king, while its 'two mouths' . . . slyly brings to mind the sources of his corpulence: to get so fat would require more than a single mouth" (332). Amit (1989) proposes that "the adjective 'fat' also fits the association of a fatted animal" (110), that is, one destined for slaughter. However, human corpulence is normally associated with the root **šmn*, as in Deut 32:15, Jer 5:28, Neh 9:25, and Ezek 34:16 (mostly figurative). In fact, just a few verses later (3:29) we read about the slaughter of every "stout and prominent" man (*kol-šāmēn vĕkol-'îš ḥāyil*).

The Hebrew *bārî'* most often applies to animals (Gen 41:2, 1 Kgs 5:3 [4:23 RSV]) or to plants (Gen 41:5) that are nice and healthy, so also to a good cut of meat (Ezek 34:3). Psalms 73:4 bemoans the bodily fitness of wicked people, and in Dan 1:15 young men who avoid the forbidden ration offered by kings nonetheless appear *ṭôv 'ûrî'ê bāśār*, "nice with healthy flesh tone." While the Targum here has *faṭîm*, "fleshy" (applied to animals), the Greek gives ἀστεῖος σφόδρα, "very handsome," using the same noun that describes baby Moses, said to be *ṭôv*, "beautiful," in Exod 2:2. My translation "a very imposing man" allows Eglon the presence that made it less necessary for him to have a full-time retinue, a crucial element in the unfolding plot.

LEFT ALONE

3 18–19. Often, Hebrew narrative style is simply not too accommodating to our needs when connecting subjects and activities, relying on pronouns when names could dispel ambiguity. Ehud is certainly the dispenser of tribute, because "once he completed presenting the tribute" simply harks back to what he was said to be doing at 3:17. If we jump ahead, to the middle of v. 18, there is no doubt that it was Ehud who requested a private audience, "O King, I have a secret message for you." What lay in between is more difficult to assign. Ehud could have dismissed (Piel of *šālaḥ*)[23] the bearers of goods, but protocol demands that Eglon be given the authority to do so. Ehud could have returned from the stone images at Gilgal, but why and when did he leave for them? Does it make sense (even if stories do not always have to follow our logic) that after delivering the tributes at wherever Eglon was quartered (and there is a hopeless debate on whether this was Jericho, Medaba in Moab, or elsewhere), Ehud goes away and then returns from the Gilgal area? Or could it be that when he was accepting Ehud's tribute, it is Eglon who had just come back from the stone monuments at Gilgal (*šāb* could be a participle as well as a perfect)? If so, it could be a sign of his control of an area that had been Israelite and where, in irony that cannot be slighted, the messenger of God gave Israel its tough warning (see the Introductory Remarks to IIA1). I would favor this approach, giving Eglon control of the movements to and from a sacral area, but also sharpening the good fortune of Ehud as he reaches his destination just as Eglon returns from his *pĕsîlîm*. The cost of such a conjunction is high, as it implies a great number of switches between Ehud and Eglon as subjects in a relatively brief sequence of clauses. My translation avoids a confrontation and (wimpishly) keeps to pronouns where supplying names might have clarified the scene.[24]

HEWN IMAGES

Here and at v. 26 the verbs associated with the *pĕsîlîm* are those of movement: *šûb min-* has the sense of "turning away, to abandon," for anger or a plan, but it refers to "returning" or "come back from" when dealing with travel or the like. The word *'āvar* (3:26) is about bypassing a place or site. So it is possible to imagine that a name of a place may be at stake (Lindars 1995: 143; Lenzi 2008: 225 n. 23). More likely, we are dealing with stone slabs that are cut into monoliths and are either cast (Isa 40:19) or capped with precious metal (Isa 30:22); they might also be shaped from clay or wood. Hebrew has a nice repertoire of these instruments of commemoration or of worship, a number of which are condemned in Lev 26:1: "You must not make for yourselves idols [*'ĕlîlîm*]. You must not erect for yourselves a *pesel* or a *maṣṣēvā*. You must not allow in your land a carved stone [*'even maśkît*] so as to worship upon it, for I the LORD am your God." Other passages also give us *'ăšērâ*, "wooden pillar" (above at 3:7 and below at 6:25). Evidently, none of these has the same configuration or purpose, yet it is possible to imagine that *pesel maṣṣēvâ* and *'even* shared functional applications, for they are often lumped conjunctively. Occasionally, they can be paired, possibly suggesting a hendiadys, as in the Lev 26:1 citation above (a "hewn *maṣṣēvâ*").[25]

Among these is the *pesel* or *pāsîl*. It could be a divine figure, whether fashioned abstractly (so a betyl or a menhir; see Mic 5:12 [13 RSV]), anthropomorphically (so human shaped, albeit with nonhuman touches such as horns or a tail; see Hos 11:2, 2 Chr 33:19), or theromorphically (so animal shaped). Philology cannot secure the precise form of what was found at Gilgal, but given the meaning of Gilgal—something round or in a circle (see the Notes to 2:1 above)—we are likely dealing with stone objects arranged circularly in the open air at higher elevations (see Ps 78:58). Such an arrangement is recalled in Josh 4:20–23: "Joshua set up in Gilgal the twelve stones [*'ăvānîm*] they had taken from the Jordan, instructing the people of Israel, 'In the future, should your children ask their fathers, "What is the meaning of those stones?" inform your children: "Israel crossed this Jordan on dry land." For the LORD your God dried up the waters of the Jordan before you until you crossed, just as the LORD your God did to the Re(e)d Sea.'" The literature on this material in biblical lore is now vast.[26] As it happens, we are also learning much about such monuments from the ancient Near East, and they involve dressed stones, mostly uninscribed and likely bearing no reliefs. We know about them from the third-millennium Ebla documents on, with details in Emar documents suggesting that a city gate led specifically to them and that they played a role in the enactment of installation rituals (many details are in Fleming 1992: 74–79). The richest attestations from one archive, however, come from Mari. There, they are called *sikkānum* (a West Semitic formation from *sakānum*, "to set up"), *râmum* (also West Semitic from *rwm*, "to raise"), and *ḫumūsum*, this last applying to a metal bas-relief (*FM* 8 38) as well as to stones piled up into a (commemorative) monument. For our purposes, the most interesting information the archives reveal is the tight connection among setting up these stones, sacred space, (cultic) ceremonies, and sacrifices.[27] A letter from a powerful tribal leader reports King Zimri-Lim's request (*FM* 8 12:3–10): "This sacrifice [for the goddess Ištar] is upon us, but there is no *sikkānum* for it yet. Promptly send a hundred men and a dependable person who can cut the *sikkānum* and have them hew at Lasqum four *sikkānātum* each of 12 cubits [18 feet!]." Another one (ARM 28 44) intimates that vassals took oaths of fealty on such stones. Once, when the king directed an administrator to recover a boulder from "Dagan's Nose" (obviously a name for a jutting cliff or the like), he faced much reluctance regarding the enterprise:

> We found that boulder and what is there is much more massive than my lord indicated to me. I took it upon myself to look into the matter, and would keep on seeking information about this site. This site is indeed "strong" (holy?) and absolutely no one wants in any way to be in contact with it. With Yasmaḫ-Addu [the previous king], there was a matter (similar) to this, and a transgression came to be associated with him because of it. I therefore came to fear this matter in my own heart, just so sooner or later my lord ought not say, "you could have made an effort to look into the matter of this site." (*FM* 8 15:5–32)

So our notice about Gilgal and its *pěsîlîm* is there not just to establish where this narrative took place, but also to explain why Eglon would be alert to communication from the divine. It is possible that Eglon was conjectured to have appropriated Joshua's stones of Gilgal as monument to his own victory over Israel. The reference might nevertheless sharpen our sense of irony, for how could Eglon hope to keep control of Israel when the *pěsîlîm* that he (or Ehud) visited were there to trigger recall of Israel (and not Moab) crossing the Jordan? Finally, it is a fine touch that the narrator sets the crucial murder scene between moves within (at 3:19) and beyond (at 3:26) these objects, as if to sharpen our focus on the macabre events within Eglon's palace (Mobley 2005: 86–101).

SECRET WORDS

With all this information on the timing and occasion of Ehud's arrival before Eglon, we are ready to unravel the plot. It is useful (albeit not crucial) to realize that Ehud is making just one statement to Eglon even if we have it recorded with slightly different vocabulary in v. 19, *děvar-sēter lî 'ēlêkā hammelek*, "I have a secret message for you, O King," and in v. 20, *děvar-'ělōhîm li 'ēlêkā*, "I have a divine message for you." The Greek (needlessly) adds "O King" to make the repetition even sharper. This statement is embedded within complementary information on how Eglon reacted: He is responsible for his own isolation ("he said 'Hush'") and makes himself an easier target for assassination ("he rose from his throne"). Describing the scene of the crime serves as a backdrop for Ehud's successful escape.[28]

Ehud declares that he wished to convey a word or an act (Hebrew *dāvār* can mean either) that is veiled or shielded (verb *sātar*). In the parallel line, this is clarified as *dĕvar-'ĕlōhîm*, which is less precise than we would like, for *'ĕlōhîm* can mean "God" or "gods," or even can be used to create a superlative, so "a grave matter" or the like.[29] In 1 Kgs 12: 22 and 1 Chr 17:3 it indeed refers to divine messages, but in 1 Chr 26:32 it simply means "divine matters." First Samuel 9:27 somewhat parallels our situation. Samuel draws Saul aside, isolating him from all, to let him hear God's *dāvār*, which turns out to be anointing him as king and proposing confirmation of his election rather than communicating to him instruction, encouragement, or warning. A good number of commentators have found irony and multiple meanings in the use of *dāvār*, because it can stand for word (hence message) or act (assassination or the like).

We can gauge Eglon's assessment of the phrase by his reaction, even if the Greek witnesses complicate it somewhat. The Hebrew has him shout an interjection, *hās*, "hush," that elsewhere in Scripture is always attached to solemn circumstances, mostly related to the divine presence. Given that the courtiers are said to leave, the inference is that Eglon is asking Ehud to remain quiet until the two are alone. Rahlfs B has Eglon explicitly ordering Ehud to "be quiet!," σιώπα (imperative), but follows with "and he had all who waited on him leave his presence," suggesting that they read *vayyōṣî* rather than the received Hebrew *vayyēṣē'*. The sequence would recall Joseph's order on wishing to remain alone with his brothers (Gen 45:1). Rahlfs A sticks with the verbal form of the Hebrew but has Eglon ordering everyone "away" from there (ἐκ μέσου).[30] Nonetheless, the notion remains that Eglon wished to be alone with Ehud. Perhaps he was hoping for a message (to him) from a foreign God? In fact, the Mari archives reveal how eager rulers were to cajole the gods (local or foreign) into revealing their intentions, whether through omens, dreams, or prophecies.[31] Perhaps he expected this Hebrew to give him information that was crucial to his continued control of Israel? That he hushed him first (Hebrew *hās* is nicely onomatopoeic, as is our "hush") gives clear insight that he was expecting to hear sensitive information. Mesopotamian omen literature is full of warnings against state secrets (*pirištum, puzrum*) being traded and treasonable acts being plotted by insiders (scribes, wives, "notables," but often enough the "cup-bearer"). One of the saddest laments on this score is cited in a note two Mari officers exchanged: "You know well how our lord [Zimri-Lim] has admonished a couple of times in meetings we attended, 'Why is it that confidential information takes to the wind as soon as I tell all of you?'" (A.158; cited in LAPO 16 #55, pp. 178–79).[32]

ALONE TOGETHER

3 20. When Ehud approached (*bā'* is best treated here as a participle) Eglon, the king was seated (*yōšēv*, also a participle). The place was a *mĕqērâ* in which there was a *'alîyâ*, the descriptions ending with juxtaposed phrases: *'ăšer lô*, "that was his," and *lĕvaddô*, "by himself." Here we have choices: With the Masoretic punctuation, we may take the two phrases as attributive to the area he was occupying: "he was sitting on the raised chamber of the reception hall that was just his." Or we may assign them as I have done serially to the space and then to Eglon, thus increasing his sense of isolation.

Much ink has been spilled on elucidating Eglon's location. The versions do not help much because *mĕqērâ* occurs only here and at 3:24. Greek gives καὶ αὐτὸς ἐκάθητο ἐν τῷ ὑπερῴῳ τῷ θερινῷ τῷ ἑαυτοῦ μονώτατος, "he himself was sitting in his own upper summer chamber," and the Targum has something similar, "in the upper room of his summer house." Most translations (*TNK* and RSV) give "cool upper/roof chamber" (or the like), deriving *mĕqērâ* from a root **qrr* that in fact has more to do with flowing (as in water, Jer 18:14, Prov 25:25) than with cooling. Realistically, such an understanding cannot be appropriate for the Jordan Valley: Upper rooms are no place for cooling off, except at nighttime (Jull 1998: 62). In fact, as we know from the construction of ice-houses in Mesopotamia, the idea is to insulate them from direct sunlight (Joannès 1994).

So we are left to our own devices to fill in the background: The phrase *ʿaliyat hammĕqērâ* of 3:20 is obviously paralleled by *ḥădar hammĕqērâ* of 3:24. Benzinger (1894: 121) is not alone in thinking of a *ʿaliyâ* as a loft, citing 2 Sam 19:1 (18:33 RSV) where, above the city gate (*ʿaliyat haššaʿar*), David took his hurt on learning of Absalom's death.[33] However, some scholars think that the difference in vocabulary between the phrases reflects architectural distinctions. Jull (1998) thinks that the *ḥădar hammĕqērâ* of 3:24 is a privy whereas the *ʿaliyat hammĕqērâ* of 3:20 is referring to the same as part of a throne room.[34]

Halpern (1988a: 43–58; see also 1988b) relies on a passage from Ps 104:3 ("[God] sets the rafters of his lofts in the waters"; see also Eccl 10:18) to reconstruct certain features of Syrian palace architecture (*bīt ḥilāni*). He proposes that *ʿaliyat hammĕqērâ* (read **hammeqārê*) is "the room over the beams," the king's private audience hall, in which are crowded his throne and, incongruously, an "inner toilet room" (*ḥădar hammĕqērâ*).[35] I think this creativity goes beyond anything archeology has taught us about any Syrian palace. Moreover, to set a toilet where one receives guests seems too far-fetched, given the sense of privacy that individuals, even in wartime, will seek when needing to relieve themselves (as when Saul goes into a cave when needing to do so at 1 Sam 24:4 [3 RSV]). What Josephus says about the Essenes' bodily scruples (*J. W.* 2.147–49) was likely prevalent since time immemorial, as suggested by Deut 23:14 (13 RSV).[36]

I take the *ʿaliyat hammĕqērâ* of 3:20 as equivalent to the *ḥădar hammĕqērâ* of 3:24. The former tells us that it was raised higher than the ground floor, so likely needing steps; the latter suggests that we are dealing with a chamber (*ḥeder*) with door panels that lock (see below). This chamber is built within the *mĕqērâ*, which (however the term is to be vocalized) simply means an audience room, a place where, in accordance with the meaning of the verb *qrh*, things "happen."[37]

So we have the following setting: Ehud comes before Eglon in an audience chamber where, on a platform Eglon sits on his throne, *kissēʾ*. Admittedly, it is difficult to decipher why Eglon rises from this throne, as we have no information that messages (secret or divine) were "heard as a Hallelujah Chorus" (to use Halpern's witticism, 1988a: 7 n. 66). It may simply be a sign of eagerness; still, this act earned Eglon a rare rabbinic approbation: "Because he rose for God, he became the father of Ruth" (Midrash *Ruth Rabbah*, 2:9; similarly, *bSanhedrin* 60a and Midrash *Numbers Rabbah*, 16:27).

The Deed

3 21. Eglon rises to his feet from his throne and thereby sets himself up for the assassination. (The Greek felt the need to open inconsequentially with, "And this is what happened: as he rose. . . .") Assassination, for political, dynastic, military, or purely personal reasons, is broadly documented in the ancient Near East. In Hebrew narratives there is a cluster of them in the works of the Deuteronomist, although they do not share the same motivation and are not carried out in the same way. We shall soon discuss Sisera's murder (at 4:17–21 and 5:24–27). Purely political is what is told about King Joash's murder by palace conspirators (2 Kgs 12:21–22 [20–21 RSV]), the weapon likely being a sword because the text says they "struck" him.[38] Also political were the murders of Governor Gedaliah by plotters with aspiration to power (2 Kgs 25:25) and of Ishboshet, Saul's heir, struck in his *ḥōmeš* (see below) during his summer siesta (2 Sam 4:5–6). Ishboshet's murderers, Benjaminites who had hoped to gain by their defection, used stealth to approach the slumbering king. (The Greek has a different scenario.) More or less the same happens to Sennacherib of Assyria, his sons striking with a sword as he worshiped his god (2 Kgs 19:37; but see Parpola 1980). Purely personal (but not without political implications) was the murder of Amnon for abusing Tamar; he was likely bludgeoned by Absalom's servants when intoxicated (2 Sam 13:28–29). The same can be said of Joab's murder of Abner, a vendetta as well as an elimination of a potential rival: "Joab took [Abner] aside within the gate to talk to him privately; there he struck him in the *ḥōmeš*" (2 Sam 3:27). Where to locate the wound is debated, with older translations (for example, KJV) favoring "the fifth *rib*," obviously because of the cardinal number *ḥāmēš* for "five"; but "abdomen" and "belly" are better choices, especially in view of our next and most instructive example.[39]

Amasa had been Absalom's main officer but, to the dismay of Joab, still retained the confidence of David, who charged him with rallying Judah troops to quell yet another rebellion. When he tarried, David sent Joab among other loyalists to engage the rebels. We pick up the story at this point (2 Sam 20: 8–12):

> As they neared the Great Stone [obviously a *maṣṣēvâ*] in Gibeon, Amasa came toward them. Joab was in military dress, over which there was a sheathed sword [*ḥerev*] tied to a belt on his waist; but as he stepped forward, it fell out. Joab greeted Amasa, "Brother, are you well?" and his right hand grasped Amasa's beard, to greet him with a kiss. Amasa was simply not on his guard against the dagger [*ḥerev*] in Joab's *left* hand, so with it he struck him to the abdomen [*ḥōmeš*], shedding his bowels to the ground. He died without *Joab* having to strike again. . . . Amasa was wallowing in blood in the middle of the road, drenched in his blood . . . ; and when [a man] saw that people were coming and milling around, he dragged Amasa from the road to a field and covered him with a garment.

There are a good deal of comments on this passage, with several explanations of how the deed was carried out; but most often we read that Joab let his sword slip out of its sheath and then snatched it with his left hand before plunging it into Amasa. More likely to me is that Joab, an experienced officer, purposely dropped the girt weapon to the ground, letting it sit there to keep Amasa off his guard. As he comes close enough for his right arm to pull Amasa by the beard, as if to kiss him, Joab completely cuts off his vision. He is now in a perfect position to have his *left* hand reach *another* weapon, this time a dagger ("sword" and "dagger" use the same word in Hebrew) with which to stab him. It should be kept in mind that in close quarters, daggers (and the like) were not held with the blade below the little finger, but with it pointing beyond the thumb, so maximizing the power of an *upward* thrust.[40] So when Joab drove his left fist upward, not only was the movement hidden from Amasa, but the blow had enough force to rip open Amasa's belly to the abdomen (*ḥōmeš*), spilling his guts to the ground and leaving him hemorrhaging to death.[41]

What happens to Eglon could not have differed much except that either because his physique made him tower over Ehud (as we learned, he was an "imposing man") or because he stood on a podium, the blow struck in the belly region, so below the *ḥōmeš*. The blade planted into his belly, a choice target, not only because there are no bones to stop the weapon, but also because it has a good chance of cutting a major blood vessel. Even if not spectacularly deep, the wound will fester as infection invariably follows, killing the hardiest survivor of the original blow.[42] The verb *ṭāqaʿ* has a number of meanings derived from the notion of pushing against something (so pitching a tent, blowing a wind instrument, even assuming responsibility). Closer to our sense are the occasions in which Jael drives a peg into Sisera's skull (below at 4:21), Joab plants darts into hapless Absalom's chest (2 Sam 18:14), and Delilah pins Samson's hair (Judg 16:13–14). The notion is of something driven deep.

"MURDER MOST FOUL . . ."

3 22. Hebrew narratives rarely indulge descriptive details, but the narrator seems to relish this particular moment, to the point of twice repeating crucial vocabulary, *lahav*, "blade"—thrice if one adds the reference to *ḥerev*, the murdering instrument. The weapon's double edges permitted it to pierce the skin and cut through the many layers of tissues with such confident penetration that it lodged deep in Eglon's belly, its pommel (*niṣṣāv*, a unique word that luckily is transparent) no longer to be seen.[43] The language to describe the disappearance of the blade is somewhat incongruous. The idiom *sāgar bĕʿad*, "to shut behind (something or someone)," almost always connotes reaching for security (Gen 7:16, Judg 9:51, Isa 26:20; but see 1 Sam 1:6) or finding privacy (2 Kgs 4:4, 21). In fact, this phrase will soon be attached to Ehud as he exits the scene of the crime. There is also mention of *ḥelev*, "fat," in Scripture most often associated with tissues that cover the entrails, kidneys, and liver. Hebrew has other words to refer to fat, for instance, *peder*, *šemen*, and *dešen*, the last two more often applied to human beings rather than to animals. The word *ḥēlev* (many references) is almost always the fat that is burned when Israel sacrifices to redress wrongs or obtain absolution; hence, together with reference to the verb *qārav* in the Ehud story (at 3:17–18), its mention has stimulated commentators to associate Eglon with sacrifice imagery. As a metaphor, *ḥēlev* serves purposes that are not easy to harmonize. Applied to plants (wine, grain, oil), or even animals, it stands for "the best." Qualifying human beings, however, it imparts arrogance, stubbornness, and insensitivity, even wickedness, all very appropriate if applicable.

When construed with a *ḥerev*, "sword" (or the like), the verb *šālaf* is about wielding a weapon or drawing it from its sheath, so the narrator may be playful here. We are not told whether Ehud did not withdraw his knife because he had lost its grip beneath the flesh or because he would not want to lug a bloodied weapon as he made his escape. It may also have plugged the wound for a brief period. From this point on, however, we meet with problems in reconstructing what happened to Eglon after the attack.

Ehud drove a double-edged dagger so forcefully upwards that it lodged completely in Eglon's innards. Reviewing the literature on abdominal injuries (admittedly as an amateur), I learned that deep knifing can severely compromise the main abdominal arteries or veins and deeply puncture or rip major internal organs (such as the stomach, intestines, kidneys, liver, or spleen). Before antibiotics, such wounds invariably led to death, from hemorrhage and resulting complications (blood clots, increased blood acidity, a drop in body temperature); if not then, eventually internal poisoning and infections developed. Still, it is difficult to imagine that such wounds would instantaneously induce shock or lead to death.[44] The victim was likely to be in severe agony at least for a brief period before losing consciousness. Yet our story says nothing about Eglon screaming, writhing on the ground, or bleeding, and nothing about how long it took for death to triumph. (See the Comments.) All we read is that, in consequence to the blow, *vayyēṣēʾ happaršĕdōnâ*.

WHAT CAME OUT

There are several proposed solutions to dealing with this phrase, none earning thorough confidence. As a verbal form *vayyēṣēʾ* can mean either that he (Ehud) or it (the *paršĕdōn*) "went" or "oozed" out.[45] This last word occurs nowhere else in Scripture; as vocalized it ends with unaccented -*â*, a directional suffix, so complicating how to treat the word. Once more, we are left to conjectures, with a large sampling rehearsed in Barré 1991 and more succinctly in Lindars 1995: 146–47. Although there are many variations on the choices, here are suggestions:

1. Follow the Targum and treat *paršĕdōn* as related to discharge, from the wound or from the anus; if from the latter, the consequence of violence (Moore 1895: 97 n. 5). The Targum seems to treat this word as combining two: *prš*, "excrement," and *šdʾ*, "to expel," so *unĕfaq ʾuklêh šĕfîk*, "his (undigested) food was expelled." Some commentators simply lop off the last three consonants of the word, ending up with *pereš*, allegedly "feces."

2. Seek a foreign etymology for *paršĕdōn*, most often via Akkadian *paraštinnu*, a word of uncertain meaning, allegedly "hole" or "something from a hole." This allows diverse scenarios with false premises:

   a. One is that the word has to do with some opening, a conduit, perhaps even a sewer system, through which Ehud made his escape (Burney 1970: 72–73; Glaser 1932; and most recently Harlé and Roqueplo 1999: 98). Naturally, this has led to some baroque scenarios, most of them realized with maximum exaggeration for the size of such items as well as minimal knowledge of how personal hygiene was carried out in antiquity. (See the Comments.)

   b. The other is that the "hole" is the anus. Because the dagger (feminine in Hebrew) could not be made subject of a masculine verbal form, there is a venerable suggestion by Meek (1929: 163–64) to emend into *vayyôṣēʾ* (Hiphil), and so have *Ehud* force the weapon through it. Barré (1991), who is fine at showing the weakness of the *paraštinnu* connection, simply promotes another root, this time *naparšudu*, "to flee or escape," with reference to excrement spilling out of the guts.[46]

3. Treat *vayyēṣēʾ happaršĕdōnâ* as so mystifying that already in antiquity it was glossed by the less ambiguous *vayyēṣēʾ ʾēhûd hammisdĕrônâ*, now opening the verse following. In fact, Rahlfs A simply omits it, while Rahlfs B has a sentence that fearlessly duplicates what follows, albeit using different vocabulary: καὶ ἐξῆλθεν Αωδ τὴν προστάδα, "Ehud exited the vestibule," using a word that sounds like the Hebrew, but with a meaning reminiscent of what later will ensue.

4. Eschew etymology and invoke the other close-quarter assassination, that of Amasa (2 Sam 20) as described above. Ehud's upward thrust tears open Eglon's belly, spilling his guts.

Despite this lengthy treatment (one easily enlarged), we come no closer to solving the meaning of the clause; hence my decision to give two possible renderings, either one of which might have been a footnote to the other. In truth, a third option is to simply excise the phrase, but I admit an aversion to removing biblical words that have stayed put for centuries.

The Escape

3 24. More or less moving from the frying pan into the fire, we continue to be challenged by the opening clause *vayyēṣēʾ ʾēhûd hammisdĕrônâ*. While *hammisdĕrônâ* is no less unique than *happaršĕdōnâ*, here we at least have Ehud as the subject of the verb. And because *hammisdĕrônâ* ends on a directional suffix, we know that Ehud was obviously heading toward or through some architectural feature, so it could be a vestibule, a veranda, a colonnade (from *sādar*, "set in a row"), or any space that stood between a reception chamber (or wherever Eglon was) and the outside.[47] Still, scholars are not easily intimidated, and proposals have been made to emend this word into *hammisgĕrônâ*, from *sāgar*, "to lock" (hence a privy, but outside the royal chamber; cited by Kraeling 1935: 208). Following an insight by D. Golomb, Halpern (1988a: 58; see also 1988b) calls on Arabic *sadira*, allegedly meaning "to be blinded, puzzled," to invent a remarkable "hidden" and hollow structure, a shaft, attached beneath the toilet through which Ehud makes his escape.

THE LOCK

How did Ehud manage to lock the room of the crime? The Hebrew gives us a two-step account: Stepping outside Eglon's throne room, Ehud shuts the doors of the raised chamber (ʿalîyâ) behind him; then, once outside, he sets the locks in. Much has been written on how Ehud achieved this, with lack of knowledge of the relevant lock system(s) contributing heavily to the reconstruction of hidden latrine shafts and the like. In fact, there were many methods to seal and lock diverse rooms, depending on whether the mechanism was installed on the outside or on the inside. While sealing is not at stake here, the mechanism for securing storerooms (verb: *ḥātam*) remained in effect for millennia all over the Levant: latches (metal, leather, or cord) tied a door to a knob on the doorpost, and the area of connection was covered with mud or clay to which a seal was stamped. Only authorized personnel could break the sealing to enter (Zettler 1987: 210–23; Potts 1990).

Perhaps whimsically (we hope), Sirach (42:6) had offered, "Where there is an evil wife, a seal is a good thing; and where there are many hands, lock things up." Palaces are places for many hands, and so we read about security mechanisms on Eglon's chamber. In biblical language, when doors (or door panels) are closed (verb: *sāgar*), a bar (*běrî°ḥ*, of timber or metal) or a bolt (*man'ûl/min'āl*) is set in place to lock (verb: *nā'al*) them. To open (verb: *pātaḥ*), a key (*mafte°ḥ*) is needed. Those keys can be large and are carried on the shoulder (Isa 22:22). King and Stager (2001) suggest that Ehud cleverly manipulated a tumbler lock to shut in his victim.[48] In use widely and deeply in antiquity, such locks are placed on the inside of a chamber but can be operated from the outside through a hole in the door (Cant 5:5). When a cleverly hollowed bar or bolt is moved into position, tumblers or nails drop by gravity into its notches, setting doors into locked positions. More dexterity is needed when a key is angled into a hollowed slot in the bolt, its matching teeth (pegs or elevations) forcing the nails or tumblers up. The key lifted, the bolt or bar is released and can be withdrawn. Unless one was experienced in manipulating blindly a key created for a specific lock, to unlock a door (let alone find the required key) must have been relatively cumbersome and time-consuming. It is not surprising, therefore, that Ehud would have ample time.[49]

What the Courtiers *Surmised*

3 24–25. Hebrew narratives (as many others) favor razor sharp conjunction of events, so no sooner does Ehud decamp than the king's (the Hebrew simply says "his") servants come to the locked chamber. It is useless to speculate why they returned at just this moment, but the fact that their focus on the locked doors was immediate is conveyed by *hinnēh* followed by a participle, phrasing that always sharpens the immediacy of an observation. The Hebrew uses a euphemism to describe what the servants *imagined* occupied Eglon: He was *mēsîk hû' 'et-raglā°v bahădar hammēqērâ*. The phrase relies on a verbal root (*skk*, Hiphil) with distinct meanings, one of which has to do with placing a cover over something, in this case "the feet/legs." It is difficult to give a precise exposition of what is at stake, the usual suggestion is that squatters are shielding themselves with their robes (see above). Since human limbs (hands, arms, feet, and legs) can be used as substitutes for the sexual organs, the phrase simply means "to defecate."[50]

The servants thought that their king was seeking privacy to answer a call of nature, and there are rabbinic comments that they were encouraged to think so because of the stink created by the spilled *paršědōn*, understood as "excrement." This statement has done much to encourage latrine-driven expositions of events. Jull (1998, see above) is not alone in seating Eglon on a latrine rather than a throne when he met his death.[51]

PRIVIES

Until the Hellenistic and Roman periods, when municipalities began building public toilets with running water and supplying sanitary sponges, for practical reasons defecating occurred outdoors at some distance from houses, with people covering their "feet" during the act with a body garment. Therefore, when in literature individuals are said to betake themselves far from view (see above), they are responding to plot demands rather than to delicacy.

Whether or not in the pre-Hellenistic Near East dwellings or even palaces had latrines or privies within walls is debated archeologically. I have scanned major contributions as well as standard reference sets for significant or undisputed details.[52] Occasionally, installations are termed "toilets," without discrimination between latrines and bath areas (the last requiring impermeable floorings or the like).[53] Nothing in this meager evidence allows us to imagine that anything else was at stake but holes over cesspits (rather than commodes over sewer lines), and perhaps under staircases rather than over them, as Halpern reconstructs (clearest in 1988b). If so, it makes no sense to locate such fixtures, of all places, near a throne. Ancient folks knew that you cannot leave fecal matter within a structure, as it invited horrid pests, let alone stenches.[54] Moreover, the amount of water they would require to retain a measure of sanitation would be beyond most ancient installations. (The toilets of my youth in 1950s Beirut were not for weak stomachs, despite being hooked up to a municipal sewer system.) Suggestions that sewage pipes lead to outside areas from second-story facilities do not find ready confirmation; such installations would be open invitations for rats and other pests to enter a home.

What Eglon was *thought* to be using, therefore, was not a fixed toilet, let alone one in his throne room, but a chamber pot.[55] We know about their use broadly, from ancient into modern times (they were good enough for Versailles kings), but identifying them archeologically is a challenge because of their shape and the material out of which they were made. There are anecdotes that play on the generic nature of their construction. A vassal of Zimri-Lim of Mari constructs a very crude image of contempt when a cup of friendship is used as a chamber pot.[56] Herodotus (Book 2 172) tells about Pharaoh Amasis teaching his courtiers a lesson by watching them worship a statue he made from a golden chamber pot (ποδανιπτὴρ).

THE PATIENCE OF COURTIERS

How long the courtiers waited is not necessary to know, but it was enough time for them to feel anxious, conveyed by the verb *ḥwl* with the adverbial phrase *'ad bôš*.[57] Elsewhere that phrase is more about time than discomfiture, as in 2 Kgs 2:17, 8:11 (see also Exod 32:1 and Judg 5:28), and it likely parallels *'ad hitmahmĕhām* in the next verse. Having to retrieve a key could not have been easy, and it must certainly have taken a bit of time to manipulate it until it lifted the tumblers (see above), giving Ehud more time to find his way to safety. What they saw on opening the door is a dead Eglon. However, the narrator crafts a description that moves beyond a mere chronology of events. This is achieved by coordinating two participial clauses, each headed by *hinnēh*, with Eglon as the subject of action. The effect is to resurrect Eglon, so to speak, and have him refuse to open his own door; when it is opened, he falls dead as his courtiers peer into the unlocked chamber. The effect is dramatic, if not also operatic—much more so here than when the same spectacle is replayed at 4:22 when Baraq finds Sisera sprawled dead in Jael's tent (see below).

The Reprisal

How the reprisal was undertaken is by no means clearly charted. If, despite clear markers, we assume that Eglon was holding court in the conquered area and then presume him to be at Jericho, we would be dealing with a bevy of activities occurring within a narrow time frame. Having assassinated Eglon, Ehud goes northeast toward the *pĕsîlîm* by Gilgal (a couple of miles from Jericho), then heads west toward the hills of Ephraim (more than a dozen miles) where he rallies his men eastward toward the Jordan (about 20 miles). We are, of course, dealing with highly motivated people, but we must not forget also that such narratives tend to surrender realism for dramatic tension. Still, it must have bothered readers who knew the topography of the area well. Josephus "solves" the problem by giving Ehud a good chunk of time to gather his followers (*Ant.* 5.194–95), for the servants who waited outside Eglon's chamber thought him asleep and did not dare wake him until the evening, a good few hours after Ehud's exit.

3 26–28. Just as Hebrew narratives indulge in scripting coincidences, not infrequently they also plot activities that are simultaneous. So, as the courtiers are fidgeting outside their lord's door ʿ*ad bôš* (see above), Ehud is decamping ʿ*ad hitmahmĕhām*. Their dawdling is conveyed onomatopoeically by a *hitpalpel* form of *mhh*, and I try to evoke it with our English "hemming and hawing." The synchronism of events is enhanced by repetition of the verb describing Ehud's action, the Niphal of *mālaṭ*, "to flee, move away from danger." There will be three references to this verb in as many verses, with the first (successful escape, applied to Ehud) and the last (unsuccessful escape, applied to Moabites) framing this particular episode.

Why we need to know that Ehud moved beyond the hewn images (*pĕsîlîm*) is difficult to judge; perhaps it is a psychological marker here: Just as he entered into Eglon's sphere of control, he now exited it, mission accomplished. We are given his direction: toward Seirah (*śĕʿîrātâ*). The Greek versions give this as a place, Σεϊρωθα (Rahlfs A) or Σετιρωθα (Rahlfs B), as does the Vulgate, Seirath, treating the directional suffix as part of a place name. There is no citation of a place by that name or by Seirah elsewhere in Scripture, and any connection with Seir (Edom) or Mount Seir (Josh 15:10) is not very helpful, given that Ehud needs to rally Ephraimites. The word is preceded by an article, however, encouraging us (as it did Rashi and others) to have Ehud head toward some bushy or woodsy area that goats (*śĕʿîr/śĕʿîrâ*) would favor.

The narrator has Ehud sounding (*vayyitqaʿ*) the shofar as soon as he reaches his destination, indulging a play on homonyms: Earlier, he had planted (*vayyitqaʿ*) the dagger in Eglon's belly; this time, however, his instrument will be even more potent. The ram's horn (shofar; Greek, κέρας, "horn") can produce a sharp sound that carries far. Although it may not be useful when plotting a revolt, as it alerts the occupiers and their spies, it is perfect to launch a premeditated attack. It is the instrument of choice for God himself, whether to champion Israel's cause (Zech 9:14) or to summon the nations of the earth to worship (Isa 27:13). People used them when happy or sad, worshiping or not, in peace and war. It can signal an attack (Judg 3:27, 2 Sam 20:1) or serve as a weapon, rousing soldiers while disheartening their enemies (Josh 6, Judg 7). In our case, Ehud is all over the hills of Ephraim (on which, see above at 2:9, where Joshua was said to be buried), a wooded area (Josh 17:15–18) noted for its pastures (Jer 50:19) but also perfect as shelter for individuals (2 Sam 20: 21) as well as for substantial numbers of armed men (1 Sam 14:22). The point to keep in mind here is that Ehud is drawing support beyond his own Benjaminites.

The phrase about all of Israel joining Ehud in coming down the mountain with him in the lead is a fine example of a *hysteron proteron* ("the latter first") construction, a rhetorical device we have met at Judg 1:7. So while there is some repetition in the verse following (3:25), what it says is by no means redundant, despite this judgment by commentators that it betrays the weaving of separate accounts or misplacement (see

Lindars 1995: 153–54). Influenced by the Greek (κατάβητε ὀπίσω μου, "follow behind me"), many emend Ehud's order, in Hebrew *ridĕfû ʾaḥăray*, by dropping a consonant and obtaining **rĕdû ʾaḥăray*, "follow me closely," emulating *rĕdû ʾaḥărāʸw* of a few words down. The sense of *rādaf ʾaḥar* is mostly "to pursue someone" (as in 1:6 above, about Adoni-bezeq, and later at 4:16; 7:23; and 8:5, 12), and it is surely too clever to imagine that Ehud is instructing Israel to deceive the Moabites by feigning a hot pursuit of a murderer. My translation is not elegant idiomatically, but it may do.

Ehud justifies his call to action by declaring God's abandonment of Moab. The phrase *nātan YHWH ʾet* (an enemy/Israel) *bĕyad* (Israel/an enemy) occurs very frequently in Scripture and needs no reference. (The closest formulation is in Deut 28:7.) For Ehud (and for Israel) the signal for the divine will was the successful murder of Eglon; in turn, Moab's defeat will also confirm God's choice of Ehud as the next judge. In a sense, the confirmation by battle of God's desire to defeat Israel's foes substitutes for the absence of a *rûʷaḥ* formula that we often see in Judges (see the Comments to IIIA, Judg 3:7–11).

The Defeat

3 29–30. The Jordan here makes its first appearance in Judges. Much has been made about its etymology (mostly from **yrd*, to "go down," said of waters), but Emar documents show it is referring to a wadi (*yardānu*; plural, *yardānātu*) rather than a water channel (Reculeau 2008a: 136–37). With his support behind him, Ehud cuts off access to the *maʿbĕrôt*, the crossings at the Jordan (mentioned also in Josh 2:7 and Judg 12:5ff.). As a result, he traps so thoroughly the forces that Moab and its allies had kept in the occupied territories that no one is able to ford the Jordan for safety. Again indulging in transposed information, the narrator first gives the number of slain warriors before describing their status. The number is high, "about ten thousand men," but in other contexts it is used to underscore sheer size (Judg 4:6 and 7:3) as well the enormity of defeats (above at Judg 1:4 and below at 20:34). The enemy is described comprehensively: Physically they were *šāmēn*, literally "fat," but more likely culled from stocky or well-fed warriors.[58] They were also drawn from the elite class, an *îš ḥāyil* being landed gentry (see Sasson 1989: 87–88). The defeated, therefore, were the crème de la crème among Moabites and Ammonites. The notice about no one escaping the slaughter (*lōʾ nimlaṭ ʾîš*) may seem placed to gloat or to contrast with Ehud's successful getaway; as likely, however, it is ironic, to underscore their steep fall. I take my cue from a passage in the "The Shipwrecked Sailor," a structurally sophisticated and thematically elaborate fantasy from Middle Kingdom Egypt (early second millennium BCE). A ship wrecks immediately after its sailors were praised: "Looked they at sky, looked they at land, their hearts were stouter than lions'. They could foretell a storm before it came, a tempest before it broke" (Lichtheim 1973: 212).

Moab is defeated. Whether or not the narrator chose to be playful in declaring its fall is debatable, but the idiom *vattikkānaʿ taḥat yad* is built around a verb that shares the same consonants as Canaan (*kĕnaʿān*, on which, see above at 1:1). Noticeable, too, is the fact that unlike the formula of success we have just read (above at 3:10), in which God facilitates Cushan-rishatayim's defeat before Othniel takes control of him, here Moab is the subject of a passive verb (so no direct mention of God), and its loss of independence is not attributed to Ehud. As in 3:11 the information that the land had peace (*vattišqōṭ hāʾāreṣ*) comes immediately after reference to Israel's control of its former enemy. This time, however, it lasts eighty years, so twice as long as the longest interval expressed elsewhere in Judges (3:11, 5:31, 8:28). (That the doubling may reflect inclusion of Shamgar's rule is possible; see below.)

At this point all Greek witnesses give καὶ ἔκρινεν αὐτοὺς Αωδ ἕως οὗ ἀπέθανεν, "Ehud judged them until he died." The clause may have occurred in the Hebrew manuscript available to the LXX translators, or it may be an expansion of what is now found at 4:1 (see below). Just as likely, however, the translators simply sensed that they needed to compensate for a startling underplay of a judge's role in the triumph against Moab.

Our episode does not give Ehud much of an afterlife, but Chronicles has the following thoroughly obscure entry in its Benjamin genealogy (1 Chr 8:6–7, about which, see Dirksen 2005: 134; *ABD*, under "Gera [Person]"): "These were Ehud's sons. They had been clan chieftains among the inhabitants of Geva (Givea?) but people exiled them to Manahath: As to Naaman and Ahijah, it is Gera who exiled them and begot Uzza and Ahihud" (other translations are possible). Al-Yaʿḳūbī credits him with the invention of the two-edged sword and, more beguilingly, adds, "in the 25th year of the reign of Ehud the 4000 years were fulfilled" (Ebied and Wickham 1970: 84).

Shamgar

3 31. The notice about Shamgar and his deeds is the most laconic we have about a judge in this book; it is so brief, in fact, that some scholars have debated whether to set him among the "minor" judges.[59] The information about him is limited to one verse, missing minimal transitions (nothing about God punishing and saving Israel; nothing about his death), and even unfolds before we read of Ehud's death (at 4:1). Nonetheless, Shamgar is also rare for being recalled beyond his own days, in material featuring another judge (at 5:6); for some scholars, this certifies his historicity (Burney 1970: 75). Naturally, scholarship has risen to the challenge and in some cases has developed scenarios remarkably full, whether or not they match anything we have about him in Scripture.[60]

HIS NAME

That Shamgar's name (Greek, Σαμεγαρ; Josephus, Σεμέγαρος) does not immediately strike the ear as Semitic, that his patronym, *ben-ʿănāt*, is evocative of Canaanite worship (see below), and that he is associated with no Hebrew tribe only increased the range of speculation. No sooner were cuneiform archives read than the name of an Assyrian vassal, Sangara of Carchemish (circa 900 BCE), seemed a fair parallel to Shamgar's. The foreign connection was deemed more plausible when the archives from Nuzi produced a flood of Hurrian names that seem to bring the correspondence closer (B. Mazar [Maisler] 1934), most often through connection with the sun-god Šimige (with variations), so something like "Šimige has given [-*ari*]." This connection has found its place in the literature ever since. But there is also the position that Shamgar may well be a Semitic name. Van Selms (1964: 299–301) is followed by Soggin (1981a: 54–55) in proposing that Shamgar is crafted as a shafel (causative) of **mgr*, found in Hebrew as well as in Phoenician personal names (Benz 1972: 339–40, who lists an unlikely name, *mgrbʾl*, on p. 137). Danelius (1963), however, proposes for the name a (hardly plausible) concoction based on Egyptian (*šm3*, "stranger") and Hebrew (*gēr*, "resident alien") elements. McDaniel, whose work must be a lampoon of Semitic philology, reshapes the name into *šām + gār*, allegedly "the attacking assailant" (1983: 69; 2003: 47–50).

Ben-ʿănāt (Rahlfs A, "son of Αναθ; Rahlfs B, "son of Δіναχ") has also received interesting speculations. Anat is the well-known name of a Canaanite deity, a major character in the myths uncovered at Ugarit. We find her name embedded in two place names in Israel, Bet-Anat and Anathoth, the last a priestly town in Benjamin and birthplace for the great prophet Jeremiah (1:1). We have already met Bet-Anat as one of the cities in upper Galilee that Naphtali was unable to control (at 1:33, the other being Bet-Shemesh, named after another deity).[61] There are proposals that Shamgar is a ruler of Bet-Anat, but van Selms has rightly argued against them (1964: 301). Suffice it to say that if narrators wanted to associate Shamgar with such a town, they might have said *bet-hăʿānātî/hăʿănātōtî*. Moreover, we might note that all other references in Judges for people called *ben* ("of someone") are to their fathers.[62] A false trail that still echoes in the literature was launched by Fensham (1961: 197–98). He proposed that *ben-ʿănāt* has to do with the Mari Ḥaneans, allegedly because they are connected with the Euphratean town Ḥanat. Actually, "Ḥaneans" is just a generic term for nomads (see Hebrew *ḥānâ*, "to camp"), while the names Ḥaneans and Ḥanat are based on completely different roots.

Anat does not occur as a personal name in Israel, but we have names in Scripture that are based on Canaanite divine names, for example, Reshep (1 Chr 7:21) and Shelah (Gen 10:24, 11:12–15). In the Amarna tablets (14 c) Anati does occur (EA 170: 43), and it is likely constructed on Anat's name. More commonly are found such names as bin-Anat, bin-Ḥanuta (the Amorite form of the same deity), and the like (collected in Layton 1990: 217–18). These parallel nicely with what we have in our passage, so it is tempting to think that Shamgar was the son of a Ben-Anat and that the word *ben*, "son," was lost though haplography (so read *šamgar <ben> ben-ʿănāt*); but that is not what our received text has, and nothing like it is supported by the versions.

HIS "ORIGINS"

The debate about establishing an etymology and a lineage for Shamgar is itself interesting because it takes for granted two postulates: (1) that to decipher the etymology of a name is to resolve the ethnic origin of its bearer, and (2) that biblical characters with non-Semitic names must own deeds that are themselves imported from their places of origin. Such notions are not always cogent. During the second millennium BCE, throughout the cuneiform world, certain classes of people owned Sumerian names when the Sumerians had ceased to exist as an identifiable group. In Mari, for example, we can establish many family portraits of people with names that come from different ethnic backgrounds. (We can do the same in our own times.) The second notion is more difficult to argue since the etymology of names is always debated. But if we accept that "Moses" (*mōšê*) was developed from an Egyptian name (and frankly I do not believe it is), then we will need to accept, as did Freud, that narratives about his early life are imported from Egypt. Ditto for "Phineas" (*pînĕḥas*), also thought to be an Egyptian name.

Still, we find in the literature some very imaginative explorations of Shamgar's deeds. Here is just a sampling:

—Shamgar was an oppressor of Israel, a Hittite, and likely the father of Sisera (Moore 1898a; Lagrange 1903: 78–79; but already proposed in antiquity, Burney 1970: 77; variation in Lindars 1995: 158; hearty sarcasm in Segond 1900: 25–26).

—He was a "convert" who took up Israel's cause (Danelius 1963).

—He was a Canaanite condottiere attacking Aegean mercenaries at the Egyptian garrisons at level VII Beth-shean (Aharoni 1970).

—He was a Canaanite warrior allied with Israel against their enemy, the Philistines (Soggin 1987: 55–56; see Boling 1975: 89–90).

—He was a Ḥap/biru mercenary hired by Pharaoh Ramses III or Ramses IV (Shupak 1989: 523; for variations see Craigie 1972 and Eissfeldt 1966).

—He was a farmer who rose to extraordinary exploits by effectively wielding an oxgoad (Snyman 2005: 128).

—He fought against marauders who were led by Sisera (McDaniel 1983: 47–51, 62–107, torturing the text into balanced tricola).

THE NOTICE ABOUT HIM

The other matter is how the notice got where it is. Here, too, there are lots of theories, most proceeding from the exceptional reference to Shamgar in Judg 5:6 ("In the days of Shamgar son of Anat / In the days of Jael / Trails are unused / Wayfarers take twisting trails"). Brettler's opinion (2002: 23–25) is illustrative: Because it is embedded in poetry and because many deem the Song of Deborah to be among the oldest surviving examples of Hebrew literature, an editor simply found a niche for a person so famous, treating him as a judge. The vignette about killing hundreds with an oxgoad was cloned from other stories of exceptional prowess (Samson's donkey jaw, for example, 15:15–17). The mention of Philistines is taken from 10:11 where God is ahead of the story by telling Israel that he had saved them "from the Egyptians, from the Amorites, from the Ammonites, and from the Philistines," the Philistines not being featured in the Judges story until Samson's days (chapters 13–16).[63] Inserting the incident with Shamgar's exploits amends this discrepancy.

Variations on this hypothesis include the suggestion that Shamgar is mentioned here simply to round out to twelve the number of judges (removing Abimelech from the count) or to create a balance between six judges with minimal accounts (the "minor" judges) and six with longer narratives (the "major" judges). Based on some manuscripts that repeat the mention of Shamgar just after Samson, there are proposals that it was shifted here simply to account for the reference in 5:6, but there are also proposals that both the Shamgar and Samson episodes belonged before Ehud's (see Moore 1898a; Amit 1999a: 40–41).

HIS PROWESS

We are next told of Shamgar's extraordinary deed: He single-handedly slaughters six hundred Philistines. The number reflects a good-sized *military* unit (Judg 18:11, 16–17; 1 Sam 27:2, 30:9; 2 Sam 15:19), but midrashic lore cuts the number to eighteen Midianites (W. Smelik 1995: 379 n. 301). The instrument is a *malmad*, associated with oxen, and it occurs only here. An old translation (Rahlfs B, ἀροτρόπους) gives it as a plowshare, a rather hefty and unwieldy tool, but putting it to use is what distinguishes heroes. (Rahlfs A simply avoids the issue: Shamgar beats six hundred Philistines, "not counting the oxen.") But the Targum, likely relying on a root, *lāmad*, offers different words for "oxgoad" (W. Smelik 1995: 379). In the literature one reads that an oxgoad was many feet long and that it could be tipped with metal on both ends, one to goad the bulls and the other to scrape mud off the ploughshare. (On the mention of Philistines, see above and also at 3:3.)

Shamgar, a Judge of Israel?

With so many suggestions and conjectures, is the matter hopeless? Perhaps not. Let us go back to the opening of the verse: *vĕʾaḥărāʾv hāyâ šamgar*. This opening is unique in Scripture, and it is taken to mean that Shamgar succeeded Ehud, especially since we have already been told about the length of Ehud's tenure. However, while in the preponderance of cases the preposition *ʾaḥar* does sequence two events, in some cases (for example, in the list of David's champions; see 2 Sam 23:11), it juxtaposes two events or people. In fact, in some contexts (see Neh 3:17 versus 3:19) the preposition is equivalent to *ʿal yad* ("someone"), always meaning "by the side of someone."[64]

We notice also that about Shamgar we are told exceptionally that "he too [*gam-hûʾ*] rescued Israel." Among its many functions when associated with a personal pronoun, the particle *gam* associates an act (or actor) with a previous one, and so what is being told about Shamgar is coordinated with the deeds of Ehud. For this reason, some traditional commentators, for example, Radaq (Kimḥi), suggest that Shamgar's rescue of Israel was not complete, and others (for example, Seder Olam), think his rule of a few months was included in the eighty years of Ehud's peace. Given the lack of markers that would establish Shamgar's rule (unlike Ehud, who has them all but the title "judge"), and given that this notice about him is sandwiched within statements about the length of Ehud's rule (3:30) and comment on his death (4:1), I would suggest the removal of Shamgar from our list of judges. We should treat his exploits no differently from those that are attached to Jael, with whom he is balanced in 5:6. I do not believe that the narrator ever meant him to be regarded as a judge, and neither should we. One more notice: An early Greek text places the Shamgar segment at the end of the Samson story (at 16:31), suggesting some doubts about a specific slot for him (see Harlé and Roqueplo 1999: 32; Cooke 1913: 31).

COMMENTS[65]

> [Ehud] became familiar with Eglon, and that by means of presents, with which he obtained his favor, and insinuated himself into his good opinion; whereby he was also beloved of those that were about the king. Now, when on a time he was bringing presents to the king . . . Ehud smote him to the heart, and leaving his dagger in his body, he went out and shut the door after him . . . On this account Ehud was dignified with the government over all the multitude, and . . . was a man worthy of commendation.
>
> —*Josephus*, Ant. 5.189–97

> And here the Scripture shows us what the Lord thought a fit message to send a tyrant from himself: a dagger of a cubit in his belly, and every

worthy man that desires to be an Ehud, a deliverer of his country, will strive to be the messenger.

—*Edward Sexby,* Killing No Murder *(advocating Cromwell's murder, 1657), 390*

These malignant devotees have incessantly before their eyes the example of Ehud, who assassinated the king of Eglon; of Judith, who cut off the head of Holofernes while in bed with him; of Samuel, hewing in pieces King Agag; of Jehoiada the priest, who murdered his queen at the horse-gate. They do not perceive that these instances, which are respectable in antiquity, are in the present day abominable. They derive their fury from religion, decidedly as religion condemns it.

—*Voltaire,* A Philosophical Dictionary *(1764), VII/ii, "Fanaticism"*

[Eglon] turns out to be a fatted calf readied for slaughter . . . [his] fat is both token of his physical ponderousness, his vulnerability to Ehud's sudden blade, and the emblem of his regal stupidity. Perhaps it may also hint at a kind of grotesque feminization of the Moabite: Ehud "comes to" the king, an idiom also used for sexual entry, and there is something hideously sexual about the description of the dagger thrust. There may also be deliberate sexual nuance in the "secret thing" Ehud brings to Eglon, in the way the two are locked together alone in a chamber, and in the sudden opening of locked entries at the conclusion of the story.

—*Alter 1981: 39*

Why is Ehud, an Israelite hero, portrayed as suffering from the physical defect of being left-handed? . . . [A] dysfunctional right hand in those days was almost certainly taken as a . . . token of improper physical hygiene and of sexual deviance. . . . By sending on the men carrying the tribute, Ehud is telling Eglon that he wants to see him in private, i.e., he is offering a homosexual liaison. . . . The storyteller would have demonstrated graphically how Ehud reached between his legs with his left hand and began to remove his clothes; and how he pulled out *a pointed sword,* which he then proceeded to thrust into Eglon's obese belly so deep that not only the sword but also the hilt (i.e., testicles) disappeared inside and could not be removed.

—*G. Miller 1996a: 114–15*

Not long ago, I enjoyed the staging of a Jacobean play, *The Revenger's Tragedy,* whose authorship is still disputed.[66] It is, as the title divulges, a retribution play, the theme in many dramas since the Elizabethan era, among them Shakespeare's *Titus Andronicus,* Kyd's *Spanish Tragedy,* and Webster's *White Devil.* This particular play knew few bounds, with murders galore (single and mass), rape, suicide, seduction, and executions. The assassination of the duke (a major character) included poisoning, physical bashing, tongue slashing, eye gouging, and throat slitting. Blood and gore flowed freely; yet from the audience, there was mostly glee and laughter. The modern staging certainly has much to do with such an incongruous reaction, but as this variety of theater is hardly expected to deliver Chekhovian subtlety, we come prepared to sit always at the fulcrum of revulsion and hilarity. So we laugh often, and our mirth is abetted by certain authorial techniques. In *The Revenger's Tragedy*, they are most powerfully delivered through the main character, who, in reacting to initial mayhem, achieves his revenge through hardly deceiving disguises, farfetched schemes, hyperbolic sentiments, and fully accommodating stock characters.

As we assess what the narrator of the Ehud story meant to convey, it is especially important not to put the cart ahead of the horse. That is, we ought not distort the words and the design with which the assassination of an enemy king is detailed because we have decided on the literary category to which it should belong. This is especially true when, arguing circularly, we rely on this slanted reading of the Ehud narrative to establish its genre.

How Ehud Was Read

Until recently, the story of Ehud was read as yet another account of the wonder-workings of and for God by God's own elect. It is true, as we have seen in the segments from Josephus's reshaping of the story, that certain aspects of the story were modified to make Ehud an intimate courtier who struck at the heart (never the belly!) of a tyrant. It is also true, however, that rabbinic lore left us less about Ehud (who is deemed a "great scholar" in Midrash *Genesis Rabbah*, 99.3) than about Eglon, who receives credit for respecting the god of the people he conquered. Sometime in the eighth century of our era, Ehud's deed inspired another tale about outmaneuvered opponents of Israel. In the "Antiochus Scroll" that once was read widely during Hanukkah, Johanan son of Hasmonean Mattathias hid under his cloak a sword "2 spans long and 1 span wide" with which he assassinated Nicanor, a governor whom King Antiochus had sent to force the Jews into impure worship of false gods. Johanan tricked Nicanor into dismissing his staff, thereby making himself defenseless.[67]

Christian fathers generally read the story mystically (especially in the use of right and left hand) or typologically (Christ conquering evil). For most readers since the Renaissance, the issue was not how Ehud accomplished his feat, but whether his deed, regicide, could nonetheless be prompted by a just God. Some issues of moral ambiguity were raised about assassinating someone whom God installed to punish sinful Israel. There was, of course, recognition of the humor of the story: in Eglon's stated portliness, in the physical effect of the murder blow (both Geneva and KJV translate "dirt came out" in 3:22), and in the way the courtiers assessed the locking of doors (Geneva: "he doeth his easement"; KJV: "he covereth his feet"). While some readers (such as deists) imagined Ehud a zealot whose "oriental" mores drove him to treason and unmanly behavior, most found in Ehud's act faithful service to God, even if not directly commanded by him. (On all this, see Gunn 2005: 38–49.)

The advent of modern biblical scholarship did indeed raise issues about the origins and reliability of the received text. The consensus has been that folk material from the Gilgal region (possibly based on some historical kernel) was reshaped by the Deuteronomist to promote a theology of divine control and of holy wars (see Moore 1895: 89–91). How historically plausible Moabite control and loss of Israel were at an early period of Israel's life was also debated inconclusively, with precious little archeological concordance to help settle the matter. Better knowledge of the languages (grammar as well as lexicography) increased the suggestions on how to interpret the many difficult words found in this relatively brief story. The most striking differences in these expositions from the traditional interpretations of the story, however, are analytic and literary, chiefly in deciding the genre to which the story belongs.

How Ehud Is Read

Especially during the post-Vietnam period, as scholarly interest in historical reconstruction of early Israel waned and appreciation of Hebraic narrative arts waxed, Ehud began to be read as satire, parody, slapstick, or even farce, with Moab (via Eglon) as its target and scatology (or coarse humor) as its mode. Alter (1981, quoted in the epigraphs above) was among the first to give a full overview of such a reading, nudging the story away from just reporting a political assassination. Through skillful manipulation of prose narrative, the story has acquired a satiric vision of the king's destruction, "at once shrewd and jubilant" (39), perfectly suited to a grotesque and lecherous ruler. A good number of studies have followed Alter's cue, and I have cited many of them in the Notes.[68] They too find humor in coarse contexts, shaping a burlesque out of a murder in the privy, with hints of Marquis de Sade perversions. Sternberg (1987: 336) finds in some scenes "a network of rather obscene connections"; Handy (1992) considers the story a fine "ethnic joke"; Deist (1996: 269) thinks it aimed at "publicly shaming [Eglon] out of his socks"; and Swanson (2012) claims his undignified behavior ("with feces on his 'bathroom hand,'" 97) makes him a parody of King David. Yet the basic premises on which the scatology and sexual innuendos are constructed are themselves flimsy. Setting aside the issues of sexuality—which can be proposed whenever one body is said to penetrate another[69]—and of feminization—which can be intimated whenever one character (especially one who is corpulent) is said to be dominated by another—the scatology that has marred recent readings of the episode is itself based on a surprisingly nonliterary appreciation of 3:24. When the courtiers see the doors of the upper chamber locked, they dally outside *imagining* their leader to be defecating (using, as most did in antiquity, a chamber pot for the purpose).

In fact, Eglon was not then so occupied, his murder having occurred when he rose from his royal throne to welcome a message that he might have thought came from Ehud's god. The courtiers' long wait is itself part of the plot, as it gives more time for Ehud to escape. (As noted above, Josephus stretches the interval further by having the courtiers wait for the king to end his sleep.) The incredibly developed literature (partially cited above) on the architecture of toilets in throne rooms is hardly reliable and often fanciful. The phrase *vayyēṣēʾ happaršĕdōnâ* (3:22) is the other one that has encouraged a "murder in the toilet" scenario; but as we have seen in the Notes, there are severe difficulties in deciding what it meant, let alone in ascertaining whether or not it belonged to the earliest versions of the story.

Without denying that the Ehud episode does contain humorous elements—the scene with the courtiers dallying outside the king's upper chamber must certainly be placed among them—I have reservations about treating it as a satire, parody, or farce.[70] Authors adopt satire when critiquing institutions, activities, or personalities, normally of their own place and time, but also those of their neighbors. Satires are by definition intentional, and they require a conspiracy of shared assumptions before they can unravel successfully: The author must own a stance from which to launch barbs, the target must to some degree be transparent and focused, and the audience must be savvy enough to appreciate when details have moved away from the descriptive to the imaginative. To welcome their audience into their art, authors of satires do rely on various levels and kinds of wit, humor, occasionally coarse, and irony; but by themselves these tools do not define the genre, and simply to catalogue absurdist manifestations in a narrative is not enough to define it as a satire.

Satire and Its Goals

So, we might ask: Who are these alleged satirists and why are they poking fun at God's own choice, Eglon and Moab, to punish Israel? Are they in fact also launching diatribes against God for such a choice? Who are the Moabites of Judg 3? Are they the same folks who were born out of incest (as per Gen 19), or are they those who sheltered David's parents when his fortunes were bleak (1 Sam 22:3–4)? As regards Eglon: Is he lampooned for being "fat" (the Hebrew, as we saw above, does not define him so sharply)? Or is it for biting the dust after crafting a coalition that occupied a territory appreciably larger than his own? Is his name ("Calf") enough to provoke parody when Israel was just led by a "Dog" (Caleb) and will soon be by a "Bee" (Deborah)?

And who is the audience that allegedly appreciated this clever jousting? The folks who witnessed Ehud's spunk? Or were they editors who massaged the story into yet another example of heroics among Hebrew ancestors but above all of the Hebrew God? Moreover, given the long and complicated textual history of the Hebrew Bible, we need to know at what stage of its development the satire surfaced. When it was first crafted orally or when first put to writing? When it was finalized as a statement against Moab, or when it was edited into a collection about judges? Such questions—and many others as well—need answers before we can label this story a satire.

Yet, there is one more thought: Also by definition satires (and their congeners) are highly inventive undertakings, compositions with the frailest attachments to reality, social or historical, and their readers recognize what they read as such. Alter (1981: 41) labels our story "fictionalized history," but Jull (1998: 73) seems to know how to harvest historical kernels from such imaginative writing, not at all the genre's likeliest products. Anderson (1987: 59) finds in it "a satiric description of the symbolic act of periodic tribute delivery"—an odd scenario for glee. Brettler (2002: 37–38) cautions us against using the Ehud story to re-create historical events during the Judges period. By implication, too, such a course also saves the modern sensibility from incriminating ancient Israel in such morally questionable activities as regicide, exacerbated in this case by the murder of God's tool for punishing Israel. But reading Ehud as satire also demands that we attribute to the Hebrew satirists and their audiences the same capacity to skewer imaginatively other targets displayed in the book of Judges. Should we, for example, assess similarly that other assassination narrative that will be featured in chapter 4? Brettler further argues that despite its lack of historicity, a satire such as developed in the story of Ehud nonetheless gave pride. Possibly; but I imagine that the pleasure derived from satiric accounts can hardly equal the pride inspired by the dispatch of a brutal tyrant when deemed true to history. Think of Purim and how its story continues to play into our own days.

IIIC

Deborah

---

1. The Prose Account (Judg 4:1–24)

4 ¹With Ehud dead, the people of Israel resumed offending the LORD, ²so the LORD turned them over to Jabin, king of Canaan, who ruled from Hazor. His army commander was Sisera, who operated from Haroshet-haggoyim. ³The people of Israel cried out to the LORD; for he had nine hundred chariots of iron and oppressed Israel brutally for twenty years. ס

⁴Deborah was a woman prophet, a wielder of flames.ᵃ It was she who was judging Israel at that time. (⁵She would sit beneath the "Palm of Deborah," between Ramah and Bethel in Mount Ephraim, and the people of Israel would come up to her for judgment.) ⁶She conveyed a message to Baraq son of Abinoam of Kedesh in Naphtali, telling him, "The LORD, God of Israel, has commanded: 'Plan to deploy at Mount Tabor, taking with you ten thousand men of Naphtali and Zebulun. ⁷At Wadi Kishon, I will deploy against you Sisera, Jabin's army commander, with his chariots and his infantry; but I will hand him over to you.'" ⁸Baraq said to her, "If you go with me, I will go; if you do not go with me, I will not go." ⁹"Very well, I will go with you," she answered; "but any glory for you will not come from the course you take, for the LORD will turn Sisera over to a woman."

Deborah arose, setting out for Kedesh to be with Baraq.ᵇ ¹⁰Baraq then mustered Zebulun and Naphtali at Kedesh. Ten thousand men marched behind his steps, with Deborah joining him. (¹¹Now Heber the Kenite had separated

---

a. Or: wife of Lappidoth.
b. Or: So Deborah arose and accompanied Baraq to Kedesh.

250

himself from other Kenites, from the descendants of Hobab, the father-in-law of Moses, pitching his tent as far as the Oak at Bezaanannim,[c] which is near Kedesh.) [12]Sisera was informed that Baraq son of Abinoam had gone up to Mount Tabor. ס [13]Sisera mustered all his chariotry—nine hundred chariots of iron— and all the troops he had, *setting forth* from Haroshet-haggoyim toward Wadi Kishon.

[14]Deborah told Baraq, "Up! This is the moment the LORD has delivered Sisera into your power, for the LORD has already taken your lead." With Baraq charging down Mount Tabor, ten thousand men behind him, [15]the LORD flustered Sisera, his chariotry, and his army, at the edge of the sword, ahead of Baraq.[d] Sisera dropped from his chariot and fled on foot. [16]Baraq chased after the chariots and the army as far as Haroshet-haggoyim. Everyone in Sisera's army fell to the sword; not even one man survived.

[17]Sisera himself fled on foot to the tent of Jael, wife of Heber the Kenite; for there was a peace accord between Jabin, king of Hazor, and the House of Heber the Kenite. [18]Jael came out to greet Sisera, saying to him, "Turn this way, my lord; turn toward me and have no fear." So he turned toward her, and into the tent. She covered him with a blanket. [19]He said to her, "Do let me have some water; I am thirsty." She opened a skin of milk, gave him drink, and covered him. [20]He said to her, "Stand at the entrance of the tent. If anybody comes to ask you if there is any man here, just say 'There is not!'" [21]Jael, wife of Heber, took hold of a tent peg and grasped a mallet in her hand. Approaching him cautiously, through his temple[e] she hammered the peg till it punched the ground. He was fast asleep from exhaustion, and so he died.

[22]Baraq just then was tracking Sisera. Jael went out to meet him, saying, "Come, I will show you the man you are seeking." When he reached her, there was Sisera sprawling dead, with a peg in his temple.[f]

[23]From that day on, God made Jabin, king of Canaan, submit to the people of Israel. [24]Their pressure against Jabin, king of Canaan, became increasingly aggressive until they annihilated Jabin, king of Canaan. ס

NOTES

Deal with them as you did with Midian, with Sisera and with Jabin
  at Wadi Kishon;
Destroyed at Endor, they became dung for the field.
  —*Ps 83:10–11 (9–10 RSV)*

---

c. *Ketiv*: The Oak at Bazeannim (see the Notes at Judg 4:11).
d. Or: *they were routed* at the edge of the sword by Baraq (see the Notes at Judg 4:15).
e. Or: jaw.
f. Or: jaw.

Jabin

4 1–2a. The introduction to the great narrative about the war of Deborah and Baraq opens with familiar material. The cycle begins once Ehud dies. With both Greek witnesses having already committed him to God at 3:30 (see the Notes there), only Rahlfs B felt the need to mention it again here. God's instrument for punishment is introduced: Jabin (*yāvîn*), king of Canaan here, but king of Hazor in 4:17. This notice opens up a number of issues, to begin with about the king himself. If based on a fine West Semitic root, **byn*, "to understand," the name would be a verbal phrase, in the causative, with a god as its lost subject. If that god is El, the name would mean "El instructs" (or the like). We could be dealing with a very old dynastic name, as Mari scribes preserved the name of the king of Hazor as Ibni-Addu, an East Semitic form that is unlikely for the area. Long ago, Cazelles (1958: 320) framed the good question: "Would the Mari scribe convert the name of a distant king into Akkadian when he would not do so for those of West Semites at closer proximity to him?"[1] Another question is whether the narrator found amusement in a name that evokes wisdom when that asset will soon prove inadequate. The other issue is about the connection between this Jabin and the king of Hazor, who organized a coalition against Joshua. The event is told in Josh 11:1–14 and I paraphrase it:

1. Jabin of Hazor summons (*vayyišlaḥ*) a number of kings, obviously belonging to an already established coalition. The immediate threat is Israel's defeat of a southern coalition of Amorite kings. They assemble by the Waters of Merom, "as numerous as the sands on the seashore—and a vast multitude of horses and chariots" (v. 4).
2. Reassured and instructed by God, Israel surprises the enemy, pursuing its tattered forces across the Galilee, to the seacoast, "letting none escape" (v. 8). Obeying God, Joshua hamstrings the horses and burns the chariots.
3. Hazor, the coalition's prime power (*rō'š kol-hammamlākôt*, v. 10), is captured and put to fire, its population slain. The other cities are emptied and occupied, their leaders slain. Israel takes much spoil and cattle.

Naturally this narrative raises the question of connection between two accounts, and in the literature one reads many approaches, complicated by readings in the Greek version of the Joshua account:

1. *These are independent narratives.* As mentioned above, Jabin is a throne name and could be used by a succession of kings (witness the string of pharaohs named Ramses in immediate sequence in early-first-millennium Egypt). Hazor, though destroyed, was in fact rebuilt, archeological records notwithstanding. Additionally, there are opinions that the Judges account occurred first, because in Joshua the king is killed.
2. *The two stories are the same*, adapted to different environments, but both with the same splendid accounts of divine control. They both deal with coalitions; they are both set in valleys; both features chariots. The broad differences, however, tend to be underplayed.
3. *The two stories leap-frog each other*, in that in Judg 4, Jabin's account simply brackets the more core narrative about the discomfiture of Sisera.

Undoubtedly there are other hypotheses, but a conjecture that persuades is not within easy reach.

Canaan was never regarded as a unit—not in antiquity, not even in Scripture—but an aggregate of areas. So the title *melek-kĕnaʿan* has certainly provoked queries. Some have suggested that because a *maqqef* separates the two words, thus setting up a construct relationship, we need to understand, "a king (that is, among many) in Canaan" (see Soggin 1981a: 60). But this is specious: The Masoretes are not consistent in using a *maqqef* after *melek*, even when syntax is considered.[2] Much simpler is to accept the notion that he is being treated as the primary king in Canaan, for the narrator quickly turns to the city that he actually ruled, Hazor.

This Hazor (Tell el-Qedah, 8 miles north of the Kinneret) is the pride of eastern Galilee and had a history that goes deep into the third millennium BCE.[3] Its second-millennium Bronze Age city covered about 200 acres and was among the most developed in Palestine, with a population (estimated at twenty thousand) about ten times larger than that of contemporaneous Jerusalem. Its traders fanned out broadly and participated in exchanges deep into the Euphrates Valley.[4] Hazor suffered major destruction during the thirteenth century BCE (by Egypt, other Canaanites, Israel?) and was not rebuilt in a significant way until the monarchic period; when, exactly, is disputed. This gap in the archeology of Hazor during an interval that is often associated with the Judges period has created no lack of argument about the historicity of events reported in Josh 11 and Judg 4.

Sisera

4 2b–3. If Jabin and Hazor had prehistories, Sisera (*sîsĕrāʾ*; Greek, Σισαρα; Josephus, Σισάρης) and his home base Harosheth-haggoyim make their appearance only from this point. (Sisera is also the name of a temple servant during the exile; Ezra 2:53, Neh 7: 55.) Sisera is Jabin's army commander (*śar ṣĕvāʾ*).[5] While kings were technically heads of their armed forces, in fact, most of them would have commanders, some a number of them, especially when they ruled empires and when warfare had become so specialized as to include diverse corps, infantry, cavalry, and chariotry. In a coalition, such officers tended to be in charge of the armies recruited locally, and when they were sent to join forces assembled by the head of that coalition, they did not surrender control of their own forces but coordinated them with those of others. Rather than a ruler in his own right, therefore, Sisera reported directly to Jabin, thus explaining why in 1 Sam 12:9 he is called "commander of Hazor's army." (RSV and others needlessly emend into "commander of the army of Jabin king of Hazor.")

In the literature, one finds many attempts at locating Harosheth-haggoyim in a fixed place with historic remains, but a corollary to the above observation is that Harosheth-haggoyim need not be a settled town but a bivouac or garrison area, explaining why it occurs only in this narrative. (The idiom *yôšēv bĕ-* can refer to bivouacking or encamping, as in 1 Sam 13:16 and 1 Kgs 11:16.) Greek versions translated it as Αρισωθ τῶν ἐθνῶν, "Arisoth of the nations" (Vulgate "Aroseth gentium"), and the Targum *bitqof karkê ʿamĕmayâ*, "in the Fort Cities of Nations," implying a fortification built by a concert of powers. A possible connection (likely because of aural proximity) to Khirbet el-Harithiyye (M.R. 161236) is not supported by the archeology of the site, and it does not help to make an equation with El Amarna's Muḥrašti (Boling 1975: 94) since we have only vague notions where to locate that town. Aharoni (1979: 221–22) is more forceful than others, therefore, when suggesting that we look not for a town, but for a forested region (Hebrew, *ḥrš*). Rainey (1983) likewise thinks of a region, "Plantations of the Gentiles," equivalent to other names such as "at Taanach, by the waters of Megiddo" (Judg 5:19) and the Gelil-haggoyim of Isa 8:23 (9:1 RSV).

Sisera's name is still a puzzler, and there is a tendency to explain it via languages and ethnic groups (once Hurrian, now mostly Luwian, Lycian, Illyrian, but also Cretan and Sardinian) that are not always fully recovered or understood, with the aim of vaguely attaching him to one of the Philistine tribes that had recently settled in the region.[6] In fact, we cannot say what kind of a name Sisera is, nor can we assume that the "children of Sisera" (Ezra 2:53, Neh 7:55) who served as temple servants (*nĕtînîm*) were his descendants; but to the Hebrews, like Eglon, he was one more tyrant trying to oppress Israel, and he shared with him an unworthy death.

Sisera controlled the area for his king by wielding an impressive chariotry: nine hundred of them.[7] (On chariots of iron, see the Notes to 1:19.) This is not an insignificant number. Here are a few examples cited in international clashes:

1. In the battle of Megiddo (mid-fifteenth century BCE), pitting Thutmosis III (Year 23) against a large Canaanite coalition led by Kadesh, the Egyptians took much spoil, including "340 living prisoners; 83 hands; 2,041 mares; 191 foals; 6 stallions; a chariot, wrought with gold, its pole of gold, belonging to that foe; a beautiful chariot, wrought with gold, belonging to the chief of Megiddo; 892 chariots of his wretched army; total, 924 chariots."
2. In the Battle of Kadesh (early thirteenth century BCE), Ramses II brought along just two hundred chariots and had to face King Muwatalli of Hatti, whose allies mustered more than three thousand of them.
3. At Qarqar (853 BCE), Shalmaneser III's two thousand chariots faced slightly more than that number, almost wholly supplied by Ahab of Israel.

In later traditions (Josephus, Pseudo-Philo), but especially in rabbinic lore, Sisera was made into a world conqueror, rivaling Alexander in prestige and achievement. He commanded more than forty thousand armies, each of one hundred thousand men. At four billion in strength, the enemy was truly worthy—for Israel, if not also for its God.[8]

Deborah

4 4–5. Her name means "bee," and she is the second person in Scripture to hold it, the other being Rebekah's nurse, who was "buried under the oak below Bethel; so it was named Allon-bakut," that is, the "Oak for Tears" (Gen 35:8).[9] There are many rabbinic comments (and some modern as well; Asen 1997) connecting her name to the insect, with its reputation for relentlessness (Deut 1:44) and swarming attacks (Ps 118:12), yet also for producing honey.[10] We are given much information about this Deborah, interestingly enough, not duplicated in the song of Judg 5:

1. Deborah is a prophet, an *'iššâ nĕvî'â*. The detail about her being a woman (*'iššâ*) seems redundant, in that the noun for prophet here is feminine (*nĕvî'â*). We shall notice that a balancing phrase is applied to a male prophet at 6:8. Unlike many neighbors, Israel did not normally allow women to have priestly function and thus to operate close to the shrines, altars, and divine paraphernalia. (Deborah will soon be

said to operate under a tree, possibly close to Mizpah, a cultic center.) But prophecy (dreams too) was always one avenue for skirting such limitations, as it permitted direct connection with God. It is true that prophets, like priests, had their own guilds, tightening privileges and requirements to members of specific families or to elites around the king; still, there was always the potential for prophets to rise from unexpected corners and circles. Miriam, sister of Moses, was deemed a prophet (Exod 15:20). She played a key role in the survival of baby Moses; she led Israel into songs, praising God for the many miracles; and she quarreled with her brother— yet it remains unclear from the narratives what exactly she did to earn this label (see S. Ackerman 2002). Isaiah's wife is said to be a prophet (Isa 8:3), but aside from bearing a child to which a symbolic name is attached, her prophetic gifts are likewise not developed. Noadiah (Neh 6:14) was called a prophet, but whether a false one or not depends on how one reads her involvement with people opposed to Nehemiah.

Aside from Deborah, about the only woman prophet who is registered as a messenger for God is Huldah (oddly, her name means "Weasel"). She authenticated the divine threats contained in a temple scroll that the high priest had discovered and delivers a Delphic oracle about Josiah (see the Notes to 2:8–10). About her, we have nice notices in 2 Kgs 22:14 (= 2 Chr 34:22): She is the wife of Shallum son of Tikvah (Tokhath), son of Harhas (Hasrah), the keeper of the wardrobe. Huldah's husband belonged to the elite. Keeping the wardrobe (of kings, not priests, as it is occasionally suggested) is a major post, with responsibilities beyond acting as the king's personal valet. Kings dispensed garments (especially those that they had worn) when trading favors with allies, vassals, and courtiers; so keeping score of such traffic also meant the ability to influence the currying of favor.[11] Huldah is also said to live in a specific quarter (the Mishneh) of Jerusalem. Why we needed to know this tidbit is not clear to me. Interestingly, the rabbis counted seven prophetesses in Scripture but had their own reasons for citing them as Sarah, Miriam, Deborah, Hannah, Abigail, Huldah, and Esther (bMegillah 14a).

2. Deborah is ʾēšet lappîdôt, "wife of Lappidoth" in most translations. That women are cited by connection to a husband is fairly normal in Hebrew narratives, especially when ʾiššâ, "wife," is in construct with a well-known personality (Nahor, Abram/ Abraham, Jacob, Amram). When the husband is not featured in narratives, as in the case of Huldah's Shallum (see above), his pedigree and/or his profession is established. Since Lappidoth is not known otherwise, the way Deborah is associated with him is anomalous (see Ehrlich 1968: 51). As a personal name, Lappidoth is based on a feminine plural construction—not usual, but known, for example, Naboth (for example, at 1 Kgs 21:1), a victim of Jezebel and Ahab, and Jeremoth (for example, at 1 Chr 7:8). (The ending in these names may, however, reflect a misvocalized abstract suffix.) However, unlike other such names, the phrase ʾēšet lappîdôt can have the full meaning "(woman) wielder of flames/torches" (see Exod 20:18; Judg 7:16–20, 15:4). This possibility had already appealed to medieval commentators, who created a whole yarn around it, best deployed in the tenth-century CE (or so) midrashic compilation known as Tanna dĕbe Eliyahu ("Lore Attributed to Elijah") but repeated in diverse versions in medieval commentaries: Deborah was married to a wick-maker, who, for the sanctuary at Shiloh, made wicks blaze as "torches."[12] In Scripture, however, ʾēšet

baʿălat-ʾôv, "a practitioner of necromancy," is *ʾēšet lappîdôt*'s closest parallel and is applied to the "witch" of Endor (1 Sam 28:7).

The lore about divination using flames comes to us mostly from Hellenistic times, and it includes a wide range of practices catalogued under "pyromancy" (divination by interpreting flames), including capnomancy (via rising smoke), daphnomancy (via a burning laurel branch), lampadomancy/lychnomancy (via wicker/candle flames), and sideromancy (via burning straw). How Deborah practiced her art is beyond us to reconstruct, but all such techniques required an expert capacity to interpret the movement of flame or of smoke, often comparatively, such as when more than one instrument was lit.[13]

3. Deborah is *šōfēṭâ bāʿēt hahîʾ*. The adverbial phrase *bāʿēt hahîʾ* can coordinate punctually ("at that precise moment," see Judg 12:6) or vaguely ("at some moment"). It might cover some of the twenty years during which Jabin was brutalizing Israel, but it does not help to explain how or under what circumstances Deborah assumed her role as judge. In fact, we are not told that God selected her for a rescue mission or that she was filled with zeal for the divine, and it may well be that we need to understand her function more concretely: She was an arbitrator, as is illustrated by the next verse. Some scholars (for example, Lindars 1995: 182–83) needlessly argue that the statement about her rule was an editorial addition, as if it is possible to decide what is original to this particular episode. True, the feminine form of *šōfēṭ*, "judge," occurs only here, but the narrator is so keen about placing Deborah among the judges that a special parenthetical clause addresses how and where she conducted her business: somewhere in the hilly area known as Mount Ephraim, between Ramah and Bethel, so beyond the main priestly centers. Our estimate of the distance between these two towns would depend on where we situate them. But if, as many topographers think, Ramah ("The Height") is at ar-Ram (M.R. 172140, about 8 kilometers north of Jerusalem) and Bethel is at Beitin (M.R. 172148, about 14 kilometers north of Jerusalem), we are speaking about a place in Benjamin near Mizpah where we will find Israel gathering to decide on a course of action against Benjamin (Judg 20:1). For Samuel, Mizpah was a stopping point at which to judge Israel.

Deborah sits (less likely, "dwells") under a *tōmer*. It is tempting to think that the word is just an oddly vocalized *tāmār*, a "palm tree," because the only other *tōmer* we know about in Scripture occurs in a difficult context (Jer 10:5) where, in some renderings, false gods are like "a scarecrow in a cucumber patch" (*tōmer miqšâ*); but the versions have entirely different understandings of the same phrase. Palm trees are not normally happy in the Judean hills, which might make this particular tree worthy of notice. As we saw above (under 2:1), there seems to be a close attachment between women named Deborah and imposing trees; but despite the proximity of this Deborah's "palm" and the oak named in memory of Rebekah's nurse (Gen 35:8), we should not assume that they were regarded as the same.[14] Rabbinic commentators (*bMegillah* 14a) have her sitting outside to avoid the hint of impropriety when meeting men within a tent—a likely contrast to where Sisera and Jael found privacy.

Unlike Samuel, Deborah seems to stay put at a specific place, allowing those with business with her to come up (*vayyaʿălû ʾēlêhā*) for *mišpāṭ*, "decision." Is this the narrator's sly comment on God's capacity to empower other than those at palaces and temples? What kinds of issues are brought to her for judgment is not said, and we may imagine them to range broadly, given Deborah's expertise as prophet, mantic, and judge. The other reference to the phrase *ʿālâ lišpōṭ* (at Obad 1:21) conveys a different sense: Mount Zion (Israel) will punish Mount Esau (Edom).

These details about Deborah were not enough for the Targum, and it expands on 4:4–5 (after W. Smelik 1995: 380–82): "Deborah, was a woman and a prophet, wife of Lappidot; it was she who was judging Israel at that very time. She lived in her town, Atarot-Deborah ["Deborah's Crowns"], making a living on her own, from palm groves in Jericho, orchards in Ramah, oil-rich olive groves in the valley, fertile land in Bethel, and white soil on the king's highway. The people of Israel would go up to her for judgment." The focus on Deborah's wealth negates the potential for bribe. (Against reality, the assumption then, as now, is that people of wealth are not corruptible.) W. Smelik (1995) shows that these notices may reveal a familiarity with Hasmonean royal holdings.

Baraq

4 6a. Deborah sends a message to Baraq (*vattišlaḥ*) with a request conveyed by the verb *qārā*, "to call, shout," the two verbs operating in hendiadys (two acting as one). The association of these verbs can form three distinct idioms.

1. *šālaḥ* + *qārā* in the infinitive means "to order (someone) to meet someone (else)"; example: "[David] dispatched men to meet [his ambassadors], for the men were greatly embarrassed" (2 Sam 10:5; see also 2 Kgs 9:17).
2. *šālaḥ* + *qārā* with direct object (via *ʾet*) means "to order the summoning of someone" and could be followed by "to say" or the like; example, "[Pharaoh] ordered the summoning of Egypt's magicians as well as its wise men" (Gen 41:8; also 2 Kgs 9:17).
3. *šālaḥ* + *qārā* with preposition *lĕ-* introducing a person in indirect object means "to convey a message to someone" and is generally followed by citing the statement. When the context is clear, the assumption is that the statement is quoted to the recipient, who is at some distance—for example, when Delilah addresses the Philistine chiefs (Judg 16:18) or when Rebekah urges Jacob to escape Esau (Gen 27:42; see also Josh 24:9 in light of Num 22:4–7).

The language of Deborah's message to Baraq belongs to the third category, the point being that she did not "summon" (as many translations—for instance, *TNK* and RSV—have it) Baraq, but had him hear a message from God. There are consequences to this understanding; least among them is to rescue Deborah from a harsh rabbinic judgment for acting arrogantly by giving orders to men (*bMegillah* 14b).

Baraq means "lightning," a name or sobriquet known in antiquity (Hamilcar Barca, Hannibal's father) as now (Ehud Baraq, Israeli politician). His father's name, Abinoam, does not occur elsewhere; this is surprising as there are many names with "Abi-," "my father," as a first-position element. Some commentators have not resisted identifying Lappidoth, Deborah's husband, with Baraq (see above), because the meaning of their names have "fire" in common (Cooke 1892: 15, and many others, before and after).

Baraq belonged to Naphtali, a tribe that failed to acquire its allotment, as detailed at Judg 1:33. He comes from one of a handful of Kedeshs (*qedeš*; Greek, Κάδης) that occur in Scripture, the repetition of the name due to its meaning "Consecrated," which easily attaches to any site with a major shrine. It is possible to decide which one is at stake in our story yet still not be certain about its place; for in locating ancient sites, we still largely depend on the survival of their names in modern garb, in our case, the many variations on the root *quds* in Arabic.

There is a Kedesh "toward the border of Edom in the South" (Josh 15:21, 23) that many have associated with Kadesh-Barnea. This one is definitely not at stake here. There is another Kedesh, a Levitical city, located in Issachar (1 Chr 6:57 [72 RSV]), possibly also cited as Kishion (Josh 21:28), and it is associated with Tell Qisan, near Mount Tabor, or with Tell Abu Qudeis (Tell Qedesh), between Taanach and Megiddo. This, too, is not likely relevant here (but see below at 4:11). There is a third Kedesh, in the Galilee, generally associated with Tell Abu Qades (M.R. 200279), not far from Lake Huleh in the Galilee, some 11 kilometers north of Hazor. Tiglath-pileser conquered it and deported its inhabitants (2 Kgs 15:29). Jonathan the Maccabee fought the Syrians nearby (1 Macc 11:63, 73), but in Josephus's time it belonged to Tyre (*Ant.* 13.154).

Baraq's home place is likely to be yet a fourth Kedesh, expressly associated with Naphtali in our passage and in Tobit 1:2, but simply Kedesh in Josh 19:33, possibly also in Josh 12:22. The most recent consensus is to place it at Khirbet Qediš (or Qedesh), on the western slope of the Kinneret (Lake Tiberias).

The Instruction

4 6b–7. The message that Deborah conveyed, likely through messengers, is God's plan for attacking the Canaanite coalition. This is by no means the only context in which God plots out the defeat of enemies (we will meet with a number of examples in Judges), but this particular case is interesting in that it is delivered through a third party, namely Deborah. The message is made up of a *header*, *instruction*, and references to divine *plan* and *intent*:

1. The *header* is a direct assertion couched as a rhetorical question, literally, "Is it not that the LORD God of Israel has commanded, 'Go . . . ?'" (GKC 474 [§150e]). This is not a statement made by Deborah, but the "envelope" (so to speak) for the message God intended for Baraq. From Mari and elsewhere such messages can take the shape of letters that an individual god sends a ruler (see "Gottesbriefe," *RlA* 3: 575–76). Since time immemorial, the notion that gods command their favorites to launch wars has been a human conceit universally (for the ancient Near East, see Altman 2010: 105–11). Rabbinic lore (*Tanna děbe Eliyahu*) proposed that Deborah knew God's will from inspecting Deut 20:1, "When you take the field against your enemies, and realize from its horses and chariots that the foe is mightier than you, do not fear them" (cited from Braude and Kapstein 1981: 156).

2. The *instruction* to Baraq seems to be composed of two parts: Baraq is commanded to gather at Mount Tabor and then to collect his armies from two tribes. In fact, we are dealing with a case of *hysteron proteron* ("the latter first"; see above at Judg 1:7). In Hebrew (and in Amorite as well), the verbs *hālak*, "to go," and *qûm*, "to rise," serve as auxiliary to the act conveyed by the verbs that follow them. When *hālak* occurs in the imperative (*lēk*), as it does here, the person addressed is urged to plan for the act described by the next imperative, in this case *māšaktā*. That verb has a broad range of meanings, most of which have to do with "drawing out," "stretching," or "dragging" something; but the context suggests military preparation, something like "to deploy" or "to muster." God is giving precise information on how many men (ten thousand)

and from which tribes (Naphtali and Zebulun) to take along as he musters at Mount Tabor, looming majestically over the land adjacent to Issachar, Zebulun, and Naphtali. The tribes called upon to supply the troops seem natural, given that Baraq is from Naphtali and that Zebulun has a stake in the Canaanite domination. But there is one element that must be kept in mind. The number of men that God wants Baraq to raise (ten thousand) seems plausible, especially in the light of numbers cited previously for fallen Canaanites (1:4) and Moabites (3:29); but such a count is dwarfed by the fallen Kedemites Gideon will slay (8:10) and the hundreds of thousands that will pit Israel against Benjamin toward the end of Judges. Given the Canaanite coalition forged by Jabin and the large number of chariots of iron that Sisera controlled, it is possible, as Josephus asserts (*Ant.* 5.202), that God is purposely playing down the army he will send against Israel's foes. In truth, he could have urged the sending of a fraction of this amount and still triumph over these foes. We shall soon read, at chapter 7, about similar tactics in the battles of Gideon.

3. God describes his *plan* by opening on the same verb used in instructing Baraq, but not the same idiom. Above, the verb did not take a direct object, but here it is construed with 'ēlêkā, "toward you" or "against you." A curiosity is whether to translate the verbal form ûmāšaktî in the future (Qal perfect with a *vav* conversive) or in the past ("I have already deployed against you"), the latter implying that God has already set the drama in motion, whether or not Baraq realized it.[15] The Masoretes often (but not always consistently; GKC 134–35 [§49h–m]) pull the accent to the last syllable of these verbal forms when the act is set in the future; they have done it here, and I follow their cue.

Together with his chariotry and his army (the word hămôn conveys huge numbers), Sisera is made to move toward the Kishon, not a river (nāhar, normally reserved for the Tigris and Euphrates) but a wadi (naḥal) that only seasonally turns into a stream and after hard rains also into torrents (so in Greek, χείμαρρος). This is important to keep in mind as we turn soon to the poetic setting of the narrative, where the defeat of Sisera is treated like the sinking of Pharaoh's forces. There is general agreement that the Kishon is Wadi/Nahr al-Muqaṭṭaʿ (renamed Kishon in modern Israel), draining the Jezreel Valley from the Carmel toward Haifa; but there is also the suggestion that equates it with Wadi el-Bira (Naḥal Tabor), which flows from Mount Tabor to empty into the Jordan. However, like most identifications that are based on naturalistic reconstruction of narratives, this last suggestion falters when explaining the other narratives involving the Kishon (1 Kgs 18:40). Elijah orders the slaughter of Baal priests there, after their Mount Carmel debacle, and it is unlikely that he traipsed them eastward to the Jordan to have it done.

4. The *intent* (ûnĕtattîhû bĕyādêkā) makes it obvious that Sisera never had a chance, whether this statement, which is also based on a perfect with a *vav* conversive, is rendered as past ("I have already handed him over to you") or future ("I will hand him over to you"); but it also sets up Baraq's decidedly equivocal answer. We have a vivid example of gods predisposing victory in a speech quoting Hammurabi of Mari before he attacked Larsa (ARM 26 385: 13'–20'): "I have consulted Šamaš and Marduk and they have repeatedly given me 'yes' for answer. I would certainly not have risen to this attack without (consulting) God." Hammurabi addressed his troops: "Go on,

may God be in your [plural] forefront. If on reaching Larsa, the city opens its gates to you, accept its offer of peace. Even if [King Rīm-Sin] had broken its oath to Šamaš and Marduk, do not [do harm] to that city."[16]

The Exchange

4 8–10. The preceding had prepared us for instant acceptance on the part of Baraq. Had we not reviewed Deborah's credentials to speak for God and for his people? She was, after all, a prophet, a diviner, and a judge, with Israel accepting her in these functions. Moreover, the message she sent Baraq contains not her words, but those of God, for whom she is just the vessel.

Ostensibly, Baraq throws a challenge to Deborah: Come with me and I will go; refuse to come and I will not go. Baraq was obviously not a subtle person, but by framing his answer from both sides, he is emulating a mode of inquiry that erases ambiguity. Still, the question arises: What was Baraq thinking when he gave her his answer? It is common to interpret his demand by evoking the many examples in which God was brought into battle, most notably via the ark (for example, Num 10:35–36, Josh 6, 1 Sam 4–7), but this is not quite the case. What is at stake is hinted at by a Greek expansion on the received Hebrew text. Both Rahlfs A and B give Baraq these additional words, "For I know not the day on which the LORD will set an angel to make me prosper." Baraq's point is that without Deborah, he would not know when to launch the war. Whether or not this sentiment was included in some Hebrew manuscript is beyond easy reconstruction, but it certainly prepares us for what Deborah does say in 4:14.[17]

Baraq, therefore, is not being cowardly or skeptical of God's promise, although we will soon meet with a character (Gideon) with an ample need for reassurance. In fact, we had already noticed the close connection between oracle taking and leadership decisions, whether military or communal.[18] We may recall here that the Mesopotamia omen takers (most prominently the *bārû*-diviners) were never satisfied to send one message on the will of the gods, however explicit, but were in constant consultation with them, especially during martial periods: when the enemy was at the gate, when battle was joined, or when troops were moving to and from a battle.[19] This is worth mentioning because Baraq is insisting on having a third party (Deborah, likely from Ephraim) call the shots. As we shall see, she does not disappoint him in this regard. (See also the Comments below.)

GOADING BARAQ

4 9–10. Deborah is willing to go. She might be irritated that Baraq remains reluctant after she had conveyed to him a detailed divine message or that he would have her perform needless augury. His doubts or lack of confidence prompts her to make a Delphic statement about *tifʾeret,* "honor, beauty, glory" (Greek, προτέρημα), and the person who would deserve it. The exception to what normally comes with victory is introduced by the conjunction *ʾefes kî* (GKC 500 [§163c]), developed idiomatically in Greek into the phrase πλὴν γίνωσκε ὅτι, "but know that": Baraq is to make no gains through his campaign (*derek,* "road, path," can have a military sense, as in 2 Chr 6:34; Akkadian, *ḫarrānum*).

Deborah's point is straightforward, built around the verb *mākar*, precisely the action attributed to an angry God delivering Israel to its foes (see 2:14, 3:8, 4:2, and 10:7). While we can be fairly positive that Baraq identified Deborah as the woman who might rob him of collecting his prize, we are less certain about Deborah's own understanding of her prediction. She might have had herself in mind, for prophets delivering two-edged pronouncements do not necessarily have a clear vision of their true application. Certainly Jonah did not realize that his prophecy about Nineveh ("Forty more days and Nineveh overturns," Jonah 3:4) allowed for its destruction as well as its rehabilitation (see Sasson 1990: 345–48). It is less clear whether Huldah realized the ambiguity of promising Josiah a peaceful entombment (see the Notes to 2:8–10).[20]

As already observed (at 4:6b–7), the verb *qûm* serves as auxiliary to the succeeding verb. But in our case, Deborah may well have "risen" from the seat she occupied under her palm. The same often applies when people "rise" from mourning before undertaking another action, explicitly in Gen 23:2 (Abraham) but implicitly in Ruth 1:6 (Naomi and her daughters-in-law). Deborah's movement is not clearly charted in the Hebrew text, as it may imply that she went with Baraq *toward* Kedesh when she should have gone *to* Kedesh to join him there. I understand the latter to be her trajectory, and my translation does not unduly tweak the Hebrew.[21] Rahlfs B "solves" this minor problem by having Deborah accompany Baraq *out of* Kedesh (ἐκ Καδης).

As Baraq had the men of Zebulun and Naphtali come to arms (Hiphil of *zāʿaq*), there seems to be a conscious strategy on the part of the narrator to parallel the moves of the antagonists, for we shall soon see Sisera do the same with his troops (at 4:13). However, whereas it is fairly common for "*běregel* someone" to be idiomatic for "following after" that person, we shall soon notice how the same construction (*běraglāyv*) differs in implication when applied to Baraq (here) and to Sisera (at 4:15). Whether or not the notice about Deborah marching with Baraq adds anything to the previous comment about her is debated; many commentators interpret a twofold reference to the verb *ʿālâ*, "to march up," as implying a move up Mount Tabor.

Parentheses: Heber the Kenite

4 11. At 1:16, we had met the Kenites with the following words: "The descendants of the Kenite, the father-in-law of Moses, marched with those of Judah from the City of Palms to the wilderness of Judah, in the Negev of Arad. Having gone there, he settled among the inhabitants." Whatever these enigmatic sentences meant to convey (see the Notes there), surely one of its goals is to tell us about the close connection between the Kenites and Judah, thus continuing the special relations established since the days of Moses. Their settlement was near Arad.

Here we learn that one branch, the budding clan of Heber, had separated from the other Kenites, moving northward and settling near where a major battle is shaping up. The Niphal of the verb *pārad* strongly implies an appreciable distancing or separation, and the participial form found here (*nifrād*) suggests an unfolding act. So we are catching an event as it is occurring: Heber was moving away from his kin—and soon enough from the loyalties his people had forged with Israel. Scripture lists about four different entities by the name Heber (*ḥever*), three from diverse tribes (Asher, Judah, and Benjamin) and this one, a Kenite.[22] The name itself is based on a clear root, **ḥbr*, but with multiple meanings: It could have something to do with forging alliances and so reminds us of the discussion earlier about the name Hebron (see the Notes to 1:13). Especially relevant here is the observation that in the Amorite tribal vocabulary recovered from Mari documents, a *ḥibrum* refers to a nomadic unit that has not yet settled down; see n. 15 to IA2 (p. 469). But the root could also have something to do with divination or charming, as in Deut 18:10–11: "Let none among you consign his son or daughter to the fire, practice divination—as a soothsayer, an augur, or a sorcerer—cast spells [*ḥōvēr ḥāver*], question ghosts or spirits, or inquire of the dead." If this is so, the notice about Heber pitching his tent by an oak (see below) may prove parallel to Deborah's location by a palm. Either way, if the name Heber is taken as a cue, then the narrator has found a way to comment on him without multiplying words.[23] Still, all that we know of Heber comes from this verse: He is the husband of Jael. Having uprooted his wife from other Kenites, he brought her into territory dominated by Jabin, a foe of people with whom the Kenites normally had links. (Jewish exegetes credit the move to divine providence.) So as we soon follow the story of Jael, let us recall the comments about Mari princesses and the issue of loyalty raised by their marriages to leaders with sympathies that may not match theirs (see the Introductory Remarks to IA2, "Achsah").

Heber had pitched his tent as far as the *'ēlôn bĕṣaʿănannîm* (*Ketiv*: *bṣʿnym*) said to be near Kedesh—which one is debated, but less likely Baraq's hometown (see above at 4:6). An *'ēlôn* (also *'allôn*) appears to be a substantial tree although, as in most other examples of flora cited in Scriptures, the exact species is not yet established. Translations often give "terebinth" (a midsized tree that is a source of tanning material and turpentine) or "oak," without indicating its variety. Although some recent translations simply treat it as part of a name (*TNK* gives Elon-bezaanannim in our case), I follow many in translating this element (arbitrarily) as "oak," if only to match what is said above about the "Palm of Deborah." B. Mazar (Maisler) (1965: 301–2) proposes that this reference to an oak gives the area sanctification.

How to parse *bĕṣaʿănannîm* has also proved slippery, whether or not its location can be fixed. Many commentators treat the initial syllable as the preposition *bĕ-*, "in, at, by," and so in most dictionaries there is a place name under "S/Zaanannim." Yet, when trees (palms, cedars, oaks, etc.) are associated with a place, or another noun for that matter, a preposition does not normally connect them: oaks of Bashan (Isa 2:13, Zech 11:2) and of Tabor (1 Sam 10:3) and cedars of Lebanon (often); oaks of "weepers" (see above at 2:1) or of "the leader" (Gen 12:6, Deut 11:30). Our closest analogue here is the *'ēlôn mĕʿônĕnîm*, "Diviners' Oak," of Judg 9:37. Whether for our passage we favor the *Qere* (likely inspired by Josh 19:33) or the *Ketiv*, we should be looking into the quadrilateral root *bṣʿn*, which may well be based on *bṣʿ*, with such distant meanings as "to make profit" or "to bring/come to an end" (Lindars 1995: 192, prefers the second but translates neutrally, "tree of Bazannim"). As it happens, the Greek versions had similar notions, with Rahlfs B giving ἕως δρυὸς πλεονεκτούντων, "at the oak of Profiteers," while Rahlfs A has πρὸς δρῦν ἀναπαυομένων, "near the Oak of the Resters." The Targum goes its own way with *mêṣar 'agānayā'*, "Plain of Ponds" (see W. Smelik 1995: 384–85). The point to keep in mind is that despite the delivery of a distinctive feature (the "oak") and the naming of a specific place (Kedesh), it is not at all wise to place Heber's tent on a map.

The Battle

4 12–16. Hebrew often uses the third-person plural for an indefinite subject; so when Sisera is told about Baraq's movements, we are curious whether he had a vast spy network reporting to him (such as plentifully recorded in the Mari records) or whether (my preference) he is being egged into action by a God choreographing his fall. That he perceived the danger to be grave explains the muster of his vast chariotry—his instrument of terror—as well as all the troops at his disposal. We notice that Sisera does not alert King Jabin of the potential trouble but heads directly to its source. Naturally, this has led scholars to discriminate between separate traditions, one pitting Sisera against a local insurrection, and one, perhaps even adapted from Josh 11:1–2, in which Jabin's Canaanite coalition faced a more massive attack.[24]

Deborah fulfills what Baraq expected of her. In fact, Baraq already had proof of God's guidance: Had Sisera not headed toward the Kishon exactly as Deborah quoted God to say (at 4:7)? This time she tells Baraq when to launch the battle, her words referring less to the day than to the moment (*yôm*) in which God had already delivered (*nātan*, a verb in the past) his enemy to him. Her statement *hălōʾ YHVH yāṣāʾ lĕfānêkā* is also a statement of divine action already taken. God occasionally does go out to battle, and the verb *yāṣāʾ* describes his advance in such (mythic) contexts as Isa 26:21, Mic 1:3, Hos 6:3, and, as we shall see, Judg 5:4.[25] In this case, too, Baraq learns that God is already winning the battle, for *lĕfānêkā*, especially when involving angels (Exod 14:19, among a number of other references) or God himself, implies that heaven is in the vanguard.[26] More or less the same language was used by Ehud (at 3:28) when summoning his people to battle. The difference, however, is that even as Baraq was leading his men to meet the enemy, God had already defeated Sisera and his men (*vayyāhom YHVH ʾet-sîsĕrāʾ*). The relevant verb *hāmam* with God as subject is used elsewhere also to describe God's throwing troops into disarray: in Exod 14:24–25, against Pharaoh's mighty army, fastening its chariotry on the Re(e)d Sea muck; and in 1 Sam 7:10, as Israel prepares for the Philistine onslaught, God thundering from above, panicking them, before they were routed by Israel. We notice that in both these occasions, the panic was launched from heaven, rather than occurring at the sight of Israel.[27]

The last of the two passages gives us a sense of the progress of a divinely designed defeat. God confounds the Philistines through violent acts of nature; they lose their composure and get slaughtered by the advancing Israel, *vayyinnāgĕfû lifnê yiśrāʾēl*. The idiom formed by the Niphal of *nāgaf* + *lifnê* (someone) is well-attested in Hebrew (see the dictionaries) to mean "defeated by someone," and it may well be that we should assume its occurrence in 4:15. Our passage, we should also note, is an excellent example of synchysis, the deliberate disorder in syntax to match the prevailing event or emotion (see Rendsburg 1998–99, who does not treat this passage). A more natural sequence (and a less-talented narrator) might have given us *vayyinnāgĕfû lĕfî-ḥerev lifnê bārāq*, "they were slaughtered at a sword's edge by Baraq." As it is, many scholars have not always appreciated this literary device and have proposed excision of either or both of the two phrases *lifnê bārāq* and *lĕfî-ḥerev* (see Moore 1895: 120–21; Boling 1975: 194–95; and Lindars 1995: 195).

We are not told why Sisera felt the need to escape on foot (*vayyānos bĕraglāyv*).[28] As noted above (see at Judg 1:19), a spooked horse can make chariot riding very dangerous.

In the other account of the battle (at 5:4–5, see below), there is mention of flooding, and one often reads in the commentaries that the chariotry of Sisera got mired in mud, much as what happened to Pharaoh's forces in the above-mentioned passage (Exod 14:24).[29] It is possible, of course; but if one holds (as I do) that unraveling a plot cannot hinge on episodes or scenes that are imported from other settings, then we must make do with the realization that a victory attributed to God hardly needs clarification, naturalistic or otherwise. In Assyrian annals, where the defeat of opponents is invariable, we read of them surrendering to face death, mutilation, or harsh tribute; we also hear frequently of leaders fleeing at the approach of the Assyrian hosts, the humiliation complete when their escape is declared as solo.[30] As it is, this notice about Sisera's escape on foot will be picked up again, at 4:17, when the focus will be entirely on his fate. In the meantime, there are only mop-up operations for Baraq to undertake (idiom *rādaf 'aḥăr* +), and they are presented in 4:16, with hardly any tension left to the drama of battle: Baraq pursues the stunned and confused army, all the way to Haroshet-haggoyim where our story began and where, just a few moments earlier, Sisera was encamped in power and security. As previously, we are told that not one of the enemies survived (idiom *lō' niš'ar 'ad-'eḥād*). At 3:29, it is *lō' nimlaṭ 'îš*.

Jael and Sisera

The entire episode that unfolds below is blocked by two references to Baraq's pursuing Israel's enemy: at 4:16 he goes after the chariotry, leaving the infantry exposed to his attacks (*ûbārāq rādaf 'aḥărê hārekev vĕ'aḥărê hammaḥănê*), and at 4:22 he is after only Sisera (*vĕhinnēh bārāq rōdēf 'et-sîsĕrā'*). The difference in the reported targets exposes Baraq's narrowing objectives, but it might also create a temporal parallel between his chase and events within Jael's tent (see also below at 4:22). How much time is meant to elapse during these activities is not easy to establish. Earlier in Judges, at 1:16 and 3:28, the interval seems brief, perhaps even not relevant. In the story of Gideon's pursuit of Midianite chieftains, however, the lapse generates a confrontation with ostensible allies (at 8:4–7). Here, from the moment Baraq pursues Sisera until he finds his corpse, time is arrested as we focus on a vital new scene.

4 17–18. Sisera's escape by foot is repeated here, picking up on where he will soon find himself. However, the syntax differs (subject–verb–adverb) here, likely coordinating a sequence similar to that in 4:16 when Baraq pursued fleeing enemies (Buth 1994: 139–40). His running here also differs by having a specific goal: Unlike his disheveled army seeking the shelter of its encampment at Haroshet-haggoyim, Sisera *meant* to reach Heber's tent. How far he had to go is not at all clear since Heber, a nomad, moved broadly, his seasonal migrations taking him close by Kedesh. B. Mazar (Maisler) (1965: 301–2) proposes that he was seeking shelter at the Oak at Bezaanannim, a potential sanctuary. More likely is what we are told: Solemn obligations for peace (*šālôm*) were drawn between the dynasty of Jabin and the House (*bêt*) of Heber the Kenite. We know enough about such concords (*salīmum/salīmātum* in the Mari archives) from the ancient world to recognize that they included pledges of military support during hostilities as well as of mutual security for the citizenry. The essence of such understanding (repeatedly duplicated at all times in antiquity) can be had from one phrase in a letter quoting an exchange between two kings (ARM 26 372: 58–59): "Be hostile to my enemy and friendly to my allies." Were it not for the jaundiced perspective we reach from observing how often firm alliances are abandoned even after the most solemn of pledges, we might even speculate (admittedly precariously) that Heber was among the forces Sisera had moved against Baraq.[31]

As luck would have it, Sisera comes first to the tent of Jael rather than that of her husband, the text specifically citing her as "Jael, wife of Heber the Kenite."[32] (The co-ordination between luck and a preordained fate is not an unknown theme in Scripture; see Gen 24:12 and Ruth 2:3.) There is nothing exceptional about a Semitic person owning a name derived from the animal world. We have met with Caleb ("Dog"), Eglon ("Calf"), and Deborah ("Bee"), and now we have $y\bar{a}^{c}\bar{e}l$, a caprid, perhaps a mountain goat.[33] For this reason, turning to the verb $^{c}\bar{a}l\hat{a}$, "to move upwards," in finding a meaning for the name Jael is needless, especially so when connecting it with male sexual activity (van Wolde 1995: 245; see Layton 1997). Also needless is paralleling $^{\prime}\bar{e}\check{s}et\ hever$ with Deborah's epithet, $^{\prime}\bar{e}\check{s}et\ lapp\hat{\imath}d\bar{o}t$, thus establishing Jael as "a woman of the Kenite community" (lastly S. Ackerman 1998: 37–38; see above).

So Heber is indeed her husband, whatever his association with Canaanites or Hebrews.[34] From Gen 31:33 we learn that each of Jacob's child-bearing women had a personal tent. Even when in a monogamous marriage, Sarah kept to her own tent (Gen 24:67). A leader of the clan that separated itself from the main group, Heber too was likely to own many tents to accommodate his wives, children, and servants; but the plot requires the tent to be off-limits to men if we are to accept Sisera's request of 4:20 (see below). In another plot, that involving the visit of angels to Abraham, Sarah needed to be in a tent behind her husband (Gen 18:9–10). I have no sure knowledge about wives of nomads living in their own tents, but we do have a number of accounts in Mari letters of nomad women having to run the household when their husbands were away to escape royal control.[35] S. Ackerman (1998: 93–102) creates a full persona for Jael as a cultic functionary, following clues B. Mazar gives on the potential sanctity of the Oak at Bezaanannim.[36]

It may be too trivial to ask where Heber was when Sisera reached one of his tents. Perhaps, as speculated above, he was escaping Baraq's troops, as were other of Jabin's allies. Or he might have been escaping Sisera, whose cause he failed to join. We are told that Jael went out to meet Sisera ($vatt\bar{e}\d{s}\bar{e}^{\prime}\ y\bar{a}^{c}\bar{e}l\ liqra^{\prime}t\ s\hat{\imath}s\bar{e}r\bar{a}$). She may not have been waiting for him to come by (as will his mother in the other telling of the event), but she certainly spied him running toward her husband's camp. From his quality outfit worthy of a leader, she was likely to know much: his affiliation (not a Kenite; not a Hebrew), his military status, and perhaps also his (high) rank. From his demeanor, she must also have known that his successes in battle were behind him. Did she know who he was? Not yet, perhaps.

Her overture is very polite, appealing to Sisera as an $^{\prime}\bar{a}d\hat{o}n$, not quite equivalent to the English vocative "lord," but more like "sir." The word went beyond simple salutation to communicate respect for someone of superior rank or class. With a first-person suffix it becomes $^{\prime}\bar{a}d\bar{o}n\hat{\imath}$, "my lord," occurring frequently in Scripture when someone is addressing kings, fathers, brothers, uncles, or husbands (see the dictionaries and Jenni, *TLOT* 1: 28). Most interestingly for our purpose, $^{\prime}\bar{a}d\bar{o}n\hat{\imath}$ is used by women when stroking the ego of a man (for instance, Abigail, who uses it excessively when facing David, 1 Sam 25:24–31) but most often when sensing they are speaking to superiors: Rebekah addressing Abraham's servant (Gen 24:18), Hannah speaking to Eli (1 Sam 1:15), Ruth seeking Boaz's favor (Ruth 2:13), and our example. So, beyond being polite, Jael is also reassuring, in that Sisera recognized her to be respectful. Her words are urgent, repeating in quick succession the crucial verb *sûr* (imperatives with ventive endings, conveying direction). The first catches his attention, but the second directs his steps. What is remarkable is her next injunction, *'al-tîrā'*, "have no fear." It is impressively cheeky! And if we had not already been prepared by encountering women of striking chutzpah (Achsah) and authority (Deborah), we might have become more aware of how incongruous it is for a tribal woman to say such words to a commander-in-chief of a powerful army. In fact, in the three dozen or so references to this phrase in Scripture, there is no other example in which a person of lower status reassures a superior with such words; rather, we often hear it used by God, to reassure patriarchs, Moses, Joshua, Gideon, and other leaders; by kings (David most often); and by prophets who are often speaking for God (see below at 6:23).

Rather than ignoring such temerity, Sisera, likely still in a shock of defeat, submits to her proposal, and in doing so he reverses the normal balance of authority between the sexes, with important consequences to the development of the story.[37] Sisera is now a client to Jael's hosting, his fate entirely in her hands. Despite the circumstances, it remains surprising that Jael does not offer refreshment to Sisera or wash his feet, hospitality requiring some such presentation, even to strangers (see the stories about Abraham and Lot in Gen 18–19 and Gen 24:32–33). Also, it may seem incongruous that Sisera has no words in reply (but see below). Her first act, instead, is protective: She covers him with a *śĕmîkâ*. This word is unique to this passage, but we are fairly sure of what it connoted because the controlling verb, *kāsâ* in the Piel, has clearly to do with covering (someone) with (*bĕ*-) something. The versions simply guessed: Rahlfs B gives καὶ περιέβαλεν αὐτὸν ἐπιβολαίῳ, "she covered him with a mantle," followed by the Vulgate, *opertus ab ea pallio*; Rahlfs A has καὶ συνεκάλυψεν αὐτὸν ἐν τῇ δέρρει αὐτῆς, "she hid him in a coarse curtain" (elsewhere δέρρις translates a hairy mantle in Zech 13:4), the last approximating the Targum's *bĕgōnakkâ* (there are other readings, see W. Smelik 1995: 388–89).[38] Some rabbis (Radaq among them) think the cover defended Jael's modesty, presumably because Sisera was in her tent rather than that of her husband.

The Reassurance

4 19–20. How long Sisera remained under cover before he asks for water is not easy to tell (but see below). Later he makes another request of Jael, but the second did not have to immediately follow on the first, and neither had to occur right after he entered. It might, however, shed light on his state of mind. Sisera is not the decisive commander; rather, he thinks in spurts, and he is no doubt still stunned by God's assault on him and his army.

Curiously, his first request, *hašqînî-nā' mĕ'at-mayim*, is reminiscent of the test Abraham's servant recalled proposing when searching for the perfect bride for Isaac (Gen 24:43). In Scripture, thirst shapes powerful metaphors, as when earth (Gen 4: 10–11) and the sword drink blood (Jer 46:10) or when the soul seeks spiritual guidance (examples at Ps 42:2–5 [1–4 RSV], 63:2 [1 RSV], 143:6; Amos 8:11–13). It also generates themes about one's duty to rescue the unfortunate (Prov 25:21) as well as reversal of fortune when appealing to God (Ps 107:5, Isa 41:17–18). In narratives, thirst is broken by water, but mostly under emergency conditions (assisted by miraculous gushes, as when Israel is in Sinai, Exod 17:3–6; Neh 9:15; or when Samson is at Lehi, Judg 15:18) or when prisoners or slaves are at death's door (1 Sam 30:11, 2 Chr 28:15). Near death after fleeing potential implication in the assassination of Amenemhet I, Sinuhe is rescued by Asiatics with water and boiled milk, the latter considered a food rather than a drink.[39]

Generally, however, in ancient Israel the drinking of water was avoided as it did not always contribute to health. In prose texts when we read of requests for drinking water, they come from strangers or suppliants who naturally may have hope for better beverages (Deut 23:5 [4 RSV]; Judg 4:19, 5:25; 1 Kgs 18:4, 13; 2 Kgs 6:22). Daniel shocks a palace official when he foregoes the king's table (delicacies and wine) for sprouts and water (Dan 1:10–16). When Nabal refuses to share even water with David, his avarice could not be more manifest (1 Sam 25:11).[40] Otherwise, wine is what is commonly served with meals, supplied to wives (Hos 2:7 [5 RSV]) or offered to palace servants (Dan 10:3). Melchizedek offers bread and wine to Abram, not for sacramental purposes, but because it would be uncivilized to offer any other beverage (Gen 14:18). When traveling, Hebrews invariably took along wine (2 Sam 16:1–2) because its alcoholic contents insured against bacterial growth and overcame the dull taste contributed by storage in skins or jars.

MILK

With all this in mind, it might be easier to understand why, after asking for water, Sisera is ready to accept another beverage. The surprise is that Jael gives him milk rather than wine. The ancient Near East was heavily invested in lactates. Because of climate, its propensity to spoil, lactose intolerance in most Asians and Africans, and the unpleasant odor it generated in the mouth, milk was not normally drunk by adults. For these reasons, we do not read in ancient documents much about it as a beverage to slacken ordinary thirst. Rather, records mention its conversion into longer lasting products: yoghurt (*laban*), sour curdles (*labne*), butter, ghee, and cheese. We occasionally see it presented at banquets (as in Gen 18:8, with other food; Sinuhe 89–95), and there is the famous prohibition against cooking kids in their mother's milk (for example, at Exod 23:19).[41] We learn from Egyptian documents that together with beer, milk was devotionally offered to the gods. Milk is well-represented in literature, particularly in Sumerian poetic myths involving Dumuzi (whose death is imaged as spilled milk; see Job 10:10) or in hymns in which deities and kings (for example, Lipit-Ištar) are shepherds, multiplying milk and fat (butter) as a symbol of their productivity and largess. Milk figures in Hebrew imagery, with the Promised Land declared as "flowing with milk and honey" and its whiteness matched with skin (Lam 4:7) and teeth and eyes (Cant 5:12).[42]

But milk was drunk, symbolically by kings from the breasts of gods (very common in the ancient world, see Isa 60:16) and actually by babies until their weaning (as late as age three, 2 Macc 7:27), coming mostly from human breasts. We know from the ancient world that women were commonly hired to nurse children (as reflected in the story of Moses) for diverse reasons, among them the mother's short supply of milk, the fear of delaying the next conception, or for bodily aesthetics.[43] In Mari, an unpublished letter reveals that the elite would send their babies for several years to the countryside for such services. As we read about Jael offering milk to Sisera, let us keep the above observations in mind as we unravel the unusual bond between the commander and the nomad's wife. Josephus, followed by many commentators (including Rashi), draw attention to the soporific effect that milk has on the tired, though Halpern (1988a: 83) disputes such an effect. Ehrlich (1968: 51) cites opinions that Jael gave Sisera fermented milk, therefore rich in alcoholic content. Rarely shying from sensuous interpretations of Scripture, rabbinic commentators had Sisera drinking from Jael's breasts, an erotic as well as a maternal image (*bNiddah* 55b). At any rate, Rahlfs A adds here a touch not available to other versions: After quenching Sisera's thirst, Jael covers his face (καὶ συνεκάλυψεν τὸ πρόσωπον αὐτοῦ), no doubt in preparation for her next deed.

Still, it is fair to ask whether Jael is covering Sisera *for a second time* once his thirst is slackened. To have done so might invest a comic touch on the whole sequence: Sisera enters the tent and does not object to Jael stuffing him under a cover. He then pokes his head out to ask for a drink. Jael gives him milk and then slips the cover over him. Soon, he will make one more request, no doubt from beyond the cover. To avoid such slapsticks, however, it may be more sensible to imagine a single act of covering that sandwiches a request. (The "again" most translations give at the end of 4:18 is not in the Hebrew.) This request would have occurred as soon as Sisera enters the tent; after satisfying Sisera's thirst, Jael covers him up. Treated as a child, Sisera will act as one when he makes his second wish.

4 20. The second request opens on a grammatical infelicity. In asking her to "stand at the entrance of the tent," Sisera uses a masculine form of the imperative, *'ămōd*, where one would have expected him to say *'imdî*. There are some examples of masculine imperatives for the feminine (GKC 325–26 [§110k]) and enough attestations for the infinite absolute (*āmōd) replacing an injunctive (GKC 346 [§113bb]) to suggest leaving the reading as is. The versions simply give the required feminine form and move on, but we may be dealing with a Sisera who is transiting from lack of coherence to forcefulness, Jael's infusion having revived him. From plaintive he turns assertive; but given Jael's earlier greeting ("turn toward me and have no fear"), his instruction seems prolix, perhaps also unnecessary. Why would he think that a woman who has treated him firmly so far would not know how to deny his presence? And if she were actually setting him up for delivery to an enemy, would his request not have fallen on deaf ears? True, a woman's tent may have been off-limits to an adult male other than her husband, but what soldier in pursuit of runaway enemies would accept unquestioningly the answer given by an ally of his foes? As it is, we will soon note that even a pursuing Baraq asks Jael no such question. Perhaps inspired by Odysseus in Polyphemus's lair, Bal (succinctly in 1988a: 145–46) treats Sisera's instruction as a riddle, with the answer he wants Jael to give *'āyin*, "there is no one," foreshadowing his own death. In effect, Sisera has his own words acted out physically by Jael.

The Murder

4 21. Lindars (1995: 199) suggests that Sisera's request gives Jael leave to secure her murder instrument. If so, the irony is not subtle. The verse itself is concerned with two issues: the act of murder and its consequence. Jael takes hold of a peg for staking a tent to the ground. (We need not imagine that she pulled one from the ground but that she took one not in use.) A *yātēd* is shaped like a nail, with a broad top and sharp bottom,

and can be used to hold segments of a structure together (the tabernacle in Exod 27:19). It can be made of metal or wood, the latter more likely when associated with looms (Judg 16:14). It is used also in the construction of metaphors, such as when speaking of Jerusalem as a tent with eternally set pegs (Isa 33:20) or of David's throne as affirmed forever (Isa 22:23; cf. Zech 10:4). A number of commentators treat it as a phallic symbol, shaping lurid scenarios for its use.[44] The *maqqevet* is a hammering instrument, used both in building (1 Kgs 6:7) and in ironwork (Isa 44:12) as well as in the refined work of jewelers (Jer 10:4). In the rabbis' opinion, Jael chose these instruments because Deut 22:5 forbad women from manly garbs and tools.

Why was it necessary for us to learn that Jael approached the sleeping Sisera *ballāʾṭ?* The adverb (based on the root *lwl'ṭ*) has to do with silent, perhaps also furtive action (so in a few contexts, including Ruth 3:7). The touch seems literary rather than realistic: Were he out cold, this information would not be necessary; had he been merely resting, she could hardly have positioned herself to strike him on his head. We have already met with two of the crucial verbs, *tāqaʿ* at 3:27 and *ṣānaḥ* at 1:14; but there, each shaped a different idiom (perhaps even represented different verbs entirely) and so had a different meaning. Here, *vattiqaʿ* is the consequence of Jael hammering with such force that the peg, cutting through Sisera's head, sinks into the ground, *vattiṣnah bāʾāreṣ*. This last verbal form is feminine, and some have suggested Jael as its subject (so, "and she drove it into the ground") rather than the peg, a suggestion that would be better if we had a Hiphil or Piel (see Soggin 1981a: 64).

What part of his head is at issue among the versions? Rahlfs A gives "jaw" (γνάθος), Rahlfs B has "temple" (κρόταφος), and the Vulgate offers *cerebrum*, "brains." The Hebrew has Jael striking at Sisera's *raqqâ*. In the only other contexts in which this word occurs, in Cant 4:3 and 6:7, this portion of the head is compared to a slice of a pomegranate and has received diverse translations, among them (most often) "temple," "brow," and "cheek," the last supported by Greek and Vulgate renderings. In our passage, Boling (1975: 98) accepts D. N. Freedman's suggestion to translate "neck," mostly for anatomical reasons; Halpern (1988a: 82) suggests "gullet." Sisera is said to be lying down, on the ground or on bedding. For Jael to approach him stealthily, it is best to imagine him on his side. Had he been on his back, Jael might have feared him to have remained alert enough to see an armed woman moving toward him. Since the Hebrew for *raqqâ* (as well as the Targum's *bĕṣidʿēh*) allows for either the temple or the cheek/jaws, I imagine that a crouching Jael attacked him from behind, driving her weapon into his skull in profile. I admit that attachment to *verismo* realization is not always the most profitable approach to interpreting literature.

How Sisera died is reported by three verbs juxtaposed to heighten an effect. The Masoretes accented the first two verbal forms as a unit, and I have followed their lead. But it is possible that we have here another manifestation of a Hebrew preference for piling on verbs (sometimes as many as five; see Gen 25:34) when sharpening effect. The first in the series, *nirdām*, is a participle, and as time sequence is not at stake in such forms, it does not reveal how soon Sisera fell into his torpor. The verb *rādam* has its closest synonyms in the verbs *yāšan* and *nûm*, both meaning "to sleep"; but when applied to prophets (Jonah 1:5–6; Dan 8:18, 10:9), they are in trance, so almost unconscious (see Sasson 1990: 101–2). The noun *tardēmâ* evokes a similar state of intense slumber, as when God turned Adam's rib into a woman (Gen 2:21) and when Abram witnessed

God (Gen 15:12). Perhaps, as S. Ackerman suggests (private communication), there is hint here of divine intervention. If so, God had not yet completed his intercession on behalf of Israel.

The remaining verbal forms, however, are both imperfects with *vav* conversives and so hint of some sequencing. The word *vayyāmot* is perfectly transparent; it is the end of the line, so to speak, for Sisera, who dies. *vayyā'af*, treated as derived from **'yf* in some dictionaries, can easily be a form of *yā'ēf*, in all its occurrences (1 Sam 14:28, 2 Sam 21:15, Jer 4:31) having to do with exhaustion (if so, see below at 8:15). This makes perfect sense if one adopts the Masoretes' punctuation and vocalization. But if there is a preference for linking them, then what happened between Sisera's deep sleep and his death becomes a point of speculation. Many scholars look for something like "collapse" or "swoon" and so promote (gingerly) some other possible roots like **'y/wp* (see Lindars 1995: 203–4; Boling 1975: 98).[45] The versions also strove for drama, with Rahlfs B offering "he fainted, darkness overtook him, and died," and the Vulgate giving "passing from sleep to death, he swooned and died." Rahlfs A, however, went further with "he went into convulsion between her knees, exhaled his last, and died" (καὶ αὐτὸς ἀπεσκάρισεν ἀνὰ μέσον τῶν γονάτων αὐτῆς καὶ ἐξέψυξεν καὶ ἀπέθανεν). This reading is obviously dependent on Judg 5:27, yet since rabbinic times it has inspired a nice body of literature on Jael as a seducer (see the Comments below). As for Sisera, despite his ignominious death, the rabbis of later times rehabilitated him (as they did Eglon) by making him an ancestor of the great Rabbi Akiva.[46]

The Aftermath

4 22. When the particle *vĕhinnê* is followed by a name, it draws attention to coordination of action or events that include that person, in this case alerting us that even as Jael was staging her sordid deed, Baraq was after his target (see above). This notice resumes what was said about Baraq in 4:16—that he was in hot pursuit of the enemy's fragmenting army—but it also informs us that Baraq is now bent on capturing its commander Sisera. (See also the Notes at 1:6 and 3:25.) This is signaled by a shift in idiom and verbal form: In 4:16 it is *rādaf 'aḥar* in the perfect, suggesting a punctual act, whereas here it is *rādaf 'et-* in the participle, implying a long-term commitment. Also, *vĕhinnê* synchronizes Jael's exit from the tent with Baraq's arrival. The choreography draws on folklore, where desired encounters are staged with minimal waste of time, as for example when Rebekah and Rachel show up on cue to set themselves for marriage (Gen 24:15 and 29:6), when Ruth finds Boaz in the field (Ruth 2), or when Boaz wastes no time in confronting the next of kin (Ruth 4).[47] In this last case, it is also very operatic, as it allows for the neatest of denouements.

The same vocabulary used earlier about Jael's greeting of Sisera is now repeated with Baraq on the scene. Here, words to Baraq open on the imperative of *hālak*, "to go," used almost as an interjection, something like "up," "come," or even "you there." Jael once more impresses by her assured tone. Earlier, she could tell a flustered Sisera not to fear; here, she knows exactly whom Baraq is seeking (*mĕvaqqēš*), no doubt because earlier Sisera had revealed himself to need hiding. S. Ackerman (1998: 92) wonders why Baraq would enter the tent of someone in alliance with Sisera. In fact, Baraq arrives as a victor, fully armed, probably not on foot, and certainly not likely to be frightened by a woman's presence. What's more, as he does not need hiding and he is never shown thirsting, there is no prospect for him to fall victim. When Baraq approaches Jael (*vayyābō' 'ēlêhā*), he realizes that he no longer need search for his foe.[48] Had he the memory for it, the same scene might well have given him the correct solution to Deborah's teaser, "the LORD will turn Sisera over to a woman" (4:9).

In this version of the story, we are not clued on any consequences for Jael. Does she receive praise for her act (as she will at 5:24)? Is she punished (or at least blamed) for breaking the oath that no doubt accompanied peacemaking between her husband and Jabin? The narrator is silent, but some commentators are not. S. Ackerman (1998: 102) assigns Jael a privileged position with the Hebrew God who "somehow" instructs her to assassinate Sisera as part of a declared holy war.

4 23. We have already met with the verb *kāna'* (in the Niphal, construed with the preposition *taḥat*) when Moab came under Israel's control (at 3:30). Ehud had instigated the turnabout, but Israel fought cleverly and carried the day. In this particular case, however, the same verb is in the Hiphil, construed with the preposition *lifnê*, with God forcing Jabin to submit to Israel. (It is particularly appropriate that the victim is from Canaan, a name that shares the same consonants as the controlling verb.) The triumph, therefore, is God's and not Israel's; in fact, the battle is conceived as a direct confrontation between God and Jabin, just as it was against Pharaoh when he would vie with God to control Israel.[49] As it happens, the other scriptural references to the same idiom also give God as the victor, with Deut 9:3 providing a fine illustration for the notion. There, Moses is admonishing Israel: "Realize now that the LORD your God is himself moving ahead of you as a devouring fire; he will have them wiped out and will make them submit to you [*vĕhû' yaknî'ēm lĕfanêkā*]. You will, by quickly destroying them, displace them, as the LORD has promised you."

McDaniel (1983: 40–45, 126–27) makes the point that in Judges (at 3:10–11 and 8:28) victory precedes the quieting of the land. Because in this context the formula about finding peace does not occur until 5:31, McDaniel would treat 4:23–24 as prologue to the song that follows. However, McDaniel's reconstruction and emendations for the opening lines of Judg 5 are so egregious that they spoil a potentially interesting notion. One might even imagine these verses to play Janus, ending chapter 4 as well as preceding chapter 5.

4 24. What is implied by the next verse about the fate of Jabin is not quite clear. Control of Jabin clearly shifts in this verse to Israel when in the previous one it was God's. In such a brief verse, the repeat of the king's name and title (*yāvîn melek-kĕnā'an*) twice seems gloating. (Rahlfs A simply gets rid of it the second time around.) The first portion implies that there was yet an issue of control of his territory even after Sisera's defeat; and so we must interpret the situation not as one in which Canaan had been conquered and was increasingly brutalized by Israel, but one in which Israel was expanding relentlessly its domination over areas as yet not overcome. (So too in the Greek version, "And the hand of the children of Israel prevailed more and more against Jabin king of Canaan"; similarly the Vulgate.) The second portion tells us of attacks that would not relent until (*'ad*) Jabin's final "destruction." *kārat* in the Hiphil implies cutting off from others or from further activities, so it is not clear whether the drama is ending with his death. Just the same, Jabin never quite realized that in his rise and fall he was but a pawn in a larger struggle about allegiance and loyalty between Israel and its God.

COMMENTS
History and Story

Our story covers much ground and moves through a number of episodes, each of which seems self-contained, albeit with the necessary connectives. A unity for the whole, however, is achieved through a framing that many attribute to the Deuteronomist: Opening on God's selection of Jabin as instrument of punishment (4:2), it ends on God forcing him to submit to a repentant Israel (4:23). Accord is sharpened by the label "king of Canaan," once in the opening and twice at the closing. This title is scarcely "historical"—that is, we do not find it in contemporaneous sources. Yet, unlike the concocted name of Cushan-rishatayim of Aram-naharayim, this fictive phrase is no invitation to doubt the historicity of events. At any rate, the narrator promptly sets us in historical mode by placing Jabin on Hazor's throne. There is, as noted above, a fairly clear effort on the part of the narrator to establish broad confrontation between the whole of Israel and the foe du jour that God promotes against his recalcitrant nation. And there cannot be a better foe than a united Canaan, more or less reprising the conflict of Joshua's time (Josh 11–12) but this time with God leading the charge. That a play on the root *knʿ* (at 4:23) may be unfolding here is plausible, but it can hardly be a controlling factor.

SISERA

We are also introduced to Sisera, enforcer of Jabin's will, his nine hundred chariots massed into one camp for quick sorties and constant intimidation. From this point on, Sisera takes over the role of antagonist while God searches for someone to oppose him. For us, this frame invites remarks on the historicity of the events. As in most moments in Israel's premonarchic history, except for those predisposed not to doubt the essential reliability of theologically garbed traditions, there is stark difference in evaluating what we are reading. This is not because Hebrews are less reliable than their neighbors in recording the past, but because we lack confirmation from outside sources and must reshuffle circumstantial evidence toward shaping plausible scenarios.

However, the period during which the Hebrews set the accomplishments of their judges (after the exodus and conquest but before the monarchy) happens to be least illumined by archeological and epigraphic finds. Of the latter, we have nothing specific; of the former we have disputed assessments and dating of destruction layers at crucial sites, such as Hazor, with the Baraq narrative set before (Aharoni 1975) or after (Liver in the *EncJud*, under "Deborah") such an occurrence. There is further complication by mention in Joshua of a major conquest involving a Jabin, and the episode there is taken as inspiring the Baraq involvement (Eissfeldt 1925: 23–33) or is independent of it (Lindars 1995: 165–66).[50] But without the mention of Hazor and its king, we are left to deal with Sisera, who has left us no trace of his existence beyond Scripture, and with Haroshet-haggoyim, which may or may not have been a place. Moreover, what is told about Sisera—his flight, his meeting with Jael, and his murder—is presented as the stuff of tales rather than of concurrent historical reporting.

Our assessment in this particular case is complicated by what we shall read in chapter 5: a poetic re-creation of the same event that may (or may not) have had direct connections with what is narrated in chapter 4, whether as source or as a dependent.

For some commentators, the style, contents, even themes of what transpires in chapter 4 duplicate what is told about Ehud in chapter 3. For others, little in chapter 4 makes complete sense without import from chapter 5, the latter deemed so crammed with realistic kernels that it has "the highest value as a historical document" (Cooke 1913: 44).[51] We shall come back to this topic presently, but we might notice here that when Ps 83:10 recalls God's saving graces ("Deal with them as you did with Midian, with Sisera, with Jabin, at Wadi Kishon"), it draws on our version of the story rather than the one from the next chapter.

DEBORAH AND DIVINATION

Between the brackets about Jabin are three episodes, and each invites comments on issues raised by the text and its interpreters. The first segment (4:4–9a) introduces Deborah and Baraq, setting them on a mission against the occupiers. Some commentators have made reference to Mari prophetesses (*āpiltum, muḫḫûtum, qammātum/qabbātum*) to accentuate the probability of Deborah's calling (Boling 1975: 99); but this confirmation is not necessary, for even when Israel made no room for women in temple functions, it did not shirk from assigning them inspiration extracultically. Besides, the role of prophets (of whatever gender) in Mari was nothing like that in Israel. The message of Mari prophets, however inspired, was destined for the king, who, in fact, had better means to ascertain the will of the gods by turning to diviners who read heaven's instruction from what is stamped on the innards of animal. Unlike prophets, diviners (and mantics) do not peddle unsolicited prognostications; they wait until a client, either personally or by proxy, comes to them with a specific query that is posed as opposite choices, much as was done via Urim and Thummim, the lots, and the ephod. Diviners do not wait for the gods to settle a message on them but use their clear vision to interpret signs embedded immemorially in time. This is often achieved by having a diviner read omens, so in a sense forcing the gods to deliver on what they are planning (ARM 26 131). This may be why Deborah is said to also be a "wielder of torches." Her ability to force answers through special inquiry and through interpretation of signs (however their mechanics) permits her to establish truths not dependent on God's assignment or timing. It is perhaps this capacity, as much as her function as judge, that brought people streaming to her palm tree.

This capacity of Deborah to make inquiry may also explain Baraq's insistence on having her with him when battling the superiorly armed Sisera. True, the message that God forwarded to him through Deborah may well have come through normal channels of prophecy: Deborah could enter a trance or have a vision in which she would receive a message for Baraq. But Baraq needed more than just to have her accompany him; he needed for her to act as a diviner, constantly searching the signs for the right moment to enter the fray.

Whether inspired directly or through her divinatory skills, Deborah fulfills this expectation; but because of his lack of faith in God's original pronouncement, Baraq loses his chance of glory on two fronts: First, there is no battle for him to win, for God had done it all; and second, there is no captive enemy commander to seal the triumph. For all these reasons, Baraq remains at the edge of Israel's memory, neither a hero nor a judge, and when the song of triumph is uttered by both Baraq and Deborah, her voice dominates the shaping of words.[52]

The second segment, from vv. 9b to 16, reports on the battle itself, and the critics have had a tough time plotting its locus and unfolding. Many have muddled the contexts further by importing details from the song as reported in the succeeding chapter, such as references to "Taanach by the waters of Megiddo" of 5:19 and to *naḥal qĕdûmîm* (see below) in Judg 5:21. If we stay with our episode, as we should, we would have to deal with the following named places: Hazor (not immediately relevant to the battle), Kedesh (multiple locales), Haroshet-haggoyim, "Oak at Bezaanannim" (or however one wants to read this locale), Mount Tabor, and Wadi Kishon. As reflected in the Notes above, except for Mount Tabor, there are no fixed opinions on where to site these locales; even the placement of the Kishon wadi is disputed. Despite all the unknowns, it is very common to find historians plotting the movements of troops with the precision of eyewitnesses.[53] Even when gathering all mentions of Kedesh under one locale, plotting them on a map (as is frequently done in biblical atlases) remains a highly speculative venture. In plotting Sisera's escape, much has ridden on where to site the "Oak at Bezaanannim" when the Hebrew is nowhere committed to it as a fixed point for Heber's encampment.

In Scripture we hear of many battles, but only occasionally are we given the details to plot them on maps. (With their many maps and assured spotting of places, Bible dictionaries and atlases give false certainty about our knowledge.) The reporting in Judg 4 is minimalist even by minimal standards. We are told that Baraq moved from his hometown of Kedesh to Mount Tabor. (Ps 83:11 [10 RSV] places it incongruously at Endor.) We read that, hearing about it, Sisera sets forth to the Kishon wadi, surely not quite the necessary direction were his chariotry to meet Baraq's troops on an open field below Mount Tabor. But this is exactly where God had planned to send him, and so we may need to assign Sisera's bizarre strategy to the divine action hidden behind the verbal form *vayyāhom* in 4:15. As it is, this *vayyāhom* is the only guide we have to the prosecution of the battle itself, and the panic that overcame Sisera's troops was less because, sheltered behind chariots, they saw Israel charging against them than because God made them predisposed to panic. That tribesmen from Naphtali and Zebulun just by themselves could achieve such a stunning reversal only reverts to God's glory. Narrators deemed this achievement so crucial that they avoid detailing how King Jabin, head of an impressive Canaanite coalition and nicely protected within Hazor's formidable walls, nevertheless loses control of the land God had once turned over to him.

JAEL (AND DEBORAH) TRANSFIGURED

Judges 4:17–21 tells about Jael and Sisera, with a coda (4:22) that brings Baraq back into the scene. We shall come back to another reading of the events in chapter 5. That Judges was edited to set Sisera's assassination just after Eglon's strongly suggests that Hebrew lore found comfort in the murder of tyrants.[54] There are differences, of course: Ehud and Eglon are both direct representatives of opponents, respectively representing Israel and Moab. Jael is not of Israel, and her motivation for murdering Sisera can be endlessly debated: Was she a Hebrew married to a Kenite? Was she displeased by her husband's abandonment of ties Jethro forged with Israel (rabbinic lore had Jael a descendant of Jethro)? Did she murder Sisera to stave off retaliation? Yet, Jael remains an outsider while Sisera's connections with Canaan are never made explicit.[55]

The scene is remarkable for its dense exposure of human senses—seeing, hearing, tasting, touching—and for its rolling display of emotions, from pride to contempt, from fear to hope, from anxiety to confidence. Here I comment on just two matters, both dealing with transfigurations of Jael: one as a seducer or sexual object, the other as a divinity. The first is heavily influenced by the rich language of the account in 5:24–27 (with powerful expansion through 5:29), and the issues those verses raise will be discussed below. This portrayal is by no means a product of our times as it is already promoted in Pseudo-Philo (*LAB* 31), whose libretto seems heavily influenced by the story of Judith and Holofernes: Sisera thinks beautiful Jael is worthy of him; she, on the other hand, has only revenge and the glory of God in her heart.[56] In the Talmud one finds similar notions: Jael's voice seduced Sisera (*bMegillah* 15a), leading him to drink from her breasts (see above). In their moments together, he had multiple occasions for pleasure, none of them shared by Jael (*bYevamot* 103a; *bNazir* 23b). Zakovitch (1981; see also Houston 1997) cites rabbinic material to buttress an accommodating argument that the account in Judg 4 repressed sexuality in favor of nobility of action.[57]

But if we limit the discussion to what is reported about Jael and Sisera's interaction in this chapter, there is nothing to encourage a sexually fraught interpretation.[58] "Turn this way" (repeated twice at 4:18) cannot be taken as the invitation of a harlot even if wisdom literature (an entirely different genre) warns men not to fall for such enticement. Heber is no cuckold that we know about. Covering Sisera (twice) is not done with Jael's body. Hammering a peg into Sisera's head must not be distorted into (a parody of) rape (Yee 1993: 116; more subtly in Alter 1985: 48). Baraq "coming to" Jael only absurdly can be read as yet another overture for a tryst. One may, however, make a case (as I would) that in harking to Jael's encouragement not to fear, in accepting her tent as shelter, and in allowing her to cover him, Sisera is acting as a dependent. The intimation is even more striking after his acceptance of milk and (a second?) tucking, for it is at that point that Sisera gives up the *qui vive* that is drilled into the soldier and, despite seeming assertive, leaves it to Jael to do the protecting. I would therefore agree with the contention of many commentators that the image Jael succeeded in conveying to Sisera in this particular chapter is not that of a concubine or a seducer, but of a mother. It does not help (nor hurt for that matter) that, in concordance with biblical reticence in furnishing descriptive details, we are given no hint of the age difference between Jael and her victim. (See further the Comments on chapter 5.)

RISING TO THE OCCASION

A woman murdering (or causing the death of) an important man is by no means unique to Hebraic lore. Beyond the biblical examples of Jael and Sisera, Delilah and Samson, Judith and Holofernes, and less directly Esther and Haman, we meet with the motif in a number of literatures, among them Hittite and Ugaritic (see Grottanelli 1999: 78–84). Often brought into comparison is the Ugaritic poem "Aqhat," in which the title character is murdered for insulting (among other slights) the goddess Anat. The deed is done by Yatpan, a henchman, and we are told about his potential murder (the text breaks here) by Pughat, Aqhat's sister. Margalit (1995) goes the farthest in connecting this with Judg 4–5, finding such parallels as a setting (alleged) by the Sea of Galilee, shared characteristics between Heber and Yatpan, and murder by trickery. Craigie (1972) links Deborah and Anat by depending on their shared attributes: Both are warriors, lead warriors, have an assistant, dominate battlefields, command the stars, and the like. In a chapter she titles "Submerged Ugaritic Myths in *Judges*," Davidson (2008: 285–52) practically reads Judges as an allegory from Canaan. Taylor (1982) shifts the connection to Jael and Athtart: They are warlike, crush skulls, and are paired with another woman, and the like. Aside from connections that are impressionistic (they are gathered hither and yon with little interest in how they function in their respective narratives), elastic (Deborah and Jael are paired only by contexts), and too easily accommodating (Jael is associated with hunting because "wild goats" are hunted), these comparisons do not address what is at stake in their transmigration into Hebrew contexts. It must also be kept in mind that what we have from Ugarit are poems featuring deities, with the usual relaxed attention to realism that obtains in myths. We might have better reasons to shape parallels with biblical accounts had we troves of narrative prose from there, with accent on the activities of mortals.

Israel has never had a problem with incorporating Canaanite deities as poetic resources (Dagan, Tiroš, Yiṣhar, and Reshep are nicely embedded there). It also had no difficulty attributing to Yahveh control of powers that were owned by Canaanite deities (such as storms, thunder, and lightning). What we read about Elijah notwithstanding—he brought fire from heaven and could run faster than chariots—Israel rarely assigned supernatural feats to ancestors or leaders. So what would Israel gain by such importation of motifs from their neighbors? Craigie (1972) and to a lesser extent Dempster (1978) suggest that by entering Canaanite motifs into its narratives Israel intensified their theological contents. Taylor (1982) implies (not clearly enough for me) that Israel was in fact doing the opposite, I assume by subordinating these memories of deities to Yahveh. I would rather have a more concrete display of Deborah and Jael as avatars of such powerful deities. Do Deborah and Jael ever behave beyond what is possible for humans? Were they ever turned, practically or vestigially, into objects or instruments of worship? Were they ever evoked in later Hebraic traditions to explain other mighty acts of valor?

We need also to ask: What are we actually saying about Israel when we posit such appropriation of figures? That there remains in Israel allegiance to Canaanite deities? That Israel had (latent) longing for Canaanite mythmaking? That Israel was so impoverished culturally that it calqued its heroines from those of others? Or is it that Israel was so patriarchal that when it wished to honor women it had to confiscate paradigms from elsewhere? Such issues need to be addressed before proposed parallels amount to more than evocative gleanings from anthologies of ancient Near Eastern documents.

2. The Poem (Judg 5:1–31)

5   ¹Sang Deborah and Baraq son of Abinoam, on that very day:
　　　²For seizing leadership in Israel,
　　　For people in full devotion,
　　　　　　Bless the LORD!
　　　³Kings, listen! Rulers, be alert!
　　　I—to the LORD, I would sing
　　　　　Would exalt the LORD, god of Israel.

⁴LORD, as you head out from Seir
          March from Edom territory
Earth quakes; heaven itself dissolves;
          Clouds too dissolve into water,
          ⁵Mountains melt, because of the LORD
                    The One of Sinai—
                    Because of the LORD, god of Israel.

⁶In the days of Shamgar son of Anat,
          In the days of Jael,
Trails are unused,
          Wayfarers take twisting trails.
⁷Hamlets vanish in Israel; simply vanish
Till I,ᵃ Deborah, arise
          Arise, a mother in Israel.

⁸As God selects new *leaders*ᵇ
          War is at the gate:
          Shield is hardly seen, or a spear
                    Among forty thousand in Israel.

⁹My heart is with Israel's magistrates.
The devoted among the people
          Do bless the LORD!

¹⁰You who ride gleaming she-asses
You who sit on *woven rugs*ᶜ
And you wayfarers—Proclaim it!
¹¹Through the din of archers,
          Between watering sites,
There, they rehearse the LORD's vindication,
          Vindication for his hamlets in Israel.

Just as the LORD's people march down to the gates,
¹²Up, up, Deborah!
          Up, up and utter a song!

---

a. Or: you.
b. Or: When (*Israel*) selects new gods.
c. Or: at a tribunal; or: on saddles.

Go on, Baraq,
And gather your spoils, Son of Abinoam!
¹³Then a survivor triumphs
      Over the mightiest people.

The LORD triumphs for me,
      Over the warriors.

¹⁴From **Ephraim**, *men* with roots in Amalek;
      After you,ᵈ **Benjamin**, among your kin
From **Machir**, down come the magistrates,
      From **Zebulun**, too, such as hold the scribe's rod.
¹⁵And in **Issachar**, commanders are with Deborah
      As Baraq, so is Issachar
            —Into the valley, sent on foot.
Among the ranks of **Reuben**,
Notables are resolved of heart:
¹⁶Why then would you stay between the folds,
      Listening to the bleating of flocks?ᵉ
Among the ranks of Reuben,
      Notables are searching souls.
¹⁷**Gilead** camps beyond the Jordan
      And **Dan**—why would he dwell on ships?
Asher stays by shore of the sea,
      And camps by its wharfs
¹⁸**Zebulun**, a people taunting itself to die,
      Naphtali also, on high terrain.

¹⁹Come the kings, set to fight:
      As Canaan's kings fight,
At Taanach, by the streams of Megiddo,
      No silver in plunder they gain.
²⁰From heaven they attack—
      The stars from their courses, they attack Sisera;
²¹Torrent Kishon sweeps them away
      A primordialᶠ torrent—the Torrent Kishon.

---

d. Or: Behind you, Benjamin.
e. Or: to the piping for the flocks.
f. Or: a raging torrent.

March on, my forceful soul!

²²Just then hammer the hooves of horses
   Through the galloping, galloping of his steeds.

²³Curse Meroz, said the LORD's messenger
   Curse bitterly its inhabitants
Because they came not to the aid of the LORD,
   To the aid of the LORD, among the warriors.

²⁴Blessed among women be Jael
   Wife of Heber the Kenite;
Among women in tents may she be blessed.
²⁵Water he wants, milk she gives
   In a princely beaker she offers soured milk.
²⁶Her hand reaches for the peg,
   Her right, for the workmen's hammer.
She hammers Sisera, crushes his head,
   Smashing, splitting his temple.
²⁷Between her feet he bends, drops, sprawls.
   Between her feet he bends, drops;
   Where he bends, there he drops—crushed.

²⁸Through the window
   She leans and frets, Sisera's mother,
   through the lattice:
Why is his chariotry delayed in coming?
   Why so tardy the rattles of his chariots?
²⁹Her wisest ladies would answer;
   (But she answers herself in reply):
³⁰They must be dividing the spoil they find:
   A breeder or two for a leader,
Spoil of dyed garments for Sisera;
   Spoil of dyed garments, embroidered
   A dyed garment, doubly embroidered,
   Round the necks of spoil.^g

---

g. Or: From the necks of spoil; or (with emendation): For his [Sisera's] neck, as spoil; For my [Sisera's mother] neck as spoil.

[31]So may all your enemies perish, L ORD
But may those loving him be as the sun on its mighty rise!

The land had peace for forty years. ס

NOTES

עורי עורי שיר דברי
כבוד יי עליך נגלה
Up, up, craft a song
The L ORD's glory blankets you
—*From Shelomo Halevy Alkabetz,* Lekha dodi *(1505–1584)*[1]

Introductory Remarks: On Hebrew Poetry

In the AB commentary to Jonah, I opened annotations to Jonah's prayer in the belly of a fish with remarks on Hebrew poetry (1990: 161–67). Because they will serve us well in discussing the glorious poem of Deborah and Baraq, it might be useful to update some notions presented there.

THE NATURE OF HEBREW POETRY

Hebrew does not diverge from other languages in that markedly different rules or conventions control the flow of words in prose and in poetry. The contrast is obvious in the language used to narrate the activities of characters from the one recording their hymns or prayers. Choice of words and verbs can differ sharply between the two modes, but above all also the syntax, that is, the order in which words are arrayed. "Prose" and "poetry" are themselves broad labels, and in the written forms in which they are received from ancient Israel (we can only guess how they differed from their oral manifestations), each category included variants. Thus, legal formulations, cultic prescriptions, and diverse manifestations of wisdom literature are commonly associated with prose, but each has its own rules of composition. The same can be said for the variety of expressions that are normally deemed poetic, and it is still a matter of debate where to place lyrical sentiments that seem to bridge the two major vehicles.

It has often been observed that some of Israel's most distinctive compositions include lines that can be found in other poems.[2] This adaption or adoption of venerable sentiments (themes and motifs as well) to create fresh verses is by no means restricted to Israel. When we locate equivalent inspiration in the literature of Israel's neighbors (Mesopotamia, for example), we find that imageries, idioms, and allusions transported easily from one century to the next. What is admired in this exchange of stimulation is how beloved phrases are recast in new settings by the displacement of words, the manipulation of metaphors, the revitalization of imagery, and the formation of new cadences. Sharp illustrations in the poem attributed to Deborah are imagery of seacoast attached to Zebulon in Gen 49:13 but to Asher in Judg 5:17 and of sheepfold assigned to Issachar in Gen 49:14 but to Reuben in Judg 5:16.

Hebrew poetry rarely achieves the concentration of the composite *cento* (from Greek via Latin *cento*, a "patchwork"), a feature of Jewish prayers and medieval Hebrew poetry resulting from the more or less artful stitching of scriptural phrases. That we do not have more of its manifestation may have to do with the relatively limited amount of poetry that has reached us. This observation does have ramifications: It warns us not to hastily set a date for one poem (or segments thereof) on the basis of similar wordings in another and not to re-create settings for diverse tribes based on evocative descriptions. But it also encourages us to notice how the linkage works and to figure how glues are applied when bonding diverse segments.

POETIC FEATURES

Almost every major biblical reference set and many special studies devote fine pages to Hebrew poetry and how its language differs from that of prose.[3] Suffice it to say that Hebrew specialists have long ago recognized that *parallelism* is the essential ingredient in Hebrew poetry. A line ("colon" or "stich" are other terms for it) is divisible into two segments, and sometimes three or more, each carrying information that may rehearse, diverge from, or supplement the others. (Some of these lines may share a thought or a pattern and so can be grouped into a strophe and the strophes into stanzas.) A change in *language* is conspicuous when poetry is launched, with an increased dependence on refrains, similes, metaphors, and a bravura repertoire in wordplay. Certain *particles* seem to be denser in prose than poetry, and their presence or conspicuous absence is thought to be diagnostic. They include the definite direct object indicator *'et*, the relative pronoun (but also as a conjunction) *'ăšer*, the conjunction *vĕ*, and the definite article *ha(n)-*.[4] Beyond our capacity to assess are the *oral effects* (altering the volume, pitch, and accent of individual words) and the *gestures* that accompanied the production or the recitation of poetry.

Whether or not *meter* regulated poetry continues to be debated, with much discussion (and disagreement) on how to identify where the stress falls and how to count relevant syllables (Watson 1984: 103–11; brief overview in Bechmann 1989: 33–43). A number of fine translations of the Song of Deborah (Burney [1970] and Boling [1975] among them) in fact include syllable counts in their presentations, finding much significance in the patterns such counts produce. But I avoid such a display, first because the vowel system that buttresses our syllabification was created centuries after a consonantal text was fixed. In fact, the Hebrew we read with so much care and admiration may well be an artifice, thus seriously compromising the reliability of any count or measure.[5] Second, a major impulse for determining the metric structure of the song is to permit manipulating its lines into the balanced pattern that was deemed closer to the original. This balancing of lines, once thought to be inherently truer to a poetic spirit, is increasingly doubted as a literary virtue, and there is now much more appreciation of what can be achieved by artful unbalance (see Lindars 1995: 217, who nonetheless counts syllables in his presentation).

THE PRESENTATION OF HEBREW POETRY

Although in ancient Israel writers and their audiences sensed the differences between prosaic and poetic expression, only in exceptional cases did a scribe feel a need to line them up differently, whether on leather, papyrus, or ostraca. At Qumran the layout is prosaic throughout. The Talmud, however, speaks of certain texts presented "in the form of a half brick over a whole brick, and a whole brick over a half brick, with the exception of this one [Esth 9:7–9] and the list of the kings of Canaan [Josh 12:9–25] which are written in the form of a half brick over a half brick and a whole brick over a whole brick" (*bMegillah* 16b). Since then, copies of Hebrew Scripture have but few examples with special layout: the Song at the Sea (Exod 15), the Song of Moses (Deut 32), the Song of Deborah (Judg 5), and one of David's psalms (2 Sam 22; hence also Ps 18).[6] Neither the testaments of Jacob and Moses (Gen 49, Deut 33) nor the oracles of Balaam (Num 23–24) are distinguished from prose. None of the poetry within the Twelve Prophets is presented in a different manner from prose. However, inspired by the study of Hebrew poetry since the nineteenth century, publication of the Hebrew Bible for academic purposes has presented acres of texts in poetic layout. The most recent edition of Judges for the *Biblia Hebraica* series (*BHQ* 7; see Marcos 2011), however, has avoided this excess.

In my translation of Judges, I have not emulated the layout that is found in early codices, if only because they differ from each other. Rather, I have almost always taken the Masoretic punctuation as inspiration. The result is by no means perfect and most certainly not "original," but I trust that the visual effect will not injure the sentiments conveyed by the poem.

THE TRANSLATION OF HEBREW POETRY

While its context is clearly linked to a glorious victory, the contents of the poem break away from servile devotion to what may have transpired. Its sentiments range broadly, its expressions turn hyperbolic, its voice fractures and multiplies, its gaze becomes intimate, its vision cosmic, and its posture judgmental. In shaping lines, the poet calls on a variety of verbal forms, some referring to completed or narrated actions (perfect, imperfect with "conversive" *vav*) and others to actions as they unravel into the future (imperfect, perfect with *vav*). Yet it cannot be said that in this sort of literature the sequencing of time is a critical concern. Everything told has an abiding, transcendent, and timeless quality that must not be compromised by an exact attachment to the verbal forms of the Hebrew.[7] I am therefore opting for the English present to translate "tense" forms that in Hebrew (as well as in most translations) are differentiated by the use of suffix or prefix pronouns. This decision in no ways contravenes Hebrew grammar: The English present works well with the poet's roaming sense of time as long as a solid context or point of view is set.

One more notice: More so than for any other segment of Judges, the literature on the Song of Deborah is vast and is swollen by much citing and trafficking in opinions and interpretation, whether to accept or critique them. I cite much less than I have inspected, as it would be unconscionable to burden the pages more than they already are. Readers will find that many of the authors I do cite have not shirked their bibliographical duties.[8]

The Label

5 1. As laid out in our received Hebrew text, this verse is treated as part of the poem, with ample space separating the mention of the heroes from the timing of their composition. Its main burden is to coordinate the great victory with the crafting of the song. It does so by stressing that the composition occurred "on that day," *bayyôm hahûʾ*. There are better ways for Hebrew to link events, for example by writing [*beʿeṣem*] *hayyôm hazzê*, "this very day," or by letting the particle *ʾāz* (with imperfect) control the coordination; but *bayyôm hahûʾ* does the trick adequately, and the notion is reinforced by its appearance in 4:23, "From that day on, God made Jabin, king of Canaan, submit to the people of Israel."[9] We need not follow, however, the charming conceit of Midrash *Qohelet Rabbah* (3.14) in gathering all events and poetry involving Deborah and Baraq into one day. Ehrlich (1968: 58) seems to know that the song was chanted not at the moment of victory, but at a cultic convocation.

Another way to synchronize victory and praise is to attribute our poem to Deborah and Baraq. (In fact, had they not been cited, their poem could have been read in the book of Joshua!) To remove any doubts about their identity or context, the name of Baraq's father is included.[10] It is useless for us to try to split them, as some have done, by treating the mention of Baraq as a later insertion that was prompted by the mention of his name in 5:12 and 5:15. To insist on doing so might imply that Deborah was once known as the poem's sole author or that scholarship can reconstruct the original ascription. Neither of these positions is easily defensible.

Undoubtedly helping the effort to single out one author is the verbal form *vattāšar*, a feminine singular, meaning "she sang." However, Hebrew does permit a verb to agree with the gender and number of the first subject, even when a string of subjects follows.[11] The word *vattāšar* is based on *šîr*, a verb likely constructed from the noun *šîr* (the category) or *šîrâ* (the individual unit), both referring to a sung, chanted, or declaimed speech. In Hebrew a number of nouns (most especially *mizmôr*, *zāmîr*, and *zimrâ*) similarly refer to musically shaped words, and efforts to establish distinctions among them have not met with success, including mode (a cappella versus instrumental), vehicle (unison versus antiphonal), contexts (secular versus cultic), and contents (diversity of sentiments).[12] We can appreciate the generic quality of *šîr/šîrâ* by noticing that a more specific connotation is achieved by construing it with another noun, for example, *šîr* YHVH, "an ode to the LORD" (Ps 137:4, 2 Chr 29:27); *šîr ṣîyôn*, "a Zion song" (Ps 137:3); *šîr tĕhillâ*, "a song of praise" (Neh 12:46); or the frequent *šîr hammaʿălôt*, "a song of ascent" (likely indicating musical scale rather than a pilgrimage context).

We (but not the ancients) have a problem in labeling what Deborah and Baraq achieved. In the literature, we meet with poem ("a poetic composition of intensity in language and intricacy of presentation"), ode ("a lyric poem, elevated in style and stanzaic in structure, often accompanied by dance"), and song ("a lyric composition, adapted for singing"). Each has merit and will not harm if selected. It will be noticed that in my commentary I do not stick to any one term.

The Invocation

The invocation is tripartite: It invites all to praise of God; it declares the poet's devotion; and it evokes divine manifestation. It includes the first of fourteen references to YHVH, "the LORD," that will be deployed tactically in this poem—the seventh at another call to praise God (5:9) and the fourteenth at the closing of the poem (5:31).

ISRAEL, THE POET, AND GOD

Israel . . .   **5** 2. The poet invites all to "*bārăkû* the LORD." Burney (1970: 105–6) takes this phrase as the title of the poem and regards the clauses preceding it as part of an envelope. However, we meet with the same invitation at 5:9, and it is tempting to imagine that the poet is thereby blocking a chunk of sentiments within these brackets (see below). The verb in this phrase is clear enough; we translate *bārak* (Piel) as "to bless" when it promotes the capacity of something or someone to create well-being. The poet is therefore not urging people to sanctify God or to confer prosperity on him; rather, the poet is summoning all to accept God as the source of blessings.

But who are all those receiving the invitation? Thrice in Ps 103:20–21 we find the same formula although there it opens rather than closes sentiments as in Judg 5:9. In Psalms, the poet adores a God whose love (of nature, of Israel) is bountiful; but to bless God, he calls not on brethren but on supernatural beings, angels, divine hosts, and the entire cosmos.[13] It may be coincidental, but when we meet with a more prosaic (in all senses) version of the formula, one with an explicit direct object marker (*bārăkû ʾet-YHVH*), the subjects are human beings (Ps 134:1, 2; 134:2; 135:19, 20; Neh 9:5). Anyone awed by God, human or supernatural, is invited to celebrate.

But why is God being praised? The Hebrew is ambiguous. When *bĕ-* prefixes an infinitive (as it does here in *bifrōᵘaʿ* and *bĕhitnaddēv*), it acts as a conjunction that confers on a phrase potentially different senses: vaguely temporal, as in "when," "just as"; somewhat causal, as in "because of"; or loosely adversative, so "even if," "though." Hypothetically, God could be praised because of certain accomplishments, at a specific occasion, or even despite some activity that was performed. The Hebrew does not make a choice easy: *bifrōᵘaʿ pĕrāʿôt bĕyiśrāʾēl* is a notorious crux since time immemorial, resulting in diverse translations. The verbal root it invokes, *pāraʿ*, is susceptible to widely divergent meanings, abetted by the temptation to pilfer from Semitic lexicons. The Greek illustrates this predicament: Rahlfs B gives ἀπεκαλύφθη ἀποκάλυμμα ἐν Ισραηλ, "a revelation was revealed in Israel," and depends on the second half of the line to advance the thought, ἐν τῷ ἑκουσιασθῆναι λαόν, "when the people offer themselves willingly." Rahlfs A, however, first offers ἐν τῷ ἄρξασθαι ἀρχηγοὺς ἐν Ισραηλ, "for leaders taking the lead in Israel," and then parallels the thought with ἐν προαιπέσει λαοῦ, "for the commitment of the people." The Targum here goes completely homiletic, expanding the translation to incorporate diverse potential meanings for the Hebrew it had before it.[14]

Recent translations cluster around two proposals. The *TNK* goes with the majority of modern translations (including NEB and NRSV) with "when locks go untrimmed in Israel." The root *pāraʿ*, "to loosen," is said of hair associated with priests (as in Lev 10:6) and Nazirites (Num 6:5), but commentators draw contexts from diverse sources, including Deut 32:42 ("I will make my arrows drunk with blood . . . of the *long-haired*[?] enemy chiefs"), the grooming of warriors in Homer and the Gilgamesh epic, and the vowing of unshorn hair (see Acts 18:18). Brettler (2002: 73) chides this reading as "fashionable."

RSV's "that the leaders took the lead in Israel" is another rendering that is widely adopted, depending on Arabic *faraʿa*, "to excel, surpass (in height)," and on an (allegedly) similar meaning derived from Ugaritic, *prʿ(t)*. A number of contexts (Exod 32:25, Prov 29:18), however, imply a "lack of restraint" and so suggest an undesirable condition. This position is followed in traditional Jewish exegesis, inspiring "when depravity had broken out in Israel" or "when vengeance is inflicted upon Israel," the perception being that praising God is especially necessary in perverse times.[15]

Truth to tell, we are left to our own devices here. The form *pĕrāʿôt* is feminine plural and, if anything, suggests an abstraction (GKC 393 [§1224a]), hence my translation.

But we must also consider whether the succeeding phrase, *behitnaddēv ʿām*, parallels, contrasts, or advances the notion. The Hithpael of *nādav* (*hammitnaddĕvîm bāʿām* in 5:9) evokes an inner striving toward a good cause, and although it comes to us elsewhere exclusively in postexilic cultic contexts, it has to do here with people dedicating themselves to a worthy act, whether for defense or in contribution to a worship. Rabin (1955) senses that it reflects a zeal to answer the call for war. I have adopted a causal reason for praising God. But the above translation is tentative, and readers should feel free to prefer others.[16]

. . . the Poet . . .   **5** 3. The invocation becomes personal as the poet, representing those with a cause to glory in God's triumph (so including Deborah and Baraq), calls on all with power to recognize God's control. The Targum removes ambiguity by expanding, "Deborah said in prophecy before Yʜᴠʜ." Yet, this poem will frequently turn to the first person as a way of dragging in the auditors (and the readers), forcing on them a sense of events observed, hence correctly related (see also at 5:7, 9, 13, and 21). It will also readily give instruction, to characters in the unfolding drama as well as to us (at 5:4, 12, 14, 16–17, and 31), effectively enlarging participation, across time and space. The latter tactic is known from neighboring literature, most famously from the prologues of the Gilgamesh Epic (earliest version from Late Bronze Ugarit), in which the poet instructs listeners on visiting the great city of Uruk.

The (synonymous) paralleling of *šimʿû*, "listen," and *hāʾăzînû*, "heed," occurs often enough, with either verb taking first position. In the most majestic of the pairings, Moses summons the whole cosmos to sing the glory of God (Deut 32:1). Occasionally, *haqšîvû*, "take notice of" (or the like), replaces one of these verbs; but it can also supplement both, as in Isa 28:23, *haʾăzînû vĕšimʿû qôlî haqšîvû vĕšimʿû ʾimrātî*, "Listen carefully to my words, hear attentively my speech." There is frequent parallelism (also in the Phoenician of the Azatiwada inscription) for those summoned: *mĕlākîm*, "kings," and *rōzĕnîm*, "sovereigns." In Prov 8:15, Wisdom claims, "By me, kings reign and *rōzĕnîm* decree what is just." Since in antiquity gods attribute to sovereigns the dispensing of justice, we are dealing with a (more poetic?) term for "kings." Greek uses the plural of σατράπης, "Satrap," a term normally applied to Persian governors. In Rahlfs A, it is also applied to Hebrew *seren*, "lord," of Philistines in the Samson story.

The "suspended pronoun" is a fine stylistic device (see S. R. Driver 1998: 268–69) that exploits the repetition of a pronoun for diverse objectives. In Gen 37:30, it plays on the sound of wailing: Jacob says, *hayyeled ʾênennû vaʾănî ʾānâ ʾănî-vâ*, "the child [Joseph] is gone! Now, where am I to go?" Here, the pronoun places the poet on either side of the only God worthy of tribute. The Masoretes accent the phrase into two distinct, yet unbalanced portions: The first, *ʾānōkî*, "I," is set apart through a major disjunctive accent, and the second is set within a fuller statement, *la-Yʜᴠʜ ʾānōkî ʾašîrâ*. This division is confirmed (contra Lindars 1995: 229) by the parallel clause that likewise ties the verb to God as indirect object. Unfortunately, a literal translation ("as for me, it is to the Lᴏʀᴅ that I would sing") burdens the English where the Hebrew is elegant.

The verbal form (*ʾāšîrâ*) that ends this clause is in the cohortative, invoking a poet compelled to intone his song. The verb that opens the parallel clause (*ʾăzammēr*), however, is a normal imperfect. The two verbs are often coupled in Scripture (for example, Ps 21:13, 57:8, 68:33), so continuing the pattern of pairings we have just met. The invocation ends on claiming for Israel this powerful god. The phrase YHVH 'ĕlōhê yiśrā'ēl is fairly frequent in Scripture, but it is especially significant that its only attestation so far in Judges was when Deborah instructed Baraq on his duties to his land and God (at 4:6). In this book we shall meet it again, but always when there is a need to emphasize divine authority (at 6:8; 11:21, 23; and 21:3).

. . . and God **5** 4–5.[17] The glorious appearance of God covers (in our count) just two verses. Here, the cosmos is in disarray, but it will catch its balance when arraying against Sisera, at 5:20–21. Manifestations of the divine are almost always traumatic to all who witness them. In many cases, they might include disturbances by winds, fire, lightning, and thunder. Humans can scarcely withstand them, fearing (perhaps even welcoming) death at their occurrences (Exod 20:18–21); animals behave incongruously; and nature loses its equilibrium (Ps 29, a parade example). God can appear at any time or place, yet there is a preference for appearances near mountains, most of them to the south of Judah—Sinai, Horeb, Paran—but also at Zion, by Jerusalem. All this is fairly well discussed in the literature and can be accessed in dictionary articles on "Theophany."

There are many circumstances behind God's revelation. When not dispensing laws or instructing leaders, he is most often a warrior battling for Israel. Occasionally, God is also saving individuals (that is, "everyman") in distress (Ps 18:7–20 [6–19 RSV] = 2 Sam 22:7–20). This militarism as an act of divine mercy is evident within the context of the song, but it is clearly set out in parallel sentiments that we find in Ps 68:8–9 (7–8 RSV):

> God, as you move ahead of your people,
> As you stride [bēṣaʿdēkā] through desolation [selâ],
>> Earth quakes; even [ʾaf] heaven dissolves
>> Because of God—The one of Sinai
>> Because of God, god of Israel

Although the two theophanies share language and parallelism, the one in Psalms is tighter. Naturally, it has inspired some commentators to trim ours, ostensibly because of its prolixity, with metric regularity and syllabic count guiding the pruning.[18] Predictably, there are suggestions for the primacy of either (which, is debated) or for the dependence of both on orally delivered sentiments. Because the Psalm version launches evocations of God's guidance of his people toward Zion, there is reason to connect these sentiments with the exodus. There is less reason to do the same here, although some very fine scholars have urged it.[19] The poet is not instructing Israel about its past or covenantal obligations when it had just witnessed a more immediate manifestation of divine power.

The pairing of Seir and Edom is natural, for the two areas are practically synonymous in the Hebrew geographic lexicon (Gen 32:4 [3 in NRSV]; 36:8ff., 21; Num 24:18; Ezek 35:15). They apply to a region below Moab, between the Dead Sea and the Gulf of Aqaba. Why God should stride from this particular region is inconclusively debated, but the issue is of matter only if climatology (storms from the south are powerful) or tradition (Yahwism arose in the South) is at stake. It might be best, however, to focus less on its details than on the poet's conceit that God would force nature into aberrant behavior when Israel's fate was endangered.

Earth contrasts naturally with heaven, but it is also a merismatic allusion, hinting at cosmic totality, as in Gen 1:1. A more earthly parallel follows (missing in Ps 68), with a two-stage liquefaction, of heaven and of clouds, linked by repetition of the same verbal form (*nāṭāfû*) and the connective *gam*.[20] That there is a reversal of creation as preserved in such texts as Gen 1 is plausible, but it must be kept in mind that such a reversal, while chaotic for human beings, is simply another aspect of God's creative acts. Soon (at 5:20–21), the cosmos will be asked to perform another function.

The contrast with mountains and what happens to them (*nāzĕlû*) might likewise be merismatic; more interesting is that the verbs in this pairing easily exchange, as heavens and clouds can *nāzal* (Isa 45:8) while mountains can *nāṭaf* (Joel 4 [3 in NRSV]:18), thus nicely sustaining the sense of topsy-turvy conditions. For this reason alone we should resist a venerable emendation into the Niphal passive *nāzōllû* ("quake"), even if inspired by Isa 63:19 (where it also applies to mountains), by the Greek's ἐσαλεύθησαν, "quaked," as well as by the Targum, *zāʿû*, they "shook."

Whatever is affecting the mountains is happening *mippĕnê* YHVH. In most translations this is given plausibly as "before the LORD" or "in the presence of the LORD." However, what would it mean that "the mountains are melting" (or whatever) "before the LORD"? I think better sense is obtained if we treat the compound preposition as causal, a well-attested usage (see *HALOT* under "*pānê*," 5d), with a nice example of our phrase occurring in Mal 3:14: "You said, 'It is useless to serve God. How did we profit by keeping his charge and by remaining despondent, because of the LORD of Hosts?'"

In both the Judges and the Ps 68 accounts *zê sînay* is sandwiched between two mentions of *mippĕnê* YHVH. Because in Judges there is reference to mountains, traditional exegetes treated it as a deictic phrase, corresponding to Sinai, citing Exod 19:18 where Sinai itself quakes at God's presence. But it cannot be so in Ps 68:9, where, if it parallels anything, it has to be references to God. One treatment depends on the Rahlfs B reading for the phrase, ἀπὸ προσώπου κυρίου Ελωι τοῦτο Σινα, "before the LORD Eloi, this Sinai," to suggest a Hebrew original that did not include the offending particle.[21] In contemporary scholarship, there are those who would simply delete the phrase as a gloss—clean breaks always solve messes.[22] Late in the nineteenth century, Grimme (1896: 573 n. 1) found an analogy with the Nabatean divine name Dhu-shara ("the One of the Mountain") and proposed to connect *zê* with the Arabic demonstrative pronoun *ḏû* (ذو), so "der vom Sinaï," even if it would not explain the consonant *he* in *zê*. Since then, such a particle has found attestations in Amorite (especially in such names as Zu-ḫadnim, Zu-dādi, Zu-baḫli, and Zu-ᵈIšḫara) and Ugaritic materials. In fact, *zê* and *zû* always had the potential of mimicking independent personal pronouns (GKC 446–47 [§138g]). At first dismissed, the suggestion has gained much momentum, especially after it was relaunched by Albright in 1936.

How Things Were

THE CONTEXT

Judge Jael? **5** 6. To open with *bîmê* (+ a name) when establishing a narrative context is rather abrupt; elsewhere we are more likely to find *vayyĕhî bîmê*, for example, at

Gen 14:1, Ruth 1:1, and Esth 1:1 (see also Jer 1:3). By itself, *bîmê* tends to be embedded midsentence, in prose more than in poetry, and it is tempting to imagine us catching the poet in midthought, as if many stories had come before this juncture. Later (at 5:24–27), we will recover a fairly detailed vision of what went on between Sisera and Jael, but Shamgar will disappear from the poet's sight. The poem (and its audience) may have had definite knowledge of what that interval was like; but for us, we must rely on previous chapters to approximate it, raising an issue of intertextual dependence that will be picked up in the Comments. Beyond that concern, are we being guided to the *interval* that separated Shamgar from Jael, however brief it may have been? Or is time not at all at stake? Rather, their juxtaposition may be accenting *activities*—in this case stressing how much may be achieved with instruments of trade rather than of war (Shamgar with an oxgoad; Jael with peg and mallet). Or we might be meeting with a *qal vaḥômer* (from minor to major) argument: If two apparently non-Israelites (or, at most, fringe Israelites) fulfilled divine command, how much more is expected from Hebrews?

However we absorb the lesson of Shamgar and Jael, we must not alter the perception we have had of the two from the previous chapters. In the Notes to 3:31, I stressed that the absence of strong markers about Shamgar makes it unlikely that he was ever considered a judge of Israel. This observation saves us either from having to declare Jael also a judge (as does Rashi, followed by others) or from expunging her mention because she was manifestly not a judge (Moore 1895: 143). Some try to have it both ways by emending her name into *Jabin (Albright 1970: 13), *Ja'ir (see Lindars 1995: 235), or the like. Also at 3:31 is discussed the curious suggestion that Shamgar was an oppressor who found his way into the poem either through faulty logic (Cooke 1913: 57)[23] or because the phrase *bîmê*-[x] allegedly introduces the name of an enemy (as in Gen 14:1; but see 2 Kgs 15:29). This is needless, for as we shall see in the stories from Gideon to Samson, a judge simply guarantees that Israel has a strong champion but not that its enemies are permanently eliminated.

Turmoil   In establishing a context for the rise of Deborah and Baraq, the accent is not on foreign control but on consistent harassment and lack of security. Chaotic social conditions as a theme is consistent in ancient literature, featured most pronouncedly in jeremiads (Mesopotamian as well as Egyptian). The accent is on internecine strife and the absence of cohesion among ethnically identified groups. Harsh occupations by foreign troops may turn Israel to God for respite, and if its people whine loudly enough, he might send them a rescuer; but when instability turns one group against another, order—indeed justice—loses its balance, and a change of heart is necessary before there can be a solution.

The controlling verb is the thrice-repeated *ḥādal*, twice with specific subjects and once with a deplorable condition as an unstated subject. The verb is mostly intransitive, referring to stoppage, of good things (merriment, Isa 24:8) and of bad (sin, Prov 10:19).[24] Here it is controlled by *'orāḥôt*, "trails, paths, roads," often needlessly emended to its more mundane metonymy *'orĕḥôt*, "caravans." (In Akkadian, a road, a caravan, and even a military campaign are called by the same noun, *ḥarrānum*.) In fact, no one emends the same noun when it occurs in the next phrase where the imagery focuses on travelers and is therefore less abstract. The *nĕtîvôt* are also "paths" and "trails," and this meaning may be endorsed by a repeat at 5:10, (*hōlĕkê*) *'al-derek*, "(travelers) on paths."

But if Ugaritic *ntbt* is related to it, we are dealing with a trading station or the like.[25] The people who used them (such as merchants) reached them painfully.[26] The verb *yēlĕkû* is imperfect with a frequentive meaning, such as is found in Deut 1:19 ("we set forth from Horeb and crisscrossed this vast and terrible wilderness"). The trails are twisted, and the poet crafts an onomatopoeic adjective full of croaky sounds, *ʿăqalqallôt*. Elsewhere, in Ps 125:5, a similar phraseology is used, but with a distinctly moral weight, "Those indulging their crookedness [*ʿaqalqallôtām*], the LORD will make them frequent [*yôlîkēm*] evil-doers."[27]

The word *ḥādal* sandwiches another description of conditions. The Masoretes break up the opening clauses by balancing three words (*ḥādĕlû pĕrāzôn bĕyiśrāʾēl*) to one (*ḥādĕllû*; on doubling of the final consonant, see GKC 73 [§20i]). For diverse reasons, many prefer to achieve a balance by shifting *bĕyiśrāʾēl* to the next phrase. Aside from achieving less imaginative poetry, the shift is not supported in the Greek versions where the same lopsided scan is displayed. The problem in this clause, however, is *pĕrāzôn*, which occurs elsewhere only a few verses down (at 5:11, see below); there, it is also attached to *yiśrāʾēl*. Etymologies galore are offered for this word, none particularly compelling. Moreover, it is in the singular when the verb is plural, so many judge it an abstract singular that stands for a concrete plural (Caquot 1986: 53).

How to translate this clause depends on how one senses the poet is moving, and there is no assured solution.[28] The versions were of different opinions. Rahlfs A translates with a Greek word that aurally replayed the Hebrew, ἐξέλιπεν φραζών, "a messenger failed/was lacking" (for reading, see Harlé and Roqueplo 1999: 113). Rahlfs B has ἐξέλιπον δυνατοί, "mighty ones failed/were lacking," likely drawing on Hab 3:14, another crux with God cracking the skull of the enemy's *perez*, conjectured as a "warrior," "horde," or "village." For our passage, some inventive translations are available in the literature, from *TNK*'s "deliverance ceased," which lacks an etymology and is a notion unmatched in Scripture, to Boling's "the warriors grew plump" (1975: 106), based on the Vulgate of 1 Sam 2:5.[29] Safest is to stay with another description of upheavals and accept a traditional "hamlets," "unprotected villages," based on a root it shares with "Perizzites" (on which, see the Notes to Judg 1:4).

ENTER DEBORAH

These deteriorating conditions lasted—we cannot tell how long—*ʿad šă-*, "until . . ." This phrase sharpens the notion of something that needed to end. The use of *šă-* (sometimes also *šĕ-*) has puzzled purists because this particle is most often found in "later Hebrew," as in the Song of Songs, Ecclesiastes (Qohelet), and Ezra. Drastic emendations are proposed to remove it, but there are also (convenient) suggestions: that it be treated as "archaic" (Boling 1975: 109), that it duplicates Ugaritic *š*, or that it is dialectal (North Israel). It might just be best not to judge it as a certain marker for an early dating of the song.

The verbal form to which it is attached (with a euphonic doubling of consonants) is (*šaq)qamtî*. It looks like a nice *first-person* form of the verb "to rise," so in a poetic context yielding "I rise." This is how most traditional translations (the Targum as well) have it, with the "I" referring to Deborah, as in 5:3. But the Greek versions are unanimous in translating it as a *third person*, implying that matters were worsening until Deborah arose. The speculation is that the Greek translator saw a Hebrew **qāmat* without a final "*yôd*" and treated it as one of the rare forms of the feminine perfect with a final *-t* (GKC 120–21 [§44ff.]). In recent days, however, *qamtî* has been translated as *second person* because there are a fair number of such feminine forms that end in *-ty* (GKC 121 [§44h]).[30] Nevertheless, the choice of person remains the audience's, depending on what role the speaker assumes in the dramatization. If Deborah is inserting her own voice here ("I rise, a mother in Israel"), it would be not just to declare her solidarity with Israel's past leaders (see at 5:9) or to take control of subsequent events, but also to appropriate for herself the title "mother in Israel." As we have seen (at 5:2), assuming a first-person voice is one of the poet's many stylistic stratagems.

The title "mother in Israel" is unusual (see Exum 1985). In Hebrew (as elsewhere in the ancient world), a "father" is a person of importance, because he has authority over many (Isa 22:21) or because his advice is heavily sought (Joseph to Pharaoh, Gen 45:8; Job 29:16).[31] I know of no citation in which Hebrew *'ēm* or Akkadian *ummum* is a metonym for an adviser, but they certainly could be. In Hebrew lore, some prophets are called "my father" (2 Kgs 2:12, 13:14) because they were capable counselors; but without that intermediary, it might be a stretch to treat *'ēm* as a marker for a woman prophet (Hackett 1985: 27–28).

If Deborah is herself crafting this title, it would not be out of arrogance (contra *bPesaḥim* 66b), but as a sign of accepting responsibility, as should any mother. But if it were the poet who is addressing Deborah ("You rise, a mother in Israel"), then two calls to Deborah would sandwich "mother in Israel," an honorific title the poet would be bestowing on her.[32] I have kept the first person, but not dogmatically so, keeping in mind that radical shifts in voice, even in the personality of voices, are readily found in Hebrew (as in much other poetry; see Sasson 1990: 164–65).[33] I will soon argue that Deborah as a "mother in Israel" offers a fine balance (contrast?) to the mother of Sisera that will close the poem.

It is generally thought that the phrase "mother in Israel," when said about a woman, is unique to this passage. But it may also occur at 2 Sam 20:19 where heretofore it has been attributed to a town. Joab is in pursuit of Sheba son of Bichri, a Benjaminite who had initiated a revolt against a weakened David. Sheba and his followers took refuge in Abel Beth Maacah, a town north of Israel, and Joab was set to besiege it.

> A wise woman ['*iššâ ḥăkāmâ*; elsewhere said of a woman from Tekoah, 2 Sam 14:2] called from the city's (ramparts), "Hey there, listen. Tell Joab, 'Approach this way and I will talk to you.'" When he approached her, the woman said . . . "People were wont to think long ago that only in Abel can they make inquiry; and so they concluded. Here I am among those seeking peace for Israel when you are seeking to bring death to a city and to a mother in Israel. Why would you consume the LORD's heritage?"[34]

The woman persuades Joab to remove his troops on delivery of Sheba's head. Most commentators assume that *'ēm bĕyiśrā'ēl* is here in apposition to *'îr*, "town," because Scripture speaks of *bānôt*, "daughters," when meaning suburbs and because *'ēm* may mean the same in Phoenician (Tomback 1978: 23).[35] More likely, in my opinion, is that the woman is speaking of herself as a potential victim of Joab, because the Hiphil of *mût* ("to seek the death") is normal with animates as direct object. The woman of Abel may not be the poet Deborah is and she may not have used the subterfuge of Jael in dispatching a potential threat, but there is a bit of each in the portrait the story achieves for her.[36]

5 8. This verse opens on a nice challenge, for the Hebrew of *yivḥar ʾĕlōhîm ḥădāšîm* allows for switches between subjects and objects. Essentially, we meet with three approaches in the literature, nicely laid out in Cooke 1892: 34–36:

1. "He chooses new gods" is one possibility, implying apostasy no matter who is the subject. The Targum follows this line, amplifying homiletically, with the House of Israel worshiping deities "made only recently, and not attracting their parents' attention" (W. Smelik 1995: 435–37). The Greek witnesses have the same notion, albeit not as frontal: "They selected [Rahlfs A: ἡρέτισαν; B: ἐξελέξαντο] new gods": Whether or not their editors saw a plural verbal form (*yivḥarû*) in the text they were translating, they simply multiplied the subject. Many translations have followed suit, sometimes cloaking the act through a passive form, for example, "when new gods were chosen" (RSV). Aside from a cavalier treatment of who is doing the selecting, such translations would set Israel on a collision course with its God, requiring the poet at least to explain how Israel earned divine forgiveness. Jerome (Vulgate) turns the issue around, with "God chose new wars" (*nova bella elegit Dominus*).

2. A second approach is to stay with the above translation but understand *ʾĕlōhîm* not as "gods," but as "judges" on the basis of passages (for example, Exod 21:6; see KJV) in which this word seems to refer to an agent of justice; so "he chooses new judges." This "solution" meets with the same problem we had above of deciding who was subject, whether singular or plural. The effect is that this clause begins the counterattack against Israel's enemies. The problem is that this understanding of *ʾĕlōhîm* as "judges" is questionable, with some scholars taking the phrase literally as vestigial for "gods" (as in figurines of the gods, for oath-taking) and others as ancestral spirits (as figurines or not). At any rate, the usage is confined to the legal material in the Pentateuch.

3. The third approach is to make *ʾĕlōhîm* the subject, so "God selects *ḥădāšîm*." One difficulty is that throughout the poem the God of Israel is Yʜᴠʜ, not Elohim; yet we have already met with its congener, *ʾĕlōhê yiśrāʾēl*, at 5:3. Another problem is that *ḥădāšîm*, "new," is an adjective without the expected noun. It cannot allude to "things," since Hebrew would have used *ḥădāšôt*. In other examples in which *ḥădāšîm* occurs by itself (as in Deut 32:17 and Lam 3:23), however, antecedents were there to suggest meanings. Here, none is obvious, although one might imagine that Deborah or the poet is thinking of new leaders. Despite these shortcomings, I gingerly adopt this approach.

The challenge presented by the opening words is exacerbated by the obscurity of the clause following. It has the following consonants ʾz lḥm š/śʿrym. Proposals galore have been offered, some hardly idiomatic to Hebrew (see the collection in Lindars 1995: 240–41). The Targum goes its own way here, waxing moralistic. The Greek scurries to make sense, with Rahlfs A offering the least complicated reading: Israel chose new gods ὡς ἄρτον κρίθινον, "as (one chooses) barley bread," so reading *leḥem śĕʿōrîm*. Rahlfs B, however, gives τότε ἐπολέμησαν πόλεις ἀρχόντων, "then leaders of cities led fight," tweaking the Hebrew perhaps into *lāḥamû śārê ʿārîm*. There is no easy solution, and at such moments, it is best to stick to the Masoretic version if only to keep faith with what we have rather than what we might prefer to have had. When so, *lḥm* becomes a noun for martial activities, likely dependent on Ps 35:1 where David begs God to "attack my foe," *lĕḥam ʾet-lōḥămāy*. In this case, *š/śʿrym* easily becomes *šĕʿārîm*, "gates," and the phrase speaks of war breaking at the gates of enemies. There is an anticipation of major shifts in fortunes, which is sharpened in this song by frequent use of the *ʾāz* (with imperfect here, but with perfects also at 5:11, 13, 19, and 22). This particle mostly synchronizes action between two events.[37] It is not necessary to make a question out of the clause: "Was there a fighter then in the gates?" (*TNK*).

Forty thousand is an imposing count for people, and it is fairly frequent in the census lists of Num 1, 2, and 26. Joshua 4:13 has this precise number of equipped troops, "parading to war before the LORD," toward the plains of Jericho. (Elsewhere, they parade before the ark [Josh 4:5, 6:7], in scenes evocative of the Red Sea miracle.)[38] Controlling an imperfect in the Niphal (*yērāʾê*), the particle *ʾim* shapes a question with a negative implication: No, never could there be found so many soldiers without defensive shields (*māgēn*) or offensive spears (*rōmaḥ*) because, after all, God is taking over the battle. This couplet is rather straightforward. Nonetheless, it has elicited emendations, none worth documenting; but I might note a curious reading in Rahlfs A, ἐὰν ἴδω σιρομαστῶν, "If I saw (protection) of halberds (among forty thousands)." The poet attributes this observation to Deborah (or to himself), so setting us into the first-person mode that we will meet in the verse following.

Affirmation

5 9. This confession from a poet's (or Deborah's) heart differs from the previous first-person expression. At 5:3, there is exultation in the victory that gives opportunity to sing God's praise. There is also determination to impose this exuberance on us and so to sweep us into the same chant. Here, however, there is a return to sentiments expressed in the opening words (at 5:2), by formulating a personal declaration of solidarity with those called to testify to God's glory. Appropriately, it includes the seventh reference to YHVH. We find devotees both at 5:2 (*hitnaddēv ʿām*) and at 5:9 (*mitnaddĕvîm bāʿām*) as well as invocations to bless God, tempting us to establish a parallel between our *ḥōqĕqê yiśrāʾēl*, "magistrates of Israel" (Greek: τὰ διατεταγμένα, "what was decreed"), and that obtuse phrase of 5:2 *bifrōᵘaʿ pĕrāʿôt bĕyiśrāʾēl*. Good poetry, however, rarely indulges our urge to balance lines.

Inducement to Battle

ONE AND ALL

5 10. The poet crafts a second invocation, ending with the injunction *śîḥû*. Moore (1895: 148) sees "no way to do anything with *śîḥû*," but it is well-attested in contexts in which there is thinking, saying, praising, musing, or even lamenting.[39] The poet addresses three groups, and the question is whether they replicate or complement each other.[40] The first addresses *rōkĕvᵘ ʾătōnôt ṣĕḥōrôt*. As mentioned above (see the Notes to 1:14), female donkeys are easier to maneuver than the male of the species. Since Amorite times, dignitaries are termed "donkey-riders" (*rākib imērī*), although as in Israel (see below at 10:4 and 12:14), the highest levels of power preferred riding mules (*perdum*, Hebrew *pered*), if only because mules are steadier, more robust, and smoother of gait. (On all this, see Michel 2004, with previous bibliography.)[41] The question is how to assess the adjective *ṣĕḥōrôt*. It occurs as a personal name, Zohar (*ṣōḥar*, among them the father of Ephron, Gen 23:8), or modifies "wool" in Ezek 27:18 (taken as a place name by some). In our context, most renderings have either "white," "tawny," or "dark," depending on which Semitic dictionary is consulted. (In Old Assyrian documents, black animals are deemed sturdier.) My translation avoids the color issue, focusing instead on the glistening skin of healthy animals. Rahlfs A has simply "donkeys," and Rahlfs B has "(riding she-asses) at mid-day," presumably reading a *he* rather than *ḥet* (see *ṣāhŏrayim*).

The second category includes *yōšĕvê ʿal-middîn*, "those who sit on [*mdyn*]." The construction, a noun in construct with a prepositional phrase, occurs elsewhere; the difficulty is in the consonantal *mdyn*. Rahlfs A has them sitting ἐπὶ λαμπηνῶν, so on some contraption that elsewhere in Scripture (Num 7:3; 1 Sam 26:5, 7; Isa 66:20) has to do with carts or chariotry (*ʿăgālâ, maʿgāl, ṣāb*). This reading has (too easily) inspired emending our phrase to *yōšĕvê ʿal-ʿăgālôt* (Floyd 1980: 20). Rahlfs B, however, has them sitting ἐπὶ κριτηρίου, "tribunal" (legal), obviously connecting *middîn* with some form of *dîn*, "to judge."[42] Many follow this reading, albeit with diverse explanations for *middîn* (Freedman, in Boling 1975: 110).[43] There is also the possibility of explaining this word from *mad*, a plush garment such as worn by Ehud (see at Judg 3:16); but since it hardly makes sense for people to sit on their garments, we meet with many translations that treat it as a woven material, either a carpet or a fancy saddle (see Ezek 27:20).[44]

The third group includes travelers (*hōlĕkê ʿal-derek*); this seems clear enough, yet the versions differ. Rahlfs A clips this whole phrase, and Rahlfs B clumsily expands into καὶ πορευόμενοι ἐπὶ ὁδοὺς συνέδρων ἐφ' ὁδῷ, "those who travel by the road of those assembled, by the road." My translation supposes that the poet wishes three contrasting groups to propagate far and wide the great events he is about to describe: dignitaries (riders of she-asses), elite (who sit on rich textiles or have places at tribunals), and merchants (who use roads). Those are precisely the folks who are mobile, traveling from one place to another, and so have occasions to spread the gospel. I do not dispute those who offer a different contrast. For example, citing Eccl 10:7, Ehrlich (1968: 54) finds a contrast between rich and poor, possibly implying a topsy-turvy world.

5 11. It must be said outright about this verse: The more detached it is from the received Hebrew or from secure philology, the more appealing is its translation.[45] The Greek versions (but not the Vulgate!) blur the demarcation between vv. 10 and 11 by attaching to v. 11 the call to proclaim the great acts about to unfold (*śîḥû*), and many commentators follow suit.[46] In truth, this shift is entirely plausible, even if we do not expect this verb to be construed with the preposition *min* that opens what we now have in 5:11.[47] We can easily understand *miqqôl* as referring to sound; in fact, a surprising number of verses (mostly in Psalms and Jeremiah) open with it. But what trips us is the word to which it is construed, *mĕḥaṣĕṣîm*. It has elicited multiple etymologies, from *ḥṣṣ/ḥṣh*, to "divide, share," to a denominative of *ḥṣ*, "arrow" (Radaq, "because of the noise slung arrows"). To give the mention of sound a better context, an emendation into *maḥăṣōṣĕrîm* is also commonly adopted, but with diverse meanings: "musicians" (RSV), "harpers" (New American Bible [NAB]), and "cymbals" (Albright 1968: 44, followed by Boling). The phrase that follows *bên maš'abbîm* is less difficult even if the word occurs only here in Scripture. It certainly refers to the instrument, agent, or place of drawing waters. G. Miller (1996b: 2310) is not alone in constructing from it traditions of itinerant female performers.

Despite these uncertainties, a contrast is being set with an event or an act that is occurring "there," *šām*. Here and at Judg 11:40 (where women commemorate Jephthah's daughter), *tannôt* has to do with broadcasting testimony, whether in tales or songs.[48] In this case, recounted are the acts of justice (*ṣidqôt*, feminine plural as abstraction) as only God can bestow (*ṣidqôt YHVH*, Ps 103:6, 1 Sam 12:7, Mic 6:5). Another sense for the same word has to do with achievement and triumph that is wrought by God's righteous deeds. This is clearly charted in such passages as Ps 71:12–23, where a series of verbs about praising, extolling, telling, and chanting (etc.) are attached to repeated references to *ṣĕdāqâ*, along with *tĕhillâ* ("praise"), *tĕšû'â* ("salvific act"), *gĕvûrâ* ("mighty act"), *niflĕ'â* ("wondrous act"), and *gĕdôlâ* ("great act"). In our context, then, *ṣidqôt YHVH* are less about judgments for individuals as about triumphal negotiation of just causes, among them Israel's deliverance. This sentiment is sharpened by clarifying that God's divine acts are duplicated by his "villagers" (see above at 5:7), so the meanest of his supporters.[49]

At this juncture (*'āz*, on which, see at 5:8), God's people march down (*yārĕdû*; always applied to Israel, as at 5:13, 14) to the gates of their enemies. This last clause brings the series of introductory sentiments to a fine conclusion. Yet because it makes linkage with expressions and vocabulary that are echoed at the end of v. 11 (the root *yrd* and the sequence *'am YHVH*), there is also the possibility that the clause is propelling us into the exhortation that will soon follow. By no means should we be lured by arguments to delete it because its words seem superfluous (Cooke 1892: 41; Lindars 1995: 248), for we must always keep in mind that, as far as words and thoughts are concerned, poetry is as often about extravagance as it is about economy.

Deborah and Baraq

5 12–13. The poet brackets his story in foreshadow, from the moment an aroused Deborah crafts her dithyramb to the time Baraq carries away the fruits of victory. All that will be told subsequently lies within this interval. Probably there is also a mocking hint as the poem closes on the spoils Sisera was to bring home. Hyperbolically, Deborah is urged to shake herself from placidity. Interesting is how Rahlfs A (but not B) felt the need to expand the focus on Baraq: "Awake, awake, Debbora! *Arouse myriads among the people!* Awake, awake, speak with a song. *By strengthening*, arise, Barak; *strengthen Barak, Debbora.* Take captive your captives, Son of Abineem."

The call to rise for the occasion (*'ûrî*, when feminine, as here; *'ûrâ*, when masculine) is surprisingly common to the Bible, with the Psalmist once bold enough to address God: "Up [*'ûrâ*]; why must you sleep, LORD? Awaken [*hāqîṣâ*], do not reject us forever" (Ps 44:24 [23 RSV]; Ps 59:5–6 [4–5 RSV]; but see Ps 121:3–4).[50] This language certainly must evoke the Near Eastern ritual services when gods are awakened with prayers at dawn. Somewhat connected (but often in a martial context) are the many occasions when God is told to "rise, move ahead" (*qûmâ*), as in this passage from Num 10:35, "Whenever the ark was set to move, Moses would say, 'Rise, LORD, may your enemy scatter, your foe flee before you.'" Similarly linked to military contexts are the occasions when arms (limbs) (Isa 51:9), Zion (Isa 52:1), or weapons (Zech 13:7) are metonymic for divine power.[51] Isaiah 51:17 gives the two verbs in sequence, "Rouse, rouse yourself; rise, Jerusalem" (*hit'ôrĕrî hit'ôrĕrî qûmî yĕrûšāla'im*).[52]

It is up to us to decide whether the poet is applying divine warrior language to Deborah because in other traditions (chapter 4) she is a judge and, as such, must be there to prompt Israel into combat, or because she was recalled as a prophet and so stands for God. In asking her to utter a song (*dabbĕrî šîr*), it is likely there is a pun on her name, as many have seen.[53] The verb "to sing" normally uses the cognate *šîr* (as in Exod 15:1, Num 21:17), with the lyrics cited as *divrê-šîr* (Ps 137:3). The aging David recites to God the words of a long thanksgiving song (*vayyĕdabbēr . . . ʾet-divrê haššîrâ hazzōʾt*), suggesting that here Deborah is being asked to declaim rather than sing. The phrase *šăvê šĕvî*, "to gather spoils," is fairly well-attested in Scripture, applying to taking away captives, but also any movable object, including animals. Some would have Baraq capturing those who would capture him (so emending to **šôbêkā*), but this is hardly a sentiment for poets and prophets who securely knew that God was on their side.

Unfortunately, the verse that follows is not easily deciphered, and the ancient witnesses are not particularly helpful.[54] A case can be made that it ends the preceding; this is especially true if we make do with the received text. But one can emend the received text to connect it with the roster of tribes that will soon follow. As vocalized, the verbal form that occurs twice, *yĕrad*, looks like a shortened imperfect Piel of *rādâ*, "to achieve dominion" (GKC 188 [§69g]), or the same of *rādad*, "to trample" (so Rashi); either might be acceptable, except that the verbs are not otherwise found in the Piel. Many commentators suggest a slight change in vowels to read it *yārad*, especially since this form occurs just above (at 5:11) where there is the same sequence (but not the same allocation) for *ʿam YHVH*. In fact, the Targum did just that (W. Smelik 1995: 451–52). The word *śārîd* means "survivor" in most attestations, although in later Hebrew it can also mean "remnant" or the like. For some, this notion seems unsuited to the context. They therefore reshuffle or manipulate the consonants to produce a mention of *yśrʾl*, "Israel," as in 5:11.[55] Kaufmann (1962: 137–38) proposes *śrym*, "leaders," and Naʾaman (1990: 424–25) takes it as a place name, "Sarid," a town in Zebulun: "Then down to Sarid he marched down toward the mighty ones." With Caquot (1986: 54–55), he has v. 18 (with its reference to Zebulun) follow immediately. An issue is with whom to associate the first-person voice that occurs in the second half of the verse. There are suggestions to shift the whole to a third person (suggesting Baraq), by emending *lî* to *lô*. The Greek versions are split on this point, giving comfort to (n)either side.

As frequently emended, 5:13 would read, "Then down marched the remnant of the noble; the people of the Lord marched down for him against the mighty" (RSV) and so open the next major block of poetry. Especially because it shares vocabulary of a previous clause that opens on *ʾāz* (see above at v. 11), there is powerful reason to find a repeat of the phrase *ʿam YHVH*. Yet, in my translation I have stayed with traditional Hebrew vocalization and punctuation, making do with the verbal forms as they are. I treat *ʾaddîrîm ʿam* as a superlative phrase even when normally we might expect the first element to be in the construct (GKC 431 [§133g]). (A generation or so ago, I might have explained by conjuring up a "ballast *m*.") I treat the last clause as emanating from the poet who, as in 5:9 above, steps out of his normally descriptive mode to exult in the achievement of his people and his God. I readily admit that, as in many segments of the song, other interpretations are possible.

The Roster of Tribes

The word for "tribe" does not occur in the poem; yet the poet summons a good number of tribes into his song, in this order: Ephraim, Benjamin, Machir, Zebulun, Issachar, Reuben, Gilead, Dan, Asher, Zebulun again, and Naphtali. Missing from the idealized list of tribal eponyms descendent from Jacob/Israel are Simeon, Levi, Judah, and possibly also Gad. Practically every reliable commentator has strong convictions on how or why the roster took this shape, but some suggestions are less credible than others. To retain the duodecimal scheme for land inheritance in tribal lore, in some lists the sons of Joseph (Ephraim and Manasseh) are accorded independent status, thus compensating for the removal of Levi, whose priestly descendants never operated from an independent territory. There will be reason to suppose that Machir and (perhaps less persuasively) Gilead may be surrogates for Manasseh and Gad (see below). This makes Simeon and Judah obvious for their absence, and scholars have not lacked suggestions to explain it, among them: (1) the song did not include southern tribes because it was forged before their integration into the tribal system (Freedman 1980: 147–60), and (2) being a lampoon against some tribes, the song chose not to criticize the future house of Judah (Caquot 1986: 68–70). In some readings (Na'aman 1990) the "historical event" involved only Zebulun and Naphtali, the remaining tribes given placement in it by later poets.

The tribes themselves do not conform to any sequence of tribal lists found in other portions of Scripture (see the Introduction and the Comments). However, Machir (at 5:14) and Gilead (at 5:17), by no means unknown in lore, are nevertheless cited here as if full-fledged tribes. (For Meroz, see below at 5:23.) Zebulun, with Naphtali the only fighters featured in the prose account of chapter 4, is mentioned twice. For many commentators the listing of the tribes either meandered (Caquot 1986: 68) or had no transparent geographic order (see Lemaire 1981: 48). Moreover, the attention paid to some of them (Reuben, for example) seems not compatible in view of the "negative" role assigned them in the victory. A majority of commentators finds a division among those who heartily took up weapons (5:14–15) and those who were, shall we say, less than eager (5:15–17).[56] Block (1999: 232–35) discriminates among "the Volunteers (5:14–15a)," "the Resistors (5:15b–17)," and "the Award Winners" (5:18). These judgments, however, rely much too often on imposing meaning on difficult or elusive language. Quite often it is not possible to establish the poet's position on a tribe's participation or lack of it. I offer a suggestion on the ordering scheme in the Comments below.

Rachel Tribes

EPHRAIM

5 14. The roster emulates administrative accounting by using the preposition *min*, "from," as well as one of its avatars, *minnî* (others are *menî* and *mimmen-*), to imply "soldiers/men from."[57] Two verbless clauses that are linked by *'aḥărêkā*, "behind you" or "after you," give pride of place to Ephraim and Benjamin. A venerable assumption is that the poet has invoked two tribes that supplied Israel with its leaders, but that also had conflict with Amalek. The Targum drives home this lesson, by expanding the equivalent segment into: "From the House of Ephraim came Joshua son of Nun. He was the first to wage war with the House of Amalek [Exod 17:9–13]. After him rose Saul, from the home of Benjamin, killing those from the House of Amalek [1 Sam 15]."[58] There have been suggestions to emend the clause concerning Ephraim, especially to account for the potentially damning association of Ephraim with Amalek, Israel's proscribed enemy. The problem was perceived in antiquity and "solved" in one of the Greek witnesses (Rahlfs A) by turning the consonants behind the noun *šoršām* into a verb, *baʿămāleq* ("in Amalek") into "a valley" (**bāʿēmēq, dropping the consonant *lamed*), and *ʾaḥārêkā*, "after you," into "your brother" (**ʾaḥêkā*, dropping the consonant *rêš*). The wholesale touch-ups yielding this translation are inspired by the Greek, "The people of Ephraim took vengeance on them in the plain of your brother Benjamin."

Modern suggestions to improve on the Hebrew are equally inventive and need not be reviewed or critiqued.[59] Instead, we might first notice that at Isa 5:24, but especially at Hos 9:16, *šoršām* is also attached to Ephraim in hardly flattering circumstances. We might then speculate that by connecting Ephraim to Amalek, the poet is reaching for an amphibolous impression that depends on whether *šōreš* speaks of ancestry or posterity (Caquot 1986: 58): It would recall heroics against a despised foe but also accusations of taint.

BENJAMIN

Sadly, this finessing does not prove helpful when dealing with Benjamin. To begin with, the shift to second person is not easily solved, whether one takes Ephraim or Benjamin as the antecedent.[60] The poet may well have broken out of the immediate context, to address Baraq (Harlé and Roqueplo 1999: 120–21, comment to 5, 14b) or perhaps even a (male) member of the audience. There is a tantalizing repeat in Hos 5:8 of *ʾaḥārêkā binyāmîn*, sarcastically recalling (a vain) call to arms, and it occurs just before Ephraim (at 5:9) is likewise shown to be impotent against divine judgment.[61]

What to do with this observation is another matter. The NEB supplies a verb to reinforce it as a quotation ("Crying, 'With you, Benjamin! Your clansmen are here'"); Caquot (1986: 59; followed by Naʾaman 1990: 426) reconstructs a Benjamin attack against Ephraim but considers the whole as an interpolation; Tournay (1996: 203) sets it as a time limit (*terminus ad quem*) for the composition of the song. Naʾaman (2009) and Rendsburg and Schniedewind (2010: 196–98) think our passage establishes cultural and social linkages between Ephraim and Benjamin.

MACHIR

The Hebrew of the next phrase, *minnî mākîr yārědû měḥōqěqîm*, is far from obscure, if only because it contains a verb (*yārědû*, "they came down, descended") and a subject (*měḥōqěqîm*) that nicely connect elsewhere with makers of laws or setters of decrees. Machir, however, puzzles: It cannot but refer to the powerful Manasseh subtribe, the portion that settled Gilead (Num 32:39–40) but whose precise territory cannot be easily fixed.[62] For example, Lemaire (1981: 46–57) has it in the Succoth Valley, south of the Jabbok, whereas Seebass (1982) locates it east of the Jordan. But what does its mention communicate about it, and how does the information about its leaders instruct us about Machir's participation in Israel's finest hour? Rahlfs B must have similarly puzzled over the implication, offering its own solution: ἐν ἐμοὶ Μαχιρ κατέβησαν ἐξερευνῶντες, "the inhabitants of Machir came down with me searching out (the enemy)," presumably reading **měḥōqěrîm* (Harlé and Roqueplo 1999: 121) something like "scouts."

Leah Tribes

ZEBULUN

The same question can be raised about Zebulun. Again, the Hebrew is tolerably clear, *ûmizzĕvûlûn mōšĕkîm bĕšēveṭ sōfēr*: From Zebulun come down (the verb is picked up from the previous clause) those who "bear," "wield," "pull," or "draw out" an instrument. We have already met with the idiom *māšak bĕ-* at 4:6 where Deborah urged Baraq to deploy at Mount Tabor (*lēk ûmāšaktā bĕhar tāvôr*); but the idiom allows for multiple meanings, including the blowing of a shofar (Josh 6:5). The instrument is a *šēveṭ*, a staff or a rod that in Scripture can be used as a symbol of power or rule, a tool in agriculture, a weapon of war, and an implement for school discipline. Only here, alas, is it a tool for a scribe (*sōfēr*).[63] Then again, through metonymy, *šēveṭ* likely stands for a "tribe." Abetted by the versions (Rahlfs A is particularly deviant), commentators have been resourceful: Some delete the last word (so nothing about scribes), others remove the last two words (so letting *mōšĕkîm* parallel *mĕḥōqĕqîm*), and still others translate *sōfēr* via diverse Akkadian nouns, for example, *siparrum*, "bronze," or *šapārum*, "to govern."

As sketched in Josh 19:10–16, Zebulun's territory abutted on Asher's to the west and with Naphtali's on the north. To the east, it touched on Issachar's land (see below), with Mount Tabor at its edge. To the south of all these tribes sat the large territory of Manasseh (and Machir). It seems possible that what binds these diverse tribes in this verse is not that they participated in the battle against Sisera by sending troops (when others soon to be mentioned did not), but that each one of them had a different contribution to make: Ephraim (and maybe also Benjamin) supplied men (although this is not at all clear), but Machir produced the adjustors, who establish the rules for the division of spoils, and Zebulun contributed the scribal staff that is most necessary in the conduct of war (for taking a census, establishing the roster of troops, recording booties and their divisions, and the like).[64] The preparation is necessary and accents the will of the people, even if the battle is God's to win.

ISSACHAR

5 15. Joshua 19:17–23 places Issachar south of Mount Tabor and west of the Jordan. Landlocked but praised for its fertile land (Gen 49:15), Issachar lay close to Zebulun and Naphtali. It bordered on Manasseh and possibly also on Asher. In Tola, it will eventually produce a judge (see at Judg 10:1). As set by the Masoretes, the first phrase, *vĕśāray bĕyiśśā[s]kār 'im-dĕvôrâ*, should translate, "And my princes are in Issachar, with Deborah." It is possible to defend it by suggesting that the poet has now adopted the voice either of Israel or of God. But even traditional exegetes (Rashi among them) realize that the Masoretes tripped over meeting a plural noun in construct with a prepositional phrase (GKC 242 [§87g]). The Targum certainly avoided a first person when translating, "And the leaders of Issachar obeyed the words of Deborah." However much they strayed from what we now have in Hebrew, the Greek witnesses also avoided a first person here.[65]

Though relatively comprehensible, this phrase and the one immediately following (*vĕyiśśā[s]kār kēn bārāq*) have elicited emendations, among them: to introduce a verb where the sentence is nominal; to alter *'im* ("with") into *'am* ("people"); to remove the phrase (via Rahlfs A); to alter the second mention of Issachar into Baraq (via Rahlfs B) or into Naphtali; and to make a verb out of *kēn* (see Caquot 1986: 61–62; Harlé and Roqueplo 1999: 122–23; and Lindars 1995: 256–57). None of these suggestions is more compelling than making do with what we already have.

What happened to Issachar is that he was "set out"—in, through, or possibly also from—the valley (*bāʿēmeq*), wherever the last was located. "How" this occurred depends on the inflection we place on the preposition prefixed to *raglāy̆v*, "his feet" (behind or via). "For what purpose" depends on the antecedent for "his" (Issachar or Baraq). "By whom" depends on whether the verbal form *šullaḥ* is emended (so maybe by Deborah). The Masoretes, as was their wont whenever they met an (unrecognized) Qal passive, treated the verbal form *šullaḥ* as a Pual, the passive form of the Piel. The idiom occurs also in Job 18:8 where an evildoer "is led by his feet into the net" (*TNK*). All these choices have champions, but in truth we are left to our own devices.

REUBEN

Many commentators think that the notice about Reuben opens a list of tribes that were reluctant to participate in the war. Traditional Jewish exegetes accented the deceit, if not also the cowardice, of a tribe that developed elaborate signals (bleating of the flocks) before committing to the battle. Speaking geographically, to feature Reuben first is eccentric, as this tribe traditionally had territory east of the Jordan and north of the Arnon, sandwiched between Gad and Ammon to the north and Moab to the south (Num 32, Josh 13:15–23). The notice about Reuben begins and ends with (almost) duplicates:

—at 5:15, **b**iflaggôt rĕʾûven gĕdōlîm ḥiqĕqê-lev
—at 5:16, **l**iflaggôt rĕʾûven gĕdōlîm ḥiqĕrê-lev

Naturally, there are opinions to remove one or the other, depending on which statement has the strongest effect (see Caquot 1986: 63 n. 56). Ancient witnesses kept both, likely swayed by the different verbs occurring in each. The only other reference to *pĕlaggôt* is in Job 20:17, where it is balanced by "streams," and one can find translations (ASV among them) that give "watercourse" or the like.[66] The Targum and the Greek, however, speak of "family," or "territorial division," presumably deriving meaning from *pālag* (not in the Qal), "to divide"; and most commentators follow suit, although some needlessly replace one or the other *pĕlaggôt* by a synonym (Floyd 1980: 242). The pun on *ḥiqĕqê-lev* (at 5:15) and *ḥiqĕrê-lev* (at 5:16) is difficult to gauge: Does it establish parallel actions (so taken by the Greek versions, albeit using different words) or rather a contrast (deception versus commitment)? The only attestation of the first formulation occurs in Isa 10:1 where it is strongly accusatory.

It is hard to avoid the mocking tone with which the poet shapes a query. It is certainly rhetorical. Reuben is taunted for staying put (*lammâ yāšavta*) between the *mišpĕtayim*. In the next verse the same interrogative will control Dan's behavior. We cannot be certain what kind of place is designated by this last word, but in Gen 49:14, strong-boned Issachar is said to crouch (*rōvēṣ*) between them. In Ps 68:14 (13 RSV), people recline (*tiškĕvûn*) also between them (*šĕfattāyim*). The image may be about indolence, but this is not clear. The versions are also puzzled. The Targum turns the whole notice about Reuben into a harangue: How could such a tribe simply sit at the borders (*bên tĕḥûmayaʾ*) while its brothers are waging war? Rahlfs A gives up and simply transliterates, "Why do you sit among the *mosfatha'im* [μοσφαθαιμ]."[67] Rahlfs B, however, gives the phrase as μέσον τῆς διγομίας, "between the double-saddles/loads" (of donkeys).

The intent of the next phrase is also ambiguous: Is Reuben, lingering behind, opening his ears only to the bleating of sheep or the whistling of shepherds? Is the tribe deaf to the din of battle that may shape the future of Israel? Or is Reuben so confident in God's victory that it sits the battle out? Again the versions go their own way. Niditch (2008: 74) follows Cross (and also somewhat Halpern) in conveniently neutralizing the issue by dissecting *lāmmâ* into an "emphatic *lamed* extended by -*ma*, known from Ugaritic," and so arrives at "Verily you dwell between the settlement." (Ditto for its occurrence in the verse following.)[68] W. Smelik (1995: 458–60) shows how the Targum may have been inspired by Exod 32:18, translating didactically. The Greek versions stuck to the Hebrew in all but the last word, offering "those who awaken" (Rahlfs A) and "messengers" (Rahlfs B).

Tribes from Concubines

GILEAD (ZILPAH?)

5 17. Unlike the previous names, that of Gilead applies not to a tribe, but to a region, a high plateau between the Yarmuk and Wadi Chesban, with the Jordan on the west—the earliest region to be settled by Israel's Reuben and Gad. Although there is an opinion that Gilead was in fact a tribe (Caquot 1986: 66 n. 65, citing Zobel), the general assumption is that the poet has simply found a substitute for Gad (see the Comments below). Still, it should be mentioned that Gilead was a name born by a son of Machir (so from Manasseh, Num 26:29–30), a name already familiar to us. Furthermore, we must keep in mind that the poet may be taking a final dig at Reuben. We shall soon have more to say about Gilead, the tribe, and about two of its famous sons, Jair and Jephthah.

DAN (BILHAH)

We have already met Dan and learned of its terrible treatment at the hands of Amorites (see at 1:34–35). Not only did the tribe fail to control the area as promised in Josh 19:40–46, but it was pushed into fairly landlocked areas, a sad fate for a once glorious tribe that supplied Israel with its second largest contingent on exit from Egypt (Num 1:39).[69] (Later, at Judg 14 and 18, we will hear more about the exploits of its members.)

For scholars who insist that poetry is grounded in history, the verse about Dan and ships is difficult. What kind of connection could there be between the two? The Hebrew itself is limpid and the grammar is clear (GKC 370 [§117bb]): The question *lāmmâ yāgûr 'oniyôt* is asked about Dan dwelling (as an alien or dependent) by or in ships. Because of Dan's distance from the sea, there is a tendency to fudge: Boling (1975: 112) is among many for whom Dan supplies oarsmen to the Philistines. If this is so, why would Solomon not turn to them when staffing his navy (1 Kgs 9:27)? Moore (1895: 155) thinks the mention of ships is metonymic for Phoenicians, a maritime folk, so the verse is making Dan subservient to them. Yadin (1968) redrafts history by locating Dan at Tell Qasile XII–XI. Amit (2004: 521) analyses *lāmmâ* "as a term of negation with an emphatic *mem*," so Dan is being chided for *not* staying on or in ships. Others analyze it differently or simply eliminate it (Caquot 1986: 67). Segond (1900: 44) finds another meaning for *'onîyôt* via Arabic *waniya* (and the like), so "why does Dan live lazily?" Soggin (1981a: 84) finds support in Ugaritic *'wn*, so "Dan lives in security." And so it goes.

I simply do not know what the poet wants us to learn about Dan and its relationship with ships. I have translated with an optative, fostering ambiguity about the linkage; yet, this would not be the only passage in which poets moved tribes beyond history or geography. In Gen 49:13, Zebulun, elsewhere always landlocked (Josh 19:10–15), is set by the seashore in control of harbors.

ASHER (ZILPAH)

The territory assigned to Asher is choice, nestled between the Mediterranean and Naphtali. But as we have already seen (at 1:31–32), at best Asher seems to have been tolerated by the Canaanites, its control not giving it much access of the seacoast. Nonetheless, the poet continues on a Mediterranean theme, using a lyrical phrase (*lĕḥôf yammîm*, as in Gen 49:13) with which to site Asher by the seashore. The poet, however, seems keener to observe that Asher is camping *'al mifrāṣā^{y}v*. As this last word occurs only here, the versions do not give much guidance. While the Greek stays circumspect (Rahlfs B, "by his outlets," ἐπὶ διεξόδοις αὐτοῦ; Rahlfs A: "by his gorge/channels," ἐπὶ τὰς διακοπὰς αὐτοῦ), the Targum goes its own way, with "they rebuilt the cities of the nations that had destroyed them, and lived in them." The Hebrew suggests something to do with "to divide," *pālag*, but as it does not give a satisfying meaning, many turn to an Arabic word that means "port" or "harbor." Yet, people do not normally camp in such areas, so we simply have to guess.

5 18. Whether or not any of the above statements are admiring or critical of the relevant tribes can be a matter of judgment, but there is general agreement that the following two notices differ in tone from those preceding and so may have differed in authorship. In the Comments below, a matriarchal scheme that obtains in the listing of tribes is presented (Table 5): If we follow it, Naphtali would complete the staggered notices on offspring from Jacob's concubines. As a son of Rachel's servant Bilhah, Naphtali helps establish a nice bracket with Ephraim, Benjamin, and Machir, all three descended from Rachel. From that angle, however, only the first mention of Zebulun would be organic to the scheme, placing him among Leah's sons. It would seem, therefore, that the second mention of Zebulun is purely didactic, possibly rehearsing a tradition that was also known to the prose version (Judg 4) in which these two tribes bore the brunt of the battle.[70]

ZEBULUN (LEAH) (AGAIN)

Zebulun makes another entrance (see at 5:14), but the sentiments here are about warriors who mock death. Elsewhere, people beg for their *nefeš* ("soul," "oneself") to end (*lāmût*), when feeling harassed (Samson, at Judg 16:16) or cruelly tested by the elements (Elijah, at 1 Kgs 19:4; Jonah, at Jonah 4:8). Here the notion is opposite. It is not that Zebulun wants death (in battle) to end it all; rather, it is that death, on meeting Zebulun's courage, had no sting. Soon (at 6:35 and at 1 Chr 12:34 [33 in NRSV]), Zebulun will prove equal to the valor. The message is conveyed through a nice verb, *ḥērēf* (Piel), that deals with taunting and the courage (or chutzpah) that goes with it. The Greek versions seem to have read *meḥārēf*, the *mem* of the 'am duplicating (Harlé and Roqueplo 1999: 125).

The Targum did not find the poet's words about these two tribes praiseful enough, so it enlarged: "Members of the House of Zebulun risked their lives against blaspheming nations. May all those on earth praise them, them and members of the House of Naphtali." It is in fact odd that Baraq's tribe gets just a short statement, itself riding on the back of the previous notice. We have here a verbless clause placing Naphtali *'al měrômê śādê*. The *měrômîm* are heights so lofty that in biblical poetry they could stand for heaven; the *śādê* are spaces as small as a field but as broad as a nation. Further, there is justification to match this phrase with *śědê těrûmōt*, the "bountiful fields" itself invoked to match the "mountains of Gilboa" in David's elegy over the deaths of Saul and Jonathan. Lindars (1995) is of the opinion that this "is the only description of the Israelite action in the battle" (264–65). If so, it would make a fine transition to what follows.

The Battle

The battle, when it finally joins, receives hardly any attention. This is conventional in Near Eastern poetic literature, as for example in the epic battle between Marduk and Tiamat (*Enuma Elish*), where tension and excitement are reserved not to describe combat, but to mount argument for the selection of the hero, Marduk. The same can also be said about Gilgamesh, of epic fame, and his battle against Humbaba. In truth, in battling Israel, the Canaanites never had a chance, for no amount of maneuvering would have saved them from disaster when the God of Israel was pitting against them powers on earth and in heaven.

5 19a and 22. We have yet another sequence of events, guided by the logical pairing of the particle *'āz*, here and at v. 22, for the horses that pound the ground by their galloping can only be those of Canaanite rulers. It is important to note that the repetition of *'āz* promotes an act that turns on itself, so looping perpetually the defeat of Canaanite kings, and more specifically of Sisera. Some Aramaic renderings (cited in W. Smelik 1995: 466) explicitly mention Sisera, "Came the kings who were with Sisera, and waged war," not trusting the reader to backtrack his presence from v. 20, where the same verbal form (*nilḥāmû*) occurs.

For once, the language in this strophe is not difficult, yet we need to decide on how to allocate it. I treat the first clause, "Come the kings, ready to fight" (*bā'û mělākîm nilḥāmû*), as a label for what will ensue, but also as contrast to the just deployed roster of Israelite tribes.[71] The narrative then opens on details of the rout, but it may be forgivable to jump ahead and consider here 5:22, a miraculous verse that plays onomatopoeically on the power of charging horses as they pull powerful engines of war. The Hebrew carries forward the notion of Canaanite kings resolved to battle Israel into submission, freezing their tenacity but also their punishment into eternity. The *'āqēv* of a horse is the fleshy portion just above the hoof, into which snakes can drive their poison (Gen 49:17); but the verb it controls, *hālam*, justifies the rendering "hoof," as it has to do with striking hard, an anvil in Isa 41:7 and soon also Sisera's skull (at 5:26). The intense noise that results from (*min*) the gallop (*daḥărôt*) and (presumably) from the clang of chariotry reminds of Nah 3:2: "Cracking whip, rattling wheel; galloping stallion [*sûs dôḥēr*], bouncing chariot."[72] The duplication of *daḥărôt* multiplies the aural assault but also replicates the rhythmic sound of horses at full gait (Moore 1895: 161). The word *'abbîr* has the pattern for nouns and adjectives displaying intense quality (GKC 234 [§84bff.]) and so applies to proud leaders as well as superb animals (stallions and bulls). The "his" in *'abbîrāyv* anticipates the appearance of Sisera.

In contrast, the versions deliver more prosaic reports, tied to the sequence of events. Their readings are followed by some commentators, traditional and modern, for whom they evoke the destruction of the Canaanite chariotry (Weinfeld 1983b: 124 n. 17). Most versions (LXX, Targum, and Vulgate) have the horses maimed in some way: In Rahlfs A the hocks are cut, whereas in Rahlfs B they are just shackled. They then both opt for a human rather than an animal sense for *'abbîr*; but where Rahlfs B has the combatants hurrying on ("his mighty one eagerly hurried,"), Rahlfs A approximates the Hebrew with αμαδαρωθ δυνατῶν αὐτοῦ, "the *amadaroth* of his powerful ones." (I am not sure I understand the intent.) Some Aramaic manuscripts enlarge in diverse ways, striving to connect with the defeat of Pharaoh (see W. Smelik 1995: 468–69).

The poet comments on human plans that go astray. The kings of Canaan had chosen well their stage for battle, in open country where their chariots could do the expected damage. They anticipated much plunder (*beṣaʿ kesef*, "gains of silver"), but as the poet dryly observes, they reaped none. Taanach (likely Tell Tiʿnik, M.R. 171214) is 8 kilometers from Megiddo (Tell el-Mutesellim, M.R. 167221). Traditions had it that it had been part of Issachar before being swallowed by Manasseh (Josh 17:11–12). But where to locate "the waters of Megiddo" remains under debate (see Gass 2005: 94–95). Following Albright's heavily historicizing conjectures (1936: 27), some commentators connect it with Wadi el-Lajjun, although from v. 21 it is natural to assume that the poet had the Kishon River in mind, or at least one of its tributaries. That the locus of battle differs from where it was placed in the prose account of chapter 4 has led to much discussion, with some (Rainey 1983; Rainey and Notley 2006: 138) simply identifying the area with the Harosheth-haggoyim featured there.

. . . AND IN HEAVEN

5 20–21. What God marshals from heaven is a targeted version of the flood. The cataclysm is universal for none but the Canaanites. The stars that enter the battle are themselves instruments of God (Isa 40:26), yet the Targum avoids any hint that they might act independently by making them markers for heaven where God is in full action: "From heaven war was waged against them from where the stars leave" (see W. Smelik 1995: 466–68). As punctuated by the Masoretes, the imagery staggers as if observed on a rotating sky: From heaven the battle is joined (*nilḥāmû*), the stars themselves not budging from their courses (*mimmĕsillôtām*), yet their wars reach (*nilḥamû*) Sisera. The poet is not indulging our scientific knowledge, and it is futile to speculate whether or not these luminaries quickened the torrents that devastate Sisera's hosts (Lindars 1995: 269; but see already Josephus, *Ant.* 5.205–6).[73] Pointless also is to find in our verse the echo of an eclipse that allegedly brought the stars into broad daylight (Sawyer 1981). Least likely, too, is to find in such sentiments clues for a premonarchic belief in cosmic orbs (Fritz 2011: 241–42). In fact, divine intervention during battles is a theme that is well-known to Israel and its neighbors (Weinfeld 1983b: 124–31), and it is not surprising that later traditions set it during Passover, evoking another clash in which the elements battled Israel's foes (see Feldman 1998: 157–58). This particular imagery also occurs in a fine Akkadian text, as was noticed by Kogan (2005: 735–36). Sargon of Agade enters a mythical land where nature treats him as an enemy: "Sargon had (barely) ventured into the land of Uta-rapaštim (when), as if he were hostile, the forest waged war against him. It set darkness in place of light of the heavens. The sun dimmed, the stars sallied forth against the enemy."[74] This episode shows no continuation in the idea, and we do not know the consequence of Sargon meeting heavenly hosts. So, with Kogan, we might once again reject a linkage between battling stars and flooding rivers. They are simply two separate motifs a poet summoned against Israel's enemies.

We do not read that the "fountains of the great deep burst apart," and we are not told that "the floodgates of heaven broke open" (Gen 7:11). Yet what happened to the Kishon had devastating consequences for the Canaanites. It "swept them away" is our conjectured meaning for *gĕrāfām*, a verbal form occurring just this once, possibly ono-matopoeic (Segond 1900: 48).[75] The unrelenting power of the waters is conveyed by their triple mention: two for the Kishon that sandwich a third, *naḥal qĕdûmîm*, the last promoting yet another uniquely attested word.[76] The Targum and Rahlfs B derive from a well-known root for something old or antique. (It can reflect direction, "eastward," or position, "in front.") Rahlfs A simply treats it as a name, "Torrent Kademim." But many scholars (since Ehrlich 1968: 85) emend into *qiddĕmām*, weakly arguing that we need here a verbal form ("it forestalled them"). But to make this conjecture make sense, they readily lop off *naḥal*. Ahlström (1977) rightly critiques this suggestion but offers a translation that is not buttressed by philology: It is the front of the river, hence its flooding segment.

ENCOURAGEMENT

At the end of 5:21, the poet breaks into personalized sentiments, akin to what is found above at 5:9 and 5:13. The thought consists of three words that have elicited many emendations and interpretations, few of them needing airing here (see Lindars 1995: 270–71 for a survey). With the poet as subject, it may have had a liturgical goal, such as is found at Gen 49:18, "I wait for your deliverance, LORD!" The controlling verb is sometimes understood via Ugaritic, implying dominance. The construction would find parallel in Ps 71:7 ("You [God] are my powerful refuge [*maḥăsî-ʿōz*]"). A number of commentators, however, follow Freedman (cited in Boling 1975: 113) and have the poet exhorting Deborah: "you shall trample the throat of the mighty" (*nefeš* is taken in its primary meaning).

The Curse of Meroz[77]

5 23. With this verse, we are certainly in transition. The battle is over, if in fact any clash that features God could ever be a real war. Yet the verses that follow are no less intrinsic to the fate that overtakes the Canaanites. And so we are compelled to follow the poet until the closing sentiments at 5:31. The sense that there is a shift here is sharpened by the contrast between a cursed Meroz and a blessed Jael.[78] In fact, blessing plays a stylistic role in the song, occurring at 5:2, 5:9, and soon twice at 5:24.

The verse makes it evident that Meroz (Maroz in Rahlfs A) is neither a person nor a tribe; rather, it is a place, since we are told about "its inhabitants" (*yōšĕvêhā*, hardly "its rulers," as sometimes suggested). This in itself is striking since this song has mentioned people, tribes, and rivers, but only one town, Taanach, where the action occurred. In Judges, Israel is recognized through its tribes, and only foreign powers are cited by their cities, even if some of them later are dominated by Israel or acquire new names either through an etiology (see at 2:5) or when occupied by Israel. Traditional Jewish commentators (among them Rashi) took Meroz as a name of a reluctant Hebrew leader (Heber?) or even the name of a star that refused to obey God's order.

Despite suggestions that Meroz may have been a clan (sometimes associated with Manasseh), it may not have formed part of Israel. Alt (1940–41) once proposed it had a treaty with Israel, which it ignored at this time, hence the curse. The curse that a divine messenger launches against Meroz is elaborate as well as specific, suggesting a more critical goal, even if it fully escapes us. But if Meroz is a place, it is otherwise unknown, although Khirbet Marous (M.R. 199271) near Hazor is often suggested for hardly any decent reason beyond on aural proximity of the names.[79] There are many suggestions to emend the consonants into a known place, such as Merom, where Jabin once gathered his allies against Israel (Josh 11:1–6), Madon (Josh 11:1, 12:19), or spellings of these sites from the LXX of Josephus.

The words about Meroz are spoken by a *mal'ak YHVH*, a phrase that occupied us earlier (see the Notes to 2:1). There, I tried to justify a translation "messenger of the Lord" that is neutral as to a human or angelic form. I am following it here because nothing in the text confirms the herald's supernatural nature. (Traditional Jewish exegeses easily identify Deborah or Baraq with this messenger.) Some scholars, however, would remove *mal'ak*, attributing the curse to God himself, because most other references to divine curses emanate directly from God and because the speech seems unmediated (see Lindars 1995: 273). But in poetry, neat transitions are hardly necessary; moreover, to assign the speech directly to God might turn awkward subsequent references to the "aid of the Lord."

What this messenger has to say is impressively resolute, with forms of the verb *'ārar*, "to curse," repeated thrice in a five-word statement, if we judge it to stop before the explanation. Twice we have the imperative (*'ôrû, 'ōrû*; with slightly different vowels), the second time construed with an infinitive absolute (*'ārôr*) to intensify the imprecation. It is up to us to decide whether the explanation that follows is part of the divine message or the poet's justification for that message.[80] I have adopted the former, but it is as reasonable to assume the latter. Yet the consequence of the choice is not trivial. If the explanation is part of the curse, then Meroz is accused of avoiding participation in a holy war, whether as a member of Israel or as its ally. While references to the help that God gives are legion in Scripture, here we are meeting with God needing help (*'ezrâ*). If, however, we assign the clarification to the poet, the argument would be about a just war, when God makes joint cause with Israel. In either case, however, the vocabulary is exceptional. The Targum, ever reluctant to imply divine dependence on human beings, chides Meroz for not coming to "the help of *the people of* the Lord."

The Murder of Sisera

The verses describing the murder of Sisera (5:24–27) and the drama taking place in his palace (5:28–30) are among the finest crafted in Hebrew, but their contents differ in focus. The first set is evocative and emblematic, yet brutal and irreversible. The second is descriptive and metaphoric, yet exudes empathy and is open-ended. A case can be made (as it has at least since Josephus and Pseudo-Philo) that to flesh out for both the circumstances and sequence of events requires importing many details from the prose version of chapter 4: Who was this Sisera, laconically mentioned in the poem earlier (at 5:20)? Who, beyond being the wife of Heber, was Jael? How did Sisera get to be with her? Was Sisera seeking shelter or just asking for water? Where was he and what was he doing when she killed him? How in fact did she accomplish the deed? What were the consequences of the murder?

Yet it must not be simplistically assumed that this reliance on the prose material necessarily establishes the direction of literary dependence. In literature, prose can be distilled into poetry, poetry can be turned into prose, or each can adapt inherited lore for its own purpose. A full appreciation of both versions, however, requires respecting the independence and integrity of each.

JAEL

5 24–25. Nothing in the poem delivers more that the briefest background information on Jael, who enters abruptly, despite mention of her name at 5:6. We learn that she is Heber's wife, that he (and likely also Jael) is a Kenite, and that at least she (if not also he) lived in tents.[81] Yet, while tents play no obvious role in this account (distinctively from the prose account), they will heighten the contrast to palaces with windows where a drama is synchronously unfolding. The main message of the initial line is that Jael deserves praise, the Hebrew itself allowing for slightly distinct renderings. Jael should be blessed, *tĕvōrak*, a conviction that repeats as first and last word of the opening verse, thus framing it. The form is passive (Pual), so inviting all to share the sentiment. As noted above (at 5:1), the verb itself, *bārak*, is more about the subject becoming the source of benefits than a vessel for spiritual riches. Jael should be blessed *minnāšîm*, "among women," so a most powerful accolade; but the phrase's construction might allow us to treat *minnāšîm* as a superlative, making Jael more worthy than the matriarchs, who likewise lived in tents. If so, the purpose of the syntactically altered repetition, *minnāšîm bā'ōhel tĕvōrāk*, would be to *limit* the range of the comparison.[82] The mention of *'ōhel*, "tent," does not move us from a martial context, for warriors also used tents (Jer 37:10); but it might sharpen the difference from the palatial surroundings of the woman who gave Sisera life: his own mother.

Once Jael is introduced, the poet concentrates on just two crystallizing vignettes: her hospitality and her murderous act, the last expanding to deliver the consequence. The disparity between what Sisera requested and what she gave (*ḥālāv*, "milk") must certainly be considered a sign of her generosity (see the Notes to 4:19–20). What exactly is the *ḥem'â* that she gave him is difficult to tell from Hebrew contexts, the more so when we search for its meaning via Semitic lexicography (as in Akkadian *ḥimētum*, likely "ghee"). The term may apply to a variety of soft dairy products: It comes from cattle rather than sheep (Deut 32:14), and it is extracted from milk (Prov 30:33). It is eaten rather than drunk, with honey as sweetener (Isa 7:22), so maybe it is buttermilk, sour milk, or *ayran* (a drink made from sheep yoghurt). Unlike the prosaic verb *nātan*, "to give," that is associated with her offer of "milk," with *ḥemʾâ* the poet uses the more ceremonial *hiqrîv*, "to present" (see above at 3:17). That Jael would present it in a beaker or chalice (*sēfel*) of utmost worth (*ʾaddîrîm*, in a superlative construction) tells us more about the quality of the deed than about her wealth. It will soon shock us to learn that Jael is capable of other gestures.

THE DEED

5 26. With no transition, a gracious scene turns murderous. It divides neatly into Jael's intentions and her action. We are free to presume that Jael had always intended to kill, but this would be an inference from the praise the poet heaped on her as well as from importation of a scene from Judg 4. We may posit that Sisera dropped his guard when Jael treated him so nicely, but nothing in the text tells us how he manifested his trust in her. If she was picking up her weapons in his full view, he might have imagined that she needed them to pitch a tent where he might rest as well as hide, but the poet wastes no words on the matter. We have met the tent peg (*yātēd*) at 4:21, but here the Masoretes have created a difficulty by vocalizing the verbal form, *tišlaḥnâ*, into a feminine *plural* for no obvious reasons. (It is difficult for the subject to be an emended "hands.") Many have simply touched up the vowels into a ventive ("energic"), *tišlaḥennâ*, so keeping Jael as the subject (see Cooke 1892: 50; Lindars 1995: 278).[83] Of more consequence is deciphering the category of the other instrument Jael sought. It is natural to imagine it as some sort of mallet (as in 4:21). The Hebrew word *halmût*, with an abstract ending, is unique here although it seems to be based on the root **hlm* that we met earlier (at 5:22), referring to the beating of equine hooves. The sense will be obvious when Jael soon hammers (*hālēmâ*) Sisera. It is not at all clear why the poet chose to qualify this hammer as that of *ʿămēlîm*. The term seems to do with labor (*ʿamal* is the regular Arabic word for "work" or the like), but some think its real meaning is "toil," hence is predictive of the nasty work it will soon do.

However, our real problem is not so much establishing precise meaning for the weapons but deciding on how Jael used them. She needed both hands to wield the tools, and it would require remarkable imagining on our part to have her use them effectively on a standing Sisera, whether frontally or from his back.[84] There are suggestions that Sisera was caught unawares, with his head deep into a curds-filled bowl; he may have been squatting or simply sitting on the ground. Some, importing a scene from chapter 4, have him sleeping.[85] But the poet seems less concerned with choreographing the attack than with displaying its savagery, devoting to it four verbs in a seven-word clause. They do not record a succession of acts but the consequence of one murderous blow (*hālēmâ*), itself playing on the shared consonants in the instrument (*halmût*) she had picked up. The remaining verbs zoom in: Jael crushes (*māḥăqâ*) Sisera's head; she splits (*hālēpâ*) his temple when she strikes (*māḥăṣâ*) it. The verbs themselves might reflect intensification of brutality or escalation of purpose, but their choice was as likely guided by their onomatopoeic or assonantic potential.[86] One verb (*māḥăqâ*) occurs only here and, in fact, may be an Aramaic version of another (*māḥăṣâ*), itself found exclusively in poetic contexts and often with God as the subject and as the target, the head, brows, or loins of a (mythological) enemy.

5 27. The poet takes it for granted that Sisera would not recover from such a mortal wound; nonetheless, there is keen interest in displaying his demise. Three verbs juxtapose without conjunctions, and they cinematically display a body as it crumples to the ground. There is also a repeat of crucial vocabulary, perhaps to "mimic Sisera's death agony" (Alter 1985: 45). The oozing of Sisera's life is told three times through two verbs, *kāraʿ*, "to break at the knee," and *nāfāl*, "to fall." Unlike the prose narrator, who readily puts Sisera out of his misery (at 4:21), for the poet death is too good for Sisera. He remains suspended on the edge of mortality through two verbal forms, the active *šākāv*, "to lie flat on the ground," and the passive *šādûd*, accentuating devastation and destruction that might lead to death.[87]

Much has been written about where Sisera falls. The preposition *bēʸn* describes an interval in time or space, so translating it *bēʸn raglêhā*, "at her feet," as is often done, is not correct. Especially in some recent writing, however, this notice is explored sensationally (see the Comments). What seems to be evoked here is a triumphal stance, one that occurs elsewhere (2 Sam 22:39 = Ps 18:39 [38 RSV]; Ps 47:4 [3 RSV]; Lam 3:34), admittedly with the use of slightly different vocabulary (*taḥat raglayim*).

A Mother's Angst

THE WINDOW

It is not necessary to suppose that the scene about to unfold in 5:28–30 synchronized with Jael's murder of Sisera, but imagining it to be so increases its pathos. Sisera's mother is nameless—not at all unusual in Scripture, as Samson's mother will soon be another example.[88] Yet she is fully identified because by now we have learned much about the Canaanite enemy and the fate of her son. The poet, as was done in 5:20, accentuates her presence by placing her mention in the second clause (Cooke 1913: 51), releasing the information about her in a sharp stagger. We zoom to her in two stages, via the *ḥallôn* first and then the *ʾešnāv*. She stands there, not to view a scene, but to relieve her anxiety. We must not imagine the *ḥallôn* as a "window" in our sense, a glassed aperture that can shut off the outside even as it allows us to view it. Rather, it is a cut (from the root *ḥll*) in the wall that permits access to the outside.[89] Joshua 2:18 suggests the existence of side studs to which ropes could be tied. For protection from the elements and from unwelcome pests, an *ʾešnav* may be installed at such apertures; that these were shutters is plausible, for they can be opened (Gen 8:6, 2 Kgs 13:7).

From a *ḥallôn* people can escape: spies, with the help of Rahab (Josh 2:15), and David, with Michal's assistance (1 Sam 19:12). Most contexts, however, have people leaning (*šāqaf*, Niphal or Hiphil) "at," "through," or "behind" (*baʿad*) it, depending on the context; but it is another verb that specifies the action they take while there.[90] God looks at the earth (*hibbîṭ*) from his holy height (Ps 102:20 [19 RSV]); Abimelech observes (*vayyarʾ*) Isaac fondling his wife (Gen 26:8); Michal watches (*vattēreʾ*) David dancing indecently (2 Sam 6:16, 1 Chr 15:29); "Solomon" sees (*vāʾēreʾ*) an adulteress's prospective victim (Prov 7:7). When Jezebel shouts (*vattōʾmer*) at Zimri from a window, he had her eunuchs fling her from it (*vayyišmēṭûhā*) (2 Kgs 9:30–33).

So Sisera's mother leans through her widow. What she does from it is not clear, hidden by a verb (*vattĕyabbēb*) that occurs only once in Scripture.[91] It must have something do to with uttering a thought or cry, and it is a guess on my part that she is fretting, if only because whining, wailing, or lamenting would not be suitable for her at this stage. The Targum simply has her "saying." What follows, however, is no parody of a lament, but the recounting of a mind grappling with anxiety.

Whether or not the form *bōšēš* (here a Polel) has anything to do with the meaning of "to feel shame" is debated (Rahlfs B, in fact, reads διότι ᾐσχύνθη ἅρμα αὐτοῦ, "It is because his chariot is shamed [or because the feet of his chariots tarry]"). As in Exod 32:1 and likely at Ezra 8:22 (Qal), here it acts as auxiliary to another verb in the infinitive to convey a delay in fulfilling an act. Sisera's mother is anxious, but by itself the adverb *maddûᵘaʿ*, "why?," does not betray the intensity of her apprehension. The poet therefore constructs a mushrooming concern, moving from the general (*rikvô*, "his chariotry") to the specific (*markĕvôtāʸv*, "his [own] chariots"); from the visually distant (they fail to come), to the aurally proximate (the clatter of his chariots). Whether the latter phrase is meant to recall 5:22 is not clear, but the poet's argument here relies on a subtle change in vocabulary as well as on striking personification: hoof beats or the clatter of wheels (*pěʿamîm* in the construct) control a normally human action (*ʾēḥar*, "to tarry, remain behind") (see GKC 171 [§64h]). The Targum, unappreciative of the poet's effort, simply puts new thoughts in the mother's mouth: "Why do the runners who would bring me the letter of victory delay?" (see W. Smelik 1995: 477–78).

LADIES IN WAITING

5 29–30. Sisera's mother is not alone at her window. Like Jezebel, who has eunuchs around her as she waits for her son's murderer (2 Kgs 9:30–33), the mother has attendants close by. Here, her retinue includes *śārôteʸhā*, not her servants, but high-born ladies such as Sisera's kin, sisters and nieces. *taʿăneʸnnâ* is third-person feminine plural of the verb *ʿānâ*, "to answer," that, despite a doubling of the last *nun* (see *tirʾeʸnnâ* in Mic 7:10), is a decent enough verbal form; yet, it does not explain to whom the ladies are answering. Many commentators (including traditional Jewish exegetes) touch it up to make it *taʿănennâ*, "she answers her," forcing a change in the subject either by emendation (*ḥakmat*, "a wise woman among"; see *HALOT*; Lindars 1995: 283–84, 295; *ḥokmat*, "wisdom of") or by appeal to alleged Canaanite forms (Boling 1975: 115). The emendation allows Ehrlich (1968: 87) to connect the wise woman with the *hîʾ*, "she," of the next phrase.

The proposed emendations may not be necessary. The purpose here of *ʾaf-hîʾ*, as in 2 Kgs 2:14 (*ʾaf-hûʾ*), is to be synchronous rather than contrastive or emphatic, the poet thus portraying a woman who, despite her multiple questions and the finest counsel around her, has ears only for her own voice. This is a psychologically perceptive appraisal of behavior during stress, and it is dispensed with the fewest of words. For this reason, we cannot tell whether the crass thoughts we shall soon read are originally those of the "wisest ladies" (hence highly ironic, given Sisera's fate) or of an increasingly distraught mother. In our case, the point may be that advisers would have offered Sisera's mother an (unwelcome) answer, but she was already there with the comforting reaction.[92] The possibility remains, however, that Sisera's mother is attributing her son's delay to the aftermath of war, when armies break up to grab as much booty as they can: an altogether realistic observation, to judge from what took place at the Battle of Qadesh, when Hittite troops preferred massive looting over the destruction of Ramses II's routed armies.

The answer that satisfies Sisera's mother is couched as a question introduced by *hălōʾ*, "Is it not the case that?" It is purely rhetorical and we are forgiven if we couch it as a statement of fact (see above at 4:6, 14). The verbs *maṣaʾ* and *ḥālaq* (Piel) are offered in sequence, but they form one continuous act: Sisera's men divide whatever they find. Both Greek witnesses, however, interpret dynamically: "Will they not find him (Sisera) dividing the spoil?" This is a very nice touch, given the mother's state of mind, but to make the Hebrew conform to its sentiments would require many emendations.

The division of booty is presented as if an extract from an administrative account, with the keyword *šālāl*, "spoils," thrice repeated. The plunder is both human (women) and artifacts (dyed embroideries). The layout of the division is concentric, with Sisera at its center. The word used for the woman is at once empathic and crude, for *reḥem* (here *raḥam*) refers to a woman's womb, from which are constructed verbal forms as well as metaphors to convey pity, compassion, and fecundity but also barrenness and the despair that attends it. In West Semitic,*rḥm* can describe a goddess (Anat) as well as a slave woman (Mesha inscription). In our context, the allusion is to captive women forced to breed slaves for their masters. So there is a need to translate with something more boorish than the usual "damsel." "Wench" (Lindars) might do, but I offer the less refined "breeder." What is interesting is that the Greek translations (both Rahlfs A and B) avoid coarseness, retaining instead a focus on Sisera's magnanimity: Rahlfs B gives οἰκτίρμων οἰκτιρήσει εἰς κεφαλὴν ἀνδρός, "displaying compassion to each person," with a slightly different Rahlfs A. Diverse Aramaic renderings also try for less vulgarity, suggesting the distribution of "a man and his household" (Targum) or a "donkey" (metathesis of *rḥm* into *ḥmwr*).

A *rōʾš geber* obtains the enslaved women. The usual translation, "for each leader/man," is defensible but cannot be confirmed. Rather, as in 1 Chr 24:4 and 26:12, where we meet with *rāʾšê haggĕbārîm*, "group leaders," it may well be that the phrase is paralleling and anticipating the mention of Sisera in the next phrase. If so, attention is directed only to him, as befits a mother's thought. The remaining evocation likewise keeps him in focus: Sisera obtains dyed garments (*ṣĕvāʿîm*, occurring only here; an Aramaism, some say) as spoils. Naturally he picks the best: something colorfully woven or embroidered (*riqmâ*), some perhaps on both sides. The final clause, however, is a problem, as the Hebrew makes difficult sense. The phrase *lĕṣavvĕʾrê* literally means "for (or, possibly, from) the necks of (spoil)." Many suggestions are made, mostly to delete the last word, *šālāl*, or to emend it either into *šōlēl*, "plunderer," or *šēgal*, "queen mother." Changes for the final syllable of *ṣavvāʾr*, "neck," are also proposed, to make it read either *ṣavvāʾrî*, "my neck," with reference to Sisera's mother, or *ṣavvāʾrô*, "his neck," thus continuing the focus on Sisera.[93] The last choice is also made in the Greek versions, but the Targum goes on its own. It speaks of a scarf around Sisera's neck, but ends on Sisera's men plundering whatever they coveted (see W. Smelik 1995: 479–80).

Jubilation

5 31. The poem ends on two sentiments that triumphantly recap those already embedded in it previously:

—At closing, *an invocation* (5:9): My heart is with Israel's magistrates. / The devoted among the people / Do bless the LORD!

—At closing, *a summons to battle* (5:13b): The LORD triumphs for me, / Over the warriors.

—At closing, *a roster of tribes* (5:21): March on, my forceful soul!

—And now, *at Sisera's discomfiture.*

Given this series, it is difficult to agree with opinions that declare these lines as liturgical comments inserted into the poem.[94] The last expression, however, differs sensibly from those in previous verses where the poet (Deborah and Baraq according to 5:1) crafted summons to great deeds. With the mission nicely achieved, we now read exultant words, albeit those that also convey gratitude. God is first addressed directly, with the poet gloating over the defeat of his enemies. There is then a sudden switch to the third person, provoking many fine commentators (Moore, Burney, Lindars) to harmonize all into an address to God (*věʾōhăvêkā*, "and those who love you").[95] Yet such shifts are by no means unknown to Hebrew poetry. Also known is the notion that misjudging God (and his people) leads to the enemy's perdition (Exod 15:6; Ps 68:2–3 [1–2 RSV], 92:10 [9 RSV]).[96]

The second sentiment uses fewer words but is more sophisticated as it assigns those who love God the power and majesty of the rising sun. Undoubtedly, the imagery is taken from cultures in which the sun is a major cosmic agent, rising daily and triumphantly from its struggles with darkness. The sun's *gěvurâ*, "power," is evoked elsewhere (Ps 19:6 [5 RSV]) in what seems to be a simile from an ode to the sun, "like a groom rising from his bridal chamber, exulting like a champion [*gibbôr*] running a course." This may be the reason why fastidious rabbinic literature (*mTeharot* 11:6, cited in W. Smelik 1995: 483) speaks of "sunburst" rather than "sun." The Targum took the occasion to expand homiletically: "All those who hate your people, LORD, should perish like Sisera. But those who love him are bound to shine in the splendor of his glory, three hundred and forty three times more, like the burst of the sun in its might."[97]

It is fitting that the poem ends on this word, as it shares the same root as *gibbôr* of 5:13 and 5:23, both referring to warriors under God's control, and as *geber* of 5:30, in a construction that alludes to Sisera himself. Nonetheless, commentators feel the need to chide such cruel glee: "Why expect knowledge of the Gospels from the author of the Song of Deborah and his contemporary when in our own days . . . people hate their enemies no less than those then?" (Segond 1900: 61).

The interval of peace, forty years, is the same as that due to Othniel's ministry, half as much as that occurring in the days of Ehud, the same as what will happen during the days of Gideon, and twice that occurring during Samson's days. One might note, too, that the number of peaceful years achieved during the rule of mostly "minor" judges (from Abimelech though Abdon) will also be eighty.

COMMENTS

Many comments come to mind at the close of our poem for, aside from indulging in incredibly difficult verses, its text covers much new ground even as it rehearses material seemingly familiar from chapter 4. In the vast literature about it, the issues tend to crystallize around two principal subjects: One has to do with the linkage between materials in chapters 4 and 5, and the other with the literary category to which the poem belongs, an issue having an implication on its dating (see Sasson 2011). In the Notes to individual verses and in the Comments for chapter 4, I have had occasion to address some of these matters. I revisit them here as needed.

The Prose and Poetic Accounts

PRIMACY AND HISTORICITY

Much does not match or compare in the prose of chapter 4 and the poetry of chapter 5, yet it is perfectly proper to speak of "versions," if only because they share protagonists, enemies, events, and the goals of reciting the saving grace of the Hebrew God. Describing discrepancies between them is broadly but also rather mechanically reported in the literature (for example, in Younger 1991, G. Ogden 1994, and Block 1999: 175–86). So as not to multiply the citations, Table 4 presents a list of the most cited differences between the two versions.

The many debates provoked by these discrepancies coalesce around the following judgments:

1. *The accounts are independent of each other.* De Vaux (1978: 789–90) articulates this notion most clearly, although Richter (1963) discussed it earlier. Originally a victory song such as found among nomadic Arabs, the poem was spliced between 4:24 and the prose words of 5:31 ("The land found peace for forty years") with minimal interpolations (such as the mention of Deborah in 5:7–12). In de Vaux's opinion, "This . . . does not necessarily mean that it is any closer to historical reality, because poetry after all modifies reality" (1978: 790). Yet, in calling it a "victory song," de Vaux, as do others (Echols 2008; see below), is imagining its composition to be close to the event. Others have labeled it a "song of thanks" or assign it a place within festal liturgy (Gray 1977, following many others). Wong (2007: 19–22; already in 2006) thinks that the polemical thrust displayed in the poem against reluctant tribes is entirely missing from the prose version, suggesting independence from each other. These, and other arguments for independent origins (Lindars 1995: 168–69), allow for more flexible imagining of the circumstances of production, but they also presume remarkable restraint from scribal interference over the generations. J. Wright (2011) promises an article in which he likewise shows that "in weaving these texts together [in chapters 4 and 5], the authors of Judges fashioned an impressive war monument that not only depicts a diversity of actors but also articulates a national identity that these actors—and the readers—can collectively embrace as their own" (521).

2. *The accounts have a single author* and are presented synchronously to enhance diverse aspects of the same story (Guest 1998, Reis 2005). Although ancient scribes were not averse to collecting diverse versions of the truth in the same library (for example, creation narratives with different exposition of how substances came to be), I am not sure there is precedence for having the same scribe purposely author different versions of a single event.

3. *The accounts complement each other.* Independent of origins (from a common source or not), the versions are juxtaposed in the final redaction of Judges to complement each other (Younger 1991, Amit 1999a). Na'aman (1994b) argues that they are there because the Deuteronomist wished to avoid making a choice. In fact, as said above, ancient scribes were remarkably tolerant of diversity. See also below at 6.

Table 4. Comparing Elements in Judg 4 and 5

	Prose (Judg 4)	Poem (Judg 5)
1. Individuals		
Deborah	—Prophet, wielder of flames, judge (4:4) —"She would sit beneath the 'Palm of Deborah,' between Ramah and Bethel in Mount Ephraim" (4:5)	—A "mother in Israel" (5:7)
Baraq	—From Naphtali (4:6) —Hesitant and argumentative —Loses glory when Jael kills Sisera	—From Issachar? (5:15) —No hesitation reported —Activities hardly mentioned
Jabin	—Rules Canaan from Hazor (4:2) —Elohim humbles Jabin (4:23)	
Jael	—Wife of Heber the Kenite (4:17)	—Wife of Heber the Kenite (5:24)
Sisera	—Commander for Jabin of Hazor (4:2) —Killed in his sleep (4:21), a mallet driving a peg into his temple (4:20–21)	—No attribution (5:26; head of the Canaanite coalition, 5:19) —Killed in standing (?) position (5:25–27), his skull shattered between peg and hammer
Sisera's mother		—Anxiously waiting (5:28–30)
2. Circumstances	—Terror via Sisera's chariotry (4:2–3)	—Deteriorating security (5:6–7)
3. Antagonists	—Jabin, "king of Canaan, ruling from Hazor" (4:2) —Sisera, his army commander (4:2)	—"kings of Canaan" (5:19) —Mention of Sisera (5:20)
4. Tribes	—Two: Naphtali and Zebulon (4:6) —10,000 strong (4:10)	—At least ten, some without fervor
5. War	—Local —Army mustered at Kedesh, attacks from Mount Tabor (4:9ff.)	—National (Israel vs. Canaan) —Battle at Taanach, by the waters of Megiddo (5:19)
6. Victory	—Yhvh flusters the enemy (4:15)	—Stars of heaven battle Sisera (5:20) —The torrent Kishon carries them away (5:21)

4. *The poetry influences the prose.* This is the majority opinion, at least until very recently. While occasionally one meets with comparisons of selected episodes or vocabulary to claim a priority for the poem (Houston 1997, Neef 1994), most of those sharing this view generally grant poetry precedence over prose, often arguing that in its oral form the song likely stored living memory of the event.[98] In setting the two "versions" into a chronological sequence, there is also opportunity to speculate on the development of Hebrew literature. Few schools took this opportunity as seriously as at Harvard where Albright's early setting for the song was nicely stimulated by Albert B. Lord's contributions on orally transmitted poetry, either whole or in fragments. Halpern (1988a: 76–103 = 1983a) gives the most entertaining, if eventually unconvincing, case that the Deuteronomist historian shaped history (the prose) from a lyric celebration (the poem). His proof depends on highly accommodating readings (for example, at v. 18 of the poem, only Zebulun and Naphtali are given combat experience, hence their roles in the prose), interpretations too clever to be plausible (the poem can be said to attribute just five thousand troops per tribe, hence the ten thousand mentioned in the prose), or bravura exegesis (the murder of poetic Sisera is simplified into that of prosaic Sisera). Halpern (1988a) had also written: "Passages shared by Kings and Chronicles . . . are universally thought to come from Kings, because Chronicles is dated later. This is a weak argument: it does not exclude the possibility of a common source" (77). He might have argued the same for the Deborah material.

5. *The prose influences the poetry.* The prose account in Judg 4 begins on a threatening note, progresses though a reversal of the menace, and ends on a note of grace for Israel. In all, it is a complete story that fits nicely into the book that tells history cyclically. The poem, however, is allusive, componental, and undirected. Remarkably, the suggestion that the prose influenced the drafting of the poem is comparatively rarely expressed. When it is, however, a major argument is that the coherence of the song, no less than its place in Judges, might be severely tested without importing information from the prose. Gilead (1988–89) thinks that the song resolves issues left open in the prose, such as the involvement of Issachar's participation in the war.

Each argument in the above perceptions has merit, but they all proceed from the assumption that neither the prose nor the verse of the received versions has lost its pristine shape despite centuries of scribal and editorial manipulation. Such reticence over the centuries would be quite remarkable. Not asked enough are the following questions: What is at stake when an inspiration goes one way or another? Do panegyrists create only on the spur of the moment or at any time they feel so moved? Are narrators more (or less) likely to distort contexts when crafting in prose? Does "earlier" mean "more reliable" whenever we extract historical or cultural information from a document? Whatever direction the crafting of either version took, as noted above, it remains true that without the prose version it is hardly possible to create a cogent script from the poem. In fact, once the names of Deborah and Baraq are excised, the poem could be set in Joshua, reference to Shamgar and Jael notwithstanding. For these and other reasons, gaining in the literature are notions that underplay the role of priority for either version, among them the following suggestions:

6. *Both versions communicate the same chain of events, inherited from a common source or shared memory.* Among writers who favor literary assessment of the Bible, there is much effort to show how the artistry of separate visions or the logic of different media permitted accentuating diverse components of shared traditions. Essentially, this approach is taken, among many others, by Alter (1985: 43–49) and, less effectively, by G. Ogden (1994). The narratives are deemed complementary, saturating characterization, enriching contexts, or sharpening distinctions. Malamat (1971: 137–40) has suggested that the prose focused on the battle while the poem on pursuit. This judgment falters because neither version details the battle or invests many words in describing the pursuit. Younger (1991) is more successful, displaying examples of Near Eastern literature that share contents and contexts but subordinate detail and impression to diversity of purpose. Webb (1987: 138–45) thinks the prose is concerned with mundane events in which individuals triumph against others. The poem assumes knowledge of those mundane events but turns the battle cosmic and the victor divine. Ackroyd (1952) invokes a study of traditions regarding Alfred the Great to suggest that a century passed since the event ("a turning point in the fortunes of the invaders; hence memorable," 161) before memories of it were integrated. The whole says more about the culture that produced it than the society participating in it.

7. *The versions have differing inspirations.* In recent feminist and womanist articulations, the comparison of the two versions has moved from ascertaining priority to discriminating between inspirations: one "male" (the prose) and the other "female" (the poem). Using different geometric metaphors, Brenner (1990, triangles and rhombuses) and Bal (1992: 95–133; see also 1988a, apparently coordinated rectangles) arrive at differing accents for the interrelationship of the two versions. Brenner locates two strata, the first (the prose) accentuating a union of politics and militarism, the second (the poem) emphasizing gender and sexual issues. She characterizes the prose as "male" and the poem as "female," by which she means essential focus without implying gendered authorship. Bal comments encyclopedically (but alas for me, hardly limpidly) about the implications of each interpretive approach current in the discipline (historical, theological, anthropological, literary) before focusing on ethnocentric and phallic readings. The difference between the narrative and the poem is the contrast between voices, that of a male warrior in Judg 4 and of a female rhapsode in Judg 5, touched by satire. A number of other commentators have followed on this characterization, but perhaps with much less daring or imagination (for example, van der Kooij 1996).

My own sympathy is with the judgment that, as far as biblical literature is concerned, priority of inspiration is irrelevant. In Mesopotamian literature, it will matter a lot whether a composition comes from the Old Babylonian or Neo-Babylonian period, because we can integrate the knowledge we extract from it into distinct cultures. With biblical works, at best we can assign individual units before or after the exile, always with the proviso that material from either side of the divide may have been shuffled during centuries of manipulation. All other subdivisions or allocations and the glimpses they offer of their cultural contexts are hardly undisputed.

Moreover, with better knowledge of ancient Near Eastern literature, we recognize that it is the burden of neither poetry nor prose to cultivate *verismo* attachment to events, at least not to the extent that one would search the lines of the other for usable historical testimonial. As we are learning from documentation across the ancient Near East, while royal epics, annals, and monumental inscriptions do provide reflections of reality, reconstructing a dependable thread of events will always depend on quilting details from excavated administrative and epistolary archives, supplemented by archeological testimony.[99] Alas, this program is not yet as available for recovering Israel's past.

MOTHERING SISERA

In reviewing Table 4, one can easily notice how few matches exist between moments detailed in chapters 4 and 5. Among the few is the scene involving Jael and Sisera, at 4:17–21 and 5:24–27. A good amount of commentary on these episodes tries to harmonize among the details, a notable exception (since much duplicated) being Alter's distinction between the "moral and psychological" account and the "emblematic tableau" in the poem (1985: 43–50).

Mothering by Jael   Since antiquity Jael has endured several transfigurations, among them as a seducer or as a sexual object. For first-century Pseudo-Philo (*LAB* 31.7), Jael prefigures Judith to Sisera's Holofernes, an association that continues to be exploited today.[100] Sisera finds her gallant and strives to make her his. Jael, however, is contemptuous and seeks revenge. In rabbinic texts, Jael's seductive voice sharpens Sisera's desire (*bMegillah* 15a). Their encounter is brief, but he drinks the milk of her breasts (inferred in *bNiddah* 55b) and rises to the occasion seven times (*bYevamot* 103a).[101] Jael, however, derives no pleasure from any of them (*bNazir* 23b; for "all the favors of the wicked are evil to the righteous"), which might explain her resolve to murder him. This accent on physical attraction is veiled in the texts themselves, but it is nevertheless heavily featured in modern treatments of the narratives, sometimes edging on the pornographic. Until we get the movie version, however, I suggest hearing the delicious opera by Ildebrando Pizzetti, *Dèbora e Jaéle*, of 1922. In it, Jael and Sisera become lovers. She adores his elevated soul but must kill him during deep intimacy to prevent his capture by a fanatic Deborah and her Hebrew mob (Leneman 2007). Luckily, the prose account is more interesting, on which see the Comments to IIIC1, where I suggest that Jael takes on the role of a mother.

The Schooling(s) of Enkidu   The motif of a woman mothering an adult who is not her own son is also featured in the Old Babylonian (OB) version of the Gilgamesh Epic from the first half of the second millennium BCE. Enkidu, a Tarzan character, mates with Šamkatu, a harlot, who is charged with changing him. Afterwards, clothing Enkidu and holding him by the hand, the woman leads him, childlike, to other human beings where he learns to eat, drink, groom, and dress.[102] By acting as an adult human being, Enkidu becomes one and is now ready to meet Gilgamesh (Pennsylvania Tablet = OB II). In this version, Enkidu's transfiguration is, more than anything else, anthropological, accompanied by the humor in watching awkward behavior.

This focus on Enkidu's move into the human world is the earliest of four we have. Two others from later in the second millennium have equivalent emphasis on the pedagogy of a woman (*ḫarimtu*), but one from the first millennium (Standard Babylonian [SB]) has a sharply different texture (George 2007). On seeing the woman, Enkidu mates with her, "for six days and seven nights," the text says. As in the OB account, there are no breaks or chit-chats; in fact, hardly any human interaction beyond the sexual occurs. The difference is all postcoital. Imagining himself unchanged, Enkidu wants to resume his frolics, but sensing him as different, his animals dart away. Enkidu tries to join them, but his body betrays him. Their rejection tells him what he is no longer. Silently, he sits at the woman's feet and waits to learn what he has become. As told, his journey is solitary, private, intuitive, and psychologically astute.

Likewise is the fate of Sisera in the Song of Deborah. The scene is abruptly set, as if plucked from the ether. There is no direct dialogue, inviting us to exploit the psychology of the moment. The poet is most focused on Jael's murderous act. Here, Sisera's fate is not at all disgraceful. Yes, he had lost his battle—not to mortals, but to stars in heaven and floods on earth.[103] There is no flight, whether by chariot or on foot, and certainly nothing about panic. Rather, we find him accepting Jael's offer of curds in a princely bowl, as befits his dignity. He does not cower, he not hide. He does not lie down, and he does not sleep. When the mortal blow strikes, he takes it standing up, preparing us for the steeper crash (in all senses) that he will soon experience. The language used here is reminiscent not of human combat, but of the savage battles at the end of time, when God dispatches Leviathan (Job 40, Isa 27, Ps 74). Sisera is struck, apparently frontally, and drops. His collapse is conveyed cinematographically, with paired verbs of motion crafting movements as if from diverse perspectives. His body lands between Jael's legs, *bên raglêhā*. In recent writing, this notice is exploited sensationally: Sisera dies as Jael is servicing him sexually, either professionally or as a victim of rape. This is far-fetched, not just because poetry does not demand so trivial a connective, but also because their positions—he standing, she about to crush his skull—would make for a gymnastic coupling.[104] The scene, however, could be of triumph, with the victim at the foot of the victor; but it could also be a portrayal or parody of birthing (Seeman 2004: 19). If so, it might offer an inferred transition to the abrupt change of scene, taking us from the tent of Jael to the palace of Sisera, with his mother on the balcony awaiting the return of her son.

A Mother's Anxiety   In the prose, Sisera is hardly given a biography. We meet him first as a redoubtable warrior with, unfortunately for him, God as his opponent. His end is ignominious: Bloodied and swathed, his body is delivered to his enemies. In the poem, Sisera acquires a nameless mother who can display infinite tenderness toward her son. And there are harem ladies as well who can recall Sisera's capacity to win wars and gain booty. The entire tableau covers two verses only and reads as if from a dirge, yet nothing in it is an "implicit woman's critique of the phenomenon of war which creates heroes but eliminates sons" (Niditch 2005: 284); Sisera's mother would have greeted joyfully the arrival of shackled Hebrews—men, women, and children. We reach her through a *ḥallôn*, a cut in the wall, inviting much incongruous comparison with artifacts showing full-faced women as if framed by a window. These women are said to be prostitutes, which is hardly the case of Sisera's mother.[105] We might find in an Egyptian text a better illustration for the description left to us. In the second monument he devotes to the subject, Pharaoh Kamose of the Seventeenth Dynasty (early sixteenth century BCE) tells us what he saw as he approached an enemy town: "I espied the women of [Hyksos Pharaoh Apophis] upon his roof, peering out of their windows toward the harbor. Their bellies stirred not as they saw me, peeping from their loop-holes upon their walls like the young of *inḫ*-animals in their holes, saying: 'he is swift!'"[106]

In striking contrast with the poem's murder scene, these verses are suffused with the anxiety that Sisera's mother bounces off her ladies-in-waiting. We must not confuse her apprehension with Ninsun's, Gilgamesh's mother, who berates Šamaš for giving her a son with a restless heart (SB GE III: ii), or with Hecuba's, who begs her son Hector not to face Achilles (*Iliad* 22.79–89).[107] Rather, it comes closest to the tragic vision Aeschylus has of Atossa, queen of the Persians and mother of Xerxes, as she awaits news of her son's triumph against the Greeks.[108] Both mothers have sons who provoked God—and pay for it dearly.

Text, Date, Structure, and Scheme

In the many pages of Scripture there is minimal recall of Deborah's powerful ode. A case is made in the literature that vv. 9–10 (8–9 RSV) of Ps 68 were inspired by it, but the direction cannot be substantiated, and it may be that both were drawing on familiar notions. Yet, when Ps 83:10 (9 RSV) cites God's victory against Sisera and Jabin at Wadi Kishon, the juxtaposition of details could only come from the prose version of Judg 4. Josephus practically ignores the poem except when he draws on it expansively to explain the victory at Mount Tabor (*Ant.* 5.205–9).[109]

TEXT

Because too many passages of the poem are obscure (at least a dozen words are unknown elsewhere in the Bible, almost as many as in the entire book of Judges), neither traditional exegesis nor reliance on ancient translations that may have depended on surer originals has adequately improved its comprehension. In modern times, advances in textual analysis and the retrieval of Semitic literature, rich in vocabulary and imagery, have given hopes of shrinking the number of difficult passages. Above all, however, after the recovery of Ugaritic poetry there also came to be confidence that a more pristine version of Deborah's effort is achievable, especially because the gap separating the two efforts was deemed to be comparatively narrow. A good deal of recent scholarship on the poem, therefore, has focused on regaining a version that is closer to a presumed original by having it fit what is regarded as the poetic style of its time. Most often this is accomplished by trimming certain lines or transposing them to achieve balanced syllabification. The efforts are many (an adequate listing is in Lindars 1995: 217–20; Caquot 1986, with bibliography), but they cannot be said to have achieved broad or even mutual acceptance.

In the Introductory Remarks I argued against striving for a better text than what is received and doubted claims that poetry can be dated by its style. Many proposals are simply driven by historicizing arguments, when our control of the historical circumstances is tenuous whether they concern the events or their transfer into a poem. They can, especially in some schools, also be motivated by a desire to set the poem soon after the battle it describes, hence investing both with reciprocal confirmation.[110] In the literature, one even finds a healthy discussion on whether the poem is celebrating one major battle or is composed from a series of skirmishes, no doubt complicating the burden of proof (see Gross 2009: 329–32). Occasionally, one meets with a stunningly precise date for the conflict; for instance, Sawyer (1981) proposes September 30, 1131 BCE. In biblical atlases (Rainey 2006: 136–37), it is possible to find intricately drawn maps with positions of armies and directions of troop movements as if constructed from military dispatches.

DATE

A good many scholars seem content to establish a relative dating for the confection of the poem, setting its production before, at, or after other Hebrew poetry thought to be of deep antiquity, such as Gen 49, Exod 15 (Hauser 1987), and Deut 32.[111] The comparison is occasionally drawn on the poetry of a Canaanite tale (the Ugaritic "Aqhat"; see Margalit 1995) or on the oracles of relatively early prophets such as Hosea (Tournay 1996: 203, 207). More frequently, however, a parallel is made with Assyrian and Egyptian triumphal odes (Craigie 1969), almost always drawn from second-millennium examples (Younger 1991). Some are content with merely shifting down a regnant dating hypothesis, with hardly any discussion of its merits (M. Smith 2009: 55–56). There is a tacit assumption that stylistic (or ideological) resemblance is temporal correspondence. This inference is not warranted. To begin with, none of the materials brought into comparison from Israel's neighbors comes from literary collections, but each is associated with a specific ruler, from whose court it is drawn. In fact, it is equally possible to make similarly profitable matching with verses praising other rulers, some earlier (Zimri-Lim of Mari, eighteenth century BCE) but many later (among them Nebuchadnezzar II of Babylon, sixth century BCE). Even then, the discrepancy between events and their heroic descriptions can be manifest.[112]

In proposing a context and date for the poem, some have drawn comparisons with other incidents from Israel's history. For example, following Mayes (1969), Soggin (1981b) finds similarity with the ark narratives (beginning in 1 Sam 4) and so places the poem at a period when the Philistines and Canaanites were allies. He conjectures that two separate strands were combined between the reigns of Hezekiah and Josiah. For Garbini (1978) the poem is early monarchic, inspired by a theomachy between YHVH and a Philistine god (represented by Sisera). Guillaume (2000) and Neumann (2002) turn to the story of Saul and Ishbaal to flesh out events. Such inferences will not likely do, for they rely on establishing narrative rather than historical conjunctions, when the historicity behind each of the elements is subject to intense debate.

Aside from such attempts at situating the poem historically, in the literature there is hardly much reflection about what kind of benefits could be drawn from securing a date for the song. We expect that setting a piece of literature within a specific interval might promote reciprocal functions: The composition illumines the times and the contexts in which it was crafted while the milieu in which it originated explains the composition's allusions and concerns. The problem we meet when treating the Song of Deborah is that we rely on its verses, imperfectly understood as they are, to fulfill both these functions, with predictably unstable consequences. Beyond allowing us access to literary aesthetics, its verses leave us with many unresolvable issues: Do the contents of the poem give reliable glimpses of the society that produced, performed, or heard it? Or must we import into it such considerations from comparative material? Do we learn from it how a culture evaluates behavior, maintains stability, establishes moral codes, or differentiates itself from the other? Might its words help us unlock a political or ideological charter, a drive to advance the cause of one particular god, group, or individual?

In themselves, successful answers to such questions might go far in satisfying our urge to set a date on any biblical text.

STRUCTURE

A more realistic concern is how to assess the structure of the song. The initial problem is to decide whether or not the poem formed a single unit, at least since it was committed to writing. Given the poem's resistance to full intelligibility, the surprising consensus in recent scholarly literature is that it does, but the reasons given differ. Some fine proposals "prove" its original unity because its components follow a specific narrative, from a call to arms to an achieved victory, or because it displays structural markers, among them refrains, repetitions, and aural plays (Vincent 2000). The intrusion of certain elements or even full verses is seen as not unduly compromising this unity, while the focus on Sisera is deemed paradigmatic and well-suited to the lesson for which the poem was striving. The poetic structure of the poem (with accent on chiastic patterns) is sometimes cited as another proof of the poem's original integrity, although how this structure is displayed differs from author to author. Among recent efforts are Globe (1974), Coogan (1978), Fokkelman (1995), and Auffret (2002), each offering individual arrangements of component units. Unity is also proposed on the basis of thematic concentration. Wong (2007) refers to a series of panels with larger segments. For Blenkinsopp (1961), theophany imposes religious control over the whole.[113] He is among (mostly continental) form critics who place the song within Israel's cultic experience, whether it is invoked at (conjectured) tribal covenant renewal ceremonies or during royal militaristic displays (Tournay 1996: 206–7). One might observe that the issue of unity is often clouded by lack of discrimination between unity that is original to the composition and one that is developed through manipulation of collected material (M. Smith 2009). We may notice here how the fourteen references of the Tetragrammaton—the seventh at 5:9, the fourteenth at 5:31—provided additional undergirding (see the Notes to 5:2–5).

THE MATRIARCHS AS SCHEME

In Judg 5, ten tribes are listed, in an order that is not matched elsewhere in Scripture: Ephraim, Benjamin, Machir, Zebulun, Issachar, Reuben, Gilead, Dan, Asher, Zebulun again, and Naphtali.[114] Machir and Gilead are cited here as if full-fledged tribes. Not surprisingly, some scholars emend the text to reach the traditional twelve, and others trim to seven, a number deemed more significant.[115] Opinions on the sequence differ sharply. Europeans tend to think it is aimless or devoid of useful historical information. Americans, with higher stakes in the poem's historicity, distribute them either by allegiance to Deborah (hence Israel) or geographically. There is virtue in most proposals; but here I examine the tribes' traditionally set ancestry (see Table 5).

In the poem (see column "n" on Table 5), first are mentioned Ephraim, Benjamin, and Machir, descendants of Rachel (indicated by "R" on Table 5), Jacob's adored wife. Ephraim is Joseph's son and Machir his grandson, via Manasseh. Next are mentioned Zebulun, Issachar, and Reuben. They are sons of Leah ("L" on Table 5), although not in the birth order they have in Genesis. There, their names and sequence are cue to the ferocious struggle taking place between the daughters of Laban. The final group of tribes is born to Zilpah ("Z") and Bilhah ("B"), surrogates respectively to Rachel and

Table 5. Tribal Lists by Descent from Matriarchs

	a	b	c	d	e	f	g	h	i	j	k	l	m	n
1st	L_R	L_R	L_R	L_R	L_R	L_R	L_R	L_Y	L_R	L_R	L_R	L_R	L_Y	R_E (J)
2nd	L_S	L_S	L_S	L_S	L_S	L_S	L_S	L_I	L_S	L_S	L_Y	L_S	L_S	R_B
3rd	L_L	L_L	L_L	L_L	L_L	L_Y	Z_G	L_Z	L_Y	Z_G	L_L	L_L	L_L	R_{Mach} (J)
4th	L_Y	L_Y	L_Y	L_Y	L_Y	L_I	L_Y	L_R	L_I	L_Y	R_B	L_Y	R_B	L_Z
5th	B_D	L_I	L_I	L_Z	L_I	R_J (E)	L_I	L_S	R_E (J)	L_I	R_J (E)	L_I	R_J (E)	L_I
6th	B_N	L_Z	L_Z	L_I	L_Z	R_J (M)	L_Z	Z_G	R_B	L_Z	R_J (M)	L_Z	R_J (MI)	L_R
7th	Z_G	R_J	Z_G	B_D	R_B	R_B	R_J (E)	R_J (E)	L_Z	R_M (J)	L_Z	B_D	L_I	Z_{Gil} (G2)
8th	Z_A	R_B	Z_A	Z_G	B_D	B_D	R_J (M)	R_J (M)	R_J (M)	R_E (J)	L_I	R_J	L_Z	B_D
9th	L_I	B_D	R_J	Z_A	B_N	Z_A	R_B	R_B	B_D	R_B	Z_G	R_B	B_N	Z_A
10th	L_Z	B_N	R_B	B_N	Z_G	Z_G	B_D	B_D	Z_A	B_D	B_D	B_N	B_D	$[L_Z]$ B_N
11th	R_J	Z_G	B_D	R_J	Z_A	Z_G	Z_A	Z_A	B_N	Z_A	B_N	Z_G	Z_A	
12th		Z_A	B_N	R_B		B_N	B_N	B_N	Z_G	B_N	Z_A	Z_A	$L_R/Z_G/M_2$	

Notes: 1st–12th indicate position in the list. The letters a–n refer to where the lists appear: a = Gen 29–30; b = Gen 35; c = Gen 46; d = Gen 49; e = Exod 1; f = Num 1:5–16; g = Num 1:20–43+; h = Num 2; i = Num 13; j = Num 26; k = Deut 33+; l = 1 Chr 2; m = 1 Chr 12; n = Judg 5.

Mach indicates Machir; Gil, Gilead.

Matriarchs and tribes are indicated by letters:

    L(eah): Reuben, Simeon, Levi, Judah (Y), Issachar, Zebulun
    R(achel): Joseph (Ephraim/Manasseh), Benjamin
    Z(ilpah): Gad, Asher
    B(ilhah): Dan, Naphtali

Leah. If we leave out the repeat mention of Zebulun, we have Gilead, Dan, Asher, and Naphtali. It is generally assumed that Gilead, which is a place rather than a tribe, is a substitute for Gad. A good hint for the switch is that Gilead occupies the seventh slot in this roster, equivalent to the value of the consonants in the name Gad: *gimel* = 3 and *dalet* = 4.[116] So the names in this last group play leapfrog with ancestry: Zilpah, Bilhah, Zilpah, Bilhah.

As an organizing device, listing tribes by descent from matriarchs is always deliberate. In fact, of about fourteen such lists, all but a handful follow this pattern, even if within these lists the inventory of eponyms does not always follow the birth order as classically laid out in Gen 29–30. However, none of the other rosters begins with Rachel. The investment in motherhood that is particular to the poem raises issues that are not easily solvable. What does it tell us intellectually and culturally about Israel that such an effort is set within a grandly martial context? The combination is certainly unusual: Deborah is touted as "mother in Israel" at 5:7, a vignette on the mother of Sisera opens at 5:28, and in between is a roster of tribes arranged by eponymous mothers (see Bal 1988b: 206–11). Yet the whole cannot be proof, as it is claimed, of gendered authorship. If so, we might assign vast portions of biblical narratives to female authors, since men in crises are rarely presented without saving women. It would be convenient—even attractive—to join a chorus of scholarly voices that attributes to women the creation of victory odes, except that I am not sure anyone knows how to control the criteria for such an attribution. It is certainly not enough to claim that women likely composed odes because biblical lore says that they chanted them and danced to them. Nor is it necessarily logical, in my opinion, that mocking and taunting, which are characteristic of the genre, should be an exclusive domain of women (Steve Cook 2009). Homer and Vergil are full of taunts and mockery, some of which are assigned to women (Hellene), but most are allotted to men (Keith 1924). And if we stay with classical testimony, we might notice that similar categories of panegyrics were composed by men (Pindar, Simonides).

While I doubt that men alone crafted biblical lore, as far as the remarkable role maternity has played in organizing the poem my observations advance a solution that does not appeal to factors outside the poem, but my conclusions nevertheless remain modest. To begin with, the listing underscores the role of northern tribes, not at all a surprise, given the context. The grouping by matriarchs warns us not to interpret their presence historically, geographically, or economically, as has been done. What is implied is that traditions about Jacob, his wives, and the personal tribulations that they experienced were available when the poem was constructed, and their knowledge proved fundamental. Additionally, the arrangement may have been crafted *before* editing had made it conventional to open such series on tribes, perhaps also before traditions on the order of eponymous birth had become fixed. At the least, therefore, these observations might give us a useful angle from which to speculate on the composition, or perhaps better, on the redaction of the poem, if not from the historical or chronological perspectives, certainly from those that are cultural or intellectual.

A Mother for Israel

Pseudo-Philo, the highly nationalistic and inventive author of *Liber antiquitatum biblicarum* who is presumed to be a near contemporary of Josephus, has the most extensive and effusive portrayal of Deborah, assigning to her some of the most moving language invented for biblical characters. In it, Israel is said to lose its sense of ancestry, consorting with Amorite women. God decides to have a woman enlighten them (*LAB* 30.2). On taking charge, Deborah rehearses God's plan for Israel. Sisera dies at the hand of a proselyte (Jael) because he planned to enslave Israelite women (31.1). As his life ebbs away, Sisera recognizes that death has turned the tables on him (31.7). Pseudo-Philo finds a way to assign the Song to Deborah alone (32.19), shifting its contents toward another rehearsal of the past and adding poignant sentiments on matriarchs and the pain they have had in raising their children (32.1–6).

For the past two sections (Judg 4 and 5), Deborah has dominated our attention. It is therefore appropriate to give her final words, as quoted by Pseudo-Philo. After forty years of judging Israel, Deborah tells the people: "I admonish you as a woman of God, and give you light as one of the race of women; obey me now as your mother, and obey my words as mortals who must die" (*LAB* 33.1). Her advice does not differ much from the usual exhortation for leading a god-fearing life; but later, when people beg her to intercede for them from the beyond (33.4), Deborah insists that they must earn their own salvation here on Earth. These are robust sentiments, but not at all inconsistent for a woman who rallies Israel and then finds the right words by which to praise the mighty acts of the Hebrew God.

Gideon

---

1. The Call (Judg 6:1–32)

6 ¹The people of Israel did what was offensive to the Lord, so he abandoned them to Midian for seven years. ²Midian so ruthlessly controlled Israel that, because of Midian, the people of Israel made for themselves *dens* that were in the mountains, so caves and fissures. ³Thus it was that whenever Israel seeded its land, Midian would rise, together with Amalek and Qedem tribesmen, to gang up against it. ⁴Setting up camp opposite them, they would ravage whatever the land was yielding, as far as Gaza, leaving nothing edible in Israel, including sheep, cattle, or donkeys. ⁵They and their livestock would come up, together with their tents, swarming like locusts. They and their camels were beyond reckoning, penetrating the land just to ravage it. ⁶Because of Midian, Israel was brought so low that its people pleaded with the Lord. ס

⁷As Israel was beseeching the Lord on account of Midian, ⁸he sent them a man, a prophet who told them, "This is what the Lord, the God of Israel, says: It is I who brought you out of Egypt, freeing you from a house of bondage. ⁹I delivered you from Egypt and from all those oppressing you. I drove them from before you and gave you their land. ¹⁰I would say to you, 'I am the Lord your God. Do not fear the gods of the Amorites, in whose land you live'; but you would not listen to me." ס

¹¹An angel of the Lord came and sat under the oak at Ophrah belonging to Joash of Abiezer. His son Gideon was then beating out the wheat in a winepress to stash it away from the Midianites. ¹²The angel of the Lord became visible to Gideon and said, "The Lord be with you, warrior." ¹³"Please, sir," Gideon replied, "if the Lord is with us, how could all this be happening to us? Where are

all those marvelous deeds of his that our ancestors related when telling us that the Lord brought us out of Egypt? The Lord has now abandoned us, handing us over to Midian." [14]The Lord faced him and said, "Go in this strength of yours and rescue Israel from Midian's control. I am empowering you." [15]"Please, lord," he said to him, "with what do I rescue Israel? My clan is the weakest in Manasseh, and I am the youngest in my family." [16]The Lord answered him, "I will certainly be with you, and you will trounce Midian as one person." [17]"If you favor me," he replied, "give me a sign that it is to me you speak. [18]Just don't move from here until I come back to set before you the offering I bring out." "I will wait until you return," he replied. [19]When Gideon came *home*, he prepared a young goat and an ephah of unleavened wheat bread. Putting the meat in a basket and its broth in a pot, he presented them to him under the oak tree as he approached. ס [20]The angel of God said to him, "Take the meat and the unleavened bread and set them on the boulder over there, but pour out the broth." He did so. [21]The angel of the Lord extended the tip of the staff he held, touching the meat and the unleavened bread. As fire shot out of the rock, consuming the meat and the bread, the angel of the Lord vanished from his sight. [22]Gideon realized that it was the angel of the Lord, ס and he exclaimed, "Aḥaḥ, Lord Yhvh; inasmuch as I have seen the angel of the Lord face to face!" [23]But to him said the Lord, "Be at peace and do not fear; you will not die." [24]Gideon built there an altar to the Lord, naming it "Lord Peace." (To this day it still stands in Ophrah of Abiezer.) ס

[25]That same night the Lord said to him, "Take the sacrificial ox belonging to your father and, with another that is seven years old, tear down the Baal altar belonging to your father and cut down as well the *asherah* over it. [26]Build a *properly arrayed* altar to the Lord your God at the peak of the fortification, then take the second ox and make a burnt offering with the wood of the *asherah* that you will cut down." [27]So Gideon took ten of his servants and did as the Lord told him. However, fearing his father's household and the townsfolk, he worked at night rather than during the day. [28]In the morning, the townsfolk awoke to a razed altar of Baal, a cut-down *asherah* (that was) over it, and the second ox sacrificed on the newly built altar. [29]They asked each other, "Who did this?" After inquiry and investigation, they concluded, "Gideon son of Joash did it." [30]The townsfolk demanded of Joash, "Bring out your son. He must die, because he has razed Baal's altar and cut down the *asherah* over it." [31]But Joash replied to those standing by him, "Is it for you to plead Baal's cause? Are you trying to save him? Whoever pleads for him shall be put to death by morning! If he is God, let him plead for himself when someone razed his altar." [32]On that very day, he called him Jerubbaal, meaning, "Let Baal rebuke him because he razed his altar." ס

NOTES

I am a poor farmer beating out wheat in his wine press. Suddenly a
black-bearded stranger appears at my elbow and shouts "I am your
God!" Well, I find this all unusual business. I do not hold everyday
traffic with gods.
—*Paddy Chayefsky,* Gideon *(1961), act 1, scene 1*

Introductory Remarks: Testing for Divinity

We have had occasion to review the many ways in which God connects with individuals,
whether directly or in their diverse stages of wakefulness, through instruments (such as
the Urim and Thummim) or via third parties, among them angels and prophets.[1] Given
how often speaking agents are deployed in Scripture, it is useful to inquire whether they
met with skepticism. Here, Hebrew lore divides into two major categories. The first
involves prophets (or the like), who might be termed "false," most often by rivals. The
second includes supernatural beings, normally angels (or even God himself), especially
when their otherworldliness is not immediately recognized. For each, a few comments
are in order.

In the Mari archives, there are many complaints about an enemy's falsehood and
provocations, but from the rich corpus of prophetic and oneiric documents, we do not
read about false prophets or deceitful prophecy. Such charges would be immaterial or
irrelevant, for not only are there multiple sources for any divine message, but truth is
seldom restricted to a single version.[2] Rather, we learn of examinations imposed on the
prophets or dreamers, not to establish their authenticity, but to ascertain whether they
ever had a message to convey. This is done by subjecting clippings from bodily hair and
fringes from outer garments to divination, for inspection of an animal's innards was
judged a superior vehicle for uncovering what has already been fated in the cosmos.
In Hebrew narratives, by contrast, the issue is alive throughout, with prophets playing
major roles in defaming each other; for with only one true God to channel messages,
how could one reverse contradictory formulations of the same instruction without im-
pugning a rival's veracity and motivations?

During the monarchy, rulers inoculated themselves from divine interference by
enlarging the pool of prophets, thus fragmenting a divine message or diluting its gist.
This is the locus for the classic confrontations that, for example, pitted Micaiah against
Zedekiah (1 Kgs 22) or Jeremiah against Hananiah (Jer 27–28). Because even venerated
prophets occasionally carried messages that were never fulfilled, how to distinguish true
from false prophecy came to be a major problem long before the exile. Yet none of the
criteria advanced in the Hebrew Bible (as well as in modern scholarship) has proved
consistently applicable for arriving at a correct judgment.[3]

When supernatural beings are featured in narratives, however, there is significant
diversity in how they interact with humans but hardly any difference whether the encounter is experienced in a dream, a vision, or during normal activities.[4] To begin with,
such beings tend to visit when an individual is isolated from others and the setting is
unusual. Consequently, the context invests intimacy in the experience, such as we find
in Jacob's uncanny confrontation at the Jabbok (Gen 32) or when Zipporah and her
husband met God on their way to Egypt (Exod 4).

In some instances, individuals, such as Abraham (Gen 18) and Lot, instantly recognize the otherworldly nature of their visitors and treat them with appropriate obsequiousness. In others, the revelation unfolds over time, as when Eli eventually realizes that Samuel is being visited by God (1 Sam 3). But even when they fail to appreciate who is facing them, individuals rarely test the visitors (but see below at 6:17) or ask them to identify themselves. (Joshua is unusual in this regard; Josh 5.) Rather, the request for identification often comes *after* individuals register reverence, awe, fear, or self-doubt, signs that they have grasped a visitor's true nature, and *after* a commission is fulfilled or a reassurance is delivered.

We shall soon find many parallels between the experiences of Gideon and of Samson's parents (at Judg 13) when they meet a stranger.[5] (For now, see Table 6.) But what they do *not* share is an urge to test the nature of the visitor. Gideon, in fact, is alone among others in similar situations in remaining skeptical until the very end of his experience with divinity. When invited to save Israel in dire times, he questions the judgment of his visitor; when he finds seriousness in proposals, he first asks whether he is being mistaken for someone else before demanding confirmation. This interrogation is in itself doubly interesting, not just because it is unusual in Scripture, but also because the narrator early on identifies the visitor as God (6:14). As a result, the narrator steps out of the normally partisan stance held about God: We are not to adopt Gideon's skepticism, but we are to keep faith in his selection as Israel's savior, at least for the duration of his tales.

The Assault

6 1. This is the briefest version of the phrase that introduces Israel's reversal of fortunes. (See the Notes to 3:7–8a; similarly at 13:1.) Missing here is the 'et particle and specifics on the kind of provocation that Israel displayed. The idiom *nātan YHVH běyad-X*, "the LORD has handed 'X' over," has so far been to Israel's advantage (at 1:4; 3:10, 28; 4:14). Here (and at 13:1), however, it is to their enemy's, the chosen instrument for chastising Israel.

The tribe called Midian (Greek, Μαδιάμ) is as yet unattested in Near Eastern sources, although it is possible to link the name with a region called Madiama/Madyan mentioned in classical and Muslim sources (Knauf 1988: 1–6). With an etymology that remains obscure, Midian is nicely featured in Scripture, its origins attributed to an eponymous son of Abraham from his second wife, Keturah (Gen 25:4).[6] In turn, Midian is said to father five eponyms. Midian and Ishmaelite traders are credited with selling Joseph to Egyptians, apparently separately (Gen 37:25–28, 36; 39:1), but they will be deemed the same in Judg 8:22–24. Gideon's story, then, is another occasion that pits Midian with Joseph, this time via Manasseh. But so many links are made with other tribal groups mentioned in Scripture (including Edomites, Kenites, and Moabites) that, long before Noth, Haupt (1909) proposed that Midian is the name of an Edomite Sinai-amphictyony, centered around Elat on the Gulf of Aqaba, a notion revived by Dumbrell (1975).

Midian's connection with Israel can be beneficial, as in traditions about Moses's father-in-law, an influential "priest of Midian" (Exod 2:16), but is more often negative, damning (Num 25:6–18), or violent (Num 31). Scholars have sought to divide, with debatable success, the material into historical phases when Midian moved toward antagonism from happy relations with the Hebrews (allegedly before 1100 BCE; Stager 1998: 143). In recent literature, Midian is often associated with northwest Arabian territory east of Aqaba (many articles to that effect are in Sawyer and Clines 1983), but it seems settled and agricultural rather than nomadic. In Hebrew traditions, however, its range is vast, on all sides of Israel's borders, and its occupations diverse, including caravaneers, farmers, and herders. We will soon meet their "kings" (Judg 8), but there is also mention of their *nāśî'* ("heads," Josh 13:21), *nāsîk* ("chiefs," Ps 83:12 [11 RSV]), and *nādîv* ("principal," Ps 83:12 [11 RSV]).[7]

6 2–5. In contrast to the brief notice on how Israel's fortunes deteriorated, the next verses give the most detailed description of its woes. As presented, Midian's success is due to Israel's sin, and it would be too historicizing to attribute it to the defeat of the Canaanites under Sisera (Aharoni 1979: 262–63). The misery that Midian forced on Israel is twofold and presented in *hysteron proteron* ("the latter first"; see above at 1:7): People become troglodytes (after three years—seven in some manuscripts—of abuse, Josephus claims; *Ant.* 5.210–12) when their harvests are destroyed and their fertile land is turned into parking lots. The language to describe what the Hebrews created when escaping the Midianites is patently etiological, explaining a phenomenon that presumably was observable. Unfortunately, the main word, *minhārôt*, occurs only here, and some very fancy etymologies have sought to pin down its meaning: from **nhr*, meaning either "light" (so subterranean chambers with cuts for light; places where fire beacons are set up, via Arabic *manhar*) or "river" (so stream beds in gorges or in mountains, also from Arabic *manhar*). Greek renderings also offered conjectures: either "shelters" (μάνδρας in Rahlfs A) or "holes" (τρυμαλιὰς in Rahlfs B). Luckily, we are given an explanation: These consisted of caves (*mĕʿārôt*) and inaccessible fissures in the mountains (*mĕṣādôt*). In Ezek 33:27 we are told that plague alone can vanquish those who hide in caves and crevices, whereas wild animals finish those who live in the open, and the sword destroys those in desolate places.

How destructive the Midianites were is elaborated in two scenes of wanton damage and permanent havoc by a coalition that includes Amalek and Qedem tribesmen. The former are the fiercest of Israel's enemies, their participation always sharpening the destructive power of a coalition. As in 3:11–14, however, their mention also heralds a change in Israel's fortune, for Amalek is hated by the God of Israel. The *bĕnê qedem* are "easterners"; the phrase is used generically to convey the East (with Egypt as the West), as when Solomon's wisdom is said to surpass those of both (1 Kgs 5:10 [4:30 RSV]); when describing Job's great wealth (Job 1:3); or where Jacob heads when escaping his brother (Gen 29:1).[8] But, as in our contexts, in Isa 11:14 and Ezek 25:4, the phrase refers to a specific tribal group, although one not known from Near Eastern documents. Missing in the Qumran fragment 4QJudg[a] is the phrase *vĕʿālû ʿālāʾv*.

The conflict is cast in classic desert and sown mode. Israel is a farming community and, as accented by the mention of camels (6:5), the enemy is nomadic, with lots of opportunities to camp and threaten terror. The attacks are not meant to rob Israel of its yield but to deliberately damage its crop (the Hiphil of *šāḥat* in 6:4 conveys this notion) any time before harvest as well as to sterilize the land. For this reason, the suggestion that the *minhārôt* of the previous verse refer to silos in which to hide grain (Lagrange

1903: 118) rather than human shelter may not be appropriate. Soon we will read of Gideon's tactic to prevent loss of harvest.

Phrases allude to the enemy's depravity. It was extensive, for it reached Gaza, so at the limits of Israel's borders. It was intense, for it included removal of livestock: sheep for food, cattle for labor, donkey for transport.[9] It was devastating, for it involved vast numbers. This is conveyed by allusion to locusts, the most relentlessly voracious creature known to the ancient Near East (Joel 1:4) and so impossible to control that only a wind from God can affect its movement (Exod 10:19).[10] It was meant to be permanent, for the foe was bringing its entire stock as well as tents.[11] This last notice is important, for the land they plan to occupy was God's gift to Israel. The enemy's presumption, as much as any appeal by Israel, is what leads God to reverse his judgment.

The Lesson

6 7–10. The construction *vayyĕhî/vehāyâ kî* can be causal ("Because the people of Israel pleaded with God") or temporal ("When/as [soon as] the people of Israel . . ."), the latter allowing for simultaneity of action. The main lesson conveyed, however, is the nature of God's response: He appoints a prophet to lecture Israel on its behavior. The phrase *'îš nāvî'*, "a man, a prophet," in 6:8 is unusual since this form for prophet is masculine. Since antiquity the distinction is often ignored in most translations, but it makes sense after mention of the similarly redundant *'iššâ nĕvî'â* (at 4:4) for Deborah. Traditional exegetes identify this prophet with Phineas, Aaron's grandson, who had been featured in anti-Midianite action (Num 25:7–8; 31), in arguing against building sacrificial altars east of the Jordan (Josh 22), and later in Judges (20) in supporting a war against the Benjaminites. Similarly, the same exegetes give Phineas a role (unrecorded) in the Jephthah story.

The message carried to Israel rehearses an important moment in its historiography, when Israel and God had arrived at an understanding: He took them out of Egypt, delivering a land to them by vacating it of its inhabitants. In return, the people were to acknowledge only him, without fearing the gods of Amorites whose land they were occupying. Previously (at 2:1–4), a "messenger of the LORD" rehearsed the covenant at Sinai and the failure of Israel to keep it. His message was so sharply worded that it provoked the people into loud self-reproach and launched the narrator into expansive argument on the necessity (but also the futility) of sending judges to rescue them (2:5–23). In our passage, Israel's rejection is delivered laconically: "You would not listen to me."

What is striking is that this episode stands as an orphan, with no response or follow-up by those being scolded, so much so that Wellhausen treated the passage as a redactional feature (1994 [1885]: 234). More, the move of God to rescue Israel though Gideon stands in sharp contrast to the obstinacy he laments about them. In fact, the whole episode is missing from a Judges fragment from Qumran, 4QJudg[a] (Trebolle Barrera 1989), and its editor has suggested that it characterizes a version of Judges that was shorter than what has reached us. The lamentable nature of the fragment (fewer than two score words are extant in full), the omissions of phrases (*v'lw 'lyv* in v. 3), the liberty taken in reshaping verbal forms (*šsprw lnw* for MT *'šr sprw-lnw* in v. 13), and the many errors it contains (there are interlinear corrections and missing conjunctions) would caution against such a sweeping judgment (see also Marcos 2003; O'Connell 1996: 147 n. 178; Tov 2012: 213–14). Admittedly, for reasons as yet uncharted, the (apprentice?) scribe may simply have skipped over a segment paragraphed within two *pĕtuḥôt* (see Hess 1997).

Still, this passage is important, for on it will be built the great frustration that God will express at the close of the Gideon-Abimelech accounts (at 10:10–16).

Naming Narratives: A. "LORD Peace"

THE VISIT

6 11–19. "Angels of the LORD" make frequent visits in Judges. We have already met with one lecturing Israel at Bochim (2:1–4) and one cursing Meroz (at 5:23). In this episode, as well as in one describing the birth of Samson (at Judg 13), they have major narrative roles, with missions that go beyond delivering messages. Gideon will not realize that the visitor is a messenger, let alone an angel, for a few more verses. Yet, as Gideon's character is shaped in the contrast between what we know about the visitor versus Gideon's unfolding discovery, I have gone ahead and translated as I have.

On reaching Ophrah, the angel places himself under an *'ēlâ*, a good place for messengers to rest (1 Kgs 13:14). It was either an oak or a terebinth, different botanical species, albeit often confused (only the former makes forests; see Gen 18:1). In either case, it was an imposing and long-living tree, and there may be some irony that Gideon's son will be proclaimed king at a similar tree (*'ēlôn*) in Shechem (Judg 9:6). Hosea (Hos 4:13) is among many to witness that sacrifice took place by them. That particular tree grew in Ophrah, one of two villages in Israel sharing the same name (see below).[12] Potential confusion between the two is avoided by linkage with the clan, Abiezer, to which Gideon belonged, along with his father Joash, whose name means "the LORD Gives ['ûš] or Heals ['āšâ]." Their clan, Abiezer ("Helper"),[13] may have kept the name of an ancestor (Josh 17:2), with a slightly different configuration in Num 26:30 (*'Iezer*).[14] What is not clear from the clause is whether it is the tree or Ophrah that belonged to Gideon's father.[15]

Gideon (we shall soon discuss his name) is beating out (*ḥōvēṭ*) wheat in a winepress, to remove the grain from Midianite attention. His aim is to beat the stems and husks so as to separate the grains or seeds from the straw. In better times, threshing would be done (verb *dû/iš*) over a large flat surface, using handheld flails or (with much less drudgery) an animal-drawn sledge (*ḥārûṣ*). Winepresses are outdoor (sometimes covered) installations that are cut into rock in open areas, although they differ in configuration. Unlike threshing floors, winepresses generally have two levels, connected by channels or tubing with filtering devices. People tread on harvested grapes on a flat area (*yeqev*). The juice collects in a vat (*gat*), a lower, generally also smaller and deeper, pool in later period with mosaics.[16] Threshing floors and winepresses need not be close to each other, but it helps to observe that they were used at different times of the year (threshing in late spring; wine-making in the fall), so Midianites would not be closely observing the area that Gideon was using. The verbal form (*lĕhānîs*, in the Hiphil) has to do with acting with speed and stealth.

One point of the notice is that Gideon could not be comfortable doing his deed in such a tight spot. Moreover, he was not acting his rank—for even in dire times, he might have used servants to do the task. From his own perspective, too, all this stealth could not be dignified, let alone heroic; hence his reaction to the stranger's greetings.

6 12–13. The idiom *rā'â* (Niphal) *'el* (someone) occurs frequently in Scripture, overwhelmingly about sudden appearances of God or angels (exceptions at Gen 46:29 and Lev 13:19). The lore about such supernatural beings is that they can choose when to be seen by mortals.[17] We recall the story of Balaam who had a donkey with better sense for angels than did this particular prophet (Num 22). How long the angel sat under his tree watching Gideon as he threshed wheat in a winepress is not told to us.[18] He opens fairly innocuously with a salutation (*YHVH 'immĕkā*, "God be with you"; see Ruth 2:4) that, despite the mention of God, has no special significance beyond goodwill. However, given that Gideon was acting in fear and behaving stealthily as he threshed, the second portion of the greeting must have seemed cutting. Without the article, the phrase *gibbôr ḥāyil* refers to men of means, normally owners of property (for example, Boaz), but it does not exclude fighters (see below at 11:1).[19] With the article, however, *gibbôr heḥāyil* alludes to well-armed warriors and occurs mostly in the plural (for example, at Josh 1:14, 6:2). In Rahlfs B the allusion is more explicit, "strong among the forces" (ἰσχυρὸς τῶν δυνάμεων).

Gideon's response flows as lava, betraying the frustration and bitterness of living under constant threat. Also, it might well have played on the name of a clan, Abiezer, with "help" as one of its elements (Garsiel 1993: 304). Gideon does not know who has addressed him, but he is polite, opening on conventional courtesy, *'ădōnî*, that is couched as if replying to a superior (see above under 4:18). The *bî* gives the phrase additional intensity, as when Judah supplicates Joseph in Egypt (Gen 43:20, 44:18) or when women beg justice from Solomon (1 Kgs 3:17). But when Gideon repeats the formula at 6:15, the sarcasm is obvious. Josephus (*Ant.* 5.213) conveys it well, "A mighty indication of God's favor to me that I am forced to use this wine-press instead of a threshing-floor!"

Gideon's first reaction is to play on the first part of the innocuous greeting; "the LORD be with you" is turned into questioning of God's presence that is more fully presented in Exod 17:7 when the rebellious Hebrews asked "is the LORD among us or not?" The balance, questioning the reliability of the inherited tradition about God's saving acts, is sharpened by the message just now carried by a prophet to Israel (above, vv. 7–10). Gideon may not have heard it, but his vocabulary for forsaking (*vĕ'attâ nĕṭašānû YHVH*) is among the most pregnant in Scripture, whether it is God who abandons Israel or vice versa, for it conveys intentionality or malice aforethought.

THE DISCUSSION

6 14–16. The Hebrew God himself engages Gideon, apparently without any physical changes to make his divinity obvious. This meeting was judged too frontal by the versions, and they inserted "messenger of" before the name of God. This piety is not necessary, for in a number of passages God and angels alternate, most famously at Gen 18–19 where Abraham addresses visitors both as plural and as singular, ending his dialogue with a tête-à-tête with God. The idiom *pānâ 'el-* occurs often enough to give the sense of turning toward (or away from) someone, and it gives an eerily anthropomorphic feel to the scene, the more to shock us at the chutzpah of Gideon that will soon surface.

God's message is crisp: You must go with the resources you already have, for I am commissioning you. The word *kōaḥ*, "force," does not apply to armies or the like, so

Table 6. Supernatural Manifestation in Judg 6 and 13

	Judg 6	Judg 13
Supernatural being (Sb)	Angel of the LORD (*mal'ak YHVH*) (vv. 11–13, 20–22); the LORD (YHVH) (vv. 14, 16); Angel of God (*mal'ak hā'ĕlōhîm*) (v. 20)	Angel of the LORD (*mal'ak YHVH*); Man of God (*'îš hā'ĕlōhîm*) (vv. 6, 8); Angel of God (*mal'ak hā'ĕlōhîm*) (vv. 6, 9)
Human (H)	Gideon	Wife of Manoah; Manoah
Setting	Winepress by Ophrah	1. Wife in [?] 2. Wife in field (v. 9) 3. Wife and Manoah (v. 11)
Status	Alone, threshing	1 & 2. Wife alone 3. Wife and Manoah
Manifestation	*mal'ak YHVH* seated under tree	*mal'ak YHVH* "appears" (v. 3)
Sb's salutation	*mal'ak YHVH*: "The LORD be with you, warrior" (v. 12)	"You're barren now, but you will conceive and bear a son" (v. 3)
H's response	"If the LORD is with us, how could all this be happening to us?" (v. 13)	
Commission	YHVH: "Go . . . and rescue Israel" (v. 14)	"You will bear a son who will be a Nazir from the womb and who will begin to deliver Israel" (vv. 4–5)
H's reaction 1	"With what? My clan is the weakest . . . and I am the youngest" (v. 15)	Wife runs to tell her husband about "man of God"; husband begs YHVH for the same messenger (v. 8)
Commission 2	YHVH: "I will certainly be with you" (v. 16)	God (*hā'ĕlōhîm*) listens; angel of the LORD (*mal'ak YHVH*) returns to repeat the message (vv. 9–14)
H's reaction 2	"Give me a sign that it is to me you speak" (v. 17)	Manoah presses a meal on the angel of the LORD (*mal'ak YHVH*) (vv. 15–16)
H asks name		"What is your name?" (v. 17)
Sb's reaction		"Why do you ask? It is *unknowable*" (v. 18)
H offers gift	"Just don't move from here until I come back to set before you the offering" (v. 18)	Manoah sets for YHVH sacrifice on rock (v. 19)

Sb's reaction	*mal'ak hā'ĕlōhîm*: "Take the meat" (v. 20)	*'umaflî la'ăśôt* (see Notes there)
Sb's acceptance	*mal'ak YHVH* touches gift with staff, fire ignites, and the messenger disappears (v. 21)	When the flame arose, the angel of the LORD (*mal'ak YHVH*) ascends into the smoke (vv. 16, 20)
H expresses fear	"Ahah Lord YHVH . . . inasmuch as I have seen the angel of the LORD face to face!" (v. 22)	Manoah: "We shall surely die because we have seen God ['*ĕlōhîm*]" (v. 22)
Reassurance	YHVH: "Be at peace and do not fear; you will not die" (v. 23)	Wife reasons that the LORD (YHVH) accepted their sacrifice (v. 23)
H offering	Builds "LORD Peace" altar	Wife bears Samson (v. 24)

Gideon must have puzzled over what (*bammâ*) exactly will be his tool for success. His response is personal (I am the least likely to succeed) and follows similar examples where modesty trumps reality, most equivalent being Saul's reaction (1 Sam 9:21).[20] We do not know whether Gideon was the youngest or least important (*ṣā'îr*, with both meanings) in his immediate family, but in fact, his clan had much prestige in Manasseh.[21] At any rate, he was no teenager (as was David) since we learn soon that he had a son who likely was (so more like Moses at the burning bush; Exod 3). Nor was he without means, for later (at 6:27), we find him able to summon ten men from his own entourage.

On the repeat of the courtesy formula, the Masoretes vocalized the second element *'ădōnāy*, normally addressing God, as in Gen 18:3 and 19:18, when Abraham and Lot specifically conversed with God when visited by angels.[22] With the Greek witnesses not displaying this difference in vocalization, it is impossible to know how the narrator (as distinguished from the Masoretes) reacted to the presence of God: Did he recognize him as divine? If so, Gideon's response would be a bargaining move, more in parallel with what obtains when Moses offers at least five objections to God's desire to empower him (at Exod 3:11, 13; 4:1, 10, 13). If not, we may assess his response as indulging the stranger's odd proposal.

The tribe to which Gideon belongs is Manasseh. Earlier (at 1:27) we had seen how it shared the fate of others in failing to conquer the territory God assigned to it. According to J. Finkelstein's survey (1988: 65–91, 352–56), Manasseh—and almost as equally Ephraim (linked by tradition as sons of Joseph)—formed the heartland of Palestine at the opening of the Iron Age (circa twelfth century BCE), with almost 70 percent of settlements within their borders. It divided into half-tribes on either side of the Jordan. To the west, Manasseh's home was the fertile highland, from Bethel north to the Jezreel Valley.

Gideon receives from God reassurance that he will support him, the line *kî 'ehyeh 'immāk*, "I will certainly be with you," also addressed to Moses (Exod 3:12).[23] This assistance will allow Gideon to defeat Midian *kĕ'îš 'eḥād*, "as one man." Other attestations make it clear that it is Midian that will suffer as a unit, but Gideon may have had heard it to apply to him, so defeating the enemy single-handedly. Although Gideon is persuaded, at this point he displays one of his more endearing traits: a healthy skepticism.

THE SIGN

6 17–19. That Gideon now realizes the elite nature of the visitor is suggested by the nice expression "if you favor me," generally posed to a superior. His skepticism has been sharpened by (what seemed to him) the outlandish proposal he had just heard, yet he could not dismiss its potential truth. It is important, therefore, not to confuse what he will request of the visitor with seeking reassurance from God about future successes; for he does not yet know what we do, that the speaker is God himself. Nor is Gideon on this occasion testing God's steadfast support. Rather, he has two concerns: He wishes to corroborate the supernatural nature of the visitor and to receive a sign (*'ôt*) that it is truly him that is being addressed.[24] The request for a sign may reflect the self-doubt that marks Gideon's personality throughout his wars with Midian. Testing for divinity, however, has Near Eastern antecedents, as developed in this brief excursus.

Near Eastern Examples   Naram-Sin, grandson of Sargon of Agade, has had many tales told about him, mostly highlighting the contrast between the two. Sargon triumphed in all enterprises since, like Moses, he survived his abandonment as a baby. Naram-Sin, however, attracted negative reaction from the gods, to the point that he was saddled (unhistorically) with bringing destruction to Agade.[25] In an episode called "Naram-Sin and the Enemy Hordes" or "The Cuthean Legend of Naram-Sin," invaders so terrified Naram-Sin's army that their human nature was questioned. Pricking them to see whether they shed blood was set as a test; but when this was done, they proved neither human nor divine, but golem creatures of the god Ea. More to our point is an episode from a Hittite narrative often labeled "The Cannibal Text" because it mentions troops eating a captured woman. In it, a battle is taking place near a city. A person called Dumu.maḫ.líl (the reading of the name is disputed) is being chased into a city, and his nature is in doubt.[26] Here is what a man named Kaniu did (after Gilan 2008: 272; Mouton 2004a: 305): "Kaniu took cooked pork and placed it before Dumu.maḫ.líl (thinking): 'If he *marks* it, then (he is) a god. If he does not *mark it*, then (he is) mortal; and so we shall fight (him).' Dumu.maḫ.líl took the pork and ate it up." The episode is far from transparent, and its import is lost to us (as happens so often) in gaps and breaks. Clear, however, is that there is a test for divinity that centers on the *marking* of a meat offering, unkosher though it may have been. The crucial verb (*ḫazziya*) has many meanings, among them, "to hit" (as with an arrow), "to pierce," to "set a mark," or even "to inscribe" (Mouton 2004b: 100). For Dumu.maḫ.líl to prove human, he needed to do something else besides "mark, hit, or pierce" the meat. He ended up partaking of it, thus disproving his divinity.[27] Let us keep both of these acts in mind as we proceed with Gideon's test.

Gideon wants his visitor to stay in place until he lays out an offering (*minḥâ*) in his presence.[28] As we saw earlier (at 3:15–17) the term has both secular and ritual contexts. The Greek versions opt for sacrifice (θυσία). However, the verb Gideon uses, *hāniyaḥ*

(Hiphil of *nvḥ*), is not as normally attached to a ritual offer as, say, *hiqrîv* or *hāvî*; so it is not at all clear what kind of test Gideon had in store for the visitor. Whether or not he stays put while Gideon prepares his elaborate meal may well be part of the test. The remarkably theomorphic notion of God agreeing to sit in wait is toned down in the Targum where he only "waits."

Preparing a banquet in which humans interact with deities is part of the lore of the ancient world (Grottanelli 1989). The occasion is more striking, however, when it is detailed in Scripture, for the Hebrew God is not meant to share human behavior. The clearest example is Abraham's catering to visitors (Gen 18) whom he knew to be supernatural, to judge from his excessive kowtowing and the amount of food he prepares: a calf and about an *'eˀfâ*-worth (12 liters) of pastry flour, curds, and milk.[29] Unlike the Genesis account, however, the amount Gideon prepares (a young goat and an *'eˀfâ*-bushel of matzah) straddles the line between a modest offer to a deity and a generous presentation to a respected guest.[30] In biblical lore, bread is offered in baskets (*sal*), not meat, so Gideon's presentation (meat in a basket, broth in a pot) does not reflect sacrifice ritual (Moore 1895: 188).[31] The verb attached to Gideon after his presentation (Hiphil of *nāgaš*) bears a cultic meaning only when a direct object clarifies the nature of the action. It is not at all necessary to treat it as a Qal and to connect it with the verse following ("when he approached, the angel of God said to him . . .").[32] So, again at this stage, Gideon's intents escape specific definition.

THE COUNTERSIGNS

6 20–21. In this segment, the angel returns to full feature and offers a series of countersigns that are meant to remove any doubts about his supernatural character. This time, however, he is called *malˀak hāˀĕlōhîm* rather than *malˀak YHVH*, as he will be again at vv. 21–22. Some exegetes therefore consider v. 20 as a later addition (see Moore 1895: 188). This is indeed possible, yet in this narrative, there are switches galore in the vocabulary for the visitor. We might also note that something similar will occur in the story of Samson. Additionally, by removing this verse, we miss Gideon's participation in the miracle (contra Lagrange 1903: 123).

Why the bread and meat need to be on a boulder (*selaˁ*, later also *ṣûr*, the latter usually more massive than the former) is made clear in the scene that follows. The angel extends the tip of a staff (*mišˁenet*), a walking instrument (Exod 21:19) that gives its owner authority, whether it be Elijah (2 Kgs 4:29–31), leaders (Num 21:18), or (metaphoric) shepherds (Ps 23:4). Its purpose is not to set fire to the offered material, but to designate where the fire coming out of the rock is to strike. This might be a first countersign, indeed the equivalent act in Kaniu's test for Dumu.maḥ.líl's divinity. The link between fire and the divine is pronounced in Scripture (as at Gen 15:17, Exod 3:2, Lev 9:24, Num 16:35, 1 Chr 21:26, 2 Chr 7:1). The motif of a fire "eating" (*ˀākal*) its target will occur again in the Samson story (at Judg 13:20) and in Elijah's (1 Kgs 18:38), but its point of origin will differ in each. Still, what they share in common, as they do with the Hittite anecdote cited above, is that gods do not eat in a human way, Abraham's midday visitors notwithstanding.[33] This may be a second countersign for the visitor's divinity.

Potentially crucial is the instruction to pour out (*šāfak*) the broth (*māraq*). The verb is one of many (*rîq* in the Hiphil; *yāṣaq*, *nāsak*, and *nātak* are others) that has to do with liquids. The word *šāfak*, however, suggests a sudden dumping and is often associated with blood, either of sacrifice or in a metaphor for reprehensible murder. So the angel is not asking for a libation. At the same time, he is not being precise enough about where to spill or on what, except that it would be done in proximity of the rock. It is tempting to think him targeting the bread and meat; if this were so, the narrator would be promoting a motif more fully shaped in Elijah's confrontation with the priests of Baal. There, heavenly fire consumes the offer on an altar after it was soaked with water (1 Kgs 18:30–38). Perhaps he is leaving it up to Gideon to decide whether or not to sharpen the test. In this case, this would be yet a third countersign, the fourth one coming soon after.

The disappearance of the angel coincides with the burning of the offering and is presented strikingly: Gideon's eyes lose track of the vanishing visitor. Yet, the abruptness of the exit is moderated by God lingering to deliver reassurances.

THE RECOGNITION

6 22–23. There may be an intentional glide from the physical eyes that lose contact and the inner eye that recognizes what has happened, the verb *rā'â* frequently carrying extended senses. Gideon's shriek of *'ăhāh* (*mappîq* in the *hê*, sounding it as a consonant) is often rendered too weakly by "alas." It is an onomatopoeic *cri d'angoisse*, and it occurs about a dozen times in Hebrew, among them its crucial reference in the aftermath of Jephthah's vow (at Judg 11:35). In the narratives and in the prophets, it is overwhelmingly (eight out of twelve times) followed by "Lord God" (or the like), accentuating the terror that comes from tasting death.[34] I follow the LXX (ἆ ἆ), which approximates the sound rather than offers a translation.[35] The compound conjunction *kî-'al-kēn* is used to deliver an observation on matters that should have been obvious. Gideon's *'ădōnāy YHVH* beautifully conveys his stunned arrival at the powerful truth, moving from the blithe "sir" (*'ădōnî*) he first used at 6:13 and by way of the "lord" (*'ădōnāy*) of 6:15.[36] I have kept the Tetragrammaton in the translation of 6:22 to communicate Gideon's sudden insight: He has seen God and must therefore die. Jacob, who survived his bout with the divine, is likewise stunned to live beyond the experience (Gen 32:31 [30 RSV]). In the lore, only Moses can face God and live (Exod 33:11, Deut 34:10). As readers (or listeners), we were aware of God's presence since 6:14, and it might please us to have Gideon catch up to our knowledge, if not also to our apprehension.

THE ALTAR

God himself calms Gideon using three asyndetic expressions that are nevertheless related. The first, *šālôm lĕkā*, "feel safe," is what strikes his ear initially and will soon provide the etiology for the altar Gideon builds. The second, *'al-tîrā'*, is one of a half-dozen expressions for reassurance that are said to frightened, wary, or doubting patriarchs, leaders, and prophets, a number of which are nicely assembled in Deut 31:6: "Be strong and resolute [*ḥizqû vĕ'imṣû*], be not afraid [*'al tîrĕ'û*] or in dread of them [*'al-tā'arṣû mippĕnêhem*]; for your God the Lord himself marches with you. He will not fail or abandon you [*lō' yarpĕkā vĕlō' ya'azvekā*]."[37] The third, *lō' tāmût*, "you will not die," is what must have relieved Gideon the most, for his fault was nothing like David's sin (marrying Bathsheba), which required divine absolution to avoid death (2 Sam 12:13).

God's calming response gives reason for Gideon to dedicate an altar to God that is said to survive the time, calling it "(the) Lord (is) Peace," with the word *šālôm* conveying a broad array of meanings: "success," "wholeness," "salvation," and "(covenantal) accord."[38] The ad hoc foundation story ignores Deuteronomistic drives to unify worship and conforms to other commemorative contexts that are mostly associated with the patriarchs, such as at Gen 26:25 (Isaac at Beersheba), Gen 33:20 (Jacob at Shechem), Gen 35:7 (Jacob at Bethel), and Exod 17 (Moses at Rephidim). Indeed, the narrative shares the same drive to authenticate holy spaces through holy stories and calls on the same props: sacred trees, divine manifestation, soothing promises, and foundation of altars (de Vaux 1961: 306). Striking, however, is that the etiology is based on a visual rather than an oral derivation, for the sequence of the two words it replays from the previous verse cuts across a disjunction that would have separated them aurally.

For the phrase ʿad hayyôm hazzê, "until this day," see the Notes under Judg 1:21. The altar is said to be at ʿofrāt ʾăvî hāʿezrî, a genitival (but see at 8:32) construction that suggests that the narrator wished to differentiate it from an Ophrah in Benjamin (Αφ[α]ρᾰ Γοφερα; Josh 18:23, 1 Sam 13:17).[39] In the Mari archives, separate towns with the same name were differentiated by the tribal elements who settled them. For example, Sippar Yaḥrurum (at Tell Abu Ḥabbah) and Sippar Amanānum (at Tell ed-Dēr) are at appreciably different locations, having been settled by different groups of the Yaminite tribes.[40] This particular Ophrah (Εφραθα) belonged to Manasseh, and in view of what we later learn about the mother of Abimelech, Gideon's son, it probably was not too distant from Shechem. By ending on ʿofrāt ʾăvî hāʿezrî, the narrator loops back to the opening of his story. The phrase will also occur at 8:32, in reference to the family tomb in which Gideon is buried.

Naming Narratives: B. Jerubbaal

THE COMMISSION

6 25–27. It is not necessary to believe that this is a second account either for the foundation of Ophrah or the call of Gideon (Moore 1895: 190). This particular episode does indeed tell of overturning one altar and establishing another, but the etiology is mostly about a second name for our hero (see the Comments below).

Given the nighttime context of Gideon's call, it is reasonable to assume that God addressed Gideon in a dream. However, the Gideon narratives about God are steeped in anthropomorphism, and we have the example of the phrase vayyĕhî ballaylâ hahû̓ at 7:9 where neither a dream nor a vision is at stake; so at the most removed, we are dealing with a vision. Although it is not made explicit, the occasion is just after the close of the previous episode.[41] Here too the urgency of the appeal and the choice of medium for divine revelation continue a connection to the patriarchal narratives (as in Gen 26:24).

The Hebrew God is never easy to fathom, and is even less so here. While the goal he sets for Gideon replays similar commands (for example, at Exod 12:3, 24:12–13; Deut 7:5, 12:3), the instrument and the path are vague. Linked words create the unique par-haššôr, a redundant construct since both terms refer to a (sacrificial) ox of unspecified age.[42] I am guessing that this ox must have been handsome enough as it is attributed to Gideon's father, a clan leader. It might be ready for stud or, more to the point, to be Joash's personal gift to Baal.[43] Such animals were carefully fattened by Mari palace workers for cultic ceremonies at which they became the king's special igisûm-gift.[44] Hittite instructions to temple officials warned against interfering with animals designated for sacrifice.[45] However, what happens to Joash's ox will remain obscure; it may well be that the challenge to the father is the only point of God's directive, and that is the inference made by medieval rabbis, for whom Joash had become an idolater.

There is then a request for a second ox, seven years old. This one is a crux, grammatically no less than coherently, and it would not help to compile the long list of emendations, since their success depends on ingenuity rather than attachment to the text.[46] Many commentators understand the phrase epexegetically (so replaying God's instruction on the first animal), thus ignoring the explicit mention of a second animal, here and at vv. 26 and 28.[47] Seven-year-old cattle are not especially prime gifts to gods, and it may well be, as medieval rabbis have suggested, that the age of the animal was a match for the period in which Midianites harassed Israel. S. Ackerman suggests that two oxen might have been yoked to pull down the altar (private communication).[48]

The instruction is to demolish the altar (*hāras*, at 1 Kgs 19:10–14 with similar application; elsewhere also *nātaṣ*). Much as the first bull, it too is attributed to Joash. Gideon is also to cut up the wooden *asherah* (*'ăšērâ*). Used for the second commission is the Qal of *kārat*, "to cut, hack, hew," also with *asherah* as a target in Exod 34:13 and 2 Kgs 23:14.[49] In this last passage, the object for chopping down is the plural of (*ha*)*'ăšērâ*, suggesting strongly that we are dealing with a cultic object, more or less a wooden pillar, and not with a figurine of the goddess herself—both of these meanings conveyed abundantly in Scripture by the same word. It is simply too bad that God did not use another verb with the same meaning, **gāda'*, when instructing Gideon to do the deed, as it might have made for a delicious play on the name of our hero (but see the Comments below).

The *asherah* is said to be *'ālā'v*. Most translations, perhaps conscious of dealing with a wooden object, have it sitting beside the altar. Perhaps the inspiration comes from Deut 16:21, "You shall plant no tree as an Asherah [*'ăšērâ kol-'ēṣ*] by [*'ēṣel*] any altar you make for your LORD." This is not at all what the preposition normally conveys, and we have this fine passage in 2 Chr 34:4 where it is said about Josiah: "They demolished the altars of the Baals in [Josiah's] presence. He had the *ḥammānîm* above them chopped down [*giddē*ª*]; he smashed the sacred posts, the idols, and the images; he ground them to bits, spreading them over the graves of those sacrificing to them." These *ḥammānîm* were frequently associated with the *asherah* (Isa 17:8, 27:9) and somehow loomed over the altar before they were cut down. Whatever they were, I doubt that they were "incense stands," as suggested by the dictionaries.

God wanted Gideon to take the second ox and immolate him on an altar *'al hammā'ōz hazzeh bamma'ărākâ*. Detailed though its words may be, the instruction is not at all clear, and some rabbis (Yosef Karo among them) simply equated this altar with the previous one. The Greek versions guessed well that the *ma'ărākâ* had to do with an array or arrangement, so offered in sequence (παράταξις); but because of the surfeit of features, they both took *mā'ōz* as a place name: Mount Maoz (ὄρος Μαωζ in Rahlfs A) and Maouek (Μαουεκ in Rahlfs B). It is possible (Lagrange [1903] and others) that *bamma'ărākâ* applies to the type of construction for the altar, and this is what I offer in translation, transposing for clarity the word order.

Gideon certainly took the instructions broadly, for he altered them in two significant ways: He asked ten men (a minyan, according to the rabbis, based on Gen 18:32) to join him. We may presume that they came from his personal household since he was acting beyond his father's knowledge. He also acted at night (the following rather than the same), not likely the most propitious time to offer a sacrifice. In fact, the rabbis were most exercised by Gideon's deed, finding in it multiple faults, for which God had to give him special dispensation: He was too young and was no priest; and he was sacrificing at night, on a cut altar, far from the sanctuary, using wood from an *asherah*, near an idolatrous shrine (*bTemurah* 28b; see Légasse 1991: 243–44).[50]

THE CONFRONTATION

6 28–32. Constructions in verse 28 are in the passive. Somewhat awkward stylistically, they are adequate grammatically and reinforce agreement between God's order and Gideon's acts. Although the gaze seems to be that of the people of Ophrah, mention of a sacrificed "second" ox suggests that it is the narrator's. The search for the culprit that they undertook is expressed through two verbs that are set parallel to the other even if they are not precise synonyms. The word *bāqāš* refers to a search for something concrete; *dāraš* is more about seeking an explanation for an event or circumstance and so is often used when the inquiry is done before a deity. When the two verbs complement each other, the sequence from *bāqāš* to *dāraš* is more frequent. Thus, Saul wants people to locate for him (*baqqĕšû-lî*) a necromancer so he can inquire through her (*'edrĕšâ-bāh*) (1 Sam 28:7). What is implied in the reversal of sequence in our passage is the extraordinary care paid to finding the culprit. The citizens inquired, likely though divination, and then investigated to make certain they got the right person. Whether the conclusion is what they concluded (as in this translation) or what they heard (as in many other renderings) depends on how *vayyōmĕrû* is parsed. I take it as part of the series of verbs in which the townsfolk are the subject.

The last time we met the phrase *'āmad 'al+* it had to with servants attending Ehud (at 3:19). Here it refers to the townsmen bringing their complaints to Joash. Following the Greek version, most translate with something like "those standing against him." Moore (1895: 195) adopts this formulation but admits that it represents a later Hebrew. "Stand by him" may give the same sense, but it also allows the townsmen a lower status than Joash, thus justifying his sharp rebuke as well as his privilege to resolve the matter. The gist of Joash's message is clear enough: Baal is mighty enough to punish the culprit; but the language is convoluted, making three references to the phrase *rîb lĕ + ba'al* that is meant to provide us with an etymology for Jerubbaal. The verb has to do with quarreling and in legal contexts with disputing. The idiom is about doing either on behalf of someone, and since in ancient times there were no professional lawyers, the connotation is of interceding (or interfering) in a dispute.[51] Joash's point is that executing Gideon is unnecessary; given that the honor of a god is at stake, meddling with divine retribution is hubris worthy of death. In effect, Joash is threatening to execute anyone who follows up on the matter, for the crime of *lèse-divinité*. Whether Joash had the authority to carry out the threat or not, it seems that no one was eager to challenge him. Potentially playful is the use of *'ĕlōhîm*, literally "gods." When clearly construed as a singular, it normally refers to the Hebrew God. There are several examples, however, of the plural denoting a pagan god (1 Kgs 11:5, Ashtoreth; 1 Kgs 11:33, Ashtoreth, Chemosh, and Milkom).

The above exchange is backdrop for Gideon acquiring the name Jerubbaal. The notice opens on *vayyiqrā'-lô*, and the subject can be Joash or impersonal, so it is a matter of choice who fashioned the new name. It could mean that over the course of time, admirers gave Gideon the name Jerubbaal. Or it could be that generically, the townsmen assigned that name, however much after the event. In that case it can hardly be complimentary, so we would need to imagine that the folks in Ophrah mean Baal to do something negative to Gideon. I would rather credit Joash with the naming, thus tightening the moment for the drama as well as making Joash commit to Gideon's future. As given, however, the etiology does not replay Joash's words to the townsmen because the idiom in it differs from the three previous manifestations attributed to him. *Rîb bĕ* + (*baʿal*) has to do with rebuking or accusing (as in Hos 2:4), the gist of the phrase being that every day that Gideon lives is an indication of Baal's ineffectiveness for failing to punish the sacrilege. This shift of vocabulary has naturally prompted scholars (Budde and Richter among them) to divorce this verse from the preceding, but if this is done, the major point of the episode is lost (see Emerton 1976: 291).

The new name assigned Gideon is Jerubbaal, and it is explained by the narrator as "Let Baal rebuke him because he demolished his altar." Such a meaning is accommodatingly etiological, for names are hardly formulated to demean a featured god. *Yĕrubbaʿal* (Rahlfs A, Ιεροβααλ; B, Ιαρβαλ) includes a verbal form and a noun. The element *baʿal* may be a noun or an epithet for a god: When the former, it means "owner, lord" and so can be applied to any (male) deity; when the latter, it refers to the Canaanite god Baal and occurs in Ugarit as a fixed epithet for the god Hadad. In the Hebrew Bible, the name can stand for any of the gods that were venerated by Canaanites and Phoenicians. Often, however, a plural form of the noun is used pejoratively (see at 2:11 and 3:7), designating powers that must not be venerated because they are false.

In the Bible, the noun *baʿal* was never an accepted substitute for the Hebrew God; yet fervent Yahwists could have personal names in which it substituted for YHVH, for example, Ishbaal (son of Saul) and Meribaal (son of Jonathan).[52] The verbal element in Jerubbaal should be related to the verb *rîb*; but because this verb features an *i*-vowel in its forms rather than the *u*-vowel, many have sought a different root: some from *yrh* (so, "Baal establishes"—Wellhausen), others from *rbh* (Piel, so "Baal nurtures"—B. Levine), *rbb* ("May Baal be LORD"—Noth; "May Baal give increase"—Albright).[53] Yet there are two verbal forms (at Judg 21:22 and Prov 3:30) that suggest the verb could have an alternative *u*-vowel. So, with Burney (1970: 201), I would stay with *rîb* as a verbal element and explain Jerubbaal as meaning "Baal contests"—an equivocal act that might fit well with the aim of the narrative. It might refer to Baal's discomfiture, but it can also reflect positively on him, reminiscent of what is said in Isa 3:13: "The LORD stands up to argue a cause [*niṣṣāb lārîv YHVH*], rises to judge people."

COMMENTS

The Texture of the Narratives

The narratives about Gideon begin on a trajectory that is familiar enough, with Israel's transgressions providing God with the justification to provoke a punishing invasion. What made the oppression of Midian and its allies (including the dreaded Amalek) so cruel was its opportunism. Like vultures waiting to feed on weakened animals, the Midianites simply awaited to despoil a defenseless Israel just as it was ready to harvest the fruits of its labors. It did not help at all that when Israel shrieked for help, the response it got from a prophet was an evocation of happier times and a lecture about the faults that were bringing it so low.

The introduction of Gideon, however, differs from all previous presentations of the prospective rescuer (*môšî‘a‘*). Except for the brief anecdote on how Othniel acquired a clever bride (at 1:12–16), itself hardly connected with his activities as judge (3:9–11), we learn nothing about how judges were selected or called to lead Israel from its doldrums. Moreover, while controlling the fall and rise of Hebrew fortunes, the Hebrew God had avoided debating personally with them; instead, messengers were sent to restate the plaints God had against Israel. Othniel, Ehud, and Deborah (and Shamgar and Baraq, for that matter) are not in direct or obvious communication with God.

Rather suddenly, the texture of the narrative changes. God enters as a character in the unfolding drama and will remain in close contact with Gideon for a good portion of the tales devoted to him. This association between a personalized God and a chosen hero readily reminds us of patriarchal narratives with resultant shrines and altars. It also evokes accounts of the election of major characters such as Moses, where reluctance is met by comforting signs, and Joshua. These links naturally evoke interest in the process by which Gideon lore found its way into Judges, with variations on the usual threefold response:

1. The stories were well-known, and their design influenced others that historiographers set as formative to Israel.
2. The stories were inserted later, even post-Deuteronomic, with an older veneer by copying patterns associated with ancestral narratives (for example, Auld 1989: 263–66).
3. The stories shared inherited archetypes for the founding of a state. Gideon is associated with Manasseh, a tribe controlling one of Israel's most heavily inhabited regions, with such towns as Shechem, Tirzah, and Samaria located within it. These sites came to be the engine that drove the kingdom of Israel since its traditional founding under Jeroboam. It might be conjectured that the stories about Gideon from Manasseh and of the failed dynastic succession of his son Abimelech (see below) may well belong to narratives about the foundation of the Northern Kingdom. If so, a conjecture would be that they parallel equivalent but better-known Judean stories featuring Saul and David. After the fall of the Northern Kingdom, the concept of a united monarchy was retrojected, with narratives about Saul and David providing an umbrella for both kingdoms. Gideon and his son lost their primacy as royal ancestors.

It is possible to argue for any of these positions (plus many others, nicely collected in Emerton 1976) because, with the dating of most biblical narratives in flux, the ground keeps shifting on their elements. Unlike most other stories with which it is compared, however, that of Gideon is also accented by seeming repetitions of motifs and by a doubling on the name assigned the hero.

The Two Altars

GIDEON'S ALTAR

Our segment has two narratives with interest in altars, three of which are mentioned. Gideon constructs one at Ophrah in gratitude for surviving his interview with God (6:12–24). On direct orders from God, Gideon destroys one dedicated to Baal and then builds one in another space, perhaps also at Ophrah (6:25–32). Since these stories also allude to two names for Gideon, there are frequent suggestions that we might be dealing with differing accounts for an Ophrah altar (de Vaux 1961: 306–7; contra Haag 1967: 309–12). Table 7 might allow better focus on the issue.

The table makes it difficult to admit that the narratives have similar objectives when about all they share are the protagonists (Gideon and God or his avatar) and the building of altars. The goals differ: In the first, Gideon decides to display his acceptance of God's charge by dedicating an altar in his name. The dialogue itself is fine preparation for the personality of Gideon that will come into focus shortly, and his election

Table 7. The Two Altars in Judg 6:11–32

	6:11–23	6:25–32
Context	Day	Night
Activity	Gideon threshing	Gideon (dreaming?)
Instrument	Angel/the LORD	The LORD
Colloquy	Angel of the LORD: Greetings. Gideon: Why abandoned? The LORD: I am empowering you. Gideon: I am not worthy. The LORD: I will be with you. Gideon: Give me a sign.	
Instruction		The LORD: Destroy Baal *altar*; build new *altar* at summit of fortification; offer a sacrifice.
Fulfillment		Gideon complies.
Reaction		Townsmen: Gideon must die.
Proof	Gideon prepares a meal. Angel of the LORD ignites food and disappears. Gideon fears death.	
Etiology	The LORD: Be at peace (*šālôm lĕkā*).	Joash: Baal should plead for himself (*yārev lô*).
Outcome	Gideon builds *altar* in Ophrah, calling it: "The LORD (is) Peace."	Joash (?) calls his son Jerubbaal, meaning, "Let Baal rebuke him [*yārev bô*] because he demolished his altar."

accentuates the freedom of God to choose the unlikely. In the second, Gideon is but an instrument of God in a drawn-out struggle against Baal, and the destruction of his altar is more in the foreground than is the construction of one for Yʜᴠʜ. Yet, the target of this particular anecdote is less about the fate of altars than about how Gideon earned the name Jerubbaal. We may stay, therefore, with the probability of separate traditions about altars at Ophrah, but not insist on recovering the reality behind each or both.

JOASH'S ALTAR

The episode in which Gideon acquires a new name is briefer than the one just preceding. Although it features a divine order that was communicated either directly, as a vision, or in a dream, and although it demonstrates Gideon's total acceptance of God's order, the main object of focus is the dialogue between irritated townsmen and an unyielding Joash. Likely more outraged by the destruction of an altar to Baal and Asherah than by consecration of a new (and unauthorized) altar, the townsmen demand Gideon's death. It has been suggested that they do not carry out the sentence on their own for fear of provoking vendettas. Much more plausible is that the altar was not theirs to defend; as it is explicitly stated in 6:25, it belonged to Joash. How individuals construct private shrines will soon be featured in the story of Micah (Judg 17). The process is strikingly illustrated in an Emar document:

> In the days of Limi-malik son of Ir'ib-Baal, Pilsu-Dagan [son of X-m]alik built a temple for Nergal-of-the-Baetyl. He made the elders of the city of Emar sit down and they wrote this tablet: "From this day on, Pilsu-Dagan is the priest [ˡᵘsanga] of the temple of Nergal-of-the-Baetyl. His sons and his grandsons will be priests of the Nergal temple forever. No other man shall raise claims against Pilsu-Dagan concerning the Nergal temple. Should some- one raise claims, he shall pay 1,000 shekels of silver. May Nergal destroy the family and descendant of anyone altering these words. (In addition), he shall build another temple, a duplicate of the temple of Pilsu-Dagan."[54]

The Emar document suggests that the building of shrines was a private endeavor, need- ing no state or priestly sanction. What the elders of Emar (a mayor is a witness as well) could do, however, is to prevent future encroachment on the individual's right to be- stow the privilege to family, setting a heavy penalty on the violator. But they could not unilaterally interfere to alter any aspect of the endeavor. Presumably, too, Pilsu-Dagan could put the building to other uses and revoke his priestly function for himself and his descendants. I am less certain whether his descendants shared this right, although there is an Emar document in which priests gave their building to a benefactor who kept them alive during famine (see van der Toorn 1995: 48).

Whatever reasons impelled the production of privately developed shrines—spiri- tuality, prestige, or economics—control of the clan through access to the gods was also very likely. Gideon's protests that his was the weakest clan in Manasseh notwithstand- ing, there are clues that Joash was a major player in it: He controlled an altar to Baal and likely the *asherah* about it; he was in possession of the (sacrificial) bull; and he had license (whether plausible or not) to decide whether or not to execute a blasphemer. We might characterize Joash as a Pilsu-Dagan, and so likely the first builder of Baal's altar. To judge from the role of the elders of Emar, Ophrah's leaders are limited to sanctioning

Joash's control over the altar. As long as the matter remains internal to the family, they have no authority to decide on the altar's well-being. And this is exactly Joash's pungently stated point. I am therefore of the mind that when God urged Gideon to make off with that bull and destroy the altar to Baal, the confrontation he was provoking was above all with Joash rather than with Joash's clan. To judge from his name, Joash came from a Yahwist stock, but he was not beyond giving tribute to Baal.

Gideon/Jerubbaal

In antiquity the destruction of temples, shrines, and altars was a political rather than a religious act, and omen texts placed such occurrences among other political instabilities (Dalley and Teissier 1992: 108, lines 26–27). When Mesopotamian kings destroy such places, their goal is to deny the defeated enemies the support of their gods, thus minimizing their opponents' capacity to rebel. The deed is prompted, therefore, by belief in the effectiveness of the relevant gods rather than by denial of their existence. Thus, the Babylonians destroyed the Jerusalem temple when it proved the locus of resistance and not because they doubted the divinity of YHVH. No civilized polytheists would ruin places for worship dedicated to gods they did not know, much as they might have coveted their wealth. Although they were Hebrews, the townsmen were apparently cosmopolitan religiously and would have felt that Gideon's decision to build a new altar was a challenge to his father, not to his neighbors. That they left it up to Joash to execute his son may mean that they regarded his offense as rebellion, perhaps against his father's own authority. The entire episode, however, is filtered through Deuteronomistic eyes, and Gideon's fault is made an excuse to judge the effectiveness of a false god. The clash that follows their demand essentially replays themes occurring when Elijah challenges the prophets of Baal at Mount Carmel (1 Kgs 18).

There is a discrepancy between the idioms Joash used when defying the townsmen and when explaining the new name he is awarding Gideon. There is also a problem in how the verbal form enters into the creation of the name Jerubbaal. These matters are discussed in the Notes above. In the literature, two other issues reoccur: the priority of one name over the other, and whether two different personalities had been merged into Gideon narratives.

NAME CHANGES

Biblical lore preserves a score of name changes for individuals, under differing circumstances. Some have names that albeit modestly modified presaged consequential changes (for example, Abram becoming Abraham); others acquire names with no linguistic connections (Jacob becoming Israel). Once given, the new name can be forgotten (Esau is just once called Edom); it can be assumed (almost) consistently after the change (Hosea becoming Joshua; Jedidiah becoming Solomon); or it can remain in use along with the birth name (Jacob and Israel). Naming agents differ. The name changes promoted by God (or delegates) are too well-known to cite fully, but they include Abram (Abraham), Saray (Sarah), Jacob (Israel), and Jedidiah (Solomon). Elsewhere, the changes are attributed to family members (Eve, from "woman" by Adam; Gen 3:20), to kings (Joseph by Pharaoh, Gen 41:45; Jehoiakim by Necho, 2 Kgs 23:34; Zedekiah and three courtiers by Nebuchadnezzar, 2 Kgs 24:17, Dan 1:7), to leaders (Joshua by Moses,

Num 13:16), to the person involved (Mara by Naomi, Ruth 1:20–21), or anonymously (Esau, Gen 25:30). In the case of Gideon/Jerubbaal, there are these observations:

1. Gideon is named in narratives about his call (chapter 6), his war against Midian (chapters 7–8), his deflection of kingship (8:22–28), and his legacy and death (8:30–34). The rallying cry for Israel in its battle is "(This sword is) for the LORD and for Gideon" (7:18, 20).

2. Jerubbaal is featured in the etiology for this name (6:25–32) but primarily in the story of Abimelech's reach for power and his success and failure (chapter 9).

3. A number of connectives attach the two names: One is direct ("Jerubbaal being Gideon," at 7:1) and, together with mention to "Jerubbaal son of Joash" (at 8:29), provides a bracket for all the Gideon material. At 8:33, reference to the disloyalty to the "House of Jerubbaal-Gideon" ends God's investment in Israel under Gideon and prepares for the disaster that Abimelech will launch.

4. Two significant references to Jerubbaal occur in the books of Samuel:
   a. On facing yet another invasion by the Ammonites, the prophet Samuel recalls past wonders God performed for his people when they acted contrite: "The LORD then sent Jerubbaal, Bedan, Jephthah, and Samuel to save you from enemies around you so that you can live in security" (1 Sam 12:11).[55] Since the roster seems to track backward from Samuel, it is possible that Jerubbaal was the name used exclusively when this tradition about past rescuers was recorded. This notion is reinforced by the next citation.
   b. In a biting report to King David on the death of Uriah, Joab anticipates David's scolding for losing many officers at the walls of the enemies: "Who struck down Abimelech son of Jerubbesheth [Greek, Jerubbaal]?[56] A woman simply dropped an upper millstone on him from the wall and killed him at Thebez! Why did you come so close to the wall?" (2 Sam 11:21). See below, notes to Judges 9:50–51.

5. Hosea 10:14 reads (*TNK*): "But the din of war shall arise in your own people / And all your fortresses shall be ravaged / As Beth-arbel was ravaged by Shalman [*kĕšōd šalmān bêt ʾarbēʾl* / On a day of battle, / When mothers and babies were dashed to death together." Many suggestions are made for Shalman, among them Shallum (one of the Assyrian Shalmanesers), a Moabite king, and the Zalmunna of chapter 8. For Beth-arbel, the Assyrian Arbela is often mentioned, but also a number of Arbelas closer to home. The Greek for the third clause, however, gives Salaman (Σαλαμαν) out of the house of Jerubbaal (Ιεροβααλ). This is mystifying, and many simply emend the Greek to read, respectively, Zalmunna and Jeroboam, or the like, without clarifying the context much.

What these observations suggest is that narratives about two separate personalities may once have floated around, and certainly so when materials about Samuel and David were taking shape. However, when Judges was achieving a final form, the two had merged even if without complete erasure of the demarcations. It is noticeable, however, that whereas the "Gideon" tales could easily sustain their place among those devoted to rescuers of premonarchic Israel, without depending on those concerning "Jerubbaal," the reverse would not have worked at all. From 6:1 through 8:35, there is as complete a cycle of horrors affecting Israel and its reversal as we are used to seeing in Judges, with as full a biography of the chosen rescuer as we have had earlier, and with all of the expected elements, including formulaic conclusions (notices about the land at peace and the death and burial of Gideon). These details would be missed if the "Jerubbaal" material is treated by itself, with its total devotion to the affairs of Abimelech (less so of Jotham) rather than those of Jerubbaal. In the literature, there is speculation on who these two personalities might have been before they were joined, many with novelistic touches that do not command repeat (see Emerton 1976: 302–8).

How these two narratives, with their separate missions, came to be cobbled together is beyond easy reconstruction. A hint may be found in the etymology of the name Gideon (gidᵉ'ôn; Γεδεων). It is based on the root gādaᶜ to which is attached the element -ôn (as in šimᶜôn, ḥeṣrôn, šimrôn, and the like). There is no explicit attempt to give an explanation for it, but a notice in the same episode that secures for Gideon the name Jerubbaal (6:25–32) may suggest awareness of the connection: When Gideon was instructed to demolish Baal's altar, he was also to cut up and use as kindling the wooden asherah ('ăšērâ) that in some way is connected with it (see above). In other contexts with a similar charge to chop up assorted wooden objects of worship, among them the asherah (Deut 7:5, 12:3; 2 Chr 14:2 [3 RSV], 31:1, 34:4–7), the Piel of gādaᶜ is used. That this verb was not used here may be conscious, due to a reluctance not to overload this particular episode with too many etiologies. If so, the episode would function less as an etiology for one name than as a contribution to a successful patching of two narrative strands.

2. Signs and Wonders (Judg 6:33–8:3)

6 ³³All Midian, Amalek, and Qedem tribesmen joined forces. They crossed over and camped in the Jezreel Valley. ³⁴Zeal for the LORD sheathed Gideon. He sounded the ram's horn and Abiezer rallied behind him. ³⁵He sent messengers throughout Manasseh, and it too rallied behind him. He then sent messengers through Asher, Zebulun, and Naphtali, and they came up to meet them.

³⁶Gideon said to God himself, "If you intend me to be the rescuer of Israel, as you once said, ³⁷I am setting this woolen fleece on the threshing floor. If dew is on just the fleece when the entire ground is dry, I will know that you will rescue Israel through me, as you once said." ³⁸So it was: When he rose early the next day, he squeezed the fleece and wrung dew from it—a bowlful of water. ³⁹Gideon said to God himself, "Do not be angry with me for speaking yet again. Let me make just one more test through the fleece: Let the fleece be dry, while there is dew all over the ground." ⁴⁰That night, God did exactly that: The fleece only was dry, but all over the ground there was dew. פ

7 ¹Next morning, Jerubbaal—that is, Gideon—and all the troops with him encamped by Harod Spring. From his angle, the camp of Midian was to the north, at Moreh Hill, in the valley. ²The LORD said to Gideon, "You have too many people with you for me to deliver Midian into their hands; Israel might take credit from me, boasting, 'My own might rescued me.' ³Therefore, tell the people openly, 'Anyone scared or anxious should turn back by taking flight from Mount Gilead.'" Among the people, twenty-two thousand turned back while ten thousand remained. ס

⁴The Lord said to Gideon, "The people are too many. Lead them to water and I will cull them for you there. Anyone of whom I tell you, 'This one goes with you,' that one shall go with you; and anyone of whom I tell you, 'This one is not to go with you,' that one shall not go." ⁵When he led the people to water, the Lord said to Gideon, "Set apart all those who lap up water with the tongue, as does a dog, *from* all those who bend down on their knees to drink." ס ⁶Three hundred was the number of lappers, with hand to their mouth, while the rest of the people bent down on their knees to drink water. ⁷Then the Lord said to Gideon, "With these three hundred lappers I will rescue you and deliver Midian to you. The people may all go home." ⁸The provisions of the people were collected, their ram's horns as well. He sent off every man from Israel, each to his tent, keeping just the three hundred men. The camp of Midian was below him, in the valley. פ

⁹That same night the Lord said to him, "Be ready to go down into the camp, for I have turned it over to you. ¹⁰Should you fear going down, then go down with your attendant Purah toward the camp. ¹¹Once you hear what they say, you will take courage and go down into the camp." So he went down with his attendant Purah to the outpost of those girded for battle in the camp. ¹²Midian, Amalek, and all Kedem were swarming on the valley plain, as many as locusts. Their camels were beyond count, as many as sand on the seashore. ¹³Gideon came there just as one man was relating a dream to another, "I just had a dream: There was a *round loaf* of barley bread tumbling in the Midian camp. It reached the tent, falling as it struck it. It spun it upwards, and the tent crumpled."ᵃ ¹⁴His companion answered, "This can be nothing but the sword of Gideon son of Joash, from Israel. God is turning Midian and the entire camp over to him." פ

¹⁵When Gideon heard the dream told and interpreted, he bowed low. Returning to the camp of Israel, he said, "Be ready, for the Lord has turned the camp of Midian over to you!" ¹⁶He divided the three hundred men into three units, equipping them all with ram's horns and empty jars, with torches in the jars. ¹⁷He told them, "Observe my action to do the same. When I reach the outpost of the camp, simply do whatever I do. ¹⁸As I and all those with me blow the ram's horn, you too will blow your ram's horn from all around the camp, saying, 'For the Lord and for Gideon!'" פ

¹⁹Gideon and the hundred men with him arrived at the outposts of the camp, at the start of the middle watch, barely after the sentries were posted.

---

a. Or: "Reaching the tent, it struck it and it fell—when it threw it upwards, the tent collapsed."

They blew the ram's horns and crashed the jars they had. ²⁰The men in three units blew their horns and broke their jars. Grasping torches in their left hands and in their right hands the rams' horns for blowing, they shouted, "A sword for the LORD and for Gideon!" ²¹While everyone circling the camp stood his ground, the whole camp began running, howling, and scampering. ²²Just as the three hundred ram's horns were sounded, everywhere in the camp the LORD set one sword against the other. The entire host fled toward Zererah as far as Beth-shittah, then as far as the outskirts of Abel-meholah by Tabbath. ²³From Naphtali, from Asher, from Manasseh, men from Israel were summoned and they rushed after Midian. ²⁴The messengers Gideon sent all over the hills of Ephraim conveyed: "Come down to face Midian, but capture ahead of them the waterways along the Jordan up to Beit-barah." All the men of Ephraim rushed and captured the waterways along the Jordan up to Beit-barah. ²⁵They captured Midian's two commanders, Oreb and Zeeb. They executed Oreb at Oreb Rock and they executed Zeeb at Zeeb Winepress, and kept after Midian. They brought Gideon the heads of Oreb and Zeeb from across the Jordan.

8 ¹The men of Ephraim censured him severely by telling him, "How could you treat us like this by not calling us when you went to fight Midian?" ²He answered them, "Have I done anything so far comparable to you? Ephraim's gleanings are better than Abiezer's vintage! ³To you God turned over Midian's commanders, Oreb and Zeeb; what did I achieve that matches you?" Their resentment against him abated once he addressed them in this way.

NOTES

Introductory Remarks: On Testing God

When Israel felt lost in the desert, its people complained, occasionally rebelled, but also sought reassurance by goading God. Their whining and backsliding is a major theme in Exodus, leading to frequent testing of God, who responds by quenching their thirst (Exod 15:22–27, 17:2–7) and satisfying their hunger (Exod 16).[1] Striking is the fact that the murmuring occurs moments after Israel had witnessed miracles on its behalf. What is apparent, too, in these narratives is that the testing is often provoked but also that the signs in response are forced on God. Nostalgic about a sentimentalized past and insecure about its future in the face of a hostile topography and aggressive adversaries, Israel goads its god into repeated drives for reassurance. With Moses successfully interceding ("Why do you quarrel with me; why do you test the LORD?," Exod 17:2), Israel manages to escape God's ire. Not surprisingly, in the remarkable elaboration of what is required for Israel to have God as its god, not testing him (*lōʾ těnassû ʾet-YHVH ʾělōhêkem*; Deut 6:16) is sandwiched between refraining from worshiping other deities and continuing to obey God's commands.

The theme of testing God is frequently addressed in Scripture. It can be argued that Abraham reverses the direction of the test when he single-mindedly marches his son to Mount Moriah (Gen 22)—for could God afford to rescind an oft-repeated promise to deliver an heir through Sarah? It can also be argued that elements in the vows of Jacob, most notably demanding safe protection while abroad, are themselves challenges for God's effectiveness beyond the borders of the Promised Land. Arresting, too, are moments when God asks to be tested. Isaiah offers Ahaz the choice on how to set up such a test, and the king (wisely) refuses to do so (Isa 7:11–12). Hezekiah seeks divine reassurance about his health, and Isaiah allows him to establish the criterion (2 Kgs 20:4–11; with variation in Isa 38:4–8, 21–22). However, none of the passages is as frontal about testing God or forcing him into delivering signs as are the many occasions involving Gideon—not only for their chutzpah (Gideon craves reassurance even after divine statements of support), but also for their frequency (at 6:17, 36–40). Most remarkable, Gideon receives signs of divine patronage even when unsolicited (twice in chapter 7).

The Hostilities

6 33–35. The narrative picks up from the notices that open the chapter, with Midian and its allies resuming their harassment of Israel, no doubt expecting the same past successes. The valley in which they camped is named Jezreel ("may God sow") and is not in Judah (Josh 15:56), but in Issachar (Josh 19:18). There, Saul camped before his fatal battle at Gilboa (1 Sam 29–31) and Ahab had a palace. Whether or not its mention here gives a clue to the apocalyptic sentiments set there by Hosea (1:5) is open to debate.

An unusual phrase is used to speak of God's investment in Gideon: His *rûᵃḥ* is said to *lāvaš*, to "clothe," him.[2] This verb is susceptible to imagery, with God and people said to be sheathed in justice, majesty, shame, or the like. In other contexts, the phrase is applied to people (an officer in 1 Chr 12:19; a priest in 2 Chr 24:20) transported by the excitement of the moment. Here, however, the sense is approximated by Mesopotamian art, in which the bodies of deities and kings are enveloped by *melammu*.[3] Although Gideon is moved to act, he is not yet ready to fight. On the use of the ram's horn (*šōfār*), see above at 3:27. Some Greek texts have Gideon calling "Abiezer, his brother" before it rallied behind him, likely reading two phrases, *'ăvî 'ezer 'eḥāᵃv* and *'ăvî 'ezer 'aḥărāyv*. The messengers are sent first to his own tribe, Manasseh, before they fan out north and clockwise to Asher, Zebulun, and Naphtali, tribes we have already met. In military contexts, the verb *'ālâ* is about rising to the challenge more than moving toward higher terrain or northward. When troops move to meet (*liqrā't*) another, only exceptionally (as 2 Kgs 1:3) is it in opposition. The phrase *vayyaʿălû liqra'tām*, therefore, balances the activity of the enemy by assembling Israel's forces (contra Moore 1895: 197).

The Twofold Sign

6 36–40. *hā'ĕlōhîm* occurs about a dozen times in Judges. In its absolute form, however, it is restricted to stories about Gideon (6:36, 39; 7:14) and Samson (13:9, 16:28 [vocative]). The article can be regarded as a mild demonstrative, "that god" (GKC 404 [§126a,b]), implying "the true God" (BDB 43b). "God himself" gives a smoother rendering, and I adopt it despite my qualms about its gender implication. Its use is attributed to E or P, but the narrator's intent here is to underscore the intimacy of contact between God and Gideon. Gideon frames the question as a challenge, despite the previous reassurance about his selection: If God intends (*yēš* [x] *bĕyad*) to fulfill his promise, he must prove himself through a prearranged test. The whole premise might be odd, given that earlier, Gideon (at 6:17) had requested to know that he indeed was

God's target. The consequent dramatic display proved the divinity of his interlocutor, but it might not have delivered the assurance he was after. Such relentless need for reassurance, not to say also mistrust of God, riled ancient commentators. Josephus and Pseudo-Philo simply ignored this particular story; the latter found their multiplicity in the Gideon sequence unseemly and told his readers (*LAB* 35:7) to search for them in the book of Judges. Still, Gideon did assume a divine charge when he summoned troops from hither and yon.

The *gōren*, "threshing ground," is selected not because it is (or is not) likely to collect dew (Burney 1970: 204), but because it is a public area (for example, 1 Kgs 22:10, Ruth 3) large enough to be converted into a place for sacrifice (2 Sam 24:21–24). As suggested by S. Ackerman (private communication), the choice may not be guided by space alone but as a reversal of the earliest setting for Gideon's debut, when he treated the grain at a winepress—a less obvious place for Midian to monitor. It does not hurt that Gideon had amassed a nice army by now. The verb *yāṣag* is about setting something for display; it will reoccur at crucial moments in Gideon's tales (at 7:5 and 8:27). Dew (*ṭal*) is a major element in Levantine climate and agriculture. Especially during the dry season (May–September) and in the hilly regions, moisture-laden winds produce dew on hitting cooler soil (Frick 1992: 119–26).[4] Wool absorbs water but does not transfer it for evaporation (wicking), so despite the dry climate of summer months, it can pull moisture from the night air. Yet neither the wool nor the stone/beaten earth floor is being cited here for how dew affects it; rather, it is to establish a sharp contrast in how they interact at each test. In the first move, the outcome is stated impersonally (*vayyĕhî-kēn*), reassuring the rabbis who, citing Hos 14:6 (5 RSV), could not imagine God desiccating Israel (Légasse 1991: 244–45). Gideon can fill a *sēfel* worth of water, a vessel mentioned elsewhere only in the confrontation between Sisera and Jael (at 5:25).[5]

Setting up a condition only to have it reversed is fairly frequent in ancient literature. We need only recall reversals attached to Moses: a rod that turns into a snake and back again into a rod, and a hand that turns leprous before becoming hale again (see Bertman 1964). Gideon's reversal of the conditions opens with a plea to resist anger. The language recalls Rachel's words as she apologizes to her father for not standing on his arrival (Gen 31:35) and Aaron's as he staves off his brother's anger for allowing the worship of the golden calf (Exod 32:22). But it reminds most of Abraham's passionate debate with God about the fate of the guilty (Gen 18). In fact, the phrase to speak (*'ak happā'am*) makes better sense in the mouth of an Abraham who had already questioned God's judgment five times (Gen 18:32) when he utters it. (We shall also meet with "yet again" in the Samson story, at 16:28.) In contrast, the phrase *raq-happā'am* when asking for a new test is unique and suggests that there will be no more requests. Undoubtedly, the result of the second test is more likely to persuade since, as I noted above, wool is a fine absorbing agent. For this reason, perhaps, God is given credit for making it happen, as requested.

A Twofold Countertest

THE SIFTING

7 1–8. As discussed in the Comments to the previous section, the equation between Jerubbaal and Gideon (*yĕrubba'al hû' gid'ôn*) transits us to a setting in which the name Gideon for our hero predominates. It will come back at 8:35 (*bêt yĕrubba'al gid'ôn*),

at which point it will disappear. Harod (ḥărōd, "Trembling") Spring occurs only here, obviously in anticipation of God's instruction that will soon follow.[6] Traditionally, it is cited at ʿAin Jâlûd near Gibeah. The same verse in Ps 83 that recalled the defeat of Sisera and Jabin by the waters of Kishon (see the Comments at IIIC1, Judg 4:1–24) mentions Midian's destruction at Endor, so a few kilometers south of Mount Tabor. Moreh Hill, whence Midian's large camp stretched, cannot be located with precision (but see Lagrange 1903: 131–32; Burney 1970: 205–7). It is presumed to be in the vicinity of Jezreel (6:33) and Mount Tabor (8:18).

Having experienced Gideon's tests, God turns the tables. Gideon is obviously vacillating (see above), renewing demands for reassurance after he had called Israel to battle. In effect, God fortifies Gideon's resolve by raising the odds against a victory, but he also exposes his own commitment to it. Gideon managed to raise 32,000 men when the enemy had massed 135,000 (see at 8:10). It might well be that the night attack God will soon devise against the Midianites demands a small force (Malamat 1953: 65), but the accent here is on the unorthodox way the unit was formed. God often battles for Israel (lastly against Sisera), but the motivation for taking charge is rarely as blunt as we see here.

The idiom lehitpāʾēr ʿal+ has to do with acquiring praise meant for someone else. Moses transfers to Pharaoh the credit for requesting God's intercession in the matter of frogs plaguing the land (Exod 8:5). The sharper example for us is at Isa 10:15. The prophet lectures the Assyrian king for attributing triumphs to his own might (TNK): "Does an ax boast over him who hews with it / Or a saw magnify itself above him [yitgaddēl ʿal-] who wields it?" The Assyrians are joining Pharaoh and many others in bragging.

The first cull cuts the number of potential warriors by more than half and might not at first be regarded as a challenge, for Hebraic law (Deut 20:8) does allow for desertion on the eve of battles: "Any man who is fearful and without courage may return home, lest he infect his comrades with his faintheartedness." Gideon is to make a public statement. The Hebrew idiom qārāʾ bĕʾōzen, literally meaning "declaim in someone's ear," draws from the world of symbolic gestures, as might also other constructions, such as "uncover the ear" (as in 1 Sam 9:15 and Ruth 4:4) and "place in the ear" (as in Exod 17:14). "Ear" may be kept in translations, as already in the ancient versions, if quaintness is a goal. Those who are fearful are to turn back (yāšōv) and vĕyyiṣpōr min-, an idiom that occurs only here but foreshadows a pun that will be deployed at 7:4.[7] With TNK ("as a bird flies from Mount Gilead"), I have it constructed on what a bird (ṣippōr) does when frightened. There is a fine passage from a Mari letter in which King Zimri-Lim defends giving protection to a smith accused of stealing jewelry from Hazor (TH 72.16): "My 'father' [King Yarim-Lim of Aleppo] has written me about this man, about returning a man who, like a trembling bird fleeing a falcon, had come to me. Is this a man I should release? If I release this man, afterwards anyone who hears, will he seek shelter as if with an interceding deity?"[8] Commentators have needlessly fretted about the mention of Mount Gilead when Gideon is closer to Mount Gilboa, and they have proposed many emendations (Barthélemy 1982: 95). The clause seems modeled after a gnomic saying and so is best left as is.

The second selection is a test of some sort, with God setting up an aural pun on ṣpr at 7:3 and ṣrp at 7:4. Gideon is to bring them to a body of water, and God will "cull them" for him (vĕ'eṣrĕfennû lĕkā), the verb drawing on a language for metallurgy. The instruction remaining in 7:4 seems strangely redundant, unless it be that God did not trust Gideon to follow instructions. The test itself is odd and is not conducted as commanded: Those who lap (lāqaq) water by using their tongue (as do dogs) were to be separated from those who fell on their knees.[9] Yet, the men who were set aside (7:4) did no such thing: They actually used their hands to scoop water so did not at all act as dogs, whose paws are of no use in drinking.[10] However, because the same verb (lāqaq, albeit a Piel) is used here as for the test act, I am presuming that the *instrument* for drinking was not at stake, but the *positioning* was: Especially when on the run, dogs remain on all fours when lowering their tongues into the water. So, men who crouched before scooping water were to be differentiated from those who fell to their knees when doing the same.

What to do with this "insight" remains an issue, for although how Gideon is told to act is clear enough, its logic is not. In the literature one reads many suggestions, none easily acceptable.[11] Josephus (*Ant.* 5.216) thought that those who drank on their knees were courageous, but those who drank "tumultuously" were few and cowardly, the better to display God's power. Malamat (1953: 62–63) cites Field Marshall Lord Wavell, who accepts the opposite explanation: Those who cupped the water were alert soldiers. Moore (1895: 202, and Assis 2005b: 62–63) finds a connection with the fierceness of dogs. Citing 1 Kgs 19:18, traditional Jewish exegetes made the kneelers potential worshipers of false gods.[12]

The few gathered the ram's horns of the many, but also their ṣēʸdâ, the latter normally referring to the rations they carried when off to war, so hardly light transport. Looking ahead to how the tale develops, many have emended this word to *kaddēʸ, "pitchers," so the remnant gathered (empty) vessels as well. Others find gratuitous difficulty in the sequence of voices (vayyiqĕḥû, "they took," and then šillaḥ, "he sent off") and so emend the first verb into a singular (Moore 1895: 204; see Barthélemy 1982: 95). As a result, just 1 percent of those volunteering for combat were selected. In truth, even those numbers were too high, for when the God of Israel fights the foe, no humans need participate. Still, having reinforced Gideon's skittishness by cutting his troops to a fraction of the enemy's, God felt the need to bolster his courage through one more demonstration of support.

THE DREAM

7 9–15. The sequence of tests and signs in this and the previous chapter gives an impression of a series in immediate conjunction, but the narrative covers an undetermined yet rather tight interval, given the danger posed by the enemy's invasion. This particular demonstration occurs after the three hundred men were selected, a notion enhanced by Rahlfs A, which adds "(go down) quickly from here [τὸ τάχος ἐντεῦθεν]." It is by far the most complex display of signs that we have, as it merges diverse divinatory processes. Moreover, within this sequence God codes a test for his capacity to deliver on a promise.

The same phrase (vayyĕhî ballaylâ hahûʾ) that opened God's instruction on destroying the Baal altar (at 6:25) is used here, and we may here also surmise that we are dealing with an anthropomorphic manifestation of God or a vision rather than a dream. It is unusual that God feels the need to prove his word just after declaring that he has granted Israel victory—"for I have turned [the enemy] over to you" (*kî nĕtattîv bĕyādekā*), a phrase that will soon echo in the mouths of a Midianite (7:14) and of Gideon (7:15). So, the question arises whether God is urging Gideon to "attack" now, as *TNK* translates the command *rēd*, or he is simply instructing him to "go down" (the normal translation of the verb) into the camp where he will find cause to strengthen his resolve (at 7:11).[13] I lean toward the second, if only to clarify the role of the acolyte accompanying Gideon; but in the process, I am extending the number of tests and signals that take place before any of Israel's enemies come to harm.

Is God goading Gideon by citing his fear (*'im-yārē' 'attâ*)? Perhaps there is realism here, given how few troops remain with him. Psychologically, telling Gideon to take along Purah (*pûrâ*; Greek, Φαρα) is astute. Purah is Gideon's attendant (*na'ar*; in military contexts applied to assistance rather than youth). Such servants tend to carry shields and weapons, but this is hardly his function here.[14] Nor is it likely that the lad is to bolster Gideon's courage, for Gideon might have done better with one of the three hundred warriors.[15] He could, of course, be another witness to what will soon occur in the Midianite camp, but we shall soon find that Gideon needs no confirmation beyond what he will fear. In fact, the narrator simply forgets about Purah.[16] Therefore, the advice to take Purah, I speculate, forces Gideon to act in conscious obedience of God. As he does so, there is sharpened motivation for Gideon to accept proofs of God's investment in his welfare.

Biblical narratives are fond of sharp conjunctions, as much to keep a story tight as to sharpen the predetermination of events. Gideon and Purah arrive just as a warrior is troubled enough by a dream to reveal it to a companion. In the ancient Near East, dreams are not normally interpreted by those who have them, but by a third party, and that is very lucky for us readers because we get to hear about them.[17] Dreams are highly symbolic and often contain a fair density of puns, leaving it to the interpretation to deliver the key. Dreams are also never less than fraught with truths that beg for decipherment. The solution might emerge promptly, as in our case, or it might take years—as well as prompting—to materialize. When Joseph dreams that eleven stars bow to him (Gen 37:9), he actualizes the vision by cruelly plotting to have Benjamin come to Egypt so that all eleven brothers can kowtow to him.

God guarantees that what Gideon hears will give him courage, in essence giving Gideon no discretion in the matter. Gideon and Purah penetrate the camp where bivouacked warriors prepared for battle, the noun *ḥămušîm* having to do with belts around the *ḥōmeš*, "the abdomen," rather than with any multiple of five (*ḥāmēš*). The danger facing them, now and in the future, is sharpened by assigning the enemy themes from 6:5 (swarms of locusts) and Josh 11:4 (as sand at the seashore).

The dream is at once transparent and obscure. What the warrior reveals is a *ṣĕlûl* (*Ketiv*) or *ṣĕlîl* (*Qere*), a word occurring only here, leading to conjectures: following the Greek, something round (μαγίς), or following the rabbis, something roasted, made from barley.[18] It was tumbling (*mithappēk*) across the camp of Midian, penetrating deep into the camp to strike *the* tent, presumably the one central to the military operation. When it hits it (the verb here is commonly used in martial conquests), it fells something (the tent or the tumbling bread?). The rest of the sentence may tell what happens next; just as likely (I give both renderings), it repeats the sequence, using the same vocabulary, as if the warrior is stunned by what he dreamed.

As happens in dream narratives (biblical or otherwise), the elucidation can be brutal. Here, however, it seems to have little connection with the elements of the dream.[19] The collapsing tent easily evokes the destruction of the Midianite camp, but it is difficult for me to recognize any play on words (or even ideas) behind the round (?) loaf of barley and the sword of Gideon. This may well be the point, for Gideon would surely be more impressed by an interpretation that bluntly cites him (plus his father, no less) as victor than by one that clarifies ambiguously. About all that can be said is that Gideon (or the narrator) drew on the interpretation to create the *cri de guerre* that we shall soon hear in the mouths of Hebrew warriors: "A sword for the Lord and Gideon" (7:18, 20).[20]

By prostrating himself (see Josh 5:14), Gideon signals that he understands both the intent of the dream (*mispar hahǎlôm*) and the significance of its elucidation.[21] The word *šivrô* is unusual here when elsewhere Hebrew uses *peter* for an explication.[22] Many explanations are offered, but none is fully convincing. Luckily, the intent is clear.

ROUT OF MIDIAN

7 15b–22. If the reader wonders why God shows so much patience with Gideon when many others might have seized the opportunity to be a champion, how Gideon routed Midian might provide an answer. Allowed few resources (three hundred men against thousands), he is left to formulate a plan. It did not hurt that Gideon returned from his night venture totally certain of victory. Displaying commendable reticence, he does not quote the interpretation he had just heard, possibly because it might rob credit from God. As it happens, in literary traditions, recognition of the divine effort is recalled: We have noted how in Ps 83:10–12 (9–11 RSV) God is urged to champion Israel as when he defeated Midian's hosts. Isaiah, too, reflects on events at the Rock of Oreb (at Isa 10:26; see below). There is also the prophet's exulting in the triumphs of God (at Isa 9:3) as repeats of the "Day of Midian" (*yôm midyān*).

Dividing a military force makes sense especially because a night sky can hide numbers. A threefold division (*šĕlōšâ rāʾšîm*) is remarkably well-represented in Scripture, and it may well have been a standard strategy.[23] No weapon is issued to the men, but each receives a ram's horn and an empty jar, with an *unlit* torch stuck in its mouth, likely to ease the transport.[24] In imitation of Gideon, each is to blow his horn and shout the war cry. As hatched, the plan was set to unfold appreciably before dawn. We can't be precise, but given that Hebrews divided the night (which seasonally differed in length) into three watches (*ʾašmōret* or *ʾašmûrâ*), this middle one (*tîkōn*) likely lasted about ninety minutes before and after our midnight.

The assault was to take place as the guards had picked up their positions, so presumably not yet fallen in to the ease of normalcy. They were still on the alert, but it obviously did not improve their cause. The Hebrews blew their horns as instructed and, following Gideon's lead, crashed their jugs, no doubt maximizing the noise. We presume that the torches they had freed from the jars were now lit. Holding them high in their left hand, they blew the horn held with the right and shouted an expanded version of the war cry that alludes to the sword that is now dedicated to a holy war. I am not at all sure why Burney (1970: 180–82, 214–18, following Budde, Moore, and others) found the scenario so problematic that he needed to split the material into two strands (J and E).[25]

Gideon's men stood their ground (literally, "they stood in their place," *'āmad taḥtāʸv*) while continuing to blow their horns, shout, and wave torches. The strategy here is to give the Midianites the impression that they still have time to save their lives. As a result, pandemonium ensues, with men running and shouting without discipline. Adding terror, God enters the fray, turning one man against the other, whether imagining each other as enemy or as someone blocking their escape. (A similar tactic appears in 1 Sam 14:20.) The direction they took mentions four place names, only one of which, Abel-meholah, can be recognized as it was the birthplace of Elisha (1 Kgs 19:16). The place was assigned under Solomon to a region from Beth-shean stretching east of the Jordan (1 Kgs 4:12). The others are either unknown (*bêt haššiṭâ; ṭabbāt*) or their mention is emended to give them a thicker profile (*ṣĕrērâ* into *ṣĕrēdâ* or *ṣārĕtān*). Unclear is whether in panic the Midian host sought escape in several directions or whether they ran out of steam at two spots (Beth-shittah and Abel-meholah) when they hoped to reach farther (Zererah and Tabbath). These obscurities have not stopped commentators from locating these places on maps, either topographically or by making conjunctions with evocative modern names, hardly delivering more sense to what is already clear: The enemy was in a rout even as no Hebrew sword was raised against it.[26]

7 23–25. The language for the rush of troops against Midian is elaborate and likely replays what is found in 6:35. The great tête-à-têtes between God and Gideon (6:36–40, 7:1–7) are thus framed, emulating parables. At 6:35, Gideon is said to send messengers to Manasseh, and it mustered (*vayyizzāʿēq*, using a passive construction) behind him. He also appealed to Naphtali, Zebulon, and Asher, and they joined forces with Manasseh. Here, minus Zebulon, these tribes are mustered (*vayyiṣāʿēq ʾîš-yiśrāʾēl*). Gideon's call to Ephraim has a syntax that gives primacy to the messengers (*ûmalʾākîm šālaḥ gidʿôn*), but it is difficult to convey in English. The same passive construction as in 6:35 is now applied to Ephraim (*vayyiṣāʿēq kol-ʾîš efrayim*), thus accenting the bracketing. (Almost the same phrase will soon occur at 12:1, with different consequences.) Ephraim is instructed to cut the escape routes of Midian as its men naturally seek shelter across the Jordan by moving ahead of fragments of the broken Midianites as they reach the natural crossing spots on the river. We have seen how Ehud tried to block the Moabites from escaping at the *maʿbĕrôt hayyardēn* (Judg 3:28).[27] With Beit-barah an unknown place, it is tempting to follow those who seek similar phrasing here, for example, Burney 1970: 225.

The commanders have totemic names: *ʿōrēv* is a raven, and *zĕʾēv* is a wolf. These can be true or acquired names. Here (and at 8:3) they are labeled *śar*, a person of authority (military or not), while in Ps 83:12 they are *nādîv*, a person of elite status. Later (at 8:6, 14, and likely also at 10:18), the label will be assigned to leaders who may not be military. Bluedorn (2001: 149) points out that in Judges the verb *hārag*, "to kill, execute," is mostly limited to the Gideon narratives. The clause *vayyirdĕfû ʾel midyān*, "they kept after Midian," is sandwiched between statements about the captured commanders. The idiom is oddly construed with the preposition *ʾel*, but the sense is clear: The executions occurred even as a mop-up operation was in progress. Etiologies follow: Oreb is killed near a rock that henceforth bears his name. Isaiah (10:26) recalls this spot as well as the Red Sea to remind Assyria of God's sword. Rösel (1976: 16, 20) is among many who consider the place as primary. The *yeqev* bearing Zeev's name is the upper level of a winepress (see under 6:11), but by metonymy it can stand for the full winepress.[28]

There may be irony, suggests S. Ackerman (private communication), that Zeeb dies at a winepress, a shelter for Gideon when escaping Midian.

Beheading is a grizzly practice, with Babylonians assigning it to primordial days, when Gilgamesh triumphed over Ḫumbaba. It is a form of desecration no less than humiliation, for in most cultures the burial of corpses made incomplete by removal of the head effectively compromises the dead's afterlife. Oddly enough, wounded prisoners are known to beg for decapitation rather than suffer the pain and shame of a triumphal display followed by public execution. Beheading is messy and is not done just to end the life of victims, as when Judith murders Holofernes (Jdt 13:6–9) or when Herod executes the Baptist (Matt 14:1–12).[29] Rather, it is used also to dispatch heads as a lesson to the living: Families receive them in revenge, allies in triumph, enemies in threats (2 Sam 4:5–7), and gods in homage (1 Sam 17:54, 2 Macc 15:30).[30] It must not be assumed (as had Boling [1975: 151] and many previous commentators) that Gideon had already crossed the Jordan when he received the ghoulish tribute.

Ephraim's Peeve

8 1–3. Ephraim is peeved for not receiving a call against Midian. Normally, the complaint is about missing the opportunity to plunder. However, unlike what is reported in a parallel incident involving Ephraim and Jephthah (12:1–6), Ephraim had as much chance to loot as the other tribes. The phrase *māh-haddāvār hazzeh*, construed with forms of the verb *ʿāśâ*, "to do," implies indignation or shock, often at discovering a slight or mismanagement. It may well be that a major goal of the episode is to bring out once more the verb that is at the core of the name Jerubbaal, but this time in the phrase *rîb ʾet* + suffix, with both legal ("they contested him") and nonlegal ("they rebuked him") implications.

In fewer than a couple of phrases, Gideon manages to inflate their egos twice. For Ephraim, what its harvesters leave behind (*ʿōlēlôt*, referring to grapes or olives) is more worthy than what Abiezer collects initially (*bāṣîr*, referring only to grapes).[31] Gideon is likely stuffing a known saying with metaphors, but his failure to cite other tribes by no means betrays the narrator's reliance on a tradition that limits the muster to this clan (Burney 1970: 227). Without giving Ephraim a chance to acknowledge the compliment, Gideon launches his second tribute, this one with a specific purpose: Whether or not they were among the first to be summoned, they were favored by God. Furthermore, their capture of the two Midian leaders must surely have yielded booty.

"A gentle response reverses anger" is what we learn from Prov 15:1. By flattering Ephraim on both the tribal and the personal levels, Gideon cools their temper and can proceed with his responsibility.[32] Such a presence of mind is nicely illustrated in a passage from ARM 26 404. During tense negotiations among vassals, when one ruler (Atamrum of Andarig) provokes supporters of the opposite side by insisting on the regional primacy of Zimri-Lim, his future ally (Asqur-Addu of Karana) saves the situation by declaring that opportunity exists for power-sharing among all competing suzerains. We shall soon have, however, an application of the other portion of the same verse: "A harsh word provokes anger." In the meantime, we might keep in mind that the town of Shechem was reckoned as much in Manasseh (17:2) as in Ephraim (Josh 7:24).

COMMENTS
Challenging God

The material in this segment is culled from three chapters in our Bible and includes many distinct episodes, yet they are glued by the contribution they make to the voyage of self-discovery that Gideon undertakes. When first introduced, Gideon is not a particularly obvious choice to save Israel. Over the years in which his world was ground down by a rapacious enemy, he had learned to hide his activities. Sarcasm came easily to him then, and it seemed incongruous to him that if there were to be miracles from his god, they would be conducted through him. The first deed asked of Gideon is not to rally the opposition and challenge the enemy, but to foment difficulties within the clan by destroying a Baal altar, leading away a bull belonging to his father and creating an altar without permission. That he obtained his father's support despite his defiance must have reassured Gideon that God's plan is already working.

This segment picks up on the threat of Midian and its allies. Filled with enthusiasm by his selection, Gideon summons kin and closest tribes; yet there is still testing to be done and signs to be read. In the first Introductory Remarks in this book (IA1), I delved into the many ways in which the will of God was ascertained, with particular emphasis on the need to multiply and collate responses to avoid false understanding of the divine message. The principle applies here also. In requesting mirror images of a specific miracle, Gideon was not only reassuring himself of God's support, but also examining his own judgment; for it was always possible that God had not intended that Gideon be the one to summon the needed force from so many tribes.

Challenging Gideon

As it happens, Gideon gets mixed grades on his effort. Yes, God complies (patiently) with the examination. Failure to do so might heighten Gideon's skittishness. Given the large number of troops mentioned on all sides (135,000 versus 32,000), realism may not be the main objective of the narrative, but delivering parabolic insights through a specific scene must certainly be a major goal. The argument developed in the Notes is ostensibly about God not wishing to share credit for the forthcoming victory (7:2), but a major goal of the arcane countertest God imposes may well have been to cultivate the leadership skills that will turn Gideon into an effective leader. Facing insurmountable odds, would he summon enough imagination (and faith) to carry out the needed attack?

The troops were to be reduced to less than 1 percent. Dividing the process into two phases might mirror Gideon's twofold test. The first stage removes two-thirds of the men Gideon successfully summoned, and they go home out of fear. It is no use to reason how the second stage was supposed to work. Josephus's idea that the remaining three hundred were selected for their cowardice has received many accolades in the literature; this cannot be correct, however, because all the cowards had already gone home, so both kneelers and lappers are faultlessly heroic. The result of this drastic sifting, however, forces Gideon to think beyond the normal approach of pitting one force against the other in open warfare, where the likelihood of defeat would be strong.

Although other biblical characters faced repeated hardship despite being favored by God (Jacob and Moses, among others), few required as many signs as did Gideon, and even fewer had the satisfaction to get them. Despite the heavy investment of divine power in bringing Israel once more on its feet, each of the signs deployed on both sides went into the construction of the capable warrior God needed in these circumstances. The dream sequence proves crucial in this formation.

Shaping a Leader

The principle behind the scene in the camp of Midian is that the best confirmation of a divine message is its duplication in as many different revelatory means as possible. In Mesopotamia, it was agreed that validation is achieved most reliably through extispicy, the reading of signs embedded in an animal's innards. Here, God reassures Gideon of victory by directing him to hear the retelling of a dream imposed on a Midianite soldier. Far more consequential is the interpretation of the dream that God forces on the dreamer's companion where little effort is made to give a plausible accounting of the imagery; rather, in the mouth of a Midianite is placed a statement on the power of God and the strength of the leader that God has selected. We might wonder (as did Moore [1895: 205–6]) how the name of Gideon, no less that of his father, reached a Midianite soldier, but Gideon took it as the sharpest indication that whatever he might plan will succeed.

We might also notice that when Gideon was devising his stratagem, God was nowhere to advise him as he did, say, Joshua at the walls of Jericho (Josh 6). And when God indeed displayed his powers, it was in a relatively unobtrusive way (Judg 6:22) as compared to, say, when he defeated Sisera (at Judg 4:15–16). Here again, the issue of cowardice is nowhere displayed, for when the enemy is in a panicked flight, Gideon did not need to summon a new batch of warriors but could rely on those mustered earlier. True, Gideon indeed does call on Ephraim to block Midian's escape routes, and the result is the slaughter of two of the enemy's leaders. The incident that follows on their success, wherein they rebuke Gideon for not including them in planning the war, reveals much about the frayed relationship of tribes during a period of see-sawing fortunes, but it also prepares for another such occasion during the rule of Jephthah. Most importantly, it contributes to a fuller portrait of Gideon as he masters the art of ruling. Much later, when the Apostle Paul movingly recalls the faith of his ancestors, he places Gideon first among the judges God selected to fulfill his will: "For time would fail me to tell of Gideon, Barak, Samson, Jephthah, of David and Samuel and the prophets" (Heb 11: 32). As it happens, he had called on heroes who were touched also by personal failures.

In the next series of episodes, Gideon will carry out his aggressive attacks against the enemy. As we shall see, he will not leave the stage without providing God with reason for ire (see below at 8:27). However, the proof of support that Gideon and Purah gathered from invading the enemy camp will prove the charm. There will be no more mutual goading.

3. Toward Kingship (Judg 8:4–28)

8 ⁴Gideon moved toward the Jordan; he crossed *it* and with him were three hundred men, exhausted yet pursuing. ⁵He told the people of Succoth, "Please give some loaves of bread to the people who follow me as they are exhausted; I am pursuing Zebah and Zalmunna, the kings of Midian." ⁶The chiefs of Succoth replied, "Are the palms of Zebah and Zalmunna already in your hand that we should give bread to your troops?" ⁷Gideon said, "Just for that, when the LORD turns Zebah and Zalmunna to me, I will flail your flesh with desert thorns and briers." ⁸From there he went up to Penuel and made the same request of them; but the people of Penuel answered the same as the people of Succoth. ⁹So he also told the people of Penuel: "On my safe return, I will demolish this citadel!" ס

¹⁰Zebah and Zalmunna were at Karkor. The army they had was about 15,000—all that remained of the entire camp of the Qedem tribesmen, for the fallen numbered 120,000 swordsmen. ¹¹Gideon marched up the road of the tent dwellers, up to the east of Nobah and Jogbehah, and routed the camp, which was off guard. ¹²Zebah and Zalmunna took to flight, with Gideon in pursuit. He captured Zebah and Zalmunna, the two kings of Midian, and threw the whole army into panic.

¹³On his way back from the battle through Potsherd Heights, Gideon son of Joash ¹⁴captured a youthᵃ from the people of Succoth and interrogated him. He wrote for him the names of the commanders and elders of Succoth, seventy-seven in number. ¹⁵Then he came to the people of Succoth and said, "Here are Zebah and Zalmunna, about whom you taunted me, saying, 'Are the palms of Zebah and Zalmunna already in your hand that we should give bread to your tired men?'" ¹⁶He took the town's elders and desert thorns and briers as well, and had the people of Succoth experience them. ¹⁷As for Penuel, he razed its citadel, killing the town's population.

¹⁸He then asked Zebah and Zalmunna, "Where are the men you killed in Tabor?" "May the same happen to you," they replied, "each had the bearing of princes." ¹⁹"They were my brothers," he said, "sons of my mother; as the LORD lives, had you spared them, I would not kill you." ²⁰He told his eldest son Jether, "Go ahead and kill them!" The youth would not draw his sword, for he was fearful, being still young. ²¹Zebah and Zalmunna then said, "Go ahead and cut us down, for manhood defines the person!" So Gideon went ahead and killed Zebah and Zalmunna. He took the crescents that were on the necks of their camels.

²²Everyone in Israel said to Gideon, "Rule over us—you, as well as your son and your grandson; for you have rescued us from Midian." ²³But Gideon told them, "I will not rule over you myself and my son will not rule over you; the LORD alone shall rule over you." ²⁴Gideon said to them, "I have a request to make of you: Each of you give me a ring from his plunder." (They had gold

---

a. Or: an administrator.

rings because they were of Ishmael.) [25]"Gladly," they replied. They spread out a garment and everyone tossed in it a ring from his plunder. [26]The weight of the gold he had requested came to 1,700 (shekels) of gold; this was apart from the crescents and the pendants and the purple robes worn by the kings of Midian or from the collars on the necks of their camels. [27]Gideon turned it into an ephod and set it up in his own town of Ophrah. All Israel lusted after it; for Gideon and his house, it became a snare. [28]Thus Midian was humbled before the people of Israel, and could not recover. The land had peace for forty years in Gideon's days. ꜱ

NOTES
Seeking Respect

8 4–9. Gideon received the heads of Orev and Zeev while still on the west side of the Jordan. With the band he used for the successful night attack, he crossed the Jordan. The syntax in Hebrew is odd, relying on a participle when a narrative tense would be more normal.[1] The intent may be to focus on him above all, and this sense is heightened when Gideon does not include himself among those needing help from Succoth. The men who followed him (*běregel*; see at 4:10) must have been famished, yet the Hebrew gives them as *ʿăyēfîm*, which has to do with exhaustion, rather than the expected *rěʿēvîm*, "famished." Rahlfs A expands with "faint" and "famished." Rahlfs B, with knowledge of Gideon's request for bread (at 8:5), also has the verb for hungering (πεινάω), and many modern translations follow suit. We must not always expect that narrators and characters be in synch about pronouncements. Hunger and exhaustion certainly march together, but Gideon may not be ready to admit to the former.

Succoth, one of two places with the same name (the other being in the Egyptian delta), is north of the confluence of the Jabbok and the eastern side of the Jordan (Josh 13:27). On his return to Canaan, Jacob builds "booths" for his cattle, providing a name for the place (Gen 33:17). There is active disagreement whether or not Deir ʿAlla (of the famous Balaam inscription) is Succoth, and there are speculations that it was a Canaanite enclave (see the dictionaries). It makes sense that Gideon would ask for loaves of bread (*kikkěrôt leḥem*) with which to feed his famished men, but not that Succoth would accept his notion that a motley crew could capture two Midianite kings who were backed by an imposing force (about fifteen thousand men, at 8:10). The absurdity of his notion is a major reason for their derision.

The kings he was pursuing have good Semitic names. Zebah (*zevaḥ*; Greek, Ζεβεε) could be given to a child born on a major feast; Zalmunna (*ṣalmunnaʿ*; Greek, Σαλμανα, Σελμανα; Josephus, Ζαρμουνής) is likely to include two elements: *ṣlm*, a north Arabian deity, and the root *mnʿ, "to prevent," so meaning something like "may Selem prevent (harm)."[2] Their names could be confected ironically or pejoratively, as was the case of Cushan-rishatayim (see the Comments to IIIA).

The leaders of Succoth (acting unanimously, with a singular subject for *vayyōʾmer*) might not have refused Gideon the food he was seeking had he not named his targets. They were in fact commanders (*śārîm*), so theirs was a military judgment. Why would they want to help someone who could bring the ire of oppressors against them? Their gibe is sharp: Show us the palms (*kaf*) you have removed from these kings and we will feed your victorious men. Unlike mutilation, which has degradation as a goal (see the Notes to Adoni-bezeq's fate, at 1:6), or the lopping off of heads to taunt the family or sponsors of enemies (see above at 7:25), cutting off hands, penises (prepuces in 1 Sam 18:25–27), and tongues is done to arrive at a reasonable count of soldiers killed.[3] We might imagine that tattoos and brands identified whether the palms were those of the defeated kings, but this is not necessary for the sarcasm to have its effect.

The word *lākēn* often introduces a response contrary to (or despite) a previously stated proposition; we shall see it operating this way again at 10:13 and 11:8. Here it introduces Gideon's threat. Using agricultural language, he vows that upon receiving God's support in capturing (*bĕtēt* YHVH *'et-*) the kings, he will return to Succoth and treat the body of the officials as harvested grain, threshing it (verb: *dûš*).[4] In Israel, three methods were available to loosen the grain from chaff, and they are neatly mentioned in Isa 28:27 (*TNK*): "So, too, black cumin is not threshed [*yûdaš*] with a threshing board [*ḥārûṣ*], Nor is the wheel of a threshing sledge rolled over [*yûssāv*] cumin; But black cumin is beaten out [*yēḥāveṭ*] with a stick [*maṭṭeh*] and cumin with a rod [*šēveṭ*]." The Hebrew for 8:7 (and Rahlfs B for that matter) suggests that victims were carded (their bodies dragged over thorns, or thorny sledges pulled over them). Although the verb *ḥāvaṭ* (see at 6:11) is not used in our context, we might nonetheless imagine that desert thorns and other spiked instruments (*barqonîm*, mentioned only here) will shape the flail used to punish the mockers.[5]

The second rejection occurs at Penuel, upstream the Jabbok from Succoth. Jacob wrestled the angel at this spot (Gen 32:23–33 [22–32 RSV]) and gave it its name, "the face of God." Gideon vows that on returning safely (*bĕšûvî vĕšālôm*), he will tear down the town's main stronghold (see below at 11:31). The verb he uses (*nātaṣ*) is familiar to us from its extensive use in the episode of the destruction of the Baal altar (at 6:25–32). On the nature of the *migdāl* he plans to destroy, see below at 8:13–17. This will explain why Gideon is said to have killed everyone in Penuel (8:17).

CAPTURING TWO KINGS OF MIDIAN

8 10–12. In contrast to the detailed accounting of how Gideon's tiny force routed the hosts of Midian, this time hardly any explanation is given for success despite the enemy's 50 to 1 advantage. Somewhat belatedly we learn that Midian had already lost 120,000 in its battle against the tribes Gideon summoned and against Ephraim. It is the highest number of losses reported in Judges, although 400,000 will be attributed to the army Israel musters against Benjamin (at 20:2, 17).[6] Some 15,000 are left at Karkor to the east of Penuel.

Karkor (*qarqōr*, perhaps "ground," as in Akkadian *qaqqarum*) occurs only in this passage. It is too far south and east to be equated with Qarqar on the Orontes where Shalmaneser battled a coalition including Ahab of Israel (853 BCE). A number of modern sites have just as evocative names and are sometimes cited in the literature (see the *ABD*, s.v.), but the consensus now is to situate it in the Wadi Sirḥan in the northern Hejaz, on the Damascus route into Arabia. However, as this location is almost 200 kilometers from Succoth and Penuel, it might stretch our imagination to bring Gideon and his brave group so far from familiar resources. It does not help that the road Gideon takes to reach Karkor is also difficult to chart. There is a Nobah (*nōvaḥ*) in Gilead, formerly Kenath (Num 32:42), but this one is likely to be a homonym farther south. Jogbehah (Jogbohah in some Hebrew manuscripts) is mentioned in Num 32:35 among towns east of the Jordan. Allocated to Gad, it is sometimes identified with either Tell Jubeihat, 24 kilometers southeast of Penuel, but other locales are equally favored.

Despite these ambiguities, the gist of the narrative is that Gideon did not take the obvious route, but one circuitous enough to provide him with the necessary surprise for success, given that the encampment of Midian was (or felt) secure (*hāyâ veṭaḥ*). Ironically, when places or people are said to feel "secure," often they are in for a rude surprise (as in Gen 34:25, Deut 28:52, and often in prophets chiding Israel). Or perhaps Gideon found another way to penetrate defenses, because when he attacked and captured the kings he was after, everyone in the camp panicked (*kol-hammaḥăneh heḥĕrîd*).

SETTLING SCORES

8 13–17. With the captured kings in tow, Gideon moves back to the town that nastily refused to help him.[7] Reference to the name of Gideon's father reminds of its invocation by the Midian dream interpreter (at 7:14). Here we have choices: Either Gideon moved through "Potsherd Heights," a name with similar construction as Potsherd Hill (see at 1:34), or, much less likely, he arrived there at dawn, since *ḥeres* is also a poetic word for the sun (KJV, "before the sun *was up*").[8] By itself a *naʿar* is a "youth," and we shall soon meet such an adolescent within a few more verses (at 8:20, and lots in the story of Samson); but when linked to a person, it refers to the service the *naʿar* is providing, the age not being a major factor: If in an administrative setting (as in Ruth 2:5), it is that of a foreman or steward; if in a military context (as at 7:10–11, see also 1 Sam 14:1, 25:5), it is that of a squire or attendant.[9] If, as in our case here, linkage is to city officials, this *naʿar* could be a scribe, for the *'ănāšîm* of a city are men of rank (see Ps 4:3 [2 RSV], 49:3 [2 RSV]), as in Akkadian *awīlū*.[10] This explains why he knew about the hierarchy there or, more remarkable, why he can write. This notice has exercised commentators since antiquity, for Rahlfs A gives ἀπογράφω, "to register, enroll," rather than Rahlfs B's γράφω, "to write," implying conveying rather than writing names (Harlé and Roqueplo 1999: 159). Yet, this reference is no indication that literacy was high east of the Jordan (see Young 1998a: 250), for Gideon was fortunate to have captured such a professional.[11]

This capture was even more fortunate for Succoth; for given what happened next at Penuel, Gideon might have simply butchered the whole town had he not worked from a list. What Gideon extracted from the man was the names of all officials at Succoth, both tribal commanders (*śārîm*) and town elders (*zĕqēnîm*), the two terms often paired, as in 2 Kgs 10:1 (Shomron) and Isa 3:14 (Jerusalem). It is surely accidental, but nonetheless ironic, that the number seventy-seven is applied to the revenge Lemech will take on his enemies (Gen 4:24).[12] Only the elders are said to be scourged, but likely the whole leadership is punished.

In presenting the captured kings to the men of Succoth, Gideon throws back on the latter an almost verbatim version of the sarcasm they had used; yet he expands by attributing to them an observation on the exhaustion of his men. In this way, they convict themselves by their callousness. Interesting is the condition of the men. The narrator had earlier used the verb **ʿyp* (at 8:4 and 8:5); Gideon instead calls on **yʿp* (*yĕʿēfîm*), which elsewhere (as in 2 Sam 16:2) has to do with the thirst that comes from wandering in arid regions. (On a possible application of the same verb on Sisera's condition, see at 4:21.)

Gideon punished as he had promised; Radaq suggests that their punishment was to teach them (and Israel) the enormity of their sin. The report on their fate is somewhat truncated, forcing the Greek versions to expand freely to harmonize with Gideon's threat. In the Hebrew (but not Rahlfs A) only the elders (*zĕqēnîm*) are assembled; but as the chiefs (*śārîm*) were the first to give offense (8:6), they were not likely spared. It is safe to assume they were subsumed under *'anšêy sukkôt*. Gideon collects also the instruments of torture and (the text says) *vayyōdaʿ*, "the victims." The verb is a Hiphil of *yādaʿ*, "to know, experience," and it has invited countless emendations or expansion of its meaning via other Semitic languages (a partial listing is in Bluedorn 2001: 159 n. 296). The Greek reprises the verbs used above at 8:7, suggesting that at least Rahlfs B read the same verb (*vayyādōš*) as in the Hebrew of 8:7. My translation stays with the received text, but it does not solve the problem. Luckily, no major complication rides on the matter.

What happened in Penuel fulfills Gideon's vow: The people died when the citadel was destroyed. Budde (1890: 114 n. 1) unnecessarily cuts the last clause because it is not mentioned in Gideon's vow. The *migdāl* (elsewhere *migdôl*) can refer to towers, in fields and elsewhere, but when it is within a city, it is the fortified segment (in Mari the *kirḫum*), where can be found the essentials for governing a town.[13] "Citadel" is a better approximation for the word than "tower," especially when citizens can move into it for protection. In postexilic Jerusalem a series of such self-contained but integrated units were built as bastions, among them the *bîrâ* of the Second Temple period (as in Neh 2:8), the Hellenistic Acra (as in 2 Macc 4:12, 27–28), and the Herodian Antonia, still extant today.

EXECUTING ZEBAH AND ZALMUNNA

8 18–21. The execution of the kings does not take place until *after* Succoth and Penuel are punished, for, aside from displaying them to refute his mockers, Gideon savored having the kings witness his power. In executing them publicly, Gideon is practicing the type of realistic psychological terror that, sadly, is well-attested in literature. (Amenhotep II, the son of Thutmosis III, was a master at this craft, long before the Assyrians.) Captured foes are slain at a spot where the people need either to know fear by witnessing execution or to gain courage by seeing an enemy degraded. The standard procedure, as noticed in the story of Adoni-bezeq (at 1:5–7), is to humiliate the defeated, inspire awe in potential enemies, and induce pride and jubilation among the victorious.

Still, we are startled by the question that Gideon sets before them and the seemingly incongruent exchange it provokes, for captured leaders are rarely left with followers to foment revenge. Gideon wants to know where (*'êfōh*) the men Zebah and Zalmunna killed are, but the puzzle is, what is he asking? Where are they buried, or what has happened to their bodies? If either, what would he do if such questions had concrete answers? Gideon and his prisoners might have known about the event at Tabor in which they were killed, but we have no clue. Tabor could be Mount Tabor, the site of some battle not mentioned as background to our texts (but see above at 6:33 [Jezreel Valley]). Or it could be Tabor, a town in Zebulun (1 Chr 6:62 [77 RSV]). Naturally, emendations have been offered: For the particle *'êfōh*, read *'êkāh*, "how, in what way," a particle, however, that controls verbs rather than nouns, as in our case; for the verb *hāragtem* ("you killed"), read **nihagtēm* ("you forcibly removed"); for Tabor, read *tabbûr* (*hā'āreṣ*) from 9:37, and so forth.[14] Traditional exegetes have Gideon ask "where are such men as those you killed?," suggesting a lament on the savage passing of great men, a theme nicely represented in ancient literature.

The answer the doomed kings give is no less puzzling. Literally they are saying, "Like you [*kāmôkā*], like them [*kĕmôhem*]," but what are they implying? And what does "each had the bearing [*tô'ar*] of princes" suggest? These renderings are followed rather closely by ancient witnesses, indicating reticence to probe deeper; but modern translations seem to go their own way, most surprisingly the normally literal *TNK*, "They looked just like you . . . like sons of a king." To capture this phrase's connotation, however, much depends not on philology, but on assessing the tone of the responses. If the kings meant to flatter Gideon, they would be praising the heroic nature of the opponents they had met—cut from the same cloth as the man who captured them. If they were into bravado, sarcasm, or taunt, the kings would be flattering themselves for their past victories over worthy opponents. But they might also be cursing Gideon: May you share the same fate as they, however noble you might imagine yourself. The last conjecture is the likeliest, because the kings will soon prove to know what fate awaits them.

Their answer must have satisfied Gideon that these kings were implicated in the death of family members. Gideon speaks of *'aḥay*, "my brothers," but as the word may also loosely apply to kinsmen or brethren, he adds that they were *bĕnê 'immî*, "my mother's sons." In this rhetorical way, he privatizes the peeve without necessarily personalizing the loss. In fact, we had no previous knowledge that Gideon's clan had lost any members to Midian, albeit this is perfectly plausible.[15] The phrase *ḥay* YHVH, literally "as lives the LORD," generally introduces oaths; but this part of Gideon's statement is also rhetorical, for what does it mean to pledge mercy to those who cannot be saved? The use of the particle *lû* on which a verb in the perfect depends introduces a condition unlikely to occur.

We know the names of only three of Gideon's seventy-one sons: his eldest Jether ("Abundance"), his youngest Jotham ("The LORD is complete"), and Abimelech ("My father is king"), the last the child of a concubine. Jether wields his own sword, but he may not have accompanied his father to Karkor. If so, then the execution of the Midian kings is taking place back home, but nothing in the text forces this contention. For Jether to kill the two kings is to acquire prestige, but for the kings to be killed by a youth is utter disgrace. Humiliation, in fact, does play a role in these macabre ceremonials. We recall that when Joshua wanted to humiliate five captured kings, he summoned his captains and, in the presence of his entire army (*kol 'îš yiśrā'ēl*), had them step on the victims' necks. The execution was carried out by Joshua, however, before ordering them impaled (Josh 10:23–27).

Luckily for Zebah and Zalmunna, youthful Jether is hesitant, not least because executions (usually followed by beheading) require mental no less than physical strength (Radaq). The youth's hesitation gives the kings the opportunity for one more taunt. When asking Gideon himself to cut them down, they avoid the language of execution he had used (*hārag 'et-*); instead, they resort to *pāga' be-*, an idiom reflecting a chance, perhaps even unacceptable slaying (see at 15:12, 18:25).[16] As many commentators have noted, for its terseness their last statement seems drawn from a proverb: A person is defined by his strength (*gĕvûrâ*). Rahlfs A matches the Hebrew, albeit with more words. Rahlfs B, however, felt the need to be less gnomic, contrasting Gideon to his son, "For your power is like that of a man [ὅτι ὡς ἀνδρὸς ἡ δύναμίς σου]." Surprisingly, some commentators (Budde, Lagrange) miss the point, emending the text into the flat "for you are heroic."[17]

There is also the possibility, however, that the comment applies to the kings rather than to Gideon. When Urtakku, a kin of the Elamite king, is fatally wounded in battle against Ashurbanipal, "he called to an Assyrian, 'Go ahead, cut off my head. Bring it before the king your lord and achieve a good reputation'" (Radner 2005: 92–93). Noting that Urtakku's name is preserved while the beheader's is not, Radner rightly makes a case that the heroism is attached to the victim rather than to the slayer. If so, Gideon's enemies would be praising their own courage.

The scene ends with a truncated list of what Gideon appropriates from the kings, with a fuller version occurring at 8:26. Here I note only that the ornaments around the necks of camels are called *śahărōnîm*, whereas at 8:26 they are *'ănāqîm*, neck rings.[18] To judge from their etymology, these *śahărōnîm* are crescent shaped, possibly because they recall the moon god Šahar, so likely a talisman to ward off evil that arises from envy.

Kingship Declined

8 22–23. The phrase *'îš yiśrā'ēl*, "man of Israel," is fairly common in Deuteronomistic lore. Its accent is on ethnic affiliation, but not on the number involved nor on rank. In Josh 10:24, the expression is contrasted with military officers (*qāṣîn*), so referring to the rank and file; this is likely the same in Judg 7:23, when Gideon summons the men from ally tribes. We have seen this expression used most effectively when the dream interpreter applied it to Gideon (at 7:14), and it will reappear a few times in chapter 20 to contrast the combatants in the Benjamin wars. Here, the stress is on the unanimity of opinion about drafting Gideon for rule.

It is not at all certain that the people were asking Gideon to become king in the sense that we know best from ancient sources, for *māšal be-*, "to govern, dominate," occurs here rather than *mālak*, "to rule as king."[19] Although many attestations for this idiom are political, occasionally even with kings as subjects (as in Josh 12:2, 1 Kgs 5·1 [4:21 RSV]), others do not share this sense. Thus, the sun and the moon control the passage of time (Gen 1:18), men manage home life (Gen 3:16), people stifle their urges (Gen 4:7), and servants administer an estate (Gen 24:2) (see the Comments for implications). That Gideon is being asked to initiate what for the people was something new may be hinted by the addition of "you, as well as your son and your grandson" (*gam-'attâ gam-binkā gam ben-bĕnĕkā*). Were it not for its modern pejorative connotation, the Latin "dictator" might be used, amended in this instance by the people's consent to follow this rule into the personal and absolute power (at least) until the third generation. It may be that it is this amendment that persuaded Gideon not to accept.

We have already met the verb used (a Hiphil of *yaša'*) in previous verses (see the Notes to 2:16–17). There is no obvious implication that the people discern the hand of God behind their choice; yet we have had references to rescue as it concerns Gideon's destiny: in the mouth of God himself (at 6:14) and in the twofold test with which

Gideon sought assurance about his selection (see at 6:36–40). There are more playful applications of the same, as when Gideon questions his own selection (at 6:15), when Joash challenges Baal's capacity to vindicate himself (6:31), and when God reserves for himself the rescue of Israel (at 7:2, 7). It may well be that Gideon has those divine sentiments in mind when he lectures Israel on who is to rule them.

THE EPHOD

Gideon wants a favor from the people whose offer he has just turned down; the idiom he uses literally means "to request [*šāʾal*] a request [*šēʾēlâ*]" (from someone). It plays heavily in the birth story of Samuel (1 Sam 1), leading several commentators to presume that the story was originally about the birth of Saul (*šāʾûl*). The *nezem* (Greek, ἐνώτιον) he requests of them is a ring that can be placed on the nostril (Gen 24:47, Ezek 16:12) or the ears (Gen 35:4, Exod 32:2–3), by men or women. Pseudo-Philo makes bracelets out of them (*LAB* 36:3). What is essential is that they be of precious metal so that they can be given as gifts (Job 42:11) or, as in the case of Exod 32, can be melted and reshaped into sacred objects. In fact, they functioned as "money" because they could be traded. Although we have already noted (see under 6:1) that the Hebrew linkage between Midian and Ishmael was fluid, it remains unclear why there is a reference to Ishmaelites here, for gold rings are associated across cultures and Ishmaelites do not play any role in Judges.[20]

That the people responded with alacrity, even when they had no idea why Gideon wanted the rings, is a fine hint that they were treating him with the respect that he once imagined was beyond his grasp. The spreading of a garment (*śimlâ*) to collect the loot is a nice touch, giving a cinematic notion of people advancing to drop their contribution into one pile. (At 2 Kgs 5:23, Naaman wraps a talent of gold in each of two garments before presenting them to greedy Gehazi.) While the number is large (Rahlfs B cuts it down to just 1,500 units), neither the unit nor the standard of measurement is given. The presumption is that we are dealing with shekels, since higher (talent and mina) or lower (a number of terms) units are likely to be explicitly cited. Shekels differed in weight depending on whether they were Babylonian or Phoenician and within Israel whether they used the "royal" or "sacred" measure. All this makes it difficult to estimate the weight, but if we take the shekel to be around 11 grams and imagine that we are dealing with rings that were twice the weight of Rebekah's nose ring (half a shekel, Gen 24:22), Gideon would have collected around 20 kilograms, or 45 pounds of gold. (Burney and Moore give twice this amount; Pseudo-Philo is astronomical, with 12 talents, so more than 700 pounds.) Given that sacred paraphernalia were rarely solid gold, but rather were encrusted, plated, or overlaid with it, this amount of gold might have produced a spectacular ephod.[21]

The catalogue of objects taken from Midian will have nothing to do with the manufacture of the ephod. While a number of commentators regard diverse (or all) portions of the list as editorial insertions because they seem superfluous, the listing does play a role in amplifying the success that Gideon had over Israel's enemies as well as establishing a basis for his wealth. If we keep in mind that rulers (and gods) received the lion's share of the plunder, especially those removed from royal opponents, we might imagine other reasons for the inventory. It included crescents (*śahărōnîm*; at 8:21 said to be around the necks of the royal camels) and pendants (*nĕṭifôt*, in Isa 3:19), listed among bracelets and veils, and wine-dark garments (*bigdê ʾargāmān*); along with those made from *tĕkēlet*, "deep violet," they are the most precious of dyed textiles. Added, too, are the *ʿănāqôt*, breastplates of rings encrusted with jewels that adorned the camel's necks.[22]

The presumption is that only the collected gold served to make the ephod; but this may not be correct. The ephod is one of a few divinatory or consultative instruments available to Israel.[23] What the ephod might be is a problem because our sources give incompatible information that is creatively supplemented by Talmudic materials.[24] In the "legal" texts (best at Exod 28), the ephod is one article in cultic accouterment. Sleeveless (but not so according to Josephus) and decorated with expensive threads, it covered the body either entirely or only in the trunk area, depending on sources. Over a blue undergarment, the ephod was worn (mostly *lābaš*) by means of a girdle and shoulder pieces crossing in the back. It had (gold) rings above and chains below that allowed the fixing of a breastplate as well as a pouch containing the Urim and Thummim. In the narratives, a linen ephod seems to identify people with access to god (many priests at 1 Sam 22:18; Samuel at 1 Sam 2:18). It must not have been too cumbersome, since David wears it when dancing wildly before God (2 Sam 6:14). This would explain why the golden ephod made by Gideon (Judg 8:27) could be denounced as a form of idolatry.

In other texts, the ephod was not worn but made (*ʿāśâ*), carried (*nāśaʾ*), or, as in our passage, set down (Hiphil of *yāṣag*), likely in a sanctuary (see 1 Sam 21:10 [9 RSV]).[25] We have met this verb twice already in the Gideon saga, once as it concerns the woolen fleece where it obviously means to lay down (at 6:37), and another as it concerns setting aside men who do not pass the water test (at 7:5). Other scriptural citations similarly divide between these two possible meanings, likely because the basic meaning is to situate something, depending on its category.[26]

There is nothing intrinsically aberrant or sinful about consecrating an ephod, since its legitimate use is frequent and sanctioned by divine commands. The narrator, however, minces no words about its abuse: Israel "lusted after it," the same language for unrestrained pursuit of false worship that we met at 2:17. Here, however, the accusation is not that Israel was abandoning God for the deities of its neighbors (say a Baal or a Chemosh), but that the ephod itself became the object of their devotion. There is here unusual anticipation of apostasy, before the death of the designated savior. Pseudo-Philo is wonderful here: God could not interfere while Gideon was alive, lest Baal get credit for avenging himself on the man who destroyed his sanctuary (*LAB* 36:4). There is also manifest parallel with Israel forcing Aaron to create a "golden calf," ostensibly an avatar for either God or the absent Moses.[27] At Judg 2:3, a prophet gave us a fine sense for the slide to apostasy: The gods of the Canaanites remaining in the land will prove too seductive, and in worshiping them Israel will have fallen into a trap (*môqeš*), for the God of Israel will not be kind to those rejecting him. It must have hurt God to deal with a people with little resistance to foreign gods, but it must have hurt him more when the snare was of Israel's own making.

As did Moab after Ehud's victory (at 3:30), Midian submitted (Niphal of *kānaʿ*), but here construed with *lifnê* rather than *taḥat* to catch the moment of this event.[28] Its defeat was so complete that it could never recover or pose a threat. The idiom used to describe its condition is very anatomic: to lift the head (*nāśā' rō'š*), that is, to find pride in one's action. The period of Israel's control under Gideon lasted forty years, the same as under Othniel (3:11) and Deborah (5:31), but half as much as under Ehud (3:30). This is the last time in Judges that we meet with the formula "the land had peace" which we had at 3:11 (Othniel), 3:30 (Ehud), and 5:31 (Deborah).

COMMENTS

In previous chapters, we had witnessed Gideon move from doubt to self-possession. Secure in divine support, he rallies his people and achieves scarcely possible victories. Finally at ease with the destiny allotted him, Gideon takes three steps to consolidate his authority.

Prerogatives

I. THE RIGHT TO PUNISH

The squabble between Gideon and two towns east of the Jordan, Succoth and Penuel, is ostensibly about failure to feed the hungry for fear of retaliation by powerful elements. The repartee is couched in sarcasm on the part of the towns' leaders. Had Gideon simply asked for food for his motley group without declaring his goal, the leaders might have finessed his request as an act of charity to a distant kin; but with Gideon open about his goal—the capture of two kings that dominated the area—the leaders may have feared retaliation. But the narrator is most interested here in aspects of the anecdote: the vows of Gideon and their fulfillment. At Succoth, he vows a horrible execution, tying it to a victory against Midian. At Penuel, he promises a destruction that is also massive, linking it to his own safe return. Only if Midian wins or Gideon dies in battle—acts requiring divine reneging—would these pledges be null and void. (We shall meet with a similar linkage of themes in the story of Jephthah.) With success already guaranteed by heaven, Gideon has found a way to absolve himself from these cruel acts. More importantly, he advances his own cause, for as we know from Near Eastern legal compilations, the shedding of blood in punishment is reserved for rulers. We have a nice Mari letter showing that this notion was realistic. A slave escapes, taking with him two female companions. His master captures them all and blinds the slave. Still enraged, the master wants the slave impaled, but he must turn to his king for permission.[29] The language in another letter (A.3862; Charpin forthcoming [15]) makes it clear that bandits and nomads create havoc through raids and skirmishes, but only kings threaten wars and dismantle fortifications. In effect, with the public scourging of leaders in Succoth and with the annihilation of Penuel's population, Gideon has appropriated roles that are normally allocated to heads of states.

2. THE RIGHT TO EXECUTE

There is a fable of Aesop, cited in many versions and widely reproduced across the Web, in which a wolf and a stray lamb find themselves in the same spot. Rather than pouncing on the lamb, the wolf makes outlandish accusations, each of which the lamb patiently disproves. No, he had not befouled the wolf's water since he was drinking downstream; no, he could not have taken his food because he lives on grass; no, he could not have insulted him last year because he was not born then. No matter, the wolf says, if it was not you, it was your father. On this, the wolf devours the lamb.[30]

The dialogue among Gideon and the two captured kings is not quite as contradictorily drawn. In history we often meet with captured kings who are taken to palaces of their conquerors, where they can be treated decently or even become respected advisers. Most often, however, their fate (or that of their kinfolk) is not enviable. Commonly, they are paraded before execution, with luck, swiftly. We have already read about the fate of Adoni-bezeq, who, mutilated, lived long enough to sing the glory of divine justice (see IA1).

Unlike their military commanders, Oreb and Zeeb, who were summarily executed by Ephraimites, Zebah and Zalmunna were kept alive and likely displayed until they were given what seems to be a hearing. Yet fairness and justice were not at all at issue, and the inquiry opens on a note so incongruous that it has often been emended. But if we stay with the received Hebrew text (rarely a rash decision), the question "where are the men you killed in Tabor?" can be seen as a trick question. It may not matter that nothing is known about what had happened in Tabor; no answer coming from the kings would have brought them mercy. What good would it have done them had they explained how they disposed of the men Gideon mentioned?

The kings, who grasped the thrust of the question better than most biblical scholars, answer sarcastically, with a savage twist: Gideon ought to share their fate. Then they add a phrase that reveals how perfectly they understood the motivation behind their "trial." The men they are alleged to have killed all had the *figure* of princes—so counterfeit royalty rather than the real thing. Having hurled such insults at Gideon, their trial could only end with the expected verdict. The failure of Jether to execute the kings allows them to make one more predictive statement: Gideon can prove worthy of them by taking it upon himself to carry out the execution. From the Narmer palette to the bas-reliefs on edifices of Roman Egypt, in which Pharaoh crushes the skull of captive rulers, we have testimony that the execution of royalty is the privilege of royalties.[31]

3. THE RIGHT TO ACCESS GOD

> Should someone take hold of a brother living in his father's house, saying, "You own a garment! Come and be a chief for us so that this trouble will be yours to solve." He will right away protest, "I will not govern. There is neither food nor clothing in my home, so you can't make me chief of a people."
>
> —*Isa 3:6–7*

In the two panels of a triptych, Gideon has acted as a head of state. What would make him refuse the offer to rule? The other usages of "men of Israel" (*'îš yiśrā'ēl*) suggest that we are dealing with acclamation rather than selection by an elite group, although we can debate whether to include all of Israel or just the local tribes (Manasseh, Asher, Zebulon, and Naphtali) that Gideon summoned earlier at 7:23 under the same rubric. We recall that Joshua executed many Canaanite kings without anyone offering him kingship. In the Notes we have observed that the idiom used, *limšōl be-*, "to rule over (people)," is not an exact equivalent of *limlōk 'al-*, "to reign over (people)." So what is it exactly that the men were proposing?

An approach that relies on tradition-historical exegesis suggests that the offer was not to Gideon, but to Jerubbaal, because the issue of kingship plays a large role in chapter 9, with references to Jerubbaal rather than to Gideon. Gideon's resistance to kingship is thought to represent a rejection of the Canaanite version of this institution (allegedly more autocratic, less divinely centered), precisely the sort of rule that Abimelech will soon adopt. All this is heavily discussed in the literature.[32] Biblical tradition, however, places Jerubbaal with Jephthah and Samuel, all of them judges, not kings (1 Sam 12:11). Also, the distinction often surmised between Canaanite and Hebrew kingship is hard to support from Near Eastern sources. In both worlds, kingship is divinely guided. In both worlds, too, royal power was bolstered less by the institution than by ability and charisma. And in both worlds, diverse notions of continuity obtained. Primogeniture was the smoothest path, of course, but it can be adjusted by a discretion kings had to name their successors; for example, David selects Solomon, and Rehoboam, Abijah. In Israel as well as in western Asia another route was election by divine grace. Thus, Zakkur of Hammath owed it all to his god, Baal-Shamayn. Oddly enough, rhetoric can mask transitions. In the Mari archives, for example, there was dynastic continuity without blood connection. Usurpers can claim "to sit on the throne of their fathers" even when the link can be metaphoric rather than physical. (They get to sit on thrones provided to them by "fathers," that is, sponsoring suzerains.) Something similar occurred in the Northern Kingdom, where bloodlines changed but kingship was continuous. In Judah, however, assassinations hardly compromised the bloodline (see 2 Kgs 11:4ff., 12:21ff., 14:5–6, 21:23ff.).

There is therefore much to argue concerning what exactly Gideon is rejecting. Less debatable are the steps that move him from displaying external authority (earning the right to punish scoffers or take the lives of kings) to demonstrating internal control. This is done through two linked actions. With the first, Gideon persuades (forces?) military officers to give up a portion of their loot; with the second, he shapes and places under his own control a medium by which to consult with the divine.[33]

Spoils of War

The sharing of booty among soldiers, officers, kings, and deities is a fixture of Near Eastern cultures, for such undertakings were the engine that gave rulers the support of a vital segment of the population. A king of Qatna tells Yasmah-Addu of Mari to join him in a war against badly fortified towns. Soldiers will gain much booty and end up blessing them (ARM 5 16 = LAPO 17 #443, p. 11). In Mari documents, the dispersal of booty (*šallatum*) was highly formalized, with shares destined for kings (*huzbātum*), deities (*šulūtum*), and combatants. For kings or gods, spoils were set aside under oath (ARM 5 72 = LAPO 17 #462, pp. 37–39).[34] Beyond the plunder, officers can expect additional gifts, thus displaying a king's largess. On conquering a town, a king writes his brother about handing out a gold ring of 10 shekels and a gold disk half as heavy to top officers, with smaller gifts, including garments, to other officers and nomad chieftains (see ARM 4 74 = LAPO 17 #541, pp. 140–42; ARM 27 161). An interesting phenomenon is that kings can demand special contributions from these gifts and spoils for special occasions. Thus, because his king's palace was short on personnel, a ranking diplomat appropriates a large number of captives that had been allocated to officers as their share (ARM 26

408). They get to keep, however, ten pots of plants that had been distributed to them. After another victory, captives are assigned to the king's choice of gods (ARM 26 436).

Matters were similar in Israel. It is possible to infer that the jewelry Jacob's children deliver to him for burial at the oak of Shechem (Gen 35:4) was looted from the city's inhabitants. When God instructs Moses about saving Israel from Egypt, he predicts that Egyptians will willingly surrender their jewelry to their former slaves (Exod 3:22). This is fulfilled (Exod 11:1–2), and Israel walks out with the spoils of Egypt. Not much later, from this same spoil Aaron demands rings with which to create the golden calf (Exod 32:2–3). Likely also from the same plunder come the precious artifacts people surrender for producing a tabernacle (Exod 35:22). The booty from Midian is treated similarly, with special contributions (Num 31:50) that go beyond assigning God his share (Num 31:28–30). Yet what distinguishes Gideon's request is that he gives the elders no clue about what he plans to do with the objects he collects. They willingly surrender their share of the booty because they imagine it as a contribution to Gideon himself. As far as they are concerned, Gideon has only technically turned down their offer. But in turning some of the spoil into an ephod, Gideon may be acknowledging that his campaign against Midian had turned into a holy war.

Cultic Paraphernalia

In antiquity (no less than today) anyone may make gifts to the deities, either because they are thankful or because they hope for kindness and mercy. Normally, however, the building and upkeep of shrines or their investment in paraphernalia (thrones, statues, ornaments, garments, and the like) is left to rulers; but see p. 343. In a polytheistic world, rulers praise their own efforts at supporting temples across their territory and are known to contribute to those beyond their own borders. Especially worthy of attention are the shrines that are built within the palace, for they afford privileged access to royalty and to palace personnel, with benefits for all concerned. In Israel, narratives associated this building program with the consolidation of the Davidic dynasty, but archeology has scant reason to agree. It must be kept in mind that to furnish cultic material is *not* necessarily to assume priestly authority, as we shall see in the story of Micah (Judg 17).

In the Comments to IIID1, there is speculation about Joash's control of the Baal altar. That he acquiesced to its destruction by his son and, more importantly, that he condoned the construction of a rival shrine dedicated to Yhvh were by themselves portents of events to come. At Judg 17:5, Micah creates for himself a shrine with an ephod and many teraphims. The ephod of Gideon belongs to this category, and although it may not have had anthropomorphic features, it was substantial enough to absorb kilos of gold. Given its value, it was likely enshrined within a safe building in Ophrah. I speculate that it was set up not too far from the altar Gideon built for Yhvh, perhaps playing a role parallel to that of Baal's *asherah* that Gideon rudely destroyed. Deciding which of the two altars Gideon built was to receive the ephod would not be fruitful.

One of the more striking aspects of Gideon's career is the ease with which he connected directly with God. From his perspective, therefore, the shaping of an ephod was not egoistic; rather, it was a fitting adornment for the altar he built to a God who meets with him physically, with the same facility accorded only to Moses. We must not mistake Gideon's act as "an assumption of priesthood" (Halpern 1978: 84–85); rather, it is sponsorship of cultic objects, with all the influence this confers on the benefactor. That in this instance the consequences were sinister might be ascribed less to Gideon's desire for immediate gratification than to a thoughtless *"après moi le déluge"* perspective; such an attitude is not foreign to a cynical or skeptical mind.

Kingship

In the literature, there are several approaches to Israel's offer to have Gideon rule, most of them judging the office to be kingship rather than any other form of government:

1. Gideon rejects it, reflecting a theocratic attitude best evoked in 1 Sam 8–12 (see Burney [1970: 183], who follows previous scholarship, itself buttressed by centuries of traditional exegesis).[35]
2. Gideon accepts kingship, but later redactors hide the reality by touching up details such as his dedication of an altar to YHVH in Ophrah or by discriminating between Gideon and Jerubbaal (see above).
3. Gideon accepts kingship but uses the language of coy refusal, in full character of the deprecatory and pious diffidence he displays in earlier anecdotes about him (see Davies 1963).[36]

The comparison above is with kingship that was known in urban settings, in Canaan as elsewhere. In those contexts, a "king" is most often a (male) individual who inherits, holds for life, and bequeaths to his child the highest temporal authority in a territory (however small), invoking divine consecration or approval. We have already met with a number of references to such kings in Judges: Adoni-bezeq at 1:7, Cushan-rishatayim at 3:8, Eglon at 3:12, Jabin at 4:2, and just now the two executed kings of Midian. However, in connection with the story of Gideon, we may need to keep in mind that tribal groups have their own form of rule. In Mari documents, where we have much information about them, the title "king" (*šarrum*) can be applied to leaders (*sugāgū*) without implying the same type of authority as enjoyed by those ruling at urban centers.[37] A major difference, as it might be in the case of Gideon (or Jerubbaal for that matter), is that while the rule might be bequeathed within a family, it is not automatic but requires renewal by other chieftains in a confederacy.

The first two prerogatives Gideon displays (the right to punish and to execute kings) incite Israel to propose him as a **mōšēl*. Encouraged, he privatizes his authority by obtaining from his people a third privilege (access to God). Missing is his assent to bequeath these privileges. This is where the next chapter will take us when his son Abimelech proposes to be that **mōšēl* (see at 9:2); instead, he is given sovereignty (*melek*). Also missing is God's concurrence. This last omission especially will control the drama that we will soon follow.

IIIE

Abimelech

---

1. King of Shechem (Judg 8:29–9:21)

8 ²⁹Jerubbaal son of Joash went to live in his own house. ³⁰Seventy sons were Gideon's—all of them his issue, for he had many wives. ³¹When also his concubine,ᵃ who lived in Shechem, bore him a son, he set his name as Abimelech. ³²Gideon son of Joash died at a ripe old age and was buried in the tomb of his father Joash at Ophrah of Abiezer. פ

³³Once Gideon died, Israel again lusted after the many Baals, setting up Baal-berith as God. ³⁴Israel had no memory for the LORD their God who delivers them from all the enemies around them. ³⁵They did not show solidarity with the House of Jerubbaal-Gideon despite the good that he had done for Israel. פ

9 ¹Abimelech son of Jerubbaal traveled to Shechem to meet with his maternal uncles. Speaking to them and to the whole clan of his mother's family, he said, ²"Speak openly to all the leaders of Shechem: Which is better for you, seventy men—sons of Jerubbaal, all—ruling you or just one man ruling you? Keep in mind that I am your own bone and flesh." ³His maternal uncles spoke openly on his behalf to all the leaders of Shechem, and they resolved to support Abimelech for they reasoned, "He is our brother." ⁴They gave him 70 shekels from the temple of Baal-berith. Abimelech used them to hire some rootless and reckless men, and they followed him. ⁵He came to his father's house in Ophrah and executed on one stone his brothers, the sons of Jerubbaal, seventy men. Only Jotham, the youngest son of Jerubbaal, survived because he went into hiding. ס

---

a. Or: secondary wife.

373

⁶All the leaders of Shechem assembled along with all Beth-millo. They went and installed Abimelech as king by the *firmly set* oak at Shechem. ⁷When Jotham was informed, he climbed to the summit of Mount Gerizim and he called out to them in a loud voice, "Listen to me, leaders of Shechem, so God may listen to you."

> ⁸The trees set out to anoint a king over themselves. They said to the olive tree, "Reign over us." ⁹But the olive tree replied, "Have I stopped yielding my wealth of oil, with which through me gods and men are honored, that I should go hold sway over the trees?" ¹⁰The trees said to the fig tree, "Do come and reign over us." ¹¹But the fig tree replied, "Have I stopped yielding my deliciously sweet fruit that I should go hold sway over the trees?" ¹²The trees said to the vine, "Do come and reign over us." ¹³But the vine replied, "Have I stopped yielding my wine, which gladdens gods and men, that I should go hold sway over the trees?" ¹⁴Then all the trees said to the thorn, "Do come and reign over us." ¹⁵The thorn said to the trees, "If in good faith you are anointing me king over you, come and find shelter in my shade; but if not, may fire issue from the thorn and consume the cedars of Lebanon."

¹⁶"Now then, if you have acted completely in good faith when making Abimelech king, if you have done right by Jerubbaal and his house, and if you have repaid him for his favors, ¹⁷as when my father fought for you, casting his life aside, to save you from Midian; ¹⁸yet you rose against my father's house that day, you killed his sons—seventy men—on one stone, and set up Abimelech, the son of his handmaid as king above the leaders of Shechem because he is your brother. ¹⁹So, if you have acted completely in good faith toward Jerubbaal and his house on this very day, then rejoice in Abimelech and may he also likewise rejoice in you. ²⁰But if not, may fire issue from Abimelech and consume the leaders of Shechem and Beth-millo, but may fire also issue from the leaders of Shechem and Beth-millo and consume Abimelech!" ²¹With that, Jotham fled; he escaped toward Beer and lived there, away from his brother Abimelech. פ

NOTES
Introductory Remarks: Fables

In Hebrew, the label *māšāl* covers a broad literary typology that includes proverbs, parables, and fables. Parables and fables are allegorical but save the hearer the effort of deciphering both because they are embedded in a context that provides clues and because they are usually followed by an explicit interpretation or an edifying moral. Parables and fables are comfortable in the Hebrew Bible, and while both share fiction as their language, we artificially distinguish between them by whether they have human characters (parables) or not (fables).[1]

In the ancient Near East, fables can be embedded within tales with broader goals, such as the "Snake and the Eagle" in the Mesopotamian *Etana* legend (Foster 1996: 437–57) and several fables in the demotic *Myth of the Eye of the Sun* (Lichtheim 1980: 156–59). Most fables favor anthropomorphic and anthropopathic animals, largely because we have better rapport with animals than with plants; but Mesopotamian literature includes a series of learned debates ("Disputations") among diverse plants in which each displays incomparable merits and virtues.[2] Some fables are embedded within narratives. The Aramaic wisdom of Ahiqar has this example: "The thorn bush had a message for the pomegranate, 'The thorn bush greets the pomegranate, What good are your many thorns for those who touch your fruit?' The pomegranate answered the thorn bush, 'You are all thorns for anyone touching you.'" Though shorn of its explanation, the point is that the kettle must not call the pot black.[3] The Qumran text 4Q552–53 (= 4Q *Four Kingdoms*) develops on a Daniel allegory on four empires, in this case pitting four trees in the contention, so likely inspired by Judg 9 (see Hogeterp 2010).

Hebrew lore preserves a plant fable that is no less tart, this one attributed to Jehoash of Israel (2 Kgs 14:8–10). Feeling his oats because he had defeated the Edomites, Amaziah of Judah foolishly posted a declaration of war to Jehoash of Israel ("Come, let us show each other up"; *nitrā'eh pānîm*). Jehoash mocks him acidly, adding this fable: "The thistle of Lebanon contacted the cedar of Lebanon, demanding, 'Give your daughter as wife to my son!' But a wild animal trampled the thistle simply by walking over it. Have you become arrogant when defeating Edom? Feel important; but stay put. Why would you court disaster, find defeat, dragging Judah with you?"[4] "Amaziah paid no heed," we are told, and Jehoash clobbered him. While by no means covering the same ground or arriving at a similar conclusion, the two Hebrew fables nevertheless share an A-B-C-B-A frame. Narrators (A) set them within historical contexts and return at the end to bring out the lesson (in Judges, developed in the next segment). Outraged individuals (B) are made to cite the fable before drawing from it a conclusion. The core of the fable itself features characters (C) that differ physically, matching their dissimilar temperaments and behaviors. Their interaction is guided by suspicion that is generated by their creators.

In Scripture, apothegms are not often labeled, not even by the almost generic *māšāl*. This is the case of Jotham's fable. In the literature, there are many conjectures about it: Did it circulate independently before its adoption into the tale of Abimelech? If so, what elements were introduced into it or removed from it as it was tailored for our context? Largely because the speculation relies on assigning priority to some of its segments over others or on reading its details as allegorical for events relayed in Israel's historical traditions, it is possible to find arguments that the fable is independent of the narrative in which it was set, that it is crafted specifically for the context, or that it postdates any other segment of the narrative.[5]

Prologue to Abimelech

8 29–32. Normally, reference to the number of years in which Israel controlled its own destiny (at 8:28) is followed by a reversal in Israel's attachment to God (see at 3:11, 30; 5:31). But in our case, the narrative is already preparing for the story of Abimelech, the son of Jerubbaal, in which, it might be said that Baal, no less than the Hebrew God, is taking his revenge on Joash's family.

How mundanely should we take the word *bayit* here? In many ancient cultures "house" also stands for dynasty. When it refers to a ruling house, however, the word tends to be followed by a personal name, unlike here; but it will soon occur exactly as that at 8:35. The allusion here may stress Gideon's refusal to accept kingship (Burney 1970: 264). We are next told about the large brood Gideon produced: seventy sons. We will soon discover, however, that the cited number is not accurate, for it will not include two sons, Abimelech and Jotham. Elsewhere we have reference to such a number. When Jacob went to Egypt, he took with him sixty-six members of his household. The text cites them as *yōṣĕᵉ̂ê yĕrēkô* (literally, "issues of his thigh") because his wives and the mothers of his grandchildren were not counted (Gen 46:26). Including him, Joseph, and his two sons the count reached seventy, a perfect number for a community.[6] Moses is asked to bring along seventy elders to meet with God (Num 11:16–17). Ahab, like Gideon, reaches the same amount on his own (2 Kgs 10:1), while a later judge, Abdon, needs another generation to compare with either (Judg 12:14). The more appropriate similarity, however, may well be with the "seventy kings" begging at Adoni-bezeq's table, in the sense that Gideon's brood depended on his largess (Judg 1:7). In our case, however, rather than a sign of future prosperity, the large number of offspring promises only trouble.[7]

"ABIMELECH"

The story of Abimelech opens on singling out one woman, his mother, because her relationship with Gideon made her different from the mothers of his other children.[8] In the same way (J. Janzen 1987), his story will end with accent on the one woman (9:53) who takes away his life. The seventy-first son of Gideon is not born to a primary wife, but to a *pîlegeš*, imprecisely translated as "concubine." The insistence that "she too" (*gam-hî'*) bore Gideon a child alerts that there will be more to say about the child (see Gen 22:20, among others.) The term *pîlegeš* is of non-Semitic origins, often attached to Homeric Greek παλλακή, παλλακίς, but without a credible route for its induction into Hebrew. It applies to a wife with secondary status, either because a man with a primary wife was legally not permitted to bring another of equal status, because she was brought in to be a surrogate to a barren wife, or because, failing to bring a decent dowry, she had little prestige. In all other ways, she was a wife, her husband being a *ḥātān*, "son-in-law," to her father. Her own children had inferior standing only when a primary wife had born children, in Israel, likely males. Presently (at 9:18), we shall note that a surviving son of Gideon will label her an *'āmâ*, often also imprecisely translated "slavewoman" or "handmaid," when it applies to a woman who cannot have primary status. In the translation, I have kept "concubine" for *pîlegeš* because circumlocutions will be just as inexact.

In many cultures of the ancient Near East, children of secondary wives can become rulers (Urḫi-Tešub of Ḫatti among them); this is what makes the name that Gideon chose for his son (8:31) so interesting: *'ăvîmelek* means "my father is king."[9] The coinage is West Semitic, and while it can be held by kings (famously Abi-milki of Tyre in the Amarna letters and a king of Gerar in biblical historiography), it can also be given to people with lesser status (see 1 Chr 18:16). Here it is also a cue name for what will transpire.[10] This is implied by the unusual vocabulary for naming the boy (*vayyāśem 'et-šĕmô*). Second Kings 17:34 and Neh 9:7 have this idiom when referring, respectively, to new names God bestows on Jacob and Abraham. In Dan 1:7, the same construction is used for giving Jewish men Babylonian names. The implication, then, is that Abimelech was *renamed* by a father who wished this son of a secondary wife to be accorded elite status, even if the sentiment does not fit someone who had just rejected kingship. Not quite analogous may be the case of Benjamin. He was bestowed a lugubrious name by the dying Rachel, but Jacob moved to better his fortunes by changing his name (Gen 35:18; S. Ackerman's observation).

SHECHEM

This concubine lived in Shechem (Greek, Συχεμ, Σικιμα; Josephus, Σίκιμα), a city that will be featured in the Introductory Remarks below. This may not at all be a statement about a type of marriage (for example, Samson's) in which a man retains visiting rights with a woman who is staying with her family. In the Old Assyrian period, merchants had separate households in different towns, and at all periods, rulers had secondary homes beyond their capitals. As we saw above (at 6:22–23), Ophrah is not easy to locate, but it could not have been more than a dozen kilometers from Shechem, not a particularly ample distance. Rahlfs B needlessly adds that Gideon died "in his own city."

To die at a ripe old age (*běśêvâ ṭôvâ*) was the lot of Abraham (Gen 15:15, 25:8), who lived 175 years. But it was also applied to David, who died at age seventy (1 Chr 29:28). We can only guess about Gideon. He already had an adolescent son (Jether) when he took on the Midianites, so he may have been in his mid-thirties, and he ruled for forty years. That he was buried in his father's tomb suggests contrastive implications. It reinforces the prestige of his father, for to own a burial space in one's own surrounding is an elite privilege (see Franklin 2003: 2; see Isa 14:18). But it might also reinforce the nonroyal status of Gideon/Jerubbaal, since presumably, dynasts inaugurated their own burial grounds in which followers may be interred.

BAAL-BERITH

8 33–35. The normal notion in Judges is that the slide toward perdition begins after the death of the rescuer or judge, for it is inconceivable that the elects of God would allow such misbehavior to occur under their watch. And this is what happens after the death of Gideon. However, the narrator might be implying that the deterioration of will was in process even during Gideon's lifetime. In Judges, we have seen the idiom *liznōt 'aḥăr-* first at 2:17, when precisely this aberration is predicted: "Yet, even the judges the people would not heed, for they would lust after other gods, falling prostrate before them." Just now (at 8:27) we saw this idiom in connection with the ephod that became a snare for Gideon's house no less than for all Israel.

The god that Israel preferred over its own was a specific manifestation of a Canaanite storm-god. Here, he is known as the *ba'al běrît*, "Lord of the Covenant," and we will soon (at 9:4) hear of his temple in Shechem. This notice implies that local shrines—even when devoted to Baal—prevailed during Gideon's days, without suggesting abandonment of Gideon's altar and shrine at Ophrah, with its precious ephod. It is possible that the phrase is shortened from **ba'al běrît šālôm*, "Lord of the Peace/Treaty Covenant" (see Ezek 34:25, 37:26, and Isa 54:10). If so, then we are not too distant from the "Lord Peace" altar Gideon built on first witnessing God (6:24).[11] Later (at 9:46) we will learn that a temple attributed to "El of the Covenant" (*'ēl běrît*) was at Migdal Shechem ("Shechem Citadel"). It is a source of much dispute whether we are dealing with two separate places, so likely also dedicated to separate gods, or the same temple under different names, hence also with the same god under different labels.[12] I gravitate (with slight conviction) toward the latter, noting that "lord" (*ba'al*) and "god" (*'ēl*) act also as common nouns.

Israel is accused of three major flaws: It first turns to Baal (whatever his manifestations) and then no longer minds the savior god (participle of Hiphil of *nāṣal*) who repeatedly protected it from fierce enemies. We notice that this particular verb, albeit common in Hebrew, makes its Judges debut at the opening of the Gideon narrative, when God complains of neglect despite his heroics on behalf of Israel.

The third error is related: Israel no longer keeps allegiance to Gideon's house. The noun *ḥesed* is ubiquitous in Hebrew but cannot be rendered easily (in English most often "lovingkindness" or the like), its nuances determined by the relationship between the parties that either display or acquire it. The words *ḥesed* and *bĕrît* are often juxtaposed (and taken in hendiadys in translations), not because they parallel each other, but because they share a similar notion about obligations. Covenants are set as obligations by treaties and alliances; *ḥesed* is established by human conventions. Thus God has a *bĕrît* with Israel, from which derive commitments on all sides; but *ḥesed* interactions among him, Israel, and diverse individuals are governed by a natural imbalance of power that allows God to be (or not) benevolent. The same discrepancy in authority on the human plane affects dispensation of *ḥesed* between rulers and vassals, rich and poor, husbands and wives, parents and children.[13] Israel's inconstancy, therefore, is not only to the God that has repeatedly saved it, but also to the human instruments for his will. Reference to the House (*bêt*) of Jerubbaal-Gideon at 8:35 comes close to admitting that family leadership has become institutionalized (see at 1:22–23).

In other previous contexts, this sort of jeremiad is followed by reference to a surge of hostile forces as instrument for divine punishment. Such a scenario will not occur until 10:7 when Philistines and Ammonites take control of Israel, setting us up for the rise of Jephthah. In our case, however, the focus will be on internal dissension, foreshadowing internecine disasters that will be featured in the closing chapters of Judges.

Seizure of Power

THE ARGUMENT

9 1–3. How long after the death of Gideon Abimelech took action is beyond us to reconstruct. We also cannot know how the family fared during the interval. We will soon learn that Abimelech was able to corral them for slaughter, so we might imagine that they had not gone their own ways, or established their own households.[14] While his mother stayed in Shechem, Abimelech likely lived in Ophrah, but with very limited chances of playing a major role in Gideon's House. As others who faced limited opportunities under the status quo (Athaliah of Judah would be a fine illustration), Abimelech decided to act. The journey he took to address the Shechemites is as much realistic (to persuade, one needs to make an imposing presence) as psychological, for it sets Abimelech away from the rest of Gideon's children, preparing us for the deed that will follow next. He does not speak directly to the people of Shechem but had his uncles relay a public message (*lĕdabbēr be'ōzen+*; so nothing secret about it) that addresses the leaders of the town (*ba'ălê šĕkem*), likely at a council.[15] He presents them with two arguments about choices available to them, both of them accentuating the singular circumstances of Abimelech's birth. The first is nicely balanced, with the same verbal forms (*mĕšōl*, "to rule") making an improbable contrast between a horde of rulers, with its likely chaos, or just one. Though perfectly reasonable as a contrast between the many unknowns and the one known individual, the argument has clout only if the people of Shechem had to be governed by someone from the family of Gideon/ Jerubbaal.

The second thrust follows on the first: Naturally they would prefer the rule of one person over the many, but would they not want someone of their own? The words *ʿeṣem*, "bone," and *bāśār*, "flesh," are frequently linked: Adam discovers the same pairing in his mate (Gen 2:23), and Laban engages Jacob into his fold for sharing them (Gen 29:14). The kingship of David is repeatedly argued on the basis of such bonds (2 Sam 5:1, 19:13–14), suggesting that Abimelech was making a "formulaic association with the royal covenant."[16] When Abimelech's message is heard as conveyed, Shechem's decision was to support him (*nāṭâ lēv ʾaḥărê*, literally, "to incline the heart toward/after someone"). Their reasoning tells us that his second argument fell on receptive ears, as expected in a tribal world.

KINGSHIP

9 4–6. What is not expected, however, is that the leaders of Shechem would open up the coffers of their temple to Abimelech. We are not told what they had in mind, but here we might recall that in some reckonings (Josh 24:7) Shechem was part of Ephraim, the same tribe that once (at 8:1–3) had groused to Gideon about not being summoned to war against Midian. Earlier, leaders from Israel displayed fealty to Gideon by surrendering hard-earned booty, but they were acting on his request (8:24–27). Here, however, it was Shechem's own idea to give him resources, yet not a shekel came from individual pockets. Instead, the leaders turned to temple treasures. We must not imagine that this funding implies religious allegiance to Baal-berith, on the part of the giver or the receiver, for in antiquity temples were bankers, being a major source of lending. The amount, 70 shekels, doubtlessly strives to balance what will ensue: 1 shekel per murdered brother—dirt cheap, given that Joseph was sold for 20 shekels (Gen 37:28).[17] The irony here is that Shechem responds to him because "he is our brother" (*kî ʾāḥînû hûʾ*), a kinship attachment Abimelech will not feel for his own. Soon enough, too, Shechem will forget this sentiment.

The men Abimelech hires are first described as *rēʾqîm*, literally "empty." These are not "outlaws" and certainly not "worthless," as is found in translations, but people unattached to a specific leader, so unemployed (Radaq). Generally, such people can be uprooted because of the turbulence of the time and cannot find gainful attachment as mercenaries (or the like) because leadership is lacking.[18] We will meet such folks when Jephthah creates his own band (Judg 11:3) and when Jeroboam creates his own kingdom (2 Chr 13:7; Irwin 2012: 339–50 would make it correspondent with our passage). They might be poor (see, metaphorically, 2 Sam 6:20 and Neh 5:13), but for them to be uncontrolled they also had to be *pōḥăzîm*, as applied to rushing water (Gen 49:4) and to treacherous prophets (Zeph 3:4). In Mari, *sarrārū* is the term that is used for such unaffiliated men (ARM 3 12 = LAPO 17 #748, pp. 510–11). The etymology accents their capacity to lie (*sarārum*), but they are not necessarily "robbers" (*CAD*, *sarrāru* A, pp. 178–79); rather, they are beyond legal control of a state and can be bought for any mercenary activity.

The number of brothers who are murdered is made to fit the amount paid for their slaughter. The artificiality of the number seventy is sharpened by not taking into account a survivor, Jotham (see above). Realism falls to style also in the account of Bar-rakib of Zinjirli. He tells us how his father Panamuwa (II) survived the murder of his own father as well as of seventy brothers (Younger 2000; Fensham 1977). The notice about the killings over one stone is not to evoke the ritual slaughter at a single rock following defeat of the Philistines (1 Sam 14:31–35; see Moore 1895: 242–43) but to underscore the savage efficiency of the act.[19] Luckily enough for Abimelech, all his brothers were at home (coincidence being a nice folkloristic touch). He rounded them up, marched them to one spot, and had them butchered. Discriminating readers of court histories may understand this fratricidal act as a claim on kinship.[20]

We assume that Jotham was the youngest (*haqqāṭôn*) not by the form, but from the tradition of focusing on the youngest. Joash of Judah was an infant (and so presumably the youngest) when he survived Athaliah's murders (2 Kgs 11: 1–2). The name *yôtām* (Greek, Ιωαθαμ) seems to play on a root meaning "completeness" (**tmm*), with an abbreviated form of God as a preformative, so something like "God completes/perfects" or "is complete/perfect." It is a far stretch to attach the name to *yātôm*, "orphan" (Boling 1975: 171; Halpern 1978: 96 n. 47), if only because it could hardly have inspired the naming of another Jotham, a moderately pious king of Judah.

INVESTITURE

Removal of all rivals turned Abimelech into the natural heir to Gideon. Why the leaders of Shechem decided to crown him king (*melek*) when he had asked to be only a **môšel* (see at 9:2) is a difficult problem, but it has allowed some commentators to divorce the two stories and others to consider Shechem a Canaanite enclave that is tied to this event. However, the notice may also be background to conflicting notions Israel will have about its fortunes without kingship (see at 17:6) or about the role God will need to play in initiating it. It might be significant that while the construction with a cognate accusative is fairly regular in Hebrew, this particular phrasing (*vayyamlîkû . . . lĕmelek*) occurs thickly in connection with Saul's failed kingship (1 Sam 8:22, 12:1, 15:11).

The language for crowning is terse but highly ceremonial: There is an ingathering by the leaders of Shechem and all *bêʸt millôʾ*. There is also a movement of the entire body toward a landmark where they make Abimelech king. This much is clear, but not so the reference to *bêʸt millôʾ*: Does it imply that the combination of two different localities was necessary to confer kingship on Abimelech? Or is it more about two different levels of society?—leaders of Shechem and people who lived in a quarter (*bêʸt*) of the terrace (*millôʾ*) where, to go by etymology, there is much earthen work, so near fortifications or the like.[21]

The landmark consists of an oak (already cited in Gen 35:4, where Jacob buried cultic paraphernalia) that is connected in some ways with *muṣṣāb*. The easiest way to deal with this last word is to follow the Greek (στάσις) that presumes *maṣṣēvâ*, "stela" (see the Notes on 3:18–19), and this is readily done in the literature, but I am not sure why any famous oak would need to be associated with a pillar for better identification. Another way is to cite Isa 29:3 where *muṣṣāb* refers to a mound or rampart—so for us an oak (atop) a mound. Perhaps it is best to stay with the form we have (a Hophal participle) and treat it as it appears in Gen 28:12, where a ladder is said to be set up with its top toward heaven. So we may be dealing with a "firmly set" oak.[22] Lagrange (1903: 165 n. 6) thinks this allusion is "absurd"; true, but it might prepare us for the world of Jotham where trees have human senses.

Jotham's Dare

THE CIRCUMSTANCES

9 7. We need not fret about how Jotham received news of Abimelech's crowning or whether he was surprised by it. Anyone who escapes mass murder of a leader's children must know that some power move is afoot. Likewise, we are not to question too deeply the contexts of the fable. It is certainly more dramatic to imagine Jotham beginning his sermon just as Abimelech received the crown, but nothing in the text encourages this.[23] It may not matter whether or not the latter was in Shechem to hear Jotham's sermon, for its leaders were just as guilty for providing Abimelech the means with which he butchered his kin.

Where Jotham stood is another puzzle. Shechem is sandwiched between Mount Gerizim (*har-gĕrizîm*) to the south and Mount Ebal to the north.[24] The two loom almost the same height (880 and 940 meters, respectively), but whereas Mount Gerizim is well-watered and groved, Ebal is not. The discrepancy is likely behind the tradition that at the former was set the blessing portion of the covenant between God and Israel (Deut 11:29; see 27:12–13). The topography of Mount Gerizim makes it difficult to know how Jotham could stand on its summit (*rōʾš*) and be heard in the valley, some 500 meters below.[25] People concerned with realism have proposed that he stood on a projecting crag, where some ruins (Tananir) are now to be found, with Boling (1975: 165, 172) going so far as to translate "[Jotham] stood on a promontory."[26] But it must be kept in mind that to bring Jotham to a place where he could intone his longish fable within hearing distance of others would certainly make him vulnerable to capture.

The invocation is set in classical parallelism: By listening to me, God will listen to you. Jotham is not equating himself with God but is assuming a prophetic stance, asserting that if the leaders of Shechem understand what he is saying, they are bound to reverse an unjust act. Such a notion seems to me Pollyannaish—for nothing in the leaders' activities so far has them siding with virtue.

The Fable

In translations, Jotham's fable is often presented as poetry, the Hebrew forced into a verse format either through baroque layout (as in the *Biblia Hebraica* series) or manipulation of its text (for example, Burney 1970: 272–75). There may be motivations for such a display, among them a readiness to attach antiquity to poetic statements or to attribute them to folk circles, but there is little in the language or the style of the fable itself to encourage such presuppositions.

ANOINTING

9 8–13. The trees are looking for a king to anoint (*limšōaḥ ʿălêhem*). Anointing with oil and fats was done to heal pains and sores. By extension, the process also sealed wooden (including divine statues) and leather products. In cuneiform documents we hear of anointing children to protect their skins, but also to ward off evil powers.[27] From Ebla on, oil was poured on the heads of brides, so not exactly anointing. In legal settings, contracting parties may anoint each other after eating and drinking beer (for example, in ARM 8 13). In Mari, women were given oil rations when healing after childbirth (*inūma išlimu*; see Ezek 16:9), but it was also dispensed broadly, including to anoint (*ana pišāš+*) diplomats, statues of the gods, altars, and so forth.[28]

The fable presumes that anointing was known to Jotham. For de Vaux (1961: 104), therefore, the tradition relied on knowledge of what he considers to be a prevailing practice in Canaan. But as far as anointing kings on investiture in the ancient Near East, the material is rich but open to multiple interpretations.[29] Especially among West Semites (the Hittites as well), leaders might be anointed, although it is not clear whether it was done just once, exceptionally, or regularly. More important, it is still to be determined what actually the act symbolized. In the Amarna tablet EA 51, a king of Nuḥašše recalls how an ancestor was anointed by Pharaoh. In EA 34, the ruler of Alašiya (in Cyprus) sends oil as a gift to Pharaoh because the latter is sitting on the throne—so evidently too late for any investiture ceremony. When Tudḫaliya of Ḫatti is anointed, it is as priest of Nerik and Ḫakmiš rather than as king. In Assyria, a substitute king and his queen, destined to ward off evil from the real royal couple, were wined, dined, and anointed—not especially a good portent, considering their destiny (State Archives of Assyria Vol. 10, No. 2). In the Mari extract cited under IA1 (Judg 1:1–7), the god Addu spreads oil from his own numinous glow on Zimri-Lim, thus sharing with him divine charisma as well as shielding the king from harm. This last example may well give us a link to how Israel appropriated the symbolism. We read in Scripture that anointed kings are endowed with the divine (1 Sam 16:13) or become invincible (1 Sam 24:6; 2 Sam 1:14–16, 19:22).[30] There is reason to suppose that the anointing of kings in Judah (and Israel) occurred only after a disputed rise to the throne, so according to the Talmud (*bHorayot* 11b and 12a). Even if we accept a conjecture by scholars that Gideon had acted as de facto king (see the Comments), it is still safer to presume that the story is retrojecting an institution that is not said to rise in Israel until Saul.[31]

The trees are said to *hālôk hālĕkû*, a fairly common cognate construction in which the infinitive absolute of a verb is positioned ahead of the conjugated form of the same verb to convey movement with a goal.[32] The trees they will approach—the olive, the fig, and the vine—are elsewhere cited together (only the pomegranate is missing here) as evidence of God's bounty (Deut 8:8, 2 Kgs 18:31–32, Hag 2:19), their absence a sign of divine disapproval (Hab 3:17).[33] In Hebrew, the fig and the vine are feminine, the olive and the last named, the thorn, are masculine; but this does not seem to be relevant to the fable's eventual lesson.

THE OLIVE TREE

The olive tree is the fable's first character, its oil likely used in anointing, so establishing a nice link between content and context internal to the fable that follows. Potentially tall but usually pruned to about 30 feet (its leaf alerted Noah that he was reaching dry land), the Mediterranean olive is among the longest living trees (a thousand years is claimed). The tree takes much time to fully mature (fifteen to twenty years) and needs much sun, but when it produces its many varieties, it can be a goldmine for its tasty fruit and fragrant oil.[34]

The response of the olive is at once proud and modest, but mostly mocking. This is clear even if the verbal form as vocalized (*heḥodaltî*) is anomalous; the possibilities are detailed in GKC 167 [§63k]. The form is best treated (as do the versions) as a Qal perfect, with an interrogative *he-*; but it must not be translated as a future (as do many versions). The olive is not refusing kingship because it will have to stop yielding its fruit when ruling. To the contrary, it will accept the crown when it is all dried up and has nothing more to contribute. As long as I am fruitful, the olive is insisting, it is through me (*bî*, syntactically emphatic) that people offer tribute (*yĕkabbĕdû*, impersonal subject) to anything in the universe.[35] The phrase *ʾĕlōhîm vaʾănāšîm*, "gods and men," is a *merismus* (opposites used to convey a whole) and is best not parsed for its theological contents. Nor must the first element be translated "God," as do many, likely following the Greek.[36]

What the olive (and soon the fig and the grapevine as well) rejects is to go *lanûaʿ*, an act that is difficult to convey in English. (I admit that "hold sway" carries the desired play on words in English rather than in Hebrew.) The Hebrew sense covers much ground, from "aimless wandering" to "fearful trembling." Taking advantage of the leeway, Rahlfs A (and the Targum) is contextual, "to rule over the trees." Rahlfs B is jocose, "to hover [κινέω] over the trees."

THE FIG TREE

The fig tree (*tĕʾēnâ*), approached next, is a handsome deciduous tree that is native to Western Asia, growing up to 30 feet but likely to be half as tall in ancient times.[37] Its branches are twisting, spreading wide, with broad leaves that are too gummy for skin contact (despite Gen 3:7). Feeding on sunshine, the tree nevertheless offers a deep shade; hence sitting under it (and under a vine) was proverbial for achieving security (1 Kgs 5:5, Mic 4:4). The fig tree alludes to its *tĕnûvâ*, a generic term for what is produced, qualified by its sweetness (*mōteq*, used attributively) and appeal (*ṭôvâ*), making it unnecessary to detail why the fig is valuable.

THE VINE

The vine (*gefen*) is a climbing plant that uses trees or poles to rise above the ground. In biblical lore the term is used almost exclusively for the variety that has grapes as its fruit.[38] In ancient Israel it was trained to rise high enough that it could provide shade. The vine here is proudest of its capacity to bring happiness to all. Its product, *tîrôš*, is a word of uncertain origin and etymology used in poetic contexts for fresh wine.

THE THORN

9 14–15. The fourth candidate to be approached by the trees (exceptional here, by "all the trees") is the *ʾāṭād*, a term among many in the Hebrew Bible that refer to a variety of plants with prickles or spines, among them *šāmîr*, *šayit*, and *ḥôaḥ*, the last occurring in the Joash fable cited above. The *ʾāṭād* here cannot be identified with any certainty among the many thorns, so I have kept it generic.[39] Whereas those that have rejected kingship (olive, fig, and vine) can give shade in the hot sun, thorns are generally too squat, their leaves too small, and their branches too sharp to afford shelter for any but the smallest creatures.

With a combination of pride yet lack of confidence that rings psychologically true, the thorn reveals its contradictory, even conflicted attitude by at once doubting the sincerity of the trees (*'im be'ĕmet*, "if in good faith") and inviting them to bask under its shade (*bō'û ḥăsû vĕṣillî*). The language of the fable, which depends on incongruity, here turns literal to achieve its effectiveness, for ordinarily to "find shelter under someone" is a fairly widespread metaphor for protection, divine or political. For example, in Isa 30:2 God rails against those who would seek refuge with Pharaoh and "seek shelter in Egypt's shade" (*laḥĕsôt bĕṣēl miṣrāyim*).[40]

Because it harbors suspicions, the *'āṭād* binds the trees to their promise through a curse: If there is no sincerity to their proposal, then a fire should come out from a lowly plant and consume the mightiest, the cedars of Lebanon (*'arzê hallĕvānôn*).[41] In prophetic lore, there are passages in which the anger of God burns forests (Jer 11:16, 21:14; Ezek 15:6), and in Ps 29 God's fury shatters the cedars of Lebanon. Occasionally, however, the fire begins in wild brushes (Isa 10:17, 27:4), before it turns into a cataclysm (Ezek 21:3; see also Jer 11:16). The thorn is no Sinai bush that can be ignited without being consumed (Exod 3:2–3); rather, the insincerity of the trees would so provoke the thorn that it would be willing to risk immolation just to destroy the others.

Jotham's Exhortation

9 16–21. The shift to the lesson of the fable is introduced by *vĕ'attâ*, "now then"; but rather than turning to the application immediately, a series of incised clauses complicate the condition. As shaped by Jotham, the fable does not carry a choice for the trees, but certain destruction. For, when read literally, the thorn cannot give shelter to such mighty trees; therefore, the matter can end only in conflagration. Jotham picks up on the thorn's emphasis on sincerity but sharpens it by adding *tammîm*, "complete" (reversed at Josh 24:14).[42] The phrase *'im-be'ĕmet ûvĕtāmmîm 'ăśîtem* is repeated at 9:19, thus bracketing a review of events that will impeach the people of Shechem.[43] Shechem's hypocrisy is brought out in a series of conjectures, each introduced by the conjunction *'im*, "if":

1. 9:16—Were you deeply sincere when proclaiming Abimelech king?
2. 9:16—Were you doing what is right with Jerubbaal and his house?
3. 9:16—Were you responding to all the favors (*gĕmûl yad*; Prov 12:14; sarcastic, Isa 3:11) he did for you? There follows an indictment that is patterned after diplomatic communications, in which an aggrieved party details the good deeds and then the evil that repays them.[44]
   a. *The good*: Jotham speaks of his own father (*'āvî*, "my father"), implying the full legitimacy that he will soon deny Abimelech. Jerubbaal fought for Shechem, here explicitly tied to Israel; and in saving its people from Midian, Jerubbaal did not hesitate to set prudence aside (*minneged* placed postpositively, as among others in Gen 21:16, Deut 28:66).[45] Citing Abimelech by name here could not but be biting, given its meaning.
   b. *The evil*: Shechem however, has done only evil. Its leaders rose (*qamtem 'al-*) against Jerubbaal's house, and on that occasion (*hayyôm*, not necessarily today) did what we already know they did. The minor difference is that Jotham speaks of

Abimelech's mother as an *'ămâ*, rather than the *pîlegeš* we saw above. In this litany, Jotham is not condemning Shechem for establishing kingship, but for selecting Abimelech, blood ties being their only reason.

With a resumptive repetition of the phrase *'im-be'ĕmet uvetāmmîm 'ăśîtem* (from 9:16), Jotham can bring his homily to its conclusion. It turns on two conditional sentences, each with a condition (protasis) that when met must lead to a specified outcome (apodosis). The first is "positive" but cannot possibly have a happy aftermath: If the people of Shechem had dealt in an honest way with both Jerubbaal (which they might have) and his house (which they absolutely did not), then should they find happiness (*śāmaḥ bĕ-*) with each other?[46] In the second construction, the condition is carried from the first, but only the formulation of its reversal is kept (*vĕ'im 'ayin*; see Gen 30:1, Exod 32:32). The consequence amounts to a curse: Fires will be launched from the implicated parties, with mutually destructive consequences.

Having had his say, Jotham escapes. The Hebrew stages his exit in two phases: *nûs* gets him off the stage while the idiom *bāraḥ . . . mippĕnē* gives direction to his flight, away from harm. Unfortunately, we cannot tell where he went for refuge, for the Moabite Beer ("a Well"), where Israel found water (Num 21:16), is not likely his true destination. It remains far-fetched, but not beyond possibility, that where he is said to settle is figurative for the water that will quench the coming fire. In the Mari archives, there are dossiers about *keltū*, men who find shelter at influential courts while keeping after the thrones they were denied. The fate of most of those we can follow in those documents was not rosy. (See n. 14 to Judg 11:3, IIIG1.) Jotham was luckier: He simply vanishes from our records. Despite the brevity of his appearance, however, he and his fable have survived well the oblivion of time.

COMMENTS

In Judges, a notice about the land having found peace for a nice interval (at 8:28, as well as 3:11, 30, and 5:31) is normally a good closing signal for events that are guided by a major personality. However, a narrator who had dexterously moved a character from self-doubt to assured leadership revisits here the quirkiness that makes Gideon such a singular personality. The tidbits that are collected as a postscript about him add texture to the portrait so far achieved. Gideon may not be a king, but he has formed a house (as had Joseph his ancestor), he has a brood, and he has taken concubines. When, after a long life, he dies, no tomb is built for him, as one might be for a dynast; rather, his remains are placed in the family tomb. His example might have taught Israel the brittle advantage of living under charismatic leadership. Israel does not need kingship, Gideon had insisted, for its God is enthroned since time immemorial. But, in creating an ephod, he had implanted in his followers the doubts he once nurtured about believing in a god most others cannot see, sense, touch, or manipulate. In his own life, he had managed to balance these potentially contradictory postures. With Gideon's body not yet cold, not much was left to emulate or perpetuate.

By ending on prospects so dire, the narrator has created a fine transition to Abimelech. He has also remained true to his effort of guiding Israel's history toward its full realization in the monarchic period. His expertise as a teller of tradition cannot be better judged than by the muddled effort of Josephus to reshape Gideon into a worthier ancestor. Josephus was eager to present Gideon as a fine prototype of Jewish leadership. He is tolerant, avoiding confrontation with Baalism; he has visions of God, but knows how to communicate their essence to his followers; "a man of temper and [one] that excelled in every virtue," he knows how to gain the loyalty of the potentially seditious; he does not punish those refusing to support his cause; he gives justice when others expect him to gain power. This Gideon has nothing to do with ephods or cultic paraphernalia. Josephus has him die a warrior, much respected, so that there is nothing in this antiseptic construct to prepare us for the rampages of Abimelech and the consequent debacle that Israel experiences.[47]

About this Abimelech: When source criticism was regarded as a reliable instrument by which to assign Hebrew literature to precise moments in Israelite history or to meaningful cultural development in monarchic Israel, there was a consensus that his story stood out of the Deuteronomistic material, but also debate whether its main resource was E (because of exclusive allusion to *'ĕlōhîm*), J (because of its alleged affinity to 8:4–21), a split between the two (with a caesura at 9:22), or a mix of both.[48] While Gideon was never called a *šōfēṭ*, "judge," there were plenty of allusions to *yāša'*, "to rescue," to set his story within the cycle of narratives about a called leader. Most striking is the drive among some of these contributors to defend the story as a stray bit of Canaanite history, documenting tension between the settling Hebrew tribes and the people they were despoiling. Ironically, the narrative was often assigned more historical value than what was told about Gideon, so full of supernatural moments were his accounts thought to be.

In contrast, what is told about Abimelech lacks interest in divine commitment either to Israel or to its foes, major ingredients in the cycle of events involving judges. Despite allusion to Israel as a whole (in 9:22; see v. 55), the story is fairly narrowly localized, as if derived from memory of local politics. If treated as an integral narrative, unconnected to Gideon's saga, in its verses kingship seems taken for granted, with little interest on following up on Abimelech's initial request and no hint that anyone doubted its application to Israel. Rather, the focus is on a conspiracy to bestow kingship on one individual. Moreover, despite suggestions to the contrary, in the tale there is no desire to condemn the suitability of a temple at Shechem (Boling 1975: 184–85) or hint of a rivalry between shrines at Ophrah and Shechem (Halpern 1978: 91–92).[49]

Jotham and His Fable[50]

For this segment of Abimelech's tale, the issues that remain constant have to do with the fable and its relationship to the crowning of Abimelech. It is commonly accepted that the trees in search of leadership represent Shechem and that the thorn that welcomes their offer is Abimelech. Yet, the premise that launches the tale does not fit the envelope reporting on the events behind it. There, initially Shechem is not looking to crown anyone; rather, it is Abimelech who asks its help. Moreover, his request is not to become its king, but to "rule" (*māšal*) over it. To find "trees" looking for leadership, we need to go back to the meeting Gideon had with the "men of Israel" (8:23), when he turns down their offer to have him rule (*māšal*). His argument then is that neither he nor his son (singular!) will rule because God is the perfect ruler they need. Here we notice that the olive and the vine—both productive trees—maintain that their devotion to pleasing "gods and people" is far more gratifying than to becoming king. (The fig is similarly satisfied with its role without citing recipients.) If the allegory is parsed for its character equivalence, Gideon/Jerubbaal would stand for any (or all) the trees that rejected kingship because subservience is gratifying all by itself. The implication is that the first portion of the fable is relying on Gideon material to drive its argument about leaving well enough alone.[51]

The introduction of the thorn carries the program further. If richly endowed trees can accept their fate, how much more should the thorn when it has much less to offer (O'Connell 1996: 165 n. 210). Yet, much like the Abimelech it mimes, the thorn needed no entreaty. If we judge its reaction by the conventions that shaped relations between rulers and ruled in antiquity, the thorn was ready to move to the binding clauses of covenantal agreements, thus cementing the trees to their choice of king. The language used is that of blessings and curses that concludes treaties between overlords and vassals or, for that matter, between God and Israel. Its gist is that the honorable will find shelter while the devious will be destroyed. In the thorn's vocabulary, retribution is a fire that can consume the mightiest cedars. It is launched from the aggrieved, but it matters little to the message whether punishment is carried out by the thorn or through a curse. The Shechemites hearing this portion of the fable will know that the threshold for loyalty is high.

THE LESSON ELEMENT

Without an appended moral, a fable will entertain, but its application might remain vague. Jotham delivers the key, turning the fable dark. However, his perspective about the most evil of crimes, the slaughter of brethren, is at odds with that of the narrator's. Jotham hardly has any interest in Abimelech; rather, his focus is on the leaders of Shechem, disputably "the trees" of his fable. How could anyone have faith in their loyalty to anything or anyone, given their capacity to turn on old allegiances? It is they, he implies, not Abimelech, who massacred the seventy brothers on one stone, the act displaying planning, savagery, and determination. It is they who made Abimelech king when he had asked for something other. There is no specific condemnation of kingship, but simply of the scheme that brought illegitimate kingship to a fratricide (Oeste 2011: 81–87, 166–67). Both parties may now be happy with the result, but given the fickleness of Shechem and the ambition of Abimelech, no pledge anyone makes is likely to stand. Sooner than later, the imprecation uttered by the thorn will find its application. Mutual destruction is guaranteed.

In Beer, "away from his brother Abimelech," Jotham will simply have to wait to hear how and when the malediction takes its toll on them all. The wait will be brief.

2. Fall of a Ruler (Judg 9:22–57)

9 	 [22]For three years, Abimelech wielded authority over Israel. [23]Then God cast such ill will between Abimelech and the leaders of Shechem that the leaders of Shechem betrayed Abimelech, [24]so that the violence against the seventy sons of Jerubbaal could be revisited and their bloodguilt could rest on their brother Abimelech—because he had executed them—as well as on the leaders of Shechem—because they had encouraged him to execute his brothers. ²⁵The leaders of Shechem set ambushes against him on mountaintops. They robbed whoever passed by them on the road. Word of this reached Abimelech. ס

²⁶Gaal son of Ebed came, together with his brethren, and they moved into Shechem, and the leaders of Shechem trusted him. ²⁷They went out into the fields, harvested and trod their grapes, and had celebrations. They entered their temples and after eating and drinking, they cursed Abimelech. ²⁸Gaal son of Ebed said, "Who is Abimelech and who is Shechem that we should serve him? Did not this son of Jerubbaal and his agent Zebul once serve the men of Hamor, ancestor of Shechem? Why should we serve him? ²⁹Were I given command over this people, I would get rid of Abimelech!" He then challenged Abimelech, "Increase your forces and head out."

³⁰When Zebul, the town's governor, heard the words of Gaal son of Ebed, he was furious. ³¹He sent messages to Abimelech at Tormah[a] to say, "Gaal son of Ebed and his brethren have come to Shechem and they are inciting the town against you. ³²Therefore, set out tonight with the forces you have with you and lie in wait in the open country. ³³Next morning at sunrise, make an early rush on the town; but once he and his people move out against you, do with him as you see fit." ס ³⁴Abimelech and all the people with him moved out by night and set up four divisions in ambush against Shechem. ³⁵When Gaal son of Ebed came out to post himself at the entrance to the town's gate, Abimelech and the people with him moved out from the ambush. ³⁶Gaal saw the people and said to Zebul, "People are marching down from the hilltops!" But Zebul said to him, "You mistake shadows made by hills for men." ס ³⁷Gaal spoke up again, "People are now coming down from the core of the earth and one division is heading from the direction of Soothsayers Oak." ³⁸Zebul told him, "Where is now your boast, 'Who is Abimelech that we should serve him?'? There is the people you belittled—go out there and fight him!" ס

³⁹So, in front of the leaders of Shechem, Gaal went out to fight Abimelech. ⁴⁰When Abimelech rushed at him, he ran away from him. Many fell wounded, all the way to the entrance of the gate. ⁴¹With Abimelech staying in Arumah, Zebul drove out Gaal and his people from Shechem where they could no longer stay. ⁴²The next day, when brethren went to the fields, Abimelech was informed. ⁴³Taking his people, he partitioned them into three units, posting them in ambush in the fields. Whenever he saw people leaving town, he pounced on them and struck them down. ⁴⁴Abimelech and the men in his unit fanned out into position at the entrance of the town's gate. Two other units rushed against all those out in the field, striking them down. ⁴⁵All during that day, Abimelech

---

a. Or: secretly.

fought against the town. He captured the town, killing the people in it. He razed the town and sowed it with salt. פ

⁴⁶When all leaders of Citadel Shechem heard about it, they went into the chamber of the El-berith temple. ⁴⁷Abimelech was told that all the leaders of Citadel Shechem had gathered. ⁴⁸Abimelech went up Mount Zalmon, along with all the people with him. Grasping some axe in his hand, Abimelech chopped off a tree limb, then lifting it, he set it on his shoulder. He then said to the people near him, "What you have seen me do, quickly copy me." ⁴⁹Each of them having also chopped a limb, they all followed Abimelech. They piled them about the chamber and set it on fire over them. In this way, all the people of Citadel Shechem also died, about a thousand men and women. פ

⁵⁰Abimelech went to Thebez; he encamped at Thebez and captured it. ⁵¹There was a fortified citadel in the center of the town. Men and women, as well as the town's leaders, hurried into it. Locking up behind them, they climbed up to the citadel's roof. ⁵²Abimelech reached the citadel and attacked it. He moved up to the gate of the citadel to set it on fire; ⁵³but some woman hurled an upper millstone on Abimelech's head, shattering his skull. ⁵⁴Immediately, he shouted to the attendant, his arms-bearer, "Draw your sword and kill me, lest it is said about me that a woman killed him." His attendant stabbed him and he died.

⁵⁵When the men of Israel saw that Abimelech was dead, everyone went home. ⁵⁶Thus God turned back on Abimelech the evil he had done to his father by killing his seventy brothers. ⁵⁷As to the evil acts by the people of Shechem, God brought them on their own head. The curse of Jotham son of Jerubbaal had indeed fallen on them. פ

NOTES

Introductory Remarks: Shechem

Shechem has had a storied history in biblical and nonbiblical material.[1] Located on a 6-acre mound at present-day Tell Balaṭa, east of modern Nablus and some 65 kilometers north of Jerusalem, ancient Shechem is near the traditionally cited tomb of Joseph and the well of Jacob. It controlled traffic through the narrow space between Mount Ebal (to the north) and Gerizim (to the south), its topography possibly inspiring its name: "shoulder" or "slope."[2] With good access to water and fertile land, the area was settled since the Chalcolithic period, prospering as an urban center at least since the early second millennium BCE, but also inviting hostile actions. In the early twentieth century, the mound was excavated by Germans (primarily Ernst Sellin), but after the Second World War by Americans (primarily George Ernest Wright). In nonbiblical texts, Shechem may be mentioned in Twelfth Dynasty records, one of which might give Ibiš-Haddu as its ruler and another mentioning an Egyptian sortie against it. It flourished during the Hyksos period, with fine fortifications, turning into a major center at the close of the Middle Bronze Age (1650–1550 BCE). Repeated destruction levels, mostly attributed to Egyptian incursions, suggest that it was an inviting target.

Shechem returns to focus in the Late Bronze Age. Archeological reports are commonly dependent on biblical material for interpretation of the evidence, with much debated results. Recovery of the burial of a quadruped (donkey) under the floor of a guardroom excited interest since it evoked reference to Jacob's purchase of a plot of land from the "sons of Hamor, Shechem's father" (Gen 33:19).[3] During the Amarna period the beleaguered king of Jerusalem accuses an adventurer named Lab'aya ("Lion's Cub") of transferring Shechem (Shakmi) to the Habirus (EA 289). Able to control much territory in the Jezreel Valley by playing one party against another and giving much grief to his neighbors, Lab'aya eventually paid the ultimate price.[4] However, the city was rebuilt, and from it was recovered a fine statue of a striding god, in bronze and silver overlay, that, not surprisingly, has been associated with Baal/El-berith. A destruction level late in the twelfth century BCE is often attributed to Abimelech.[5]

It is difficult to know how much the Deuteronomist knew of the narratives that involve the patriarchs with Shechem. The tradition that Jacob purchased a plot in Shechem from "the sons of Hamor, the father of Shechem, for a hundred qĕśîṭâ" (see the Notes to Judg 9:4–6) where he established an altar to "El, god of Israel" (Gen 33:19–20) was certainly available because almost the same notice is used in Josh 24:32, when Joseph's bones were given their final rest, and possibly because of the altar Joshua built at nearby Mount Ebal (Josh 8:30–35). Later in our story (Judg 9:28), we will read of the "men of Hamor son of Shechem." Possible too is the recall that the story of Joseph's rise to one of the highest offices in Egypt began at Shechem (Gen 37:12), as well as the enigmatic reference in Gen 48:22, "I am now assigning to you one side [šĕkem 'aḥad; LXX, Σικιμα] over your brothers, that I have taken from the Amorites through my sword and bow." The rape of Dinah (Gen 34) by Shechem son of the chieftain (nāśî') Hamor and the consequent sack of the town by Simeon and Levi are not rehearsed, and there is speculation that the narrative was part of an aborted attempt to assign the area to these tribes (de Vaux 1978: 171–72). Reference to Jacob's burial of foreign gods by the oak at Shechem (Gen 35:4) is not developed elsewhere.

In Joshua, Shechem is assigned to Manasseh in 17:7 but to Ephraim in 20:7, where it was set as a city of refuge (21:21). The great covenant ceremony at the close of Joshua's career is said to occur at Shechem, possibly in recall of it being a stepping stone into Canaan by the patriarchs (Gen 12:6, 33:18–19) as well as in amplifying on Mosaic instruction on recognizing God's bounties (Deut 26:1–11). There is to be, then, a recall of past traditions.[6] Shechem is featured in one other major incident. Rehoboam, accepting kingship there (1 Kgs 12:1), insults tribes hoping for treatment less harsh than Solomon's. As a result, ten tribes revolt and join Jeroboam, who fortifies it into a royal stronghold (12:25) before moving his court to Tirzah. Shechem loses its importance, and while it has moments of great prosperity, archeology testifies to its decline and destruction (by John Hyrcanus, 107 BCE). A new version of the town was created by Vespasian, a couple of kilometers away, who called it Flavius Neapolis, the name still with us today as Nablus.

Although it is commonly repeated in the literature (and likely influenced by archeological interpretations), nothing in Hebraic lore about Shechem treats it as a Canaanite enclave in Manasseh, especially not after Jacob's children destroyed it (Gen 34). There is nothing specifically Canaanite (or un-Israelite) about the narrator's perception of Abimelech and his activities. This is the point made long ago by Lagrange and bears repeating now that the narrative about Abimelech and his putsch for kingship is about to progress.[7]

Ill Will

9 22–25. In introducing the steps that lead to Abimelech's demise, the narrator is careful not to characterize his rule by verbs that might suggest acceptance of his rise to power. So rather than the *mālak*, "to reign," used by Shechem, and *māšal*, "to rule," as proposed for Gideon by Israel as well as by Abimelech for himself, we meet with the verb *śārar*, with a more ambiguous meaning. We have met the noun *śar*, "commander," at 4:2 (Sisera) and 5:15. The information about Abimelech presented here is an abbreviated version of a formula that will be standard when describing the rule of Hebrew kings, the closest parallel being the notice about the reign of Saul (1 Sam 13:1).[8] This is quite unlike what we have seen about Israel's judges, for we learn about the extent of their leadership only as they exit from the stage. It is tempting to reckon that the three years of control may have been assigned to him after the book of Judges had become stable, for with it added to the computation in Judges, Israel will be said to control its enemies for three hundred years. As we shall see, that number comes back, albeit for a different purpose (see at 11:26).

Biblical lore has it that innocent blood has powerful claim to vengeance, as in Gen 4:10 in which God addresses Cain: "What have you done? The clamor from your brother's blood cries out to me from the ground!" The *rûʷaḥ rāʿâ* God sends to kindle discord between Abimelech and Shechem is an agent that is featured in other narratives with similar aim. Elsewhere it might be called *rûʷaḥ šeqer* ("deceiving spirit," 1 Kgs 22:22 = 2 Chr 18:21), *rûʷaḥ tardēmâ* ("lethargic spirit," Isa 29:10), *rûʷaḥ ʿivʿîm* ("distorting spirit," Isa 19:14), or even simply *rûʷaḥ* (as in 2 Kgs 19:7). They all share a capacity to lodge in individuals, turning their minds against their own best interests. To judge from 1 Sam 16:15–16, everyone knew that such humors came from God, and it is possible that they were associated with the demonic world.[9] They are there to overturn conditions, deflecting them from their normal courses toward unexpected conclusions. As narrative components, they act as dei ex machina, in our case short-circuiting events to get to the meaty part of the story.

The *rûʷaḥ* may deflect the narrative or make it economical, but the verse that follows is obtrusive. By explaining why God found it necessary to introduce this ill will, the narrator dramatically influences our judgment on the development of characters and events. Such narrative interference is relatively rare in Hebrew literature, so we must assess this particular instance as reflecting a strong antipathy on the narrator's part to what Abimelech represented. However, by also reminding us that the leaders of Shechem were heavily implicated (*ḥizzēqû ʾet-yādāʸv*) in this murderous scheme, the narrator brings them back smartly into a drama that will launch by the reversal of their support. We are not shown why and how matters soured for Abimelech and Shechem, but Shechem is credited with breaking the trust (*vayyivgĕdû . . . baʾăvîmelek*) that had bound them. Perhaps its citizens were peeved that Abimelech did not choose to make Shechem his seat of power, settling elsewhere (see at 9:41, maybe also at 9:31) and treating Shechem as a vassal land to be handled by an appointed administrator (see at 9:30).[10]

The Hebrew for the incised sentence justifying the introduction of discord is messy, but it can make sense without the many proposed emendations, none meriting detailed reporting. The language is metaphoric, with violence (*ḥamas*) and bloodshed (*dāmîm*) taking active roles. A single act, the murder of the seventy brothers, unleashes avenging powers with two targets: Abimelech, for doing the deed, and the leaders of Shechem, for aiding and abetting his actions. Especially by involving Shechem, the narrator is embracing Jotham's reading of events, as developed in the moral of his fable (see at 9:16–20). It might be important to note here, too, that for the narrator the crime is not in Abimelech assuming the kingship that Gideon rejected (with Shechem goading him to it), but in stooping to a thoroughly dastardly crime against kith and kin (Gerbrandt 1986: 132). There is of course irony in that, having wiped out all but one member of his family, Abimelech has no kin to discourage assaults against him and so is left to his own devices.

The effect of the ill will is instantaneous, with Shechem launching the series of deceitful acts that force Abimelech into murderous retaliation. In itself this is interesting, for the scenario is nowhere reflected in the series of royal abuses registered elsewhere (1 Sam 8:11–18) as reason to regret the establishment of kingship. Rather, we learn that Shechem initiates the conflict by laying ambushes (*mĕʾārĕvîm*, Piel from *ʾārav*) on mountaintops. These are set against Abimelech (*vayyāśîmû lô*) and not, as suggest some commentators, "to his hurt/damage."[11] Were they out just to rob his caravans or to kill him? Shechem bandits had no compunction about robbing (*vayyigzĕlû*) anyone who was traveling; in this way, they also damage Abimelech's reputation as a provider (usually for a fee) of safe passage.

The matter was revealed to Abimelech, so the ill will is now infecting all parties.[12] It is possible that in some earlier manipulation of the story, this notice (*vayyuggad laʾăvîmelek*, "Abimelech was told") connected directly to 9:47, with the same phrase picking up the thread.

Gaal

9 26–29. Enter Gaal. The meaning of his name (*gaʿal*; Greek, Γααλ) is pretty obscure, and some have dipped in Semitic lexica to come up with meanings, mostly prejudicial, "dung beetle" or "small/ugly man."[13] Unlikely is that the name plays on "Baal." Another problem is how to interpret the *ben-ʿeved*. Ostensibly, Gaal is the "son of Ebed."[14] As vocalized by the Masoretes, the phrase could mean "the son of a slave," and it may well be that this was their opinion of him. But it might have been read Obed, "worker," which is a reasonable name (Ruth's son had it), meaning "laborer" or a shorter version of Obadiah or the like. Either way, the narrator will soon (at 9:28) have a fine occasion to play on the word.

He brings along "his brothers," *ʾeḥāʸv*, no doubt kinsmen; but with "brother" finding almost a dozen repeats in the Abimelech segment, it would not hurt to stay literal here. This Gaal and his band may not have sunk as low as the men Abimelech hired, but they equally were looking for fortune, more or less precursors to the bands assembled by Jephthah, the Danites (Judg 18), and David. We are not told what it is they did to earn the confidence of the leaders of Shechem—simply that they joined the Shechemites at their temple.

While *vayyaʿavrû biškem* may be rendered (as is commonly done) "and they passed through Shechem," it is jarring to find it sandwiched between coming to Shechem and obtaining its trust. (It is dropped in Rahlfs A.) The phrase is likely technical for incorporation into a political unit. What may have occurred, therefore, is that Gaal was accepted as a Shechemite, whatever his past. This joining of groups is implied in the story of Dinah and Shechem son of Hamor (Gen 34), but an actual case is documented in the Mari archives. A high official reported (A.981; see Sasson 1998a: 105; Durand 1992: 117–20) on shifting the allegiance of a clan from one tribe to another by slaughtering a donkey. (Text cited above at IA2, note 15 to Judg 1:8.) Shechem is said to put its trust in Gaal (*vayyivṭēḥû-vô*)—an ironic notice, given the lack of loyalty in this story.

Verse 27 delivers the scene that turned Gaal into a member of Shechem. The ceremony stretched over a few days. First there was harvesting and pressing the grapes, allowing for thanksgiving and praise-giving ceremonies (*hillûlîm*; see Lev 19:24).[15] Then they banqueted at their temple (*bêt 'ĕlōhêhem*, "house of their gods").[16] Combining drinking and eating (often presumed) with covenantal behavior is a widely observed ancient lore, with a fine example reported in Gen 26:26–30.[17] Thereupon, the citizens did not "revile" (*TNK* and others), for they hardly needed to be in a temple to do that. Rather, they cursed Abimelech (*vayyĕqallĕlû*; so also the Greek versions) before every god they worshiped, in effect renouncing him as king. Cursing someone by or before the gods is a very powerful imprecation (1 Sam 17:43, Goliath "cursed David by his gods"), an act that is worthy of death because it carries its own fulfillment.[18]

It is important to realize that as a result of his absorption into Shechem, Gaal is now a full-fledged Shechemite, perhaps no less than Abimelech. Gaal's speech drips with sarcasm, but in citing it, the narrator seems needlessly to repeat the name of Gaal's father ('*eved*). Yet three verbal forms of the same root are impressively brought out within words of each other. Gaal is trading on the "taunt," a convention as old as Gilgamesh and Agga.[19] His words divide into four segments (see Boling 1963):

1. *The target of the taunt*: Who is Abimelech and who is Shechem (*mî 'ăvîmelek ûmî šĕkem*) that we should serve him? The pairing is not of equivalence, as in 1 Sam 25:10, "Who is David; who is the son of Jesse?" Rather, it is contrasting two poles, as is made clear in the next segment.[20]

2. *The reason for the taunt*: The notion is clear here: Abimelech and his officer were once taking their orders from the leaders of Shechem. Why should it be otherwise now? The Hebrew is complicated by a plural imperative verbal form, '*ivdû*, "serve (the people of Hamor!)" that seems out of place. The Greek witnesses take it as a noun, "his servant" (so reading *'avdô*), yielding an awkward conjunction of phrases: "Is (he) not the son of Ierobbaal? And Zeboul his supervisor is his slave, along with the men of Hemmor." Most exegetes, therefore, emend the vowels to '*avĕdû*, "they served," with Abimelech and Zebul as subjects, and I adopt it. In other contexts, *ḥāmôr*, "Hamor" ("Donkey," for toughness and determination), is the "father of Shechem," both literally (Gen 34) and figuratively (Josh 24:32). It serves little to treat the phrase as a gloss (Lagrange 1903: 173 and others).

3. *The pledge*: The phrase *mî-yittēn*, literally, "who might give," introduces wishes that have good potential of being fulfilled: If only he could be trusted with men, he would get rid (*'āsîrâ*) of Abimelech.

4. *The dare*: The Hebrew gives the impression that Gaal's speech ended with a wish for soldiers and implied that he got his desire, for next he is quoted as launching a challenge to Abimelech. The Greek, however, is less awkward, reading the verbal form as first person, "I will tell Abimelech/him," so inserting the whole within

Gaal's speech.[21] By egging on Abimelech about needing to increase his forces (*rabbeh ṣĕvāʾăkā*) because he will need it, Gaal is being purposely insulting. He might be inciting Abimelech to leave his fortified area; more likely, he is playing to the Shechem crowd, not expecting his words to bear wings.

Zebul

9 30–33. Zebul ("Prince") seems to be an abbreviated version of a name that likely included a divinity, such as Baalzebul (the famous Baalzebub!). Just earlier (at 9:28), he was titled a *pāqîd* of Abimelech, which means that he was his officer. It is difficult to fix exactly what kind of function Zebul had. Here he is called *śar-hāʿîr*, the town's mayor. Such bureaucrats with double responsibility (not to say also allegiance) may report to the town's rulers (in this case, the elders of Shechem), but more likely to a king whose authority he represents (in this case, Abimelech). In Mari, such delegates of the king are called *šākinum* or *ḫazzānum*. They can be foreigners who are appointed to reside there or can be selected from the population. We find both categories in the Near East, with an excellent example of the latter pattern in the case of Ṣidqum-lanasi, a major officer in the court of Carchemish, who nevertheless sold his expertise to Zimri-Lim of Mari (B. Lafont, 1991).

We may assume that Zebul was none too pleased at the expansion of Gaal's authority. The remarkable matter is that Gaal did not send him packing. But it should be told that during politically unstable conditions, when power behaves like an amoeba and rulers play lethal versions of musical chairs, bureaucrats survive by bartering their loyalty. Such a state of affairs is well-documented for us in the Mari and Amarna archives and no doubt was applicable to moments with an absence of central authority. Zebul ostensibly accommodates Gaal, but his allegiance to Abimelech is not impaired.

So on hearing Gaal's boasts, with the insulting implication heaped on him, Zebul is said to react badly: *vayyiḥar ʾappô*, in Hebrew most often an idiom reflecting anger, as is likely here, but elsewhere also anxiety and even depression. Zebul calculates that Gaal was a big mouth, with only a slight chance of carrying out successful operations despite the band following him. Abimelech, on the other hand, was no bragger: He could butcher dozens of brothers in one maneuver and still make it to a coronation. Zebul's message to Abimelech is sent *bĕtormâ*, a word occurring only here.[22] In the literature, this puzzling word was commonly taken either as an otherwise unknown place name, Tormah (so *TNK*), or as a badly transmitted **bêt [ʾa]rûmâ*, "Beth Arumah." The latter would approximate the Arumah that we shall meet in 9:41 as Abimelech's stronghold.

The versions find their own meanings for the Hebrew: Rahlfs A has "with gifts" (obviously connecting with the Hebrew *tĕrûmâ*); Rahlfs B, "secretly" (via *rāmâ*, "to deceive); Targum, "secretly"; and Peshiṭta, "treacherously." When a Mari inscription cited Yaminite tribesmen as TUR-*mi-im*, its first editor (Dossin 1955: 27) normalized the cuneiform as *turmim*. Relying on the Greek and Latin understanding of *bĕtormâ*, he translated the Mari reference as "perfidious, treacherous."[23] Circularly, many biblical dictionaries now repay the compliment by turning to Mari to validate the versions' meanings. However, Zebul could be treacherous only to Abimelech, his sponsor; so if taken as a noun rather than a place, something like "stealthily" or "secretly" would fit best.

Zebul is alerting Abimelech about Gaal's machinations. He uses participial forms that have no attachment to a specific time, perhaps to avoid explaining why he waited to dispatch messengers. It might be surprising that couriers can be readily exchanged, but in politically fluid times, movement tends to be chaotic and so freer. The phrase *ṣārîm ʿal+* occurs a fair number of times and is mostly about laying siege to a city or pressing something against another (see Song 8:9), which may mean that they are strengthening the inner citadel against him.[24] But as this meaning is difficult to defend here because of the absence of the preposition *ʿal+*, some have emended rather implausibly to *mĕʿîrîm*, "are stirring up" (Burney 1970: 282 among them) and others, just as improbably, to *môṣĕʾîm*, "bringing out" (Lagrange 1903: 174).[25] Zebul's advice is for Abimelech to take up spots (Qal of *ʾārav*) in the open areas, likely also wooded (*baśadeh*). There is urgency, and this is communicated, oddly enough, by the lack of an article on *laylâ* (as in Exod 12:30).

The instruction is for Abimelech to begin a forced march that very night so as to pick up a good position to trap Gaal and for a raid against the city (*ûfāšaṭṭā ʿal-hāʿîr*; see Job 1:17). Zebul knows the folks in Shechem: Given their previous treatment of oaths and covenants, they were bound to let him front any difficult battle. He also knows Gaal: Given his boast, Gaal will be forced to take the fight to Abimelech. Zebul does not need to instruct Abimelech further on how to deceive Gaal, but he is confident that Gaal's vanity would not let him remain behind the safety of walls. Aided only by his own troops (*hāʿām ʾăšer ʾittô*), he will rush toward his own destruction. Finally, Zebul also knows Abimelech, and by telling him to act as he pleases with Gaal, he must have an idea about Gaal's fate. Ridding himself of the intruders could not be against Zebul's own interests.

THE TRAP

9 34–41. Trusting Zebul, Abimelech developed his plan, breaking his forces into four units (*ʾarbāʿâ rāʾšîm*). The idea is to trick Gaal into underestimating the array against him. In antiquity, pitched battles were fought mostly among major national powers. (The battles in Judg 4 and 5 were configured as such.) When confrontations were local or tribal, however, raids or skirmishes predominated, with numerous ambushes and counterambushes. The bloodiest confrontations occurred near a city's fortifications, with dangers for the besiegers no less than the besieged. Siege engines (towers, rams) were expensive to create, maintain, haul into position, and deploy. Mining walls and creating tunnels were too time- and energy-consuming; in certain areas they also could be too obvious to the opposite side. Armies rarely had enough resources to maintain a siege for long, the lack of water becoming a problem as a siege lingered into the summer. The Mari evidence about setting sieges involves powers significantly more evolved than those at Shechem. Nonetheless, they illustrate the same deployment of martial techniques and clever stratagems.[26] Besiegers and besieged tried to take advantage of each other's miscalculation. With besiegers thinning their forces to encircle a town, the besieged would unexpectedly make sorties, attacking the besiegers at weak spots.[27]

The tactic Abimelech espouses would give the impression of limited military resources. He threatens Shechem, but he also gives it (and Gaal) hope for victory against what must seem to them weak forces. This is why he breaks up into four units, and the older literature is wrong to label it a gloss (Lagrange 1903: 175). Rahlfs A opens the coordinated events "in the morning [πρωὶ]." Just as Gaal and his followers, with Zebul at their side, come out to stand by the city gate, Abimelech brings his unit out from hiding on higher ground. It is not at all clear to me why Zebul tricks Gaal into misjudging the attack by Abimelech. Most suggestions are that Zebul is insinuating that a coward will see a foe when there is none (Moore 1895: 260). But if Gaal had conjured up enemies, he would not have moved beyond the gate. Soon, in fact, he will see enough to rattle him. Here, however, the accent remains on Zebul's motivation. He favors a clash between Abimelech and Gaal and so may be buying time, keeping Gaal outside the gates long enough to misjudge Abimelech's power when seeing only a fourth of it streaming from the mountain. It is possible, too, that the shadow of the mountains (ṣēl hehārîm) that are said to seem like men (kāʾănāšîm) is meant to evoke the shadow of the thorn in the fable. Boling (1975), who knows the archeology of Shechem, has them all standing by its east gate (see his figure 5).

It does not take long for Gaal to repeat his observation, this time with finality: One group comes from ṭabbûr hāʾāreṣ. It would not do at all to regard the phrase as a place name, as in TNK's "Tabbur-erez."[28] Nor is it helpful to identify it with the distant Mount Tabor, with which it shares consonants. To judge from Ezek 38:12, where the phrase highlights Gog's insatiable ambitions, and from Isa 40:22, where a similar phrase (ḥûg hāʾāreṣ) discloses God's sovereignty, Gaal invokes the phrase metaphorically: People are welling up as if from the pit of the earth, so an exaggeration of the forces stacking up against him. The Greek, in fact, extends this imagery, giving the sea as its ultimate destiny (ἰδοὺ λαὸς καταβαίνων κατὰ θάλασσαν ἀπὸ τοῦ ἐχόμενα τοῦ ὀμφαλοῦ τῆς γῆς, "Look, people are coming down toward the sea from the area near the navel of the Earth").[29] It is difficult to imagine Gaal waxing poetic under stress, but the narrator may well have assigned him such language to grant him awareness of his dire situation.

Gaal continues to find reason to move behind protective doors. He sees another unit coming from a specific direction, this time via the road that leads to ʾēlôn mĕʿônĕnîm, an oak tree that is connected with activities of diviners. Whether or not this is to be identified with other oaks with similar attachments is debatable. Earlier (at 9:6) we had an oak tree witness the crowning of Abimelech, and this one may be another.

Sensing loss of will on the part of Gaal, Zebul taunts him by turning his words on him, for it was crucial to keep him beyond the gates. The double particle ʾayyê ʾēfô (with "where" plus "how") gives finality to the query, here about Gaal's "mouth," that is, his "trash talk." Zebul cites Gaal's words accurately, except for deleting mention of Shechem, likely to keep him focused on what he needs to do. The phrase māʾas bĕ- is normally about rejecting or refusing someone, but here it must have a most biting connotation. Zebul's ploy worked. Stung, Gaal goes out to meet Abimelech, lifnê baʿălê šĕkem; this does not mean that he was leading Shechem elders to battle (NIV and others, "So Gaal led out the elders of Shechem"), but that the confrontation was taking place within the sight of leaders who placed so much hope in him. Certainly he had followers—for many will fall (vayyippĕlû ḥălālîm rabbîm). Sallying forth from the gate area gives defendants the element of surprise, and, if they are brave, they can inflict much damage on besiegers, as is told in the story about Uriah's death (2 Sam 11:14–17). But this is not what occurs here. The sequence of verbs sharpens the scene: As Abimelech rushes at him (*vayyirdĕfēhû*), Gaal takes fright and seeks to escape (*vayyānos*), the scene a much paler version of Hector's last moments at Troy's gates (*Iliad*, Book 22).[30] Whether or not Gaal survives is ambiguous, but many of his followers are not fortunate enough to reach the gate for protection.

RAZING SHECHEM

9 41–45. Wherever we need to look for Arumah, it cannot be too distant from Shechem. For phonetic reasons, some might identify it with Khirbet/Jabal el-ʿUrma, 4 kilometers southeast of Shechem, but no precise location is possible. Debated are connections with Rumah of 2 Kgs 23:36 (in lower Galilee, home of King Jehoiakim's mother) and of Josh 15:52 (near Hebron).[31] The better point is that after humiliating Gaal and wounding (likely killing) many of his followers, Abimelech is happy to leave Zebul in control of events. Zebul drives Gaal and what is left of his minions out of Shechem, according to Josephus, by accusing him of cowardice. Once this is done, Zebul disappears from our story, and the focus returns to Abimelech.

With Gaal gone, Shechem imagines itself rid of retaliatory threat and can return to normal times, among which is to resume tending fields. (Josephus has its citizens caring for their grapes.) This is the reason for confidence rather than disarray in a text that once connected the destruction of Shechem with the banditry of its citizens mentioned above at 9:25 (Moore 1895: 262–63). The false assumption is that Abimelech would not destroy his own town just because it displayed lawless entrepreneurship. What proves catastrophic to Shechem is that it never realizes how much of a true scion of Gideon its former king was, for Abimelech, too, is not likely to let an affront go unpunished. Perhaps Shechem may not have had knowledge of the fates of Penuel and Succoth.

Once again, anonymous information is passed on to Abimelech, and once again, he follows his preferred stratagem. To net as many victims as possible, he divides his men into units, evoking his father's ruse against Midian (at 7:16). Is Zebul the source of the latest intelligence? Or has Abimelech simply lumped him among his intended victims? This, we cannot know; what is clear is the savagery with which Abimelech carries out his purge. The verb *pāšaṭ* controls the action, first as an auxiliary to *ʿāmad*, "to stand," but then in the idiom *pāšaṭ ʿal+*, which, as we have seen at 9:33, conveys a forceful act. Incongruous is the mention of "units" (*rāʾšîm* in the plural) directly under Abimelech when the other two (of three) are dispatched to the field and in all there should be just three of them. Rahlfs B "solves" the problem by translating the element **rʾš* as "leaders" (οἱ ἀρχηγοί); similarly, Radaq assigns many leaders to the unit under Abimelech.

Not content with killing those outside the city, Abimelech treats Shechem as his father acted toward Penuel, with the same verb (*nātaṣ*) applied to the destruction of its constructions. In this case, however, with Shechem having infringed on oaths that normally accompany a crowning ceremony, the punishment is more brutal. Seeding ground with salt is said to destroy its fertility, but recent research is of many minds on this, not so much on its effectiveness, but on its likelihood.[32] To begin with, the processing of salt was too costly to waste the immense amount of it needed to cover razed towns. Moreover, reports that salt was spread on the ruins of devastated cities (among them Carthage) are proving to be inventions of modern research.[33] In Semitic languages, processed salt has names (*melaḥ, ṭabtum*) that accentuate a positive quality, suggesting that symbolism (religious, covenantal, or magical) may be the most likely explanation for Abimelech's move (see Honeyman 1953 and Gevirtz 1963).

BURNING THE CITADEL

9 46–49. Not content with razing the town's wall and massacring its citizens, Abimelech goes after its leaders, who were safe in their citadel (see at 8:17). Within it was the temple dedicated to El-berith (see the discussion at 8:33–35 and 9:4).[34] The problem here is to decide what is the *ṣĕrîᵃḥ* into which the leaders gathered and where to locate it: Is it part of a fortified area near the temple (ὀχύρωμα in Rahlfs A), a large assembly area in the temple (συνέλευσιν in Rahlfs B), or neither? Is this structure above (Radaq) or beneath (Rashi) the ground? At 6:2 we saw the Hebrews cringing in mountain hideouts. In 1 Sam 13:6, frightened Hebrews hid in natural spaces (caves, crevices, and clefts in rocks) and human-created ones (*ṣĕrihîm* and cisterns). So it is natural to think of some sort of chamber that is part of a temple, but one that stands out from the others and is possibly flammable, because soon we will learn that Abimelech's men readily accessed it to stack timber all about it. I therefore have doubts that it is an underground chamber or a crypt. (See *HALOT* s.v. for diverse opinions.) Perhaps it is the chamber where cultic paraphernalia could be stacked rather than where the cultic image is to be found, the latter requiring a smaller space.[35]

Who gives Abimelech details on where the leaders had gone to hide may be worth asking, even if we realize that a motif is replaying in this narrative. Earlier, Jotham learned about the convocation to crown Abimelech king (at 9:7, Hiphil conversive imperfect with impersonal subject), and Abimelech found out about Shechem's dastardly betrayal (at 9:25). Although information seems to leak in such unstable conditions, there is reason to credit the ill will God commissioned (see at 9:23).

What is Mount Zalmon (*har ṣalmôn*, "Mount Darkish") is also a question. Given the topography of the region, we are likely dealing with a nickname.[36] If so, it might be appropriate for the wooded Mount Gerizim from which Jotham launched his fable (at 9:7). Boling (1975) credits Father Tournay for equating it with Ebal, a mountain associated with covenantal cursing, yet turns incongruously realistic by adding "the argument . . . cannot appeal to the convenient location of the northwest gate at Shechem, which was apparently unused in the Late Bronze and Iron I periods" (181).

Abimelech takes an axe and cuts down the wood he will use against the offenders. In Hebrew, *garzen* is the word for axe; occasionally, *barzel* stands metonymically for that instrument by citing its iron blade (2 Kgs 6:5, Isa 10:34). Here, however, we meet with *qardummôt*, a word likely of non-Hebraic derivation, possibly connected with *qulmum/ qalpum*, one of many Akkadian names for an axe. (Other associations are also made, via Arabic and the like, but none as convincing.) The tool is featured in Jer 46:22, with soldiers coming against Egypt "like hewers of wood," bearing *qardummôt* (see also at Ps 74:5 and 1 Sam 13:20). In all but the Samuel passage (where it might be defectively written), the word ends on -*ôt*, often a marker for the plural. The oddity in our passage is that the noun apparently occurs in the plural and is attached to a definite article ("so he grasped the axes by his hand"). The latter phenomenon is not at all unusual; we have already met two examples at 4:21 when Jael "took hold of a tent peg and grasped a mallet in her hand," and at 19:29 we will come on a dastardly act done with "a knife." As for the use of the plural, several explanations are possible: (1) the grammars offer examples of plurals connoting the (poetic) singular of abstractions; (2) a single instrument was passed on multiple times for use by others, and most attractively; and (3) it is a "false plural," the *-ôt* ending actually reflecting an *-ât*.[37] None is a perfect clarification; luckily, how the instrument was put to use is not in question.

What he cuts are the *śôk*s of trees. The word occurs only in this context (both as feminine and masculine), and while it is something that is part of a tree, we must guess what is intended. I would happily connect it, again via Arabic, with "thorns," especially since it revisits one of Gideon's more notorious acts, which was to use thorns and briers when flaying the elders of Succoth (at 8:16), and it recalls Jotham's fable about the consuming thorn (9:15). Yet, thorns do not transport happily on shoulders, and it may be prudent to follow the Greek, which gives either "some brushwood" (Rahlfs A) or some tree limbs (Rahlfs B). To learn that Abimelech (and his men) carried what they cut on their shoulders (*ʿal šikmô*) may seem superfluous, but with this tidbit the narrator was making one final play on Shechem's name.

Abimelech orders his men to do as he does, thus expanding on the language his father used when giving instruction on how to terrorize Midian (7:16–18). Whether the victims died of asphyxiation or fire is not clear; we have only the phrase *vayyaṣîtû ʿălêhem ʾet-haṣṣĕrîʿah bāʾēš* to suggest that the fire was set "over" or "against" them.[38] The use of fire is here certainly tactical, but let it also be noted that in Mari documents, burning is the fate allotted to traitors and their families.[39] It boggles the mind that any chamber (or cave, or tunnel) with a fortified area would have room for a thousand refugees, but the number is not exorbitant by the standard of Judges.[40]

A Pretender's End

9 50–51. The sorry end of a schemer comes at a place that was not even mentioned previously, unless one accepts an emendation at 8:18 (for which, see above). But over time, Thebez and Abimelech become a pair, so much so that in 2 Sam 11:18–21 Joab recalls the ignominious end of Abimelech (son of Jerubbeshet) when reporting on the death of Uriah.[41] (See the Comments to IIID1.) The location of Thebez (*tēvēṣ*) is a guess, with most commentators placing it at the superficially similar sounding Ṭūbās, a village a dozen miles from Nablus, despite its lack of Late Bronze or Iron Age remains. Rainey and Notley (2006: 140) would emend the Hebrew to read "Tirzah"; Gass (2005: 333–34) offers other choices.

Why Abimelech takes the battle to Thebez is a mystery, unless it is because the rebellion against him was general (not improbable) or because the town had a pact with Shechem. This last is implied in Rahlfs B, as it has him proceed to Thebez from the Shechem temple. Once there, he meets no resistance. Rather, the citizens of Thebez hope to withstand the onslaught by hiding behind strong doors. For Abimelech, the same technique that gave him success was worth applying. He might have wished to encourage his men to pile more brush at the gate, but this time the results are different, for "some woman" (*ʾiššâ ʾaḥat*, literally "one woman") brings his career to an end. There might be irony in the use of the cardinal number here; earlier (at 9:2), Abimelech persuaded Shechem that it was to their advantage to back just one person (*ʾîš ʾeḥād*). This woman cracked (*vattāriṣ*) his skull.[42]

There is a report (A.350+) in the Mari archives about Susu, the king of Apum (upper Ḫabur), who suffered a disputed death while resisting the onslaught of Zimri-Lim. Some report he died from a disease ("God's water"), others say a stone crushed his head by a town's wall, and still others claim that he died a natural death.[43] Whatever the cause, it could not surprise that death can be served by a stone during a siege.[44] What makes the fate of Abimelech worthy of recall is that he actually died a suicide (albeit by a third hand) because his ego would not allow him to credit his death to a woman, a dreaded disgrace already discussed as it concerned Sisera (chapter 4). We need not imagine that the millstone was cast by Wonder Woman (of comic book memory), for the millstones of antiquity divided neatly between those women operated in private homes and those turned by animal labor at larger installations.[45]

The stones generally came in pairs, the more substantial and stationary of the two placed below while an upper stone was manipulated to grind the grain. There is broad testimony from cuneiform sources that millstones came in a great variety, were made from a wide diversity of stones, and may (or may not) have had handles.[46] Biblical lore is in agreement, with diverse words applied to instruments for grinding—the dual noun *rēḥayim* being most descriptive, while our *pelaḥ* (meaning "slice"; see Greek κλάσμα, "a portion") requires qualification to indicate whether it was the lower millstone (*taḥtît*) or, as in our case, the upper one (*rekeb*, "the rider").[47] Again here, there might be irony in the mention of stones in the death of yet another of Gideon's sons (Boogaart 1985). As we recall, Abimelech butchered his brothers on a single stone (see 9:5 and 9:18).

We are not told how Abimelech knew who cast the stone on his skull, but the fact that the grinding of grain in a home was the task of women (Exod 11:5, Isa 47:2 [humiliated Babylon]) must have allowed him to draw his conclusion.[48] A subtle touch here is that Abimelech could credit death to an unknown woman while Sisera could not foresee it coming from the last woman he met. Abimelech's suicide is assisted by his *naʿar* ("attendant"), here, unlike what is said about Gideon's (at 7:11), explained as *nōśēʾ kēlāyv*, the "arms-bearer." Abimelech asks him to deliver the final blow (*môtĕtēnî*; the Polel of *mût* has this intensive notion, as in 1 Sam 14:13 and elsewhere), with Rahlfs B giving "draw *my* sword." Abimelech's attendant obliges, unlike that other scene in which a mortally wounded Saul ends his own life because his attendant would not kill a king (1 Sam 31:4–7, with interesting contrast at 2 Sam 1:1–16). However, while Saul's arms-bearer followed his master's example by taking his own life, Abimelech's slayer apparently had no qualms resuming his private life. In both scenes, the narrators remain morally neutral about the act but not, as in our case, on the circumstances that led to such a dire decision.

In sharp contrast to the notice about the brood his father left behind, nothing is said about Abimelech fathering any children, though he was an adult and had ruled for a few years.

THE LESSON

9 55–57. On Abimelech's death, Israel disbanded its force: *vayyēlĕkû ʾîš limqōmô*, "everyone (in Israel) went back home." Despite what was said about the sway Abimelech had over Israel (at 9:22), this statement nevertheless seems especially incongruous, given the local nature of the fight between Abimelech and his ex-allies. So much so that some commentators (Moore, Burney, following Wellhausen) attribute Canaanite sentiments to those rebelling against Abimelech: They once welcomed him as one of their own but discovered quickly enough that he remains Gideon's son. Yet the reference to the scattering of Israel's forces recalls, above all, Judg 7:7–8. There, a similar phrase (*věkol-hā'ām yēlěkû 'îš limqōmô*) is used when God instructs Gideon to dismiss his troops, to sharpen the miracle about to unfold.

The coda stands out from the narrative and might, frankly, be needless had it not provided the moral necessary to complete Jotham's fable: Both sides in the unholy alliance are shown to get the retribution they deserve—Abimelech for dishonoring his father when murdering his brothers, and Shechem for participating in the crime.[49] Fire did indeed roll out of Abimelech, destroying Shechem as well as Abimelech, who dies as he was deploying it. The lesson is as old as that told in the action of Nadab and Abihu, both sons of Aaron, who discovered (Lev 10:1–3) that the most dangerous fires are not those launched from heaven, but those that are brought to accomplish human designs.

COMMENTS

> Rescuers [*môšî'îm*] shall come up to Mount Zion to judge [*lišpōṭ*] Mount Esau; yet kingship shall be the LORD's.
> —*Obad 1:21*

Abimelech in Hebraic Tradition

In Judg 10:1, the first verse of the chapter that immediately follows on our section, we will be told, "Stepping up to rescue Israel after Abimelech was Tola son of Puah son of Dodo, of Issachar." The syntax of transition is important, for it accents the rescue of Israel after a change of rulers, in this case after Abimelech has had his chance to help Israel through its difficulties. Only at 10:2 are we invited to assess Tola's contribution to the experiment: "He was judge in Israel [*vayyišpōṭ 'et-yiśrā'ēl*] for twenty-three years." (See the Notes and Comments there.) If correctly perceived, this notice surprises, for this rescue is set to follow Abimelech, whose salvific virtues had been nil, rather than Gideon/Jerubbaal, who, while never termed a judge, had had memorable têtes-à-têtes with God. Because of what we already know about Abimelech's striking demise, this "after Abimelech" (*'aḥărê 'ăvîmelek*) is ambiguous: It can be sequential ("after Abimelech had been the rescuer") or consequential ("after the mess that Abimelech created").

Whichever way it is read, this notice suggests that, his ignominious end notwithstanding, Abimelech had a fuller afterlife than most other major personalities in Judges. We have already mentioned an anecdote, set in the days of David, wherein Joab invokes Abimelech's death to illustrate the danger of combat near fortifications, suggesting a readiness to set Abimelech within a sequence of leaders of Israel. This is startling because in the chapter devoted to his story, there is no hint that he participated in that continuity. Since the death of Gideon, Israel had shown little remorse for its attachment to Baal-berith; therefore, it gave God no cause to rescue it from its plight (8:33). Unlike what transpired in the days of Gideon, when God and his selected champion repeatedly egged each other on when shaping an opposition to Midian, in the ample story about Abimelech, God is hardly more than an instrument for revenge in a rather local morality play. Israel itself is not attacked by any outside force, and not a tear is shed as a result of oppression.

Abimelech in Current Scholarship

It is obvious therefore that in the story of Abimelech we are tackling issues and subjects that do not easily mesh with others so far promoted in Judges. Yet, the narrator was willing to accord much space to this anomalous account. Table 8 shows a rather expansive (if also hardly "scientific") verse count in the received account.

We notice that the narratives about Gideon/Jerubbaal and Samson are the longest, with the story of Abimelech just behind them in length. Whereas the other narratives assemble episodes with markedly different goals, Abimelech's story is comparatively narrowly focused, even if one includes the fable. In scholarship (both traditional and modern), therefore, there is interest in understanding how what is told about Abimelech fits in Judges. Was it shaped after a Canaanite tale? What were its constitutive elements? How did it find its niche among Gideon tales? The literature on these matters is vast and, as is normal in scholarship, not always of lasting significance. Fortunately, that literature has been nicely (and comprehensively) reviewed, among others, by Bluedorn (2001: 15–56) and O'Connell (1996: 345–68). Suffice it for me to pick up on some of its strands.

More so than other efforts dealing with personalities in Judges, assessing the import of the Abimelech episode has been closely linked with approaches current at the time of the speculation, the reason being that the stories about him seem only um-

Table 8. Verse Count in Narratives About Judges

Judge	Title	Verses	Source
Gideon/Jerubbaal	*môšîᵃ‘*	100	6:1–8:32
Samson	*môšîᵃ‘/šōfēṭ*	96	15–16
Abimelech	*[môšîᵃ‘]*	64	8:29–9:57
Jephthah	*šōfēṭ*	60	10:6–12:7
Deborah	*šōfēṭ*	24	4:1–24
Song		31	5:1–31
Ehud	*môšîᵃ‘*	19	3:12–30
Othniel	*môšîᵃ‘/šōfēṭ*	7	3:5–11
Abdon	*šōfēṭ*	3	12:13–15
Ibzan	*šōfēṭ*	3	12:8–10
Jair	*šōfēṭ*	3	10:3–5
Elon	*šōfēṭ*	2	12:11–12
Tola	*šōfēṭ*	2	10:1–2
[Shamgar	*môšîᵃ‘*	1	3:31]

bilically attached to what precedes them while little that follows depends on them. In the Comments to the previous segment, I observed that through the First World War the documentary hypothesis held sway on assessing the Abimelech story. Since Noth's monumental work on the Deuteronomist (beginning in 1930), in which preexisting lore about tribal leaders was integrated with lists of judges (our "minor" judges) to produce a chapter in a developing history of Israel, there have been significant attempts to rethink the development of Judges traditions. Few of these have been as productive or as influential as the works of Richter (1963, 1964). He reconstructed the remnants of what he called a "Book of Saviors" (*Retterbuch*), now preserved mostly in Judg 3–9—accounts that took shape in the Northern Kingdom of the Jehu period, as hinted by reference to the murder of the seventy sons of Ahab (2 Kgs 10:7) that inspired the notice about the murder of Gideon's seventy sons. By identifying the latter with Jerubbaal, the Abimelech story got grafted to that of Gideon. (See also the relevant commentary in the Introduction.)

While the proposals of Noth and Richter continue to play as *basso continuo* in any discussion that exploits inner biblical exegesis, new formulations on the Abimelech episode continue to be offered. Guillaume (2004: 55–74), as one example, has an elaborate theory on how the story of Abimelech, by condemning kingship as well as revolting against it, is actually teaching acceptance of Assyrian rule. For Becker (1990: 140ff.), Abimelech's rule is the Deuteronomist historian's brutal lesson on the failure of kingship, especially when contrasted with Gideon's rejection of it. Moralistic and legal touches (at 8:24–27, 9:16–17, and 9:56–57) were inserted by others in the Deuteronomistic circles (DtrN). Fritz (1982) breaks it up into two units: the Gaal episode, and the rise and fall as king of Shechem, both before the ninth century BCE. He also identifies two stages of Deuteronomic reworkings, one that added the fable and another that gave Abimelech control over Israel. Fritz is sharply critiqued by Boogaart (1985: 47).[50] In turn, Boogaart proposes (simplistically) that "retribution" is the theme that glues the narrative: Abimelech kills on a stone, and he is killed by one.

Those who treat the story synchronically, however, rely on the archeology of Tell Balaṭa (Shechem) to give historicity to events as well as to affirm a date for the events around the twelfth to the eleventh centuries BCE. It is possible to read reports on the excavation that explain the topography of the area via the Abimelech story or to attribute the destruction of certain levels (XI) to "Abimelech."[51] Other efforts to explain the thrust of the Abimelech tradition rely on Amarna archives to read it as "a page out of a Canaanite history notebook" (Block 1999: 308–9). Abimelech is cast as a period chieftain (Reviv 1966), and the earliest strands of his story are set in that age (de Castelbajac 2001). Such efforts assume a Canaanite status for Shechem, hence partially also for Abimelech, so that between him and Shechem the strife was ethnic—if not also religious when references to the temples of Baal and El are taken into consideration.

Yet, the experiences of Abimelech and Lab'aya are not exceptional, for the rise and fall of opportunistic leaders can be rehearsed whenever there is a lack of strong regional control. Thus, after the death of the imperial Samsi-Addu of the Mari archives, territory around kingdoms such as Kurda, Andarig, Ašnakkum, and Karana shrank or swelled at a moment's notice. One need only to review the brief careers of Samsi-Eraḥ in the Yapṭurum region (Guichard 2011) and Ibal-Addu of Ašlakka (Sasson 2013a, "'*It is for this reason*'") to recognize that in troubled times men rose high and fell from grace in less than a decade, leaving trails of havoc and destruction in their wakes. The same parties that championed Samsi-Eraḫ also brought him to an end, while Ibal-Addu's life story also featured reliance on *ḫabirū*s, more or less matching that of Lab'aya.

ABIMELECH, THE *UNHEILSHERRSCHER*

In lore about the deeds of past leaders, there are traditions about a distinct type that scholars now term an *Unheilsherrscher*. It applies to rulers whose actions (whether naive or calculated, beneficial or detrimental) were judged in antiquity to lead (them) to misfortune, so they were leaders marked by and for disaster. For the typology to apply, the source of the calamity was not particularly relevant, although self-induced personal errors (hubris, impiety, excessive courage, etc.) hardened their fall.[52] For Mesopotamia, the parade example as drawn in antiquity is Naram-Sin, although modern scholars might include others, such as Ibbi-Sin of Ur, Sargon or Sennacherib of Assyria, and Nabonidus of Babylon. Naram-Sin slights the gods and, despite a name that means "beloved of (the moon god) Sin," pays for his hubris by losing political prestige. His own arrival to the throne is not without markers. Omen traditions had it that his predecessors—his uncle Rimuš and his father Maništušu—were both assassinated, the latter likely also a fratricide. Naram-Sin's capital, Agade, is abandoned by the gods and is devastated. This assessment is not always consistent, and it is certainly far from historical; for while he countered numerous revolts during his reign, we know that Naram-Sin's successor, Šar-kali-šarri, ruled from a relatively prosperous Agade for a quarter of a century and was himself followed by successors. Moreover, the memory of Naram-Sin was kept alive in private devotions for centuries. What is interesting, therefore, is that the same circles that created the image of a failing king likely also knew the reality of his reign. Their interest in a literary portrayal that deviated from historical knowledge was prodded by theosophic concerns that are not always obvious to us now.[53]

In biblical scholarship, Saul, Manasseh, and more obviously Jeroboam are deemed *Unheilsherrscher*s.[54] Ceded a generous portion of Solomon's kingdom because (according to the prophet Ahijah) of the sins of the latter, Jeroboam first reigned from Shechem. He quickly earned condemnation for creating a center of worship away from Jerusalem, for installing in Dan and Bethel avatars for the Hebrew god that scarcely pleased God, and for shuffling the cultic calendar to suit his priesthood. As a number of scholars have argued (among them Van Seters 1983: 313–14), the accusations likely were Deuteronomistic polemics, for the brunt of the message is that God cannot be dismissed, mocked, or reconfigured.

Yet, as drawn in native traditions, what enhanced Naram-Sin's status as an *Unheilsherrscher* as much as his self-propelled fall is the contrast drawn between him and Sargon—actually his grandfather, but often presented as his father to sharpen the contrast. From his fairytale survival as an abandoned child and his selection by the gods to establish a dynasty centered in Agade, the Sargon of legends could hardly falter. He was pious, daring, and visionary. His military drives went deep into the enemy's territory, and his energy bolstered the confidence of his troops. It is in the opposition of traits and achievements of father and son, rather than just because of his shortcomings, that Abimelech can be proposed as an *Unheilsherrscher*. We may judge Gideon to be skittish in adopting God's charge, but for the narrator, God was behind Gideon's every move. Not so for Abimelech. Divine censure is hinted in Jotham's fable, of him no less than of Shechem. This disfavor is formulated as an imposed ill-will soon after the opening of Abimelech's career; it is also delivered as an apothegm when his life is ebbing away. The narrator turns Gideon's repeated reluctance to take on divine assignments into as many occasions for God to display commitment to Israel. In turn, Abimelech's faults are tracked as starkly personal, from the moment he accepts funds from the temple of Baal-berith with which to massacre his brothers. Gideon's disinclination to take up kingship is contrasted with Abimelech's ready adoption of its trappings.

This contrast between related rulers with opposite fates is enhanced by a rehearsal of differences in behavior that is attributed to Jotham (9:16–20). Less obtrusive is the paralleling of activities or situations that are assigned to each:

—Both Gideon and Abimelech *were not the most prominent in their father's eyes*: the former in his own estimation (6:15), and the latter because of his mother's status.

—They both *had difficulties with members of their extended families*: Gideon provoking anger when destroying clan altars (6:25–32), and Abimelech being rejected by the leaders of Shechem, a reversal of fortune attributed to a "spirit of discord" (9:22–23).

—*They are both offered authority* that they did not request: Gideon famously refusing it (8:22–23), and Abimelech readily accepting coronation (9:6).

—*They both have arms-bearers*: Gideon's Purah accompanies him in a test of God's support (7:9–11), and Abimelech's takes his life to save him from shame (9:54–55). As Purah's role is vestigial (in fact, the narrator forgets about him when he returns Gideon alone to the Hebrew camp), it may well be that he is there also to balance the more important role assigned to Abimelech's *na'ar*.

—*They both favor a martial technique of dividing forces* to maximize attacks: Gideon uses it to attack Midian (7:16–18), and Abimelech does the same first against Gaal (9:34) and then against Shechem (9:43).

—*They both are targets of taunts*: Gideon by the men of Succoth (8:6) and the kings he captures (8:18–21), and Abimelech by Gaal (9:28–29).

—*They are both vengeful*: Gideon scourges the men of Succoth (8:16) and destroys the tower of Penuel, killing its citizens in the process (8:17), and Abimelech is relentless, razing Shechem and massacring its people before torching those taking refuge in its citadel (9:43–49). He was readying to do the same to Thebez.

These touches do not amount to repetitions and none is obvious by itself, but cumulatively, they do create a backdrop by which to keep the comparison alive. The goal is to drive home what is obvious: Men of the same flesh and of many similar characters are destined for opposite reputations when they do not share the affection or support of the God of Israel. The lesson buttresses God's unpredictable control of events, a characteristic that, as proposed in the Introduction, the book of Judges actively promotes.

"Minor" Judges, Major Rift
(Judg 10:1–16)

---

10 ¹Stepping up to rescue Israel after Abimelech was Tola son of Puah son of Dodo, of Issachar. He lived at Shamir in the hills of Ephraim. ²He was judge in Israel for twenty-three years. He died and was buried at Shamir. ס

³After him, Jair of Gilead stepped up and was judge in Israel for twenty-two years. ⁴He had thirty sons who rode on thirty colts. Thirty villages were theirs. To them even now is applied the name "Hovels of Jair," in the territory of Gilead. ⁵Then Jair died and was buried at Kamon. ס

⁶The people of Israel resumed offending the LORD: They worshiped the many Baals and Ashtaroth, as well as the gods of Aram, the gods of Sidon, the gods of Moab, the gods of the Ammonites, and the gods of the Philistines. They forsook the LORD and did not worship him. ⁷Incensed against Israel, the LORD turned them over to the Philistines and to the men of Ammon. ⁸They crushed and oppressed the people of Israel in that year for eighteen years—all the people of Israel across the Jordan—in the Amorite territory of Gilead.

⁹The men of Ammon crossed the Jordan to make war on Judah, Benjamin, as well as the House of Ephraim. Israel suffered terribly. ¹⁰The Israelites pleaded with the LORD, "We have sinned against you, by forsaking our God and worshiping many Baals." ס

¹¹The LORD said to the people of Israel, "Was it not that when Egypt, the Amorites, the Ammonites, the Philistines, ¹²the Sidonians, Amalek, and Maon oppressed you, you cried out to me and I indeed rescued you from them? ¹³Yet

you have abandoned me and worshiped other gods. Just for that, I will not keep on rescuing you. [14]Go and beseech the gods you have chosen; these might rescue you in this time of trouble." [15]But the people of Israel told the LORD: "We have sinned. Do to us whatever you wish; only save us just now!" [16]They removed the alien gods from their midst and worshiped the LORD; but he lost patience with Israel's behavior. ס

NOTES

Introductory Remarks: The "Minor" Judges

The phrase "minor judges" was created in modern scholarship to refer to five judges with brief notices attached to them (see Table 9). Despite the many good objections against alluding to it in such a way, the phrase remains in heavy usage.[1] The roster is set on either side of the Jephthah story: two (Tola and Jair) at 10:1–5 and three (Ibzan, Elon, and Abdon) at 12:8–15. These notices are formulaic, brief, and minimalist, with Elon's the tightest and Abdon's the broadest. Each is introduced by attachment to a previous account ("After . . ."). A name is cited next, with (or without) the name of a father and/or home/tribe. Oddly enough, these names are duplicated (perhaps even culled) from other lists in the Hebrew Bible.[2] An anecdote may follow before the posting of length of rule. Death and place of burial are recorded last. The moralistic line about Israel sinning and having to deal with punishment before receiving absolution is not there at all.

For at least the reasons detailed above, biblical scholarship has long discriminated between these "minor" judges and the richer narratives about Othniel, Ehud, Deborah (and Baraq), Gideon, and Samson. Jephthah is said to bridge the two categories, not so much because of length, but because of mixed language drawn from both formulas. There is dispute over whether or not a Deuteronomistic hand was implicated in their introduction.[3] Following Alt, Noth claimed that these minor judges were tribal magistrates trusted to adjudicate disputes between the leaders of other members of the Israelite amphictyony. Hence their authority is closest to what we might consider arbitrators or interpreters of legal issues, based on their personal integrity (Scherer 2007). This material was drawn from an official list of such officers. The more elaborate narratives that include warfare (internal, national, or international) involve charismatic leaders, such as Ehud, Deborah and Baraq, Gideon, and Samson, who took power at moments of crises. The members of these two groups differed in origins and function, even if they shared vocabulary, such as *šōfēt*, or occasionally phraseology, such as notices about length of rule or recall of burial place.

Noth's construct ruled the scholarly debate for almost a generation. It fell partly to the side after Richter offered an alternate understanding of the development of traditions that concern the so-called major judges. More harmful to Noth was the collapse of his amphictyony theory, making it difficult to present the minor judges as national magistrates or to maintain distinctions between them and the major judges, aside from the obviously richer tapestry of anecdotes about the latter. In recent literature, the trend is to evaluate the material as antimonarchic and as originating in the Northern Kingdom, with unsubtle claims for the viability of the rule by judges (lastly Nelson 2007;

Table 9. The "Minor" Judges

Judge	Text	Sequence	Father	Home/tribe	Rule (yrs)	Anecdote	Burial
Tola	10:1–2	(vayyāqom ʾaḥărê Abimelech . . . vayyišpōṭ)	Puah son of Dodo	Shamir in the hills of Ephraim/ Issachar	23		Shamir
Jair	10:3–4	vayyāqom ʾaḥărāʾv . . . vayyišpōṭ		Gilead	22	30 sons on 30 donkeys; 30 towns in Gilead (Havoth-Jair)	Kamon
[Jephthah]	11–12:7	vayyišpōṭ yiftāḥ	Gilead	Gilead	6[a]	narratives	"cities of Gilead"]
Ibzan	12:8–10	vayyišpōṭ ʾaḥărāʾv		Bethlehem	7	30 sons, 30 daughters; interclan marriages	Bethlehem
Elon	12:11–12	vayyišpōṭ ʾaḥărāʾv		Zebulon	10		Ayyalon in Zebulon
Abdon	12:13–14	vayyišpōṭ ʾaḥărāʾv	Hillel	Pirʿaton	8	40 sons, 30 grandsons, riding 70 donkeys	Pirʿaton in Ephraim on Amalek Hill

[a]Rahlfs B: 60.

contra G. Miller 2011: 240–44). What we are left with, therefore, are anecdotes of dubious value (or perhaps better, with dubious objectives) as attached to Jair, Ibzan, and Abdon. About them, what we learn replays a fixation on the number of children they had (thirties and forties) and the number of towns and donkeys they owned (thirties and seventies). These numbers hardly lead to developed narratives, but they do sharpen the drama that will overtake Jephthah, who famously had just one daughter.

Judge Tola

10 1–2. The transition from Abimelech is abrupt. None of the normal features—Israel's depravity, God's resolve to punish Israel, the enemy's rampage, and Israel gaining God's mercy—is deployed. Tola is the first of the minor judges to be listed as well as the seventh judge (by some calculations but not others) in our received compilation. As mentioned in the Comments to the previous segment, much is unusual about this opening line. The sequence of verbs *vayyāqom . . . lĕhôšîaʿ ʾet-yiśrāʾēl* is unique for Tola, and since his mission as judge (*šōfēṭ*) is not introduced until the next verse, we surmise that there is an attempt to connect with the narratives about Gideon/Jerubbaal where almost half of all forms of *yāšaʿ* occurring in Judges are embedded. The surprise here is that the sequence is said to continue after Abimelech rather than after Gideon/Jerubbaal. (But see a contrary suggestion in the Comments below.) As vocalized, *vayyāqom* gives Tola control of his own actions, mildly implying a power grab. This verbal form is repeated for Jair at 10:3, but not for the series of judges that will come right after Jephthah. In some Greek manuscripts, God is given control of events, suggesting a reading of *vayyāqēm (after 2:16, 18), but also there is an attribution of ancestry that goes its own direction (see Moore 1895: 273 for details).

Tola (*tôlāʿ*; Greek, Θωλα) has a name that means "worm" or "caterpillar"—more precisely, according to Astour (1965: 349 n. 31), "the kermes insect from which crimson dyes were extracted." He is said to be the son of Puah (*pûʾâ*), with a name that has to do with madder (*rubia tinctorum*, red dye). In Num 26:23, the roster of "sons" (that is, clans) belonging to Issachar includes this notice: "*To* Tola *belonged* the Tola clan; to Puvah [*puvâ*], the Puni [*pûnî*; Greek, Φουαϊ] clan." So in Greek the name of Tola's father (Φουα) reflects both his name in Hebrew and the spelling of his clan as recorded in the Greek of Numbers.

It Hebrew lore, it is not uncommon to give leaders an ancestry that goes back several generations, but in Judges it occurs only with reference to Phineas, "son of Elazar son of Aaron, the priest" (at 20:28).[4] Likely for this reason, following the LXX, *bēn dôdô* is taken literally, that is, as "the son of his paternal uncle" (υἱὸς πατραδέλφου αὐτοῦ). The same occurs in some Targumic readings (W. Smelik 1995: 534). If in 10:1 the antecedent for the phrase is Abimelech, Gideon's son, it would mean that either Tola or his father Puah was his cousin. Though startling, despite different tribal affiliations this connection is not in itself impossible, as it would mean continuity from Joash's descendants. However, in some Semitic languages (for example, Mari Amorite) *dādum* refers to the mother's brother; this would be hardly likely, given our previous story. Because in Scripture there are a couple of occurrences of a person by the name of Dôdô/Dôdî (for example, at 2 Sam 23:24), I am sticking with Tola having a grandfather by that name, as suggested in traditional Jewish exegesis, but it is obviously not beyond challenge.

As a personal name, Dodo would be based on *dwd*, which means either "love" (*dôd*) or "uncle" (*dôd*).[5] However, in Arabic *dûd* means "worm," and in rabbinic lore Solomon built the temple with a "shamir" (see just below), a tiny (but mythical) worm that was said to cut stone and engrave solid metal (for example, at *bPesahim* 54a; Maimonides, *Commentary on Abot* 5.6).[6] What to make of all these names in one family that have connections with insects or annelids is difficult to say. Astour (1965) found in them reason to believe that this Issachar clan, because of its proximity to Phoenicia, shared a name that was later associated with Phoenicia and Punic Carthage.

Tola is said to belong to the tribe of Issachar. The tribe, occupying a landlocked but fertile area south of Mount Tabor, receives favorable attention in the Song of Deborah (see at 5:15).[7] He ruled from Shamir (*šāmîr*). Not to be confused with a homonym in Judah (Josh 15:48), this Shamir in the hills of Ephraim is so unknown that Rahlfs B offers the better known Σαμάρεια, Samaria, normally *šōmrôn* in Hebrew. Because the building of that fortress was attributed to Omri, scholars dismiss this identification. Yet, kings in the ancient world claimed to be builders of cities when they simply made major renovations to them or built up their walls. In this case, however, the Greek is simply offering a known for an unknown.

Judge Jair

10 3–4. The name Jair (Greek, Ιαϊρ, Ιαηρ) duplicates a verbal form *yāʾîr* (Hiphil of *ʾwr*) that translates as "he will give radiance," occurring in such passages as Job 41:24 and Ps 139:12. Doubtless, God is the subject, the notion being that the birth of the child is the parents' great blessing. His father's name is not recorded; this is not unusual since only the first and last of the minor judges are so identified. He is, however, termed a man from Gilead, a tribal area named after a significant offshoot of Machir, itself a component of Manasseh (see the Notes at 5:17). Gilead will soon play a major role in the Jephthah story.

The anecdote attached to this Jair has two edges: the thirty sons he had ("of good character," according to Josephus) and the control he had over thirty towns.[8] The bountiful number of offspring is also a feature in the brief notes attached to Ibzan (who additionally had thirty daughters; at 12:9) and Abdon (who had forty sons but also thirty grandsons; at 12:14). Earlier we had read about Gideon's seventy sons, and their wholesale massacre gave a clue to the monstrosity of Abimelech, and of Shechem as well. Here, as noted, this remarkable surfeit will make for an instructive contrast with Jephthah's descent.[9]

Jair's thirty sons rode on thirty colts (*rokĕbîm ʿal-šĕlōšîm ʿăyārîm*). Elsewhere the donkey that is ridden is either a male (*ḥămôr*) or female (*ʾātôn*) donkey.[10] Here, however, *ʿăyārîm* is obviously introduced to craft a pun on the next segment of the boast, for Jair (or his sons) had thirty towns (*ʿăyārîm*, spelled identically).[11] The reference to riding colts has little to do with the animals' "special sacral significance" (Boling 1975: 188, citing Pedersen); rather, it has to do with status, especially among Amorites. In Mari, ranking diplomats trafficked so often among capitals that they were simply labeled *rākib imērī*, "donkey riders."[12] The impression here is that Jair is set to be in control deep into the generations following.

The target of the pun is an association with a circle of villages that over time had gotten the name *ḥavvôt yāʾir*. What are these *ḥavvôt* is difficult to say. The Vulgate avoids deciding by transliterating it (*avothiair*; Old Latin, *aoth*). In 2 Sam 23:13, there is reference to thirty [*sic*] of David's warriors, among whom three were brave enough to penetrate a Philistine shantytown (?) (*ḥayyat* [*ḥavat?*] *pĕlištîm*) from where to draw water. There are five other references to *ḥavvôt yāʾir*. At Num 32:41 and Deut 3:14, in the days of Moses, Jair son of Manasseh (son of Joseph) captures the whole of the Argov district in the Bashan region, an area across the Jordan once ruled by Og, and renames it after himself, "Hovels of Jair." This allusion to the occupation of Gilead territory during Israel's heroic period will soon come back in the story of Jephthah. The name *ḥavvôt yāʾir* is said to be still in effect in traditions regarding Solomon (1 Kgs 4:13). In Josh 13:30, the number of towns is sixty, so double what we have in Judges. The reference in 1 Chr 2:22–23 has its own goal: Jair is now the son of Segub, born of Hezron, grandson of Judah, and of a sister of Gilead. This Jair had only twenty-three towns in Gilead but lost much to Geshur and Aram, some to towns including the Hovels of Jair. It is hardly possible to create harmony out of all these details, but explanations are not lacking (see Lagrange 1903: 187–88).

Jair is buried in Kamon (*qāmôn*). The place is doubtless in Gilead, but it occurs nowhere else. In Greek it is given as Ραμμω (Rahlfs A) and Ραμνων (Rahlfs B). There are, however, other Greek manuscripts that give it as Καμων. Josephus's Καμὼν may have been taken directly from the Hebrew. Many identifications since Eusebius are offered, most based on similarity of sound, but none is beyond guessing.[13]

The Offense This Time

10 6–9. We have had already several references to Israel's offensive behavior (*laʿăśôt hāraʿ bĕʿênê YHVH*) at 2:11, 3:7, 3:12, and 4:1, with one more forthcoming at 13:1 (Samson). Such observations are not unexpected, given the transformations that cyclically overtake Israel during this period. The examples divide between two types. Type A (at 2:11, 3:7, and 6:1) opens on *vayyăʿaśû vĕnê yiśrāʾel hāraʿ bĕʿênê YHVH* ("the people of Israel did what was offensive to the Lord") (Table 10). Two of the three examples of Type A have phrasing that amplifies on the offense before turning to Israel's punishment (italics in Table 10), the exception occurring at 6:1, where an explanation for Israel's woes is carried by a prophet (see at 6:7–10).

Type B offenses (3:12, 4:1, and 13:1) begin with *vayyōsifû vĕnê yiśrāʾel laʿăśôt hāraʿ bĕʿênê YHVH* ("the people of Israel resumed offending the Lord") (Table 11). This is immediately followed by notice of divine retaliation (italics in Table 11). The language at 10:6 opens on a Type B formula but turns into Type A in contents. Resumption of offense is followed by a development that finds its closest parallel in 2:11–14 (Type A), in effect dwelling longer initially on the fault before moving to the punishment. As a result there are more opportunities to enlarge on God's anger. While at 2:11–14b the accent is on Israel's failure to remember God's wonders on its behalf, in our passage, the focus is on Israel's indiscriminate choice of foreign gods—seven of them, as Rashi noticed. These are not the gods of major powers such as of Egypt; rather, they are generic seducers, plus the gods of nations most of which are slated to be vanquished, subdued, or neutralized by Israel and its God.[14] As a result, an angry God unleashes enemies whose oppression is conveyed through onomatopoeic verbal forms (*vayyirʿăṣû vayyĕrōṣĕṣû*).[15] As given, the duration of the repression is syntactically awkward and is simplified in Rahlfs B by eliminating *baššānâ hāhîʾ*, "in that year."[16] The reference to the "Amorite territory" and to "Gilead" anticipates Jephthah's argument of 11:21–22.

Table 10. Type A Offenses

2:11–14 (Type A)	3:7–8a (Type A)	6:1–2 (Mixed)
[11]The people of Israel did what was offensive to the LORD: *They worshiped the many Baals;* [12]*they forsook the LORD, God of their fathers, who had brought them out of the land of Egypt; they committed to other gods, from among those of people around them, bowing down to them. So they provoked the LORD* [13]*by forsaking the LORD and worshiping Baal and the Ashtaroth.* [14]Incensed against Israel, the LORD . . . turned them over to their enemies on all sides.	[7]The people of Israel did what was offensive to the LORD: *They forgot the LORD their God and worshiped the many Baals and Asherahs.* [8]Incensed against Israel, the LORD turned them over to Cushan-rishatayim.	[1]The people of Israel did what was offensive to the LORD, so he abandoned them to Midian for seven years. [2]Midian so ruthlessly controlled Israel that, because of Midian, the people of Israel made for themselves *dens* out of the caves and fissures in the mountains.

THE CONSEQUENCE

10 9–16. The war opens with the Ammonites (without any Philistines). Not unusually, it is made to include a good portion of Israel. The jeremiads that ensue on both sides follow predictable lines. Israel's is short and generic: We have sinned, not just by abandoning you, but by adopting foreign gods. God's response seems instantaneous, even dispensing with the normal media. Unlike the relatively soothing complaint reported by a divine messenger (at 2:1–4) or God's own justification for the unconquered territory (at 2:20–22), or even the comparable grievance conveyed via a prophet (at 6:8–9), this outburst is attributed directly to God.[17] It is mercilessly critical, with a fractured syntax (anacoluthon) that effectively approximates bursts of anger.[18] The language replays what had been expressed in 6:8–9; but whereas in that context, the narrative moves immediately to the story of God's wonder on behalf of Israel (and Gideon), in this case the outcome will be different (see Table 12). God is said to have rescued Israel from seven powers, a significant (potentially a symbolic) number that discourages trimming. Three of them (Ammon, Philistia, Sidon) had gods that seduced Israel (at 10:6). Rahlfs A expands by adding Moab, but it (and Rahlfs B as well) gives Madian (Midian) for Maon, likely because the Maon mentioned in biblical sources was much too insignificant a town in Judah.[19]

Unlike previous examples, this indictment is God's bill of separation: He will not save them this time, so that their misery can only persist. God encourages their

Table 11. Type B Offenses

3:12 (Type B)	4:1–2 (Type B)	10:6–7 (Mixed)	13:1 (Type B)
[12]the people of Israel resumed offending the LORD; *so the LORD emboldened Eglon, king of Moab, against Israel because its people did what was offensive to the LORD.*	[1]With Ehud dead, the people of Israel resumed offending the LORD; *[2]so the LORD turned them over to Jabin, king of Canaan, who ruled in Hazor.*	[6]The people of Israel resumed offending the LORD: They worshiped the many Baals and Ashtaroth, as well as the gods of Aram, the gods of Sidon, the gods of Moab, the gods of the Ammonites, and the gods of the Philistines. They forsook the LORD and did not worship him. [7]*Incensed against Israel, the LORD turned them over to the Philistines and to the Ammonites.*	[1]The people of Israel resumed offending the LORD; *so the LORD abandoned them to the Philistines for forty years.*

disloyalty, for their continuing perdition can only confirm the falsity of foreign gods. God is being sarcastic, of course, accentuating the vapidity of Israel for appealing to its ancestral God only when the going gets tough (*bĕ'ēt ṣāratkem*). Normally, when God is asked to do *haṭṭôv bĕ'ênāyv*, "as he wishes" (as in 1 Sam 3:18; 2 Sam 15:26), there is acceptance and resignation, but also hope that there might be forgiveness. In this case, however, the sense is of despair, akin to someone with a toothache begging for instant relief from any source, so not exactly a fervent conversion. As the people clear their shrines of alien gods and resume worshiping God, we are told about God that *vattiqṣar nafšô ba'amal yiśrā'ēl*.

The versions did not treat this clause lackadaisically. In Targum Jonathan the Hebrew was not rendered into Aramaic, likely because it was attached to a list of passages whose translation was forbidden, for doctrinal or pietistic reasons. In some traditions, however, the clause was emended into an expression of deep love.[20] Rahlfs A, however, offers a complicated reading that seems to double up on the same clause, with contrasting implications. The first clause, καὶ οὐκ εὐηρέστησεν ἐν τῷ λαῷ, "he found no pleasure in the people," obviously reads *vattiqṣar nafšô *bā'am*. The second clause, καὶ ὠλιγοψύχησεν ἐν τῷ κόπῳ Ισραηλ, repeats what is found in the Hebrew; it centers on

Table 12. Divine Rebuke, Then and Now

6:8–10	10:11–14
[8][God] sent them a man, a prophet who told them, "This is what the LORD, the God of Israel, says: It is I who brought you out of Egypt, freeing you from a house of bondage. [9]I saved you from Egypt's grip and from that of all those oppressing you. I drove them from before you and gave you their land. [10]I would say to you, 'I am the LORD your God. Do not fear the gods of the Amorites, in whose land you live'; but you would not listen to me."	[11]The LORD said to the people of Israel, "Was it not that when Egypt, the Amorites, the Ammonites, the Philistines, [12]the Sidonians, Amalek, and Maon oppressed you, you cried out to me and I indeed rescued you from them? [13]Yet you have abandoned me and worshiped other gods. Just for that, I will not keep on rescuing you. [14]Go and beseech the gods you have chosen; these might rescue you in this time of trouble."

Israel's suffering and takes recourse in a verb (ὀλιγοψυχέω) that was applied earlier (at 8:4) to Gideon's exhausted troops (*'āyēfîm*).[21] Rahlfs B follows the Hebrew but arrives at an accented meaning, "his soul diminished because of Israel's trouble."

Qāṣar nefeš The idiom *qāṣar nefeš* (and congeners as well, among them *qāṣar rûʷaḥ*), literally "the spirit/throat constricts," does not suggest a generosity of spirit; to the contrary, it connotes lack of patience or displeasure.[22] A passage in an Ugaritic liturgy (*KTU* 1.40 [*CTA* 32]: 22, 31–32) suggests the sharpest definition, as the idiom is set in parallel with "anger" (*'ap*) and "vexation" (*qṭṭ*). King Keret (Kirta) is accused by his son of "ignoring the legal suit of a widow and not judging the case of a vexed person [*qṣr npš*]" (*KTU* 1.16 [*CTA* 16]: VI: 33–34]). Biblical examples support this notion, with the sharpest example applied to Samson (Judg 16:16): "Finally, after [Delilah] nagged him and pressed him constantly, *he was wearied to death.*"[23]

In our passage, the cause of God's reaction is the *'āmāl* of Israel. The word has to do with action and its effects, positive as well as negative, depending on the context and on unambiguous words with which it is often paired (see Schwertner in *TLOT* 924–26). Thus *'āmāl* may convey the distress of people in trouble (as in Gen 41:51) or in need (Deut 26:7), but it may also reflect injustice (Ps 7:17 [16 RSV]), misfortune (Job 15:35), or deceit (as in Ps 7:15 [14 RSV]). In Judg 10:16, we lack parallel words to calibrate its import. Following the versions, most commentators have leaned toward the first and so imagine God as so moved by Israel's plight that he essentially loses patience with his own lack of patience. As a result, despite his decision at 10:13, God once again succumbs to kindness and moves toward rescuing Israel. However, because contextual guidance is wanting, I have opted for a more neutral rendering for *'āmāl* as "behavior," and so stayed with the main thrust of *qāṣar nefeš*. While a few exegetes have reached a similar sense for the passage (for example, Block 1999: 349; Webb 1987: 46; Gunn 2005: 167), they have not developed its full implication.

COMMENTS

The Introductory Remarks above make it obvious why what is said about Tola and Jair cannot be discussed separately from those about the three other minor judges that will be detailed at 12:8–15; by then we would have followed the story of Jephthah, from his rise until his less than glorious end. The five form a unit not only because the notices about them share contents and lack the normal details and expansions applied to a judge, but because the odd numbers allotted to their rule amount to just seventy years (23 + 22 + 7 + 10 + 8), a figure suggesting completeness of group or time units. This number is the same in the LXX, suggesting that it antedates the adjustment of lifetimes allotted to the ancestors that occurred during the Maccabean period. Again, it is worth noting that this round sum is achieved only *by excluding* Jephthah, who is said to rule six years (Greek, sixty), thus confirming that his portrait was spliced within.

The bigger story here is contained in the verses that seemingly replay the cycle of commitment and rejection that overtakes both Israel and God. In fact, the round of divine accusation and Israelite promise ends on a sharp turn on the part of God. He turns sarcastic and, exasperated by Israel's lack of effort to regain his trust, promptly moves to alter its expectation.[24] This is reported in the crucial 10:16. Lulled by the standard pattern of a God who eventually mollifies, translators have commonly rendered this clause as "he could no longer bear Israel's misery," thus implying a merciful change of heart. In fact, it has the opposite sense: God actually "loses patience with Israel's behavior," suggesting that he will leave Israel to its own devices. In effect, just before Jephthah, God pulls out of the rescue business. As it concerns tales about the judges of Israel, we will have just one narrated episode, the story of Samson. It will find him actively involved in Israel's fate, but it will veer steeply from the familiar paradigm. The consequence of God's withdrawal of favor is crucial, not just for Jephthah, who will actually thrive in this power vacuum, but—as we shall see—also for the remaining chapters of Judges where the case for a new vision of political reality is constructed.

What is striking here is that God should let pass forty-five years and await the death of two judges before his patience comes to an end. With no clue, we are left to our own devices. It is possible, of course, that Tola and Jair did their jobs fairly well and Israel practiced its foibles only in the intervals. Worth conjecturing, however, is that God's anger explodes, not after the death of Jair, not even after that of Abimelech, but at the close of Gideon/Jerubbaal's life, with this chapter's jeremiad fitting very nicely after 8:35. This would confirm what others have proposed about the intrusion of the Abimelech episode, but it would also suggest that the sequence of minor judges and the narrative about Jephthah do not have much in common, despite suggestions by Richter and his followers. (But see an alternative suggestion at 10:1–2.)

But why was the Jephthah story inserted right after Jair rather than after any of the other minor judges? Let us recall that this sequence of minor judges opened on Abimelech, the son of a concubine, whose father, Gideon, famously had begotten seventy sons. With Jair, a Gilead connection is established. Let me speculate that this judge, who famously fathered thirty sons and held sway over much territory, may have had one more child allotted to him. Jair would have spawned Jephthah on a local prostitute, a son who came to be despised by his siblings: a nice launch into one of the more richly textured stories in Judges.[25]

Jephthah

---

1. Jephthah's Challenges (Judg 10:17–11:28)

10 ⁱ⁷The men of Ammon were summoned and camped in Gilead while the men of Israel assembled and camped by Mizpah. ¹⁸Among the people, the commanders of Gilead said to each other, "Whoever is first to fight against Ammon shall be chief over all the inhabitants of Gilead." ס

11 ¹Jephthah of Gilead was well-born, the son of a harlot; Gilead begot Jephthah. ²Gilead's wife bore him sons and when the wife's sons grew up, they drove Jephthah out, telling him, "You must not share in our father's property, for you are the son of another woman." ³So Jephthah fled from his brothers and settled in the Tob Land. Rootless men were drawn to Jephthah and they joined with him. ס

⁴Soon after, Ammon attacked Israel. ⁵And just as Ammon was attacking Israel, the elders of Gilead went to fetch Jephthah from Tob Land. ⁶They said to Jephthah, "Come be our general so that we can fight Ammon." ⁷Jephthah told the elders of Gilead, "Did you not hate me and drive me out of my father's house? Why would you come to me now, just when you are in trouble?" ⁸The elders of Gilead told Jephthah, "Just so! We now are turning to you. Go with us and fight Ammon; you will then be our chief, over all the people of Gilead." ⁹Jephthah said to the elders of Gilead, "If you are bringing me back to fight Ammon, once the Lord delivers them to me, I am to be a chief for you." ¹⁰The elders of Gilead told Jephthah, "The Lord is witness between us that we will do just as you have said." ¹¹So Jephthah went with the elders of Gilead. The people made him chief and general over them. Jephthah repeated all terms pertaining to him before the Lord at Mizpah. ס

¹²Jephthah then sent messengers to the king of Ammon, saying, "What have you to do with me that you come against me, to fight in my land?" ¹³The king of Ammon replied to Jephthah's messengers, "Well, Israel seized my land when coming out of Egypt, from the Arnon to the Jabbok, as far as the Jordan. Now, then, restore all of it peaceably." ¹⁴Jephthah once again sent messengers to the king of Ammon, ¹⁵saying to him,

> Thus says Jephthah: Israel did not seize the land of Moab or the land of Ammon. ¹⁶For, as they left Egypt, Israel followed the desert to the Red Sea and on to Kadesh. ¹⁷Israel then sent messengers to the king of Edom, saying "Allow me to pass through your country." But the king of Edom would not approve. Israel also sent (messengers) to the king of Moab; but he refused. So Israel remained at Kadesh. ¹⁸Then, taking the desert, Israel skirted the land of Edom and the land of Moab. Keeping to the east of the land of Moab, Israel camped across the Arnon. So, with the Arnon as Moab's border, Israel never went within Moab's territory.
>
> ¹⁹Next, Israel sent messengers to Sihon, king of the Amorites and king of Heshbon. Israel said to him, "Allow us to pass through your land to my place." ²⁰Sihon would not trust Israel to cross his border.ᵃ Instead, Sihon rallied all his people, camping by Jahza. He then attacked Israel. ²¹But the LORD, the God of Israel, handed Sihon and all his people over to Israel, and they defeated them. Israel occupied all the land of the Amorites, the inhabitants of that land. ²²So *the people of Israel* occupied all the territory of the Amorites, from the Arnon to the Jabbok, from the desert to the Jordan.
>
> ²³Therefore, now that the LORD, the God of Israel, displaced the Amorites on behalf of his people Israel, are you to occupy it? ²⁴Whatever your god Chemosh displaces for you, you must surely occupy. So too, whatever the LORD our god has displaced on our behalf, we must occupy. ²⁵Moreover, are you any better than Balak son of Zippor, king of Moab? Did he start a quarrel with Israel let alone go to war against them? ²⁶With Israel now having settled for three hundred years in Heshbon and its dependencies, in Aroer and its dependencies, and in all the towns along the Arnon, why has none of you regained *them* at any time then? ²⁷While I have not wronged you, you are doing me harm to fight against me. The LORD is the judge to decide now between the people of Israel and the people of Ammon! ס

²⁸But the king of Ammon would not listen to the words that Jephthah sent him.

---

a. Or: to pass through his territory.

NOTES

Introductory Remarks: Declaring War

From Near Eastern lore, we learn of armed raids galore—by bandits, rogue armies, tribal groups, even by occupiers of stable thrones—but they rarely flare up into active wars. We also know of conflicts that seem to break out suddenly, such as rebellions on the death of a leader, contentious fights for a vacated throne, and occupation of disputed territory or of coveted properties. Most of these give no justification, leaving us with the burden of re-creating causes or of shaping background for them—political, religious, ethnic, economic, or the like. If fortunate, we might have the evidence to do so.

When conditions to avert wars are set by attackers, we find them couched in ultimatums, the most effective among them being those delivered when an army is already at the gates of its enemy.[1] Near Eastern archives have produced a fair amount of ultimatums, and they tend to be drafted by powers with obvious military advantage over their targets. In such cases, the senders calculate that they can obtain what they wish (or at least most of it) by mere threats, for even when forewarned, the adversary will not be able to mount a useful defense. Of the many fine examples in the Mari archives, I cite a diplomat's letter sent to Zimri-Lim (A.6 = LAPO 17 #556, pp. 170–73) in which is embedded a copy of a letter the Marshall (*sukkalum*) of Elam had sent to Hammurabi (of Kurda): "So says the Marshall [of Elam] to Hammurabi: My servant Atamrum (of Andarig) took you as his son (vassal). Yet I keep hearing that you are constantly sending your letters to Babylon and to Mari. You must not again send your letters to Babylon and Mari. If you again send your letters to Babylon and Mari, I will *move aggressively* against you." We can reconstruct that when posting its threat, Elam was still flush with its victory over mighty Ešnunna and so felt particularly prone to bully lesser powers. Such warnings occur in many archives and from our earliest periods of documentation; for example, Sumerian epics about Gilgamesh, Enmerkar, and Lugalbanda are well-stocked with instances, albeit hardly realistic. They are also especially thickly embedded in historiographic documents, among them annals and prologues to treaties, in which incidents of gallant behavior ("I gave them a chance to surrender") were thought to please the gods.

Rarer to survive are declarations of war, by which senders give their opponents no terms for surrender or set conditions for resolving disputes; instead, they declare themselves determined to fight and even fix the moment for initiating the hostilities.[2] Why examples from this category are scarce will be developed in the Comments below.

Searching for a Leader

10 17–18. The notice serves as an introduction to the emergence of Jephthah as leader and may be read as a summarized resumption of what was said in 10:8–9. Ammon had moved aggressively into Gilead and was making devastating raids to the west of the Jordan: "Israel suffered terribly" (10:9). The verbs used to describe the muster of Ammon and Israel are paired. The first set is similar in goal but nuanced to give the Ammonites a more disciplined assembling ("they answered a summons," *vayyiṣāʿăqû*) than took place with the Israelites ("they assembled," *vayyēʾāsĕfû*). In view of the situation that will soon be described about Israel, the contrast is intentional. The second set is the same ("they camped," *vayyaḥănû*). The two Greek renderings agree on the activity of Ammon ("they went up and camped in Galaad"), but they differ in describing Israel's. Rahlfs A has them "coming out and camping in Massepha," while Rahlfs B offers "they assembled and camped at an observation point [ἐν τῇ σκοπιᾷ]," the latter obviously taking *miṣpâ* as a noun rather than a place name.

Mizpah is one of several places so named because they are set at elevations that allow surveillance of surrounding areas, in Benjamin (the most heavily represented), Judah, Moab, and Gilead.[3] The place name is generally distinguished from the common noun by the article to which the latter is attached (*hammiṣpâ*). The place will be an arena for the story of Jephthah.

The syntax of the clause at 10:18 opens oddly on *hāʿām*, "the people," likely to accent what had been said at 10:9, that all of Israel was challenged by Ammon.[4] Quickly, however, the perspective shrinks back to Gilead and its officers (*śārê*; see the Notes at 7:25), who make a consequential pledge: They will accept a *rōʾš*, "chief." While its nuance will shift depending on the context and organization (such as a tribe, army, or group), the term *rōʾš* is applied to the top officer in any enterprise, whether military, tribal, or administrative (see the dictionaries and Bartlett 1969). In our case, as it is offered by regional elders, it implies significant authority regionally over Gilead, although not necessarily over all of Israel. The terms of empowerment are not detailed, so whether or not it lasted until hostilities ceased or during the lifetime of its holder is unknown.

How this authority is achieved is curiously stated: Whoever is first to take up arms (*yāḥēl lĕhillāḥēm*) will receive the accolade. It is as if the leaders, having met with their own solid lack of resolve to battle, are desperate for anyone from within to become such a leader. The vocabulary is reminiscent of Judg 1:1, where deciding on who would lead the charge against the Canaanites was in question. On that occasion, however, Israel addressed God. Here, Israel is ready to let courage be the hallmark of the individual. Perhaps it had come to realize that God was not likely to cooperate.

Enter Jephthah

11 1. Jephthah is cited by a phrase, *yiftāḥ haggilʿādî*, "Jephthah of Gilead," that is repeated at 12:7, thus bracketing his story. His name (Greek, Ιεφθαε) is based on a shortened verbal sentence meaning "He opens," the "He" being a deity given credit for opening the womb of a woman who might have been sterile (Gen 29:31, 30:22); but God is also known to open the lips of poets (as in Ps 51:17 [15 RSV]) and the mouths of prophets (Ezek 3:27). The full version of the name might have been *yiftaḥ-ʾēl*, actually a place that was likely named after an ancestor (see Josh 19:14, 27). Another form might be *pĕtaḥyâ*, the name of a Levite (Ezra 10:23).

Jephthah is introduced in spurts. The first presentation retains its shock value, as much for its unusual sequence of presenting the parents—first the mother and then the father—as for its stark contrast between his genteel status, acquired from his father, and that of his mother, a prostitute. (The irony is sharper in this translation.) He is called a *gibbôr ḥayil*, a term that is applied to people with status, whether military (brave, powerful, said of Naaman at 2 Kgs 5:1), administrative (able, said of Jeroboam at 1 Kgs 11:28), or wealth (landowner, said of Boaz at Ruth 2:1).[5] Worth observing in contrast is the multiplicity of labels used when David is first brought to Saul's attention (1 Sam 16:18): "he is skilled in music [*yōdēʸaʿ naggēn*], well-born [*gibbôr ḥayil*], a warrior [*'îš milḥāmâ*], discreet [*nĕvôn dāvār*], and fine-looking [*'îš tō'ar*], the Lord being with him." While Jephthah will prove to be a fighter, at this stage it is best not to attach to him such titles as "knight" and to treat him as a warrior (*TNK*; Amit 1999b: 194). It would be too much to classify him as "one trained in upper-class combat, and who furnished his own equipment as well as a squire and/or a unit of soldiers" (Boling 1975: 197; see already Josephus at *Ant.* 5.257, "on account of that army which he maintained at his own expense").[6]

Yet Jephthah's mother was an *'iššâ zônâ*. What a *zônâ* was is subject to debate, especially in recent discussions. Bird (2006) is among those arguing for nuanced distinctions among promiscuity, adultery, and prostitution, the last a sex occupation.[7] In legal material, Hebrews were prohibited from turning their daughters into a *zônâ* (Lev 19:29), and women were not to become so in fulfillment of a vow (Deut 23:18–19 [17–18 RSV]). In the narratives, the *zônâ* can have a place within society, some attaining heroic status (Rahab of Jericho). Prominent Hebrews frequented them (Judah, at least by intent; Samson). The tale of the women seeking Solomon's judgment (1 Kgs 3: 16–27) indicates that pregnancy was a hazard for the profession.

In Mesopotamian literature, the *ḥarimtu* (Sumerian, kar.kid) has an equivocal fate, at once satisfying and sordid (Gilgamesh VII). The goddess Inanna (Ištar), who occasionally deemed herself a *ḥarimtu*, charged her customers different rates for different services. Yet, while the sale of sexual favor was not envied, it did not bear the moral opprobrium or the sense of sin that obtains in our culture. According to law codes, which themselves are literary products, a *ḥarimtu* may marry (LL 27, 30; CH 181; MAL A40, 49, 52), but in actual legal documents she may lose her children to male members of her family.[8]

In our context, I use the word "harlot" because it is less specifically associated with a paid profession. The Greek versions are categorical, labeling her a πόρνη, a "prostitute"; but the Targum was more charitable, treating her as a *fundqêtā'*, an "innkeeper, hostess."[9] Later, when Jephthah's brothers force him out of the clan, they justify their action not because the mother is a *zônâ*, but because she was an *'iššâ 'āḥeret*, indicating an anomaly about her status. (The Greek versions have her there as a ἑταίρα, a "courtesan.") The phrase is applied elsewhere (1 Chr 2:26) to the secondary wife of Jerahmeel, ancestor of a clan that was absorbed into Judah, and it may be that the accent here is on intrusion from beyond the tribe, hence justifying the *TNK*'s rendering "outsider" for *'iššâ 'āḥeret*. Worth recalling is the status of Abimelech's mother, who is associated with Shechem, thus not sharing Gideon's background.

Gilead is said to beget Jephthah. Gilead is normally a region, discussed last in connection with Jair (at 10:3), but in lists of eponyms, Gilead is connected to Joseph via Manasseh's son Machir (see the Notes to 5:17 and 10:3–4).[10] The language here, with *yālad* in the Hiphil, is documented in lists (mostly at Gen 5 and 11) where the focus is exclusively on male pedigree. The peculiarity of the phrasing was met in the Greek versions through paraphrase: the prostitute "bore Iephthae to Galaad." Feigin (1931: 188) invents the meaning "adopt" for this verbal form to resolve the problem of Jephthah's murky status. Marcus (1989: 98) simply assumes its occurrence to clarify the dispute between Jephthah and the elders (see below). In rabbinic tradition this phrase underscores Jephthah's paternity and thus sharpens the injustice that will overtake him.

Above, I have speculated that there may have been interest in linking this father with Jair of Gilead (see the Comments to IIIF).

11 2–3. The drama opens on a violent act, the language oddly distancing Gilead from the action of his sons, with the focus on wives and on sons. It is difficult to evaluate the status in Israel of children other than from a wife.[11] Clearer is the issue of how inheritance is decided in Israel, where normally it is patrilineal. When Sarah presses her husband (at Gen 21:10) to oust Hagar and Ishmael, "for the son of a handmaid must not share the inheritance with my son [Isaac]," she was being disingenuous, because Ishmael in fact was her own child, born through a surrogate. The same can be said of Jacob's sons from his wives' maids.

That Gilead's legitimate sons forced Jephthah out (*vayyĕgārĕšû ʾet-yiptāḥ*) is itself a legal problem, since such a decision is normally a father's privilege.[12] It may be that aside from the brothers reaching adulthood, they also awaited the death of their father to make their move. What is plausible is that the brothers appealed to the elders of Gilead to rid themselves of Jephthah, for later (at 11:7), Jephthah chides the elders (not his brothers) for driving him out because "you hated me." The brothers were not simply dispossessing their brother but were intent to harm him; for the idiom that tells us about his escape (*bāraḥ mippĕnê* [someone]) is invariably associated with threats of violence, among them Hagar from Sarah, Jacob from Esau, David from Saul, and Jeroboam from Solomon, and just above (at 9:21), Jotham from Abimelech.

Jephthah ends up in Tob, not a city, but a land (*ʾereṣ ṭôv*), so meant to give him protection because he would not be within the jurisdiction of his family's clan or tribe. In 2 Sam 10:6 and 8 we are told that mercenaries could be hired from Tob (*ʾîš ṭôv*), but where to locate it is a problem. During the Amarna period, a ruler of Ṭubu declares his readiness to assist the Pharaoh (EA 205), and his land is associated with a Ṭubi recorded among the conquests of Thutmoses III (Rainey and Notley 2006: 72, #22), as well as with our Tob.[13] No doubt because of aural similarity, modern scholars guess that it should be found at Tell et-Ṭayyibeh, not far from Derʿa (Edrei) in Jordan (Rainey and Notley 2006: 140; Gass 2005: 494–96). The rabbis also speculate that it was associated with Susitha, somewhere in the Bashan, but they found irony that Jephthah would escape harm in a land called "Good." That there might be a play on Israel's plea (at 10:15) that God should do as he pleases (*kĕkol-haṭṭôv bĕʿênĕkā*) is likely far-fetched because the language here is idiomatic.

Abimelech used funds from the temple of Shechem to hire "rootless and reckless men" (at 9:4). In Jephthah's case, the men were just rootless (*ʾănāšîm rêqîm*), that is, people like him who had lost their places in their communities, but they were not as irresponsible. The verbal form (Hithpael of *lāqaṭ*) gives a sense of (voluntary) linkage taking place over time—not at all how Abimelech raised his little army. *yāṣāʾ ʿim* simply means to join with someone (as in Ruth 2:22, 2 Chr 22:7). That their goal was raiding and marauding is more than possible, as they operated in the interstices of power. This is illustrated in a letter exchanged between two leaders a generation or so after the collapse of Mari (so around 1725 BCE): "Aya-abum, a man from Yamutbal, has set himself up in Zurra as a *ḫābiru*. Ever since there has been internal peace in the land, he has led outlaws and, taking or kidnapping people from Yamutbal, he had them cross though Kaspatum in Idamaras territory because he was not allowed to enter Zurra (with them)" (cited from Eidem 2011: #42, pp. 111–13). In fact, the Jephthah narrative replays a theme from lore (Abimelech, David, Idrimi) and from real life: Men with little future create it elsewhere by collecting equally dislocated riffraff.[14] Normally, established leaders avoided them; but in unsettled times, chutzpah yielded them standing. An official writes Zimri-Lim of Mari (A.2939 = LAPO 16 #296, pp. 462–64; Fleming 2012: 267): "Now there is a man, Iṣi-Nabu by name, from Yamutbal, who has 30 Yamutbalian rootless men [*ḫābirū*] at his command. He wrote me as follows, 'muster an army of 500 to 600 men. Come here by night and I will deliver (the city) of Ašnakkum to you." The governor is wary of the offer.

The Negotiation

THE OFFER

11 4–6. After a brief interlude in which to introduce Jephthah, the narrative resumes with the tension between Ammon and Israel. Linkage is achieved through *miyyāmîm*, in which the plural of *yôm*, "day," is attached to the preposition *min*. We will meet with multiple references to this compound in Judges (also at 14:8, 15:1) as well as with variations, *miyyāmîm yāmîmâ* (11:40, 21:19) and *layyāmîm* (17:10), each with its own nuance about the passage of time.[15] *Miyyāmîm* is vague yet implies the passage of a negligible amount of time. In the Targum this is given as *lizman yômîm*, "a few days' interval." There seems to be a surfeit of references to the hostilities, so Rahlfs B tightens by gliding over v. 4 entirely, possibly by *homeoteleuton* (skipping the repeat of a phrase), but likely intentionally.

That the elders formed a mission to Tob is a sign of despair no less than of swallowing pride. Earlier, no one had had the courage to respond to their appeal for a successful champion who would then be appointed as *rōʾš* ("chief"). What they offer Jephthah is a different office: They would welcome him as their *qāṣîn*. In Mic 3:1 (and again at 3:9) the two titles are paired. The prophet appeals to the "chiefs of Jacob [*rāʾšê yaʿăqōv*] and officers in the House of Israel [*ûqěṣînê bêt yiśrāʾēl*]." While Jacob and the House of Israel are obviously synonymous, *rōʾš* and *qāṣîn* are not meant to be the same (contra Marcus 1989: 97; see Willis 1997). They indeed cannot be equivalent when at 11:11 Jephthah is given both titles at the same occasion. The word *qāṣîn* certainly has a military connotation in Josh 10:24 and in Isa 22:3 as well, where they are said to run as cowards. A Ḥorvat ʿUzza ostracon has a tribal *qṣn* second to the top commander (Aḥituv 2008: 168). Isaiah 3:6–7 clarifies that a *qāṣîn* is not born but is proclaimed, and in Prov 6:7 the title is differentiated from a tribal and an urban leadership. In all, it is reasonable to presume that the elders of Gilead are offering Jephthah leadership that has value mostly during combat; in the context, therefore, a translation of "general" or "marshal" might suit best.

RAISING THE STAKES

11 7–8. The syntax of Jephthah's accusation sharpens his intent to raise the ante against those who could scarcely afford to contradict him. When, eager to settle disputes over control of wells, Abimelech of Gerar and his officers come to Isaac, Isaac greets them with a charge (Gen 26:27), "Why do you come to me when you have so hated me that you have driven me away from you?" By questioning the motivation behind Abimelech's voyage (*maddûᵘaᶜ bāʾtem ʾēlāy*) before accusing him of acting in hatred, Isaac actually gives Abimelech an overture to explain himself. Abimelech eagerly takes the opening: Even when Gerar pushed Isaac away, it did so without malice or hostility. The terms of agreement are therefore clear, and Isaac could resume his well-digging activities.

Jephthah's address differs sharply. He is frontal with the elders, opening on two strong accusations: You "have hated me [*śēnēʾtem ʾôtî*]" so much that you drove me out of my father's house. Hatred is a powerful emotion, often linked with such an intense desire to hurt that biblical law forbade its manifestation among Hebrews (Lev 19:17). In biblical lore, Joseph can incite his brothers to hatred (Gen 37), Amnon can loathe the woman he once obsessively desired (2 Sam 13), and Ahab can despise the prophet who demeans him (1 Kgs 22). Jephthah is intentionally hyperbolic in using this language against the elders, for whatever the disposition that led his brothers to disinherit him (from jealousy to greed), it could not be initiated by the elders, who merely sanctioned his expulsion.[16] They therefore have no language with which to respond, especially not when they wished to secure his help. At this point, Jephthah can end with *ûmaddûᵘaᶜ bāʾtem ʾēlāy ᶜattâ*, "Why would you come to me now?," knowing full well that the main burden of the elders is to answer the broadly targeted charge of hatred rather than to negotiate terms for his cooperation.[17] The elders' only response to Jephthah's accusation, therefore, is *lākēn*, "Just so." Curt though it may be, it tells all.[18] But they also sweeten the prize, offering Jephthah the same deal that was available to any Gileadite who took up his weapons against Ammon: becoming a *rōʾš*. In this way, the elders explicitly reverse themselves, treating Jephthah as one of theirs.

Having thrown in the towel, the elders are all business, and what they say next must not be taken as yet another proposal, as does, for example, the *TNK* ("If you come with us and fight the Ammonites, you shall be our commander over all the inhabitants of Gilead"). Yet, in their statement, there is a slight shift that is hard to assess. When they first approached Jephthah, at 11:6, they asked him to join their battle (*vĕnillāḥămâ bivnê ᶜammôn*). Now, however, they ask him to turn back and fight Ammon, apparently on his own (*vĕnilḥamtā bivnê ᶜammôn*). The difference may be accidental (Rahlfs A simply ignores it), but if not, it opens up an excuse for an additional statement of Jephthah that may, at first meeting, seem superfluous.

BRINGING GOD AS WITNESS

11 9–10. Many commentators are puzzled by Jephthah's statement. The elders have just offered him the post unconditionally. He needed only to go back with them to battle Ammon, and he is their chief. So why does he complicate matters by making his accession conditional? Does it foreshadow his lack of self-confidence, which will soon make him utter a famous vow (11:30–31)? Some translations make a question out of Jephthah's words, as if he could scarcely believe their offer; for example the KJV gives them as, "If ye bring me home again to fight against the children of Ammon, and the LORD deliver them before me, shall I be your head?"

In fact, having already forced the elders to accept him back into the fold, Jephthah is now negotiating for a permanent leadership. The elders may believe that their offer is linked to the immediate circumstances. With or without their help, Jephthah was to lead his forces against Ammon. He could hardly expect them to keep him at his post if Ammon defeats him, but what will happen beyond a victory? Would he, like the early patrician of Rome Lucius Quinctius Cincinnatus, go back to his previous life once danger is averted? Given the lack of trust between the two parties, Jephthah is aiming to secure his future. The declaration itself is made up of three clauses. The first establishes a condition already agreed upon, using a participial form (*'im-mĕšîvîm 'attem 'ôtî*). The second invokes a stipulation set for the future, using an inverted perfect (*vĕnātan YHVH 'ôtām lĕfānāy*). It is important to observe how Jephthah brings God into this provision, when he could have easily left him out.[19] (He will do so again in his argument with Ammon, see at 11:27.) Also worth notice is how Jephthah personalizes the victory (*lĕfānāy*), excluding the elders from any achieved triumph. As shaped, the fulfillment of the condition accents the individual: It is I (*'ānōkî*)—Jephthah—who shall (continue) to be your leader.

Jephthah obtains his desire. Explicitly citing YHVH as arbiter and using a sequence of verbal forms, the elders immediately and permanently place themselves under oath (*yihyeh šōmēya' bênôtênû*), inviting dire consequences on themselves should they fail (*'im-lō'*) to follow his proposal (*kidvārĕkā*), provided, of course, that Jephthah brings them victory.[20] To be safe, Jephthah secures the pledge by repeating all the terms he had proposed (*vayyĕdabbēr . . . 'et-kol-dĕvārāᵞv*) before God's shrine at Mizpah, likely in the presence of the elders themselves. Oath notwithstanding, distrust was never fully erased between them.[21]

Exceptional is what happens as the emissaries return to their camp at Mizpah, having successfully coaxed Jephthah to follow them. The people (*hā'ām*) confer on him both titles, "chief" (*rō'š*) and "general" (*qāṣîn*), in reverse order of what was proposed. This is a stunning development, but to grasp its implication it need only be recalled that acclamation by the people was one of the ways in which Saul came to be Israel's first national king; however, he earned it after a display of exceptional military skills (1 Sam 11:1–15).[22] It might also be recalled that despite Samuel anointing him king on God's behest, David accepted the allegiance of all the tribes (2 Sam 5:1–3). That the elders of Gilead take these steps before entering the shrine at Mizpah and before a battle is admittedly odd. Still, Jephthah has managed to earn, however temporarily, two offices—one civil, the other military—thus almost attaining the prerogatives of a *šōfēṭ*, "judge." The missing component is acquiring *rûʷaḥ YHVH*. That step is taken in the next tableau.

The Exchange with Ammon

THE FIRST DELEGATION

11 12–14. A leader of a motley band of fugitives and ne'er-do-wells, Jephthah nevertheless displays remarkable control of diplomacy. As was the norm, the negotiation is first assigned to diplomatic missions, but with Ammon already in Gilead, diplomats did not need days to shuttle between antagonists. Jephthah shows patience but also persistence, acting for all intents as the equal of the king of Ammon.[23] Moreover, as do other monarchs in the ancient world, Jephthah personalizes the confrontation (*mah-lî vālāk*) as if it is just a dispute between two leaders. The phrase *mah-lĕ vālĕ* occurs fairly frequently in Scripture, always accusatorily and always implying an unjustified breach of etiquette or protocol. Jephthah continues to force the focus on himself: You come *against me* to fight *in my land*.[24] Although Ammon is demanding land east of the Jordan, for Jephthah, *’arṣî*, "my land," is no longer the Tob (*’ereṣ ṭôv*) of 11:3, nor is it "the Amorite territory of Gilead" (at 10:8), for Ammon had been occupied now for eighteen years. Rather, it is also "Judah, Benjamin, as well as the House of Ephraim" that Ammon aims to conquer. Jephthah is acting now as a national leader.

In responding, the king invokes history, thus providing Jephthah with a good occasion soon to correct his interpretation of the past. The king may have erred by opening on Israel's exit from Egypt (*baʿălôtô mimmiṣrayim*), for this evocation plays into Israel's strongest argument: that the God who helped break Israel's bondage would not leave it without a homeland. The king claims territory east of the Jordan bounded by two rivers that serve as boundaries: to the south, the Arnon, with a gorge (Wadi Mujîb) that empties into the Moabite plateau; to the north, the Jabbok (Nahr ez-Zarqa), emptying into the Jordan some 40 kilometers above the Dead Sea. (On this area, see below.)

He wants them returned *bĕšālôm*, which I have translated "peaceably," but the semantic range of the word *šālôm* is broad and includes elements of completeness, safety, and health. The king is demanding the return of every acre of land, without any resistance. In effect, he is asking Israel to vacate the area or, if not, to submit, the latter normally including the payment of tribute and possibly the acceptance of forced labor. (The verbal form *hišlîm*, "to submit," refers to the status of those accepting subordination; see Josh 10:1, 4; 2 Sam 10:19.) Since troops from Ammon are already in Gilead, the king's reply to Jephthah is, in effect, an ultimatum. (Rahlfs B completely misunderstands the issue when, to the king's reply, it adds "and I will leave.")

Jephthah could accept Ammon's terms, risking the posts he has just obtained, or he could begin hostilities. Such a negotiation can sometimes involve many exchanges, as does, for example, Ben-Hadad's attempt at shaking down Ahab (1 Kgs 20); but in assigning his diplomats another mission, Jephthah made certain that it will fail.

THE SECOND DELEGATION

11 15–22. The communication opens on an expression that cites the addressor, Jephthah, *kōh ’āmar yiftaḥ*. This formula allows for a message to be delivered orally, as were the divine messages of Moses and Aaron to Pharaoh (for example, at Exod 4:22, 5:1) and the many messages prophets delivered to Israel. Or it may suggest an invitation to the king's scribe to read a written document, likely on parchment, as is implied by the letter David had Uriah deliver to Joab. Given its length and its sequences of rehearsed history, the written form is more probable, but the issue must not be pressed.[25]

HISTORY DEBATED

With his first statement, Jephthah rejects the king's demand. A good portion of the message is commentary to that rejection, but there is also a closing of the doors to any reconciliation. No, Israel had seized neither Moab nor Ammon. The argument is that land claimed by Ammon had come to be Israel's because of other circumstances.[26] The information Jephthah communicates is partially known to us from other sources detailed in Num 20–21 and Deut 2, but the three do not entirely match, likely because each source has its own motivation and goal for drawing on traditions about Israel's conquest. With extrabiblical information lacking on these events, scholarship has no means to adjudicate among them even when doubts are not cast on historicity. As a result, in scholarly literature we find diverse assignment of priority, largely influenced by divergent approaches to biblical texts.[27]

Jephthah reviews history, naturally, from Israel's perspective. He opens on the same page as the king of Ammon—after Israel left Egypt—and uses, as is conventional, the verb *ʿālâ*, to "move upwards," associated with exiting Egypt (and later Babylon) toward the Promised Land. He highlights the high spots: the Red Sea, where God defeated the Egyptian host, and Kadesh, where Israel prepared to enter the Promised Land.[28] He also covers the entire forty years of travel for Israel to reach its destiny. Such notices could not have interested the king of Ammon—why would he want to know about Israel's triumphs or travails? They could certainly be more appropriate as prologue to treaties, but not to avert imminent war. In our case, however, they build an argument and, not incidentally, give pleasure to Hebrews aware of the traditions.

Jephthah focuses on a series of past incidents that contrasts the failure of foreign belligerence with the success of Israel's ethical behavior. On reaching the borders of Edom and then of Moab, Israel sought permission to cross their territory (*ʾeʿběrâ-nnāʾ věʾarṣekā*) to reach its destination; neither nation allowed it, the language of rejection conveyed by negated verbs (*lōʾ šāmaʿ . . . lōʾ ʾāvâ*) that are frequently paired in Hebrew. Israel was forced to stay put in Kadesh until it decided how to proceed. Two matters need notice here. The first is that none of the other sources (Numbers and Deuteronomy) has anything to say about discussion with Moab, and only Numbers discusses negotiation with Edom. Scholars have debated whether it was omitted from those sources or added in Judges. Whatever the judgment, mention of Moab will be crucial to Jephthah's argument. The second has to do with the omission of details reflected in the other sources, among them the fact that God had explicitly forbidden Israel to conquer Edom, Moab, and Ammon (Deut 2).

Israel was forced to make a long detour (*vayyāsov ʾet-ʾereṣ*) around those countries, moving to the east of them, where the sun rises (*mimmizraḥ-šemeš*), until they reached the Arnon River from the north, where they camped, so respecting Moabite territory on the other side of the river.[29] Scruple aside, Jephthah is making a case against Israel's willful seizure of Ammonite territory that Ammon wants returned.

SIHON'S AGGRESSION

The core of Jephthah's review of history is contained in the account of Israel's conquest of all Amorite territory.[30] It is balanced by other sources, with interesting differences (see Table 13). Jephthah never bothers to explain to the Ammonite king how Sihon ended up controlling precisely the area under dispute. Yet, in labeling Sihon (Greek, Ση/ιων; Josephus, Σιχών) king of the Amorites (as in Num 21:21) and of Heshbon (as in Deut 2:26), Jephthah assumes this merging of territory, for Heshbon (Greek, Εσεβων) was, according to Num 21:26–31, conquered by Sihon from Moab. This is a key detail in his argument.[31]

Israel is cited as wishing to reach its destination (*ʿad-měqômî*) but also as giving Sihon no reassurance where its endpoint might be found. This may well explain his reaction: He does not trust (*heʾěmîn*) Israel's motivation. The verb is unusual, and many emend it to the less interesting *vayyěmāʾēn, closer to verbs of rejection found

Table 13. The Exchanges with Sihon

Num 21:21–26, 31 (TNK)	Deut 2:26–37 (TNK)	Judg 11:19–26
²¹Israel now sent messengers to Sihon king of the Amorites, saying,	²⁶Then I sent messengers from the wilderness of Kedemoth to King Sihon of Heshbon with an offer of peace, as follows,	¹⁹Israel sent messengers to Sihon, king of the Amorites and king of Heshbon. Israel said to him,
²²"Let me pass through your country. We will not turn off into fields or vineyards, and we will not drink water from wells. We will follow the king's highway until we have crossed your territory."	²⁷"Let me pass through your country. I will keep strictly to the highway, turning off neither to the right nor to the left. ²⁸What food I eat you will supply for money, and what water I drink you will furnish for money; just let me pass through— ²⁹as the descendants of Esau who dwell in Seir did for me, and the Moabites who dwell in Ar—that I may cross the Jordan into the land that the LORD our God is giving us."	"Allow us to pass through your land to my place."
²³But Sihon would not let Israel pass through his territory.	³⁰But King Sihon of Heshbon refused to let us pass through, because the LORD had stiffened his will and hardened his heart in order to deliver him into your power—as is now the case. ³¹And the LORD said to me: See, I begin by placing Sihon and his land at your disposal. Begin the occupation; take possession of his land.	²⁰Sihon would not trust Israel to cross his border [or: to pass through his territory].
Sihon gathered all his people and went out against Israel in the wilderness. He came to Jahaz and engaged Israel in battle.	³²Sihon with all his men took the field against us at Jahaz,	Instead, Sihon rallied all his people, camping at Jahaz. He then attacked Israel.

(continued)

Table 13. The Exchanges with Sihon (*Continued*)

Num 21:21–26, 31 (TNK)	Deut 2:26–37 (TNK)	Judg 11:19–26
		²¹*But the Lord, the God of Israel, handed Sihon and all his people over to Israel, and they defeated them. Israel occupied all the land of the Amorites, the inhabitants of that land.*
	³³*and the LORD our God delivered him to us and we defeated him and his sons and all his men.*	
		²²*So the people of Israel occupied all the territory of the Amorites, from the Arnon to the Jabbok, from the desert to the Jordan.*
	³⁴*At that time we captured all his towns,* and we doomed every town—men, women, and children—leaving no survivor.	
	³⁵We retained as booty only the cattle and the spoil of the cities that we captured. ³⁶*From Aroer on the edge of the Arnon Valley,* including the town in the valley itself, to Gilead, not a city was too mighty for us; the LORD our God delivered everything to us.	
²⁴*But Israel put them to the sword, and took possession of their land, from the Arnon to the Jabbok, as far as Az of the Ammonites, for Az marked the boundary of the Ammonites.*		²³Therefore, now that the LORD, the God of Israel, displaced the Amorites on behalf of his people Israel, are you to occupy it?
²⁵*Israel took all those towns. And Israel settled in all the towns of the Amorites, in Heshbon and all its dependencies.*		²⁴*Whatever your god Chemosh displaces for you, you must surely occupy. So too, whatever the LORD our god has displaced on our behalf, we must occupy.*
	³⁷*But you did not encroach upon the land of the Ammonites,* all along the Wadi Jabbok and the towns of the hill country, just as the LORD our God had commanded.	²⁵Moreover, are you any better than Balak son of Zippor, king of Moab? Did he start a quarrel with Israel or go to war against them? ²⁶*With Israel now having settled for three hundred years in Heshbon and its dependencies, in Aroer and its dependencies, and in all the towns along the Arnon,* why has none of you regained them at any time then?
²⁶*Now Heshbon was the city of Sihon king of the Amorites, who had fought against a former king of Moab and taken all his land from him as far as the Arnon.* . . . ³¹*So Israel occupied the land of the Amorites.*		

Note: Italics indicate passages in Judg 11:19–26 that find equivalence (not necessarily verbatim) in Num 21:21–26, 31 and Deut 2:26–37.

in the other accounts, especially at Num 20:21.[32] However, if one drags the Deuteronomy version of events into Jephthah's rendition, the notion of trust finds perfect background in God's hardening Sihon's heart (Deut 2:30), as he had Pharaoh's when his doom was being choreographed. Sihon therefore not only masses his troops defensively, but from Jahza (Jahaz), he attacks Israel (*vayyillāḥem ʿim-yiśrāʾēl*).[33] His fate is sealed, but more importantly, all the *Amorite* territory that he once controlled, including chunks of Moabite land, falls into Israel's control by right of conquest. Jephthah reprises the language the king of Ammon had used in his ultimatum in describing the disputed land, but specifically calls it Amorite. For good measure, however, he enlarges on the conquest, stretching it from the plateau east of the Jordan toward that river (*min-hammidbār vĕʿad-hayyardēn*).

11 23–24. About a third of the Judges references to the verb *yāraš* ("to occupy" in the Qal and "to displace" in the Hiphil; see discussion at 1:19) are embedded in the Sihon episode of Jephthah's address, bringing us to the heart of his case. He offers two separate arguments, each of which is introduced by *vĕʿattâ*, an adverb that is used whenever a practical conclusion is to be drawn on the basis of positions just stated. The first has to do with the powers of the gods to control history and the second with accepting conventions in political life. For the first, the reasoning is simple: Gods allot victory to rulers they favor. When such gifts are made, it would be inconceivable for rulers to reject or deflect them. The play on verbal tenses here is subtle, reinforcing arguments: At 11:23—God has already driven out the Amorites in favor of Israel (*hôrîš*, a completed action), so how could you expect to win out (*tîrāš*, a contemplated action)? At 11:24—If Chemosh conquers for you (*yôrîšĕkā*, a potential event), then you should take advantage of it (*tîrāš*, a consequential action); but now that God has already conquered for us (*hôrîš*, a completed action), we are now (and presumably forever) in control (*nîrāš*, a consequential act).[34] The contrast shapes a dare: We are now enjoying the result of our God's power while your own success will depend on your god making a move that he has not yet attempted. The premise itself depends on theological positions fairly well-accepted in ancient historiography—that the rise and fall of empires on earth mirrors decisions that are taken in heaven, as a result either of confrontations among the gods (*theomachy*) or of a coordinated decision taken in heaven to shift power among the gods, hence also on earth.[35]

We must not cite this passage to debate Jephthah's attachment to monolatry (the potency of a deity within its own borders), Yahvism (the superiority of the Hebrew God), or monotheism (the uniqueness of Yнvн). He might well be sarcastic, doubting the efficacy (let alone the existence) of foreign gods; yet, in a diplomatic exchange, he was bound to engage foreign powers on their own terms. Given that divine success is couched hypothetically, Jephthah could well afford taking that position. The big issue raised in this segment is Jephthah's discordant citing of the Moabite god Chemosh as Ammon's god, when Milkom would be correct. Chemosh is heavily cited in Scripture as the god of Moab. In Moabite doctrines (as conveyed in the Mesha inscription), he is no less an activist god than is Yнvн.[36] The explanations for the misidentification are many; they can be arranged by whom to credit for the oddity—the editor, Jephthah, or the narrator.

Editor Transposed episode: Given the placement of the disputed territory (between the Arnon and the Jabbok), Jephthah's war was always with Moab and was applied to Ammon to suit the frame. Alternately: The war was with Ammon, but the narrator inserted material that concerned a now lost war with Moab (Burney 1970: 298–99, with previous literature).

Transposed god: Chemosh is cited because the territory in question was Moabite but is now under Ammon's jurisdiction; hence Chemosh can now be cited as the god of the king of Ammon, much as Marduk can be cited as Cyrus's god (Boling 1975: 203–4).

Jephthah An Israelite, Jephthah is rather nonchalant about foreign gods, perhaps intentionally insulting his antagonist (Block 1999: 362).[37] Yet Chemosh had a following in Israel centuries after Solomon built for him a shrine (1 Kgs 11:7; see 2 Kgs 23:13).

Narrator The error is unintentional and it slipped into the text (Lagrange 1903: 200).

The error is intentional and is a clue for those familiar with Hebrew traditions that what they are reading need not be taken as historically accurate but that it carries verities just the same.

None of these suggestions is fully convincing (see the Comments).

JUSTIFICATION: CONVENTIONAL BEHAVIOR

11 25–26. The second *'attâ* opens Jephthah's next argument. It is twofold: No other regional king has chosen to retrieve land lost to Israel; the status quo was accepted from time immemorial. That Jephthah has selected Balak to illustrate a point is as much because he played a role in Israel's early struggles to establish itself as because he is alone among named potential adversaries (the others being Sihon and Og of Bashan) who did *not* fall to Israel's sword. For the first part, Jephthah uses the interrogative particle *'im* to construct a "let alone, not to mention" sequence indicating that because the first element did not happen, then certainly the second could not.[38]

Traditions about Balak are linked to those about Balaam, a diviner-prophet whom Balak hired to curse Israel (Num 22–24). We cannot tell which aspects of the rich Balak-Balaam traditions inspired Jephthah (and his narrator), but those we know do not support his argument. Joshua 24:9 explicitly credits him with initiating an attack against Israel (*vayyillāḥem bĕyiśrā'ēl*) by turning first to imprecations and curses. The language in Joshua is but a variation of what Jephthah denies has happened. But while it is possible to agree that Balak never actually crossed arms with Israel and that he was not successful in mounting magic forces against it, Jephthah is certainly going against the vast Balaam traditions to claim that Balak had no quarrel (*hărôv rāv 'im yiśrā'ēl*) with Israel.[39] By asking the king of Ammon whether he imagines himself better than Balak (*hăṭôv ṭôv 'attâ mibbālāq*), Jephthah is not denigrating him (Block 1999: 362) but simply offering him a good example to follow.

Jephthah also argues for affirmation that centuries of status quo are providing. The three hundred years he cites are defended for accuracy in rabbinical exegesis, among them Rashi and Radaq (depending on the late-Roman-period *Seder Olam Rabbah*), who arrive at the needed figure by including (not always consistently) the years of foreign subjugation within the years of domination by individual judges.[40] Scholarship with investment in biblical veracity has followed suit. It must be noted, however, that in Near Eastern literary documents and formal inscriptions, rounding numbers is not equated with peddling untruths.

We have met Heshbon above; here it is listed among towns settled by Israel, together with its dependencies (*bānôt*, literally, "daughters"), normally in its environment. Aroer (*'arʿôr*; Rahlfs B, Αροηρ) and its vicinity are also mentioned. With a name meaning "Juniper," it is not surprising that several localities are similarly called.[41] Because of the mention of the Arnon in the same verse, this particular Aroer is associated with it, so at its northern bank, in Moabite territory. If so, Aroer could have been cited several times in the narratives and occasionally assigned as the capital of Sihon (Josh 12:2). Traditions differ whether it was allotted to Reuben or to Gad. In his inscription, Mesha of Moab speaks of fortifying it. Rahlfs A, however, has Ιαζηρ instead of Aroer, and both Greek versions give the Jordan as the river along which Israel settled. Jazer (the location is still disputed, but generally is considered to be by modern Amman; see Josh 13:25) is cited as one of the Ammonite cities of Sihon captured by Israel (Num 21:24). Scholars differ on which of these readings is primary, an issue not likely to be settled easily. The location of Aroer is not helped by what we shall soon read about Jephthah's victories (at 11:33).

The punch line comes now: With all these years, how come Israel's control was not challenged? The phrase *bāʿēt hāhîʾ* often has a punctual meaning, "at that specific time" (contra Moore 1895: 298), but there are occasions when it covers an entire period, among them at 4:4, when Deborah is said to have judged Israel during the time of Canaanite oppression.[42] The form (*hiṣṣaltem*) is plural and applies to all past rulers, Ammonites, Amorites, Moabites, or whatever. Despite Rahlfs B's reading, it makes no sense to revocalize as a singular (**hiṣṣaltām*, "why did you not regain them?"), presuming the king of Ammon as subject, since it would accord him a superhuman longevity. Moreover, the presumed form would have a masculine object, when "cities," the obvious antecedent, is feminine.

BRINGING GOD AS WITNESS, AGAIN

11 27–28. Jephthah returns to his earlier message (at 11:12) in which the confrontation was between him and the king of Ammon. The demarcation is sharp: Jephthah is innocent of any offense; his opponent is a fiend for attacking him. This is no longer a war between two powers, but a conflict between the opposing motivations. The crucial line comes now: Yhvh, the Hebrew god, in his capacity as judge (*haššōfēṭ*), is called on to judge (*yišfōṭ*) between the two adversaries.[43] It is striking and possibly deliberate that God is alone in the book of Judges to be labeled a *šōfēṭ*, "judge." The word *hayyôm*, "today, now," is an invitation for God to exercise judgment this very moment rather than a notice about God asserting this authority just for this occasion (both translations are grammatically possible). In fact, Yhvh dispenses justice eternally and to all creation (Gen 18:25), a theme that is developed in Hebrew poetry, with the splendid Ps 82 displaying him forcing justice on judges. In the narratives, however, there are occasions in which God is asked to decide between two parties. With Hagar carrying the child of her husband, Saray (Sarah) sinks into despair at the confirmation of her sterility and accuses her servant of insolence (Gen 16:5). She wishes God to stand as witness to her husband's fault. Abram, in full retreat, avoids the confrontation. David asks for God to ascribe fault between him and Saul (1 Sam 24:13 [12 RSV]).

With Chemosh previously invited into the argument about retaining conquered territory (at 11:24), it is striking that Jephthah would call just on the Hebrew god to determine the virtue of two opposing parties. How could Ammon believe in the fairness of such a course when its own god (indeed any other god in addition to Yнvн) is not party to establishing what is just? In fact, when Laban and Jacob had agreed on a modus vivendi, each appealed to the god(s) of his ancestors to witness their future attachment to the pact (Gen 31:53). This course is common, especially when agreements are ratified; but this is not such a case. The Comments below will attend to this seeming oddity.

The king of Ammon, it is said, would not listen to Jephthah's word. He is not speechless because he could not refute Jephthah's arguments (O'Connell 1996: 193) but because war is already launched.

COMMENTS

Two matters about Jephthah's rise invite comments: how he managed to assume leadership among a people that had rejected him, and what he achieved by sending messages to the king of Ammon when the latter's troops were already in Gilead.

Jephthah's Goals

Jephthah's story covers less than two full chapters and divides neatly into four tableaus, two of which have occupied us here. His career is steeped in hostility and alienation, opening on personal dislocation and closing on internecine warfare, with an episode soon to enfold involving his daughter that will become emblematic of him, his personality, and his career as a judge of Israel. As Jephthah enters the stage, God has nearly given up investing in Israel's future. Even as he invites Ammon (and later the Philistines) as instrument of punishment, God leaves Israel to resolve its own mess. With no divinely set judge (*šōfēṭ*) or rescuer (*môšîᵃ‘*) to save them and with no one rising internally to face the challenge, the leaders of Gilead pin their hopes on a man who had achieved armed success when ousted from their circles. As set forth in the Notes, the ensuing negotiation gives crucial insight into Jephthah's tactical control of arguments. Suffice it to observe here that with Jephthah setting forth the terms before God at Mizpah, he not only amassed civil and military authority, but set God to arbitrate their permanence through victory over Ammon.

These first tableaus give a clue to the character that the narrator (or editor) wants to shape about Jephthah: He whines and allots blame, but only for tactical purposes. He haggles, but only for assured advantage. He uses the language of diplomacy, yet his target is not the king of Ammon but the Hebrew God he wishes to draw out of political hibernation. The exchanges he has with the king of Ammon ostensibly are about the integrity of Israel's territory, but they are also about arguing the necessity for God to interfere on Israel's behalf. The longer message that Jephthah posts to Ammon is key to achieving this goal. Its closest analogues are not the entreaties for peace, but the declarations of war.

Jephthah's War Declaration

The message comes after receiving an ultimatum from Ammon, itself in response to a challenge issued by Israel. With it, far from arguing a peaceful solution to the territorial dispute, Jephthah is delivering a declaration of war. In fact, he is likely to have already taken the battle into territory occupied by Ammon.[44] The format follows a fine example of the genre that was recovered in the Mari archive.[45] Its author is Yarim-Lim, father-in-law of Zimri-Lim of Mari, who reigned in Aleppo, likely the most powerful regional capital during the first half of the eighteenth century BCE. He is writing to Yašub-yaḥad, king of Dēr, a city on the other side of the Tigris River, so hundreds of miles away from Aleppo. The Sin-gāmil he cites is king of Diniktum, a city likely to be in the Diyala Basin (so north of Baghdad). The gods he invokes are Šamaš (Sun), arbitrator for justice; Addu (Storm), executor of divine decrees; and Sin (Moon), mediator for truth:

> Tell Yašub-yaḥad; Yarim-Lim, your brother, says:
> Šamaš ought to investigate your conduct and mine and come to judgment. While I have acted as father and brother toward you, toward me you have acted as villain and enemy. What good was it that, by means of the weapons of Addu [Adad] and Yarim-Lim, I saved the city of Babylon and gave life to your land and to you? Were it not for Addu and Yarim-Lim, fifteen years ago, the city of Dēr would have been cast to the winds as if it were chaff; one would never have found it and you could not have treated me like this.
>
> Certainly, Sin-gamil, king of Diniktum, very much like you would keep answering me with hostility and provocations. Having moored five hundred skiffs in Diniktum's quay, I *sank his land* as well as him for twelve years!
>
> Now, as to you being like him: You are continually responding to me with hostility and provocations. I swear to you by Addu, my city's god, and by Sin, my personal god: [may I be punished] should I ever go away before annihilating your land and you!
>
> Now therefore, I shall come at springtime and shall pitch camp at your city's gate. I shall have you witness the galling weapons of Addu and of Yarim-Lim.

It might be profitable to make these comparisons with the letter of Jephthah:

1. *The appeal*: Despite calling Yašub-yaḥad a "brother" (that is, his equal), Yarim-Lim is not writing to soothe his soul. There is a dispute between them that must now be left to Šamaš, god of justice, to decide. In Jephthah's letter this call on divine intercession is left to the closing lines ("The LORD is the judge to decide now between the people of Israel and the people of Ammon!").
2. *The grievance*: Yarim-Lim next attends to another point: I have acted correctly; you have been evil. Here, too, Jephthah leaves the grievance to the closing lines ("While I have not wronged you, you are doing me harm to fight against me").

3. *The case history*: Yarim-Lim calls on history to bolster his grievance. His god Addu had made it possible for Ḥalab's weapons to save not just his opponent's city, but also Babylon. Unlike Jephthah, Yarim-Lim is not claiming control of land because of his god's interference in history, but simply because Dēr ought to continue paying allegiance to him.

4. *The example*: Yarim-Lim reminds his opponent of the unhappy results overtaking an offending Sin-gāmil of Diniktum. In Jephthah's retelling, Balak is alleged to have made a better choice by not offending Israel.

5. *The oath and war declaration*: These features do not find equivalent in Jephthah's letter, since Ammon is already in Gilead and its intent to war was linked to Israel's refusal to accept its authority.

I have dubbed Yarim-Lim's letter a "declaration of war" because, unlike an ultimatum, it makes no demands for change but uses the lesson of history as a backdrop for announcing hostility.[46] Gods are not invited to judge between causes when there is yet room for bridging differences; to the contrary, they enter the fray to give victory to the just. As observed earlier, ultimatums are delivered within earshot of the foes. The same attitude obtained in Israel. In Hebrew legal tradition, Israel at war is charged with giving an ultimatum (Deut 20:10): "As you approach a city and prepare to attack it, you must first offer it terms of peace [věqārā'tā 'ēlêhā lěšālôm]." This also occurred with troops ready to strike, for it makes little sense to alert your enemy about your hostile plans too far in advance.

WAR DECLARATIONS AS GENRE

Despite our noblest sentiments about the decency of declaring wars, the genre existed only post-factum, embedded in historiographic monuments (such as those about the Lagash-Umma conflict in Sumer), in annals (such as those of Mursili II of Ḥatti and Ashurbanipal of Assyria), and in literary texts (such as Gilgamesh's letter recovered from Sultantepe). My assessment of the material is that declarations of war were literary rather than realistic creations. I derive confirmation from the fact that Yarim-Lim's letter was recovered from Mari—not a party to the dispute—rather than from Dēr, where it was destined to reach, or from Aleppo, where a copy of it could have been kept. Moreover, despite their incredible loquacity, the Mari archives have yet to deliver any information about a Yašub-yaḫad. Similarly, the nice anecdote I have cited about Jehoash of Israel mocking Amaziah of Judah's war declaration tells us much about the use of the genre in historiography (see the Introductory Remarks to IIIE1).

What this observation suggests is that it is not at all necessary to argue for or against the authenticity (however defined) of Jephthah's letter to the king of Ammon, for in the diplomatic lives of ancient states, declarations of war were not generated as a crisis was unfolding. If they took shape at all, it was only in the hands of historiographers and creators of imaginative encounters, their main goal being pedagogic or evocative of moral superiority. In the case of Jephthah's message, we might suppose that a narrator would have delighted in one of Israel's leaders confronting one of its major enemies. It might well be, too, that falsely citing Chemosh as Ammon's god or Balak as holding no animosity to Israel hints that the truth conveyed by the message is much more trustworthy than the facts embedded in it.

But there might be a more direct purpose for its creation: With an appeal to divine justice at its core, Jephthah's challenge is effectively pushing God into entering the fray on Israel's behalf, that is, also on Jephthah's. The argument is not that Ammon is being despicable now—after all, it was God who incited its troops in Gilead—but that Ammon is threatening to annul results achieved in Moses's days. If there is any validity to Moses's conquests, God had better take Jephthah's side.[47] This obligation, more than any agreement Jephthah has had with his brethren, is what will lead God to bestow his *rûʷaḥ* on him. In turn, the expected victory and the consequent fulfillment of promises by the elders of Gilead will make Jephthah a judge of Israel in all the important ways, even if his call is generated on earth rather than in heaven. The narrator is certainly compiling facets in shaping a character for Jephthah. The portrayal will be completed in the next two scenes.

2. Jephthah's Daughter (Judg 11:29–40)

11 [29]Endowed with zeal for the LORD, Jephthah crossed Gilead and Manasseh, passed through Mizpeh of Gilead, and from Mizpeh he marched into Ammon. [30]Jephthah made the following vow to the LORD, "If you deliver Ammon into my hands, [31]then whoever comes out, leaving the doors of my home to meet me on my safe return from Ammon, will be the LORD's and I will have him offered as a burnt victim." ס

[32]When Jephthah marched into Ammon to fight against it, the LORD handed its people to him. [33]From Aroer as far as Minnith, he devastated some twenty towns, all the way to Abel-keramim—a crushing blow. Ammon was humbled because of Israel. [34]When Jephthah approached his home in Mizpah, there was his daughter coming out to meet him, with drums and dances. There was only her, a beloved child; beside her, he had no son or daughter.[a] [35]On seeing her, he rent his clothes and said, "Ahah, daughter! You have devastated me utterly and are among those tormenting me! For I have opened my mouth to the LORD and I cannot turn back." [36]"Father!" she said to him, "you have opened your mouth to the LORD; do with me as has come out of it, now that the LORD has executed vengeance for you against your enemies from Ammon." [37]She said to her father, "This should be done for me: Leave me be for two months as I go away. I will move down the hills and there weep over my maidenhood, my companions and I." [38]He said, "Go" and sent her on for two months. She went—she and her companions—and bemoaned her maidenhood upon the hills. [39]At the end of two months, when she returned to her father, he did to her as he had vowed. She had never known a man. So it became a tradition in Israel:[b] [40]At set moments, daughters of Israel would go out four days a year to commemorate the daughter of Jephthah of Gilead. ס

---

a. MT reads *mimmennû*, so "from him, there was no (other) son or daughter."

b. Or: she set an example in Israel.

J'ai vu s'élever contre moi,
les dieux, ma patrie et mon père.
  —*Christoph Willibald Gluck,* Iphigénie en Tauride *(act I, scene 1)*

Introductory Remarks: Vows

When setting off to war, beyond organizing a large and disciplined army and invest-ing in decent spies, good generals consult the gods, sacrifice to them, and take them as talisman out to battle. More economical, however, is to petition a god with a specific goal in mind, pledging gifts or services in return. The petition, the condition, and the promise are essential components of a vow—*neder* in Hebrew—but they operate dif-ferently depending on their application.[1] Legal documents and prayers carefully itemize what is promised, including gifts, services, increased devotion, or adoption of atypi-cal practices. In such material, the uncertainty is not about whether to discharge the pledge, but whether heaven will act favorably on the condition. Vow-makers hope that God will accept (*šāma'*, "listen to") their vows. Occasionally, we are told that God has indeed done so (Num 21:2–3).[2] Except for vows made by women who depend on men, itself the subject of legislation (Num 30), there is no indication that the terms of a vow needed to meet common sense before they become obligatory.

In narrative, however, the reverse is at stake. There is hardly any doubt that the condition will be met by the petitioned deity; instead, whether or how the pledging individual resolves the pledge generates the plotline and gives shape to the character of the person involved. When Absalom cites a vow he allegedly made when in exile as reason for going to Hebron (2 Sam 15:8), we (but not necessarily David) are clued to its contrivance because of its vague terms ("If the LORD has me return to Jerusalem, I will serve the LORD") no less than of its patent incongruity.[3] In Ugaritic lore, King Keret loses control of his future when he forgets a promise to an unforgiving goddess. In Genesis, Jacob uses the vow to bind a God who had just made him a fervent promise. Jacob's fortunes in fact begin to decay when he neglects to fulfill components of this cheeky vow (for more, see below).

In the narrative that we follow here, a vow launches events that end in a ghastly way. It is the linking of two separate human acts—the pledge and its fulfillment—that has captured the imagination of poets, composers, and artists, no less than of theolo-gians and researchers.[4]

The Vow

11 29–31. Regarding *rûªḥ YHVH* and how it affects its recipients, see the Introductory Remarks to IIIA (Judg 3:7–11). With Jephthah resolved to take the battle to Ammon, this occurrence of the phrasing seems more detached than others in Judges. This is not a God who had planned to deliver support in this way, but one maneuvered into do-ing so. Three actions are assigned to Jephthah, each using the same verb, *'āvar*, twice with the same idiom (*'āvar 'et-*). Hebrew heightens intents by staying with the same constructions, forcing focus on their objects. The opposite is true for English where good style requires avoiding repetition.[5] The verbs I offer here mean to bring Jephthah's fight aggressively not just into areas within Ammon's expansion into Gilead (see the previous section), but possibly also into Ammon, so forcing it to defend its territory by pulling its troops out of Gilead. Recovering the precise strategy depends on identifying the towns cited at 11:32–33. Nevertheless, it is difficult to figure out the literary effect. The presumption is that Jephthah posted his diplomats from Mizpah, where the covenant was sealed. The other presumption is that Mizpah (at 10:17) and Mizpeh (twice here), with different vowels, are the same; yet at 11:34 Mizpah reoccurs as the location of Jephthah's home. Since *mišpâ* or *mišpeh* can also be generic for any great height (and is taken as such in the Greek), all sorts of reconstructions are possible, none totally convincing or even necessary.

THE LANGUAGE OF THE VOW

At this point Jephthah utters his famous vow, with two conditions and a set of related promises. These components are not juxtaposed by types, but leapfrog each other. The narrator's introduction is unexceptional, using a cognate accusative construction that is common to Hebrew and attaching to it the name of the addressee, *vayyidar nēder laYHVH*. It might be best to deal with these components serially.

Condition No. 1 In other biblical vows set in narratives, the condition may be focused, as in the example attributed to Absalom (2 Sam 15:8): "If the LORD brings me back to Jerusalem . . ." It could be deployed over several segments but with essentially an unambiguous demand, as in Hannah's plea for a child (1 Sam 1:11): "LORD of Hosts, if you notice the suffering of your servant, and keep me in mind so as not to forget your servant, and give your servant a male child, then . . ." Or the condition may itself be a series of coordinated requests, as in Jacob's vow (Gen 28:20–21): "If God stays with me, protecting me on this journey on which I am setting; if he gives me food to eat and clothing to wear; and if I return in safety to my father's home . . ." In this vow, the conditions cannot be fulfilled by one single act (victory or the birth of a child) but are drawn out over a potentially longish interval and require a diversity of implementation: safe travel, fine upkeep, and safe return—any of which could have sufficed as stipulation. Remarkable, too, is that this vow comes after God had assured Jacob of guidance and protection (Gen 28:13–15).[6] We shall soon notice that Jacob's promise is yet the most striking segment of this vow. In all cases, the promises follow the conditions.

The first condition Jephthah sets out is for an achieved victory over Ammon (*ʾim-nātôn tittēn . . . bĕyādî*), with another cognate construction with the main verb in the imperfect. The language duplicates what occurs at Num 21:2, when Israel speaks as one in hoping for victory against Arad.

Premise A preliminary exposition of the promise follows, and it is introduced by *vĕhāyâ*, "it shall be." The language is somewhat belabored, *hayyôṣēʾ ʾăšer yēṣēʾ*, literally, "the one coming out, who comes out." In an episode of the Jericho narrative at Josh 2:19, the phrasing is simpler in using *kōl*, "all/whoever," without compromising the open choice that it requires: *vĕhāyâ kol ʾăšer-yēṣēʾ middaltê bêtēk*, "Whoever comes out through the doors of your house" will be at fault if he or she is killed.

Condition No. 2 The second condition is sandwiched between repeats of *vĕhāyâ*. It is brief but expands on the previous term, *bĕšûvî vĕšālôm mibbĕnê ʿammôn*, "upon my safe return from Ammon." This phrase is often rendered something like "when I return with victory (or triumph or successfully) from the Ammonites." In fact, this is the same language that Gideon used when vowing to punish the men of Penuel (at 8:9) and that Jacob formulated at Bethel (Gen 28:21). In all cases, they are stipulating making payment only *after* a safe return from a dangerous mission.[7] This is a perfectly natural wish, given the many traditions of leaders not coming back home from campaigns (for example, Saul, Ahab, and Josiah), but given the promise Jephthah will make, this extra request will prove lugubrious and grotesque. It is therefore mistaken to dismiss the clause as an expansion of Jephthah's initial pledge.[8]

Promise   A second *věhāyâ* takes up the promise. In Absalom's recalled vow (2 Sam 15:8), the promise is clear-cut: (If God allows my return home), "I will serve the LORD." Similarly brief is Israel's pledge to put Canaanite cities under ban (Num 21:2). The offer, however, may consist of parts, themselves not necessarily related. Jacob pledges himself to God, to turn a pillar into a shrine, and to donate a tenth of his future fortunes (Gen 28:22). Hannah's consists of two but related offers: The son will be God's, and his head will never be sheared (1 Sam 1:11). Jephthah's promise would be full if it stopped at the same: Whoever comes to meet him will be God's (*věhāyâ laYHVH*) and will bear signs of such a dedication. But Jephthah's offer shifts to the sinister: *věhaʿălîtihû ʿōlâ*, "I will have him offered as a burnt victim." The anticipated victim is identified as male by the suffix. One must not read too much into this because Hebrew used masculine as the default suffix; still, the gender might be kept in mind.

The Daughter of Jephthah

11 32–34. The notice about Jephthah's campaign picks up from the final clause in 11:29. The area under control of Israel as a result of Jephthah's crushing blow (*makkâ gĕdôlâ*) is described with large strokes. It is said to include at least twenty towns, within parameters created by the farthest points of Jephthah's conquest. There is much conjecture in the literature as to how to identify and where to locate the mentioned sites—Aroer, Minnith, and Abel-keramim—but there is no doubt that the battles were within a limited arena, suggesting a Blitzkrieg triumph.[9] We learn from this passage that Jephthah had a home in Mizpah, the seat for a YHVH shrine, indicating that he had fully assumed the functions assigned him by Gilead's elders by the time he completed his victories.[10] One Greek manuscript adds, "Looking as he went" (Harlé and Roqueplo 1999: 190).

Jephthah's daughter leaps into the story totally unannounced, her entry sharpened by a *hysteron proteron* presentation ("the latter first"; see above at 3:26–28, 4:6–7, and 6:2–5). In biblical lore, when individuals are slated to play a role in a developing narrative, they are generally introduced earlier, if only to identify them by name. For example, Rebekah is cited long before God chooses her as Isaac's bride (Gen 22:23); Laban is introduced much before he duels mischievously with Jacob (Gen 24); and David's children are listed before they begin their murderous competition (2 Sam 3:2–5). Jephthah's daughter, however, makes her debut like a supernova, with nary a hint of her existence previously. Nothing is said about her mother (although Radaq readily invents a life for her), and she remains so famously nameless that Pseudo-Philo (and many commentators since) felt the need to assign her one ("Se'ila").[11] Later (at 11:40) she is identified as *bat-yiftāḥ*, "daughter of Jephthah," itself not an impossible personal name.[12] Still, this notice about a daughter, unmarried yet able to participate in welcome ceremonies, tells us that Jephthah was already into firm adulthood when he achieved his triumph.

It is vital not to fudge on how she is first presented: *věhinnēh bittô yōṣēʾt liqrāʾtô vĕtuppîm ûvimḥōlôt.* Here is how *TNK* has it: "there was his daughter coming out to meet him, with timbrel and dance!" Many translations offer a precise image of a single woman, with instrument in hand, dancing toward her father, the implication being that she was alone to greet him, so hardly a glorious reception.[13] But this is not what text and custom prompt us to imagine. The *tôf* was not a timbrel (as often translated), as it was not known in Israel until the Hellenistic period. More likely, it was a shallow and rather small drum (Greek, τύμπανον), certainly without any jingles cut into the frame (as in the tambourine) and no trailing body.[14] It was held in one hand and struck with the other, producing the beat to accompany the string (*kinnôr, nevel*) or wind (*ḥālîl*) instrument with which it is often paired. The *māḥoll/mĕḥōlâ* is a group dance (Greek, χορός), with dancers either in a single file or facing each other (Song 7:1), likely responding to the beat of drums and the sound of other instruments. In Judg 21:21, the "girls of Shiloh" are to be kidnapped before they join such bands.

Exodus 15:20–21 gives us a sense of how it worked. As Moses and other men sang a great victory song, Miriam picked up a drum and, with other women contributing to the beat or engaging in dancing, took up the lines in response (antiphon).[15] First Samuel 18:6 offers a similar image: Women surge from diverse towns, singing and dancing and accompanied by musicians with drums, jubilation, and sistrum (or cymbals). From the Bible and elsewhere, other passages report on the festive atmosphere and on the crowds during triumphal processions. Later on, we learn that the daughter had many women companions, as befits a woman of standing. So, we are not likely dealing with a greeting party limited to just one member of the household; had this been the normal practice, Jephthah might not have needed to be specific about the sequence of greeters or risked the consequent disaster. In contrast, the point of having a large party moving out of the compound is to accentuate the oddity of Jephthah fixing his sight just on his daughter when she was joined by other celebrants.

Having set the scene, the narrator inserts crucial information, belaboring a single point: *raq hîʾ yĕḥîdâ,* "there was only her, a beloved child." Given the prominence of barren wives as theme, there is lore in Scripture about the beloved son (*yāḥîd*), most obviously Isaac.[16] In contrast, this is a unique reference to an only daughter. As if two notices about the daughter's uniqueness are not enough, the narrator attaches yet another qualification: *ʾēn-lô mimmennû bēn ʾô-vat.* The word *mimmennû,* normally "from him," has been corrected to "from her" as early as the Greek versions; indeed, using masculine for feminine suffixes is nicely represented in Hebrew (GKC 440 [§135o]).

A FATHER'S HURT, A DAUGHTER'S CONSOLATION

11 35–36. Jephthah's response to the tragedy is shock. No sooner does he spot his daughter than the immensity of the self-inflicted catastrophe strikes him. In Scripture, tearing one's clothing is a mourning act, but it is also associated with frustration when facing an unfurling tragedy.[17] But it is his shriek that conveys the depth of agony: *ʾăhāh,* ending on a heavily accented aspiration of the final *he* as a full consonant. This "Ahah" is an onomatopoeic *cri d'angoisse*, carrying with it none of the resignation associated with our "Alas."[18] In the narratives and in the prophets, ʾăhāh is overwhelmingly (eight out of twelve times) followed by "LORD God" (or the like), indicating that it is directed to God.[19] For example, Joshua pleads (Josh 7:7) "ʾăhāh, LORD God! Why would you have this people cross the Jordan, just to deliver us to the Amorites for destruction?" We have also seen how it is invoked by Gideon (6:22), shocked by realizing with whom he was conversing. Consequently, although Jephthah may seem to direct his words to "my daughter" (bittî), he is addressing the god who has done him wrong. The blame he will soon lay on his daughter can equally be meant for God.

For the daughter, who must have been stunned by her father's reaction, Jephthah has a reproach and an explanation. The reproach includes two phrases with a play on words (kr‿/‿kr) that complicates meanings, hakrêaʿ hikraʿtinî and vĕʾat hāyît bĕʿōkrāy. The sense of the first phrase is that she has brought him to his knees, the Hiphil of kāraʿ always giving the sense of a forced submission. The second phrase, featuring the verb ʿākar, is about generating the trouble or torment that harms others. It is difficult to know with whom Jephthah is associating his daughter, but it would not be out of character if he is recalling his brothers' slights (Lagrange 1903: 205).[20] That there is self-pity too cannot be dismissed, although translations such as "you have made me miserable and wretched" (Block 1999: 394) seem lame.

Jephthah's own explanation for the reaction is missing, but we notice, too, that he neither cites his vow nor labels it as such (neder). The verb pāṣâ has to do with opening widely. With the mouth (or lips) as object, most attestations are not flattering: The earth opens widely to accept innocent blood (Gen 4:10) or rebels (Num 16:30, Deut 11:6). People do so to state vapidity (Job 35:16) and to threaten the innocent (Ps 22:14 [13 RSV]; Lam 2:16, 3:46). The intimation here is that Jephthah is admitting to a gross blunder, akin to our "opening a big mouth." Moreover, by stating lōʾ ʾûkal lāšûv, "I cannot turn back," he comes closest to disclosing that a vow was at stake.[21] Still, with the Qal of šûv, the idiom is concrete (as in 1 Kgs 13:16) rather than metaphoric, and so Jephthah may (also?) be lamenting his incapacity to step back, from his home perhaps, rather than in pulling back his vow.

THE DAUGHTER'S RESPONSE(S)

The daughter, still nameless, opens on a vocative ʾāvî, "my father," that must certainly have torn a hole in Jephthah's heart. She disregards the double-dosed onus Jephthah has set on her.[22] Subtly censorious, nonetheless, she uses her father's own language to affirm the need to fulfill any pledge to God.[23] By repeating her father's words, she avoids demanding to know what exactly is at stake. Yet, it tells us much about her knowledge of her father that she grasps at once that he had bargained something precious for his victory.

The daughter reasons why her father must do what he had intended. The phrase ʾaḥărê ʾăšer is a compound conjunction that focuses on the next stage of events. The daughter is not establishing an effect after a cause (implied by many translations such as "since," "inasmuch," or "given that") but is drawing a conclusion based on an un-contestable occurrence. She also balances between what the father must do (ʿăśê lî, "do to me") and what God has already done (ʿāśâ lĕkā YHVH nĕqāmôt mēʾōyvêkā). What the "God of Vengeance" (Ps 94:1) has done is to execute retribution, nĕqāmôt given here in what grammarians term the "plural of amplification."

11 37–38. In Hebrew, direct quotations are commonly introduced by forms of the verb *ʾāmar*, "to say," and if there is a string of them in a dialogue, they tend to be separated by pertinent responses, also similarly introduced. This pattern is by no means universal, but when it is broken, attention is being drawn or gaps are being ignored.[24] We will never know whether or how long the daughter waited for an answer, perhaps hoping for some comfort or reassurance. But Jephthah is no longer into opening his mouth. For the daughter it must now be clear that something terrifying is awaiting her, but the narrator is not yet revealing whether she is fully aware of what her father has bartered. She continues as if no interval had elapsed but is not confrontational, as she uses a passive form (*yēʿāśeh-llî haddābār hazzeh*) to shape her request.[25] The request, however, is meant for Jephthah, and it opens on an idiom, *harpēh mimmennî*, that elsewhere implies annoyance, as in Deut 9:14 when God wants Moses to stay back so that he can punish Israel: "Leave me be [*heref mimmennî*] to destroy them." Whether or not the daughter shares this emotion is up to us to decide, but it does not seem as if she is begging for the surcease. Why two months (*šěnayim* [*šěnê* at 11:38] *ḥŏdāšîm*) is a riddle, for unlike the "three months" that is mentioned fairly often in Hebrew literature, this interval does not seem especially meaningful. It would be trivial to speculate when the actual count begins, but a Greek manuscript gives "two full months" to avoid suggesting two new moons (Harlé and Roqueplo 1999: 191), which might potentially stretch the interval into three months.

Another puzzler is the sequence of activities the daughter wants to accomplish: *vě ʾēlěkâ věyāradtî ʿal-hehārîm vě ʾevkeh . . . ʿal-bětûlay.* In other contexts where "to go" and "to descend" occur together, the setting is a mountain (Sinai, see Exod 19:24, 32:7). One might follow Radaq, who placed Mizpah at some height, given the meaning "observation point" (see Barthélemy 1982: 104).[26] Other exegetes have found instances in which *yārad* simply suggests a movement (as in the frequent "descending to Egypt") or propose that another root is at stake, many of them in difficult contexts: *rûd*, "to wander," as in Ps 55:3 (2 RSV); or *yārad*, "to fall," said of the wailing (?) accompanied by tears, as in Isa 15:3. Many emendations are proposed, by medieval commentators among others, and they are collected in Orlinsky (1942), who would dispense with the verb altogether.[27] The *TNK* is not unique in fudging: "I will go with my companions and lament upon the hills and there bewail my maidenhood." Marcus (1986: 30) raises the important issue of whether the movement on the mountains is at stake here at all; the daughter may simply be asking for a time of solitude with her companions. Later, at 11:38, there seems to be a connection between the wailing and the mountains where it occurred, although it is easy for us to romanticize such a setting.

The Masoretes placed a strong disjunctive accent over *ḥŏdāšîm* right after the daughter had requested a surcease, suggesting special focus on what follows. Orlinsky (1942: 93–94) has noticed the odd syntax in which two cohortatives (*vě ʾēlěkâ . . . vě ʾevkeh*) sandwich a perfect conversive (*věyāradtî*). I note that a *vě ʾēlěkâ* with a strong disjunction occurs at Gen 30:26 (Jacob, "Give me my wives and children for whom I have served you that I may go") and also at Num 23:3. I therefore translate our passage as if the accent were set over *vě ʾēlěkâ*, leaving us with the more plausible series of two verbs, a perfect conversive followed by a cohortative. The consequence is that the main brunt of the daughter's request will come only after her request for delay and leave.

Whatever the direction or purpose of the daughter's move into the mountains, her activity during that period is clear: Together with her companions, she will weep ʿal-bĕtûlay. The plural may seem odd when applied to "virginity," but it is not at all uncommon when reflecting a state, such as "youth" (bĕḥûrîm), "old age" (zĕqûnîm), or the like. A bĕtûlâ is a nubile young woman, who might very well be a virgin in our sense. It is commonly recognized in the literature that Hebrew does not have a single word equivalent for the English "virgin" and must add the circumlocution "no man has known her" to refer to a young woman whose hymen has not been broken (below at 11:39; Gen 19:8, 24:16).[28] It is not at all clear on which side of the divide the daughter feels herself to be: Is she saddened by the prospects of not attaining that stage, in which case she has foreboding about death? Or is she bewailing an arrest in the normal fruition of life now that she has reached that phase, in which case she fears seclusion? We will have more to say about these prospects in the Comments. P. Day (1989) has followed the opinion that bĕtûlîm does not refer to a stage in the daughter's life but "rather specifies when the lament takes place . . . Jephthah's daughter requests and is granted permission to perform a bĕtûlîm lament" (60).

Who these companions are is not clear. The written form (Ketiv) is raʿyōtāy, plural of raʿyā; but scribal instruction (Qere) urges us to read rēʿôtāy, plural of rēʿâ, likely because of the latter's occurrence at 11:38. The two terms both convey the same meaning, that of close companions or attendants. We are not told why these young women would want to join the daughter, but they could belong to the same age group, hence sharing the same experience as they enter nubility. They may also be attached to her because of her father's status.

Jephthah's answer is one word (lĕkî), as if dismissing a servant. (He might have achieved a more tender reply by repeating a less accusatory bittî, "my daughter," as in Ruth 2:2.). Still, he is in full authority as he dismisses her. The language here is not quite as stark as when Amnon tells his attendant about the bĕtûlâ he had just raped to "rid me of this one outside" (šillĕḥû-nāʾ ʾet-zōʾt mēʿallay haḥûṣâ) (2 Sam 13:17), but the two may share the self-loathing that prompted the hurried reaction.

The Deed and Its Aftermath

11 39–40. When the daughter returns at the end (miqqēṣ) of the two months, Jephthah fulfills his vow.[29] The verbs used in such events include šillem ("to pay up"; very common), pillēʾ ("to fulfill," as in Lev 22:21), and nāśāʾ ("to bring over" to God, as in Deut 12:26). Here, Jephthah is said "to do something" to his daughter (vayyaʿaś lah), the verb suggesting a very physical act. It may be a hint that the other example of its association with a vow is at Jer 44:25, when God tells idolaters: "You and your wives confirmed by deed what you spoke in words, 'We will perform [ʿāśōh naʿăśeh] the vows that we have pledged, to burn incense to the Queen of Heaven and to pour libations to her.' Go ahead, make vows and perform them!"

What exactly Jephthah did to his daughter has been the subject of speculation for centuries, and it will be taken up in the Comments. The narrator has two remarks: The first is that the daughter "did not know a man," a phrase that is a shortened version of what we find at 21:12 about locating many an adolescent girl (bĕtûlâ) who has "not known a man through male intercourse" (lōʾ-yādĕʿâ ʾîš lĕmiškav zākār).[30] It is perfectly reasonable that young women are described this way when their futures are ahead of them (Rebekah, Gen 24:16) or to plot out a story (Lot's daughters, Gen 19:8), but what is the point of this notice? Is it to tell us that when Jephthah carried out his vow she was still a virgin (in our sense)? Yet this remark would seem unnecessary, given that the daughter still lived in her father's home, neither a widow nor a divorcée. Might the purpose then be to give us a glimpse at her future as a consequence of Jephthah's deed? Those who argue that the daughter was consecrated to a celibate life favor this last interpretation.[31] If so, we might have had a construction that looked to the future, as was told of Tamar after her rape: "Tamar remained in her brother's house, a spinster [šōmēmâ]" (2 Sam 13:20).

The second notice has to do with what came to be associated with the daughter. The relevant phrase is set Janus-like, depending on what precedes (having experienced her father's resolve, *vattĕhî ḥōq*, she came to be a *ḥōq* in Israel) or what follows (because she became a *ḥōq* in Israel, this is what came to be).[32] A *ḥōq* is a prescribed regulation, mostly with the force of law, but also a norm or a custom developed over time though practice. In Israel's historiography, it became conventional that all the laws that Israel would ever need were dispensed during the Sinai wanderings, with two exceptions: when David made it unacceptable to murder an anointed of God (1 Sam 30:14–16) and when he set a fixed precedent (*vayyĕśîmehā lĕḥōq ûlĕmišpāṭ*) that warriors must share the spoils with noncombatants in an army (1 Sam 30:21–25). So, in the *ḥōq* pertaining to Jephthah's daughter, we are not likely to be speaking of anything enforced by royal or priestly authority.

Haran (1969) has clarified the meaning of *miyyāmîm yāmîmâ*; it has to do with regularity rather than circumstance or periodicity and so may not have to coincide with any festival. In this way, the narrator did not need to expand on an occasion with such an obviously ad hoc origin. (The Greek simply calques on the Hebrew.) The *bĕnôt yiśrā'ēl* are young women of marriageable age. They are called upon to shed tears over Saul and Jonathan, who had supplied them with finery (2 Sam 1:24). However, here they are *lĕtannôt lĕvat-yiftāḥ*. As we saw earlier (at 5:11), this verb has to do with broadcasting testimony, whether in tales or songs, so a form of commemoration with the daughter (not Jephthah) specifically in mind.[33] Four days a year seems a good chunk of time, so not likely during harvests or shearing.

In the cultic cycle of ancient Israel, there is no mention of such a celebration. Could the narrator simply have conjured it up to divert attention from a distasteful ending?[34] Did it reflect a living institution that was slighted in a male-oriented Bible? Or might it be, as argued in the literature, an etiology for puberty, a lament for the death of youth, a prenuptial ceremony, each and all reflected in classical literature?[35]

COMMENTS[36]

Shall I offer my first born for my transgression,
The fruit of my body for my personal sins?
—*Mic 6:7*

Thus said the LORD of Hosts: Ponder this and summon the dirge-songstresses, let them come. Send for the skilled women, let them

come. Let them quickly start a wailing for us, that our eyes may run
with tears, our pupils flow with water.

—*Jer 9:16–17 (17–18 RSV)*

Jephthah's Vow

Most commentators propose that Jephthah's vow to sacrifice the first person meeting
him on his triumph was flawed because it was unnecessary. This is true, not just because
in narrative there is hardly a doubt that the gods will fulfill a petitioner's request (see
the Introductory Remarks), but also because biblical narrators rarely challenge a character's privileged knowledge of God's decision. As noted, however, Jephthah embedded
a second condition in his vow. He would deliver on his promise, he says, on his "safe
return from Ammon." Here this extra request engages two aspects of the sensibility that
has been shaped for Jephthah: He may trust in God, but like Gideon he sees no harm
in bolstering the chances for a happy ending. More subtly, Jephthah wants to return
not to Tob, where he controlled ruffians, but to Mizpah, where those who rejected him
probably lived and where God witnessed his consecration as a de facto judge.

This setting in Mizpah inspires yet a third provision that Jephthah builds into
his pledge. God must select his own gift by motivating a victim to step out first from
Jephthah's compound. Since antiquity, the suggestion has been that Jephthah meant
to include animals among the potential greeters, and some translations give "whatever
comes from my doors" for "whoever" does so.[37] Without challenging the likelihood that
animals were kept within the confines of a home, this scenario is far-fetched: Hebrews
did not grant animals the will to lead victory parades.[38] In the example of Josh 2:19
cited above, the phrasing applies only to humans, so it is likely the case here as well.

What is significant, however, is that the choice of victim reinforces the gambling
personality created for Jephthah. Biblical lore knows of other occasions in which God
is forced into decisions—for example, when Abraham's servant maneuvers God into
selecting a bride for Isaac (Gen 24).[39] Here, however, Jephthah has selfishly pledged a
quid pro quo: the life of another human being as a warranty for his own. Sordid as the
offer might be, it would not have jolted us as much had Jephthah simply stopped at the
first clause ("whoever comes out . . . , will be the LORD's"). The pledge would have been
to deliver a member of his household to God, as Hannah did when she begged for the
future Samuel.[40]

By adding that extra clause ("I will have him offered as a burnt victim"), however, Jephthah consigned the victim to a particularly loathsome fate. When animals are
offered as *ʿōlâ* (Greek, ὁλοκαύτωμα; elsewhere, ὁλοκαύτωσις, "holocaust"), violence
never slackens: The trussing is brutal, the bleating is shrill, blood spurts everywhere,
limbs jerk, and the bowels let go. Then there is the cracking of bones, the ripping of
organs, the screeching of fire, and the acrid stench of burning flesh. These steps cannot
be less dramatic with humans as victim. Naturally, there is much speculation on where
Jephthah, or more precisely his creators, drew inspiration for such a violent offer.

HUMAN SACRIFICE[41]

There is much discussion in the literature on whether Jephthah was impervious to Hebrew traditions that forbade human sacrifice, especially as reflected in Deuteronomistic
writing, or whether he was simply imitating vile Canaanite practices.[42] The premises

themselves are flawed. From Canaan, there is as yet practically no incontestable record of its practice. In Hebrew narratives, albeit not necessarily in real life, ritualized killing is scarcely condemned, with reference to the extermination of prisoners; the exposition of disarticulated reprobates, "for the LORD, facing the sun" (Num 25:4); the hacking of kings "before the LORD" (1 Sam 15:33); the immolation of Hebrew princes; and the construction of fortifications over the corpses of immolated brothers.[43] It might even be argued that human sacrifice opens human history, as Cain tried to emulate Abel's success by offering his brother as a precious blood gift to God (Gen 4) (Maccoby 1982: 11–40). Most famously, there is also the near sacrifice of Isaac, itself demanded by God. Table 14 presents the biblical testimonies by their approximation to elements in Jephthah's tale.

1. Closest to what obtains in the story of Jephthah and his daughter is the narrative about Saul (1 Sam 14) and the damning oath he imposed on his army to secure victory against the Philistines. Unknowingly, his son Jonathan breaks the oath. Saul was ready to strike him down, but he is saved by the people. Eventually, Jonathan (like Jephthah's daughter) does pay with his life for his father's intemperance; furthermore, Jonathan's seed never comes to rule Israel. The remaining testimonies differ, each in its own way.

2. Mesha of Moab organizes a military sortie to escape a Hebrew coalition set to conquer the last of his cities. It fails and in despair he offers his firstborn as a ʿōlâ in full view of the enemy. Second Kings 3:27 explicitly credits this act with achieving Mesha's objective, forcing commentators ever since to debate how.

3. It is told in 1 Kgs 16:34 that in the days of Ahab, a king adept at vexing God, Hiel of Bethel wished to fortify Jericho. There was a curse against such an undertaking (Josh 6:26), demanding human sacrifice for reversal. Hiel does so. The narrator is noncommittal about it all.

4. All but the last item in Table 14 (Isaac) deal with sacrifices offered probably to foreign gods: no. 5 by foreigners, nos. 6–7 by kings of Judah (Ahaz and Manasseh) regarded as sinners by the narrator. While we cannot know how much is true in their polemics against these kings, it is certain that the narrator is not informing us about "ritual singeing by fire," as occasionally claimed.

5. I have left to the last the famous Akedah, because it has little to compare with the Jephthah story: The sacrifice is inspired by God; the potential victim (Isaac) is identified from the first; the potential immolator would have accomplished the deed without complaints and a substitute is advanced. Most commentators who make the comparison set up the issues accommodatingly, if not also confessionally. Thus Block (1999: 371–72) turns Jephthah, who was mortified for what he was about to do, into a "paganized deliverer-hero"; in contrast, Abraham is a "saintly patriarch," obeying God and agonizing over the fate of his victim (hardly in the text). Jephthah's daughter is said to lack love, going to the mountains accompanied by companions rather than family; Isaac, instead, was loved deeply by a father who accompanied him to the place of sacrifice (an odd conjunction, for how else was the test to function?). Abraham's trial "confirmed the faith of the sacrificer" and the faithfulness [sic] of God while that of Jephthah confirmed the faithlessness of the sacrificer and the withdrawal of God. And so forth . . .

Table 14. Human Sacrifice in the Hebrew Bible

	Victim	Parents	Context	Why?	Immolator	Deity	Substitute	Outcome	Text
1	Jephthah's daughter	Jephthah	Battle	Vow	Jephthah	Y<small>HVH</small>	None	Battle success	Judg 11
2	Jonathan (potential)	Saul	Battle	Oath		N/A	N/A	Battle aborted	1 Sam 14
3	Firstborn of Mesha	Mesha (of Moab)	Battle	Despair	Mesha	Chemosh (?)	None	Israel withdraws	2 Kgs 3:26–27
4	Abiram Segub	Hiel of Bethel	Jericho walls	Curse	Father	Y<small>HVH</small> (?)		?	1 Kgs 16:34 (see Josh 6:26)
5	Children of Sepharvites		?	?	?	Adrammelech and Anammelech	N/A	?	2 Kgs 17:31
6	Son of Ahaz	Ahaz (king of Judah)	?	?	?	?	N/A	?	2 Kgs 16:3
7	Son of Manasseh	Manasseh (of Judah)	?	?	?	Molech (?)	N/A	?	2 Kgs 21:6
8	Isaac (potential)	Abraham and Sarah	Test from God	Y<small>HVH</small>	Abraham	Y<small>HVH</small>	Ram	Abraham deemed faithful	Gen 22
9	[Abel	Adam and Eve	God deemed to favor blood sacrifice	Jealousy	Cain	Y<small>HVH</small>	N/A	Cain is banished	Gen 4]

Still, it can be asked, could the Jephthah narrator have poached on non-Hebraic, especially Greek, traditions where there is a rich repertoire of tales about the sacrifice (or near sacrifice) of human beings? While the story of Iphigenia is most often brought into comparison, it is commonly acknowledged that, with its multiple settings for Agamemnon's vow and its diverse resolutions, none of its versions has a sequence that matches the steps found in the Jephthah account: (1) a request to be fulfilled by a divinity, for which there is (2) a pledge to sacrifice a human being, and (3) a stipulation on how the victim is to be singled out.[44] There are, however, three examples that compare well, all from late antiquity. Pausanias (*Description of Greece* 9.33.4) tells of a Boeotian king who, facing a drought, accepts Delphic advice to kill the first person he meets on his return home from the oracle. His son Lophis is the victim, his spurting blood turning into the needed water on hitting the soil. Pseudo-Plutarch (*De Fluviis* 9.1) offers another etiology for the upwelling of a body of water. To gain a victory, Maiandros pledges an unspecified victim that will meet him. His entire family does. According to some versions, he felt such remorse on killing his kin that he let a river bear away his body— and his name. The last example is taken from Marius (Maurus) Servius, a late-fourth-century CE commentator on Virgil's *Aeneid* (3.121 and 11.264). Caught in a storm, King Idomeneus of Crete pledges the first person to meet him on his safe landing. His son does, but the resolution is certain only in Mozart's opera *Idomeneo* (K. 366). Servius lived among Christians, some of whom attributed materials to him. So, through them he may have drawn on Jephthah's story to accent the pathos of his setting. All of the above examples from the classics are interesting in a Stith Thompson *Motif-Index* sort of way, but despite frequent allusions to them in biblical scholarship, they are hardly the stuff that might seriously contribute to shaping a Hebraic tale.

The Choices in the Vow

It would not be out of character for Jephthah to neglect the possibility that his only daughter might stick out in a crowd. Had Jephthah's eyes alighted on another person, the results would be no less horrifying, but we would certainly not have experienced the pathos so powerfully developed in the exchange between father and daughter.[45] The irony here is profound: Jephthah may have wished God to choose his own reward; yet, betrayed by his own eyesight, Jephthah ended up making that choice just the same. The way Jephthah's sight settled on his daughter is ripe for a psychological explanation; instead, the narrator turns it into one element in his continuing construction of Jephthah's portrait. Earlier, in his meeting with the elders and in his letter to the Ammonites Jephthah had proved to be a kvetcher, but one with a talent for using perceived victimhood as a basis for concessions. Jephthah had also drawn God into his battle against Ammon by alluding to divinely sponsored victories in the days of Moses. (See the Comments to IIIG1.) At this occasion, Jephthah pushes his luck further. He wants his victory against Ammon, but he also wants to live to enjoy the fruits of his machinations.[46] So he gives God the ultimate choice in selecting his own reward for keeping him whole. That reward must be worthy, and—I have argued—in Jephthah's mind it could come only at the expense of another life. Let God, however, decide which one: Jephthah would go eyeball to eyeball with God, fully expecting him to blink first— just as God did for Abraham when the life of Isaac was at stake. Facing the dilemma of having to identify a victim, God may have made the only choice that might deflect

Jephthah from his sordid plan: Surely he would not go through with it when the life of his only daughter is at stake. Let Jephthah absorb the onus of a broken vow. But God has not counted on Jephthah's obduracy. Even as he senses his gamble lost and is cut to the quick by events, Jephthah remains fully in character. Saying "You have devastated me utterly and are among those tormenting me" (11:35), he lays reproach and blame on his daughter. Moreover, by claiming that his pledge is beyond retraction, Jephthah once more deflects on God the responsibility of justifying his poor judgment.

If in narratives vows are tracked mostly for the resolution of pledges, then our narrator had several options for concluding the story. Since Roman times, commentators have assumed that the daughter was sacrificed, scathingly indicting Jephthah's deed and character. Artistic depictions and scholarly assessments largely have followed suit. Especially in recent years several inspired feminist contributions have sharpened the daughter's status in culture and in memory. Nevertheless, a venerable minority opinion has argued that, whether intentionally or accidentally, the daughter was consecrated to divine service rather than sacrificed.[47] The arguments for both conclusions are nicely charted in David Marcus's careful study of 1986. While he gravitates toward a nonsacrificial resolution of the daughter's fate, Marcus credits the narrator with "devising a deliberately ambiguous ending" (53).

There is something to Marcus's opinion, but I would not term the plotting ambiguous, at least not in any rhetorical sense, in which a word, expression, or idea is open to multiple interpretations. What we have here, instead, are conflicting clues that lead to incongruous yet individually coherent endings. The narrator relies exclusively on dialogue, thus constricting all potential solutions to what the characters, by their words, allow us to consider.

THE JEPHTHAH SOLUTION

Jephthah knew what he had pledged and was most reluctant to dishonor it. Had there been an ending consistent with Jephthah's understanding of the pledge, the tale would have cut directly to its atrocious conclusion at v. 39. Following immediately on his grief-stricken lecture to his daughter, we would have learned that "[Jephthah] did to her as he had pledged. She had never known a man (or: she was not to know a man)."

THE NARRATOR'S POTENTIAL RESOLUTION

To avoid exalting a perverse act of piety as well as exposing God's passivity, the narrator might have sought another path, which is to rely on several dei ex machina available to Hebraic traditions. A substitute animal could have manifested itself, as happened for Isaac (Gen 22). The Gileadites could have prevailed on Jephthah to change his mind, as was done for Saul's son, Jonathan (1 Sam 14). The narrator could have given Jephthah refuge in redemptive acts, known already to Mari Amorites and later codified in Lev 27:1–8. In fact, Jephthah was criticized in rabbinic lore precisely for that failure.[48]

THE DAUGHTER'S UNDERSTANDING

The daughter's initial reaction to her father's overwrought charges is restrained but delicately critical: "Father!" she says, "you have opened your mouth to the LORD; do with me as has come out of it, now that the LORD has executed vengeance for you against your enemies from Ammon" (11:36). What, in fact, is there for an unmarried daughter to say when learning that both her father and her God had agreed to make her the price of her people's victory? It is just as well, therefore, that Jephthah keeps shut the mouth that is costing him so much; instead, he listens to a proposal with two premises, one of which he knows to be false.

The daughter wants two months during which, with her friends, she will bewail her "virginity." If with her own words the daughter is lamenting not achieving the normal life of a young woman, then she must certainly have grasped her father's brutal plans and can only ask for a surcease in which to prepare for its end. However, if she fears consecration, then she is imagining a confined life, with no hope of bearing the child that might normally memorialize her—or her father for that matter. What would strengthen assigning her this second reflection is to know something about consecrating women to religious organizations in ancient Israel, as we do about the *gubabātu* of Kanesh and the *nadâtu* of Mesopotamia.[49] These women were cloistered as in-laws of diverse gods: Some were celibate; all were not to have children. In the Bible, the *ṣōvĕʾōt* (Exod 38:8) were connected to sanctuaries, and in one passage those who slept with them were labeled sinful (1 Sam 2:22), so operating as vestals. The devotees of Tammuz in postexilic Jerusalem may have belonged to the same institutions (Ezek 8:14; see Dan 11:37). We know, too, that the fertility of certain women was controlled, especially after abnormal activities. Tamar, raped by Amnon, was forced to live in seclusion in Absalom's home (2 Sam 13:20).[50] We are left, then, without a clear notion of what the daughter expected her future to be. For her, the two months of incertitude must have been beyond bearing. For us, we have the narrator's comment on what transpired.

The Aftermath

Jephthah gives his daughter permission to do as she requests. She returns two months later, and her father fulfills his promise. It is at this point, after her immolation, that we learn that "she herself had not known a man" (11:39). Given her father's resolve, it does not much matter whether this tidbit is circumstantial (what she was at death) or consequential (how she died as a virgin).[51] Yet the narrator must certainly want us to recognize the horror of the daughter's fate, for, as Ramban long ago noted, it would not do for the women of Israel to gather four days a year to memorialize a young girl just because she was forced to die a spinster.[52] I will have more to say on the narrator's elegiac ending in the Comments to the next episode regarding Jephthah.

3. Jephthah's Flaws (Judg 12)

12 [1]Ephraim was summoned to a man and crossed the Jordan to Zaphon. They said to Jephthah, "Why did you move to fight Ammon and us you did not call to go with you? We will set your house on fire with you in it!" [2]Jephthah answered them, "I was intensely in conflict with Ammon—my people and I. I pleaded with you, but you would not rescue me from them. [3]When I realized that you are no rescuer, I took life in hand and moved against Ammon. The LORD handed them over to me. So why do you rise against me just now to fight me?" [4]Jephthah gathered all the men of Gilead and fought Ephraim. Gilead defeated Ephraim, for having said, "You are but survivors from Ephraim, Gilead, in the midst of Ephraim as in Manasseh's." ⁵Gilead barred the fords of the Jordan from Ephraim. Should a survivor from Ephraim say, "Let me cross," the men of Gilead would ask him, "Are you an Ephraimite?" On saying "No," ⁶they would press him, "Say Shibbolet!" "Sibbolet," he would say, not managing to voice it that way. Seizing him, they would slaughter him by the fords of the Jordan. In that instance alone, from Ephraim forty-two thousand fell.

⁷Jephthah was judge in Israel for six years. When Jephthah of Gilead died, he was buried in the towns of Gilead. ס

IBZAN

⁸Judging Israel after him was Ibzan of Bethlehem. ⁹He had thirty sons. He sent thirty daughters beyond *the area* and had thirty daughters brought for his sons from beyond *the area*. He was judge in Israel for seven years. ¹⁰Then Ibzan died and was buried in Bethlehem. ס

ELON

¹¹Judging Israel after him was Elon of Zebulon; he was judge in Israel for ten years. ¹²Then Elon of Zebulon died and was buried in Ayyalon, in the territory of Zebulon. ס

ABDON

¹³Judging Israel after him was Abdon son of Hillel of Pirʿaton. ¹⁴He had forty sons and thirty grandsons, who rode on seventy colts; he was judge in Israel for eight years. ¹⁵Then Abdon son of Hillel of Pirʿaton died. He was buried in Pirʿaton, in the territory of Ephraim, on Amalek Hill. ס

NOTES

Introductory Remarks: Languages, Dialects, and Articulations

It is hardly necessary to document the rich warehouse of languages that was the ancient Near East. Beyond the main families that include Semitic, Hamitic (which may have once belonged together), Indo-European, Hurrian, and Elamite languages, there were other constellations that are not yet fully charted or understood.[1] Many of these families are known to us by a broad selection of languages, and some of them can be further distinguished by dialects. Hebrew belongs to the Semitic family of languages and is most often classified within a West Semitic cluster of dialects that includes Ammonite, Moabite, Phoenician (many subcategories), and Edomite.

The Hebrew that we now parse with so much care is a composite, an artificial creation. Consonants come from an infinitely earlier period than the vowels. The grammar that controls the vocalization established by the Masoretes was more in tune with that of the mishnaic than the monarchic or postexilic period. Despite efforts to keep an oral tradition of the earlier forms of Hebrew, it is likely that over time much in our received text was harmonized or homogenized.[2] Nonetheless, a number of scholars have found evidence for distinct speech patterns within each dialect, among them divergent soundings of consonants, stresses on syllables, formations of idioms, even verbal usages. There are many articulations of these views, and they do not always garner undisputed support; but the subdialects or jargon detected in the received Hebrew text are most often allocated to two groups: "Israelian" in the North (featured in the Samaria ostraca) and "Judahite" in the South (featured in finds from Arad and Lachish).

So much is what modern research tells us. What the Hebrews themselves say about languages and dialects differs. For them, languages forked when ambitious men sought to storm heaven by building a tower just after God had graciously allowed Noah and his children to survive the flood (Gen 11). Yet, despite an elaborate categorization of languages as associated with diverse folk (Gen 10) and recognition of the diversity (Esth 1:22, 8:9; Dan 1:4, 5:19, 6:26 [25 RSV]) and incomprehensibility (Ps 81:6 [5 RSV]) of foreign languages, Hebrew narrative art recognizes distinctions among them only when important to the plot: Joseph speaks through interpreters to avoid recognition by his brothers (Gen 42ff.), and Sennacherib's chamberlain, who can speak Hebrew, is urged toward Aramaic lest people in Judah understand what he says (Isa 36:4–11). Otherwise, everyone speaks lovely Hebrew: Pharaohs and Philistine rulers turn to it when conversing with patriarchs; Potiphar's wife has no problem with it even when addressing her slaves (Gen 39); Jonah uses it to warn the Ninevites (Jonah 3:4); Babylonian and Persian dignitaries do the same when they address exiled Jews. Words taken from other languages slip in, but their origins are hardly acknowledged (as in Gen 31:47; 41:43, 45). At the end of days, it was thought, God will make it so that foreigners will understand the divine message even if couched in Canaanite or Hebrew (Isa 19:18, Ezek 3:4–7).

With Hebrew narrators displaying little interest in acknowledging language distinctions despite the opportunity to do so, the anecdote featured in the verses below is doubly striking. First because it shapes a whole incident on what seems to us a linguistic (actually a voicing) peculiarity that is scarcely acknowledged elsewhere in Scripture, and second because it explains the nature of such differences in a manner that tests our capacity to resolve. Nevertheless, we must try to elucidate the notice as well as its role in the context.

War with Ephraim

12 1–3. It would be good to cite the other occasion in which Ephraim complained of neglect. Gideon had just won his stunning victory when we read (at 8:1–3): "The men of Ephraim censured [Gideon] severely by telling him, 'How could you treat us like this by not calling us when you went to fight Midian?' He answered them, 'Have I done anything so far comparable to you? Ephraim's gleanings are better than Abiezer's vintage! To you God turned over Midian's commanders, Oreb and Zeeb; what did I achieve that matches you?' Their resentment against him abated once he addressed them in this way." There are differences, of course, in the contexts. Gideon had called on Ephraim to help corner the routed Midian. Its troops crossed the Jordan River, captured two major commanders, and executed them. So they had likely taken many spoils but were angling for the larger share they would have gotten had they joined Gideon earlier. In the days of Jephthah, however, the only knowledge we have about

Ephraim is that it was one of the many major tribal areas in Israel invaded by Ammon (see at 10:9). The presumption is that they were too cowed to attack the invaders. And it may be that vengeance, no less than greed for plunder, prompted them to wish that they had participated in turning the tables on the enemy. So they pressed Jephthah; alas for them, he was no Gideon. When flush with victory, Jephthah seems to lose his cunning. The manipulative skills with which he negotiated with the elders of Gilead and the diplomatic dexterity that helped earn God's support evade him when dealing with the demands of Ephraim. It might be that fulfilling his vow unsettled his senses (but see below for a suggestion on the chronology of these two events).

Zaphon (ṣāfōn; Rahlfs A, Σεφινα), "North," is likely an abbreviated form of a place (or clan) name, in Gad's territory not far from Succoth (Josh 13:27). It has been (falsely) identified with Ṣapuma (EA 274) and has invited many suggestions as to its location.[3] The essential point is that it lay across the Jordan, so taking Ephraim out of its space and into areas now controlled by Jephthah. Nothing in the text permits locating Jephthah's home there, as is occasionally proposed, and there is no reason to posit a personal confrontation between leaders; such exchanges are done via messengers, as we have already learned.

The exchange between the two parties is bellicose, but it is not clear what Ephraim hoped to gain. It does not make a demand but declares itself ready to burn down Jephthah's home, with him in it (bêtĕkâ niśrōf ʿālêkā bāʾēš). The Philistines will similarly menace Samson's wife, and actually carry out the threat (at Judg 14:15 and 15:6), but a more vivid realization is at 1 Kgs 16:18 where the regicide Zimri sets on fire the palace he had little time to enjoy, dying in the conflagration. We might also keep in mind that in Judges, fire is an instrument of vengeance. It is cited as such in Jotham's fable (9:15, 20) and applied against Shechem (9:49).[4] Jephthah may have sensed that Ephraim is being blustery, but rather than investigating how to sooth its hurt, he makes accusations that cannot be substantiated in the inherited narrative.

Jephthah opens, as before (at 11:15), on a historical note. By stating ʾîš rîv hāyîtî ʾānî vĕʿammî . . . mĕʾōd, he is not boasting of being "a contentious man" or parading his struggle with his own people; rather, he is emphasizing the private nature of the struggle he had with Ammon, with repeated accent on the first-person pronoun, even on ʿammî, "my people."[5] The argument is that Jephthah had appealed to the men of Ephraim (Qal of zāʿaq, here with ʾet+ rather than the usual ʾel+) to save him, but they would not respond; had they done so, he would have been personally indebted to their weapons. But Ephraim did not; so Jephthah, continuing to personalize the matter, claims, "I placed my own life in my palm." The idiom (lāśîm nefeš bakkaf) is about taking enormous risk, most strikingly when David faced Goliath (1 Sam 19:5) and when the "witch" of Endor practiced necromancy in the presence of the king who had forbidden it (1 Sam 28:21). It might be attractive to imagine that Jephthah is reflecting on the colossal chance he took in making his vow, for there is a hint of it in the way he attributes his victory and his personal safety to a bargain with God. Yet, with Jephthah having framed similar reasoning in his message to Ammon, it might be too charitable to find him introspective here.

Jephthah throws the onus on the people of Ephraim: By invading his space, they have brought war on themselves.

He struggles, searching, and then says, "Shibboleth. Faith is the true Shibboleth."

—*"Sibboleth," The West Wing (season 2, episode 16; November 22, 2000)*

12 4–6. The verb *qābaṣ* is associated with mustering troops, and in the Qal the subject is given control on how to do it and whom to draft. Jephthah is in full charge of Gilead now and will not hesitate to use his power. We are told that Gilead beat Ephraim, followed by a *kî*-clause that ordinarily gives explanation, whether for cause ("because") or to set a condition ("in case of"). It is not at all clear here how to treat it, for the quoted words are laconic, *pĕlîṭîm* are survivors of massacres (rather than fugitives or immigrants), and the Masoretic punctuation can be shifted so that the crucial *ʾattem* can address either Ephraim or Gilead.[6] One may ask, therefore, who is being cited when it says *kî ʾāmĕrû?*

> —Ephraim? If so, we might be dealing with a taunt against clans originally from Manasseh: Gilead, you are but fugitives *from* Ephraim, (hiding) in Ephraim and Manasseh. This is the most accepted suggestion. Rabbi Karo thinks Ephraim is shocked that Jephthah was made head without its approval.
> —Gilead? If so, it might read as impertinence: You are nothing but dregs from Ephraim; Gilead will take over Ephraim and Manasseh. This is a less likely interpretation.
> —An indefinite subject? If yes, then we might have a saying: "For it was said, 'You will always be fugitives from Ephraim, Gilead, whether in Ephraim or Manasseh.'" This reading would be the least likely.

Whatever is meant by this difficult clause, the narrative backtracks to illustrate how *one portion of the slaughter* unfolded. A battle seems to have already occurred in which Ephraim was mauled, and we are learning now what happened to survivors trying to escape by crossing the Jordan back to safer territory. We knew how dangerous such a venture could be when Ehud's men cut off the escape of Moabites by the Jordan crossing points (at 3:29).[7] The story supposes that no one but escaped soldiers from Ephraim would be crossing the waters, for otherwise, members from the eleven other tribes would also have had to submit to a test since they too could not be *ʾefrātî*.[8] Above all, it depends on a stated or alleged inability of soldiers from Ephraim to hear or pronounce the sibilant *sh* in the word *šibbōlet*; instead, they would give it as an *es* sound.[9] The incident is ignored by Josephus and Pseudo-Philo, but since rabbinic times, it has generated a flood of scholarship that, among others, raises the following issues:

1. *What might "shibbolet/sibbolet" mean and what is its etymology?* Hebrew gives a choice of meanings: either "ear of grain," a word nicely represented in the literature (Rahlfs B, στάχυς), or the slightly attested word for a "water stream" (as in Ps 69: 3 [2 RSV], 16 [15 RSV]).[10] The meaning ultimately may not matter, but for some exegetes it would make sense that the test word evokes the river setting: The men of Gilead would have pointed to the water and asked the escapees to say what it is. This

is certainly more likely than setting the trial by pulling out a stalk of grain from a knapsack. But what if the answer they give is one of a handful of Hebrew words for water and streams, none with a sibilant? In truth, people do not pronounce correctly what they hear, even after much prompting. (I cannot duplicate certain diphthongs in English even as a native speaker mouths them before me.)

2. *What is the implication of the difference in pronunciation?* We are told about the escaping soldier that *vĕlōʾ yākîn lĕdabbēr kēn*. The verbal form is often emended into *yāvîn*, "he understood" (after the Greek), or into *yākôl*, "he is able" (after the Syriac).[11] However, the Hebrew that we have makes good enough sense: Soldiers from Ephraim simply could not manage to shape the sound familiar to those from Gilead. Here the narrator became obtrusive in a stark way: To advance the point of the anecdote, a word was purposely (or not) misspelled by using the consonant *samekh* (ס) instead of the expected *shin* (שׁ). The scribe might have had another option, which was to use the *śin* (שׂ), but avoided it, at least because it was orthographically undistinguishable from *shin* and might have compromised the thrust of the story.

Given the Hebrew narrator's lack of interest in developing issues based on language differences, let alone intradialect distinctions, this whole episode could be anecdotal. Speiser (1967: 146) said as much, but equipped with a fine feel for linguistic authenticity, he joined many others (before and since) in reconstructing the distinct sounding of Semitic sibilants in Gilead and Ephraim and in charting their divergent development over the course of time.[12] The choices are at least four (Block 1999: 384 n. 157, with bibliography):

1. Proto-Semitic *s_1 (as in s_1blt) became *š* in Gilead, but *s* in Ephraim (Faber 1992).
2. Proto-Semitic *t̠* (as in *t̠blt*) was preserved in Gilead, but turned into *s* in Ephraim (Rendsburg 1988; Speiser 1967).
3. Proto-Semitic *s* (as in *sblt*) was turned into *š* in Gilead, but was preserved in Ephraim (Beeston 1979, 1988).
4. Proto-Semitic *š* (as in *šblt*) was preserved in Gilead, but turned into *s* in Ephraim (often).

All of these proposals have a fair amount of circular reasoning, with the massacre at the Jordan a source as well as an explanation for the reconstruction. A challenge is to find nonbiblical collaboration for any of these alleged shifts. In recent days, such an instance has been advanced (lastly by Rendsburg 1988; Hendel 1996) when an Ammonite seal with the likely royal name *bʿlyšʿ* (so **Baal-yāšaʿ/yišʿa*, with *shin*) was deemed equivalent to a *Baʿălîs* (with a *samekh*), the name of a king of Ammon cited in Jer 40:14 as implicated in the murder of Gedaliah.[13] This seems a reasonable resolution of the matter, except for the fact that in the Ammonite lexicon so far compiled, words with *shin* have the same phoneme in their Hebrew equivalence, whereas words that contain a *samekh* show the same correspondence in Hebrew.[14] This is not very encouraging. For this reason, it might be wiser to accept the suggestion that if there is any reality beyond the anecdotal, the same sibilant was pronounced distinctly by inhabitants on either side of the Jordan.[15] At the least, this approach might curb the gush of hypotheses that rely on this single notice to reconstruct tribal movements across the centuries (Lemaire 1985) or establish dialectical differences (Rendsburg 1988; Hendel 1996) that are hardly sustained by other biblical material on Ephraim and Gilead.[16]

SLAUGHTER

Whatever we decide about the meaning and implication of the incident, the immense slaughter is what the narrator would like us to notice.[17] Forty-two thousand (*’arbā‘îm ûšĕnayim ’ālef*) soldiers are said to have died *bā‘et hahî’*. This phrase bears a slightly different nuance when used to open a narrative sequence, setting the time in a general way (at 4:4, for example). Here it ends it and so serves to accent results specific to an occasion. We have seen such a usage at the conclusion of the Ehud story (at 3:29), with striking parallel.[18]

How many more of Ephraim died before the bloodbath on "this occasion" is not told. This particular number is beyond authentication, for testing and killing one person per minute would have taken a full month of twenty-four-hour slaughter. Still, such numbers favor effect over realism, and it would hardly serve the story to trick it into reading "forty-two *leaders*" (*’arbā‘îm ûšĕnayim *’alûf*).

A Final Notice on Jephthah

12 7. On this note ends the story of Jephthah. We are not told that he kept the land secure during his rule. God's absence remains conspicuous as the series of "minor" judges resumes (see Table 9). The formula is unusual here, not just because it occurs at the end of his rule—we will find an even more oddly placed instance midway in the Samson story, at 15:20—but because it is the only occasion when Jephthah is connected with judging (*vayyišpōṭ yiftāḥ ’et-yiśrā’ēl*). It is possible, therefore, as others have noted, that the language was picked up from what was applied to the minor judges.

Jephthah is given six years of reign, the briefest of any judge, so this is possibly a comment on his unsuitability as judge. Rahlfs B turns the number into sixty, possibly a confusion between the Greek ligature-number 6 (*stigma*) and 60 (*xi*) (Harlé and Roqueplo 1999: 195). An odder notice is about his burial place, literally among the "cities of Gilead" (*bĕ‘ārê gil‘ād*), fine Hebrew but difficult sense.[19] Unlikely is a parallel with Richard the Lionheart, whose organs (heart, entrails) and corpse were buried at diverse sites. With deft stroking of the Hebrew (*bĕ‘îrô bĕgil‘ād*), it is possible to match the Greek, with its "he was buried in his city in Galaad." Modern scholars are more precise, suggesting he was buried in Mizpeh, following the lead of Josephus (*Ant.* 5.270), who had him entombed in Sebee of Gilead, and of a number of Greek minuscules that locate the burial in Scph(e) (see Moore 1895: 310; Barthélemy 1982: 106).

The Masoretes broke into a new line at this point (*pĕtûḥâ*), thus framing events at the core of Jephthah's rule that collected since 11:32. They included victory against Ammon, the fateful vow and its consequence, and his massacre of Ephraim. There will be similar markings before 12:11, 12:13, and 13:1, effectively blocking out the few tidbits about the judges that follow.

The Other "Minor" Judges

When Tola and Jair, the first minor judges, were introduced at 10:1–5, two clauses were associated with their rule. The first, *vayyāqom ’aḥăr+* ("stepping up after" [someone]), presents the name of the judge; the second, *vayyišpōṭ ’et yiśrā’ēl* ("he was judge in Israel"), tells how long he was in power. Anecdotal material was sandwiched between them.

In this series, however, there is a slight shift, in that the verb *šāfaṭ*, "to judge," occurs in both clauses. This observation might suggest that the expansive formulation purposely discriminated from the previous series and as such was adjusted *after* the Jephthah narratives were inserted between them. The names of all three in this series of judges likely has an *-ān/ôn* expansion, a feature in Hebrew name creation that will continue with Samson's.

IBZAN

12 8–10. At least since Josephus, Ibzan of Bethlehem is associated with Judah (see Gass 2005: 349–52). (Vaticanus gives it as Βαιθμαν rather than Bethlehem.) The reference to Bethlehem encouraged rabbis to equate Ibzan with Boaz, husband of Ruth and ancestor of David, with many remarkable stories.[20] In fact, although both have names with difficult meanings, they share only one consonant (*bet*). *'Ibṣān* (Αβαισαν, Εσεβων) may simply mean the man from Ebez (*'eveṣ*), a town in Issachar, according to Josh 19:20. Given that the other minor judges were recruited from northern Israel, scholars feel encouraged to bring him out from Bethlehem, not of Judah, but of Zebulon, as located there in Josh 19:5, by the border of Asher. It might be noted that at 10:1–2 Tola is deemed to be from Issachar, and at 12:11–12 Elon is said to come from Zebulon. To avoid repetition of origins, many commentators assign Ibzan to Asher (for example, Boling 1975: 215–16). It would not be productive to dismiss (or defend) any suggestion.

The anecdote about Ibzan resumes the thread we have seen earlier concerning Jair of Gilead (at 10:4), about the great number of offspring he had: thirty sons and thirty daughters. To send daughters outside (*šillaḥ haḥûṣâ*) and bring women from outside (*hēvî' min-haḥûṣ*) is idiomatic for creating marriages outside one's family and clan.[21] The accent is not just on the good marriages he had for all of them, but that he used them to establish political connection beyond his area of control, as did rulers of the time. Ibzan's rule is not particularly long, but while the number "seven" mostly evokes good associations, this may not be one of them. Josephus praises him blandly (*Ant.* 5.271): "He did nothing in the seven years of his administration that was worth recording, or deserved a memorial. So he died an old man, and was buried in his own country."

ELON

12 11–12. Elon (*'êlôn*; Αιλων, Αιλωμ) was from Zebulon. He had a name with a meaning ("oak," see at 4:11; or an expansion of *'ayil*, "ram") that made it, with slight orthographic variations, favored by others—among them, interestingly enough, another man from Zebulon (Gen 46:14, Num 26:26). He gets a minimalist treatment, with mention only of the length of his rule and his place of burial, Ayyalon, "Deer Park," thus making a play that is more obvious in the Hebrew consonants (*'ylwn* = Elon; *'ylwn* = Ayyalon). There may indeed be a play on the names of the judge and his burial place, and it is not resisted in Rahlfs B, where both are given as Αιλωμ. The oddity is that the Hebrew weakens the pun by spelling the judge's name this time around *'êlôn*, so minus a *yôd*. We had already met a homonym (at 1:35), an Amorite town that the tribe of Dan failed to capture but that played a nice role in Hebrew historiography (see the dictionaries, often under "Aijalon"). Josephus (*Ant.* 5.272) has nothing much to say about "Helon," but Pseudo-Philo (*LAB* 41.2) has him take twelve cities from the Philistines. Interestingly, he is said to follow Addon, presumably Abdon.

12 13–15. The final judge in the series is Abdon (ʿavdôn; Αβδὼν).[22] As in the case of the first judge, Tola, his father (*hillēl*) is also cited. Several Abdons are mentioned in the Hebrew Bible (the name is based on ʿeved, "worshiper, slave"), this one being the most famous. He is said to come from Pirʿaton (Pirathon in most translations) (*pirʿātôn*), a town generally associated with Farʿata, a village about 6 miles southwest of Shechem (Gass 2005: 352–55). Spellings in Rahlfs A (Φρααθων) and B (Φαραθων) suggest slightly different pronunciations of the name.

The notice about Abdon is odd. It cites forty sons for him, from whom he had thirty grandsons. They were all important officials. (See above at 10:4 on the significance of riding colts.) Beyond the nice balance between the numbers of descendants and the colts (seventy), it is striking that Abdon produced this brood during his rule and that it included fewer grandsons than sons. For Pseudo-Philo (*LAB* 41.1), Addon, "son of Elech of Praton," replays Jephthah's conflict with Ammon; but this time it is Moab that sends out an ultimatum. Moab is bested in a war that costs it forty-five thousand souls.

Abdon is buried in his hometown, said to be in Ephraim territory. But there is also one more detail: It was in highlands named after Amalek dwellers (*har hāʿămālēqî*). Whether this tidbit conveys triumph against a hated foe or is a sinister signal cannot be assessed. Once more going its own way, Rahlfs A gives it as "in the mountain of Lanak." Because some Greek manuscripts also speak of it as in "the land of Sellem," an association with "the land of Shaalim" of 1 Sam 9:4 has been defended (Lagrange 1903: 220), but also dismissed (Burney 1970: 335).[23]

COMMENTS

In the Hebrew text, Jephthah is said to rule six years, but as already noted, this is sixty in one of the Greek versions—extreme numbers both. He is said to be buried not in Mizpah or even Tob, but in "the towns of Gilead," so lacking the precise location normally attached to other judges. Needless to say, such a riddle gave free rein to the rabbis (*Genesis Rabbah* 60.3), who had Jephthah die either in battle or from some disease that seriatim dropped his limbs in one city after another—a small price to pay for his bad judgment. Yet, on facing another invasion by the Ammonites, the prophet Samuel cited the great wonders God performed for his people, singling out Gideon and Jephthah among them (1 Sam 12:11).[24] It may therefore be that in some traditions Jephthah's reputation was much more appealing than what our narrator drafted for him. The portrait achieved in Judges, however, is what is retained over the centuries, and it is from it that we must reconstruct his character.

We draw that image of Jephthah from two full chapters (11 and 12) in the book of Judges that cover four scenes. In combination they provide a layered display of his character. As we have seen in the preceding segments, the first two scenes are about personal dislocation and adroit diplomacy (see the Comments to IIIG1). The third focuses on his vow and the last on fratricidal warfare, deeds that prove centripetal, displaying him at extreme edges of his traits. As such, they prove emblematic of him, his personality, and his career as a judge of Israel.

The Character of Jephthah

The sacrifice of Jephthah's daughter carried with it the death of his hopes for the future. There can scarcely be a more powerful indictment of Jephthah's conduct than the laconic comments on the commemoration of his rashness rather than his victory. Jephthah's story could have ended there, with the expected notice about his length of rule and place of burial. Yet, in attaching lore about Jephthah's war with his brethren, the narrator had more to say about his failures. That tradition, famous for its "shibboleth" incident, is sequenced after Jephthah's triumph over the Ammonites and relies on it for context. The Ephraimites, obviously seeking a share of the spoils, accuse Jephthah of warring without them. In the days of Gideon, the same tribe had a similar complaint, but Gideon knew how to mollify. Jephthah, instead, first accuses them of abandoning him and then attacks them. Even after defeating them, he corners and butchers an astronomical number of their fighters (forty-two thousand).

The confrontation, therefore, makes best sense if staged to occur at the end of the war with the Ammonites, and although I fail to find in its telling the literary vestiges for its timing, I am moved to propose that the narrator is setting the events not *after* the immolation of the daughter as vowed, but *during* the two-month surcease he gives her. If this is so, the episode would reveal how little Jephthah learned from his experience and how true to form the narrator has kept him to the last.[25]

Such a portrayal provides coherence to another of these interesting personalities that we find in Judges, but it also gives occasion to mull over the problem of power when there is a spiritual vacuum. Jephthah's story is framed between two series of short notices about minor judges and thus stands removed from the more substantial tales of Gideon and Samson on either side. Together with the involuntary support that God maintains during Jephthah's rule, the series of episodes acquires a parabolic texture. Jephthah, much like Saul, can display all the signs of success, but because he could not rise above the scars of rejection, he remains a troubled personality throughout. Opportunistic, he can grasp power although it is not his to have—but truth to tell, it is also not Israel's to give. Controlling, he imagines himself capable of manipulating Israel's God. He plans selfishly, and in one scene that distills his many faults as well as his few virtues, he makes a vow that illustrates his incapacity to adjust to life as a national leader. To the last, the narrator rigidly keeps Jephthah in character: During the two months in which his daughter resolutely faces a gratuitous death, Jephthah never summons the resilience to break his vow or the fortitude to risk himself in its consequence.

After Jephthah

Even after Jephthah dies, God's continued uninterest in Israel is made evident by the absence of the usual notice about sin, punishment, and deliverance that normally separates the rule of each judge. Three of them are said to lead Israel for a total of twenty-five years, not one of them challenged by the usual enemies God sends to discipline Israel. They seem simply happy with producing children and making nice *schiduch* for them. Ahead are stories about Samson, an adult with the hormones of an addled teenager, and about Eli and Samuel, priest-judges who would delegate authority to flawed sons; which is also to say that the experiment in giving rule to Israel via God-selected judges was running its course. Kingship will not be too far ahead.

Notes

Introduction

1. "An outsider came to Shammai and said to him, 'Convert me; provided that you first teach the whole Torah while I stand on one foot.' Shammai pushed him away with a builder's stick he had in hand. He then came before Hillel who converted him. He told him 'What is hateful to you, do not do to another. This is all the Torah, entirely—the rest is its commentary [זו היא כל התורה כולה ואידך פירושה הוא]. Go and study.'" A fine analysis of this anecdote is in Jospe 1990.

2. Eli and Samuel are both designated as judges, the first for forty years (1 Sam 4:18) and the second "during his whole lifetime" (1 Sam 7:15). Eli's corrupt sons never succeeded their father, God actually acting as a judge to end their hopes (1 Sam 3:13). Samuel guides Israel for a good amount of time. As he aged, he tried to bestow his office to his sons (1 Sam 8:1–3); by then, however, the run of judges had ended.

3. The book is often dated to the first century CE but seems to fit nicely in the Byzantine period. Its material likely developing over the centuries, with several manipulations; see Satran 1995 but compare with Schwemer 1995: I/65–71, both citing earlier scholarship.

4. In the commentary I have cited a number of them, under their customary names:

Ibn Kaspi:	Yossef (ibn) Kaspi or Yossef Kaspi (L'Argentières and Tarascon, 1279–1340)
Karo:	Yosef ben Ephraïm Karo (Toledo and Safed, 1488–1575)
Mitrani:	Yosef di Trani, the Younger (Safed and Istanbul, 1573–1644)

Other rabbis cited are called by their traditional acronyms:

Radaq:	David Kimḥi, also Kimchi or Qimchi (Narbonnes, 1160–1235)
Ralbag:	Levi ben Gershon, also Gersonides (Bagnols-sur-Cèze, 1288–1344)
Rambam:	Moshe ben Maimon, also Maimonides (Cordova and Fustat, 1135–1204)
Ramban:	Moshe ben Nachman, also Nachmanides (Gerona and Acres, 1194–1270)
Rashi:	Shelomo Yitzchaki (Troyes, 1040–1105)

5. In Judges we meet with about fifteen *hapax legomena*.

6. Barthélemy 1982: 73–127 is a fine analysis of readings from diverse translations, and I acknowledge its contribution. The Judges fascicle in the *BHQ 7* (Marcos 2011) gathers many suggestions from him and from other scholars. Incredibly insightful even when occasionally esoteric (not to say bizarre) are the many suggested readings of Ehrlich in both his German and Hebrew annotations to the book of Judges (republished in 1968 and 1969).

7. Good overviews (with bibliographies) of the literature on the Septuagint are available in Bible dictionaries or the like. A fine example is Melvin Peters's essay in the *ABD*. See also O'Connell (1996: 369–73). A wishful expectation that there once existed a prototype for all Greek translations of Judges is commonly conveyed, tellingly without much accord on how, when, or where.

8. Bodine (1980) has shown the difficulty of assigning the B text of Judges to any specific LXX family. The same can be said about Esther, also displaying diverse receptions in Greek.

9. Harlé and Roqueplo (1999) offer introductory pages with notices about their textual development. They also attend to textual comparisons among the versions and the Hebrew text. Good judgment on the issues is in Lindars 1986.

10. This is generally accepted, although there are counterarguments to the persistence of Hebrew as a living language well into the Roman period. No doubt, then as now, people had practical control of several languages. The issue is discussed extensively by W. Smelik (1995: 1–23).

11. See also the comments of O'Connell (1996: 373–82).

12. A more developed version of this section is in Sasson 2010.

13. These numbers will differ in the Greek versions of Judges. To obtain three hundred, we will need to include the rule of Abimelech, following Gideon's control that lasted forty years. In the accounting itself there is reliance on forty-year sequence, a conventional interval that covers a period between the birth of a male and that of his grandson.

14. This lack may be a primary reason for prompting Josephus and the slightly later midrashic chronograph, the *Seder Olam*, to fold their tenure within the harsh days of Cushan-rishatayim. *Seder Olam Rabbah* ("Sequence of the World," large version) is a midrashic tractate that may have had its earliest phases in the Talmudic period, as it is ascribed to the second-century *tanna* Yose ben Halafta. It likewise binds beginning to end: "In the days of Cushan-rishatayim occurred the idol of Micah . . . and the concubine of Gibeah [Judg 18–19]"; cited from chapter 12 (pp. 52–53) of the online scanning of D. B. Ratner's edition (Vilna 1897; see http://www.hebrewbooks.org/14282). Translation and commentary in Guggenheimer 1998: 121–23.

15. Whether kingship is actually experienced or merely recalled by the narrator's audiences can be debated, the issue of consequence on setting a pre- or postexilic date on this particular segment of Judges.

16. Most often cited is WB 444, manuscript "G" in Glassner 2004: 117–26 (English). A composite of diverse recensions is available at the ETCSL, http://etcsl.orinst.ox.ac.uk/cgi-bin/etcsl.cgi?text=t.2.1.1#, with a translation at http://cdli.ucla.edu/P384786. Some very fine studies on the Sumerian King List include Michalowski 1983, Wilcke 1989, and Marchesi 2010. A late-third-millennium forerunner dispensed with the prediluvian segment.

17. Shamgar must not be regarded as a true judge; see the Notes and Comments to IIIB, Judg 3:12–21.

18. "Hence it may be asked: What was the special character of Deborah that she, too, judged Israel and prophesied concerning them? In regard to her deeds, I call heaven and earth to witness that whether it be a heathen or a Jew, whether it be a man or a woman, a manservant or a maidservant, the holy spirit will suffuse each of them in keeping with the deeds he or she performs" (*Tanna děbe Eliyahu*, cited from Braude and Kapstein 1981: 152).

19. "One might call the Bible a chronicle of human rebellion. The history of Israel from beginning to end is motivated by defiance of God" (Kaufmann 1960: 295). Rabbinic lore has the following: "The plain fact [is] that of the four hundred and ten years God dwelt in the First Temple, for only twenty years of its existence was he alone worshiped there: during the remaining three hundred and ninety years the kings of Israel and the kings of Judah worshiped idols" (adapted from Braude and Kapstein 1981: 435). The twenty years of purity of worship likely matched those in which Josiah purified the sacred precincts.

20. The most succinct version, in fact, is given in a grand paean attached to the returning exiles in the days of Nehemiah (9:26–28): "Defying you, [the Israelites] rebelled; they cast your teaching behind their back . . . ; they committed great impieties. You delivered them into the power of their adversaries who oppressed them. In their time of trouble they cried to you; you in heaven heard them, and in your abundant compassion gave them saviors [*môšî˓îm*] who saved them from the power of their adversaries. But when they had relief, they again did what was evil in your sight, so you abandoned them to the power of their enemies, who subjugated them. Again they cried to you, and you in heaven heard and rescued them in your compassion, time after time."

21. This is the point as attributed to Moses himself. When in one of the many moments during Israel's trek in Sinai God threatens destruction of Israel to the people, Moses tells God, "If you kill this people to a man, the nations who have heard your fame will then say, 'because the Lord could not bring that people into the land he had pledged to them, he slaughtered them in the wilderness'" (Num 14:15–16).

22. According to the church fathers Eusebius and Cyril, Jews copied Judges and Ruth on one scroll so as to reduce the number of books in the Hebrew Bible from twenty-seven to twenty-two, equivalent to the consonants in the Hebrew alphabet; see Harlé and Roqueplo 1999: 21–22; Moore 1895: xiii.

23. The tradition is developed further in 2 Chr 35, with several innovations from the pentateuchal formulations, at Exod 12, Lev 23:5–8, Num 28:16–17, and Deut 16:1–8. The Passover in Hezekiah's time (2 Chr 30) is not known from any other sources, is celebrated in the second (rather than the first) month, lasts longer than what is prescribed elsewhere, and has a national rather than a family character.

24. They are preserved in Books 7 and 8 of the *Apostolic Constitutions*, among them this one: "Gideon, upon the rock and the fleeces, before his sin / Manoah—and of his wife—in the field / Sampson, in his thirst before his error / Jephthah, in the war, before his unwise promise / Barak and Deborah, in the days of Sisera . . . [added as an afterthought] Jael in praises"; cited from Fiensy and Darnell 1985: 684–85. It is interesting to note that the petition-prayer *mî šě˓ānâ* ("He who answered [followed by the name of an ancestor]") traditionally recited during the Yom Kippur service, skips from the miracle for Joshua at Gilgal (Josh 10) to the one for Samuel at Mizpah (1 Sam 7:9).

25. See Nickelsburg 1984: 33–87. A nice study of most of this material is Wills 1995. A good amount of midrashic lore in Talmudic material belongs here.

26. A serviceable online translation is at Internet Sacred Text Archive, http://www.sacred -texts.com/bib/bap/index.htm. Useful studies on Pseudo-Philo are that of Murphy

(1993) and the massive commentary of Jacobson (1996). DesCamp (1997) has a useful table comparatively displaying the biblical and Pseudo-Philo's takes on Deborah (68–70). Burnette-Bletsch (1998) studies the Sisera episode in Pseudo-Philo.

27. See also Josephus, *Ant.* 5.184, where Kenaz takes the place of Othniel. The two are pretty much in agreement that Kenaz uses an oracle in coming to the aid of Israel, but they say so for different reasons. In the pseudepigraphic *Lives of the Prophets* (§10) Jonah is said to be buried in the Cave of Kenaz, "who became judge of one tribe in the days of the anarchy."

28. The name for Saul, Ṭâlût, may have been crafted in paired assonance with Jâlût.

29. The Divinity School Library at Vanderbilt maintains a website that is helpful in reviewing liturgical citations of Scripture (http://lectionary.library.vanderbilt.edu/). I am grateful to my colleague Father Bruce Morrill for helping me navigate its information. Father Gregory Hohnholt of Holy Trinity Greek Orthodox Church (Nashville, TN) patiently answered my inquiries.

30. a. The Song of Deborah (Judg 5) is chanted as a *hafṭārâ* to supplement the synagogue reading of *pᵃrašat bᵉšallaḥ* (Exod 13:17–17:16), because the latter features the Song at the Sea. The two extracts celebrate the greatest of God's many acts on behalf of Israel. Ashkenazi Jews actually begin with chapter 4, giving them the longest reading in the cycle of *hafṭārôt*.

b. Jephthah's rise to power and his victory over Ammon (Judg 11:1–33) is placed in parallel with *pᵃrašat ḥuqqat* (Num 19–22:1), because the latter refers to Moses's request to pass through Edomite and Amorite lands. (See the Notes esp. to Judg 11:15–22.) It is interesting that when calendric adjustments (lastly in 2009) require the reading of this *pᵃrāšâ* jointly with *bālāq* (Num 22:2–25:9), the choice is to read the latter's *hafṭārâ*, Mic 5:6–6:8.

c. The annunciation to Samson's parents (Judg 13) is read in conjunction with the Nazirite laws of *pᵃrašat nāśōʾ* (Num 4:21–7:89). The accounts are made to complement each other in that neither displays full details on the practice.

31. The Service of the Salutations to the Most Holy Theotókos features odes chanted at Small Compline on the Fridays of Lent. Ode Six includes an *irmos* (είρμος) that poetically connects with Judg 6. It addresses Mary: "From you has dripped the refreshing dew, undoing polytheism's fever, and we therefore say to you: Rejoice, the fleece that was wondrously bedewed, O Holy Virgin, which Gideon foresaw"; cited from the Great Orthodox Archdiocese of America, http://www.goarch.org/chapel/chant/akathist.

32. Cited from Nabokov 1980: 207–8.

33. A fine entry into this rich load is dispersed in diverse chapters of Gunn 2005.

34. Chapters on diverse methods of analyzing the Bible are in McKenzie and Haynes 1993. A charming exploration of, as well as engagement with, many of these issues is in J. Collins 2005. Bal (1988b and 1992) explores how "disciplinary codes" control perceptions, applying her insights to the interpretations of two accounts of the murder of Sisera. Sakenfeld (2008) subjects the Jael episodes to a postcolonial reading. A borderland figure—neither of Israel nor of Canaan—and wife of another borderland figure (Heber), Jael is forced to decide between unappealing choices.

35. See O'Connell's Excursus One, "Compilation, Redaction, and the Rhetoric of Judges" (1996: 345–68).

36. Moore contributed a lighter version of his Judges commentary to the Holy Bible Polychrome Edition (1898b), in which the composite structure of the book was displayed in color, alas now fading in the copies I have seen. Before a consensus was achieved in the

wake of Wellhausen's sequence of sources, critical scholars discriminated among contributions made before, during, and after Deuteronomy; see O'Connell 1996: 348–49.

37. Others (among them Eissfeldt 1925) continued calibrating the influence of the sources. Simpson's contribution to the debate (1957) is practically a caricature of the method, with multiple subdivisions of the familiar sigla, diverse combinations of some of them under redactional control, as well as the identification of new sources (C). What stuns is the certainty of purpose as words and phrases are surgically cut and reassembled on the basis of highly subjective criteria.

38. O'Brien (1989: 3–23) and, more accessibly, Römer (2005) review the complicated story of how this theory was formulated and what has happened to it since its launching in 1943 (Noth 1981). See also Latvus 1998 and the nice collection of essays in de Pury, Römer, and Macchi 2000. In an introductory chapter, van Bekkum (2011: 7–92) has a nice overview of this past century's scholarship on "Historiography and Settlement Debate," covering many issues germane to recent studies of Judges.

39. See Liverani 2005: 292–307. Levin (2012) recognizes two steps: (1) Accounts of individual judges that first circulated orally reflect Iron Age I culture (so at the end of the second millennium). (2) A Deuteronomistic process that gave envelope to a written version of these tales. Van Bekkum (2011) also finds memory of Iron I culture in Judg 1 despite the manipulation of the text over time.

40. Guillaume 2004: 261.

41. The matter is not as clear cut as one would like, first because in the argument for sending judges at 2:16–18 verbal roots for both are juxtaposed. Additionally, both the first (Othniel) and the last (Samson) judges are known by both terms (or by derivative formations), as are several of the "minor" judges (see Table I). Writing about the same time, Beyerlin (1963a, 1963b) separated traditions by the formulation of Israel's outcry against oppression.

42. Gross's massive German commentary (2009) follows up on many of these matters. The Judges commentary by the late Barnabas Lindars was left incomplete in 1995. It likewise would have made for a very fine historical-critical contribution.

43. See Knauf (2010, table at 147), who lays out a stunningly exact procession for the accretion of written traditions, from as early as 875–850 BCE (the Song of Deborah, from the Omride court) to as late as 325–250 (Judg 1:22–26, depending on Samaritan traditions). Guillaume (2004, table at 255–56) similarly allocates Judges traditions to six stages (with substages), the latest at 150 BCE.

44. "Rather than attempting to resolve problems, I have tried to point them out and to indicate possible lines of approach. Rather than doing theology and making the texts present a message for our time, I have preferred to show what the texts are concerned to say and the problems with which they tried to cope" (Soggin 1981a: xii).

45. More accessible version of this work, with illustrations from Near Eastern texts and artifacts, is Block 2009.

46. "What is new is our access to early Israel's provisions for civil defense, that is the Yahwist variation upon institutions of the military muster, as known from Mari, together with its related conceptions of land tenure (inheritance) and regulations for distribution or restriction of booty (ḥerem)" (Boling 1975: 116; see pp. 15–17). Fleming (2012) has a more informed—but no less quixotic—application of Mari evidence in evaluating the traditions of early Israel.

47. Boling (1975: 29–31) reconstructs four stages, the first of which was orally communicated. The second was an eighth-century BCE pragmatic collection that, for brief gaps,

covered the story from 2:6 through Samson's death. There was also a seventh-century BCE "Deuteronomistic framework" (2:1–5; 6:7–10; 10:6–16; 16:1–18:31) and a sixth-century BCE "Deuteronomistic framework" (1:1–36; 19:1–21:25).

48. The numbers are disputed or guesstimated in many cases, but they include the desert wandering (forty), the conquest (more than five), Judges (see numbers above), Eli (forty), Samuel (more than ten), Saul (two, before the anointing of David), David (forty), Solomon (four, before the temple). The numbers are replayed in many publications; see, for example, Burney 1970: l–liv.

49. A. Mazar offers similar notions, albeit with different scenarios for the occupation, in Finkelstein, Mazar, and Schmidt 2007: 85–98. As others are doing (for example Redford 1992: 275–79 and Rainey 2008), Mazar suggests a link with the Shasu group, about which see at 2:14–15. In another study Bloch-Smith (2003) suggests a "Tell-Tale" approach that eschews "culture areas," in favor of setting up markers that distinguish Israel from the Philistines: "Circumcision, sporting a short beard rather than a clean-shaven face, and abstaining from eating pork" (422). While acknowledging that none of these may have been exclusive to Israel, she dates these "contextually meaningful practices" from the twelfth to the early tenth centuries BCE. Since her evidence for them comes from the Bible, Bloch-Smith proposes "that the process of 'narrativization,' of forming the 'collective memory of former unity' began in the twelfth or eleventh century B.C.E." All this is somewhat circular, relying on the very biblical evidence for distinctions (and dates of distinctions) that cannot be certified by archaeological means.

50. Halpern (1983b: 90–91; *ABD* 5: 1132–35) speculates that Israel developed out of elements from Egypt that picked up Yahwism from Edom. Entering Canaan east of the Jordan, they joined with hill natives recalled as "Israel" in the Merneptah stela. R. Miller (2005) introduces anthropological modeling (undervaluing the tribally rich Mari records) to re-create "chieftain kingdoms" for the Judges that, he eventually admits (pp. 22, 112), fits neither the archaeological nor the biblical evidence. Fritz (2011) gives a fine overview of the issues, albeit accenting the authenticity of biblical traditions on the conquest.

It is interesting to note that the same sort of dilemma on how to assess ancient evidence on tribal implantation confronts the study of the settlement of Amorite tribes in the Mari era, notwithstanding the availability of a relatively rich assortment of contemporaneous documents; see Whiting 1995 and Charpin and Ziegler 2003: 29–32.

51. An overview of the topic is in Niditch 2005.

52. See also Talmon (1993).

53. Niditch (2008) offers two translations (modified from Everett Fox's approach) that differ from each other by the level of attentiveness to Hebrew characteristics, both renderings meant to emphasize rhetorical patterning and to preserve the aurality of the literature. By wielding a "poetic prose" that blurs prose and poetry, Niditch wishes to reveal "the texture of Israelite 'ethnic genres'" (2008: 20). However, most of her clues for laying out the text in quasi-poetic format (possibly in reaction to Talmon's criticism) are based on the punctuation set by the Masoretes, the last hardly carriers of the bardic or the theological voices that, in her opinion, inform Judges. The halting, repetitive, heavily conjunctive language she produces risks archaizing the Hebrew, turning it quaint and distant. Moreover, converting English into a stilted language just to dramatize the peculiarities of a conjectured original Hebrew does not seem to me a useful strategy. With such blurring of phrasing, how does one recognize the shift into (and out of) a poetic mode when reading the Song of Deborah?

54. An estimate that I once read, but can no longer cite just now, is that over the centuries Europe has produced about four hundred artifacts (mostly paintings) that draw on the story of Jephthah. I would not doubt that a similar volume of production can be associated with the story of Samson, and likely also the murder of Sisera when linked to the thematically related killing of Holofernes. Useful compilations are gathered, under the name of each personality, in Jeffrey 1992. See also Müller, Ehninger, and Fess 2005, and del Olmo Lete 2000: 61–63.

55. A digest of Gunn's observations is available in Beal and Gunn 2009.

56. The discrepancy likely widened when the Masoretes attached vowels and punctuation a few centuries later. See also the Introductory Remarks at IIIG3 (Judg 12).

57. I have developed some notions about the use of Mari in biblical research in Sasson 1998a. The basic study on Mari and its history is *FM* 5 (Charpin and Ziegler 2003). Brief surveys of its culture are available in diverse biblical dictionaries and encyclopedias, but the richest review is in the *Supplément au dictionnaire de la Bible* 14: fasc. 77–78 (Paris: Letouzey and Ané, 2008), pp. 17–466. Durand's LAPO 16–18 form an indispensable set of collated translations, with magisterial overviews and incisive comments. Heimpel (2003) translates into English a vast number of Mari letters, essentially those published in ARM 26 and 27, plus a few others.

58. It is interesting to note that from the same material Kaufmann had argued that after Joshua the Canaanites were no longer a factor in Israel, even when Sisera's war is taken into account; Kaufmann 1960: 253–54; see also Kaufmann 1953: 87–91.

59. For explanation see Notes to 1:8–11.

60. See the notice under Judg 3:7–8a.

61. The singular "daughter" before a geographic name actually personifies that town, as in *bat ṣîyôn*, often rendered "daughter of Zion" (Isa 1:8, among others) when it simply means "Zion."

IA1. The Southern Tribes: Adoni-bezeq (Judg 1:1–7)

1. A fuller exposition of these issues is in Sasson 2008. Veldhuis (1999: 209) is helpful in understanding the process in Mesopotamia of reading divinely set signs. Thelle (2002) gives a very fine review of diverse practices and techniques in Israel for ascertaining God's wishes.

2. See also Num 12:6. Essentially, these are the same routes that are followed in Hittite Anatolia. Hoping to survive a virulent plague, Muršili II (late fourteenth century) begs the Ḥattian storm-god, "If, on the other hand, people are dying for some other reason [than my father's guilt], either let me see it in a dream, or let it be found by an oracle, or let a prophet declare it, or let all the priests find out by incubation whatever I suggest to them" (*ANET*[3], 396a).

3. It was possible to obtain responses by inquiring of a "curse" (Job 31:30) or of "Abel" (name or noun, 2 Sam 20:18). What is at stake here is not clear. The idiom is obviously instrumental when applied to teraphim (Ezek 21:26 [21 RSV], judged a pagan practice), a block of wood (Hos 4:12, sarcastically), and ghosts (1 Chr 10:13, denouncing Saul). Greek construes the verb ἐπηρωτάω, with either διά or ἐν to achieve a similar meaning (Harlé and Roqueplo 1999: 72). Targum, as is wont, avoids potential anthropomorphism by rendering *ûšĕʾîlû . . . bĕmêmĕrāʾ daYY* (W. Smelik 1995: 329). A somewhat similar range of meanings applies to the phrase *dāraš be-* (seldom also *dāraš le-*); see S. Wagner, *TDOT* 2: 302–3.

4. See comments in Sasson 1990: 108–10 and the article "*gôrāl*" in *TDOT* 2: 450–56 (W. Dommershausen). The major study on all aspects of the procedure is van Dam 1997. On Num 27:21, see Noort 1999. Note esp. 1 Sam 14 in which lots are cast to establish a reason for God's silence on how to proceed with battle. Saul shortens the search by setting Israel on one side and the royal line on the other as potential bearers of guilt. The (Old) Greek gives a more elaborate version of the procedure (quoted from *NETS*): "And Saoul said, 'O Lord God of Israel, why is it that you have not answered your slave today? If this guilt is in me or in my son Ionathan, O Lord God, give *clear ones* [Greek δῆλος = *'ûrîm*], and if this is what you say, "In your people Israel," give, now, *holiness* [Greek ὁσιότης = *tummîm*].' Ionathan and Saoul were indicated by the lot, and the people were cleared." (I have added the italics.)

5. See also 2 Sam 2:1: David asks God whether to select a town in Judah from which to rule. When encouraged to do so, he asks God to tell him which town to select.

6. David's anxiety duplicates that of Zimri-Lim, king of Mari, when fearing that his troops would be detained by his ally, Hammurabi of Babylon. Zimri-Lim asks his wife to pose the following questions to diviners or prophets: "For now, inquire about Hammurabi of Babylon: 'Will this man die? Will he be honest with us? Will he battle against us? If I go north, will he besiege us? What?' Inquire about this man. Once you inquire, do so again and send me a report about him on all you inquire" (ARM 26 185b = ARM 10 134 + 177). Perhaps from the same context, we have a dispatch by Erib-Sin, a diviner for a Mari army aiding Hammurabi of Babylon. He writes from Babylonia (near Sippar): "I made another round of omen-taking (inquiring as follows), 'My lord's army, which he sent Hammurabi: this army, will Hammurabi not stir it to revolt; not exterminate it; not have it exterminated? Will he keep it captive, for harm or good? Having left Mari's gate intact, will its men reenter Mari alive?'" (ARM 26 100b). Repetition as a means of narrowing ambiguity is by no means confined to the Semitic world. For Ḫatti, see Beal 2002: 32–33. A particularly striking example occurs in an Egyptian inscription of Neferkare Amunemnisu (Twenty-First Dynasty, 1043–39): A priest places before the god Amun a series of (seven!) inquiries on whether to permit the return of banished palace officials (Ritner 2009: 124–29).

7. Commentators have unappreciatively excised parts or the entire original query; for an example of trimming for historicity, see Veijola 1984.

8. The phrase is not to be confused with *vĕ'aḥar môt-* (+ name), in 1 Chr 2:24.

9. The Greek, however, calls on the equivalent formula καὶ ἐγένετο μετὰ τὴν τελευτὴν (name) only in opening Joshua and Judges. But it is also found in 2 Chr 24:17 (for Hebrew *vĕ'aḥărê môt* [name]) and in 1 Macc 9:23.

10. Ehrlich 1968: 67 treats *lānû* as a partitive.

11. Fuller and more exact listing is in Weippert 1976–80.

12. On all this, see, Na'aman 1994a and Rainey 1996, as well as exchanges between Lemche 1998 and Na'aman 1999.

13. For a more nuanced description, see Na'aman 1986a: 244–51 (with bibliography).

14. There is even disagreement whether to treat Judah as a personal or a place name; see Zobel, *TDOT* 5: 483–86.

15. The idiom is found in nonmilitary contexts in Gen 50:14 (Jacob's sons join Joseph in returning to Egypt after burying their fathers) and Exod 12:38 (rabbles joining the Hebrews exiting Egypt).

16. For that matter, the same lack of extrabiblical attestation and surplus of idle scholarly speculation attends the Girgashites and Jebusites. From Ugaritic evidence we know that

the Rephaim were no race of giants or preconquest Levantine warriors, but the shades of dead leaders. See the dictionaries under each of these names, and also Ishida 1979.

17. Na'aman (1988) depends on this solution to unnecessarily place a late date on this tradition.

18. See Zertal's discussion in the *ABD* 1: 717–18; but see also Dorsey 1991: 173; Welten 1965; and Gass 2005: 9–11.

19. *Ant.* 5.121: "[The Canaanites] expected the Israelites with a great army at the city Bezeq, having put the government into the hands of Adoni-bezeq, which name denotes the *Lord of Bezeq*, for *Adoni* in the Hebrew tongue signifies *Lord*." Some commentators, for example Boling (1975: 55), adopt this rendering.

20. Lindars 1995: 16 cites and rejects Noth's opinion that the name was original there.

21. On all these points, see esp. Moore 1895: 14–17; Burney 1970: 4–6; and G. Wright 1946.

22. Note *bYoma* 22b, "Whence do you know that the word 'bezeq' is here used in the sense of being broken [i.e., pebbles], perhaps it is the name of a place, as it is written: And they found Adoni-bezeq in Bezeq."

23. For good measure, they also struck her with epilepsy.

24. Mutilation follows long after a body has turned to dust, as it has been increasingly noticed since Nylander (1980) discussed the mutilation of Sargon's copper head. Note also Assurbanipal's statement, "I cut off his [i.e., the statue of an Elamite king's] nose, which he had turned into a seer" (cited from the *CAD* Š/1, 370b).

25. Relying on the Amarna tablet to judge the prominence of Bezeq versus Jerusalem is not a reliable method for evaluating anecdotes. At any rate, Jerusalem was a bit more than a hovel then; see below at Judg 1:8.

26. The Targum (see also the Vulgate) needless adds *laḥmā*, "bread"; see W. Smelik 1995: 332.

27. In Ps 97:7 we have the oddity of foreign gods prostrating themselves before the Hebrew God (*hištaḥăvû-lô kol-ʾĕlōhîm*).

28. Cited from Frame 1995: 293.

29. We shall revisit this device several times in Judges, among them at 3:26–28, 4:6–7, 6:2–5, and 11:32–34.

30. According to 1 Sam 17:54, Goliath's head was displayed in Jerusalem. This notice anticipates the city's future centrality. For the burial of an enemy's head far from the scene of his death, see ARM 6 37 (= LAPO 17 #635, pp. 326–27). The head belonged to Qarni-Lim of Andarig, an ally of Zimri-Lim; see note 30 at IIID2 (Judg 6:33–8:3).

31. The verses are cited in the Comments to Judg 1:22–36 (IB1). See also Aharoni 1967: 211–17.

32. This is a paraphrase of a good portion of a text that is published in Durand 1993 and has since then been the subject of numerous studies. An accessible English rendering (with discussion) is in Sasson 1994a: 314–16.

IA2. The Southern Tribes: Achsah (Judg 1:8–15)

1. See the fine studies of Pintore 1978, Schulman 1979, Maier 2000, and Liverani 1990: 274–82. Hebrew lore reports many such marriages in which brides are given to vassals (Jehoram of Judah marrying Athaliah of Israel) and to rising chieftains (David marrying Merab/Michal). They are also given to cement tribal connections (Shechem wishing to marry Jacob's daughter) and to strengthen mutual agreement between local chieftains

(David marrying a princess from Geshur) and powerful states (Ahab marrying Jezebel of Tyre).

2. Luckily, a merchant manages to retrieve this wealth (not clear how), earning a temple sinecure for himself and his descendants. A recent review of this text is in Durand and Marti 2003: 145–49. They cite Neo-Assyrian examples (pp. 145–46 n. 22).

3. SH891; see Eidem, *SA1* 78: 9′–15′, and below on 1 Kgs 9:16. For *ana šarrak[ūt] mārtīya*; perhaps read *ana šarratūt mārtīya*, "for my daughter in her status as queen."

4. A fine overview is in Lafont 1987, but the major study of the dossier is by Ziegler 1999. An earlier study is in Batto 1974. A number of letters of princesses are translated into French in LAPO 18 #1221–50, pp. 426–79. Bodi has exploited some of the dossiers in his study of Michal (2005) and of David's kingship (2010).

5. Naramtum, married to Šarraya of Eluḫut, a strong supporter of Zimri-Lim, writes to her father: "I have no other father beyond you; beyond my lady, I have no mother. Here, now, the palace's maidservants are gathering against me, saying, 'There, in your father's house, nobody knows or worries about you. Should we, then, honor you (here)?'" (ARM 10 46 = LAPO 18 #1237, pp. 455–56).

6. That both Atamrum and Ili-Ištar met violent ends should not affect our assessment of the sisters' capacity to take charge of their world. We do not know what happened to either princess after the fall of their husbands; they either entered the harem of the victors, not necessarily for sexual access, or were consigned as priestesses in a temple.

7. This letter is tricky in that Inbatum speaks of her father and of her husband as her "lord." To clarify matters, I have substituted "my father" and "my husband" as appropriate.

8. On these matters, see Perrot 1969; fine online comments and bibliography by J. M. Oesch at WiBiLex (www.wibilex.de), http://tinyurl.com/ayg2n4r.

9. Qumran fragment 4QJudgᵃ skips over Judg 6:7–10, a passage that is set between two *pĕtûḫôt* in the MT. On this basis, Trebolle Barrera (1991: 94) proposes that these symbols drew attention to sutures in the text for inserted material. Unfortunately, the lamentable nature of the Qumran fragment as well as the absence of spacing (*vacat*) where 6:6 and 11 are linked weaken his proposal; see further the Notes to Judg 6:7–10.

10. The narrative in Josh 10 is so highly reminiscent of Gen 14 (Abram fighting a coalition that threatens Sodom, where his nephew Lot has made a home) that tradition made a link between Jerusalem and Salem (Gen 14:18, Ps 76:3), and so have many scholars. There are also many proposals to emend the reference(s).

11. See any biblical dictionary. Boling and Wright (1982: 167) have made a no longer tenable connection between Jebus and Yabasûm (from a root *bsʾ* rather than *ybs*), a Simʾal clan (*gāʾum*) mentioned in the Mari archives, and this is repeated in many dictionary entries. There are also efforts to separate Jerusalem from Jebus, attributing the misidentification to scribes or editors; see, as one example, J. Miller 1974.

12. Collected attestations are in Otto 1976–80. Maeir 2011 offers a good review of Jerusalem before the Hebrews. The execration texts are translated in *ANET*³, 328–29. Examples from the Amarna tablets are translated on pp. 487–89, but see Moran 1992 for new renderings. Widely reported in 2010 was the recovery of a small cuneiform fragment that dates to the same period; see Rollston Epigraphy, "Reflections on the Fragmentary Cuneiform Tablet from the Ophel," http://www.rollstonepigraphy.com/?p=90.

13. The spelling *yrvšlym* occurs in Jer 26:18, plus four more times in Chronicles; note also *yĕrûšālaymâ* in 2 Chr 32:9.

14. Similar imagery is found in Greek, ἐν στόματι ῥομφαίας. For the Targum's *lepitgam dĕḥārav*, see W. Smelik 1995: 332–34.

15. The word *ḫibrum* seems to refer to a nomadic unit that has not yet settled down or is not linked by blood ties, for in one juridical text (ARM 8 11) the term is contrasted with the behavior of settled folk. It often occurs in the phrase *ḫibrum ša nawêm* and so is associated with transhumant flocks. Comparative anthropology notwithstanding, a Mari document shows that we are yet to fully grasp how the tribal system worked in Mari, let alone in Scripture where it was an institution perceived though utopian filters.

> . . . the elders of Dabiš [a Benjamin town] came here and said, "In origins, we were not *yaradum* among the Yaḫurra-tribe; but in the encampment [*nawûm*] we have neither a *ḫibrum* nor a *ka-di*. We are therefore *zurûḫātum* for/at the Yaḫrur-tribe. We want, therefore, to move into the Sim'al-tribe itself, among the people of Niḫad, and slaughter a donkey-foal.
>
> When I answered (them), "I must write, to the king," they said, "Do so!" I kept them waiting a full day and after I questioned them (again), they said, "Do write, to the king!" A third time I asked them and still they answered me in a similar vein. Now then, the God of my lord should declare whether because the towns of Ura, Šakka, and Puzurran slaughtered a donkey-foal, Dabiš, Ilum-Muluk, and Samanum ought to do the same. And if I am to slaughter the donkey-foal of Dabiš my lord should promptly convey a reply to my tablet. (A.981: 32–53, cited from Durand 1992: 117–18)

The elders of Dabiš were feeling a loss of status among the Yaḫurra, a component of the Bin-Yamina, a tribe recorded in the Mari archives that, some have argued, was a direct ancestor of the Hebrew Benjaminites. Having lost their status as *yaradum*, they now lacked an authoritative body (the *ḫibrum*) to give them support. They consequently wanted to move out of their tribe and join the Bensim'al confederation. To do so, they needed to sacrifice a donkey, a ritual that seems confined to tribal groups from Mari, although it is featured in *kispum* rituals for ancestors (Jacquet 2011: 202–9). That people could shop around for a tribe to which to declare allegiance through a sacrifice is a notion that is as yet unattested from ancient Near Eastern documents.

Amorite *ḫibrum* can also have formed the base for a personal name, in this case Ḫibran (Durand 1997: 643 n. 578). There will be comments soon on Heber the Kenite (at Judg 4:11). Admittedly, it is possible that Amorite *ḫibrum* is related to *ʿbr*, verbal forms of which now occur in Mari documents (ARM 14 50: 14 and 72: 18). See Anbar 1991: 77–79, 161–66.

16. In Egyptian sources, Tanis (San el-hagar in the northeast Nile delta) was said to be founded during Ramses IX's nineteenth year (circa 1087 BCE). However, earlier, Ramses II had set its inception four hundred years before Sethy, then an official (*ANET*³, 252–53). See Geoffrey Graham's entry in the *OEAE* 3: 348–50.

17. In 1986, a portion of an Akkadian cuneiform tablet was discovered at Jebel er-Rumeyde, a hill just west of Hebron, so possibly its site at one time. (Even when fortified and the locus of a temple, a named town can move from one hill to another over time, and this might explain the dearth of Late Bronze material in Hebron itself.) It is an administrative text, with the mention of a king occurring several times. The personal names cited were West Semitic and (one) Hurrian. The tablet is judged to come from the seventeenth or sixteenth century BCE; see Anbar and Naʿaman, 1986–87.

18. In Gen 35:27 Greek gives εἰς Μαμβρη εἰς πόλιν τοῦ πεδίου ("at Mambre, at a city of the plain") for the Hebrew *mamrēʾ qiryat hāʾarbaʿ*.

19. The Anakim are yet another folk that Hebrew traditions place in Canaan before the conquest and that are as yet not attested extrabiblically. Some scholars, however, find them in the Egyptian execration texts (*y'nq*) of the early second millennium (*ANET*³, 328–29). In biblical lore, they are said to be a race of giants, mostly in the Judean hills but, according to Josh 11:21–22, also everywhere else.

20. Midrash *Genesis Rabbah* (58:4, Soncino edition):

    It had four names: Eshcol, Mamre, Kiriath-arba, and Hebron. Why was it called Kiriath-arba? Because four righteous men dwelt in it: Aner, Eshcol, Mamre, and Abraham; and four righteous men were circumcised in it: Abraham, Aner, Eshcol, and Mamre. Again, four righteous men were buried therein: Adam, Abraham, Isaac, and Jacob. Four matriarchs were buried therein: Eve, Sarah, Rebekah, and Leah. Or, on account of its masters, who were four, viz. Anak and his three sons. R. Azariah said: Because from there went forth Abraham, who pursued four kings, each a mighty ruler. Further, because it fell to the lot of four: first to Judah, then to Caleb, afterwards to the priests, and finally to the Levites.

21. On such formations in Judah nomenclature, see already the comments of Burney 1970: 9–10.

22. It is possible for us to "recover" the name of king who was defeated by Joshua if we transpose a phrase in Josh 10:3 to read "Eglon, king of Debir," since "Debir" as a personal name occurs only here. Admittedly, "Eglon" occurs as a place name as well as a personal name, but see Barr 1990, who finds such a solution too simplistic.

23. *Sefer* can have this meaning (*DNWSI* 800; see Boling and Wright 1982: 293, "Town of the Treaty-Stele"). I don't see the advantage of changing the vowels of the second element into *sōfer* just to obtain "Scribe City," despite Talmudic equivalence between Aramaic *spr'* and Persian *dbyr*, "scribe"; *bAvodah Zarah* 24b, taken up by Radaq. For the Targum *qiryat 'arkê* and its proper rendering, see W. Smelik 1995: 335. In some commentaries, there is reference to a Bet-sofer ("Scribe House") that occurs in P. Anastasi 22: 5 (*ANET*³ 477) and that, interestingly enough, is mentioned next to Qart-'anba (i.e. "Grape City"), a name reminiscent of Anab, a nearby town mentioned in Josh 15:50. But as long as we do not know their exact locations, no equivalence can be proposed. On the testimony of Jerome (cited in Abel 1938: 2, 422) the name "Cariatsepher" was still alive in his days.

24. Num 13:30; but with Joshua in 14:6–9. There is a great deal of discussion in the literature on how to discriminate between a Caleb son of Jephunneh (said to be a descendant of Qenaz) and, at 1 Chr 2:18, a Caleb son of Hezron (said to be a descendant of Perez). (There is even a "Caleb son of Hur" in 1 Chr 2:50, but the phrase is almost always split, and the two names are distanced from each other.) This is not easy, as our genealogical sources, especially those by the Chroniclers, are prolix enough to instill confusion. Compare, for example, statements about Caleb (occasionally also Chelubay) in 1 Chr 2:18–24, 42–50, and 4:11–20. The lists can repeat homonyms within several generations, adding to the suspicion that even in antiquity no one had it easy. Luckily, the issue is not of major import to us here. See the dictionaries under "Caleb," "Kenizzites," "Hezron," "Jephunneh," and the like.

25. This is preferred over "raging with canine madness," as proposed in Zadok 1988: 70, via Nöldeke. Names taken from the animal world (Leah, Rachel, Hamor, Tola, Deborah, Nahash, etc.) can also be totemic and are common to Near Eastern onomastica. Com-

paring someone to a dog may indeed be insulting (see *kalbu* in *CAD* K, 72), but it can also be said in admiration. Ishbi-Erra, who outfoxed his Ur III masters to become king of Isin, was reputed to have had "the cunning of a dog." Rabbinic literature was not pleased with the canine explanation, offering instead, "They called him 'Caleb' because he turned [*pny*, a pun on Jephunneh] his heart [*lbyh*] from the advice of the spies" (Targum to 1 Chr 4:15, cited in W. Smelik 1995: 338). A variant explanation is cited below.

26. In Achsah's case a bangle or the like; see by-forms of the root in Prov 7:22, Isa 3:16–18, and Stamm 1967: 328 [= 1980: 124].

27. In fact, there is rabbinic discussion on the issue (*bTemurah* 16a; see also *bSotah* 11b and Midrash to Num 13:6), complicated by a notice that connects Othniel with Jabez:

> But was Caleb the son of Kenaz? Was he not the son of Jephunneh?—The meaning of the word Jephunneh [*ypn*] is that he turned [*pny*] on the root [*klyb*, pun on Caleb] from the counsel of the spies. But still was he [Caleb] the son of Kenaz? Was he not the son of Hezron, since it says: And Caleb the son of Hezron begat Azubah? [1 Chr 2:18]—Said Raba: He [Caleb] was a stepson of Kenaz. This can also be proved, since it says: Caleb the son of Jephunneh the Kenizzite, but does not say the son of Kenaz. [That is he was his stepfather.] A Tanna taught: Othniel is the same as Jabez [see 1 Chr 2:55]. He was called Othniel because God answered him, and Jabez because he counseled and fostered Torah in Israel. And what was his [real] name? Judah the brother of Simeon. And whence do we derive that God answered him?—Since it says: And Jabez called on the God of Israel saying, Oh that thou wouldst bless me indeed and enlarge my border, and that thine hand might be with me, and that thou wouldst keep me from evil that it may not grieve me! And God granted him that which he requested [1 Chr 4:10].

28. Block (1999: 96–97) is anachronistic when he speaks of Kenaz, Caleb, and Othniel as proselytes who became "thoroughly integrated into the faith and culture" of Israel. Requiring religious allegiance did not harden until the Hellenistic period. Moreover, as we saw above (at 1:10), movement in and out of tribal units was not restricted.

29. In the Mari archives "brother," when not a blood kin, is metaphoric for *political* equivalence, apparently not at stake here; see Sasson 1998b: 462–64.

30. The ceremony of bringing the bride to the groom (occasionally vice versa, as implied in Judg 14:11, possibly also at Cant 3:9–11) is recorded in the literature, especially when it involved the elite and required long-distance match-making; see Gen 24:67 (on a camel); Ps 45:14–16 (on foot); and 1 Macc 9:37–39 (large retinue). At Mari, the procession was termed *ḥuddušum*; see A.1124 (= LAPO 18 #1014, pp. 179–80), sent by a Mari official to his king: "I have had the bride enter (the home) of my lord's servant (the groom). As for news of the marriage procession . . . (it takes place) within 4 days."

31. The readings are reviewed in detail in Barthélemy 1982: 35–37; see also Harlé and Roqueplo 1999: 76 and Lindars 1995: 28–29. Hess 1999: 144 cites "ambiguity" in legal terminology to explain the discrepancy on whether Othniel or Achsah initiates the request. It is hardly that.

32. Mosca (1984) has a faulty understanding of Hebrew syntax in rendering our phrase "When she arrived, she beguiled him [Caleb], asking from her father arable land." Minimally, such a reading would require us to have *vattišʾal rather than *lišʾôl*. Also why have "her father"? Ehrlich (1968: 46) suggests (not quite idiomatically) *vattesîrēhû*, "she made him take her side."

33. The Targum goes its own way by speaking here and in v. 15 about an *'aḥsontā*, "property, inheritance"; W. Smelik 1995: 338–40.

34. The Judges version, in fact, has *"the* field" (as in most Greek versions) and so encourages the notion that we are dealing with Hebron. It is possible that the article in Judges is the product of dittography, the scribe simply doubling the "he" from the preceding word *'ābîhā*, "her father," and attaching it to *śādeh*, "field," which may not have had an article; see Harlé and Roqueplo 1999: 76–77.

35. In a nice note dating to just after Hammurabi's reign, King Aqba-Ḥammu of Qaṭṭara writes to his wife, Iltani (*OBTR* 66 = Dalley, Walker, and Hawkins 1976: 65–66),

> I have heard the letter you sent to me. You wrote to me about your sister saying, "No donkeys are available for me to convey her to my lord." But you also wrote about travel to Rabātum. I have now conveyed donkeys to you. You are to ride them to Rabātum. Once you reach Rabātum, let [your sister] ride these donkeys and convey her to me. As to your provisions about which you wrote to me, I have collected money, donkeys, and the donkey drivers who are headed to the king [Hammurabi?]. I will send them to you following this note.

36. Most translations do not distinguish between genders, simply giving "ass" or the like. The word *ḥămôr* can generically apply to a jenny (2 Sam 19:27); see In der Smitten *TDOT* 4: 465–70 and Borowski 1998: 90–99. Yet when wealth is said to include donkeys, it involves jennies (1 Chr 27:30; Job 1:3, 42:12). Male donkeys, unless castrated, tend to be unreliable, as they are likely to drive heedlessly toward a female in heat. Deborah Cantrell suggests to me that, rather than sex difference, "ass" and "jenny" refer to different breeds of donkeys, some more suitable for riding than others.

37. There are scholars who suppose that the multiplicity of textual readings permits reconstructing the "original" text; not surprisingly, they differ in results; see Lindars 1971, Grossfeld 1973, and Nicholson 1977.

38. *bTemurah* 16a: "What does the word *wa-tiznaḥ* mean? Raba reported in the name of R. Isaac: She said to him: Just as an ass when it has no food in its trough immediately cries out [play on *ṣvḥ* or *ṣr*] so a woman when she has no wheat in her house cries out immediately [as it says: And Caleb said unto her: What wouldst thou?]."

39. Criticizing a philology that observes traditional interpretations, Bal has Achsah clapping her hands. Not only is the derivation from Arabic for *vattiṣnāḥ* (allegedly *ṣaḥana*) doubtful, but Hebrew is particularly rich in idioms for the clapping of the hands (*kāp*, "hand palm" as object of a number of verbs: *nākā, sāfaq, māḥā', tāqa'*), reflecting a broad range of emotion (anger, derision, exasperation, joy), none of which easily fits Bal's "phatic" application of drawing attention.

40. See, among many others, Gibson 1976.

41. Contra Joüon and Muraoka (1996: 442 [§125ba]). Ehrlich (1968: 46) simply suggests emending the text accordingly. See Lemos 2010: 55–56, who collects a number of interpretations.

42. Adopted by the New Revised Standard Version (NRSV) and the Revised English Bible (REB); see Lemos 2010: 55–56.

43. Rights over water resources have launched conflicts from time immemorial and are central to a number of narratives, including the Sumerian Gilgamesh and Agga stories (Katz 1993; Civil 1999–2000). See also Gen 21, 26.

44. The adjective *'illît* occurs only here, but *taḥtît* is fairly well-represented, frequently as an attributive to Sheol and its epithets (Deut 32:22, Ezek 31:14–18). The Joshua equiva-

lent to the anecdote gives the attributes as ʿillîyôt/taḥtîyôt, which superficially look like an adjectival plural, so harmonizing with gullōt. The last also superficially, looks like a feminine plural noun. In fact, the -ôt is acting like an abstract ending, as is clear from several occurrences of taḥtîyôt (ʿillîyôt is unique), most referring to the lowest reaches of the Netherworld (for example, Ps 88:7; Isa 44:23; Lam 3:55; Ezek 26:20, 32:18–24; see GKC 397–98 (§124d,f). For unclear (to me) reasons, Albright 1968: 42–45 treats these terms as "archaic."

45. Hallo (2004) makes an incongruous connection among the leeches of Prov 30:15, the Arabic names of wells near Khirbet Rabûd (allegedly recalling leeches, but other meanings are possible), and Achsah's behavior. Pseudo-Philo's *LAB* (29) may preserve a garbled account of this story in the tale of Zebul, successor to Kenaz as Israel's first judge (see above), who gives land to his daughters, one of them, Odihel, possibly Othniel; see Jacobson 1996: 822–27.

46. See also Rainey and Notley 2006: 15–16.

47. There are places that have slightly different spellings of their names, especially when cited in different books; for example, Qiryat-yearim (Josh 9:17 and others) is called Qiryat-arim in Ezr 2:25 (see Kiriathiarius in 1 Esd 5:19). This is common in antiquity, as both scribal spelling traditions and phonemic writing differed.

48. Such double names are not unknown; see Woestenburg and Jagersma 1992 and Charpin 2003.

49. Westbrook (1991: 143) cites the dowry of a woman from Sippar. Rich though it may be, the list cannot compare to the luxury accompanying a princess-bride as reported in the Mari archives; see Lafont 1987: 118–19. Lemos (2010) distinguishes between two phases in the application of marriage gifts: bridewealth was accented in preexilic literature while dowry came to predominate in postexilic documentation. Building on the work of Jack Goody, she argues that the shift was affected by social changes that occurred in ancient Palestine during the same period. Ancient Near Eastern material does not support a linear evolution in marriage gift exchanges but indicates differences depending on status and individual circumstances. Lemos struggles to sustain coherent conjunctures when even in its paucity the material is not wholly supportive; see 2010: 230–36. A rich storehouse of accessible information on these subjects is in Westbrook 2003 (see index).

50. On such matters, see Westbrook 1991: 142–64, esp. 147–48. For a fuller treatment of the Mesopotamian material, see Westbrook 1988: 29–34, 99–102. For the Neo-Babylonian period, see also Abraham 1993 (basing herself on Roth 1989a, but also citing Greek and Hellenistic features). A large number of articles on the topic well worth inspecting are in Lesko 1989. It should be admitted that the vocabulary for marriage transactions is rather slippery, possibly because of regional and temporal differences.

IA3. The Southern Tribes: Chariots of Iron (Judg 1:16–21)

1. Much has been written on this topic. For succinct reviews, see de Vaux 1961: 258–67. Lohfink (*TDOT* 5: 180–99) is especially careful with the vocabulary and reviews potential parallels from Greece, Rome (*devotio*), and ancient Europe. The classic study of von Rad (1991) is now translated into English, with a good review of the history of the discussion (by B. C. Ollenburger) and a nice bibliography (by J. E. Sanderson). Von Rad's opinion is succinctly challenged by Gottwald in the *IDBSup*, 942–44. J. Collins (2003: 4–10) assesses ḥērem among other acts of violence related in the Bible. Otto (1996) sets it within ancient Near East contexts.

2. Internecine wars can also be divinely guided, as when denial of God is at stake; see Deut 13:13–18.
3. Routledge 2004: 150.
4. Deut 7:1–2 and 20:17; the last is minus the Girgashites. Among the battles are those against Canaanite Arad (Num 21:1–3), Amorite Sihon and Og (Num 21:21–35), and the Midianites (Num 31:1–54). On the destruction of Canaan in Hebrew literature, see B. Schwartz 2004.
5. Somewhat similar conclusions are offered by Hoffman 1999. Among the more bizarre justification for the *ḥērem* is that it was an instrument for controlling epidemics, for example, in Jericho as carried by snails (Boling 1983).
6. M. Liverani has stimulating chapters on this topic in 1990: 115–79. The mythologization of conflicts as a major component of the *ḥērem* is exploited by P. Stern 1991, but his thesis is heavily criticized in Mayer 1995.
7. King Mesha (but most probably via his son) tells us that he "killed all the townsfolk [from the tribe of Gad] as *libation* for Chemosh" (11–12) and that after taking Nebo, "I killed its complete population—7000 males and *boys*, women and *girls*, maidservants too—for I devoted (the town) to Ashtar-Chemosh. But I took all of YHVH's vessels and displayed them before Chemosh." (The number seven thousand is obviously symbolic.) The Mesha stela is widely quoted, for example in *ANET*³, 320–21, and *COS* 2: 137–38. A readable study (with nice bibliography) is K. Smelik 1991: 29–50, 171–72; but see also K. Smelik 1992. Fine contributions are in Liver 1967 and Dearman 1989. Green (2010: 95–135) discusses the ideology of kingship, here most concerned with erasing shame and restoring honor.
8. See Charpin 1997, but also van der Toorn 1985. The eating of the *asakkum* (an herb) finds its closest equivalent in Num 5, when a potion is imbibed to decide on the fidelity of a married woman.
9. Writes the god Šamaš: "Before the defeat of the enemy, I had sent you Kanisanum regarding the consecrated portion [*asakkum*] of the god Addu. Collect the entire portion and have it brought to the Aleppo temple of Addu" (ARM 26 194: 13–17). There is even a passage that, because it is set within a prophecy, gains hyperbolically. The goddess Annunitum tells King Zimri-Lim: "Even when you neglect me, I shower you with love [Durand, "I massacre on your behalf"]. I hand your enemy over to you. As for those who rob me, I seize them and give them over to the belly/camp/destruction of the goddess Belet-ekallim" (ARM 10 8 = LAPO 18 #1138, p. 316). P. Stern has a good discussion of this text (1991: 67–70) although he treats "those who rob me" as the name of a city.
10. Eduard Meyer emended to read "Cain, the brother-in-law of Moses," and for a while was followed by some critics; see Moore 1895: 31–33, who is relentless on this topic, citing much and many.
11. Speculations are not lacking on how to decipher the connection among the diverse Jethro, Hobab, and Reuel; see Albright 1963, B. Mazar 1965, and Mitchell 1969.
12. Some scholars suggest revocalizing the first clause in Deut 33:3 to read **ap ḥōbāb ʿimmām*, "Hobab indeed among them."
13. Segments of the Negev were expressly associated with diverse tribes, for example, Judah, Jerahmeel, and Qeni in 1 Sam 27:10; Kereti, Judah, and Caleb in 1 Sam 30:14.
14. See Burney 1970: 15–17, with developed explanations.
15. Boling (1975: 51) follows Albright (1968: 40–41) in proposing: "The people of Hobab the Qenite, Moses' son-in-law [*sic*], had gone up from Palm City with the Judahites to

the plain south of Judah, going down from Arad . . . And they went and lived among the Amaleqites!"

16. The Greek versions are not always consistent in how they render the Hebrew place name Hormah. Elsewhere it also occurs as Herman (Num 14:45), Herma (Deut 1:44; Josh 15:30, 19:4), Hermath (Josh 12:14), and, strangely enough, Ierimouth (1 Sam 30:30), so approximating its pronunciation.

17. A few more examples of the phrase have ʿim rather than ʾet (Exod 18:19, 1 Sam 20:13, 1 Chr 22:16, 2 Chr 19:11), but only exceptionally (at 2 Chr 17:3) do they have the same application. Whether it is coincidence or not, we notice that the phrase construed with YHVH is linked to those with YHVH in their name (perceived as such in the name Judah, Gen 29:35), and the one with Elohim is attached to a name with El (observation of Daniel Sasson).

18. Dahood (1979) weakens this resolve by unnecessarily emending lōʾ into lāʾâ, allegedly meaning "to fail."

19. Lindars (1995: 47) stays with the MT. See also Rake 2006: 35–42 and above at 1:8. Harmonizing contradictory pieces of information by drawing them into close proximity is known elsewhere in Scripture. As an example, in Gen 10 Cush is attached to three distinct regions with the same name; see the Notes below at 3:7–8a.

20. In Judges, this phrase addresses the names of places (at 1:26, 10:4, 15:19, and 18:12), cultic presence (6:24), and anthropological observations (1:21, 19:30); see also Block 1999: 64–65.

IB1. The Northern Tribes: Stratagems and Reality (Judg 1:22–36)

1. Along with dictionary entries, see the good surveys by Whiting 1995 and G. Schwartz 1995.

2. Samsi-Addu wrote to his son Yasmaḥ-Addu, "Now that Išar-Lim has had brought to you messengers from Hazor and from four Amorite kings [4 lugal amurrîm], assign these messengers to [someone] . . . to escort them to Qatna" (adapted from Durand, LAPO 16 #375, p. 574 [A.2760]). On Mari material about Amurru, see Sasson 1998a: 121–23.

3. Among them are Num 21:26–30; Deut 2:26–35; Josh 12:2, 4–5; 13:10, 12, 21, 27; 1 Kgs 4:19. See also below at Judg 11:19–22.

4. CAD B, pp. 293–95. This usage may seem obvious as simile for a royal household, but in fact it feeds on a fiction of a common ancestry for royal houses of Amorite background. Trying to stave off potential conflict with Mari, Hammurabi of Babylon writes Zimri-Lim (ARM 26 449): "Has this House, then or now, ever transgressed against Mari? Furthermore, has there ever been a single conflict between Mari and this House? Mari and Babylon, then as now, are one House—and one finger—that cannot be divided."

5. Possibly perplexing are the many ways in which bêt is put to use in Hebrew as well as other Semitic languages. It does stand for "house," physically and metaphorically ("property"); but among other constructions, it readily joins with other substantives and names to label temples (bêt and deity), tribes (bêt and eponym), and cities (bêt and attribute or characteristic feature). Unusual is bêt YHVH to represent the Promised Land in Hos 8:1.

6. The last observation is by S. Ackerman.

7. Greek is euphemistic here: οὕτως ποιήσω ὑμῖν οἶκος τοῦ Ισραηλ, "I will do thus to you, O House of Israel" (Hos 10:15).

8. Rainey and Notley 2006: 116–17; Rainey 2006; Finkelstein and Singer-Avitz 2009; Gass 2005: 71–76. Livingston (1994) has sited it closer to Jerusalem, at el-Bireh.

9. Budde once proposed that both readings went back to a יהשוע, "Joshua," original; see Burney 1970: 22, who approves.

10. The text is A.3552 (LAPO 17 #456, pp. 29–31).

11. See above at 1:10, on the name of Hebron, and the Comments to IB.

12. On distinguishing between the Late Bronze and Iron Age Hittites and their recall in the Bible, see B. Collins 2007b. Somewhat similar is Gerhards 2009.

13. From the Mari archives, we know of refugees naming new shelters after their place of origins, see Charpin 2003: 13. A medieval (ninth-century) epic, *Historia Brittonum*, tells how a Brutus, a grandson of Aeneas of Troy, eventually settled what was to become Britain. A tidbit for us is that his voyages are synchronized with the Philistine capture of the ark, so at the tail end of Judges.

14. See Z. Herzog, "Cities (Cities in the Levant)" and "Fortifications (Levant)," *ABD* 1032–43 and 844–852, respectively.

15. It is possible that the Luz episode is but a harbinger of what we will learn later (Judg 18) about the fate of Laish (Dan), a city so secure in its own future that it took few defensive measures.

16. See also Josh 17:11–13, with discrepancies detailed in Lindars 1995: 56–58.

17. See also Josh 16:10, where is added, "the Canaanites living among them, but performing forced labor."

18. In Qumranic exegesis, Akko is the point of entry for Armageddon, with ʾšr (Asher) read as Assur (= the Romans), leading the charge; see Jassen 2011.

19. See the dictionaries. Guillaume speculates (2004: 94–103; see also Guillaume 2001) that the absence of Tyre in this notice is evocative of conditions when Sennacherib conquered westward, giving him a date for the composition with Judg 1. Scribal vagaries among cuneiform scribes no less than manipulations among biblical editors warn that omissions and additions of places or people are hardly ever the best justification for dating episodes.

20. Kallai (1986: 71–72) thinks it is a regional name.

21. This is one of a handful of occasions in Judges where the Greek opts to translate a geographical name by parsing its Hebrew components. The others are at 2:1, 5 ("The [place of] Weeping" for [*hab*]*bōkîm*), 6:24 ("The father of Esdri" for *ʾăvî hāʿezrî*), 15:17 ("Lifting of Jawbones" for *rāmat-leḥî*), and 15:19 ("Well of Invokers" for *ʿên-haqqôrēʾ*). The remaining names (about eighteen more) are transliterated from the Hebrew. In some cases the latter may display differences between the A and B texts. In all, almost 130 place names occur in Judges, about a third occurring nowhere else; see Harlé and Roqueplo 1999: 63–34.

22. See the Comments to IA1 (1:1–7) and IIA3 (3:1–6). Some scholars uncover more elaborate structure in Judg 1 than others; see Younger 1994 (more or less the same in 1995), who offers somewhat accommodating charts. Citing previous scholarship, he reads the pattern as emblematic of the dissolution that (allegedly) characterizes the entire book.

IIA1. What Went Wrong: Accusation (Judg 2:1–5)

1. *New York Times*, February 3, 2009, "A Good Cry Isn't for Everyone," http://www.nytimes.com/2009/02/03/health/03iht-03mind.19888964.html. Cited in Fögen 2009: 1.

2. A good overview of the subjects, as well as a dialogue among scholars regarding some crucial passages, can be found in *TDOT* 8: 308–25 (מַלְאָךְ), by D. N. Freedman, B. E. Willoughby, H. Ringgren, and H.-J. Fabry.

3. Gen 18:16–17; see also Gen 21:17–19 when an angel comes and God talks, and the Comments to Gideon's experience with a divine messenger at IIID1.

4. W. Smelik (1995: 349–50) offers fine comments on the Targumic translation of *mal'āk*.

5. Followed by the *Seder Olam Rabbah*, a medieval compilation attributed to the second-century Yose ben Halafta. Ehrlich (1968: 70–71) argues that angels do not appear before groups and are not normally said to come from a specific town. Rashi thinks it was the High Priest Phineas, who will be featured in Judg 20:28.

6. See also below, at Judg 6.

7. See also the Introductory Remarks to IIID1 (Judg 6:1–32).

8. A similarly delayed explanation of a name occurs in Gen 12:8 when Abraham stops at Bethel, a place that is not said to acquire its name until Gen 28:19.

9. A fine review of the steps taken to arm a covenant in the Old Babylonian period is in Lafont 2001a: 262–83.

10. The procedure is often compared to reports in Gen 15 and Jer 34:18–20. See good lexical discussion by Kutsch, *TLOT* 1: 256–66 and 2: 635–37; and general overviews in Mc-Carthy 1978.

11. Similar notions are found, among other occasions, in Exod 34:13–14 and Deut 12:3. Rake (2006: 102–24) argues for the precedence of the Judges passage.

12. *Ṣiddîm*, having to do with "side, flank," is difficult, and some restore *ṣārîm*, "adversary," allegedly based on the Greek εἰς συνοχάς, "in distresses." Others adapt from Num 33:55 and Josh 23:13, "thorns [*ṣinnîm*] to the sides." There are more suggestions, based on ransacking Semitic dictionaries, and they are reviewed in W. Smelik 1995: 353 n. 168 and Barthélemy 1982: 76.

13. The Mari evidence is that decorum sharply circumscribed private grieving and contained public demonstration that goes beyond the expected period; see Jacquet 2012. On weeping during sacral periods, see Ghouti 1991.

14. Elsewhere the verbal form is often followed by details, such as about its purpose (most often plus *šĕlāmîm*, "for well-being"), its reoccurrence (plus *hayyāmîm*, "regularly"), its destination (plus *mišpāḥâ*, "clan"), or its locus (plus *babbāmôt*, "high places"). Consult the dictionaries (under "sacrifice") and online at WiBiLex, http://www.bibelwissenschaft.de/nc/wibilex/das-bibellexikon/details/quelle/WIBI/referenz/24240/cache/f28ac8ea5a1a3afa8f3fbe99f4e08019/. A fine philological overview, with notices of Egyptian and Mesopotamian sacrifices as well as a large bibliography, is in *TDOT* 4 (1980: 8–29). For an overview, see de Vaux 1961: 415–54.

15. A nice Mari document may be used as illustration to a comparable situation, albeit not as similarly cataclysmic. A high official (Ašmad) from Zimri-Lim's early tenure writes: "When the nomads met in a campsite (*maḫanûm*), because of the rain that fell, we began to weep before Addu and offered sacrifices for the well-being of our lord [the king]. Two kinsmen of Ḫali-ḫadun [a tribal leader] came before us to say, 'you have been removed from your [Ḫali-ḫadun] office and your home has been ransacked.' On hearing this, he broke into weeping, his kinsmen as well." (A.1191, cited in Durand 1988: 492).

16. That it presumes Israel in assembly has encouraged speculation that this event had been moved from tradition before Joshua dismissed the people (Josh 24); see, among others, Rake 2006: 125–31. Such consistency of setting is perhaps too much to expect from ideologically driven narratives.

IIA2. What Went Wrong: Judges for Israel (Judg 2:6–23)

1. Allegorized encapsulation of the judges period from the *Book of Dreams*, likely late Hellenistic period; cited from Isaac 1983: 67.

2. The *Amidah* (also termed *Shmoneh Esreh*) is a core prayer in Jewish daily service. It gathers eighteen (later nineteen) benedictions, some of which were inspired by post–Bar Kochva devotions. This benediction is appealing for the reinstatement of divine kingship with judges as human deputies. A later benediction (the fifteenth) often regarded as a later interpolation prays for the restoration of David's dynasty. In some prayer books, "sorrow [*yāgôn*]" and "groaning ['*ănāḥâ*]" are glossed as "Samael" and his mate "Lilith."

3. Exhaustive treatment is in Niehr 1986; compressed version of the same is in Niehr 2006.

4. On all this, see G. Liedke (1971) in *TLOT* 3: 1392–99. A similarly broad range of meanings develops from the LXX. There the noun most often used for *šōfēṭ* is κριτής, derived from a verb (κρίνω) that has a very broad semantic range: "to select, think, approve, resolve," but also "to have or pass judgment."

5. When Jethro gave his son-in-law advice on installing helpers who can duplicate Moses's role (Exod 18:21–26), they are to "judge" (*šāfaṭ*), but they are called *šōfēṭ* only in Deut 1:16.

6. We never find a feminine term, even when applied to Deborah!

7. There is an enormous literature on the Mari *šāpiṭum* as well as on its potential comparison with the biblical institution, but anything written before the mid-1980s is likely to be superseded. The best appreciation of the material is through Birot's 1993 edition of the correspondence of governors from one particular province, Qaṭṭunan. Lion 2001 is another seminal study. Brief but authoritative notices are in Durand 2008 and Reculeau 2008b. On the *merḫum*, see Durand 2008: 308–10. For more on this occupation, see Sasson 2004.

8. Previously, his title was that of "Moses's acolyte [*mĕšārēt*]"; Exod 24:13, 33:11; Num 11:28; Josh 1:1.

9. On the ambiguity of this passage, see Sasson 1990: 346 n. 35.

10. This interpretation is disputed by some scholars, among them B. J. Alfrink (1943, 1948), who believes it pertains to reunion in Sheol rather than in tombs. Why could it not be in both?

11. Not just the generation of Moses and Joshua, Kaufmann 1962: 95.

12. Rahlfs A gives the odd phrase "and they worshiped the she-Baal" (καὶ ἐλάτρευσαν τῇ Βααλ), here, at 3:7 and 10:6, 10. Harlé and Roqueplo (1999: 88–89) suggest that attaching a feminine article to Baal displays contempt.

13. To avoid the discrepancy, scholars have resorted to needless emendations or to elastic interpretation of the preposition *lĕ-*; see Lindars 1995: 103.

14. The Hebrew vocalization of the singular form, '*aštōret*, may hide a diatribe as it duplicates the vowels in *bōšet*, "shame"; if so, the change is after the Roman period, as the Greek seems to preserve the likely pronunciation, Ἀστάρτη.

15. But see the Greek for the relevant phrase: τὰ ποίμνια τῶν προβάτων σου, "the flock of your sheep."

16. For people, see examples in Deut 7:24, 21:10 and Judg 3:28; for land, see Josh 2:24; Judg 1:2.

17. In the Mari records, where the verb *šūzubum* (causative of *ezēbum*) is associated with saving political victims from their predators, kings who are trusted to fulfill such a function

are called *mušēzibum*, semantically equivalent to our *môšîʸaʿ*. Yet there is this fine letter where it is turned sarcastic. Ibal-Addu of Ašlakka—a fine precursor to Aziru of Amurru for shrewd ambition and to Rib-Addi of Gubla for persistent neediness—lectured Ibal-El, Zimri-Lim's chief nomad officer (*merḫûm*) (A.3194; Guichard 1999: 28–29):

> Who has grasped the hem of your lord and saved himself?
> —Sabbuganni, king of Amaz, grasped the hem of your lord, but he was
>   brought to an end . . . without finding a savior [*mušēzibum*]. Why did
>   your lord Zimri-Lim not save him?
> —Sammetar, king of Ašnakkum, who even married Zimri-Lim's sister, people
>   . . . wrapped him in leather and delivered him to Elamite power. Why did
>   your lord, Zimri-Lim, not save him?
> —Yawi-ila, king of Talḫayum, whom Zimri-Lim set for kingship; an enemy
>   brought him to an end in his own home. Why did your lord not save
>   him?
> —Now Šubram as well as his people, who is (still) grasping the hem of your
>   lord; well, Samsi-Eraḫ, a (mere) commoner, has already plundered his
>   household and goods! Why did your lord, Zimri-Lim, not save him?
> As for me too, one of these days, might you save me? Who has grasped your
> hem and saved himself?

18. The Targum, as usual, moves away from God changing his mind without hearing Israel's prayers, *mĕtív YY mimāʾ dĕʾāmar ûmqabēl ṣĕlôtĕhôn*, "God reversed what he said, accepting their prayers"; see W. Smelik 1995: 364–65. Depending on the conjugation, the root *ⁿḥm* realizes different meanings. In the Piel it means something like "to comfort"; but in the Niphal (as it is here), it seems to be about "repenting," "regretting," but also simply about "changing one's mind" (Stoebe in *TLOT* 2: 738–39; Barr 1961: 116–18). When the activity influencing God's response is in the past, "regret" may be the best rendering (for example, at Gen 6:6–7, 1 Sam 15:11, 2 Sam 24:16, Jer 42:10); but when the activity is projected for the future, "changing one's mind, relenting" may fit better. Our context, however, reports on habitual action that is set to occur in the immediate future, causing ambiguity; see Sasson 1990: 263–64.

19. On this topic see Latvus 1998 and the treatment of Judg 2 on pp. 36–49. On the connection between the two attestations of the phrase in this chapter, see the Comments below.

20. The term can be found in Amorite vocabulary among other words for polities, such as *nawûm, gaʾum/gāyum*, and *ummatum*, and these are frequently compared to Hebrew *nāvê, gôy*, and *ʾummâ*. Yet, a careful study of the Mari contexts shows that function need not follow etymon. Thus, the Amorite ethnic unit *gaʾum/gāyum* ("clan") seems closest not to Hebrew *gôy*, but to *mišpaḥâ*. Hebrew *gôy*, which seems to refer to the largest unit of people, tribal or otherwise, finds its best parallel in Mari's *ummatum*; see Sasson 1998a: 104. The term has nothing to do (as some authorities allege) with *gav*, "back," and kindred words.

21. When it does occur (as during the Amarna period), an insistence on serving a specific god exclusively tends to be imposed by rulers (Akhnaton) rather than urged by the people.

22. The literature on ancient Near Eastern prophecy is immense. A recent good monograph is Nissinen 2000; see also the overview of Vanderkam 1995.

23. Among these are male circumcision within a week of birth, implementation of the Sabbath (as a recurring seventh-day celebration), exclusion of women from the priesthood as

well as from legal forums, codification of a restricted diet and of purity taboos, and bans on aspects of dressing and grooming.

24. See Buccellati 1995.

25. Contra Block 1999: 131.

26. The formula is nicely dissected in Halpern 1988a: 121–45.

27. Good review of earlier proposals is in Lagrange 1903: 43–45 (often dismissive) and in Burney 1970: 52–55.

28. The Greek version has additional notices: At 31a, there is record of the burial with Joshua of flint knives used in the circumcision at Galgala (Gilgal); at the closing of 33 there is reference to the priesthood of Phineas, who dies and is buried with his father. More startling is what follows (33b): "And the sons of Israel departed each to their place and to their own city. And the sons of Israel worshiped Astarte and Astaroth and the gods of the nations round about them. And the LORD delivered them into the hands of Eglom, the king of Moab, and he dominated them eighteen years" (NETS, 194). On this basis (and on the odd phrasing in the Damascus Covenant 5:4 regarding the sealed book of the Law, "for it was not revealed in Israel from the death of Eleazar and Joshua, and of the elders who worshiped the Ashtarot"), some have argued for a Hebrew version that led from Joshua directly to the story of Ehud in 3:11; discussion in Tov 2012: 297–99. More likely is that the Greek has taken liberties, as it does in many other segments of Joshua. In fact, no Greek text of Judges is known to me that opens on the Ehud episode.

29. The proposal is sharpest in Brettler 1989. The transfer was facilitated because Joshua and Judges may have shared the same scroll. See also Amit 1999a: 136–41.

30. Talmon (1978) is generally credited with reviving interest in this literary technique. His study remains valuable for arguing that synchroneity, simultaneity, and contemporaneity (go to pp. 17–18 for distinction) essentially are authorial tools. Much has been written on its application since, among them by Fishbane (1985: 44–65) and Levinson (1997: 17–20). Amit's comments on this technique are illuminating (1999a: 136–41).

31. Sweeney (1997) allocates Judges into just two blocks, the second of which begins at chapter 3. Where to end the prelude is disputed, with arguments also for a break at 2:5, 10, or 25; see Irwin 2012: 444 n. 5.

32. The reign of Jehu of Israel (840–815 BCE) is offered as a plausible occasion because of a resemblance between the murder of princes in Judg 9:5 and in 2 Kgs 10:7.

33. For recent discussions and evaluations, see Lindars (1995: 98–100), who essentially follows Noth; Guillaume (2004: 5–26), who champions Beyerlin and assigns Judg 1–3 to circles around Manasseh and Josiah; O'Connell (1996: 135–66), who proposes a double prologue to explain the need to expel natives while maintaining intertribal loyalty; and Amit (1999a: 120–66, 363–83). For Amit, the early chapters form a pre-Deuteronomistic Judahite "exposition" to guide discerning readers toward the creation of (an imperfect) kingship.

IIA3. What Went Wrong: Lands Not Taken (Judg 3:1–6)

1. Other words also deemed Philistine likewise have disputed derivations, for example q/kōva', "helmet," in this case either from Hittite kupaḫ(ḫ)i or from Greek κύμβαχος "dome, crown, top of a helmet."

2. Remarkably inappropriate is the equation between the Aḫḫiyawa of Hittite texts and the Hivvites (Margalith 1988).

3. See the dictionaries under "Hivvites" as well as "Horites," since there is a fair amount of confusion between the two as far as LXX and Hebrew Bible testimonies are concerned.

4. The Targum here avoids reference to Baal, *miṭṭûr mêšar ḥarmôn*, "from the vale of Her-mon." For similar reasons Rahlfs B simply has "Hermon."

5. They include Agade, Ur, Eridu, Nippur, Uruk, or, generally, Sumer and Akkad. A sub-genre that survived into Seleucid time is the balag (presumably because it was accompa-nied by a balag instrument) that treats the destruction and reconstruction of temples in cosmic imagery; see Dobbs-Allsopp 1993 or Hallo 1995.

6. Remarkably, the occasions are not few when leaders lay their calamities squarely on them-selves or their parents. For generations, Hittite kings recognized the fault of a powerful ancestor (Suppiluliuma I) who slighted oaths and covenants with other parties; see the dossier in Singer 2002. Few texts, however, match the pathos conveyed in a letter sent by a Mari ambassador to King Zimri-Lim. In it, Yarim-Lim of Ḥalab (Yamḥad) reviews a divinely choreographed personal tragedy: "When Sumu-epuḥ, my father, feared God, he achieved his goal. No other king matched him. When he coveted that which (the god Addu?) gave Samsi-Addu, my father Sumu-epuḥ did not enjoy old age. Because he attacked the land . . . that (Addu) gave Samsi-Addu, Addu had him killed" (from *FM* 7 8: 12–22, after Durand 2002a: 24–28). Similar sentiments are expressed by Sennach-erib when striving to learn the cause of his father Sargon's ignominious death (Tadmor, Landsberger, and Parpola 1989).

7. See comments to Jonah 4:2, Sasson 1990: 275–83. The dictionaries have fine articles on this topic, generally under "Wrath/Anger of God" or under such verbs as *ḥārâ, kāʿas, qāṣaf* and such derivatives and nouns as *ʾaf, ḥārôn, ḥēmâ, qeṣef, ʿevrâ,* and *zaʿam.* The ar-ticle by Gary Herion in the *ABD* is recommended, and the monograph by Latvus (1998) succinctly reviews the literature.

8. Elsewhere, a contributing argument explained the durability of the enemy (Amorites in Gen 15:16) as expressly designed to enhance its iniquity; so the other side of the same theme.

IIIA. Othniel (Judg 3:7–11)

1. Waldman (1989) argues that the intent of the divine manifestation is to overwhelm the chosen leader.

2. RIMA 2 A.0.99.2 (after Grayson 1991: 147); the same notion is also attached to Tukultī-Ninurta II (p. 165).

3. A number of attestations of *rûʷaḥ* YHVH*ʾēlōhîm* are to "wind," including the famous occurrence at Gen 1:2. Presumably, it was also YHVH's wind that transported prophets across vast space (1 Kgs 18:12, 2 Kgs 2:16, Ezek 37:1).

4. Martin (2011) claims to detect distinct differences in each manifestation of the *rûʷaḥ* in Judges.

5. It is difficult to assess whether the *rûʷaḥ ʾēlîyāhû* that settled on Elisha originated in God (2 Kgs 2:15).

6. We read of divine spirit that leads someone (*nāḥâ be-*) toward the level path (Ps 143:10) and that it takes over the power of speech (*dibbēr be-,* 2 Sam 23:2).

7. See above, regarding Adad-nārārī's transformation. Many other Akkadian terms, each with its own nuance and occurring in diverse documents or periods, are also attested for the phenomenon, among them *rašubbatu, namrīru,* and *namurru/namurratu.* A fine overview of the subject is Cassin 1968. There is much discussion in the literature on the linkage between the Mesopotamian manifestations of divine radiance and Israel's *kāvôd* YHVH*ʾēlōhîm* (Kutsko 2000: 77–100), but less so on the connection between the latter and *rûʷaḥ* YHVH*ʾēlōhîm.*

8. The Targum gives *vělāʾ pāsqîn*, "they would not stop," implying the opposite.

9. On all the above, see most recently Levine 2009: 30–36, who finds reasons to date the Judges manifestations to the late ninth or early eighth century BCE: "This interpretation builds on the most salient feature of the early material in Judges (and in 1 Samuel), its distinctive application of the phrase רוח יהוה ('the spirit of Yahweh'). Elsewhere in the Hebrew Bible, this all-important phrase identifies diverse gifts, all divinely endowed, including the spirit of prophecy and related forms of esoteric enlightenment, skill, and wisdom. Only in the heroic literature of the Hebrew Bible, however, does the spirit of Yahweh manifest itself as physical prowess in combat" (30). Actually, this is very accommodating, both in the interpretation of the evidence and in establishing criteria for discriminating among diverse manifestations of the phenomenon. Why is the term not applied to Joshua? And where else besides the books of Judges and Samuel are we given narratives about heroes rising to the occasion?

10. Phrases in boldface accent obvious textual discrepancies.

11. On the names of the relevant deities and the discrepancy resulting from citing them from different contexts, see above under 2:11. Research on the Asherah (in all manifestations of the term) has been stimulated by the discoveries at Kuntillet al-ʿAjrud of pottery shards with cartoonish pictures and with captions about Yahweh and Ashera that might or might not refer to the cartooned figures. The enormous literature that has ensued includes profitable searches to recover the mention of *ʾăšērâ* (in the plural as well) in published documents, to catalogue standing poles near cultic installations, and to reevaluate the evidence, from Harran to Elephantine, on the existence of a consort for the Hebrew God. The issue is rehearsed in most recent biblical dictionaries. A fine overview is by N. Wyatt in the *DDD* (under "Asherah"). Older literature, relying on the LXX (ἄλσος) and Vulgate (*nemus*), generally gave the "groves" in translation.

12. On the three Cushs, see my note in Sasson 1980: 212 n. 3. The wife of Moses who is labeled a Cushite (Num 12:1) is evidently Zipporah, daughter of Reuel of Midian, and not another wife from Ethiopia.

13. Dossin (1982) makes the startling suggestion that Cushan is a scribal play on "Guzanu," the name of a town (presently Tell Halaf) in Syria.

14. One might adapt this solution by declaring it a nickname, as in "the Cruel" for France's Louis XI or for Castille's Peter I. A delicious listing of such cognomina is available at Wikipedia, http://en.wikipedia.org/wiki/List_of_monarchs_by_nickname.

15. Worth noticing is Josephus's effort to cast Israel's delivery in human terms. Inspired by God to take charge, Othniel does so, rallying a few behind him. When he succeeds in driving Cushan back to his Assyrian home beyond the Euphrates, the people select him as judge; text cited below, p. 216. In his *LAB* Pseudo-Philo (first or second century CE) treats Kenaz (Cenez), rather than Othniel, as Israel's first judge (chapters 25–28). A son of Caleb, Kenaz is chosen by lot to follow Joshua, and his activities are woven into an elaborate romance—in length almost as long as what Pseudo-Philo has to say about Moses—displaying a favorite theme: God is in perfect control of history and so can be trusted to save Israel. The portrait of Kenaz draws on lore from Joshua, midrashic Abraham, and (apocalyptic) visions but also the author's imagination. The most accessible English translation is Harrington 1985, and I normally cite relevant passages by its book numbering; but the fullest study is Jacobson 1996. (Earlier translations are readily found on the Internet.) A fine discussion of the portrait of Kenaz is in Levison 1995: 305–14, with more elaborate comments in Jacobson 1996: 757–822.

16. Among other arguments that fail to inspire confidence, Oded (1996) claims that "Cushan reminds of Kish, father of Saul" (92*). The initial consonants in both names are not the same.

17. Malamat (1971) offers a less precise version of the theory: "Would it not seem more likely that [the invasion] was directed against Egypt, the war against Israel being ephemeral? Further, it would appear that Israel's deliverance by Othniel the son of Kenaz is to be linked with the general defeat of this foreign invader of Egypt, at the hands of Setnakht, the founder of the Twentieth Dynasty" (26–27).

18. In 10:14, Israel is said to appeal to 'ĕlōhîm, "foreign gods." The idiom must not be confused with zāʿaq or ṣāʿaq 'et (as in 4:10, 13), which has to do with summoning help, or with the same verb in the Niphal, which suggests rallying around a leader, such as at 6:34–35, 4:13 (nizʿaq), 7:23, 10:17, and 12:1 (niṣʿaq).

19. A classic passage with cause and effect is Exod 2:23–25: "During these many days (while Moses was in Midian), the king of Egypt died. Israel groaned [Niphal of 'ānaḥ] under the bondage and cried out [zāʿaq; 'el is implied]; and their plea for relief [šavʿâ] from it reached God himself. God heard [šāmaʿ] their moaning [nĕ'āqâ] and, minding [zākar] his covenant with Abraham, Isaac, and Jacob, God looked upon [rā'â] Israel and God took notice [yādaʿ]."

20. See Sasson 1990: 233 n. 15 and for units other than year, EncJud 12: 1258.

21. Josh 5:6 links the forty years' duration to a shift that is crucial to God's purposes: "(No one had been circumcised . . .) for the Israelites had traveled in the wilderness forty years, until the entire nation—the men of military age who had left Egypt—had perished; because they had not obeyed the Lord, and the Lord had sworn never to let them see the land that the Lord had sworn to their fathers to assign to us, a land flowing with milk and honey" (TNK). Ezekiel gives a parallel experience (29:11–13) in which Egypt undergoes tribulations and restorations during sequential forty-year units.

22. Ironically enough, given the laconic information about him, this sequence obtains only in the case of Abdon (12:15 to 13:1–2), and here too its completeness is compromised by a deliberately paced introduction of the next rescuer (Samson).

23. I have developed this possibility in my comments to Jonah 3:6, regarding the nonhistorical title "King of Nineveh"; Sasson 1990: 247–50.

24. Some very fine Mari specialists have found plausible echoes in the Mari age when Elam leap-frogged Mesopotamia to support (morally rather than militarily) Amut-pi-el of Qatna; see Sasson 2006b.

IIIB. Ehud (Judg 3:12–31)

1. After Kramer in ANET⁵: 617; see also Michalowski 1989: 59, lines 364–70. Dobbs-Allsopp (1993, 2000) explores the relationship between the Mesopotamian and biblical displays of the genre.

2. See the comments of Knauf 1991: 31–32, who collects possible congeners even if ultimately he opts for a topographic interpretation of the name, allowing him to re-create with much gusto ("there is no doubt that ʿAjlûn is the Canaanite toponym Eglon in Arabic garb"; p. 32) a conflict between an area in Gilead and a Benjaminite clan (for him, Ehud is also a toponym).

3. Eglah, one of David's wives (2 Sam 3:5), holds a female equivalent of the name, but there are lots more such formations. In Judges alone they include Caleb, "dog," Deborah, "bee," and Jael, "ibex"; see Stamm 1967: 329–30, with bibliography. Many of the kings

of Kish in the Sumerian King List have animal names, and not all are ferocious, such as Kalibum ("dog"), Kalumum ("lamb"), Zuqaqip ("scorpion"), and Arwium ("lion"); cited from ETCSL, http://www-etcsl.orient.ox.ac.uk/section2/tr211.htm. Examples from the Mari archives include Ayyalum, "deer," a Benjaminite leader; and Šēlebum, "fox," a prophet.

4. Why the Greek gives this name as Εγλωμ is not clear to me. However, we read also about a city by that name captured by Joshua (Josh 10:23, 34) and allotted to Judah (Josh 15:39), with a king named Debir, the last a "mythical monarch," in the opinion of Barr 1990. In this case, the Greek for the town Eglon varies: Οδολλαμ, Αιλαμ (Rahlfs B) and Εγλωμ, Αγλων (Rahlfs A). On the town Debir, see the Notes to 1:11.

5. Alter 1981: 39, "[who] turns out to be a fatted calf ready for the slaughter, and perhaps even the epithet *bari*, 'stout,' is a play on *meri*, 'fatling,' a sacrificial animal occasionally bracketed with calf"; Amit 1989: 110, "The name of the king . . . hints of a ritual, whether as the subject of adoration (a calf ritual) or as an offering." In contrast, few find satiric potential in the name of his opponent, Ehud.

6. *bSotah* 47a. *bSanhedrin* 105b expands, "For as a reward for the forty-two sacrifices offered up by Balak, he was privileged that Ruth should be his descendant, [as] R. Jose b. Huna said: Ruth was the daughter of Eglon, the grandson of Balak, king of Moab." For a different attribution, see *bHorayot* 10b, "R. Jose son of R. Hanina said: Ruth was the daughter of the son of Eglon who was the son of the son of Balak the King of Moab."

7. Aside from entries *sub voce* in fine dictionaries (*ABD, EncJud*, and the like), there is now Routledge 2004, who gives archaeology and inscriptions (rather than, say, biblical evidence) primacy in controlling Moab's history and culture. Kitchen 2007 reviews the extrabiblical documentation, but the most developed assessment is in Timm 1989. Timm also considers biblical traditions regarding Moab, but oddly enough, he avoids the juicier narratives (Lot's daughters, Ehud and Eglon) when making room for those woven from similar cloth about Sihon and Balaam.

8. Verbal sequencing in English permits fudging, as in *TNK*'s "Eglon brought the Ammonites and the Amalekites together under his command, and went and defeated Israel and occupied the City of Palms."

9. Midrash *Genesis Rabbah* (99.3) interprets Jacob's line about Benjamin being a ravenous wolf (Gen 49:27) as foreshadowing Ehud. Josephus (*Ant.* 5.188) turns him into a hero, not a sissy, fit for Roman appreciation, and gives him a place of birth to justify his nationalism: "There was a young man of the tribe of Benjamin, whose name was Ehud [Ἰούδης] the son of Gera, a man of very great courage in bold undertakings, and of a very strong body, fit for hard labor, but best skilled in using his left hand, in which was his whole strength; and he also dwelt at Jericho."

10. The same name is applied in the LXX to *'ōhad*, a son of Simeon (Gen 46:10, Exod 6:15), curiously enough next to another son, *yāmîn*. Josephus calls him Ἰούδης, close enough to Judah (Ἰούδας) to stimulate some scholars in deriving both names from the same Hebrew verbal root. Pseudo-Philo (*LAB* 34) has a take on Aod, a Midianite magician who seduces Israel into following him, but he comes after Deborah. Who knows whether he belongs here or not?

11. Opposite conclusion by Lindars 1995: 140–41. Fortunately, given that no traditions are preserved about Gera himself, not much rides on whether we attribute the name to a person or to a clan. As we shall soon see, it will be otherwise when discussing the Anat associated with Shamgar.

12. For example, "lame of his right hande" (Geneva Bible). Many Jewish understandings of the phrase have depended on the Targum, *gubrā' gĕmîd bîdêh dĕyamînā'*, "a man with a withered right-hand." In Soggin's opinion (1987: 49), "everything dictates that we are dealing with a real physical defect, one that could seriously affect the capacity of a fighter such as to make him seem less dangerous." The Greek has ἄνδρας ἀμφοτεροδέξιος, "an ambidextrous man."

13. "Ehud is a left-handed man in a symbolic world in which the 'normal' preferred side is the right" (Niditch in Foley 2005: 282). An almost parodic misuse of this lore is in G. Miller 1996a: 113–17 (cited in the Comments). Unfortunately, he is not alone to do so; for recent examples, albeit with lesser reliance on a casual misreading of the text, see Alter 1981: 38–41 and Brettler 1991: 294–99. Jobling (1989) waxes exuberant on the theme of left-handedness, allegedly in response to Amit's restrained essay on Ehud (1989, also 1999a). Grottanelli (1999: 52) believes he found a parallel story in Roman lore about Gaius Mucius, nicknamed Cordus in some versions but in others Scaevola, for being left-handed. Mucius sought to assassinate Lars Porsenna, an enemy of Rome, but ended up killing Porsenna's secretary. Gaius earned his left-handedness, however, not by military training, but by burning his right hand after the botched attempt; see the nice overview "Gaius Mucius Scaevola," by Jona Lendering at http://www.livius.org/mu-mz/mucius/scaevola.html.

14. See the good pages on this topic in Halpern 1988a: 40–42, who nonetheless keeps referring to the left-handedness of Ehud.

15. For Kraeling (1935: 206–7), Ehud was "acting like the common run of traitors in seeking a private interview" with a tyrant. He is following Josephus here (*Ant.* 5.189–97), cited in the Comments below. Christiansen 2003: 62–63 turns him into a classic loner in the Clint Eastwood or James Bond mold.

16. Verbs *šālaḥ* in 2 Kgs 20:12 = Isa 39:1; Hiphil of *nāgaš* in 1 Kgs 5:1; Hiphil of *bô'* in 1 Kgs 10:25.

17. Verbs *nāśâ* in 2 Sam 8:2 and 8:6; Hiphil of *šûv* in 2 Kgs 17:3 and Ps 72:10; Hiphil of *bô'* in 2 Chr 17:11; and Qal of *nātan* in 2 Chr 26:8.

18. A discriminating discussion between different types of hand weapons in the Assyrian period is in Barron 2010: 46–78. See also Maxwell-Hyslop 1946, Yadin 1963: 1/10–11, Shalev 2004, and *ABD* under "Weapons and Implements of Warfare." Many good and illustrated pages, mostly from the classical period, can be found in the *DAGR* under "Gladius."

19. "My lady confronted the mountain range [Ebiḫ]. She advanced step by step. She sharpened both edges of her dagger. She grabbed Ebiḫ's neck as if ripping up esparto grass. She pressed the dagger's teeth into its interior. She roared like thunder" (lines 138–43 at ETCSL, http://etcsl.orinst.ox.ac.uk/cgi-bin/etcsl.cgi?text=t.1.3.2&charenc=j#).

20. The word for the edge of a blade is *pê*, "mouth," and we have already met this personification in the expression *lĕfî ḥerev* (see above at 1:25).

21. See LAPO 16 #312, pp. 493–94 (A.2721), in which taxes from a specific town are offered as tribute of allegiance. Knoppers (1993) studies a fine Ugarit document (KTU 3.1) in which Niqmaddu of Ugarit offers Suppiluliumas of Ḫatti and the sun goddess of Arinna a rich list of gifts, no doubt requiring many tribute bearers.

22. See C. Smith 1977. The relevant caption reads, "I received the tribute of Jehu of Ḫumri: silver, gold, a gold bowl, gold cups, gold buckets, tin, a staff of the king's hand, and spears." A feature with a photo of the obelisk can be found at the British Museum website,

http://www.britishmuseum.org/explore/highlights/highlight_objects/me/t/black
_obelisk_of_shalmaneser.aspx.

23. Via Freedman, Boling 1975: 86 would translate the verb here by "escort" on the basis of Gen 12:20. But this meaning is obviously depending on the clause preceding, "Pharaoh put men in charge of him," and is not inherent to the verbal form itself. The same argument can be made for Gen 31:27, a reference that likewise is called upon to affirm such a meaning.

24. In Mari documents, kings frequently summoned vassals to meet them at specific shrines where they renewed allegiances and no doubt accepted tributes. Perhaps Eglon and Ehud traveled together from the hewn images area?

25. I follow a suggestion of S. Ackerman.

26. See the dictionaries, under such words as *maṣṣēbāh* or "pillar"; the *ABD*'s compact notice (by D. W. Manor) is quite useful, citing archeological recovery of sites (Gezer, Hazor, and Arad, to which one may add Dan) where a number of such objects were found. Recent studies include Graesser 1972, Mettinger 1995, LaRocca-Pitts 2001, Avner 2001, and almost any work that deals with Ashera, since they treat pillars as side issues. In older literature, there was a tendency to declare all such set stones as "cultic," if not also "phallic" (hence "Canaanite"). Recent research has shown how ubiquitous they were in Hebraic lore, functioning as boundary markers (Gen 31:44–49), memorials (Gen 35:19–20), votive statements (2 Sam 18:18; see de Moor 1995), or avatars (Judg 17:5).

27. These are differentiated from the *narûm* (stela) and *bērûtum* (mounds of enemy cadavers). For an informative study of the cuneiform evidence as well as comparative evidence, see Durand 2005. A nice overview of the second-millennium material from Syria is Marti 2011. See also Canby 1976 (for Assur and northern Syria) and Shaw 1989 (for Crete, perhaps influenced by Phoenicia).

28. Amit 1989: 113 (= 1999a: 188–89) and elsewhere offers justification for two different statements. Josephus (*Ant.* 5.190–91) as elsewhere expands on the circumstances: "It was then summer, and the middle of the day, when the guards were not strictly on their watch, both because of the heat, and because they were gone to dinner. So the young man [Ehud], when he had offered his presents to the king, who then resided in a small parlor that stood conveniently to avoid the heat, fell into discourse with [Eglon], for they were now alone, the king having bid his servants that attended him to go their ways, because he had a mind to talk with Ehud."

29. We might have had fewer doubts had it been the more ubiquitous *děvar-YHVH*, in Scripture very commonly associated with the prophetic divine command.

30. Similarly (via Freedman) Boling 1975: 86, citing Amos 6:4 and Hab 2:4. The Targum gives *salēq*, "go away," addressing the attendants. For a full discussion of how the versions treated this episode, see Barthélemy 1982: 76–77 and O'Connell 1996: 456–57.

31. One of King Zimri-Lim's administrators wrote, "When my lord was about to set out on a campaign, he charged me, 'You are living in the city of God. Report to me whatever oracle that you *hear occurring in God's temple*'" (ARM 26 196; see Nissinen 2003: 26–27). Those same archives make it clear that kings did expect the gods of other lands to interfere (for the better they hoped) in political matters. Lenzi (2008: 224–27) reviews the formulations in light of his study of hidden knowledge and the gods, concluding that "divine oracles were considered secret even as they were being revealed" (227).

32. See Jeyes 1989: 17–18, supplemented by Durand and Marti 2004: 7–10. There is also a wonderful note (ARM 2 124 = LAPO 17 #554, pp. 168–69) in which a drunken general reveals that the king's assistant and other insiders as well are betraying the king's

deliberations. On reaching the throne, new kings forced all officers, palace workers, and diviners to take loyalty oaths; see Durand 1991a.

As is his wont when addressing his Roman audience, Josephus (*Ant.* 5.192–93) expands, "[Eglon] was now sitting on his throne; and fear seized upon Ehud lest he should miss his stroke, and not give him a deadly wound; so he raised himself up, and said he had a dream to impart to him by the command of God; upon which the king leaped out of his throne for joy of the dream."

33. See also Neh 3:31–32. The virtuous Shunamite asks her husband to build for Elisha a ʿalîyat-qîr, something like a walled loft (that is, one made of packed earth, for permanence), and Josiah destroys the altars on the terrace, a grouping known as "Ahaz's loft" (ʿalîyat ʾāḥāz). From Jer 22:13, we might presume that many luxury houses included such a structure.

34. Should the privy not have been called *haḥeder **bĕ**ʿalîyat hammĕqērâ?*

35. For Halpern's architectural reconstruction, see his 1988a: 37–75 or, more accessibly, his 1988b. The inspiration for a beamed room seems to come from Stager 1985: 16, 29 n. 7.

36. "You should carry around a digging instrument in addition to other gears, so that should you need to be outside, you use it to dig a hole, then turn back and cover your excrement." God should not have to stumble over excrement when moving around the camp.

37. Perhaps *maqrê*, a *maqṭēl* formative from which are constructed such a noun as *maṣṣēvâ*, "pillar."

38. Citing the laws of Moses (likely Deut 24:16), his son Amazia avenges his father without also executing their children (2 Kgs 14:5–6).

39. It is obvious, however, that the spot is given as such because earlier (2 Sam 2:17–23), Abner had killed Asahel, Joab's brother. Hotly pursuing Abner, Asahel would not desist, so "Abner struck him in the *ḥōmeš* with a backward thrust of his spear and the spear protruded from his back. He fell there and died on the spot."

40. Maryon 1961: 175–76. Through the Renaissance, artists almost exclusively displayed the hold in this way. In Near Eastern art, we meet with essentially three poses. In some contexts that involved piercing the victim, the hilt of a small, thin dagger (equivalent to our "punch-" or "push-" blades) is held between the middle fingers, with a double-crested pommel resting inside the palm; see Pinnock 1997. Mostly in attack poses, a dagger is wielded with the blade below the little finger. To use it effectively, the blow has to penetrate the chest despite frequently hitting the ribs. The third pose is the one used by Ehud.

In Hebrew literature the direction of the hand is normally not stated unless there is reason to do so, as in our Ehud narrative. In a stylized image of a lion hunt, a brave Assyrian kings holds a leaping lion by the throat while thrusting a dagger upward into its belly (see The Kingdom of Lions, http://lionkingdom.nl/lb002e.htm). The same pose is taken on an Old Babylonian plaque from Tell Khafaje (Tutub) (Art Resource, http://tinyurl.com/76ky767).

41. Something similar may have taken place in 2 Sam 2:16, when two sets of champions grasped each other by the head and plunged their knives into their opponents.

42. Halpern (1988a: 59) uses smart prose to re-create what the text never said happened: Ehud strikes from above a *seated* Eglon, preventing him from rising from his seat and delivering a "sic semper tyrannis" message from God. Josephus (*Ant.* 5.193) has Ehud stab Eglon in the heart, a deed more worthy of heroes.

43. For this phrase, the Peshiṭta substitutes "and the abdomen followed the wound"; see W. Smelik 1995: 374 n. 282.

44. When the anarchist Santo Ironimo Caserio plunged his dagger deep into French President Sadi Carnot's lower abdomen (24 June 1894), he left him about four hours of life despite surgical intervention.

45. The subject can hardly be the weapon (feminine) or its parts.

46. Barré (1991: 4) does not explain how this very East Semitic word got to Hebrew. Also unexplained is how, according to him, got attached "the common -ôn . . . termination," not to say also a directional suffix.

47. A number of commentators connect to *śědērōt*, "pillared porches," of 1 Kgs 6:9 and elsewhere. Midrash *Genesis Rabbah* 99:3 has these comments on *misdĕrônâ*: "R. Judan said: It means, 'into the public square.' R. Berekiah said: It means, 'The place where the ministering angels sat in ordered fashion (to protect Ehud).'" The Targum uses an aurally close word, *'ăksadrā'* (ultimately from Greek ἐξέδρα), "portico, arcade." Rahlfs A offers καὶ ἐξῆλθεν Αωδ εἰς τὴν προστάδα, "Ehud left through the vestibule," a slightly different reading of what we had in Rahlfs B of the earlier verse. Rahlfs B, however, inserts a notice not in the Hebrew, καὶ ἐξῆλθεν τοὺς διατεταγμένους, "[Ehud] moved beyond appointed (guards)."

48. See their comments in King and Stager 2001: 31–33 and more fully in Stager 2003a: 240*–44*. Fine reviews of how locks worked according to Neo-Assyrian texts are in A. Fuchs 1998: 97–107 (reference courtesy M. Stol) and Radner 2010: 270–71. For other mechanisms, see Eras 1957 and Wulff 1966.

49. Kraeling (1935: 209–10) needlessly imagines that the verb *nā'al* (because a homonym has to do with shoeing someone) requires the pull of a leather thong to secure the bolt. But his solution is more or less what King and Stager (2001) suggest. Somewhat similar is the opinion of Ehrlich 1968: 49–50.

50. For "foot/leg" used euphemistically, see Exod 4:25; Deut 11:10 ("[Canaan] is not like the land of Egypt which you have just left and where you might plant your seed then urinate on it for a vegetable garden"); Isa 6:2, 7:20; 2 Kgs 18:27. Marvin Pope gives every possible example of euphemism in the *ABD* 1: 720–25.

51. For Halpern's reconstruction, see above. See also Hübner 1987 and Deist 1996. Many ribald readings of the assassination scene are premised on *kissē'* being a "seat" rather than a "throne," thence a "commode" or "toilet." (The verb *yāšav* is used for both sitting and squatting; see Deut 23:14 [13 RSV].) Only in Talmudic times, when Roman toilets were introduced, do privies acquire the euphemism "the house of the seat" (*mTamid* 1:1; *bBerakhot* 25a).

52. See Aurenche 1981, Kempinski and Reich 1992, Daviau 1993, Stager 2003a: 242*–44*, and Fink 2008; or under such headings as "Sewers," "Latrines," and "(Personal) Hygiene" in reference sets. For Mesopotamia, assemblages in Ešnunna, Tello, and Old Babylonian Ur are occasionally labeled as such. They are said to be under staircases or cut above vertical shafts, suggesting urban cesspits that must be periodically cleaned rather than a maintained sewage system (Krafeld-Daugherty 1994: 94–124, esp. 96 n. 453, 11, 116–17). Lebeau (2005) makes a case for a seated latrine on the second floor of a temple in mid-third-millennium Tell Beydar, with drainage cut into the outside wall—a highly unlikely solution. Relying on textual evidence, George (1999: 551) challenges the opinion that latrines and public toilets were lacking in Mesopotamia and suggests there is evidence (not yet fully assembled) to the contrary. Some interesting Hittite material on the topic is gathered in Ünal 1993. Soldiers on duty were not permitted to fulfill their

needs, presumably because they would stray from their guard spot; royalties defecated at special stops (*šinapši*). There is, of course, an enormous literature on the subject from Qumran (Magness 1998: 37–40; Harter 2004) and from the Roman period (Neudecker 1994; a fine collection in the old *DAGR* 3: 987–91, under "Latrina"). Underreported is the role that pigs and dogs played in ancient hygiene. Even into our own days, they keep latrines and cesspits from becoming major health hazards. For their service, however, they were broadly considered (then as now) as ritually unclean. (On the above, I have benefited from consulting with Sara Tricoli, David Gimble, and Benjamin Sass.)

53. See Jull 1998: 70, who cites Iron II stones with centered holes in areas E3 and G ("house of Ahiel"). Worth noting are the Mishnah's notice about special latrines built to serve priests (*mTamid* 1:1) and the Talmudic alert against having privies too close to human habitation (*yEruvin* 5:1). On privies and toilet practice in Second Temple and rabbinic periods, see Neis 2012.

54. A Mari incantation warns against the scorpion in the lavatory: "a drain gave birth to it: an envoy of death"; cited in Cavigneaux 1994.

55. Hittite: ^{duig}*kalti-* (see Ünal 1993: 126–28); Sumerian: kisi; Akkadian: *karpat šīnātim*. Greek lore on chamber pots is in Sparkes 1975: 128.

56. The passage (*FM* 2 122: 34–44) reads as follows: "On another matter; why does my lord not write to Kaḫat about Akin-amar. Is this man, Akin-amar, just my enemy but not also my lord's enemy? Why does he remain in good terms with my lord? Once, this man sat by my lord and drank a cup (of friendship). Having elevated him, my lord reckoned him among worthy men, clothing him in a garment, and supplying him with a wig. Yet, turning around, [Akin-amar] dropped his excrement into the cup he used, becoming hostile to my lord!"

57. Some emend the verbal form to *yôḥîlû*, from *yḥl* (Piel), as in Gen 8:10; either way, the sense is clear. The Targum simplifies with *vě'ôrîkû 'ad sagî*, "they waited a long time."

58. While this attribute is not used for human beings, there are a couple of derivatives that are: *'ašmān* in Isa 59:10, and *mišmān* in Ps 78:31 (parallel, *baḥûr*; "choice" of Israel). Rahlfs A simply refers to the combatant status of the slain, while Rahlfs B is literal but comes closest to the sense with πᾶν λιπαρὸν καὶ πάντα ἄνδρα δυνάμεως, "all those with vigor and valor"; see Lindars 1995: 155. *Metsudat David* (commentary of Rabbi David Altschuler, eighteenth-century Galicia) suggests that Moab had sent its best to the conquered territory.

59. Beem (1991: 158–62) discusses the issues and firmly decides to avoid them altogether.

60. Among the scholarship are articles by B. Mazar (Maisler) 1934, Fensham 1961, Danelius 1963, van Selms 1964, Aharoni 1970, and Craigie 1972. Countless notices about Shamgar are embedded in diverse studies on Israel's early history. McDaniel (1983: 295–96) gives a succinct review of earlier opinions on Shamgar's ethnic affiliation.

61. Bet-Anoth of Josh 15:59 may be a third, but less likely, such place name.

62. Othniel b. Kenaz (1:13; 3:9, 11); Joshua b. Nun (2:8); Ehud b. Gera, b. Hayyemini (3:15; possibly ethnic, because of the article); Shamgar b. Anat (3:31, 5:6); Baraq b. Abinoam (4:6, 12; 5:1); Gideon b. Joash (6:29; 7:14; 8:13, 29, 32); Abimelech b. Jerubaal (9:1); Jotham b. Jerubaal (9:5, 57); Gaal b. Ebed (9:26, 28, 30, 31, 35); Tola b. Pu'ah b. Dodo (10:1); Balak b. Sippor (11:25); Abdon b. Hillel of Pirathon (!) (12:13, 15); Jonathan b. Gershom b. Manasseh (18:30); and Phineas b. Eleazar b. Aaron (20:28).

63. McDaniel (1983: 98–99, 143–44) emends them out of existence.

64. Josephus (*Ant.* 5.197) has, "After him Saagaros [Σαάγαρος] the son of Anath [ὁ Ἀνάθου], was elected as their governor, but died in the first year of his government." Similarly,

some traditional commentators (*Metsudat David* among them) have Shamgar judge and die the year of Ehud's death.

65. A fuller version of these comments is in Sasson 2009.

66. Earliest printing of the play is from 1607. The full play is available at http://www.tech .org/~cleary/reven.html

67. For a discussion on the "historical background" for this unhistorical narrative, see Kasher 1981.

68. Among others are Sternberg 1987: 331–37; Amit 1999a; Barré 1991; Brettler 1991, more nuanced in 2002; Christianson 2003; Halpern 1988a, 1988b; G. Miller 1996a; Jull 1998; Block 1999: 158–59; Guillaume 2004: 27 n. 62; Mobley 2005: 80–86; and Miles 2008.

69. One goes too far when the opening and closing of Eglon's doors are read sexually, as is done by Brettler (1991: 293). He cites material from an erotic literature (Song 5:26), where such symbolism is warranted. (I would not want to find whimsy in the doors opening in Judg 19:27.) It is discouraging, too, how easily the reading of sexuality into the Ehud story has emboldened caricatures of homosexuality (G. Miller 1996a: 113–16) or false connections with other biblical traditions about Moab (Brettler 2002: 33).

Occasionally cited as parallel (Shanks 2012) is the murder of King Henri III of France (1574–89), allegedly as he sat on a *chaise-percée*, by a monk (Jacques Clément) who claimed to be bearing secrets. This version, contradicted by court testimony (Le Roux 2006: 17), is obviously a calque on the Ehud story. The earliest illustrations have Henri facing the monk as a dagger is plunged into his belly. Worth noting too are the many historiographic references to Henri's effeminacy and homosexuality.

70. See the comments on these categories in Sasson 1990: 331–34.

IIIC1. Deborah: The Prose Account (Judg 4:1–24)

1. We know that Ibni-Addu was an Akkadianized name for Yabni-Addu, since these spellings are attached to the name of a king of Tadûm. On Hazor in the Mari documents, see Bonechi 1991. Especially interesting is A.8140 (pp. 11–13) listing garments exchanged during a four-year interval. A fragment of a damaged cuneiform text found at Hazor with information about the conveying of a young woman is addressed to an Ibni-[xx]. It is tempting to restore the name *Ibni-Addu. Because the tablet likely comes from at least a century or so after the end of the Mari archives, it might give one more testimony for the use of this dynastic name. On the tablet, see Horowitz, Oshima, and Sanders 2006: 77–78. A fuller treatment is in Horowitz and Shaffer 1992.

In a startlingly historicizing (and hardly convincing) study of a gold ring from a Megiddo tomb, Shea (2004) finds the names of Jabin and Sisera (*ybn wśśrʾ*) over two registers that show the Kishon (with a fish) flowing toward the Mediterranean. Albright (1966: 11) had proposed reading the same signs as *lʾšt bkʾy*.

2. Compare "king of Sodom" (Gen 14:8 vs. 14:2), "king of the Philistines" (Gen 26:1 vs. 26:8), king of Egypt (Gen 40:1 vs. Exod 1:15), "king of the Amorites" (Num 21:21 vs. 21:34), and "king of Moab" (Judg 3:12, 14 vs. 3:15, 17). "King of Canaan" occurs also in Jub 46:9 carrying on a fantastic war against Pharaoh.

3. The Hebrew University's Hazor excavation project maintains a fine website that is updated. Its reading of Hazor's history is enlightening but also highly dependent on biblical narratives: http://unixware.mscc.huji.ac.il/~hatsor/hazor.html. A fine overview of MB Hazor as known from the Mari archives is van Koppen 2007.

4. A Mari letter (TH 72.16 = LAPO 16 #248, pp. 388–90) tells a story involving a Hazor caravan that was robbed in Emar; see also Sasson 2007: 465–68.

5. In Scripture, only occasionally are "army commanders" cited without narratives attached to them: Abimelech of Gerar drags his officer Phicol around (Gen 21:22, 32; 26:26), conferring gravitas to his relationship with Hebrew patriarchs. More often these commanders become the focus of attention, for example Abner, Joab, and Amasa in the early monarchy. Omri is one commander who usurps the throne (1 Kgs 16:16). We get a juicy story once about a foreign commander (Naaman, at 2 Kgs 5). Closest to our story line, minus the lively details, is the episode about Hadadezer of Aram sending his commander Shobach against David. (Shobach loses his life, 2 Sam 10:16–19.)

6. See Soggin 1981a: 60, and the Notes to 3:31. For Luwian names, see Albright 1970: 15; for a Cretan (Linear A no less!) derivation, see Garbini 1978: 20–21. For a Sardinian link, see Zertal 2002. It is telling that those who make such proposals are not always specialists in those languages or cultures. There are some fictional histories that ply similar routes, for example, Williamson 1999.

7. Josephus enriches the threat posed to Israel: Jabin "had in pay three hundred footmen, and ten thousand horsemen, with fewer than three thousand chariots. Sisera was commander of all his army, and was the principal person in the king's favor. He so sorely beat the Israelites when they fought with him, that he ordered them to pay tribute" (*Ant.* 5.198–99). Pseudo-Philo assigns eight thousand chariots to Sisera (*LAB* 30.3)

8. See Feldman 1998: 155–56.

9. Establishing a Luwian etymology for Deborah's name (McDaniel 1983: 108–3) can hardly be taken seriously.

10. Bees also carried negative connotations, some of which later tradition attached to Deborah; see Feldman 1998: 154–55. At least since Hellenistic times, honey was more likely derived from dates. Bedenbender 1997 is a good example of the danger (and occasional promise) of interpreting stories by treating names as cue (Bee, Torch, Lightning, etc.).

11. In the Mari archives of Zimri-Lim, Dariš-Libur was in charge of the king's garments; perhaps because his occupation required the confidence of the king, he was often sent on some very sensitive diplomatic missions.

12. See Braude and Kapstein (1981: 153): "Deborah's husband was completely illiterate [and so unable to study Torah]. So his wife said to him: 'Come on, make wicks, and take them to the Holy Place in Shiloh. Your portion may thus be with men of worth . . . and you will have life in the world-to-come.' And because he used to make thick wicks whose light was ample, he was called by the name Lapidoth, a name which means 'Bright Lights.' In fact, he had three names—Barak, Lapidoth, and Michael: Barak, because his face had the livid look of lightning; Lapidoth, because he used to make wicks which he took to the Holy Place in Shiloh; and Michael, which was his given name." In *Megillah* 14a, however, it is Deborah who made wicks (so too Rashi). Some traditional Jewish translations take their cue from Rashi and translate the phrase a "fiery woman," potentially a misleading connotation.

13. In Mesopotamia, the omen series *šumma ālu* (for its incipit, "if a city is set on a height") devotes tablets 91–94 to divination aided by flame, torches, and smoke; see S. M. Maul in "Omina und Orakel. A," *RlA* 10: 60, 87. Its antecedents go back to the second millennium BCE. (Reference is courtesy A. Annus.) But detailed information comes mostly from Demotic papyri—so Hellenistic or Roman—although some have moved their manifestations to the pharaonic periods while others limit their origins to the Ptolemaic

period; see generally D. Ogden 2002 and specifically Dieleman 2005. (J. Dieleman graciously helped me with the bibliography here.) In early China, fire would be used to crack shells, which were then read by diviners.

14. Some commentators connect also with the "Oak at Tabor" of 1 Sam 10:3; see Moore 1895: 113.

15. Lindars (1995: 186) offers a convoluted (yet faulty) analysis of the verbal forms in question.

16. Many other examples come to mind, from Assyria to Hamath (Zakkur); see conveniently Block 1994: 244–47. What he cites can be multiplied, but the point is made.

17. Fine discussion of the versions is in Barthélemy 1982: 77–78. J. Ackerman (1975: 10) simply presumes that the Greek expansion was once original to the Hebrew, to the point of analyzing its nonexistent Hebrew vocabulary. Josephus (*Ant.* 5.203) has Baraq insisting that Deborah share military power with him.

18. See the Introductory Remarks to IA1 (Judg 1:1–7). J. Ackerman (1975: 9–10) has some good pages on this topic but cites Mari prophecies when Mari divinations are more applicable to the situation.

19. King Zimri-Lim was repeatedly warned never to undertake campaigns without taking the omens (for example, *FM* 7 38; see ARM 10 54 = LAPO 18 #1097, p. 280). As grizzled a warrior as was Samsi-Addu (the father of Zimri-Lim's predecessor on Mari's throne), he would nevertheless not make a move without consulting them. There is a letter (A.1195 + ARM 1 85 = LAPO 17 #449, pp. 19–23) in which he lectures his son Yasmaḫ-Addu on a proper way to set off for battle, among them making sure to take diviners ready to take omens (and so also many sheep).

20. Assis (2005a) argues for a demonstration of Deborah's prophetic gifts. Yee (1993: 114–17) thinks that Deborah is into shaming Baraq rather than into nurturing ambiguity.

21. The adverbial suffix *-he* occurs with many verbs of movement, including *hālak*, as in Judg 16:1.

22. Rahlfs A: καὶ οἱ πλησίον τοῦ Κιναίου, "the kin of the Kenite."

23. Soggin (1981a: 62–63) is among commentators for whom *ḥever* is a tribal unit rather than a personal name, to the point of speaking of "Yaël, une femme du groupe" in 4:21, a very awkward rendering. (Hebrew might simply have had something like **ʾešet qînîm* or, as unlikely, **ʾiššâ qênît.*)

24. See Myers 1953: 712–15.

25. On God's presence in battles, see Mann 1977: 252–61, who assembles the vocabulary relevant to our episode on pp. 253–54.

26. The motif also occurs readily in Near Eastern literature, especially in the myths and in the annals of kings, for which see Part I of Mann 1977 as well as his pp. 245–51 (for excerpts). The notion is also available in prophetic literature in which gods either reassure kings that they stand ahead of him (*ana maḫrišu*) or hand him their own expert weapons with which to achieve victory; see the Mari text I cite as a final Comment to IA1, "Adoni-bezeq."

27. It is slightly different in Josh 10:10 where Israel's night attack might have accompanied God's offensive. While obviously a feature in ancient mythmaking (think of the Mesopotamian *Enuma Elish*) and in epic literature (think of Homer or the Tukulti-Ninurta Epic), the theme of divine involvement in human conflicts is commonly reported in royal annals, where it reflects divine anger at the enemy's perfidy or desertion of treaty oaths. In Mesopotamian prophetic texts, however, their involvement can be startlingly

displayed. Locked in a dreadful fight against Elam, Ashurbanipal is in Arbela for the feast of Ištar. He reports:

> The very same night as I implored her, a visionary [*šabrû*] lay down and had a dream. When he woke up, he reported to me the nocturnal vision shown to him by Ištar: "Ištar who dwells in Arbela entered, having quivers hanging from her right and left and holding a bow in her hand. She had drawn a sharp-pointed sword, ready for battle. You [Ashurbanipal] stood before her and she spoke to you like a mother who gave birth to you. Ištar, the highest of the gods, called to you and gave you the following order: 'You are prepared for war, and I am ready to carry out my plans.' You said to her: 'Wherever you go, I will go with you!' But the Lady of Ladies answered you: 'You stay here in your place! Eat food, drink beer, make merry and praise my godhead, until I go to accomplish that task, making you attain your heart's desire. You shall not make a wry face, your feet shall not tremble, you shall not even wipe the sweat in the tumult of war!'" She sheltered you in her sweet embrace; she protected your entire body. Fire flashed in her face, and she went raging away, directing her anger against Teumman, king of Elam, who had made her furious." (Nissinen 2000: 147–48)

It is important to note that Ashurbanipal does not do as told; in fact, he carries the war to the Elamites and crushes them utterly. Nonetheless, the victory is Ištar's just the same as if she had fought the enemy single-handedly. The discrepancy between the rhetoric of divine support and its actual application is always an issue in evaluating ancient historiography.

28. Pseudo-Philo has him escape on a horse (*LAB* 31.3).

29. Josephus (*Ant.* 5.205–6) fills in the background as follows: "So the battle began; and when [the armies of Israel] were come to a close fight, there came down from heaven a great storm, with a vast quantity of rain and hail, and the wind blew the rain in the face of the Canaanites, and so darkened their eyes, that their arrows and slings were of no advantage to them, nor would the coldness of the air permit the soldiers to make use of their swords; while this storm did not so much incommode the Israelites, because it came in their backs."

30. The notices are too common to warrant listing; in Sennacherib's famous prism alone we hear such reports about Ispabara of Elippi ("fled to distant parts"), Lulê of Sidon ("fled into the midst of the sea"), Šuzibi of Chaldea ("fled alone like a criminal"; he does the same again a bit later), Merodan-baladan ("fled like a bird"), Manniae, king of Ukku ("fled to distant parts"), and Umman-menanu of Elam and his allies ("fled like pigeons"). No doubt there is a theme here that is exploited, but realism lies behind them all.

31. Fine pages on all these matters can be found in B. Lafont 2001a: 246–50, 297–301. Halpern (1988a: 85–86) claims that Heber was a double agent, steering Sisera into destructive moves. This is possible, but what would be left for God to do?

32. See the discussion above about this attribution. It is tempting to contemplate a gnomic pun on Jael's name ʾ*ešet midyānîm ûvêt ḥāver*, "contentious mistress of spacious houses" (Prov 21:9, 25:24). We recall the close association between Midian and the Kenites.

33. It is not very useful to promote other derivations, such as connection with Yāʾil, a place within Mari's control (Boling 1975: 97), or with Yāʾilanum, a tribe that gave fits to Mari kings.

34. Speculations on his status are many; see Margalit 1995: 633.

35. A district governor writes King Zimri-Lim: "In the Yaminite encampments on Terqa's outskirts, numerous are the women who are wives of the enemy—(that is) all those whose husbands have fled to be with the enemy; and they are living in my own district. For this reason, the enemy causes me troubles all the time. Five to six men would often assemble; by night, they would cross into these encampments (to visit) their wives and then would leave. They gather complete reports about us, carrying them back to their accomplices. Because of this, the presence of the enemy is constant here." (ARM 3 16 = LAPO 17 #682, pp. 425–27).

36. B. Mazar himself does not push a cultic function on Jael although he does attribute to Rashi (Notes to 5:6) the claim that she was a prophet (see B. Mazar 1965: 302 n. 27). In fact, Rashi (as some other traditional commentators) has Jael a judge, much like Shamgar, not a prophet.

37. It did not hurt that, according to rabbinic lore, Jael had grace and beauty, with men's desire surging at the mere sound of her voice (*bMegillah* 15a).

38. A. Cohen (1924: 182–83) reviews lexicography comparatively and arrives at "thick coverlet." Wilkinson (1983) is brutal to the Hebrew, splitting *śĕmîkâ* into two words to obtain the philologically suspect "[Jael] overwhelmed him with perfume." Reis (2005: 29) "clarifies the narrative" by having Jael cover Sisera with her body. After Sisera drinks, Jael services him again "in the sexually superior position" (30).

39. Lines 26–27; I cite Sinuhe from Lichtheim's translation in *COS* 1: 78–82.

40. Greek actually has "wine" rather than water in 1 Sam 25, misunderstanding the topos. On wine in biblical lore, see Sasson 1994b. Pseudo-Philo has Jael serve Sisera twice, the second time milk mixed with wine so as to deliver him into the arms of Morpheus.

41. I argue (Sasson 2002) for a sensible husbandry advice not to cook a kid in fat (*ḥēlev*) rather than milk (*ḥālāv*).

42. For milk in cuisine, see Sasson 2002; for milk and beer in Egyptian presentation, see King Antef (II)'s hymn to Re, Lichtheim 1973: 94–95; for dairy products in Mesopotamia, see Jacobsen 1983: 196–98 and Stol, "Milch (Produkte)," *RlA* 8 (1993–97): 189–201. For the mention of milk in ancient literature, see Grottanelli 1994.

43. A nice collection of articles with the raising of children in Mesopotamia as its theme is in Lion, Michel, and Villard 1997.

44. Many are collected in Reis 2005: 32–33, who adds her own excesses. See also Niditch 1989.

45. Radaq notes that the Masoretes avoided this root by not vocalizing the form *vayyā'ôf*.

46. The rabbis engaged in a mass rehabilitation of tyrants through their descendants (*bSanhedrin* 96b): "The Rabbis taught in a Baraita: Naaman was a resident convert. Nebuzaradan was a righteous convert. Descendants of Sisera learned Torah in Jerusalem [i.e., R. Akiva]. Descendants of Sancheriv taught Torah to the masses. And who were they? Shemaya and Avtalyon. Descendants of Haman studied Torah in B'nei B'rak, and there were even descendants of the wicked Nebuchadnezzar whom the Holy One, blessed be He, tried to bring under the wings of the Shechinah."

47. Such conjunctions must not be confused with what occurs when Jephthah's daughter comes out to greet her father, as it is necessary for the plot rather than decorates it; see at Judg 11:34.

48. When a man is said to "come to a woman," the idiom is most frequently a euphemism for having intercourse. In our passage, such a meaning is totally incongruous, but see the Comments. Ehrlich (1968: 79) proposes a substantial emendation into *vayyāvō' hā'ōhĕlâ* (see Exod 18:7). Many simply avoid any misconception by translating "he went into her

tent" (RSV) or "he went inside with her" (*TNK*). However, Reis (2005: 34–35) has Jael sexually favoring Baraq, apparently her third coitus (or more) of the day.

49. See also Wellhausen 1994: "In the song [Judg 5] the campaign is prepared with human means. . . . In the narrative, on the contrary, the deliverance is the work of Jehovah alone; the men of Israel are mere dummies, who show no merit and deserve no praise" (241).

50. The scholarly vocabulary is that this episode does not "belong to the tradition," the phrase intimating that we can confidently establish what was part of the tradition.

51. See also Cooke 1892: "the whole song glows with the passionate enthusiasm of a poet who was keenly interested, and perhaps took part, in the heroic deeds of which he sings. The antiquity of the poem, then, may be taken for granted, and its value as historical evidence must be admitted at the same time" (1); similarly, Cooke 1913: 44.

52. 1 Sam 12:11 reads, "The Lord then sent Jerubbaal, Bedan, Jephthah, and Samuel to save you from enemies around you so that you can live in security." Much ink is spilled on identifying Bedan, with suggestions to equate him with Baraq (LXX, followed by many), with Samson (rabbinic lore), and with Abdon (H. Ewald; see Jacobson 1992, 1994). Zakovitch (1972) proposes that it is a doublet for Jephthah, offered as a gloss in our passage, but he is challenged by Day (1993) and others. Heb 11:32 obviously depended on the LXX version of this verse. See also the Comments to IIID1 (Judg 6:1–32).

53. Zertal 2002 decorates the biblical text, creatively setting it in a context full of charioteered but slow-footed "Shardana" (Sea People) from Harosheth-haggoyim (= el-Ahwat). They come down the Aruna pass, led by Sisera, "whose name originated in Sardinia," but are caught in an ambush by Hebrews.

54. It is important to recognize that women in ancient Israel were no pacifists and that they sent their sons to war with all the pride, hopes, fears, and pains that accompany any national effort. Yet it stretches our information to reconstruct a place for women among Israel's military by invoking such figures as Rahab of Jericho, the woman of Thebez (Judg 9: 50–53), Judith, and the like; see Yee 1993: 117–21.

55. It seems to me far-fetched that Jael murders because Sisera abused her husband's hospitality when demanding from her drink and guard-duty (Matthews and Benjamin 1992). They interpret her words of 4:18 as a warning rather than an invitation. Interesting is S. Ackerman's suggestion (2000) that Delilah, a non-Hebrew who might have been a heroine to the Philistines, is a mirror image to Jael.

56. See the nice study of Burnette-Bletsch (1998).

57. In the vast lore of the Talmud, bawd occasionally overcame taste, as in the portrayal of Rebekah, normally a venerated matriarch (Poorthuis 1998).

58. Reis (2005) reviews and multiplies many of the arguments in which Jael is a *vagina dentate* with murderous phallic impulses. Interesting notices on the Jael story in modern literature are in Wallhead 2001.

IIIC2. Deborah: The Poem (Judg 5:1–31)

1. This couplet addresses Queen Sabbath, an avatar for the Shekhina, a mystical archetype for Israel. The poem is chanted at Friday night services wherever Jews worship. The language draws on Judg 5:12, with a fine play between (*šîr*) *dabběrî*, "craft (a song)," and the name Deborah.

2. I give an instance of how one poem may be crafted from inherited phrases in a study of Jonah's poem, Sasson 1990: 168–201; see also pp. 207–8, n. 66, where other examples are diagnosed.

3. Among specialized studies, see Watson 1984, a good general guide to the techniques; O'Connor 1980, a brilliant and original effort to establish new measures and criteria toward understanding the poetic idiom; and Kugel 1981, an overview on the history of scholarship on Hebrew. Alter (1985) offers interesting chapters on diverse types of biblical poetry.

4. A longer list of markers is available in Goodwin (albeit to refute them) 1969: 53–79, some of which have already disappeared from recent discussions. They include, among others, enclitic *mem*, the particle *hem*, *'ek* and *mā* as adverbs, ablative *be-*, demonstrative pronoun *zeh/zû*, vocative *lamed*, and preposition *lamed* meaning "from." In fact, several biblical poems (Deborah's song among them) contain a healthy number of conjunctions and definite articles (see below). They are often removed by critics reaching for their allegedly more pristine "original" versions.

5. See Sasson 2002: 9–10: "We know from Assyrian and Greek transcriptions that some famous people had names that sounded different from their Hebrew version. For example, Kings Menahem and Jehu of Israel answered to the names 'Menihimmu' and 'Yaw'a', respectively. Of more consequence, the Masoretes . . . did not know that certain verbal forms (for example the *qal* passive) existed, and so vocalized them differently (as *niphal* for the imperfect and as *pual* for the perfect)." See also the Introductory Remarks to IIIG3 (Judg 12).

6. In his sixth homily, devoted to the Song of Deborah, Origen speaks of a special scroll that collects these poems, another by Moses (Num 21:17–18), and one by Hannah (1 Sam 2:1–10).

7. In fact, a survey of how the RSV translates diverse verbal forms reveals great subjectivity in choice; see Watke and O'Connor 1990: 459 (§29.2ff.).

8. Bechmann 1989 uses forty tight pages just for a Deborah bibliography. A more selective list is in Becker-Spörl 1998. A fairly comprehensive bibliography is available on the Internet and is attached to McDaniel's highly eccentric study of 2003.

9. Contrast the vaguer connotation of *bā'ēt hahî'* at 4:4, said about Deborah's tenure as judge.

10. W. Smelik (1995: 391–92) cites a Targumic insert here, "because of the miraculous redemption experienced by Israel."

11. For similar constructions, see Num 5:1 and Gen 33:7. In our passage, Rahlfs A gives the verb in the singular ("Deborah sang as well as Baraq"), and Rahlfs B has the plural form ("Deborah and Baraq sang").

12. We occasionally meet with such phrases as *'āšîrâ va'ăzammĕrâ* (Ps 27:6, 57:8 [7 RSV], 108:2 [1 RSV]), which indicates a distinction between the two modes, even if probably it was reaching for a single notion (merismus), something "I shall chantingly sing," or the like.

13. In Deut 33:11 we have the same formula deceptively, for *bārēk* is transitive, "Please God bless [Levi's] substance."

14. Here is W. Smelik's rendering of the verse (1995: 392): "When the House of Israel rebelled against the law, the nations came against them and expelled them from their cities. But when they returned to keep the law, they prevailed against their enemies; they drove them out of the territory of the land of Israel. Thus, because of the retribution of Sisera's shattering and that of his army, and because of the miracle and the redemption that was performed for the sake of Israel—when the Sages sat down openly in the synagogues again and taught the people the words of the law—therefore bless and give thanks before

the Lord." The Peshiṭta also has a different take, "In the vengeance that Israel avenged (in the praise of the people, praise the LORD)"; see Weitzman 1999: 25, 37.

15. Amusing is R. Miller's original solution (2008). Seduced by the shared consonants (*pr‘*) in the phrase in question and the noun for "pharaoh," he arrives at "when the Pharaohs pharaohed" by appealing to mumbo jumbo philology, yet by making "no claim for the song to be a historical account from the Late Bronze Age of Israelite exploits" (654).

16. The absence of a definite article before ‘*ām* (but also before a few other nouns where it might be expected) is often taken as a sign of the poem's great antiquity; see the Introductory Remarks. In fact, these presumed absences tend to cluster in the invocation portion of the poem: *rōzĕnîm, mĕlākîm* (both vocatives at 5:3), ’*ereṣ* (5:4), *šāmayim* (5:4, 20), ‘*āvîm* (5:4), and *hārîm* (5:5). Elsewhere they occur readily (see vv. 16, 20, 28 [two times], and 35). Predictably, this clustering can be used to argue the composite nature of the poem.

17. Many interesting insertions are featured in diverse Targumim, and what they say is nicely reviewed by W. Smelik 1995: 398–412. Basser (2005) nicely reviews the debate among medieval rabbis on treating the theophany as a victory hymn or as a celebration of the gift of Torah at Sinai.

18. See McDaniel 1983: 68–169 for a notice on the suggestions and results. Cross (1973: 101 n. 35) would remove all allusion to waters, ostensibly because some of it is "metrically impossible." Caquot (1986: 51) cites de Wette's opinion that the song dates after David because of this affinity with Ps 68.

19. See Moore (1895: 139–38), who cites and refutes the claim.

20. In the flush of Ugaritic discoveries, when it was realized that *g* meant "voice," some examples of *gam* were treated as adverbs, for example, Ps 137:1, "By the streams of Babylon, there we sat, weeping loudly [*gam bākînû*] when thinking of Zion." Boling (1975: 101, 108) accepts such a sense here; but with hardly any sound at stake, he arrives at an awkward "with Thunder the skies rained, with thunder the clouds rained water." In the parallel description of Ps 68:9 (8 RSV), ’*af* takes the place of *gam*, and only dangerously could it be associated with a homonym for "nose, face." M. Smith (2009: 48–49) finds an echo of waters below, at 5:21.

21. Floyd 1980: 238 n. To account for the particle's existence, Floyd proposes a complicated series of steps that would not be profitable to review.

22. Yet glosses do not normally accrue except under obscure contexts. Moore (1895: 141–42) would keep it parenthetically, judging it an explanatory gloss, so "(that is Sinai)." Lindars (1995: 233–34) follow others who suggest it as a gloss, "(This means [the theophany] of Sinai)." The suggestion harks back to haggadic material in the Targum; see W. Smelik (1995: 414–30), who painstakingly reconstructs it. As suggested above, however, a reference to the exodus is doubtful here.

23. Cooke (1913), who believes that the historical Shamgar was an oppressor, writes, "When once Shamgar had been treated by late interpreters as an Israelite champion (iii. 31), the words *in the days of Jael* were probably inserted to mark the period more exactly" (57).

24. There is an enormous discussion about the exact meaning of *ḥdl*; see Schloen 1993a: 21–25. At stake for the debaters is how to eke out historical information as background for the song's inspiration.

25. See Sasson 1966: 136–37, where I suggest translating *ntbt* by "trading concession." Ugarit specialists translate the word "trail," "path," or "caravan."

26. Azatiwada contrasts the days in which there were "places which formerly were feared, when a man feared to walk the road" with those after his rule in which "a woman can

walk alone with her spindles" (*COS* 2 §2.31, p. 149; trans. K. Lawson Younger, Jr.). Nothing in the poem, or in the prose narrative of chapter 4, accentuates such conditions, and we may wish to treat them as echoic on a mundane level the chaotic conditions evoked in 5:4–5.

27. The versions differ slightly. The Targum sticks close to the Hebrew except that it opens startlingly on "when they sinned in the days of Shamgar," doubtless to transit from the Sinai context it promoted in the previous verse to a lamentable situation (W. Smelik 1995: 430–31). Rahlfs B is also very close; but Rahlfs A is not, at least in one of its clauses: "In the days of Samegar . . . , with kings lacking [ἐξέλιπον (ἐξέλειπον) Βασιλεῖς]"; see Harlé and Roqueplo 1999: 113 for a possible explanation.

28. Cooke (1892: 32–33), Lindars (1995: 237), and Barthélemy (1982: 79) are among many scholars who collect diverse suggestions.

29. Freedman's understanding is similar (1980: 150).

30. This feature is regarded as an Aramaism, lastly by Waltisburg (1999: 218–19), but this is disputed as such by Rendsburg (2003: 123).

31. Later in Judges (17:10, 18:19), a priest is a "father" to a worshiper. Especially in Akkadian from Mari, an *ummum* is also a woman who nurses a child from birth.

32. A trivial argument is that the reference should be deleted because a poet would not be "awakening" (5:12) Deborah when she had already "risen" (see Cooke 1892: 34).

33. In the song we meet with the following (with changes occurring within verses): first person (singular), at 5:3, 7(?), 9, 21; second person (singular), at 5:4, 12 (feminine), 12, 14, 16, 31; and second person (plural), at 5:2, 3, 9, 10, 23.

34. 2 Sam 20:16–19. The passage is full of difficulties, but luckily they are not germane here; see Pisano 1984: 146–49; Barthélemy 1982: 297–99.

35. Greek has a nice calque here, μητρόπολις, "Metropolis" (lit., "mother city"). However, this word is used elsewhere for *'avî*, "father of," *hā'ănāq/hā'ănôq* of Josh 15:13 and 21:11. Akkadian is known to use *ummum* figuratively: the Diyala being the "mother" of rivers and the scribal arts the "mother" of disciplines (*CAD* U/W, 130).

36. A different understanding of the context and allusions is in Camp 1981: 27–28 (reference is courtesy of S. Ackerman). Camp makes a parallel between *naḥălat YHVH*, "the Lord's possession" and a "mother in Israel," when the former phrase (as elsewhere) simply refers to Israel.

37. See Rabinowitz 1984. Na'aman (1990: 424) assigns *'āz* a role in segmenting the song into five major stages. His analysis is highly accommodating, especially when there are difficulties galore in interpreting what the song says.

38. There is not much profit in comparing this number to the ten thousand men mentioned in 4:6, as each has its own implication within its genre; but see Halpern (1988a: 80), who does just that, deriving the implication that the prose depended on the poetic version.

39. In Ps 105:2 the verb occurs in this sequence: "Sing [*šîrû le-*] to (the Lord), hymn [*zammĕrû le-*] to him, Proclaim [*śîḥû bĕ-*] his wondrous acts."

40. Targum adds one more category, "those who abandon their tasks," *mevaṭṭĕlîn 'isqêhôn*.

41. There is a nice exegesis in the Talmud (*bEruvin* 54b): "'You riders on white asses' refers to Torah scholars who wander from town to town and from province to province to study Torah and clarify its words, making them as lucid as noontime (white). 'You who sit on rich cloths [*middîn*]' refers to halachic authorities whose rulings [*dîn*] reflect the absolute truth. 'You who walk' refers to the students of Scripture." See also Braude and Kapstein 1981: 163.

42. Lagrange (1903: 88) thinks that victors are sitting on the garments of those they defeated.

43. Albright 1968: 44 emends, *metri causa* and relying on an Ugaritic phrase, to *mdn ʿr* and then proposes loss of the last by haplography, "Ye who sit on caparisoned <male donkey> (?)." Burney (1970: 122–23) competes with the Hebrew poet by offering a wholesale emendation of the verse, in parts nonidiomatically.

44. Whether or not the word has an Aramaic plural ending is disputed; see Rendsburg 2003: 123.

45. Cooke (1892: 39–40), Burney (1970: 125–29), and Lindars (1995: 245–47) are among fine commentators who review earlier proposals.

46. For Rahlfs A and B and their possible Hebrew inspiration, see Harlé and Roqueplo 1999: 117–18. In fact, in its own way, each witness struggles to give sense, with Rahlfs A much more detached from the Hebrew than Rahlfs B. The Vulgate similarly diverges, with "Where the chariots were dashed together, and the enemy host was choked," *ubi conlisi sunt currus et hostium est suffocates*. The Targum continues to paraphrase imaginatively (W. Smelik 1995: 447): "From the place where they assaulted them and took what was in their hand—the abode of publicans and the residence of rovers over cisterns in a watering-place—there they gave thanks for the righteous deeds of the LORD; for the righteous deeds of the one who lives in the unwalled cities in the land of Israel. Then the people of the LORD went down from the fortified cities to live in the unwalled cities."

47. There are proposals to emend the consonants at the end of v. 10 and the opening of v. 11, *ś/śyḥ m+*, into plausible verbal forms such as *śmḥw*, "be happy," or *šmʿw*, "listen"; see Cooke 1892: 39. There are also suggestions that rely on dislodging (yet another) enclitic *mem* from a succeeding word; Boling 1975: 110.

48. Whether this verb betrays Aramaism or not is debated, but hardly conclusively. Needlessly, a verb in Exod 32:18 (*ʿannôt*) is sometimes emended to make a third example of the form.

49. Traditional exegetes (*bPesaḥim* 87b) read **pizrōnô* for *pirzōnô* and interpret it as praising God for dispersing the Jews, for better survival.

50. Similar sentiments are at 2 Chr 6:41. Segond (1900: 60–70), citing Lamartine and Lady Anne Blunt, draws on Arab lore to create a charming image of Deborah, atop a camel in a howdah, inciting warriors to fearless battle.

51. On this motif, see the material and comments of S. Amsler in *TLOT* 3: 1140.

52. On Alkabetz's appropriation of language from 5:12 for his *Lekha dodi*, see the epigraph to the Notes above.

53. The Greek differs from the Hebrew, most starkly by opening on verbal forms that urge Deborah to awaken others rather than just herself. Moreover, just before Deborah is said to shape a song, Rahlfs A has her awakening "thousands among the people" (ἐξέγειρον μυριάδας μετὰ λαοῦ). Naturally, some scholars would emend the Hebrew into harmony with it (see Lindars 1995: 249), but the Greek is certainly an expansion, so we should resist spoiling a perfectly reasonable Hebrew text. For issues raised by Rahlfs A's version of the song, see Tov 1978, and for this verse, pp. 230–31. Tov shows that our version of Rahlfs A may have been compromised by frequent copying and liturgical adaptations.

54. The Greek traditions differ, with Rahlfs B closer to what we have, "Then went down a remnant to the strong, the people of the LORD went down for him among the mighty ones." Rahlfs A is more distant: "His power was then exalted. LORD, do humble for me

those stronger than me"—the last likely attributed to Baraq. See the good notes of Harlé and Roqueplo 1999: 119–20.

55. See, for example, Halpern 1988a: 100 n. 6; Cooke 1913: 60; and *HALOT*, under שריד.

56. See Halpern 1988a: 80 and Amit 2004: 520–21. Wong (2007) offers a sustained (if philologically uninvolved) argument for the poem's polemics against tribes reluctant to join the cause of Yнvн. Stager (1989; more detail in his 1988) gives an economic reason for their reluctance: They depended on Canaanites for their own welfare. The war was fought by tribes that were independent. Meroz had no excuse not to fight, hence its curse. Weaving a full story out of the troubles in the days of Shamgar (v. 6), Schloen (1993a) has them rising against profiteers from tolls on caravans. For G. Miller (1996a), the song, with its listing of tribes, is a "ledger in an oral culture for the recordation of inter-tribal obligations" (1996b: 2295). It was kept alive beyond the years of tribal confederacy as an argument for the superiority of the monarchy.

57. Boling (1975: 111) has the right notion but incorrectly defines the function of the preposition as "partitive." See Rahlfs A, cited below.

58. After W. Smelik 1995: 453–54. The Peshiṭta here goes its own way: "After you, Benjamin, in your love"; see Weitzman 1999: 294.

59. See partial listings in Cazelles 1974; McDaniel 1983: 203; Caquot 1986: 57 and n. 31; and Block 1999: 232 n. 391. Lindars (1995: 252–53) favors a proposed Egyptian (!) etymology (from *srs*, "an officer").

60. As we saw, Rahlfs A has Ephraim as antecedent. Rahlfs B reflects the Hebrew ambiguity. Caquot (1986: 59 n. 36) patiently reviews modern reactions.

61. On the much emended passage in Hosea and its connection with Judg 5:14, see Na'aman 2009: 221–22.

62. Lindars (1995: 254) makes a mercenary group out of it.

63. The Targum, followed by Radaq, makes a "pen" (*qulmas*) out it, translating the phrase "those who wrote with the pen of a scribe"; W. Smelik 1995: 456–57.

64. From the Mari records we have an appreciation of the role of diverse specialists, including scribes who participated in the conduct of war. Especially interesting was the major function of the *ṭupšar amurrîm*, "Amurru scribe," a post that seemed to be second in authority to the general, as far as the muster of troops is concerned; see Durand 1998, esp. 331–416 ("Les armées et les militaires").

65. Rahlfs A (drops the first phrase, though expansive otherwise): "Issachar, with Deborah, has sent forth by land. Why, are you living in the midst of the shoreline? He stretched forth on his footsteps; in the divisions of Reuben—great plumbing of the heart." In Rahlfs B, we have: "And the princes in Issachar (were) with Deborah and Baraq; so Baraq sent out in the plains in his footsteps; in the portions of Reuben—great scrutiny of the heart."

66. Whether the word is of Aramaic coinage is debated; see Waltisberg 1999: 222 and Rendsburg 2003: 124.

67. The same context is rendered μέσον τῶν κλήρων, "between the inheritance," at Gen 49:14.

68. More philological surgery on these verses by Cross (and Halpern) to involve Reuben and Dan in the war against Canaan is countered by J. Wright 2011.

69. Dan, the city, had a more interesting fate, both in tradition and in archeology. See the dictionaries.

70. Halpern (1988a: 79–81) imagines that he can judge the priority of material shared in both the prose and the poetic segment on the basis of the double mentions of Zebulun

and of the numbers of men said to participate. These arguments are specious, for they treat both materials as equal vehicles for historical information, without rhetorical allowance for the genres in which the information is carried.

71. The LXX avoids repetition of the verb by offering παρετάξαντο, "they deployed," possibly reading *yaḥanû*; Lagrange 1903: 97.

72. For *dhr, the dictionaries needlessly distinguish between two roots, one allegedly "borrowed" from Egyptian. Also needless is the widely proposed transfer of the *mem* in *middaḥărôt* to the previous word, *sûs* (Ehrlich 1968: 85). Tournay (1996: 205) cites another instance of poetic linkage between Judg 5 and Ps 68:13, when the enemies of God, "rulers of hosts, run helter-skelter" (*malkê ṣěvāʾôt yiddōdûn yiddōdûn*).

73. Rabbinic lore indulged in some fancy re-creations: The stars descended on Sisera's armies, heating up his iron chariots such that his hosts went into the Kishon to cool off. Obeying a divine command, the stream then swept them off into the sea; *bPesaḥim* 118b.

74. Lines 57–64, translated in Westenholz 1997: 69–71. Block (1999: 236–37) finds an analogue in the Gebal Barkal stela of Thutmosis III: "When (the guards) were just about to come in order to meet at night and to keep the regular watch, it was at the second hour, a star appeared to their south. Never had the like happened. It flashed against them to him. None could stand there . . . none of them offered resistance . . . and none looked back. They no longer had horses, which had bolted in." However, the parallel falters, as earlier in the text Thutmosis himself is described as "a star that crosses the sky."

75. Joel 1:17 may contain another form of the same root, *megrěfōtêhem*, its meaning disputed.

76. Some commentators falsely imagine that the final clauses require a verb and offer emendations, none of which is necessary. Floyd (1980: 243, 249) ignores the syntax in the repetition of *nḥl* by treating its second mention as a verbal form, "to inherit, possess": "The Kishon retook its age-old course."

77. In the sermons delivered during the American Revolutionary War, the curse against Meroz was the most heavily cited of all scriptural passages. The analogy was made with those who not "only failed in their duty; they did not arm to recover their liberties when wrested from them by the hand of tyranny"; from Nathaniel Whitaker's sermon, "An Antidote Against Toryism." This information is courtesy of my colleague James P. Byrd.

78. Some exegetes, among them Ackroyd (1952: 161), think this segment was imported from an earlier tradition of the battle, perhaps even from an entirely different tradition.

79. Proposals, without solutions, are in Neef 1995.

80. It is interesting to note that the two major Greek renditions of Judges differ on this point. Rahlfs B parallels the Hebrew, whereas Rahlfs A definitely assigns the clause to the poet, "for they did not come to the aid of the LORD; our help is the LORD, powerful among the warriors."

81. Many commentators would strike out the reference to Heber as a later addition, imported from 4:17, claiming that it spoils the balance of couplets. Boling (1975: 114) resists doing so, albeit with little ardor.

82. The rabbis fretted about this possibility; see W. Smelik 1995: 472. Deborah was exempted from the comparison because she lived under a tree (4:5).

83. The Targum took the opportunity to moralize: Jael acquired the hammer to "shatter the wicked and the robbers," so depending on a meaning of "trouble" for *ʿāmāl*; W. Smelik 1995: 474–75. Rahlfs A (but not B) strives for some aural play (εἰς ἀποτομὰς κατακόπων' her hand "toward bits of those weary"); Harlé and Roqueplo 1999: 129.

Both Rahlfs A and B, however, unnecessarily supply a "left hand" to balance "the right hand" of Jael. In poetry, anatomic precision is optional.

84. Most commentators urge avoiding a realistic reconstruction of how Sisera met his maker, but they nevertheless display a good amount of ingenuity in doing so; see the comments of Cooke 1892: 14, Moore 1895: 165–66, and the review of Globe 1975.

85. Why we are told that he was stuck in the temple is not easy to explain once we move from the prose mode; see Burney 1970: 80, who certainly wastes much imagination on the matter.

86. Here, too, Rahlfs A goes its own way: Jael cuts up Sisera, severing his head (καὶ ἀπέτεμεν Σισαρα ἀπέτριψεν τὴν κεφαλὴν αὐτοῦ). She mutilates it further by crushing and piercing his jaw (as per Rahlfs A at 4:21).

87. Israel is said to "crouch and lie down" like a lion in Num 24:9, obviously for an effect that is opposite for what we have here; see Tournay 1996: 205.

88. Pseudo-Philo (*LAB* 31.8) gives her the name Themec, for which, see Ginzberg 2003: 871 n. 87.

89. No connection can be made with the *bīt ḫilani* of cuneiform sources, referring to a palace structure with tripartite arrangement and portico. *meḥĕzâ* (1 Kgs 7:4), *ʾărubbâh* (often), and *kavvâ* (Aramaic, Dan 6:11) are other terms for such openings.

90. Rahlfs A expands, "Through the window leaned the mother of Sisera, through a lattice she searched for those returning with Sisera." Rahlfs B is closer to the Hebrew.

91. The verb is known in Aramaic; see W. Smelik 1995: 477–78. On its basis, the rabbis (*bRosh HaShana* 33b) decided that the lady was uttering piercing cries, emulating a shofar's *tĕrûʿâ*. It is frequently emended into the less interesting *vattabbēṭ*, "she observed"; see Lindars 1995: 283–84, who argues learnedly for it. It is hard to explain how a scribe would move (lexically, if not also orthographically) from a fairly innocuous verb to one so rare. Exum (1995) has her waiting in dread for the ultimate fruits of war.

92. Soggin (1981a: 86) offers an opposite idea: The ladies express words expected by the queen, more or less following the Targum and the Greek versions, with Rahlfs B being somewhat more belabored than A.

93. Diverse proposals are in Cooke 1892: 52–53. In 2 Sam 1:24, David urges the young women of Israel to bewail the death of Saul, for he clothed them in finery and bejeweled garments, no doubt from spoils.

94. See the discussion in Tournay 1996: 206–7.

95. Boling (1975: 115) finds "an enclitic *kāf* in the middle of a constant chain" in the first clause ("Thus may they perish / All enemies of Yahweh!"), betraying an exuberant exegesis that is very suspect now.

96. In Jewish liturgy, the Song of Deborah is read during Saturday prayers as a *hafṭārâ* (additional reading) to *pārašat bĕšallaḥ* (Exod 13–16) that features the Song at the Sea; see Introduction, n. 30. The poems praise deliverance from potential destruction.

97. See W. Smelik's fine pages (1995: 480–85) on the eschatological dimension of this expansion.

98. Caquot (1986) is critical, if not also disdainful, of such opinions, without quite rejecting them. His pages are worth inspecting for their sly comments.

99. This is generally true for Near Eastern royal panegyrics as well. From the fragments of the not yet fully published "Zimri-Lim Epic," for example, it is obvious that his bards began praising him within a few months of his usurpation of the throne, when his achievements were strictly survivalist. Not surprisingly, the notices are not easily matched to the details we have about his royal career. Good comments on the issues are in Floyd 1980:

233–35, 263–66. Not surprisingly, Seale (1962: 343–47), an Arabist, thinks that the comparison is best made with the *qasida*, both displaying the "manly virtue of the desert" (what desert?). Seale allows, however, that in contrast our poem is "shot through with genuine religious fervor" (343).

100. The association seems embedded in the book of Judith; see White (Crawford) 1992. (Reference is courtesy of S. Ackerman.)

101. See Ginzberg, who collects much rabbinic lore (2003: 868–69 and 871 nn. 84–86).

102. The relevant passage (GE OB II: 73–76; edition George) reads, "Holding his hand, she leads [Enkidu] like a god [*kīma ilim ireddešu*] to the camp of shepherds, the site of the sheep-pen." Many understand that the harlot is acting like a goddess, leading a suppliant to the gods. It is more likely, however, that *ilum*, "god," refers to Enkidu, the harlot having cajoled him earlier by saying "I look at you Enkidu, you are like a god" (53). Moreover, it would not do to make a parallel between sheepherders and gods.

103. Perhaps this is why the rabbis rewarded him by making him an ancestor of the great Rabbi Akiva: "The Rabbis taught in a Baraita: . . . Descendants of Sisera learned Torah in Jerusalem [i.e., with R. Akiva]" (*bSanhedrin* 96b).

104. "Terms such as 'kneel' and 'lie,' and the phrase, 'between her legs,' found in Judg. 5:27, create the double-entendre in a traditional Israelite medium" (Niditch 2005: 284). Sharon (2007) choreographs a series of allusions into circumstantial evidence for the rape: "rather than a calculated and premeditated action motivated by political loyalty, Jael's murder of Sisera is a spontaneous response to unexpected private threat" (269). In almost all these carnal expositions, there is hardly enough speculation on whether or not a soldier in retreat (as opposed to one in triumph) would have sex on the mind when negotiating an escape. Nor is there plausible discussion on the capacity of women in missionary (or any other) position to effectively wield weapons in both hands.

105. Much literature connects this scene to a motif about seductive women lurking behind windows for passing (and passive) victims. The motif is evoked in cuneiform texts and is associated with goddesses in omen literature; see Suter 1992, Rehm 2004, and Lisella 2005. As far as its application to biblical literature is concerned, scholars have made (too) much from fragments of texts and sundry artifacts, among them ivory pieces with a woman's head in a frame, to evoke seduction by courtesans. Whatever their merits as comparative studies, they have nothing to do with the contents of our poem: Sisera's mother (or Michal or even Jezebel for that matter) is no strumpet and is not at a window to accost clients. Despite its lengthy coverage, Seeman's study (2004) is not the less off target when, relying on highly accommodating comparative tables, he concludes that "men and women who gaze from windows signal the appearance of distinctive forms of danger—unmediated sexual desire for men [alleged about Abimelech], and the shifting fortunes of patrilineal regimes for women" (38).

106. Cited from Redford 1997: 14.

107. For an excellent review of women facing wars in classical myths and epics, see H. Foley 2005, esp. 109–11.

108. Cited by Tournay 1996: 205; see http://www.ucalgary.ca/~vandersp/Courses/texts/aescpers.html (lines 159–214). Death, it turns out, overtakes only the dreams of Xerxes.

109. "So the battle began; and when they were come to a close fight, there came down from heaven a great storm, with a vast quantity of rain and hail, and the wind blew the rain in the face of the Canaanites, and so darkened their eyes, that their arrows and slings were of no advantage to them, nor would the coldness of the air permit the soldiers to make

use of their swords; while this storm did not so much incommode the Israelites, because it came in their backs. They also took such courage, upon the apprehension that God was assisting them, that they fell upon the very midst of their enemies, and slew a great number of them; so that some of them fell by the Israelites, some fell by their own horses, which were put into disorder, and not a few were killed by their own chariots."

110. Linking a composition to the war it witnessed has venerable antecedence in biblical scholarship; see Moore 1895: 132–36. Lagrange (1903: 105) is lyrical on the poem: "Ce n'est pas un poème épique, ce n'est pas non plus un simple cantique d'actions de grâces; ces deux genres peuvent naître longtemps après l'événement. C'est la louange et le blâme, la bénédiction et la malédiction distribués aux braves et aux lâches. Ce besoin de dire à chacun son fait est caractéristique, Il respire les passions excitées par la lutte, la sympathie accrue par le péril commun, la colère longtemps contenue contre ceux qui sont dérobés au danger. C'est un genre littéraire tout spontané, tout à fait dans l'esprit des Sémites . . . Il faut don considérer le cantique comme contemporain des faits." A recent avatar of this approach is in Echols 2008. For him, the poem was a heroic victory hymn that was crafted soon after the event but was later theologized by attributing the triumph to Yhvh. What is heroic (or not) in this hymn and how to define the genre are issues that take up much space in Echols's study.

Yet equally venerable are the ascriptions of a "late" date for the song, with explanations that appeal for evidence to Aramaism, (pretentious) archaisms, and anachronisms; see most notably Vernes 1892, who is challenged (with much scorn) by Moore 1895: 130–31. Many of Vernes's points are taken up by Waltisberg 1999, and he too is refuted (not always successfully) by Rendsburg 2003: 123–26. Waltisberg's case is compromised by attributing to a fifth-to-third-century author much versatility in crafting purposely archaizing syntax. How would these authors learn such clever tricks without having at their disposal authentically ancient poetry? Writing in the 1920s, Burney collects Aramaisms in the song but decides that in the twelfth century BCE, when he presumes the song was written, distinction between Hebrew and Aramaic was not yet sharp (1970: 171–76). In assessing his suggestion, it does not help that we practically have no Aramaic before the tenth century.

111. It might be noted here that of the "markers" that are said to be missing in early biblical poetry (see the Introductory Remarks above), only the absence of the direct object 'et can be confirmed for the received version of the song: The word 'ašer occurs at 5:27; there are many examples of the conjunction vav and of the article ha- (see above), more so of the latter if one takes the Masoretic vocalization into account. Objectively, it is hard to argue for or against the diagnostic usefulness of these particles for dating Hebrew literature as long as we do not have evidence of their introduction into poetry or prose in excavated documents.

112. Good comments on the issues are in Floyd 1980: 233–35, 263–66.

113. Coogan (1978: 154) offered arguments for unity. M. Smith (2009: 55) suggests that any theological perspective "is a product of the composer, imposed in substantial measure upon the body of the poem." He proposes that older chunks of material were added by a later writer striving for a new version of the composition, one in which the prologue played a controlling interpretive role for the remaining segment of the poem.

114. For those lists, see Sasson 1978: 180.

115. De Moor (1993: 483–94) emends Judg 5:13–14 disconcertingly and interprets other verses recklessly to arrive at twelve tribes. Manipulating the poetry in 5:13–18, he arranges the resulting tribes into four triads that correlate with what is found in Gen 49

and Num 2 and 10. For Freedman (1980), the song "reflects the actual state of affairs at the time [twelfth century BCE], namely, that there was a ten-tribe league which bore the name of Israel" (153). Not until after the eleventh century were there to be a twelve-tribe federation. Guillaume (2000) trims the number of involved tribes down to seven.

116. Gad takes up the seventh slot in lists "a" (Gen 29–30) and "c" (Gen 46) in Table 5. In the latter, Gad is allotted seven sons and forms part of a community of seventy individuals who went down to Egypt.

IIID1. Gideon: The Call (Judg 6:1–32)

1. See in particular, the Introductory Remarks to IA1 (Judg 1:1–7), IIA1 (Judg 2:1–5), IIIA (Judg 3:7–11), and soon also at IIID2 (Judg 6:33–8:3).

2. True, there are judgments about lies and falsehood, especially as they become part of a rhetoric concerning power and its misuse; but they are applied to rulers rather than to prophets or administrators; see Pongratz-Leisten 2002. There is a stunning report about the reception of a prophet of Marduk who makes inflammatory accusations in the heart of Hammurabi's Babylon (ARM 26 371; see Nissinen 2003: 73–74). People simply ignore him.

3. The discussion on this subject is huge and is nicely handled in Crenshaw 1971. In the literature, scholars readily apply the term "false prophets" to individuals who are never labeled as such in the Hebrew text. The practice is in the fine tradition of the LXX, where in a good number of cases ψευδοπροφήτης replaces nāvîʾ (Crenshaw 1971: 1).

4. Savran (2003: 141) makes a table out of nineteen such encounters and offers fine comments on the phenomenon. My remarks here depend on his. See also the Notes to 2:1.

5. Stanley Cook 1927 assembles the manifestations in both.

6. Most often cited is an etymology for Midian based on the root *dyn. The connection between Midian and Mēdan is still debated, despite mention of both as descendants of Keturah in Gen 25:2, largely because of Gen 37:36 where mĕdānîm is given for the earlier midyānîm (Gen 37:28). The same can be said about references in Joshua (11:1 and 12:19) about mādôn. An alleged Anatolian origin for the Midianites (Mendenhall, lastly in IDB under "Midian," followed by Boling 1975: 122) has little merit.

7. Essentially, this is the same breadth (or confusion) of titles as we find in the Mari archives as applied to the Yaminite tribes.

8. Also treated as a vague geographical entity to the east is mention of Kedem/Kedme in the tale of Sinuhe (line 29, Lichtheim COS 1: 78).

9. There is slightly different language in 4QJudgᵃ (שׂה שׂור), likely because it ran the series of livestock right after miḥyâ, with bĕyiśrāʾēl having been left out before it was inserted interlinearily.

10. On locusts and the havoc they create as revealed in Mari letters, see Lion and Michel 1997. This excerpt from a Mari governor is illustrative (A.3816+; see Durand 1990: 109 and n. 26.): "The locust is now at Der [one day from Mari] and no one knows what to do. I have tried to chase them away, but I could do nothing at all. Here, through their voracity, [they] have badly diminished the bottomland and crops. My lord must send to help me the entire working force of the palace and other people, so that I could save the crop."

11. Movements of animals and tents use personalized verbs, inciting scholars to emend to the Hiphil, especially as it concerns tents (so also Rahlfs A), for which the MT has both a Ketiv (יבאו) and a Qere (ובאו).

12. The name Ophrah may be derived from a number of roots having to do with its sloping shape ('ôfer, "deer"), the quality or color of its soil ('āfār), or perhaps the taste of its water ('ôferet, "lead"). Where to locate it has been a vexed matter, see Gass 2005: 270–78, who favors eṭ-Ṭayyibe, about 6 miles northwest of Beth-shean. Many speculations are based on etymological dexterity and historical speculations, and they are reviewed in Niesiołowski-Spanò (2005), who tentatively proposes Ramat-Rahel as its site.

13. The element 'abî is not likely theophoric or even instrumental ("possessor of"). In either case, the final yod does not reflect a pronoun ("my f/Father) but is a connective (ḥiriq compaginis).

14. It is likely mentioned in the Samaria ostraca (nos. 13 and 28) as a personal name rather than a settlement; see Aḥituv 2008: 273, 286.

15. Given the repetition of the phrase "Ophrah of Abiezer" at 6:24 and 8:32, perhaps the clause should read, "under the oak belonging to Joash at Ophrah of Abiezer" (taḥat hā'ēlâ 'ăšer lĕyô'āš 'ăšer bĕ'ofrâ 'ăvî hā'ezrî). For other issues raised by this phrase, see Emerton 1976: 310–11.

16. A nice example from Malta is at "Gozo rock holds ancient wine presses," http://www .timesofmalta.com/articles/view/20100112/local/gozo-rock-holds-ancient-wine-presses. A Bronze Age example from Migdal haemek (Israel) is at Wikipedia, http://en.wikipedia .org/wiki/File:MigdalHaemek5.jpg.

17. Josephus (Ant. 5.213) labels the messenger a φάντασμα, "specter."

18. Pseudo-Philo has the angel meet Gideon as he returns from hiding in the mountains (LAB 35.1).

19. bMakkot 23b refers to the second portion of the Gideon greeting to justify divine support for Boaz. See also mBerakhot 9.5.

20. On Samuel declaring him Israel's hope, Saul replies, "I am from Benjamin, the smallest of Israel's tribes, and my clan is the least from any in the tribe of Benjamin."

21. Pseudo-Philo has him as the mightiest among his brothers, thus recognizing the rhetoric for what it was (LAB 35.1).

22. The Greek versions make no distinction in both formulae by using κύριος, with a very broad meaning. The Targum shows the same variation as in the MT, but manuscripts differ; see W. Smelik 1995: 489.

23. Boling (1975: 132) finds mention of a divine Ehyeh (via Exod 3:14), both here and at Exod 3:12 where, however, it would be prematurely uttered.

24. In Rahlfs B, Gideon is more frontal: "You will do for me today all that you have told me." Pseudo-Philo has Gideon asking for signs, as did Moses (LAB 35.6). Scholars have found a clue for both an early (Halpern 1988a: 121) and a late (Auld 1989: 265) dating in the use of the particle šĕ (rather than 'ăšer) in šā'attâ.

25. There will be more on this subject as we discuss Abimelech (Judg 9); in the meantime, see the accessible overview of Franke 1995. For discussion of Hittite analogues and their variation, see Mouton 2004a: 305–7.

26. It is not relevant to us that others read the name as "Son of [the god] Enlil." Mouton (2004a) collects occasions in which tests are set to distinguish divinity from humans.

27. For de Martino (2004: 56–57), the matter centered on whether or not Kaniu would eat pork, an animal that he claims was prohibited in certain areas of Anatolia. This seems far-fetched to me since the pig was widely used in Anatolian sacrifices. The text from which he draws his inference is a ritual for cleansing a person who dreamed of eating some plant or of coming in contact with pigs.

28. The scene is practically duplicated (albeit with different props and a more leisurely pace) in the pseudepigraphic *Joseph and Aseneth* (16–17); see Burchard 1985: 228–30.

29. We shall soon have another example of largess in the Samson story.

30. The phrase ʾēyfat-qemaḥ maṣṣôt need not be emended (Ap-Thomas 1940), as it has a fine parallel in ʾēyfat haqqālîʾ hazzeh in 1 Sam 17:17.

31. Rashi sets the whole episode during Passover, because of the mention of unleavened bread.

32. Discussion in Barthélemy 1982: 90–91.

33. Mouton (2004a) draws several more examples from Greek texts to prove the same point.

34. An exception is Joel 1:15. In 2 Kgs 3:10, as in our passage, the appeal to God is presumed.

35. The Lucianic version gives the standard οἴμμοι, "alas, woe."

36. The Greek doubles up on the vocatives, "LORD, LORD," while the Targum uses the *Qere* "LORD God" for this combination.

37. The reassurance is occasionally given during a theophany (Gen 26:24; Exod 20:20; Dan 10:12, 19). The equivalent lā tapallaḥ is equally well-attested in Mesopotamian texts; see Weippert 2001 and Nissinen 2003. We need to contrast this usage of the expression with Jael's cheeky address to Sisera in 4:18.

38. Following the LXX, the phrase is taken as a genitive construction, "the LORD of Peace," but this is not likely correct; see Moore 1895: 189. The Masoretes placed a disjunctive accent under the second Tetragrammaton in the verse, encouraging a translation "and the LORD named it 'Peace.'"

39. The one in Benjamin is written with a gamma in some Greek transliterations, suggesting that it was heard as beginning in a *ghayin* rather than a ʿ*ayin*.

40. Many examples are collected in Charpin 2003: 8–9, 15–16.

41. Moore's notion that this episode follows immediately on the prophet's reproof (1895: 190, 191), thus leapfrogging vv. 12–24, hardly makes for a smooth transition between the two.

42. However, it is no less redundant than the very frequent *par ben-bāqār*, normally rendered "ox of the herd." Rahlfs B offers "calf-ox" (λαβὲ τὸν μόσχον τὸν ταῦρον), while Rahlfs A offers an obviously emended "a fattened ox."

43. We may derive a parallel in the narrative about David's purchase of Aruna's threshing floor where pestilence against Israel was stayed (2 Sam 24:10–25). Instructed to build an altar there, David arrives at an acceptable price for it (50 shekels), but with the floor, he was forced to purchase the oxen as well as the threshing gears no longer needed by Araunah. The oxen, because they were specially connected with the site, came to be David's first offer in the space in which his son built the temple.

44. The fattening process was apparently tricky, and we have a case (ARM 14 5 = LAPO 18 #972, pp. 117–19) in which a bull became unhealthy and feared lost for a proper sacrifice.

45. See McMahon 1997: 221 (§18).

46. See the long note of Barthélemy (1982: 91–94), who reviews many suggestions but explains that the "second" refers to (an allegedly better) animal born in the spring rather than the fall. Emerton (1978) assumes that just one bull is at stake and suggests that Gideon is being instructed to take "the finest bull." Rudman (2000: 101–2) speculates that the second ox is a sin offering for the people while the first is for the priest. For him the phrase is a gloss on Lev 4:21 and Num 8:8 (2000: 102). There will be more such conjectures; see Bluedorn 2001: 90–96.

47. For Boling (1975: 134) the clause instructs a "slow" Gideon to sacrifice an older ox, an indication of "considerate and gracious administration in this story of domestic reform."

48. S. Ackerman refers to Blenkinsopp 1997: 97–98 n. 42, who deduces that Samuel may have been weaned at age three because his mother offered a three-year-old bull (1 Sam 1: 24) (private communication).

49. With *bĕrît* as its direct object, this verb conveys the notion of covenant making. On the *asherah*, see above at 3:7 and 2:13.

50. The Hebrew text is at http://www.biu.ac.il/JS/midrash/VR/outfiles/OUT22-09.htm.

51. Rahlfs B uses diverse forms of δικάζω, "to condemn, judge." Rahlfs A, however, turns to two other related verbs, ἀντιδικέω, "to plead a case," and ἐκδικέω, "to avenge, punish"; see Harlé and Roquepло 1999: 144. The Targum also stays with the same verb (Hithpael of *pr*) but expands: "Whoever shall try to avenge him shall be killed, *but a postponement shall be granted for him* until the morning."

52. The name *bĕ'alyāh* (1 Chr 12:6 [5 RSV]) means "Lord Yahveh" rather than "Yahveh is Baal/Lord." On these names see Fowler 1988: 55–63.

53. Levine 2000: 488; bibliography in Emerton 1976: 290–91.

54. See Arnaud 1991: 143–44 (text no. 87). This rendering is adapted from van der Toorn 1995: 48; discussion is in Avalos 1995. Other Emar documents tell us that such religious edifices and offices were bartered.

55. See note 52 to IIIC1 (Judg 4).

56. The root *bšt* is here vocalized *bešet* for the more normal *bōšet* commonly used to mask the name of Canaanite Baal (not the Egyptian Bes, as some maintain). The root has less to do with "shame" than with "(sexual) power," as in Akkadian *baštu*; but see Tov 2012: 247–50.

IIID2. Gideon: Signs and Wonders (Judg 6:33–8:3)

1. Among many passages are Num 11:4–6, 16:13–14, 20:2–5, 21:4–5; Ps 78:18, 41, 59.

2. Often treated as a later notion; see Ehrlich 1968: 94.

3. See the Introductory Remarks to IIIA (Judg 3:7–11). The Greek versions differed in rendering: Rahlfs A is literal (ἐνδύω) whereas B gives ἐνδυναμόω, "to empower."

4. On these elements in the story, see Beck 2008. In the Levant, the interval between the threshing of grain (especially wheat) and the manifestation of nightly dew was narrow. This may well be a clue for the tight sequencing of events.

5. The church fathers favored reading the episode typologically (Gideon as Christ) or allegorically (fleece impregnated with dew is a form of mystical conception), with a rich repertoire of perceptions; see Légasse 1985: 172–78.

6. The Greek versions ignore the potential pun, transliterating *ḥārōd*: Αρωεδ (Rahlfs A) and Αραδ (Rahlfs B).

7. Long discussion is in Burney 1970: 207–9, with proposed (and unnecessary) emendations, as per Ehrlich 1968. See also Barthélemy 1982: 94–95.

8. Recent treatment is in Sasson 2007: 465–66 n. 36, with bibliography. The two Greek versions agree on having Gideon speaking directly to the people to those who might be afraid: "Turn back!" (ἀποστρέφω; ἐπιστρέφω). Rahlfs A, however, apparently read *vayyispōr* and treated the second verb as part of the reaction, "twenty-two thousand set out [ἐξώρμησαν] from Mount Galaad and returned home from the people."

9. The Hebrew is somewhat terse but understandable in what is to be done with the kneeler; Rahlfs A compensates by adding "you shall put him by himself," likely taking a cue from the verse following. Boling (1975: 145–46) reconstructs (via the Greek versions) what

he imagines was an original text that was mutilated by scribal lapses. His translation (p. 142) is fluid but is not what we have in the Hebrew.

10. Many treat *bĕyādām ʾel-pîhem* ("with hand to their mouth") as a gloss, given the disjunction between *lāqaq*, "to lap up," elsewhere said about dogs lapping up shed blood (1 Kgs 21:19, 22:38), and its Piel application to people. They would move it to the end of the previous verse. They may be missing a point. Daube (1956: 156–58) follows the cue by having the men symbolizing the lapping of blood, allegedly a magical act.

11. Nice discussion in Burney 1970: 211–12; Moore 1895: 201–2; Gunn 2005: 105–6; Daube 1956; Assis 2005b: 60–65. Naturally, explanations based on reconstructed texts are better at making sense of difficult passages.

12. Légasse 1991: 245–46; for allegorical treatments of Christian fathers, see Légasse 1985: 178–85.

13. We have already encountered the phrase for "handing the enemy over" several times in Judges, both to encourage Israel to war (as at 1:2; 3:10, 28, etc.) and to declare its fall to an enemy (as at 1:4, 2:14, 6:1, etc.). Surprisingly, the occasions in which there is a command to act toward a goal are in Judges and Samuel: Ehud urges his people to "pursue [Moab] after him" (at 3:28), Deborah presses Baraq to "rise" against Sisera (at 4: 14), and our example at 7:9. Our best parallel, however, is at 1 Sam 24:3, when God urges David to attack Keilah (see the Introductory Remarks to IA1, Judg 1:1–7). In all these occasions, the verb *yārad* is about attacking.

14. The meaning of the name is uncertain; given the context, it would offer no clue to the episode. Garsiel (1993: 309) goes beyond speculation when he connects it (along with an element *yrbʿl*) to the phrase *prw wrbw* (be "fruitful and multiply"). Perhaps it replays all but the first consonant of Ophrah (ʿprh), but to what end? I offer one more suggestion in the Comments to the next section.

15. Burney cites *Iliad* 10: 220–24, where Diomedes asks for a companion before infiltrating the Trojans' camp: "When two men are together, one of them may see some opportunity which the other has not caught sight of; if a man is alone he is less full of resource, and his wit is weaker."

16. Orphaning characters is not unknown to Scripture, the most famous case being unsacrificed Isaac, left on Mount Moriah to feed our speculation (Gen 22:19).

17. The literature about dreams and their interpretation is immense, in print as well as online; see most recently Noegel 2007, with a large bibliography, and "Dream Interpretation" at Ancient Divination and Astrology on the Web, http://www.isidore-of-seville .com/astdiv/3.html.

18. Boling insists it was "moldy" (1975: 146).

19. Far-fetched would be a connection between *leḥem*, "food, bread," and *milḥamâ*, "battle," especially when the latter is not explicitly cited in this story. Josephus must have sensed this gap and so places a long explanation in the mouth of the dream interpreter: "Now the other soldier explained this vision to mean the destruction of the army; and told them what his reason was which made him so conjecture: That the seed called *barley* was all of it allowed to be of the vilest sort of seed, and that the Israelites were known to be the vilest of all the people of Asia, equivalent to the seed of barley, and that what seemed to look big among the Israelites was this Gideon and the army that was with him. Since you say that you saw the cake overturning our tents, I fear that God has granted the victory over us to Gideon" (*Ant.* 5.220–21).

20. The Targum lengthens the battle cry, "The sword from the LORD and victory through Gideon," thus enlarging on God's role and deflating Gideon's. See W. Smelik 1995:

505–6. Josephus has similar intents, "Victory to Gideon, with God's assistance" (*Ant.* 5.225). Schmitz (2008: 172–73) finds an equivalent formula in an ostracon from Tel Miqne, "For Baal and for [king] Pady"; their use, however, cannot be the same.

21. In the Targum Gideon simply thanks God rather than prostrate himself, as does David (2 Sam 9:8); see W. Smelik 1995: 505. We have a fine parallel in Gen 24, when Abraham's servant bows twice (at 24:26 and then at 24:52), affirming that a divine message has indeed been received and correctly deciphered; see Sasson 2006a: 256 and n. 51.

22. Albright (1970: xvi) indulges in linguistic mumbo jumbo to explain the form.

23. Gideon's son, Abimelech, divides his men into three to ambush Shechem (Judg 9:42–45); Saul so divided his (large) army, successfully defeating the Ammonites (1 Sam 11:11); Philistine forces split into three columns to devastate Hebrew territory (1 Sam 13:17–18).

24. Moore (1895: 207–8) is one of many earlier commentators who question the manner in which horns, jars, and torches were handled. They all presume that the torches, lit from the outset, required both hands, making it impossible to also carry the horn. It actually does not make sense that three hundred men would move toward an armed camp with lit torches. Moreover, horns can be tied around the neck.

25. In those days, allocating biblical material into documents was a key to solving problems, most often created for the occasion. The approach is hardly justifiable today.

26. The commentaries (Burney, Budde, Lagrange, and others) go through great length to sharpen our vision of the route taken by the routed army, with strong dependence on speculations and emendations; see Barthélemy 1982: 96. Detailed discussion on the topography of Gideon's wars is in Rösel 1976: 10–24. A map with conjectured movements is in Boling 1975: 121; another, but with different conjectures, is in Rainey and Notley 2006: 139.

27. The Targum simply uses "ford"; see W. Smelik 1995: 507. See also below at 12:5–6 where ironically, it is Ephraim who is prevented from using these escape hatches.

28. Zimmermann (1952: 111–13) reads the whole passage as depending on a "grim and rustic humor" involving vintage. He would have Oreb killed at the *gat* (*bivṣîr* rather than *bĕṣûr*) named after him, balancing the winepress of Zeev. He ignores the reference to the former in Isaiah and must assume a loss of a *beth*.

29. The rabbis discussed the proper instrument for beheading: sword or cleaver (*mSanhedrin* 7.3)

30. The most infamous display surely belongs to Ashurbanipal's palace. In it, a frieze has king and queen toasting the head of an Elamite enemy as it dangles within sight. The literature on this topic is now large, turning to textual as well as artistic references of beheaded enemies. A number of papers on this subject are printed in the proceedings of the 49th (London) *Rencontre Assyriologique internationale* (Collon and George 2005). There is also a healthy literature on the mutilation or beheading of the *statues* of an enemy's ancestors. See note 24 to Judg 1:6 (IA1).

31. The Targum elucidates by contrasting the weak of Ephraim with the strong of Abiezer, missing Gideon's intent; W. Smelik 1995: 508.

32. As we saw earlier (at 5:8, 11, 13, 19, 22), the particle *'az* synchronizes two events.

IIID3. Gideon: Toward Kingship (Judg 8:4–28)

1. Zimmermann (1952: 112) treats *ʿōver* as a gloss.

2. The element *ṣelem* can also be understood as the personified divine statue. There are other etymologies, based on *ṣēl*, "shadow," but also "shelter." Burney (1970: 228) and others

suggest "shelter withheld." Garsiel (1993: 308–9) reads metaphors behind these names. In Num 31:8 and Josh 13:21 are given the names of Midian chieftains killed by Moses in response to the Baal-Peor incident. Evi, Rekem, Zur, Hur, and Reba all have Semitic names, albeit not always easy to translate. Zur ("Rock") is mentioned in Num 25:15 as the father of Cozbi ("Sexpot"), the prime seducer of Hebrews. His title there reveals him to be a tribal leader (*rōʾš ʾummôt*).

3. Ahmose son of Ebana has left us an account of his rise in the armies of the Egyptian New Kingdom. Repeatedly he alludes to cutting off the hand of enemies to prove his prowess and for which he receives rewards. Here is one of the references:

> Then I conveyed King Djeserkare (Amenhotep I), the justified, when he sailed south to Kush, to enlarge the borders of Egypt. His majesty smote that Nubian Bowman in the midst of his army. They were carried off in fetters, none missing, the fleeing destroyed as if they had never been. Now I was in the van of our troops and I fought really well. His majesty saw my valor. I carried off two hands and presented them to his majesty. Then his people and his cattle were pursued, and I carried off a living captive and presented him to his majesty. I brought his majesty back to Egypt in two days from "Upper Well," and was rewarded with gold. (See Lichtheim 1976: 13–14)

In images taken from the same relief at Medinet Habu, scribes of Ramses III are taking counts of (uncircumcised) phalluses and (right) hands. For obvious reasons, collecting penises to keep count of dead soldiers gives a more accurate count than gathering limbs. (See http://www.vonluxornachabusimbel.de/Theben/Medinet/Beweispenisse .jpg and http://t2.gstatic.com/images?q=tbn:ANd9GcSymvLlx-siLSEaw6Yy24pg4Wrk wzp9VgOftisjotYCZn6GmeR0.)

4. The Greek offers two choices: καὶ καταξανῶ, "I will shred" (Rahlfs A), and καὶ ἐγὼ ἀλοήσω (Rahlfs B), the latter more often paralleling Hebrew "to thresh." The Targum and medieval exegetes approximate rather than translate the threat. The issue is retaken below at 8:16. See Barthélemy 1982: 97.

5. A flail is a wooden handle that has a short club attached to it with a thong for smart swinging. In the Hebrew Bible, prickly plants are often paired with mention of *dardar*, *šāmîr*, and *šāyit*. Perhaps *barqôn* may not be a plant but some sharp or cutting object. The Greek witnesses simply transliterate the Hebrew (Rahlfs A: βαρκοννιμ; Rahlfs B: αβαρκηνιν). Moore (1895: 225) cites classical and later texts in which victims were so carded.

6. These are by no means the highest numbers mentioned in Scriptures (see 2 Chr 13:3, 17). Numbers of defeated foes seem to rise sharply when Midian is Israel's foe; see Num 31.

7. Some Hittite treaties require vassals to provide their suzerains with food during wartime, and others permit warriors to punish sinful cities by killing their males. Malamat (2004) uses such material to illustrate what happened at Succoth and Penuel as well as to assign a second-millennium date on the event. Yet, a major point of the narrative is that these cities did not feel themselves obligated to Gideon.

8. The word *Maʿāleh* is not used in the Hebrew Bible for the rise of orbs.

9. Ziba, majordomo of Saul's estate (*naʿar bêt šāʾûl*), had fifteen sons and twenty servants, so hardly a youth; 2 Sam 19:18.

10. For a full discussion, with notices on *nʿrn (a military unit in Pharaoh's army) and the many seals of monarchic period officials bearing this title, see H. F. Fuhs in *TDOT* 9: 474–85. On semantic proximity to Akkadian *ṣuḫārum*, see Naʾaman 2004.

11. The assumption is based on the relative simplicity of the Hebrew writing system, so Albright (1960: 123) had no doubt that "there were many urchins in various parts of Palestine who could read and write as early as the time of the Judges." In the same volume Speiser labels Gideon's captive a "juvenile delinquent" (119). On the fallacy of such assumptions, see Rollston 2006: 48–49.

12. The number cited is not for the whole free male adult population (Wolf 1947: 99), for Gideon hardly would have needed a list of officials had he planned a mass extermination.

13. See de Vaux 1961: 235.

14. See Barthélemy 1982: 98.

15. Perfectly plausible, too, is that the language foreshadows events associated with Abimelech, who calls on his mother's kin (ʾăḥê-ʾimmô) to sustain his power grab. See below at 9:2–3.

16. More examples are in Hubbard 1984.

17. On all these choices, see Barthélemy 1982: 98–99.

18. The Targum adopts here the latter meaning, "neck chain," possibly to avoid idolatrous connotations (see W. Smelik 1995: 514–15). Depictions of camels in Neo-Assyrian reliefs (ninth to the seventh centuries BCE) show ropes around their necks, but no jewelry; this may largely be because their ornaments had been are confiscated (see Mitchell 2000). We do know that around the necks of horses were very elaborate breastplates (Winter 1980), and there is no reason why camels would not be similarly fitted.

19. In fact, we will not meet with mālak until Shechem decides to crown Abimelech (9:6) when, as we shall see, he had asked only to govern (9:2).

20. In Mari many items of clothing or of adornments are associated with (or named after) their areas of origins. It is less likely here, however, that it is the rings that are of Ishmaelite manufacture.

21. It is difficult to estimate what this amount would have purchased, first because the value of gold to silver fluctuated appreciably (from 4 to 1 to 15 to 1), and second because in the Bible most of the prices placed on purchased objects were controlled by other than realistic criteria.

22. The Greek versions had problems translating these terms. Rahlfs A simply transliterates some of them; see Harlé and Roqueplo 1999: 161–62.

23. The others were the Urim and Thummim, the lots, and occasionally, the teraphim; see the Introductory Remarks to IA1 (Judg 1:1–7). According to Mari documents (Sasson 2001b), teraphim were statues of divinities/ancestors that were consulted by professional inquirers, with the statues in a prone position.

24. On the ephod see the dictionaries or, despite its conclusion, Burney's fine long note (1970: 236–43). The Greek versions simply transliterate (Rahlfs A, εφουδ; Rahlfs B, εφωθ) rather than translate. Connections with Ugaritic and Old Assyrian textiles are interesting but not enlightening. Pseudo-Philo (*LAB* 36.4) makes it simple: Gideon created "idols."

25. In 1 Kgs 2:26 Solomon spares Abiathar's life because he once carried the ark. Because elsewhere Abiathar is associated with an ephod (but see 2 Sam 15:24–29), there is venerable speculation that the two have similar functions.

26. Bluedorn (2001: 170–75) is too rigid when he relies on a restrictive meaning for *yāṣag* to decide that the ephod is a vestment.

27. This parallel is widely noted; see Sharon 2006.

28. God is said to do the same to Canaan (Hiphil of *kānaʿ*) at 4:23.

29. A.1945, edited by S. Lafont (Démare) (1997), is sent to King Zimri-Lim: "A servant of Ḥardum, the nomad, led away two women companions and fled to Šubartum. [Ḥardum] overtook and seized him in Šubartum. In his anger [*ina appīšu*, a West Semiticism], he plucked out [?] the eyes of his servant [*ina appīšu īnī* lú.tur-*šu ugallil*, lines 9–11]. He came and told me, 'I want to kill this man, let him be impaled so people learn from his example.' When he told me this, I answered him, 'You must not do anything without my lord['s permission]. I will write my lord and do as he tells me.' This is what I answered him. My lord should instruct me one way or another."

30. Saul murders the priests of Nob after a similarly rhetorical inquiry (1 Sam 22:11–19).

31. Bluedorn (2001: 160–63) has written perceptively on this scene, concluding, "With the execution . . . Gideon not only attains his goal of personal revenge, he also publicly demonstrates that he himself is capable of exercising power over foreign kings and he thus publicly qualifies himself as king" (163). We must not confuse Gideon's act with Ehud's crass assassination of Eglon. The personal fate of Jabin (at 4:24) is ambiguous.

32. Reviews of the debate, with bibliography, are in Lindars 1995, Emerton 1976, and Oeste 2011.

33. Van Midden (2001: 202–3), who thinks Gideon "stands for king Solomon," argues that there is no rejection of kingship but makes highly superficial connection between the two.

34. A memorandum from early-eighteenth-century BCE Tuttul (Tell Bia) records oaths taken during the disbursement of spoils (Durand and Marti 2003: 168–70): "Re: Mortal oath: Amatpiel (of Qatna), Yaḫdullim (of Mari) and Amunapiḫ (of Tuttul) swore (as follows): The selected number of cattle taken from Tupḫi was 1350, from a total of 1665. This (is the status of the) spoil that my servant revealed, as well as Merimel, servant of Yaḫdullim said. There is no lie (in it). Ask and investigate."

35. Bright (2000: 180): "[The offer Gideon] is said flatly to have refused—and in a language thoroughly expressive of the spirit of early Israel." See G. Miller 2011: 241.

36. "Gideon's words are not a refusal: they are a protestation: a protestation of the kind of kingship he would exercise, an avowal that his kingship and that of his family will be so conducted as to eliminate any personal and tyrannical element, and to permit of the manifestation of the divine rules through his own" (Davies 1963: 157). Halpern (1978), oddly enough, finds his argument "stylistically too subtle and historically too precarious to carry weight" (84 n. 12).

37. In the Amorite vocabulary of the Mari age, the root *mlk* is reserved for deceased people of royal blood (excluding the king, who remains *šarrum*). They receive funerary offering *ana malikī*; see Jacquet 2002. Titles can shift depending on the language in which they were operating. The ruler of Guzana (Tell Fakhariya) is a governor (*šakin māti*) in Akkadian whereas he is king (*mlk*) in Aramaic (Abou-Assaf, Bordreuil, and Millard 1982: 64). Whether a changing perspective is also at stake can be debated.

IIIEI. Abimelech: King of Shechem (Judg 8:29–9:21)

1. A fine overview is in Akimoto 2010. A list that does not incorporate a number of allegories commonly mislabeled as parables (for example, Ezek 19:1–9, 10–14) would include the following:

   > Judg 9:8–15: Jotham's fable of trees seeking a king
   > 2 Sam 12:1–4: Nathan's parable of the poor man's lamb
   > 2 Sam 14:4–11: The woman of Tekoa's parable of two sons

1 Kgs 20:39–43: The prophet's parable of the escaped prisoner
2 Kgs 14:9: Jehoash's fable of the thistle and the cedar
Isa 5:1–6: The parable of the vineyard
Isa 28:23–29: The parable of the farmer
Jer 18:1–10: The parable (?) of the potter (explained?)
Ezek 17:3–10: The fable of the two eagles and the vine
Ezek 24:3–5: The parable of the boiling pot
Ezek 34:1–10: The parable of the dry bones

2. "The Date Palm and Tamarisk" is an example with a particularly long life. The genre occurs in Arabic *mufaḥara/muḥawara* disputes and the *tenson* of Provençal literature. An arresting example in Middle Persian, "The Fable of the Babylonian Tree," is edited in Brunner 1980. Echo of the genre (minus the pugilistic flavor) is Ben Sira 24:13–21 where Wisdom likens herself to diverse plants, each with its own virtue. Plant fables were likely more common than extant, with echoes in omen phraseology, as in "If bundles of reed walk about the countryside"; Reiner 1998: 651. The Aesop fable that Guillaume (2004: 56–59) brings into comparison with Jotham's is nothing but a touched-up Greek version of our fable as it entered the Aesopian collection in the Middle Ages.

3. Ginsberg in *ANET*³, 429–30. The anecdote is available online on the Comprehensive Aramaic Lexicon Project at http://cal1.cn.huc.edu/. Annalisa Azzoni kindly discussed this apologue with me.

4. I have quoted this fable from 2 Kgs 14:8–10. The same fable is in 2 Chr 25:18 but provided with a fuller background to stress Amaziah's hubris.

5. Recent representations of these positions are in Bluedorn 2001: 212–30 and Lindars 1973; Guillaume 2004: 60–64; Schöpflin (2004).

6. The registry includes Dinah and Jacob, but not Er and Onan, deceased sons of Judah. Leah has twice the number of descendants (thirty-two) than her maid Zilpah (sixteen) and so does Rachel (fourteen) compared with Bilhah (seven).

7. For more allusions to units of seventy, see Halpern 1978: 88–89.

8. We shall meet the same motif in the story of Jephthah. Josephus (*Ant.* 5.233) gives her the name Drouma.

9. See (excessively) Bluedorn 2001: 191–94, Boling 1975: 162–63. The "father" in *'ăvîmelek* may well apply to God, thus sharpening the contrast in expectations about what it implies: For Gideon, "God is king"; for Abimelech, "my father is king."

10. In Israel's lore, a good two-thirds of name bestowals are done by women (mothers, but see Ruth 4:17). The attribution by gender, however, is as much realism as literary. The rivalry between Leah and Rachel (Gen 29–30) is charted though names the mothers bestow on their babies. Earlier (Gen 4–5), fathers name ancestors and patriarchs their sons.

11. In Gen 14:13, the plural form *baʿălê běrît* means people under covenant obligations. The Greek differs slightly, with Rahlfs A more expansive (καὶ ἔθεντο αὐτοῖς τὸν Βααλβεριθ εἰς διαθήκην, "they made themselves Baalberith for a covenant") and Rahlfs B less so, "that he should be a god to them." Rabbinic lore connected this Baal-berith with "Zevuv, the idol of Ekron"; *bShabbat* 83b. Guillaume (2004: 65 n. 177) gives credit to E. A. Knauf for suggesting that Baal-berith "may be nothing else but the images of Yʜwʜ, the god of Israel, guardian of the vassalage treaty that bound the kings of Israel since Jehu." The absence of the dire consequences that 2:11–19 predicted for apostasy may indicate that, whatever its flaws, Abimelech's conduct was not assessed as an abandonment of the Hebrew God, despite 8:33–35.

12. See the succinct (albeit inconclusive) discussion in Mulder 1995: 266–72. A more ful-some study is that of Lewis 1996, who collects much evidence, epigraphic as well as archeological, to suggest that the El-berith refers to the great Canaanite god while Baal-berith is the god when sponsoring covenants. Lagrange (1903: 164) more or less had the same notion, but he would emphasize that Baal-berith is a pejorative application. Albright (1970) has this to say: "The identity of Baal-Berith and El-Berith is still uncertain, but the most plausible explanation is that it identifies Yahweh as lord of the tribal confederation [under Joshua] with the old chief divinity of the city, whose earlier name is not otherwise known" (20).

13. The literature on *ḥesed* is immense and can be accessed though articles in decent theological dictionaries, such as J. Stoebe in *TLOT* 449–64 and H. J. Zoebel in *TDOT* 5: 44–64.

14. As do other storytellers, Hebrew narrators normally stage carefree banquets as a setting for mass murder. On such an occasion, the rapist Amnon dies (2 Sam 13:28–30) and so do King Elah son of Baasa of Israel (1 Kgs 16:9) and Holofernes (Jdt 13:1–2).

15. These are not simply "citizens" of the town; see below, at 9:51, where "men and women" precede "leaders of the town." *lĕdabbēr be'oznê*+ is always about a statement made openly, sometimes even followed by "people, community," or the like to cover extent; see Gen 20:8, 23:13; Deut 31:28–30, etc. A Qumran fragment (1QJudg, 3–4) is more explicit: His uncles address Abimelech (אליו . . . [וידברו]) in front of the elders.

16. Halpern 1978: 89–90. We say "flesh and blood" and so did the Amorites. A chieftain sends this note to another: "I am your bother; your own flesh and blood am I. A foe can be hostile; but I stand by your decisions. Now you must listen to my request and make me worthy in the eye of the Amorites" (cited in Whiting 1987: 49–50; see also *CAD* Š/3 šīru 2, p. 118). In Mari the language is similar, with "heart" sometimes standing for "blood" (Marello 1997: 455–57).

17. Twenty shekels is the same amount for which a male slave was sold in Mari (ARM 8 10). Women went for 15 shekels (ARM 21 219), but price depended on sex, age, experience, and health. During the Neo-Assyrian period, however, prices shot up, with male slaves fetching up to 60 shekels, women a third less. This amount comes close to what is reported in Lev 27:3 (about 30 to 50 shekels for slaves in their prime). The value of land is better attested, but the numbers are not always realistic: 400 shekels for Machpelah and its surroundings (Abraham; Gen 23:15); 100 *qĕśîṭâ* (sheep?) for land near Shechem (Jacob; Gen 33:19 = Josh 24:32); 50 shekels for a threshing floor, oxen, and gears (David; 2 Sam 24:24); and 17 shekels for a field in Anatoth (Jeremiah; Jer 32:9). In 1 Kgs 10:29, a nice chariot went for 600 shekels, while a trained horse sold for 150.

18. Bands of armed mercenaries occur readily in Near Eastern contexts, especially so in the Mari and Amarna archives. Astour (1964) highlights their antiroyalism. Na'aman (2000) comments that almost ten such units are cited in the Bible. Doak (2011) reviews the same material to argue that "the phrase may have originally indicated *those without property*, while it could also, by extension, be transferred to the ethical realm of values to refer to moral emptiness or a vacancy of social value generally." However, there is nothing to support his contention that such "parasocial" groups reflect "what is currently known about the existence of certain changes following the collapse of societal structures in the ancient Near East." In fact, his material comes from a period (Late Bronze Age) of political but not necessarily social instability—certainly not everywhere at any rate.

19. See also below at 9:53, and Boogaart 1985.

20. The narratives about the monarchy in Israel are rich in the murder and assassination of rulers. They are sometimes told apologetically (for David and Solomon), but brutally when they concern nonroyal usurpers who seize the throne in the Northern Kingdom (for example, Baasa, Zimri and, with special venom, Jehu). There are also notices about those who purge members of their own family (according to the Chronicler): Jehoram of Judah, and his wife Athaliah. On all these matters, see the dictionaries. Murdering kinfolk as one reaches the throne is by no means a rare phenomenon. It is the stuff of myths (Seth and Osiris; Romulus and Remus) as well as the chatter in most archives. Slaying brothers was the accepted practice of Ottoman rulers, beginning with Mehmet II, famous for conquering Byzantium (fifteenth century CE). Tenderer of heart, Ahmed I (seventeenth century) replaced fratricide with ("bird cage") imprisonment.

21. There is much discussion on what this unit might be, mostly dependent on deriving a meaning from *millē'* of "to fill, stuff"; see Soggin 1973. Fritz (1982: 135–36) wonders whether it refers to a locale that was absorbed into Shechem. Solomon raised a labor levy on his people because he needed to build in Jerusalem a temple, a palace, a *terrace* (*hammillô'*), and its walls (1 Kgs 9:15). It was repaired by Hezekiah (2 Chr 32:5). So it is a major component of the walled portion of a city. The quarters (*bēt*) in this area of Jerusalem were where Joash was murdered by his servants (2 Kgs 12:20).

22. Albright (1968: 166) thought the language can apply "to a dead tree or a post replacing an original tree."

23. See Halpern (1978: 92), who follows others in making good comments about a potential conjunction.

24. The modern name, Jebal aṭ-Ṭūr, is abbreviated from Ṭura Brikha, "blessed mountain," because on it Samaritans built their holiest temple.

25. Rahlfs B has Jotham also "weeping" (καὶ ἔκλαυσεν), either because of internal corruption of verbal forms (Harlé and Roqueplo 1999: 166) or through misunderstanding of an idiom (*nāśā' qôl*) that is often followed by *bākâ*, "to weep" (see at Judg 2:4).

26. See already Lagrange 1903: 166 n. 7.

27. In Assyrian treaties, the oil that penetrates the flesh can also turn into a curse for those breaking vows; Reiner 1969: 540 (line 622).

28. For the above and much more, see M. Worthington, "Salbung," in *RlA* 11: 574–75. In Egypt, there is no direct testimony for anointing as a component of crowning, but it is often inferred from treatments of divine and royal statues; see Eva Martin-Pardey, "Salbung," in the *LÄ* 5: 367–69.

29. See lastly Mettinger 1976: 208–28 and Viberg 1992.

30. De Vaux 1961: 103–6 gives a compact account.

31. The Targum avoids the issue by giving "to appoint" rather than "anoint." Every king during the united monarchy period was anointed, including Absalom, all under especially stressful situations. The same tense background explains mention of anointing in Israel (Jehu) and in Judah (Joash, Jehoahaz).

32. The same construction is at 4:9. A different sense is achieved when the forms are switched, with the phrase acting as an auxiliary to another act, for example, at Gen 26:13, Isaac "grew increasingly rich." That the phrase opens the story is no evidence that it is plucked from a longer narrative (Bartelmus 1985: 108–10).

33. For Pseudo-Philo (*LAB* 37) the roster includes the fig, the vine, and the apple (or the myrtle), each with an opinion on Abimelech's fate—no olive and no cedar trees.

34. The scent of Middle Eastern oil is much lighter than that released by the olive of southern Europe.

35. Emending *bî* into *bô* (as does Rahlfs B) is hardly necessary; in fact, it turns a sharp retort into a flabby statement; see Barthélemy 1982: 99.

36. Predictably, the Targum takes this occasion to enter into a polemic contrasting divine honor and human vanity. See W. Smelik's comments (1995: 522–25) on different Targumic renditions of the same phrase in 9:9 and 9:13.

37. In both Josephus and Pseudo-Philo, the order of the trees differs from that of the Hebrew and Greek texts: Their sequence is fig, vine, and then olive. It is difficult to evaluate the significance and the origin of these switches.

38. On viticulture in the Bible, see Sasson 1994b.

39. Tatu (2006) has made a case that it is the *Ziziphus spina-christi*, "Christ thorn," an evergreen tree that in Israel is confined to lower elevations. This plant actually grows to 7.5 meters tall and produces a fleshy edible fruit with medicinal value; see Dafni, Levy, and Lev 2005, who give much lore about it. Tatu's plausible equation strains when he proposes that, when applied to the people of Shechem, accepting the offer forces them into an irony of dilemma: "Death is all they can get out of their unfortunate covenant with Abimelech. While being in office they will end up intoxicated by his leadership, while out of office they will be consumed by his falling circumstances" (123–24).

40. With God as protector: Ps 36:8, 57:2. For Akkadian examples, see *CAD* Ṣ 190–92 (*ṣillu*) and 242–43 (*ṣullulu* A). On seeking the shelter of a Mari king, see TH 72.16, cited in the Notes to 7:1–7.

41. We must not treat the reference to the cedars as sudden and inexplicable, for the contrast between polar opposite plants was natural enough that it played in Joash's fable; see Simon 1964. Nielsen (1955: 145–53) had needlessly presumed an earlier version of the story in which the trees failed to secure the leadership of the cedar, the noblest of the trees. Lindars (1973: 358–60) proposes that the allusion is to a proverb ("fire comes out of the bramble and consumes the cedars of Lebanon") that was inserted in the fable.

42. S. Ackerman (private communication) suggests a play on the name Jotham, also based on the same root, *tmm.

43. This repeat is resumptive (*Wiederaufnahme*), but it must not be assigned to a later scribe eager to substantiate the indictment that follows: see among many others Anbar 1988: 391.

44. A fine example from Mari is the declaration of war (early eighteenth century BCE) that one king sends to a former ally. For an exposition, see the Comments to Jephthah's war declaration (under IIIG1).

45. There is absolutely no need to emend into *minnegdô* (Lagrange 1903: 169).

46. Rahlfs A reads "may you be blessed."

47. On Josephus's portrait of Gideon, see Feldman 1998: 162–76.

48. The allocation of such sources is discussed in all the major commentaries until the Albrightian era; see, for example, Moore 1895: 237–39, Lagrange 1903: 181–85, and Burney 1970: 266–68 (first published in 1918). In those pages, diverse portions of the narrative were largely assigned to E, with some segments (often including the Gaal and the Thebez episodes) attributed to J. Building on Wellhausen, Lagrange proposes a unity for the whole, with a Deuteronomic insertion at 9:22.

49. Josephus (*Ant.* 5.234–40) has an interesting take on Abimelech. He has him murder his brothers and become a tyrant: "[He] constituted himself a lord, to do what he pleased, instead of obeying the laws; and he acted most rigorously against those who were the patrons of justice." Jotham waits for a public festival to shout out his fable that calls on the fig tree, the vine, and the olive to turn down kingship before it was offered to the

brier (with "the sort of wood for kindling"). Jotham assures Shechem that his tale is "no laughing matter," and they take his call seriously enough to repent of the crime and drive away Abimelech. Abimelech's resentment of their behavior (and not divine interference) is what sets him on the rampage against Shechem.

50. Interpretations are collected in Jans 2001: 165–71; see Bartelmus 1985.

51. Maly (1960) argues that the fable is not directed against kingship, but against those who turned down the burden for insufficient reasons. The implication is that Jotham has found fault with his own father.

IIIE2. Abimelech: Fall of a Ruler (Judg 9:22–57)

1. There is much literature on Shechem in the better biblical dictionaries. The overviews by Lawrence E. Toombs (*ABD* 5: 1174–86), Joe D. Seger (*OEANE* 5: 19–23), Edward F. Campbell (*NEAEHL* 4: 1345–54), and Gass (2005: 299–305) are especially useful. For interpretation of the biblical material, see the remarks of de Vaux (1978: 636–40, 800–806); Fritz 1982.

2. As also *kātēf* in such names as Ketef Ekron of Josh 15:11.

3. The name Hamor means "donkey." The evocation is promoted by Mari documents where the ritual killing of donkeys so helped to cement agreement between parties that by extension the phrase *ḫayaram qaṭālum* ("to slaughter a donkey foal") simply meant to establish treaties or the like; see B. Lafont 2001a: 262–93.

4. His dossier is conveniently collected at http://fontes.lstc.edu/~rklein/Documents/labaya_files/labaya.htm but is best reviewed in Moran's Amarna edition (1992). Adamthwaite (1992) would move Lab'aya and his area of control across the Transjordan, at Pella (Pehel). He also disputes the regnant interpretation of EA 289.

5. A fine description is in Stager 1999.

6. Van Seters (and others) have turned the Shechem convocation into a post-Deuteronomistic insertion; for him (1984), the text is crafted by the Yahwist, a theologian no less than a historian, calling the tribes to the faith of the fathers.

7. "toute l'histoire qui suit est inintelligible si la population de Sichem n'avait été très mélangées d'Israélites, et si de fait ils n'avaient eu la prééminence" (Lagrange 1903: 163).

8. This passage about the reign of King Saul is difficult and much discussed, and many authorities since antiquity have tinkered with it, relying on the notice about David (2 Sam 5:4) to recover Saul's age when he came to rule. It is my sense that the passage is referring to the length of his rule rather than his age at accession. Somewhere between his first and second year of unquestioned kingship (*bēᵉn šānâ . . . ûšētê šānîm*), David was anointed as king. Though he suspected it all along, only as he interviewed Samuel's ghost, at 1 Sam 28:17, does Saul come to learn of what had really happened. He then goes willingly to his fate.

9. See Hamori 2010.

10. On Josephus's reading of this episode, see note 49 of the previous section, IIIE1.

11. For example, see Burney 1970: 277 and Moore 1895: 253–54, who explain how the ambushes harm Abimelech's cause. Ehrlich (1968: 112) would read *lāhem*, the leaders of Shechem set up ambushes for their own benefits. Ambushes (Akkadian *šubtu, šūšubtu*, from *wašābu*, "to sit") are frequently cited in cuneiform documents, as much to gain military advantage as to rob caravans. In Hebrew *mĕᵓārĕvîm* is treated as a Piel participle by the Masoretes when it likely was a *maqtil* noun. The root (Qal) will occur three times in our story and several times in Samson.

12. Rahlfs B sharpens the distrust by bringing the news to "King Abimelech."
13. Josephus gives it as Γυάλης, suggesting to many that he read it *gōʿal*, which does not solve the problem of meaning.
14. The Greek gives the father's name as Αβεδ (Rahlfs A) and the difficult to explain Ιωβηλ (Rahlfs B).
15. Rahlfs A has "performed dances." Similar is the Targum, "ועבדו חנגין," and Josephus (*Ant.* 5.240). Rahlfs B gives "made *elloulim*." The consumption of wine at religious and social occasions hardly needs referencing. In Mari, wine is drunk at sacrifices, before the images of deities, and during processions (Chambon 2009: 39).
16. The phrase occurs also at 1 Chr 10:10 and Amos 2:8. It is possible that the plural "gods" suggests that making the circuit of diverse temples may be at stake. In Mari, many ceremonies were conducted by moving from one temple to the next. Yet, it must be recalled that among polytheists, more than one god shared the same shrine, albeit just one would be primary in it. A display of deities under one roof attests to the wealth of a community—but also its ostentation. There is a nice letter from Mari (A.3609 = FM 8 1) in which King Samsi-Addu excoriates his son for ordering the crafting of several divine statues, as they drain the treasury both in their manufacture and in caring for and feeding them.
17. Abimelech of Gerar tells Isaac: "We realize now that the LORD has been with you; so we have decided that there should be a sworn treaty between the two of us. So let us make a pact with you: 'You must not harm us, because we have not abused you but have only treated you fairly and sent you away in peace. Now therefore, you be the LORD's blessed!' Then [Isaac] made for them a feast, and they ate and drank." See also Gen 31:45–55; Exod 18:12, 24:11, and many other passages. Mesopotamian material is gathered in Glassner 1987–90 and Charpin 1997. Note how ARM 26 404: 60–65 summarizes the ceremony: "Once Atamrum [of Andarig] and Asqur-Addu [of Karana] came to mutual agreement and made a pact, the donkey-foal was immolated. They made each other take divine oaths and sat to toast (each other). Upon drinking their cups, they exchanged gifts between themselves; then, Asqur-Addu set out for his land and Atamrum set out for Andarig itself."
18. See 2 Sam 19:22 (21 RSV) (about Shimei) and Exod 21:17 (about a person who curses his parents). Exod 22:27 (28 RSV) equates cursing god with cursing a leader.
19. We have already noted the taunts by the leaders of Succoth (at 8:6) and those of Midianite kings at 8:18–21. Yassi-Dagan, a Mari general, cites the taunts and false information that Zaziya, a Turukku leader, was using to peel vassals away from Zimri-Lim. He would ask the rulers: "Where is Zimri-Lim whom you are seeking as your 'father' and behind whom you march while he himself rides a palanquin? Why has he not come here to save you?" (A.1025 = [LAPO 17 #545: 13–19]). A more vivid taunt takes place at the base of the rampart of Ašnakkum, a city in the upper part of the Habur River. At the moment of writing ARM 28 98, Ili-Sumu, a vassal of Zimri-Lim of Mari, was trying to remove Ašnakkum from the control of Terru of Urgiš: "When I approached Ašnakkum for combat, the king of Urgiš shouted to me from the rampart, 'When did a minion [*šaknum*, literally, "vassal"] of Zimri-Lim ever set up a king at Ašnakkum?' But I answered him, 'As to the kings of Elam—when, O when did they ever install a king in Ašnakkum? The whole land belongs to my lord.'"
20. Both Greek versions adopt this understanding by expanding into "son of Shechem," which is hardly an idiomatic expression in Hebrew. Boling (1963: 483) needlessly (and unidiomatically) emends into *šikmî*, allegedly "the Shechemite."

21. For diverse solutions to the problem posed by *vayyō'mer*, see Barthélemy 1982: 100–101.
22. See the good discussion in Barthélemy 1982: 101–2.
23. See also Dossin 1957. The cuneiform is now read DUMU-*mim* (once: *ma-ar-mi-im* in ARM 11 43: 20), a scribal abbreviation for Yaminite tribesmen, so hardly reminiscent of *tormâ*. Gevirtz (1958) suggests that the root for both is **trm*, now available to mishnaic Hebrew.
24. See Moore 1895: 259–60 for the difficulty. The witnesses do not help much, with "besiege the city [πολιορκοῦσιν] against you" (Rahlfs A); somewhat similar is Rahlfs B and the Targum.
25. See Barthélemy 1982: 102
26. A wily old king, Samsi-Addu, writes this to his son and his advisers (ARM 1 5 = LAPO 17 #517, pp. 115–17): "To wipe out the enemy, you [pl.] improvise tricks and maneuver against him; but the enemy likewise improvises tricks and maneuvers against you, just as wrestlers use tricks against each other. This is just like the old proverb, 'In her shuttles back and forth, a bitch bore blind puppies.' Now you must not act like this for fear the enemy maneuvers you into a trap."
27. A fine overview of military tactics in the Mari age, when most reported confrontations occurred at a city's gate, is in Durand 1998: 283–310. In Sasson ("Siege Mentality," forthcoming), I feature a Mari text that combines stratagems, tricks, braggadocio, and taunts, couched in a prose that comes closest to the Hebrew narrative style. The text is ARM 14 104+, reedited by Charpin 1993: 199–200 and translated as LAPO 17 #548, pp. 158–64. It is also discussed by Vidal 2009 and Eph'al 2009: 107–13. A provincial governor reports to Zimri-Lim on news conveyed by three soldiers, escapees from the army of Atamrum of Andarig. Aided by troops from Ešnunna and Elam, the latter is besieging Razama and its king, Šarriya:

> An army reached Razama, and as it did so, a contingent from the town came out and *routed* seven hundred Elamite warriors and six hundred Ešnunna men. They let ten days pass, then the elders came out before Atamrum and told him, "We want peace; as soon as the army moves away into its campsite at a half mile, I [Šarriya] shall deliver the money." However, Atamrum answered them, "In fact, you have decided, 'Let us deceive him with words and when he moves away into his campsite we can put an end to tribulation in Idamaraṣ.' If you really want peace, why has Šarriya not come out to meet me? Just keep on fighting and strengthen your town!" But the townsmen answered him, "This town belongs to Zimri-Lim and the levied army has followed him [to Yamḥad]. Stick around, until the town's lord [Zimri-Lim] catches up with you!"
>
> So, he [Šarriya] took charge and strengthened his town. Periodically, he would come out and *rout* Ešnunna troops while he [Atamrum] would pile up against the town an expanding ramp. Once the top portion of the ramp reached the parapet of the outer fortification, the townsmen *broke out from inside the town* and made two big holes, right and left, at the ramp's front sections. Having moved at night to the front of the ramp via the cuts, at dawn the town's soldier surged out and routed half the army (of Atamrum). They plundered their bronze lances and shields, taking them into town. (The goal for these townsmen is to remain loyal only to my lord!)
>
> This is what Atamrum contrived to do: He supplied thirty charlatans with bronze lances and they provoked the townsmen, "Why do you keep being loyal

to Zimri-Lim? Is it not so that his soldiers are (actually) besieging you now?" But the townsmen answered him, "These are charlatans that you have equipped and you have had them come near (us)! Yes, within five days the armies that are with Zimri-Lim will catch up with you. You will see . . . !"

28. Boling (1975: 178–79) thinks it is "an old poetic designation for the geography of the Shechem area . . . a particular reference to one of the two mountains flanking the Shechem pass."

29. Here and in Ezek 38:12, the Targum avoids such an implication by using the pedestrian "strength of the land." Lagrange (1903: 175) cites the *Iliad* (XI 34), where ὀμφαλός can suggest a rounded object, so a hill. On the Peshiṭta's reading, see Weitzman 1999: 108; Wilkie 1951.

30. Qumran's version (1QJudg, 7–8) is less heroic: Abimelech pursues the whole group.

31. Among the towns that Tiglath-Pileser III reports ravaging in the Galilee is ^{URU}*a-ru-ma-a*. While this notice bolsters a connection between Rumah and Arumah, it lies too far north from Abimelech's Arumah; see Eshel 1990: 104–5.

32. Compare Powell 1985 with Artzy and Hillel 1988.

33. The fullest review of the evidence is Ridley 1986. Gevirtz (1963) collects it from cuneiform sources that mention the spreading of minerals (*ṣīpu*) as well as seed of aggressively invasive plants (*kudimmu, saḥlu*); see also Streck 2008 for fuller details.

34. Rahlfs A simplifies by dedicating the temple to Baal-berith, as previously. Rahlfs B simply transliterates the Hebrew, Βαιθηλβεριθ.

35. Based on archeological remains of the Shechem Late Bronze temple, Stager (1999, 2003b) suggests it is a corridor between inner and outer walls of a temple. Josephus (*Ant.* 5.248) has them at a strong rock where they intended to build a wall.

36. The darkish shades of Zalmon are evoked in Ps 68:15–17, to speak of a lofty height in Bashan where snow contrasts with pitch blackness: "When the Almighty scattered the kings there, it seemed like a snowstorm in Zalmon. O majestic mountain, Mount Bashan; O jagged mountain, Mount Bashan. Why be envious, O jagged mountains, toward the mountain God covets for his dwelling? The LORD must want to remain there forever" (after *TNK*).

37. The last explanation is Koller's (2013: 40). The noun therefore would have two forms in the singular: *qardummôt* (also at Jer 46:22 and Ps 74:5) and *qardōm* of 1 Sam 13:20. For him the tool is a double-headed mattock, with one side an adze, the other an axe, with examples found at Tell Qasile and elsewhere.

38. The idiom seems the same, with (at Jer 11:16) or without the preposition ʿal-. On the use of fire in sieges, see Ephʿal 2009: 22 n. 44.

39. ARM 3 73 (= LAPO 18 #1067, pp. 242–43) and ARM 28 20, a letter from Carchemish. For more on this motif, see Holm 2008: 88–89.

40. For Josephus (*Ant.* 5.250) fifteen hundred men died, "and the rest were a great number also."

41. Interesting but highly speculative is Shalom-Guy (2010) on the differences between the two accounts of Abimelech's death and their adaptation to the David context.

42. The verbal form (but not the meaning) is ambiguous—either a Qal or Hiphil of *rāṣaṣ*.

43. To find out what really happened to Susu, see Sasson 2001a. The letter itself can also be read in Durand's LAPO 16 #333, pp. 518–20.

44. Sieges make for hostile territories. Simon of Montfort, scourge of the Cathars, was killed (1218 CE) by a stone cast by a mangonel (type of catapult) from the Toulouse fortifications. Another brother, Guy, was killed at the siege of Castelnaudary in 1220 CE.

45. This is made clear by diverse home inventories or dowry lists that included millstones, on which, see B. Lafont 2001b. In a Mari ordeal, diverse personnel are to survive plunging into a river while carrying a millstone, obviously somewhat smallish. Unnecessary is Boling's explanation: "She must have 'dropped' it, and probably had help, as a single individual could hardly manage to throw one" (1975: 182). Still the size must have troubled because both the Targum and Pseudo-Philo (*LAB* 37:5) have her casting *half* a millstone.

46. See Milano 1995 and Ellis 1995 for nice overviews.

47. Other terms exist for pounding: *mĕdōkâ* (pestle) and *ṭaḥanâ* or *ṭĕḥôn* (grinders); see van der Toorn (1992).

48. That women were the grinders of grain is the point of this Hittite notice: "I, the Great King Tabarna [Ḫattušiliš I of Ḫatti], took the hands of (the enemy's) slave girls from the handmills, and I took the hands of his (male) slaves from the sickles, and I freed them from the taxes and the *corvée*. I unloosed their belts (fetters?), and I gave them over to My Lady, the Sun-Goddess of Arinna"; CTH 4 iii 15–20, cited from B. Collins 2007a: 92.

49. This may not quite be an application of *lex talionis* (O'Connell 1996: 168). While the destruction of perpetrators of a crime is indication of justice fulfilled, the punishment must not be self-imposed (suicide) or mutual (as in our case), but meted out by those harmed by the crime. In the Mari records, God is always there to punish those who break covenants. We have this letter sent to Zimri-Lim about the death of Samsi-Eraḥ, an ambitious opportunist who betrayed and was betrayed as fortunes shifted (A.1026, cited from Guichard 2011: 73–74): "[The gods] Dagan and Iturmer are my lord's partners. The gods of my lord are bringing to account anyone who transgresses against my lord. My lord therefore remains firmly on his throne. Now then, Samsi-Eraḥ, who has stirred so much trouble in Yapṭurum, was killed in Ulaya City. In the past, I have myself kept after this man and even *urged* my lord to kill him; so now my lord's God settled his account. My lord should rejoice."

50. "If Fritz's analysis of the textual history of Judges 9 were correct, then it would not be possible to discover within it any plot . . . any organization of incident to achieve a single purpose."

51. For example, see the entry of Toombs in the *ABD*.

52. The type was identified by H. Güterbock (1938) when studying the literature about Agade leaders.

53. Handy overviews are available in Franke 1995 and in J. Westenholz 1983. Full account of the material is in J. Westenholz 1997, with historical contexts fleshed out in A. Westenholz and Sallaberger 1999: 29–59.

54. Best developed in Evans 1983; see also Holder 1988.

IIIF. "Minor" Judges, Major Rift (Judg 10:1–16)

1. Amit (1999a: 81–85) and others (Berlin, Brettler, and Fishbane 2004: 554) prefer the more descriptive but neutral term "consecutive judges." Occasionally, one reads of six "minor" judges (including Shamgar) to balance the six "major" judges (excluding Abimelech).

2. Moore (1895: 270–71) nicely argues this point.

3. On what follows, see Hauser 1975, Mullen 1982, Scherer 2007, and Nelson 2007, with many bibliographical details. See also the Introduction, the Comments to IIIE2, and the Notes at Judg 12:6.

4. The second *ben* in Ehud's pedigree (at 3:15) has to do with his Benjaminite background.

5. Wide speculation on whether there was a Near Eastern deity with a name based on this root (allegedly part of the consonants in *btdwd*, "Temple of Dôd," in the Tell Dan inscription) and whether the Hebrew God was occasionally called by that name need not concern us here; see Barstad in *DDD*, pp. 494–98.

6. We must not be surprised if this creature is named after a town associated with Tola.

7. The other Issachar tribesman to acquire fame (notoriety) is Baasha, third in line to rule Israel (around 900 BCE), after assassinating Jeroboam's son, Nadav, thus fulfilling a prophecy. He ruled from Tirza just over two score years, but his own son was assassinated while drunk.

8. The Greek versions assign him thirty-two sons, with a like number of colts and towns. No explanation is likely to make full sense.

9. Tsevat (1983) has cited a Hittite fable that has reached us with a few gaps, in which the queen of Kaneš gives birth (in a single year!) to thirty sons. She abandons them in greased containers to a river, but the gods take them into Zalpa where they grow into sturdy men. The queen then gives birth to thirty daughters. Eventually, the men mistake their sisters for potential brides but are warned by their youngest against this sexual crime. (A Hittite king excoriated a neighboring king for practicing such marriages; Beckman 1996: 27–28 [§§25–28].) There is mention of one donkey that is to climb an inner chamber; there is presentation of hostility between Hattuša and Zalpa. The connection between the Hittite and Hebrew anecdotes about Jair, Ibzan, and Abdon are intriguing but also too superficial to argue direct absorption into Hebraic lore. The Hittite tale is available in *COS* I, 181–82 (Hoffner).

10. See Notes to 1:14 and 5:10.

11. The second reference to *ʿăyārîm* is widely emended to *ʿārîm* ("cities") because of contexts, but in Middle Hebrew a plural *ʿăyārôt* also exists. Rashi (followed by others) explains that these towns do not have fortifications. The aural pun is also preserved in Greek (. . .ἐπιβεβηκότες ἐπὶ . . . πώλους καὶ . . . πόλεις αὐτοῖς). The *TNK* resorts to a very cute pun, "burros" (via Spanish) and "boroughs" in imitation. I have avoided the temptation. In truth, Hebrew just bristles with such plays on words. Later (at 12:14) Abdon's descendants are said to ride seventy colts. However, in that context, *ʿăyārîm* is not paranomastic, and it may well be that it depends on the Jair reference for inspiration. Remarkable is that Tola does not receive the same attention, given that his tribe Issachar is recalled as "a strong-boned ass, crouching among the sheepfolds" (Gen 49:14). One of the mysteries of Judges is how little that tribe is reflected in its lore.

12. See S. Lafont (Démare) 2000: 213–15 (with slightly different interpretation of Mari material) and Michel 2004. Mari kings, who normally ambulated in palanquin, traveled on a lagu-donkey when accompanying deities to shrines, so as not to obviously lord it over them. Throughout the second and well into the first millennium BCE, from Egypt (Sebait el-khadim and Bani Hassan) and Canaan, the iconography of nobility included images of men riding donkeys; see the material collected in Staubli 1991. Zechariah 9:9 records the image of a justified and triumphant, yet humble, king riding into Jerusalem on "a donkey, a colt foaled by a jenny."

13. For a selection, see H. O. Thompson in the *ABD*; Gass 2005: 347–49. Jair had an interesting afterlife, especially in Pseudo-Philo (*LAB* 38). There, he becomes a Baal-worshiping fanatic who readily throws kinfolk into the fire for refusing to offer pagan sacrifice. In a replay of stories about young Abraham and old Lot (themselves rehearsed in earlier pages

of Pseudo-Philo), an angel saves them, striking their tormentors blind. How Jair and his instrument of worship are burned is taken from the story of Gideon. The whole is fine testament to the Jewish imagination of the first century. See Murphy 1988.

14. The Greek versions offer different sequences: Rahlfs A has "[They] served the she-Baals and the Astaroth and the gods of Sidon, the gods of Moab, the gods of the sons of Ammon and the gods of the Allophyles (Philistines)." Rahlfs B has "[They] served the Baalim and the Astaroth and the gods of Arad, the gods of Sidon, the gods of Moab, the gods of the sons of Ammon, and the gods of the Phylistiim." Ehrlich 1968: 116 suggests reading "Amorite" instead of Aram, citing Josh 24:15.

15. The mention of the Philistines is obtrusive here, as they will not play a role until the Samson story, but it could be anticipatory (Lagrange 1903: 189).

16. Rashi, however, connects "that year" with the time of Jair's death.

17. Traditional exegetes (such as Ralbag) convey the message through Phinehas the priest (see at 20:28).

18. The difficulty here is that the indirect preposition *min* ("from") is attached to the first three powers (Egypt, Amorites, and Philistines), so duplicating "I brought you out (of Egypt)" from 6:8 would work for "from Egypt," but not from the remaining entities. Many simply edit them out; see Lagrange 1903: 190–92. So it may be best to let God repeat himself by inserting "to rescue."

19. See Barthélemy 1982: 103, who offers a convoluted explanation.

20. See W. Smelik 1995: 538–41. Judges 10 may have been included among the *haftarôt*, perhaps as prelude to Judg 11, which is now found attached to *parashat ḥuqqat* (Num 19–22:1).

21. The comments of Harlé and Roqueplo (1999: 180–81) are very fine on the issues raised by the Greek of 10:16.

22. Haak (1982) collects many of the references discussed below, arriving at somewhat different conclusions.

23. See also Num 21:4: "(The Hebrews) set out from Mount Hor by way of the Sea of Reeds to skirt the land of Edom. *But the people grew restive on the journey*"; Zech 11:8: "I lost the three shepherds in one month; *then my patience with them was at an end*, and they in turn were disgusted with me." More nuanced, because of its rhetoric, is Job 21:4: "Is my own complaint (not) against an individual? *So, why would I not be vexed?*"

24. There are many occasions in which God loses patience with Israel, a good number of them occurring as Israel made its way to the Promised Land. Luckily, Israel had Moses as intercessor. In one such moment, when Israel provokes God by questioning his competence to successfully deliver a land full of giants (Num 14), Moses dampens a divine urge to wipe out Israel by citing the potential loss of God's prestige among the nations should there be no people to whom to deliver the promise. This type of intimacy that we know to obtain among God, the patriarchs, and many prophets (and which makes biblical narratives at once primitive and sublime), is only associated with Gideon. So that when at this juncture Israel badly needs an intercessor, there is diminishing likelihood that someone will stand in the breach.

25. Feigin 1931: 194–96 arrives tortuously at a similar suggestion.

IIIG1. Jephthah: Jephthah's Challenges (Judg 10:17–11:28)

1. This is confirmed widely, as when Turukku tribesmen offer peace (*salīmam našûm* +) to a besieged city for the surrender of its king (ARM 26 518 = ARM 2 42 = LAPO 17 #599, pp. 259–61). Hammurabi of Babylon charges to his troops as they near Larsa: "Go on;

may God be in your forefront. If on reaching it, a city opens its gates to you, accept its offer of peace." A fuller passage from ARM 26 385 is cited at the Notes to Judg 4:6–7. On Deut 20, see below.

2. Under these circumstances, miscalculation can be costly, and we have this almost comic staging reported in a letter (RS 34.165) to the king of Ugarit (perhaps Ibiranu IV) in which an Assyrian king (perhaps Tukulti-Ninurta I) recounts past events. (The latest study is in Dietrich 2003, with previous bibliography.) A Hittite king (Tudḫalias IV) had once posted the Assyrians a declaration of war, accusing them of harassing one of his vassals ("Come, and let us join battle; if not, I will myself come against you for battle"). The Assyrians reject the challenge ("What? Why have you come? I myself have come against you") and move troops toward a city (Taidi) in a neighbor's land. Their threats having misfired, the Hittites send a diplomatic mission bearing two tablets (*ṭuppātu ša nukurti*), likely an ultimatum and a register of terms. Once again, the Assyrians balk. Three days later, the Hittite mission arrives with peace terms (*ṭuppu ša šulmi*), but matters had deteriorated, leading to a battle (at Niḫriya) for the control of disintegrating Mitanni. Worth noting is the anecdotal nature of the report, reflecting on events that likely transpired during the reign of a preceding king (Shalmaneser I).

An anecdote in 2 Kgs 14:8–10 preserves a declaration of war that uses a similarly aggressive language; see the Introductory Remarks at IIIE1 (Judg 8:29–9:21). Unusual is the incident in which the Ammonite king Nahash besieges Jabesh-Gilead (1 Sam 11). Its residents offer to surrender but are given such baroque terms (gouging out the right eye of all besieged) and counter with such an outlandish proposal (if they are not helped in seven days they will surrender) that we know we are dealing with the stuff of folklore. The anecdote is used as backdrop to the rise of Saul to kingship. A similar sequence of events is reported in a first-century BCE Greek inscription from Lindos (Rhodes) reporting miraculous interventions by deities over many previous centuries: Besieged by Darius's Persian fleet, Lindos asks for a five-day respite and of course is saved in the nick of time; backdrop in S. Cohen 2010: 170–71; see Eph'al 2009: 43 n. 27.

3. On Mizpah and its many potential locations, see Gass 2005: 481–84.

4. The ungainly words (*hāʿām śārê gilʿād*) are often shortened (Lagrange 1903: 192), simplified (Boling 1975: 194, after Rahlfs A, "The captains of the force of Gilead"), or emended, some with serious reshuffling. Burney (1970: 307) would read "the people of Israel" (**ʿam yiśrāʾēl*), thus seriously missing the restriction in perspective that is relevant to Jephthah's story.

5. On *gibbôr haḥayil* as referring to a well-armed warrior, see also at 6:12. In 1 Sam 10:26–27 there is potential contrast between "the principled men [*haḥayil*] whose hearts God touched" and the scoundrels (*běnê vělîyaʿal*) "who scorned him by not bringing him gifts."

6. The Greek tries to be literal by parsing each word; Rahlfs A gives "powerful in strength" and B has "exalted (from *gābāh*?) in power."

7. The debate is followed with even more shading in Assante's review (2007) of the book in which Bird's study appeared. Assante's opinion is that native labels we today render as "prostitute" actually refer to women living outside of male control, from virgins (spinsters) to prostitutes.

8. See the overview in Cooper 2006, with details and bibliography. A handy compilation for all these legal codes (LL, CH, and MAL) is M. Roth 1997.

9. The Old Greek of 3 Kingdoms (= 1 Kings) has interesting expansions on Jeroboam, among other details, making him the son of Sarira, a prostitute (24b). Thereafter, it

adds, that he built Sarira (Greek for Zareda), that he controlled three hundred chariots, and that he married a princess of Egypt—much myth-making. In the Hebrew Bible (1 Kgs 11:26) she is called Zeruah, so "scabrous," but there she is a "widow." Neither version seems to hold Jeroboam in high affection.

10. Feigin (1931) offers a fine defense of diverse segments of the Hebrew that, because of their hiccuppy delivery or unusual phrasing, have been judged glosses and/or were mercilessly emended by Budde, Moore, and other exegetes.

11. The *mamzēr* of Deut 23:3 (2 RSV), who is prohibited from active participation in Hebrew worship, is not a child of prostitution (despite the LXX's understanding); rather, the child is produced by a Hebrew and a member of an unacceptable ethnic group (such as Amalek).

12. One version of the *Tosefta*-Targum expands here: "This is the law in Israel from of old, that heritage does not turn around from tribe to tribe [see Num 36:5–13]. And therefore a man is not able to take a wife which is not from his own tribe. And whenever a woman loves a man, she leaves the wife's family without inheritance, and people will be calling her a hostess [*fundqêtā'*]—who loves a man who is not from her own tribe. And so it happened to [Jephthah] and his mother"; cited from W. Smelik 1995: 542–43. Pseudo-Philo (*LAB* 39.2) reverses the narrative: Jephthah is thrown out because he was jealous of his brothers.

13. Interestingly, Pseudo-Philo (*LAB* 39.3) calls it the land of Tobi.

14. See also above, regarding Abimelech's experience. Much has been written about the motif of the rise of an exiled son; see Greenstein and Marcus 1976: 75–77. Schloen (1993b) has nice material on this motif but misapplies it to Ugaritic myths. The Mari archives have much detail about men individually labeled *keltum* who covet the throne occupied by usurpers. Many of them were children of rulers who lost their thrones and, with luck, could bide their time in another court; see under IIIE, Notes to 9:16–24. Often enough, it does, Zimri-Lim being an excellent example of such a turnaround; see Sasson 2007.

15. W. Smelik (1995: 544–46) has a nice note on how these phrases are rendered in the Targum.

16. Marcus (1989: 98) argues that Jephthah is hectoring the elders "because they had previously rejected his case in court, and had annulled an adoption agreement that his father had made in his favor." Needless to say, there is much invention in such a scenario. Craig 1998 offers a finely tuned layering of the discussion among all the parties, including an ironic narrator.

17. Worth noticing is a vocabulary (*ka'ăšer ṣar lākem*; "just when you are in trouble") that reminds of God's angry retort at 10:14.

18. We have already met with a similar usage of *lākēn* in the Gideon story (at 8:7) and in God's rejection of Israel (at 10:13). Rahlfs A has οὐχ οὕτως, "Not so!," suggesting a reading *l' kn*. Misjudging what is at stake, Boling (1975: 198) follows suit. On the function of *maddu^wa'* and *lākēn*, see Marcus's good comments (1989: 97–99).

19. Pseudo-Philo (*LAB* 39.5) is remarkably subtle here: Jephthah claims that being human, he—unlike God—has good reasons not to withdraw his anger or forgive.

20. The Vulgate turns the language around, with the elders pledging to fulfill their promise (*quod nostra promissa faciamus*). Ehrlich (1968: 118) cuts *yihyēh* as duplicating the word preceding it.

21. A contrast might be noted here between the way Abimelech and Jephthah obtain their power, when neither had proved his mettle beyond making mischief. The leaders of Gilead are led step by step into accepting much more than they were initially offer-

ing. They accept Jephthah's terms and, given his military success, never felt the need to rebel against them. Those of Shechem surrender to Abimelech much more than he ever expected. They hardly draw any advantage from their (rash) move. Rather, they end up paying dearly for it once they change their minds. By then, however, God was orchestrating their mutual destruction.

22. For the circumstance, see above, note 2. As a result of taking the fight to the Ammonites, Samuel willingly anoints the victorious Saul. In fact, having experienced the rush of God's spirit (*rûᵂaḥ ʾĕlōhîm*) and vanquished his foes, Saul could easily have been a judge had Samuel not been one already. True, the narrative of Israel's history (at least as recalled) was by then centering on the rise of kingship.

    The other two avenues for Saul's kingship are divine choice (1 Sam 9–10) and selection by lots (1 Sam 10:17–27). In fact, God had instructed Samuel to anoint Saul as a *nāgîd* (1 Sam 9:16), a difficult expression to pin down, but one that probably might not entail continuity.

23. Pseudo-Philo (*LAB* 39.8) gives the name of the king as "Getal." Having just attributed many exchanges of pious sentiments to Jephthah and the elders of Gilead, Pseudo-Philo removes God's wrath precisely at this point.

24. This point is missed in translations that pluralize the pronouns, for example, Block 1999: 356: "What do you have against us that you attacked our country?"

25. It is piquant to note that in Sumerian lore, writing was invented precisely for this function. A messenger of Enmerkar of Uruk (Erech) tires of shuttling communications to the king of Aratta (an imagined mirror of Uruk): "[Enmerkar's] speech was substantial, and its contents extensive. The messenger, whose mouth was heavy, was not able to repeat it. Because the messenger, whose mouth was tired, was not able to repeat it, the lord of Kulaba [Enmerkar] patted some clay and wrote the message as if on a tablet. Formerly, the writing of messages on clay was not established. Now, under that sun and on that day, it was indeed so. The lord of Kulaba inscribed the message like a tablet. It was just like that" ("Enmerkar and the Lord of Aratta," lines 500–506; cited from ETCSL, http://etcsl .orinst.ox.ac.uk/cgi-bin/etcsl.cgi?text=t.1.8.2.3#). A nice appreciation of the literary context is in Michalowski 2011: 14–21.

26. Early Neo-Assyrian kings (from Assur-dān II on) would justify the capture of territory on the grounds that their ancestors (Middle Assyrian kings) had once conquered them, however long ago the conquest had occurred. Consequently, the defeated were rebels who deserved punishment.

27. See Van Seters (1972, 1980), Sumner (1968), and Bartlett (1978). When Judas Maccabeus moved from Gilead to Judah, he posted essentially the same request to the people of Ephron (1 Macc 5:48–51): "And Ioudas sent a message to them with peaceful words, saying, 'We will pass through your land to return to our land, and no one will do you harm; we will only pass by on foot.' But they did not want to open to him. And Ioudas gave the order to announce to the army for each to camp in the place where they were. And the men of the force camped, and he made war on the city all that day and all night, and the city was delivered into his hand. And he destroyed every male by the edge of the sword. And he demolished it and took its spoils and passed through the city over those who had been killed." The incident is revisited in 2 Macc 12:27–29, minus the request for a peaceful passage but plus mention of divine interference.

28. This is Kadesh Barnea, an oasis in the wilderness of Zin/Paran, eleven days distant from Mount Horeb. The place has gathered many traditions and occasionally is cited as En-Mishpat ("spring of verdict" in Gen 14:7) and "waters of Meribah" ("conflict" in, among

others, Num 20:13, 24). The name Kadesh, having to do with holiness, is attached to other sites. We have already met with Kedesh Naphtali by Mount Tabor, birthplace of Baraq (see at Judg 4:6). A Kadesh that is not mentioned in the Bible is a major city on the Orontes River in Syria where, among many other famous events, Pharaoh Ramses II confronted a coalition led by Muwatalli of the Hittites.

29. In Hebrew, *gĕvûl* means both the border of a state and the territory that stretches on the other side of it.

30. On the Amorites, see the Introductory Remarks at IB1 (Judg 1:22–36).

31. Heshbon is widely associated with Ḥisbān in the southern Belka (Transjordan); see Gass 2005: 484–87.

32. They are doubtless encouraged by Rahlfs A, "Seon did not want Israel" (καὶ οὐκ ἠθέλησεν Σηων).

33. Jahza (*yāhĕṣâ*; Greek, Ιασσα/Ιασα) cannot be located with any precision (see the dictionaries and Gass 2005: 488–92), but as it is mentioned in the Moabite phase of Israel's itinerary to the Promised Land and as it is cited in prophetic literature as a Moabite locality, it cannot be too distant from Heshbon or Dibbon. Jahaz/Jahza was allotted to Reuben. Mesha (ninth century BCE) claims to have taken it back into the Moabite fold.

34. The word *yôrîšĕkā* need not be emended; the Hiphil verbal form occurs with a suffixed object in Exod 15:9 and Num 14:24, among others.

35. See the material cited under the Introductory Remarks to IIIB (Judg 3:12–21). Theomachy, or battle for supremacy among the gods, is nicely represented in all Near Eastern mythology, perhaps best in Enuma Elish. In the literature, it is usually assigned to creation legends. Echoes of the cosmic battles are found in poetic lines that pit such forces as Rahab, Yam, and Tannin against the Hebrew God.

36. On Chemosh and potential antecedents, see the nice article of Müller 1995.

37. O'Connell (1996: 193) has Jephthah satirizing the king. Pseudo-Philo's Jephthah mocks his adversary for worshiping stones (*LAB* 39.9). The Targum ungallantly speaks of "Chemosh, your idol [*ṭaʿûtāk*]." One manuscript offers something quite different, clearly addressing the matter of a Moabite god: "Surely there is no use in Chemosh, your idol! Sihon drove them away, and now you plan to repossess it?"; after W. Smelik 1995: 550.

38. Similar usage is at Num 11:12, in which Moses tells God, "Was it I who was pregnant with this people, let alone birthed it?"; more examples are at BDB.

39. While documents from Mesopotamia (and especially Mari) do tell us about political arbitration between parties that include river ordeals (S. Lafont [Démare] 2000), not every mention of the verb *rîb* evokes a legal setting; contra O'Connell 1996: 195.

40. The count may (Radaq) or may not (Rashi) need to include Jephthah's six years of rule. Three hundred years happens to be the interval within which Israel is said to subjugate its enemies during the Judges period; see at 9:22. Luckily we need not deal with the sixty years the Rahlfs B recension of the Greek Judges allots Jephthah; see Moore 1895: 296–97. We meet with the same complications in other assessments of major historical phases, most famously the 480 years separating the exodus from the building of the temple (1 Kgs 6:1). The interval is most likely achieved by multiplying twelve generations—from Moses to Solomon—by forty. We have the fine example of Samsi-Addu (Shamshi-Adad) who claims: "The temple Emenue . . . which Man-ištūšu son of Sargon, king of Akkad, had built, (that temple) had become dilapidated. The temple which none of the kings who preceded me from the *fall* of Akkad until my kingship, until the capture of Nurrugu—seven generations have passed—had rebuilt"; after Grayson 1987, RIMA 1 0.39.2). Samsi-Addu's scribes, who invested heavily in chronicles and in *limmu* lists,

knew that this statement could not be chronologically correct. See M. Cogan's good assessment in the *ABD* (under "Chronology").

41. On Aroer, see Gass 2005: 473–76.

42. The same can be argued for another Judges passage (at 12:6).

43. With the Mesopotamian material about calling on divine judgment not known in his days, Ehrlich (1968: 120) found the epithet *haššōfēṭ* too odd to remain without emendation. Elsewhere, the verb calling on God's judgment is *hôkēᵃḥ* (Hiphil of *yākaḥ*), as in Gen 31:42 and 1 Chr 12:18.

44. About the fate of the messengers charged with the mission, nothing is said. While sentiments are expressed on the immunity of diplomats, reality was not always kind to them; see Elgavish 2000 and Sasson 2007: 461 n. 24. In 2 Sam 10:2–4 is recorded the humiliation experienced in Ammon by David's diplomat—yet they were there just to convey condolences!

45. The text is A.1314 = Dossin 1956. The letter is now translated with collations by Durand, LAPO 16, #251, pp. 394–97. I have studied this letter on two occasions: 1985 and forthcoming ("Casus belli").

46. It is not at all surprising that O'Connell (1996: 194–96, following Harvey 1962) finds in Jephthah's letter many features associated with the *rîb* genre of "royal covenant disputation." He appends a list of Mesopotamian documents he deems equivalent in goals.

47. Moses uses a somewhat similar stratagem (Num 14) to influence God into acting beyond his intentions. Trying to deflect God's resolve to destroy rebellious Israel, Moses argues that foreign nations will deem such an act as evidence of God's incapacity to fulfill his promise.

IIIG2. Jephthah: Jephthah's Daughter (Judg 11:29–40)

1. The legal premises for vows are stated in Num 30:3–17, but it has taken a whole Talmudic tractate (*Nĕdārîm*) to unpack their application. A vow differs from a *šĕvûᶜâ*, "oath," essentially an unconditional vow, in that it does not generally include a curse. Presumably a vow has a term limit and becomes void if the condition is not fulfilled. Vows can include promises to act positively or to abstain from certain acts, the most relevant manifestation of which in Judges will be discussed in connection with Samson's *nāzîr* status.

It is often the case that we hear about the making of vows *after* individuals fulfill their promise, an example being this statement by King Samsi-Addu: "When (the god) Itur-Mer, having heard my vow and my petition, gave me complete control of the land of Mari, the Banks of the Euphrates, as well as his dominion, I dedicated to him and offered as worthy of his divinity a large throne of *ušû*-wood, crafted in gold with much artistry" (Charpin 1984: 42). We also learn that vows of the elites were publicly stated, no doubt to increase the likelihood that they would be fulfilled. We do have this remarkable letter from Old Babylonian Tell Leilan reporting on the vow of Mutiya of Šeḥna: "In the past, before he could ascend his throne, Mutiya kept on making the following vow, 'If I were to ascend my throne, I shall donate silver, gold, cups of silver, cups of gold, and skillful maids to Belet-Nagar, my Lady!' This is what he kept on vowing. (Yet) when this man did ascend his throne, he totally ignored the goddess and did not even visit her once!" (I analyze this text in Sasson 1997 and discuss other unfulfilled vows.) While a Mari document intimates that kings sometimes forget that they had made a vow (ARM 26 84), in Mutiya's case we know that his goddess was unforgiving, for soon after, she removed him from his seat. Seminal studies on vows include Wendel 1931, Parker 1979, and Cartledge 1992. On Jephthah's vow in particular there is Marcus's fine 1986 study.

2. Job 22:26–27 gives us the full sequence: "When you seek the favor of Shadday, lifting your face toward God you will entreat him. He will listen to you and you will pay your vows."

3. If "I will serve the LORD" means more than just being a follower of the Hebrew God, Absalom had had ample time to fulfill his vow ("forty years," according to the previous verse). That David falls for this excuse is commentary on his cluelessness, a major theme in the narratives about his relationship with his sons.

4. A list of the literature (easily expandable) on the theme is in del Olmo Lete 2000: 62. Rich lore is collected in Gunn 2005: 133–69 and R. Miller (2005: 120–33).

5. Interestingly, the Greek versions stayed with the verb twice, albeit differing in each (διαβαίνω, "pass over," versus παρέρχομαι, "pass through/by"), but treated the third occurrence as if based on the noun ʿever, "the other side" (of Ammon).

6. Cartledge (1992: 166–75) makes the point that the sequence suggests that Jacob has found a way to bind God via the vow.

7. The Greek versions imply the same with ἐν εἰρήνῃ, "in peace." See also Josh 10:21, 11:13. The meaning of the phrase is sharpest at 2 Chr 18–26, an episode expanding on what is reported in 1 Kgs 22. Micaiah had predicted doom for Ahab. Annoyed, the king of Israel instructs to keep him jailed and abused until "my safe return," thus hoping to guarantee that happy ending. The idiom and verbal form are different at 11:13 (hašîvâ ʾethen běšālôm) when the king of Ammon demands the return of coveted land; still, there might be an intentional play on the words.

8. Cartledge (1992: 147): "The phrase . . . has been understood by some as an implied condition, but a return in peace is to be assumed if the Ammonites are defeated, so this adds nothing new to the condition." Cartledge is disagreeing with Wendel (1931: 109).

9. Essentially, the matter depends on whether to locate Jephthah's conquests in Ammon or in Gilead/Gad territory. Aroer (ʿărôʿēr; Greek, Αροηρ) may or may not be the town cited as ʿarʿôr in Jephthah's message to Ammon (at 11:26). Many associate it with the Aroer of Josh 13:25, placing it near Rabbah (more or less modern Amman). Abel-keramim (Rahlfs A, Αβελ ἀμπελώνων [literal]; B, Εβελχαρμιν [phonetic]) may be a topographic designation ("Vineyards Meadow") rather than an urban space. If the latter, suggestions for its location differ, but generally also around Rabbah. Knauf (*ABD*, under "Abel-Keramim") forcefully connects it with Saḥab, around the same area, but with a Canaanite rampart. Minnith is known (if the same) as an exporter of grain (Ezek 27:17); many follow Eusebius in locating it between Heshbon and Rabbah, with diverse identifications. However, the Greek renderings simply got rid of it, with Rahlfs B offering "he struck them from Aroer until as far as Arnon [River]," while Rahlfs A has the defeat reaching to Σεμωιθ, "Semoith." On these places, see MacDonald 2000: 166–68 and Gass 2005: 465–79, each with many suggestions.

10. Some argue that his home was at Zaphon where Ephraimites headed to confront Jephthah (12:1). But despite Josh 13:27, it is not certain that the passage is alluding to a place rather than a direction. Rahlfs B reads as the latter, while Rahlfs A gives it as a place, Sephina. One Greek text for Judg 12:7 says that Jephthah was buried in "Seph(e) of Galaad." Speculation on all this is found in Barthélemy 1982: 106.

11. In Byron's versed tragedy *Jephthah's Daughter* she is Thyrzah. (Byron's elegy on the death of his beloved John Edlestone was expressed as if "To Thyrza.") In Handel's glorious oratorio named after her father, the girl is called Iphis. The name may have reminded his librettist (Thomas Morell) of Iphigenia's plight, but more likely, it comes from Ovid, who tells of another Iphis with problems surviving her father. For good measure, Handel's

librettist gives the name of her mother (Storgè), and even creates a potential lover for the daughter (Hamor); see Rooke 2012: 207–26.

12. In contemporary scholarship, the name *Bat-Yiftaḥ is sometimes assigned the daughter, for example in Exum 1995; see further Bauks 2007, with a fuller study in Bauks 2010. Similarly constructed are the names of Bathshua, wife of Judah and daughter of Shua, and likely also of Bathsheba. Bathsheba's father is given as Eliam in 2 Sam 11:3 or Ammiel in 1 Chr 3:5, but some have conjectured that she might be the daughter of Sheva who rebelled against David (2 Sam 20:1). Yet the *bat-bĕtû'ēl* of Gen 24:47 turns out to be Rebekah, and *bat-lēvî* of Exod 2:1 is later identified as Jochebed and so must be taken as an attribution, "a Levite woman." This manner of identifying without naming a woman is fairly common in Hebrew, with *bat* constructed with a father's name (as above), with a kinship term (as in *bat-'aḥ+*, "niece," Gen 24:48) or with a position (as in *bat-par'ō*, Exod 2:8–9).

13. Much has been built on this premise; see Trible 1984: 101 and Block 1999: 371 n. 113.

14. See the good article of C. Meyers (1991), with nice illustrations.

15. Some suggest that in fact the verses are vestiges of a tradition wherein she, rather than (or perhaps in addition to) Moses, is the singer of a victory hymn. (Comment of S. Ackerman.) On the tradition of victory celebration by women, see Poethig 1985.

16. Perhaps influenced by Greek translation of the term in Gen 22:2, 12, 16, Rahlfs A adds αὐτῷ ἀγαπητή, "his beloved." Ehrlich (1968: 121) is correct to point out that *yĕḥîdâ* is a noun, not an adjective, and that it has to do with favoritism and love rather than singularity, the last being the object of the clause following. The story of Jephthah is as much about destroying one's future as about self-inflicted emotional wounds.

17. Among the attestations for the latter are Reuben, on discovering the disappearance of Joseph (Gen 37:29); Jacob, on seeing his son's bloodied garment (Gen 37:34); a man mourning the death of his king (2 Sam 1:2); and Tamar, reacting to her rape (2 Sam 13:19).

18. Rahlfs A uses the standard interjection οἴμμοι; Rahlfs B, however, approximates the Hebrew sound: ἇ ἇ.

19. An exception is in Joel 1:15. In 2 Kgs 3:10, as in our passage, the appeal to God is presumed.

20. The Greek versions had their troubles with it, with Rahlfs A offering "you have blocked my way, becoming a thorn [σκῶλον] in my eyes," and Rahlfs B giving a somewhat closer rendering, "you have greatly troubled me and it is you who has troubled me."

21. Deut 23:22–23: "When you make a vow to the LORD your God, you must not delay fulfilling it. The LORD your God will require it of you (just the same) but you will have incurred guilt, whereas you incur no guilt if you refrain from vowing. Be careful with what crosses your lips and fulfill exactly what you have vowed voluntarily, having made the promise with your own mouth." Neef (1999), who surveys nicely the many understandings of what was at stake in Jephthah's vow, thinks that the story illustrates the consequence of the Deuteronomic legislation. Bauks (2011) reflects on Qumran and Talmudic expositions on biblical vows and their application to Jephthah's.

22. Insensitive readers have latched on to her answer to turn her into a manipulative masochist: Ostensibly a daddy's girl, Jephthah's daughter forces her own death to avoid being married out of home (Reis 1997: 290; Ryan 2007: 91).

23. Rahlfs A offers a less docile reading: "If it is about me that you have opened your mouth to the LORD."

24. Some commentators, Budde (1890: 126) among them, imagine a loss of text here.

25. In the Greek versions, however, the father is addressed: Rahlfs A, "Do also this matter for me"; Rahlfs B, "Let my father do this thing."

26. Lagrange (1903: 206) tentatively would amend to Miṣibṭa, allegedly a "plateau."

27. "In fine, וירדתי should be excised from the text as impossible both contextually and syntactically, and as having had its origin in an erroneously twice-written ורעתי," so "I would go with my friends on the mountain." Orlinsky (1942: 96 and n. 21) cites Albright's reaction with yet another proposed reading to reach the same noun. The result, either way, would be a surfeit of "friends" and inelegant repetition.

28. See Wenham 1972 and Frymer-Kensky 1998. For Mesopotamia, see Cooper 2002.

29. We are not told what happened during this surcease, but if curious, we can turn to Pseudo-Philo (*LAB* 40.5), who assigns her a powerful lament that she utters on "Mount Stelac," the first of many such imaginings, some of which are collected in B. Miller 2005. See also Trible 1984: 108–9.

30. The phrasing may seem perfectly redundant, but it is to stress the unassailable virtue of the woman under discussion: She had been subject to no sexual contact whatsoever. In addition, the language places her totally under the control of her father, since she had belonged to no other man. Variations on the phrasing occur at Num 31:17–18, 31, 35. Boling (1975: 209) is oddly censorial: "biblical narrators were seldom so dull."

31. This is the position of Marcus 1986.

32. The Hebrew is anomalous, as one would expect it to read *vattĕhî *lĕḥōq*. Both Greek renderings give an impersonal subject, "and it became an ordinance [πρόστιγμα] in Israel." Many commentators emend the Hebrew accordingly; see Lagrange 1903: 207. Burney (1970: 324–25) offers an example of *vattĕhî* in a neuter sense. Marcus (1986: 34) is tempted by a Peshiṭta reading to translate, "she became an example in Israel." The Targum clarifies by expanding: "And it became a decree [*vahĕvāt ligzĕraʾ*] in Israel that no one may offer up his son or his daughter for a burnt offering, as Jephthah the Gileadite did, who did not ask Phinehas the priest; for if he had asked Phinehas the priest, he would have rescued her with a monetary consecration" (after W. Smelik 1995: 555, with comments).

33. Already noted by Burney 1970: 325; see also W. Smelik 1995: 557 n. 1379; P. Day (ed.) (1989: 67 n. 4). The idiom here (unlike at 5:11) is construed with a *le-*; but it is difficult to assess its import; see Moore 1895: 303–4. The Greek versions both use θρηνέω, "to bewail," for the translation. For Exum (1993: 139) the phase implies retelling the daughter's tragedy. Landers (1991), who would save the daughter from sacrifice, argues a meaning "to console," rather than "to lament" for this verb; so already Radaq, for whom the daughter is confined.

34. Biblical historiography readily explains historically sacred sites (for example, Bethel and Achor) and institutionalized practices (for example, circumcision and Passover). Some customs are given gratuitous or incongruous etiologies. For example, the priests of Dagon do not tread on their thresholds because the ark of the Lord decapitated that god's statue (1 Sam 5:5). Or, the blind and the lame cannot enter the temple because David hated them (2 Sam 5:8).

35. See Bauks 2007; P. Day (1989: 60) has this to say about the purpose of this occasion: "What I would reconstruct . . . is an annual ceremony at which young women were socially recognized as having left childhood behind and entered *bĕtûlîm*, physical maturity. This ceremony included a ritual lament which . . . acknowledged the 'death' of one stage in life in preparation for entry into a new stage." Olyan (2010) reviews what is known about rituals for women in a family context.

36. In the Comments I have drawn freely on my contribution in Sasson 2013b ("Jephthah: Chutzpa and Overreach").

37. In his commentary, Boling (1975) offers a number of house plans to illustrate our episode (after p. 170). One of them (8c) has the following caption: "Reconstruction of a typical house in Old Testament times. Because there were rooms on three sides of a court, there was plenty of space to house such animals as sheep, cows, goats. It was reasonable, therefore, for Jephthah to assume that the first creature to wander out of his house when he returned would be an animal acceptable for sacrifice, and not his daughter." But why not include among them unacceptable (for sacrifice) animals, such as donkeys, mules, dogs, and cats that presumably also took shelter there? In fact, Pseudo-Philo (*LAB* 39.11) has God retaliating against Jephthah precisely because a dog may have trotted out from his gates.

38. I imagine that God might be unimpressed by the sacrifice of any acceptable animal, a giraffe possibly excepted. Of course, there would be no story at all had Jephthah simply pledged to offer God a hecatomb for a victory.

39. For this argument, see Sasson 2006a.

40. Or even when, after its first defeat at Hormah (Num 14:43–45), Israel pledged that town to God were he to give them victory over their enemies (Num 21:3).

41. The literature is immense, albeit highly repetitive. A nice bibliography is attached to Steinberg 1999. It is important to distinguish our theme by its linkage to vows. It is not always kept in mind that literarily, it makes a difference whether a narrative opens on a human sacrifice that generates subsequent events (as in, say, Shakespeare's *Titus Andronicus*) or ends on it (as in our tale). In most examples of the latter, the sacrifice is averted, by interference (deus ex machina) or by substitution (as in the famous Akedah).

42. Logan (2009: 668–70) believes that "there is a good deal of evidence that human sacrifice was accepted practice in Canaanite and Canaanite-derivative cultures." She accepts that children were sacrificed in Carthage, when fine scholarship has suggested it was a libel; see del Olmo Lete 1995. Logan refers to an Ugaritic vow to sacrifice a child when the text is broken at a crucial spot (see Sasson 1987). She also cites Hebrew and classical sources with morbid attachments to the practices of others. I do not deny that during moments of panic and despair, societies do horrible things to themselves and to each other; but if we are speaking here of a regular cultic event, then we should be able to trace such events in economic and bureaucratic records rather than in the memory of enemies. When it comes to the Canaanites, Phoenicians, and Carthaginians, it is evident that nasty accusations against them never die; they simply get recycled.

43. The two are sons of Hiel of Bethel (1 Kgs 16:34; see Josh 6:26).

44. The comparison is often discussed; see Marcus 1986: 38–49; P. Day (ed.) 1989: 60–62; Römer 1998 (contra D. Janzen 2005). Rich lore about human sacrifice in Greek literature is in Hughes 1991, with diverse sequences. Much appreciated is a theme in which an individual singled out for death (for many reasons) is replaced by a beloved, the stories of Dumuzi/Geštinanna (Mesopotamia) and Admetus/Alcestis (Greek) being fine examples.

45. Exum (1989) speaks of it as a manifestation of a tragic vision, a dimension of biblical literature.

46. Gerstein (1989) argues that Jephthah hoped his vow would enhance his status as judge. Comparing him with several characters in Genesis, Shemesh (2011) assesses Jephthah as both victim and victimizer, a casualty of a particularly nasty period: "Thus Jephthah and the people of Israel are shown to deserve each other, and the Lord's silence indicates

His displeasure with Israel, with the leader it chose, and with the entire sequence of events" (131).

47. The Karaite al-Qirqisani seems the first to suggest consecration rather than sacrifice (Brock 2011: 7). For Landers (1991) the sacrifice of a female would not have been acceptable in Israel.

48. Fine discussion on all these topics is in W. Smelik (1995: 555–57). Hebrew narrators are generally reluctant to draw on legal traditions to solve literary problems, provoking us into endless debates why this is so. E. Fuchs (1989) argues complicity on the part of the narrator no less than the audience in reinforcing stereotypes of women and reaffirming male control of cultural traits.

49. On the former, see Michel 2009. For the latter, it might be sufficient to look at Harris 1964. The women consecrated to Šamaš may have been celibate; those to Marduk could marry but might not give birth.

50. On the basis of 2 Sam 14:27, I argue that Tamar was raped by her uncle (not her brother) Amnon and ended up living in the house of Absalom her father (not her brother); see Sasson 2001c.

51. The latter is one argument made by those who have her consecrated rather than sacrificed; see Marcus 1986: 33–34.

52. The debate is well-charted throughout Marcus (1986), Gunn (2005: 133–69), Bauks 2010, and (somewhat scattered) B. Miller (2005). Josephus had no doubt about her fate: "Accordingly, when that time was over, [Jephthah] sacrificed his daughter as a burnt-offering, offering such an oblation as was neither conformable to the law nor acceptable to God, not weighing with himself what opinion the hearers would have of such a practice" (*Ant.* 5.266). *Genesis Rabbah*, a midrashic text likely from the sixth to seventh centuries CE, disapproves of Jephthah but is not explicit about the nature of his deed; text cited above, at 1:12. For more on rabbinic lore regarding the daughter, see Kramer 1999.

   In the Middle Ages, Jewish commentators were almost unanimous in arguing that the daughter was not sacrificed, with notable exceptions. In his comments to Lev 27:29, Ramban (Nachmanides 1974) argues that she was indeed killed, Jephthah being ignorant of *halachic* laws that would not permit such severe restriction on a human being (479–83). Centuries later, during commemoration for the winter solstice, Jews recalled the blood that dripped from Jephthah's knife: "The *tekufah* of Tevet, why? During this *tekufah* Jephthah made his vow concerning his daughter, and for four days during this *tekufah* the daughters of Israel mourned her. When Jephthah slaughtered his daughter all the waters turned to blood. And since it says *Every year for four days in the year* (Jgs 11.40), we observe all four *tekufot*"; cited from Baumgarten (2007: 197), who also quotes R. Judah the Pious's twelfth-century CE *Sefer ha-kavod*.

IIIG3. Jephthah: Jephthah's Flaws (Judg 12)

1. Section 9 of *CANE* (Sasson 1995: 2097–419) is devoted to "Language, Writing, and Literature." The terms "language" and "dialects" are not clearly demarcated, even by linguists.

2. See also the Introductory Remarks to IIIC2 (Judg 5).

3. Rahlfs B is literal, with they "passed on to the north." For Zaphon, see the dictionaries or Rainey and Notley 2006: 141.

4. There will be other examples in later chapters of Judges; see also at 1:8.

5. The psychology and intents are otherwise when Jeremiah calls himself "a man of conflict and strife," cursed by all (Jer 15:10). It is possible that the narrator chose the root to remind of Jerubbaal (Gideon), famous for pitting himself against Baal, a notice sharpened by Rahlfs A in which Jephthah presents himself as an ἀνὴρ ἀντιδικῶν, "a man in opposition," recalling its only other LXX usage at 6:31 (Harlé and Roqueplo 1999: 192–93). *mĕʾōd* ("force") occurs mostly as an adverb, normally close to the word it qualifies. There are exceptions, including this passage. Rahlfs A creates a verb to back it: "The sons of Ammon were humbling me greatly [οἱ υἱοὶ Αμμων ἐταπείνουν με σφόδρα]."

6. See Barthélemy (1982: 104–5) for a number of suggestions. Some commentators simply drop the whole clause as a gloss, encouraged by the absence of portions from many Greek manuscripts and suggested by a replay of words from the opening of 11:5, *vĕhāyâ kî yōʾmĕrû pĕlîṭê ʾefrayim*. Lagrange (1903: 209) labels any attempt at comprehension a "cause désespérée."

7. It might be kept in mind that in ancient times people hardly swam and so had no choice but to ford at shallow waters. In Assyrian reliefs, we see scenes of (naked) soldiers holding on to inflated goat skins when reaching for the other side of a river; see Ataç 2010: 20–22.

8. This is Willesen's point (1958), but he draws the conclusion that we are dealing with Judean Ephrathah.

9. We are not speaking of a password, despite Rahlfs A, which presumes it is exactly that (σύνθημα) and despite the attestation of passwords in the ancient world. (Moses was to use the real name of the Hebrew God as one; see Exod 3:13.) In today's English, a "shibboleth" has many meanings, among them a "commonplace saying," a "platitude," or a "marker of distinctiveness."

10. Scholars have succeeded in tracking the word in its "ear of grain" meaning across Semitic languages, but doing the same for "water stream" has proved elusive (see below), complicating their resolution of the issue that follows. A fair number of witnesses simply give approximation of the Hebrew words; see Weitzman 1999: 143–44.

11. Barthélemy 1982: 105–6.

12. A handy chart is also in Hendel 1996: 70. Lemaire (1985) collected a good sampling of recent arguments, with the major commentaries providing additional (especially earlier) suggestions. Faber (1992) is the most thorough pursuer of the linguistic issues.

13. The equation is so taken for granted in MacDonald and Younker (1999: 16, 41) that they cite the king only as Baalis. Yet the problems for the Jeremiah reference remain on many fronts; not least among them is an available name (consonantal Bʿls; syllabic Baʿlisi) in the Ugaritic onomasticon and the widely divergent Greek readings (LXX, Josephus) for the royal name; see Weippert 2010: 374–76.

14. Jackson 1983: 93–95; Aufrecht 1989: 356–76.

15. This is suggested by earlier exegetes such as Moore (1895: 308) and recently championed by Emerton (1985). Often cited is an incident during the Sicilian Vespers (1282) when the Angevin invaders tripped on sibilants they could not pronounce. There is an (apocryphal?) anecdote that during the Second World War, the Dutch would trip up Germans by having them pronounce "Scheveningen," the name of a town. The Germans would say it with an initial *sh* rather than the correct *ske*; so the reverse of what happened in our story. All the instances cited feature people of different nationalities, where presumably other means of detection might have been just as effective. Our case, however, involves people that share ethnic and dialect environments.

16. Lagrange (1903: 210) has this comment, "Il est difficile d'admettre qu'Éphraïm eût dès lors prononcé tous les שׁ comme des ס." Marcus (1992) "solves" the problem (surely too neatly) by positing a satire at work, the test serving to ridicule the men of Ephraim for their stupidity or linguistic thickness.

17. Midrashic lore played on the consonants in "shibboleth" to turn the test into a rejection of idolatry; see W. Smelik 1995: 559–60.

18. On an appeal by Ehud, Israel "came down with him and captured all the fords of the Jordan leading to Moab, allowing no one to cross. On just this occasion [bā'et hahî'], they killed about ten thousand men; they were all stout and prominent, yet not a single man escaped."

19. The phrase occurs also with an article before Gilead, at Num 32:26 and Josh 13:25.

20. This notice is too delicious to skip. It comes from *bBava Batra* 91a:

> Rabbah the son of R. Huna said in the name of Rav: Ibzan is Boaz. . . . Boaz prepared for his sons one hundred and twenty wedding banquets, for it says, "And he [Ibzan] had thirty sons, and he sent out thirty daughters; he brought thirty daughters for his sons from without. He judged Israel for seven years" (Judges 12:9). For each of his sixty children he made two feasts [one on their betrothal and one on their marriage], one in his own house and one in the house of the in-laws. To none of these feasts did he invite Manoah [eventually, Samson's father] because he said: How could this barren mule ever pay me back? [In punishment,] all of his sixty children died during his lifetime. And this is meant by the popular saying: If you had sixty children, but they all died in your lifetime, what good were they? Marry again, and father one that will be more stalwart than the sixty." (Boaz begot Oved from Ruth, and he survived.)

See the discussion of W. Smelik 1995: 560–62, citing minor variations of the same tale.

21. Many translate "outside the clan." So as not to imagine that Ibzan was importing sisters for his sons, Rahlfs A says he brought in thirty "women."

22. Rahlfs A calls him Λαβδων son of Σελλημ.

23. Much speculation on the place is in Gass 2005: 355–57.

24. "And the LORD sent Jerubbaal, and Bedan, and Jephthah, and Samuel"; on this passage, see note 52 to IIIC1 (Judg 4).

25. Rabbinic lore blamed the slaughter on Phinehas the priest who, they say, had the choice of intervening but did not; see Braude and Kapstein 1981: 168.

Index of Subjects

Index of Modern Authors

Lenzi, A.	66, 230, 486n.31	Malamat, A.	69, 155, 216, 315, 352, 483n.17, 511n.7
Le Roux, N.	66, 490n.69		
Lesko, B. S., ed.	66, 473n.50	Maly, E.	69, 518n.51
Levin, Y.	23, 66–67, 463n.39	Mann, T. W.	69, 492n.25, 492n.26
Levine, B. A.	67, 340, 482n.9, 508n.53	Marais, J.	69, 151
		Marchesi, G.	69, 460n.16
Levinson, B.	67, 480n.30	Marcos, N. F.	xviii, 6, 69, 138, 139, 282, 331, 460n.6
Levison, J. R.	67, 482n.15		
Lewis, T. J.	67, 515n.12	Marcus, D.	69, 441, 448, 422, 526n.16, 526n.18, 529n.1, 532n.31, 532n.32, 533n.44, 534n.51, 534n.52, 536n.16
Lichtheim, M.	67, 132, 137, 241, 475, 494n.42, 505n.8, 511n.3		
Liedke, G.	67, 478n.4		
Lindars, B.	67, *and passim in Notes and Comments for* Judg 1–5 (121–372), 460n.9, 463n.42, 467n.20, 471n.31, 472n.37, 475n.19, 476n.16, 478n.13, 480n.33, 484n.11, 489n.58, 492n.15, 497n.22, 498n.28, 499n.45, 499n.53, 500n.59, 500n.62, 502n.91, 513n.32, 514n.5, 517n.41	Marello, P.	69, 515n.16
		Margalit, B.	70, 275, 319, 493n.34
		Margalith, O.	70, 480n.2
		Marti, L.	xviii, 70, 159, 486n.27
		Martin, L. R.	70, 481n.4
		Martino, S. de	70, 506n.27
		Maryon, H., et al., eds.	70, 487n.40
		Matthews, V., and D. Benjamin	70, 495n.55
		Maxwell-Hyslop, R.	70, 485n.18
Lion, B.	67, 478n.7	Mayer, W.	70, 474n.6
Lion, B and C. Michel	67, 505n.10	Mayes, A. D. H.	70, 319
		Mazar, A.	70, 166, 464n.49
Lion, B., et al., eds.	67, 494n.43	Mazar (Maisler), B.	70, 156, 242, 262, 264, 265, 474n.11, 489n.60, 494n.36
Lisella, A. R.	67–68, 503.n105		
Liver, J.	68, 474n.7	McCarthy, D. J.	70, 477n.10
Liverani, M.	68, 463n.39, 467–68n.1, 474n.6	McDaniel, T. F.	71, 243, 244, 271, 489n.60, 489n.63, 491n.9, 496n.8, 497n.18, 500n.59
Livingston, D.	68, 475n.8		
Logan, A.	68, 533n.42		
Loprieno, A.	27, 68	McKenzie, S. L., and S. R. Haynes, eds.	70, 462n.34
Maccoby, H.	68, 445		
MacDonald, B.	68, 530n.9	McMahon, G.	71, 507n.45
MacDonald, B., and R. W. Younker, eds.	68, 535n.13	McNutt, P. M.	71, 156
		Meek, T. J.	71, 236
		Mendenhall, G. E.	25, 71, 142, 143
Machinist, P.	68, 202	Mettinger, T. N. D.	71, 171, 486n.26, 516n.29
Maeir, A. M.	68, 468n.12		
Magness, J.	68, 488–89n.52	Meyers, C.	71, 531n.14
Maier, S. A.	68, 467–68n.1	Meyers, E. M., ed.	xix, 71, 166, 518n.1

Index of Ancient Sources

9:22–57	387–89	10:8	425
9:22–25	391	10:8–9	418
9:23	398	10:9	164, 192, 419, 452
9:24	223	10:9–16	412
9:25	397, 398	10:10	190, 217, 478n.12
9:26–29	392	10:10–16	330
9:28	390, 392	10:11	202
9:28–29	405	10:12	217
9:30	391	10:13	190, 361, 526n.18
9:30–33	394	10:13–14	14
9:31	391	10:14	483n.18, 526n.17
9:33	397	10:15	421
9:34	405	10:16	524n.21
9:34–41	395	10:17–11:28	416–17
9:37	262, 364	10:17	437, 483n.18
9:41	391, 394	10:17–18	418
9:41–45	397	10:18	187, 355
9:42–45	510n.23	11:1	419
9:43	405	11:1–33	462n.30
9:43–49	405	11:2–3	421
9:45	140	11:3	379, 425
9:46	166, 377	11:4	353
9:46–49	398	11:4–6	422
9:47	392	11:6	423
9:49	452	11:7	421
9:50–51	399	11:7–8	422
9:51	235, 515n.15	11:8	361
9:53	376, 515n.19	11:9–10	423
9:54–55	405	11:11	331, 422
9:54–57	219	11:12	431
9:55–57	400	11:12–14	424
9:56–57	133, 403	11:13	530n.7
10:1	219, 298, 401	11:15	452
10:1–2	409, 415, 456	11:15–22	425, 462n.30
10:1–5	407, 455	11:19–22	475n.3
10:1–16	406–7	11:19–26	427–28
10:2	189, 261, 401	11:19–28	159
10:2–3	219	11:21, 23	286
10:3	410	11:21–22	411
10:3–4	410	11:23–24	429
10:4	475n.20	11:24	432
10:5	189	11:25–26	430
10:5–7	219	11:26	391, 530n.9
10:6	189, 190, 191, 202, 478n.12	11:27	186, 424
		11:27–28	431
10:6–9	411	11:29	219, 438
10:6–16	463–64n.47	11:29–30	436
10:7	191, 202, 378	11:29–39	19

18:27	154	3	350
18:27–29	140	3:7	269
19:1	8–9	4	270
19:1–21:25	463–64n.47	4:4	351
19:10	139	4:17	514n.10
19:10–11	151		
19:27	490n.69	I SAMUEL	
19:29	398	1:6	235
19:30	475n.20	1:11	437, 438
19:47	174	1:15	265
20	329	1:20	122
20:1	256	1:27	122
20:2	361	1:28	122
20:16	227	2:1–10	496n.6
20:18	125, 126, 166	2:5	289
20:18–28	123	2:12	189
20:23	125	2:18	367
20:26	166, 180, 183	2:20	122
20:27	361	2:22	449
20:28	409, 524n.17, 477n.5	2:35	192
20:31	166	3	327
20:34	130, 241	3:1–4	177
21:2	166, 180, 182	3:13	459n.2
21:2–4	183	3:18	413
21:3	286	4	319
21:12	442	4–7	260
21:19	422	4:9	190
21:21	32, 439	4:10–12	136
21:22	340	4:18	218, 219, 459n.2
21:25	8–9	5:1	219
		5:5	532n.34
RUTH		5:6	173
1:1	14, 287–88	5:11	173
1:2	143	5:9	123
1:6	261	6:18	129
1:8	133	6:19	204
1:9	182	7:4	191
1:14	182	7:9	461n.24
1:20–21	345	7:10	263
1:22	126	7:15	219, 459n.2
2	270	8–10	219
2:1	419	8–12	372
2:2	442	8:1–3	459n.2
2:3	265	8:11–18	392
2:4	331	8:20	122
2:5	362	8:22	380
2:13	265–66	9:4	457
2:22	421	9:15	351

Maimonides (Rambam)	410, 459n.4	ARM 5 72 (LAPO 17 462)	155, 370
Nachmanides (Ramban)	74, 449, 459n.4, 534n.52	ARM 6 37 (LAPO 17 635)	467n.30
Radaq (David Kimḥi)	161, 169, 205, 245, 266, 293, 363, 364, 379, 397, 398, 431, 438, 441, 459n.4, 470n.23, 494n.45, 500n.63, 528n.40, 532n.33	ARM 8 10	515n.17
		ARM 8 11	469n.15
		ARM 8 13	382
		ARM 10 8 (LAPO 18 1138)	474n.9
		ARM 10 46 (LAPO 18 1237)	468n.5
		ARM 10 54 (LAPO 18 1097)	492n.19
Ralbag (Gersonides)	459n.4, 524n.17	ARM 10 84 (LAPO 18 1232)	137–38
Rashi (Shelomo Yitchaki)	182, 240, 268, 288, 295, 298, 305, 398, 411, 431, 459n.4, 477n.5, 491n.12, 494n.36, 507n.31, 523n.11, 524n.16, 528n.40	ARM 10 98 (LAPO 18 1239)	138
		ARM 11 43: 20	520n.23
		ARM 14 5 (LAPO 18 972)	507n.44
		ARM 14 50: 14	469n.15
		ARM 14 72: 18	469n.15
		ARM 14 104+ (LAPO 17 548)	520–21n.27

Ancient Near Eastern Texts

CUNEIFORM DOCUMENTS

RIMA 1	528	ARM 21 219	515n.17
RIMA 2	151, 212, 481/2	ARM 26 84	529n.1
RIMA 3/2	151	ARM 26 100b	466n.6
LL 27, 30	420	ARM 26 131	273
CH 181	420	ARM 26 185b	466n.6
MAL A40, 49, 52	420	ARM 26 194: 13–17	474n.9
		ARM 26 196	232 (486n.31)

MARI PERIOD

		ARM 26 214: 5	166
ARM 1 5 (LAPO 17 517)	520n.26	ARM 26 216: 1'–2'	166
ARM 1 77 (LAPO 18 1005)	164	ARM 26 229: 6–7	166
ARM 2 124 (LAPO 17 554)	486n.32	ARM 26 280	155
ARM 3 12 (LAPO 17 748)	379	ARM 26 312: 36'–39'	132
ARM 3 16 (LAPO 17 682)	494n.35	ARM 26 371	505n.2
ARM 3 73 (LAPO 18 1067)	521n.39	ARM 26 372: 58–59	264
ARM 4 74 (LAPO 17 541)	370	ARM 26 385	524–25n.1
ARM 5 16 (LAPO 17 443)	153, 370	ARM 26 385: 13'–20'	259–60
		ARM 26 404	356
		ARM 26 404: 60–65	519n.17

Index of Keywords

Hebrew
WORDS

ʾădōnî	265–66
ʾăhāh	336, 439–40
ʾāḥ	127, 146
ʾelef	130
ʾĕlōhîm	133, 291
ʾelôn	262, 330
ʾiṭṭēr (yad)	227
ʾûrîm vĕtûmmîm	122
bāʾ ʾel-	271, 494n.48
bākâ	182
bārak	283–84
bĕrākâ	149
bārîʾ	229
bĕṣaʿănannîm	262
bĕʿālîm	189–90
(hab)bōkîm	180
gam	193, 245
gam-hēm	165
gam-hîʾ	376
vĕgam	182
gôy	193
gōmed	228
gullōt	149–50
hammisdĕrônâ	237
hāqîm (*qwm)	192
hiqrîv	227–28, 229
vayyĕhî	123
vayyĕhî ʾaḥărê	123–24

zāvaḥ	183
zônâ	420
ḥāzaq	223–24
ḥallôn	308
ḥālāv	267–68, 306–7
ḥēlev	235
ḥōmeš	234–35
ḥērem	140, 153–55. See also Warfare: Holy wars in Index of Subjects
ḥerev	228
lĕfî-ḥereb	140
Yhvh (name)	31–32
yāraš (Qal vs Hiphil)	159
yātēd	268–69
laḥaṣ	173
migdāl	363
mad	228
malʾāk	178. See also Communicating with God: Angel/Messenger in Index of Subjects
minḥâ	227–28, 334–35. See also Sacrifices and Offerings in Index of Subjects

Ugaritic

'wn	301
g	497n.20
l'k	178
ntbt	288–89
pr'(t)	284

Akkadian

amurrû	163–64
awīlū	362
baštu	508n.56
biltum	229
bītum	164
isqum	129
ḫarimtu	420
ḫarrānum	260, 288
ḫibrum	469n.15
ḫimētum	306
karpat šinātim	489n.55
mandattum	229
melammu	213, 349
namrīru/namurru/ namurratu	481n.7
paraštinnu	236
qaqqarum	361
qulmum/qalpum	398
rašubbatu	481n.7
siparrum	298
ṣillu	517n.40
ṣuḫārum	511n.10
ṣullulu	517n.40
šakin māti	513n.37
šapārum	298
šubtu/šūšubtu	518n.11
tamartum	229
ummum	290, 498n.31, 35

Greek

ἄγγελος	178
γαμβρός	155
δῆλος	466n.4
ἐξέδρα	488n.47
κέρας	240
κύμβαχος	480n.1
ὁσιότης	466n.4
παλλακή/ παλλακίς	376
πενθερός	155
πνεῦμα	212
τύραννος	202

Hittite

dugkalḫi	489n.55
kupaḫ(ḫ)i	480n.1

Sumerian

kisi	489n.55
kar.kid	420
mar.tu	163
me.lám	213